WORLD
ECONOMIC
GEOGRAPHY

C. LANGDON WHITE
Professor of Geography
San Jose State College and Stanford University

PAUL F. GRIFFIN
Professor of Geography
Oregon College of Education

TOM L. McKNIGHT
Associate Professor of Geography
University of California at Los Angeles

WORLD
ECONOMIC
GEOGRAPHY

WADSWORTH PUBLISHING COMPANY, INC.

Belmont, California

First printing, January 1964
Second printing, August 1964

L.C. Cat. Card No.: 64–11795

Printed in the United States of America

PREFACE

A course in economic geography can contribute much to the student's appreciation of the world and man's role in it. It deals with *current* issues that permeate our daily lives and cannot be bypassed—issues concerning natural-resource depletion and population explosion as they affect both developed and underdeveloped lands.

This textbook, written with the student in mind, approaches economic geography by commodity, because experience has proved that this is the most effective and most interesting way of presenting the subject. Furthermore, the early chapters deal with minerals, inanimate energy, and manufacturing, rather than with agriculture. There are several reasons for this organization:

1. In most educational institutions, the course must be completed in a semester or a quarter; and invariably, with past texts, the class seldom gets beyond agriculture or, if it does, must cover minerals, manufacturing, transport, and trade very superficially at the end of the course.

2. The United States, the countries of Western Europe, and Japan have emerged as predominantly industrial nations. This is not to say that agriculture is less important in these lands than in the past, but that through scientific agriculture, and the use of inanimate energy and labor-saving equipment, fewer people now produce more food, fiber, and other items.

3. Even the underdeveloped countries (the predominantly agricultural countries) in our problem-clotted world now regard manufacturing as the panacea for their economic ills. Those living in the people-packed lands particularly are being made increasingly aware that the population in an industrialized nation like the United States is often preoccupied with the problem of how to live *luxuriously*, whereas they themselves are still preoccupied with the problem of how to live *at all*.

4. It is the industrial countries of the world, with only 10 per cent of the globe's population, that possess approximately 88 per cent of its wealth. It is they who wield most of the world's economic and political power.

This being the case, it appears logical that a college economic-geography text should begin with minerals and manufacturing (although this book is so organized that the instructor can make rearrangements or omissions that he deems necessary). Of course, agriculture is not neglected. Quite the reverse; for as population becomes more urbanized, it knows less and less about what lies beyond the faucet and the crammed refrigerator. Every student should realize that the foods on his table at nearly every meal have come largely from all parts of the nation and some even from the far corners of the earth. Further, he should be made aware of the hard work, the cost, the transportation, and the trade involved; the many hands through which these commodities have passed before they reach him.

Throughout this book, *principles are stressed*. Even the illustrations tell a story that exemplifies the application of one or more principles of geography. No effort is made to present the physical background, since, it is hoped, most students using this book will have had the introductory college geography course. Students who have not had the introductory course may wish to consult the following as supplements dealing with world climatic regions: P. James and H. V. B. Kline, Jr., *Geography of Man* (New York: Ginn and Company, 1959); G. T. Trewartha *et al.*, *Elements of Geography: Physical and Cultural* (New York: McGraw Hill, 1957); C. Langdon White and G. T. Renner, *College Geography* (New York: Appleton-Century-Crofts, 1957). In addition, since no textbook can include the many economic maps the student should consult, the authors strongly recommend that every student obtain a copy of *The Shorter Oxford Economic Atlas of the World* (2nd ed.; New York: Oxford University Press, 1959); this book is available in an inexpensive paperback edition.

Bold-face items in the text indicate that the item is defined in the glossary at the back of the book. We believe that this is the first economic-geography text containing such a glossary.

Finally, the authors have not hesitated, when justified, to include materials not strictly economic and not strictly geographic. Our principal aim has been to educate young minds—to teach students *how to think* and to enable them better to appreciate the world they are living in and their own place in it.

ACKNOWLEDGMENTS

In writing on a subject of such broad scope, the authors have necessarily drawn upon the works of many economic geographers, past and present, and on every continent—particularly the notable and original contributions of J. Russell Smith, professor emeritus of geography, Graduate School of Business, Columbia University; and of the late O. E. Baker of the U.S. Department of Agriculture, professor emeritus of geography, University of Maryland.

It is impossible to express more than a general appreciation to hundreds of geographers. Grateful acknowledgment is made to Lise Hofmann, of Stanford University, who has contributed to the book far more than these few words can indicate. Our deep appreciation is extended also to Stephen Jurika for his critical reading of Chapter 3, "Petroleum and Natural Gas," and of Chapter 7, "Nonferrous Metals"; to Alfred Fingulin, a former editor of *Steel*, for his critical reading of Chapter 10, "The Iron and Steel Industry"; to John H. Hindle, of Fairleigh Dickinson University, for suggesting the inclusion of a glossary; to Lionel A. Walford, U.S. Fish and Wildlife Service, who searched long and hard to supply the photographs for the chapter on fishing, and to the countless other persons and organizations who supplied outstanding photographs; to Jack Blok, who drafted most of the maps; and, finally, to the staff of the Wadsworth Publishing Company for their assistance and enthusiastic and friendly cooperation.

C. Langdon White
Paul F. Griffin
Tom L. McKnight

CONTENTS

PART ONE::

INTRODUCTION

CHAPTER ONE::

As far as is known, man has been on this earth for about a million years. During this time, he has become the dominant form among all land animals, primarily because he alone is endowed with the power of conceptual thought. Because primitive man was a thinking animal, he was able to do two very important things: he could alter his natural environment, up to a point; and he could adjust his own way of life to the natural environment. After many generations in his primitive state, he overcame certain obstacles to his progress and could improve his way of living. As a pastoralist, he found he could live better than as a hunter; and, as a farmer, he could live better than as a pastoralist. But his most rapid advancement came when he substituted on a large scale inanimate energy for that of his own and of his animals' muscles (see pp. 17–18). Without a doubt man's greatest resource has been his own resourcefulness.

MAN IN THIS

About 1831 the number of human beings on earth had reached the one-billion mark; by 1961 this figure had skyrocketed to approximately 3 billion. Thus, in 130 years mankind trebled its numbers. This phenomenal growth resulted from a combination of circumstances:

1. Marked progress in the conquest of disease, greater life expectancy at birth, and a worldwide drop in the death rate—a decline of more than 25 per cent in most countries and as much as 50 per cent in some.

2. Remarkable advance in the science and technology of agriculture, involving (a) plant and animal breeding; (b) ability of crops to expand deeper into the cold, dry, high, and hot humid lands; (c) wider use of insecticides and fungicides (Fig. 1-1); and (d) greater employment of commercial fertilizers.

3. Wider utilization of energy from fossil fuels, with more universal adoption of labor-saving equipment and development of transportation to all parts of the globe.

4. Rapid and wide expansion of the world's arable area.

5. Notable extension in general education.

6. Increased use of minerals.

7. Impact of industrialization and urbanization.

DISTRIBUTION OF POPULATION

Figure 1-2 and Table 1-1 show where the world's people are and where they are not. To explain these patterns is the most important task of the economic geographer; for human interests have meaning only as they are projected against the encompassing background of population and its growth. Figure 1-3 re-

ECONOMIC WORLD

Fig. 1-1. Swarming locusts plaguing man with the plow. Even before Old Testament days, the desert locusts ravaged sections of Asia, the Middle East, and Africa, stripping the earth of everything green when they paused. Only recently have coordinated control methods been inaugurated in countries with breeding grounds. The United Nations plans complete extermination of the locust. (Courtesy of United Nations.)

veals that about one fifth of the earth's land surface is too cold to permit effective settlement; another fifth is too dry; still another fifth is too rugged or too high; and a tenth is too infertile.

SPARSELY POPULATED REGIONS

With the exception of parts of South America and Inner Asia, sparsely populated regions occur in the so-called **restrictive environments.** In these environments there are such

serious obstacles to any notable increase in population that, by and large, man presently has only outposts in such places.

HIGH MOUNTAINS

Rugged surface, shallow stony soils, restricted flat land, and inhospitable climate (at the highest elevations) limit population to very small numbers in mountains everywhere on earth—except in the tropics, where elevation may furnish a truly "temperate" climate.

TABLE 1-1

WORLD POPULATION 1700-1960

(in millions)

	1700	1750	1800	1850	1900	1950	1960
Anglo-America	1	2	6	26	81	165	203
Middle America	6	5	10	13	25	51	63
South America	6	6	9	20	38	111	140
Europe (excluding Soviet Union)	106	117	156	214	303	392	422
Asia	362	438	547	793	973	1,330	1,618
Soviet Union	17	27	37	60	126	201	215
Africa	98	95	90	95	120	198	217
Oceania	2	2	2	2	6	13	15
World	596	691	857	1,223	1,672	2,461	2,893

SOURCES: *United Nations Demographic Yearbook; Encyclopaedia Britannica;* and others.

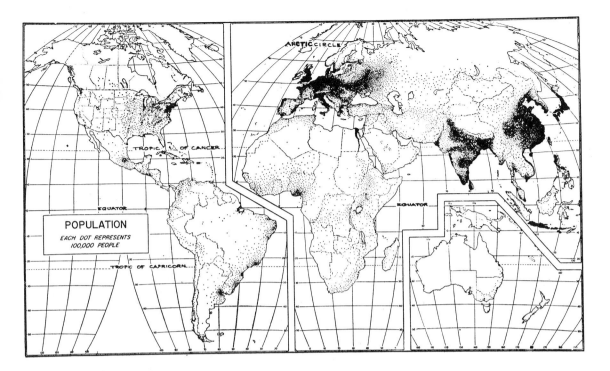

Fig. 1-2. Distribution of world population. The world's 3 billion people occupy less than half the earth's land surface. The lands of densest population all are in the Northern Hemisphere. Note the three major centers: the intensively cultivated agricultural lands of Eastern and Southern Asia, and the highly developed industrialized Western Europe and eastern Anglo-America. (Courtesy of U.S. Department of Agriculture.)

The farther man goes from the equator, however, the more inhospitable high mountains become as a permanent habitat, and in high latitudes they are wholly unoccupied.

DESERTS

The world's deserts rank among the most sparsely populated of all lands. Only a fraction of most deserts is under cultivation—a situation that promises to persist for the most part, since there is little water available. In most deserts the small numbers of people are pastoral nomads, ever on the move in search of feed and water for their animals. Mining camps with small numbers of people also exist here and there. Finally, in some areas (for example, in Egypt) irrigated oases may sustain many persons per acre or square mile and a large over-all population; but they constitute mere dots in the vast dry wildernesses.

ICE CAPS

Antarctica, most of Greenland, and some smaller ice-covered areas have no permanent inhabitants. Since Antarctica is the coldest place on earth and almost entirely covered with ice and snow, it is difficult to see any economic basis for settlement ever.

TUNDRAS

Tundras cover millions of square miles in the Arctic, but human numbers there are small. Agriculture is largely ruled out by the short growing season, the infertile soils, and the terrible isolation. **Permafrost** and poor drainage also present problems. No doubt the growing of crops will reach slightly into the tundras, but how far will depend on the results of future research and national politics. In all probability, only hardy and quick-ripening crops will succeed there. For the most part,

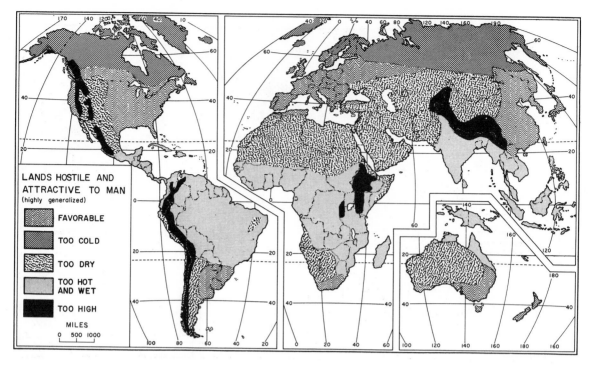

Fig. 1-3. The world's land areas—those that are attractive to man and those that are hostile to him.

man in the tundras either is a hunter and fisher (the Eskimo) or a pastoralist (the Lapp). Since each hunter in the tundras requires from 70 to 200 square miles to sustain him, it is not surprising (as Figure 1-3 shows) that the tundras are largely devoid of human beings.

WET TROPICAL LOWLANDS

In many of these lands (for instance, the Amazon Basin), man has not yet learned how to cope with the environment properly. Consequently—because of disease, enervating climate, poor water supply, infertile soils, dense forest cover, poverty, dearth of implements, lack of incentive, and reluctance to change customs—a sparsity of native peoples over sizable areas of the wet tropics persists. The white man, too, has been generally unsuccessful in hot, rainy lands. Such lands are too hot and humid for comfort and progress, and many of the same obstacles that impede the native population are applicable to the white popula-

tion. Moreover, Caucasians generally prefer a cool climate to a hot one.

DENSELY POPULATED REGIONS

The four principal regions of dense population on earth are (1) central and eastern China, peninsular Korea, and insular Japan; (2) the Indian subcontinent (India and Pakistan); (3) Western, Central, and Eastern Europe—from the Atlantic Ocean in a narrowing wedge extending into the Ukraine; and (4) southeastern Canada and northeastern United States. These four regions, with only one tenth of the land surface of the globe, sustain two thirds of the earth's people.

ORIENTAL REGIONS

About one half of the world's people inhabit Southern and Eastern (monsoon) Asia; and by the year 2000 the continent of Asia is expected to have 60 per cent of the world's population.

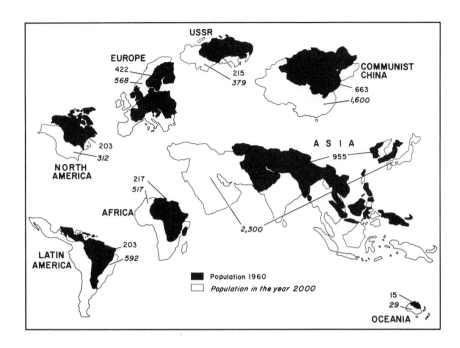

Fig. 1-4. World population in 1960, and projected population for the year 2000. (Figures represent millions of people.) The size of the areas is proportional to the estimated populations, based on the estimated average rates of population increases. Note that the major population growth is befalling the very countries that can afford it least—the ones that are economically underdeveloped. (Map modified from one made by Hugh Moore Fund.)

The majority of these people are rural dwellers and are engaged in agriculture. Only in Japan is a really appreciable part of the population occupied with manufacturing and trade. The problem of feeding this enormous population, as will be shown, is acute.

OCCIDENTAL REGIONS

Western and Central Europe and eastern Anglo-America are also densely settled. Both manufacturing and agriculture are important. But whereas most farmers in the Orient are of the subsistence type, those in the West are engaged largely in commercial agriculture. In Europe the farms, which are considerably larger than those in the Orient, are in turn much smaller than those in the United States and Canada. It is in the large, numerous, and populous cities and their environs, however, that more than three fourths of the inhabitants of the Occidental regions dwell.

THE POPULATION EXPLOSION

Mainly because of declines in infant mortality and in the death rate, world population is increasing at an unprecedented rate—about 95 persons per minute, 140,000 each day, and more than 50 million a year. At the present rate of increase, the earth is expected to have about 6 billion persons by the year 2000 (Fig. 1-4). Unfortunately, some of the poorest countries (for instance, China and India) head the list in the over-all increase, though not in percentage increase per annum.

The population explosion, however, is not confined solely to underdeveloped nations. Some developed lands also are involved. Thus the United States in 1963 had a population approaching 190 million—29 million more than it had a decade before. The explosion means a net increase of one person every ten seconds. Such rapid growth inevitably means more crowding, frustration, and regimentation for the more fortunate countries; for underdeveloped peoples it can portend only increasing poverty and malnutrition.

FOOD PRODUCTION AND POPULATION

The population explosion would be less serious if all people could enjoy a satisfactory diet (quantity and quality), a reasonable life expectancy at birth, good health, and some amenities of life. The stark facts are, however, that about two of every three people on earth go to bed hungry each night, that the overwhelming majority of mankind seldom gets a "square meal," and that the future holds little promise for the majority as long as numbers soar and incessant poverty prevails.

The majority of students of population and agriculture believe that in the race between a growing population and the food supply, the former will win. Geographers particularly point out that, as far as commercial agricultural development is concerned, the surface of the globe is limited. They declare that only about 10 per cent of the earth's surface is highly suitable for farming. Although science and technology will undoubtedly raise this percentage, the world map of land cultivation (Fig. 1-5), in its main features, is established for many decades—if not centuries—to come. Moreover, man himself is responsible for an annual loss of millions of acres of productive land through overgrazing, soil erosion, soil depletion, careless logging and waterlogging of soils, and through expansion of cities and suburbs, airports, highways, parks, golf courses,

and industries. This loss is about equal to what man adds to the arable area annually.

Is the world capable of providing satisfactory diets for the 3 billion persons living today and for the billions soon to be added? One agricultural economist, Colin Clark, points out that the Dutch, who are the best farmers in Europe, produce a very good and varied diet on the equivalent of two thirds of an acre of land per person; he believes that if all land suitable for agriculture throughout the world were equally well cultivated (assuming also that the entire world would eat as well as the most prosperous countries do now), provision could be made for 28 billion people, or almost ten times the 1960 population. Furthermore, according to Clark, if the Japanese standards of cultivation and of diet (best in Asia) are used, the world could provide for three or four times as many again.[1] Another agricultural economist, S. E. Johnson, says that for the first time in history it is physically possible to provide adequate food for all the world's people. His remedy is improved technology.[2] These are challenging ideas.

However, the authors are less optimistic. It should never be forgotten that only in the thirty industrialized nations of the Northern Hemisphere plus Australia, New Zealand, and Argentina in the Southern Hemisphere is there an assured permanent food supply. These are the countries that presently have the science, technology, financial resources, management, ability, and national vigor to meet requirements. Even if we accept the thesis that it is physically possible to provide food supplies for the inhabitants of the underdeveloped countries, this will not happen automatically. In all these lands there are shortages of management, technical skills, and capital. To satisfy the desired nutritional standards for the people of Southern Asia alone for a single year in the 1960s would have required about 29 million tons of wheat over and above the amount from domestic production and imports. To produce

[1] Colin Clark, "Do Population and Freedom Grow Together?" *Fortune*, 62:137, December 1960.
[2] Sherman E. Johnson, "The Agricultural Paradox," *Foreign Agriculture*, 25:14, November 1961.

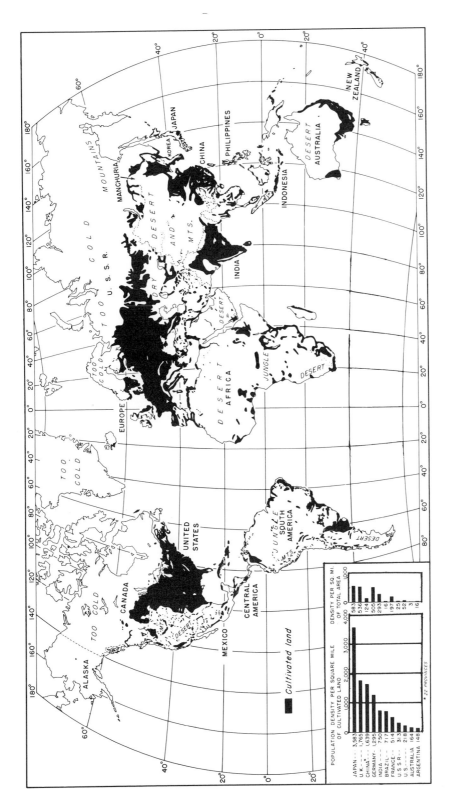

Fig. 1-5. *The world's cultivated area. Actually, the area on which man grows his crops is surprisingly small—only 8 per cent of the total land surface of the globe. About two thirds of this land lies in the so-called "temperate zone," the remainder in the tropics. Some authorities insist that 12 per cent more could be farmed—a total of 20 per cent, nearly half of which would be in the tropics. Note particularly how well this map and that of world population coincide when one is superimposed on the other. (Courtesy of Office of Foreign Agricultural Relations.)*

this tonnage would have required 3 million tons of chemical fertilizer; and to build the plants to produce it would have cost 1.65 billion dollars. There is also the problem of getting farm people to adopt new ways of farming—to break with tradition—a difficult and slow task at best. Moreover, no major industrial development or emigration ever has relieved the population pressures on food supply in that part of the world.

It is thus apparent that food shortages in Asia will be overcome only by higher farm outputs, which can be secured only by (1) vast capital investment, (2) country-wide education, (3) more scientific farming methods, (4) improved transport systems, (5) replacement of subsistence farming by commercial farming, and (6) higher per capita income. These are difficult goals for underdeveloped, rapidly growing lands to meet, even with foreign aid. It appears to be a truism that rapid population growth, at least in the underdeveloped lands, will continue to cause hunger, poverty, and misery for hundreds of millions of people.

AGRICULTURE IN DEVELOPED AND UNDERDEVELOPED COUNTRIES

We have seen that most countries cannot produce enough food for their own populations. The United States, Argentina, Canada, and Australia are exceptions; they not only produce enough food for domestic demand but have enormous surpluses for export. It is they who contribute most of the imported food to the hungry peoples of Eastern and Southern Asia, the Middle East, and large parts of Latin America.

A DEVELOPED COUNTRY: THE UNITED STATES

In 1860, one American farmer could raise enough food for himself and four other persons; some 100 years later, he could feed himself and twenty-five others. Moreover, whereas in 1860 nine out of every ten Americans were rural and agricultural, today only one in each

eight lives on a farm. Only about 8 per cent of the total labor force is engaged in agriculture. And yet the American people have never eaten so well. How is this possible? Machines utilizing petroleum are the farm producers today. Through machines (in addition to chemical fertilizers, weed killers, pesticides, hybrid seeds, and feed supplements) the farm output per hour of human labor has doubled since 1937. However, farm equipment is costly —the investment presently being about 12 billion dollars. In order to purchase it, the farmer must keep it employed; and thus the American farm has increased in size. Simultaneously, the farm population, the number of farms, and farm employment have declined (Fig. 1-6).

AN UNDERDEVELOPED COUNTRY: EGYPT

Unlike the United States, underdeveloped Egypt is primarily an agricultural nation despite the fact that it is overurbanized; 70 per cent of the working population is engaged in agriculture. In trying to comprehend the picture in Egypt, we should first of all realize that Egypt really is not the large area depicted on the political map, but rather the valley and delta of the Nile. In this area of 347 million acres, less than 3 per cent is used for agriculture, 97 per cent of the total area being unproductive desert. Yet about 85 per cent of the Nile's water flows wasted into the Mediterranean Sea.

On this riverine area dwell approximately 27 million people—more than 1,800 per square mile—one of the highest population densities in the world. What is more, this population is increasing at the rate of about 600,000 persons (3 per cent) per annum—again, one of the fastest rates in the world. This rapid population growth has taken place over the past century and a half; however, since Egypt is poor in minerals and other raw materials for industrialization, the economy has been unable to expand its nonagricultural sector proportionately.

Threatening soil exhaustion has been met by much use of commercial fertilizers and waterlogging by drainage and pumping. The

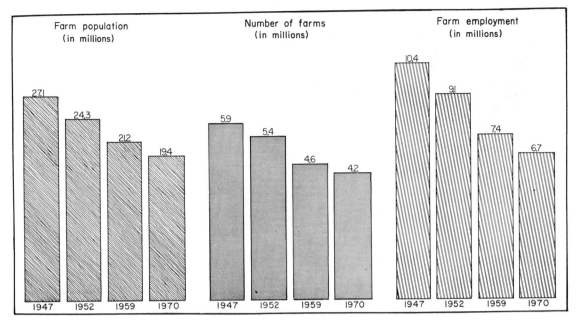

Farm population (in millions)

Farm employment (in millions)

Number of farms (in millions)

1947	27.1
1952	24.3
1959	21.2
1970	19.4

1947	5.9
1952	5.4
1959	4.6
1970	4.2

1947	10.4
1952	9.1
1959	7.4
1970	6.7

Fig. 1-6. The changing face of the United States. In just twelve years (1947–1959), the number of farms dropped from 5.9 million to 4.6 million. Figures have been projected to 1970 on bases of recent trends. Agriculture is today relatively less important than manufacturing. (Courtesy of U.S. Department of Agriculture and U.S. Department of Commerce.)

delta marshes have been reclaimed and sown mainly to rice. Fortunately, the fertile river soil, the ideal agricultural climate, and controlled irrigation give Egypt high per-acre yields. Moreover, double and even triple cropping of the same piece of land (all-year cropping) prevails. This brings the harvested area up to about 9.5 million acres.

Unfortunately, the irrigable area cannot be expanded except at a cost far beyond Egypt's financial resources. However, construction of the Aswan High Dam 430 miles south of Cairo is under way. It is estimated that the dam will permit an additional 100,000 acres a year to be put under cultivation over a twenty-year period.

Will it do for the Egyptian standard of living what the people expect it will? Probably not. For by the time the dam is completed, the rapidly growing population will have radically increased the demand on the food supply. Because of the restricted irrigable area, poverty of industrial raw materials, and the great popu-

lation pressure, the **fellah's** level of living is one of the lowest in the world.

DEVELOPED AND UNDERDEVELOPED LANDS: CONTRAST, CONFLICT, AND COMPETITION

In the present world, the developed countries are the haves, the underdeveloped countries the have-nots (Fig. 1-7). The student is quite well informed about the developed lands but often knows little about the underdeveloped ones—that is, those countries that have not reached the level of economic development characterizing Northwest Europe and Anglo-America. In these underdeveloped countries most of the inhabitants live under conditions approaching misery, and there is chronic mass poverty that is not the result of a temporary calamity; the people are poor be-

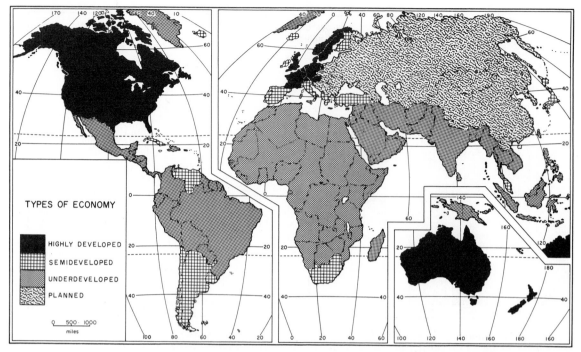

Fig. 1-7. Types of economy over the earth. The level of living between the peoples in the highly developed and the underdeveloped countries is worlds apart. Those within developed lands generally get enough of the right kind of food for health and energy. The big problem in every underdeveloped country is the race between people and food. The gap between the economies of the highly developed and the underdeveloped countries is currently widening, not narrowing.

cause their lands contain so little capable of being developed; well over half the gainfully employed males are engaged in farming, hunting, and forest gathering; the inhabitants employ backward and obsolete methods of production and utilize little inanimate power; the lands are overpopulated with respect to the resources available, the amount of arable land, and the raw materials for industry; there is a high ratio of agriculture to other forms of employment, but the diet on all counts is inadequate; the social system often is static and rigid; disease is rampant, life expectancy is short, and illiteracy is commonplace.

The underdeveloped lands are exceedingly important: they possess 50 per cent of the world's land surface and 46 per cent of the world's population (exclusive of the countries in the Communist bloc), as well as a disproportionate share of the world's minerals and the bulk of the tropical products.

They are, however, problem areas. Most of their people live in poverty, illness, and ignorance. Since they hold in their hands the future balance of world power, they are being courted by both the Free World and the Communist bloc.

Underdeveloped peoples believe their weakness and poverty stem from their overdependence on agriculture (Fig. 1-8) and from specialization in basic enterprises (raw materials), which were long owned and worked by foreigners and still are in many countries. They have come to regard industrialization as the magic wand that can and must raise the productivity of their labor. Industrialization will also, they believe, enhance national prestige. They have come to associate agrarianism with debasement, and industrialism with progress and a high level of living. In short, they have come to regard industrialization as the principal path they must follow if they are to

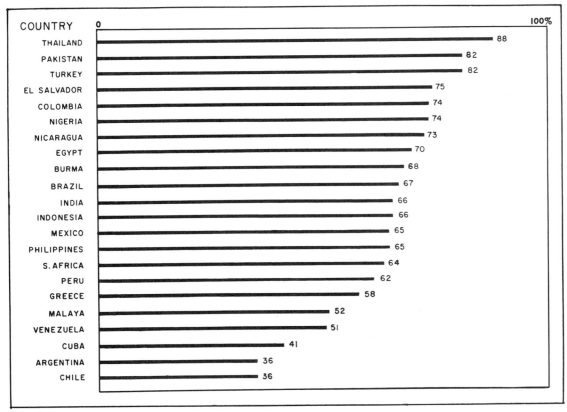

Fig 1-8. *Percentage of the total population engaged in agriculture in selected countries (countries where farming is the predominant occupation). Paradoxically, the peoples of many of these lands, though preponderantly engaged in production of food, are increasingly being compelled to "tighten their belts" still more. (After graph in* Focus, *published by the American Geographical Society.)*

emerge from economic and social backwardness. But is industrialization by itself the panacea? Many persons prominent in education, politics, and economics argue that it is. On the other hand, more and more people are beginning to suspect that too many underdeveloped countries are building walls and roofs to their economic structures without laying solid foundations—that industrialization alone is not sufficient; that a nation's well-being results from the contribution of many kinds of economic enterprises.

Moreover, such nations cannot readily industrialize because they have major deficiencies in capital, transportation, skilled labor, technological know-how, purchasing power of the population (wages are invariably low), and sometimes in resources—particularly fuel

and power. These many weaknesses often are augmented by a complex of inhibiting cultural factors (such as dietary taboos) and by a general unwillingness of local capital to invest in industrial enterprises, although changes are occurring in this respect.

The developed countries are on the whole firmly settled in a pattern of continuing economic progress. Among the poorer of the underdeveloped countries, economic progress is much slower. Some nations are even losing ground if per capita income and daily caloric intake are the test. Actually, the economic inequalities between developed and underdeveloped countries appear to be widening.

The underdeveloped countries positively cannot raise themselves by their own bootstraps. With an average per capita income of

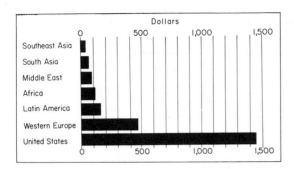

Fig. 1-9. Annual per capita income for different parts of the earth. Income per person averages less than $150 in underdeveloped areas; in many it falls as low as $50.

only $150 (United States dollars) per year, they simply cannot generate sufficient savings to provide needed capital equipment (Fig. 1-9). They must have help. Aid can come from two sources: the Free World—particularly the United States but also the countries of Western Europe, Canada, Australia, New Zealand, and Japan; and the Communist bloc—largely the Soviet Union but also Czechoslovakia and China.

The capital requirements for most industries are high. It is estimated that in the United States, $12,000 of capital are required to employ each factory operative. In the iron and steel industry the figure is very high—$90,000 for tools for each of the 5,000 production workers at the Fairless Works of the United States Steel Corporation when the plant opened in 1952. And the Bethlehem Steel Corporation in 1959 declared that from an over-all standpoint the company had more than $27,-000 invested for every employee.

Finally, the basic difference between developed and underdeveloped lands is that in the first the people have harnessed modern science; and in the final analysis it is science that enables people to grow more food, manufacture more products, use more inanimate energy, and have more leisure time.

NATIONALISM

Nationalism is the determination of peoples the world over to preserve their independence—to be absolutely free of foreign political and economic dominance. This profound sentiment is today probably more intense than ever before and is applicable to approximately three fourths of the globe. All underdeveloped countries, for example, are highly nationalistic; over considerable periods in the past, nearly all were ruled politically by some outside power. Hence nationalism serves as an outlet for long-pent-up feelings of humiliation and resentment. It reflects envy, suspicion, and fear of the wealth, power, and influence of the developed countries—particularly the United States, though also Great Britain, France, and other so-called colonial powers. In some parts of the world, as in Latin America, the word "nationalism" means anti-Yankeeism.

A specific example of nationalism will clarify the matter and show how it sometimes operates. Brazil, the largest nation in Latin America as well as the most populous, is undoubtedly the richest in natural resources and appears to have the brightest future. Yet today Brazil is in a very poor condition financially, mainly because she depends too strongly upon imported petroleum products; Brazil uses fully a third (250 to 300 million dollars annually) of her badly needed foreign exchange for such purchases. Perhaps Brazil has large reserves of petroleum, but her highly nationalistic laws will not allow foreigners to explore for oil. In short, the industry is nationalized by a control board called *Petrobrás*. This situation would be less serious if Brazil had the investment capital, the technological know-how, and the transport facilities to proceed independently, and if she were not constantly seeking loans. In this instance Brazil must be regarded as an excellent demonstration of how to be poor in the midst of plenty. Since only large corporations with ample financial resources and skill can engage in this hazardous enterprise, Brazil probably will be unable to supply her own market with oil as long as this nationalistic law remains in force.

Nationalism and politics often force foreign governments to ask for ever higher shares of company earnings, irrespective of the economic facts of life. This is the situation over most of the rich Middle East oil region and in

Venezuela (which today gets about 69 per cent of the total oil-company profits).

Some underdeveloped countries are so nationalistic that they want to curtail the exportation of such raw materials as natural rubber, bauxite, iron ore, petroleum, sulfur, or copper —thereby forcing foreign or domestic interests, or a combination of the two, to manufacture them within the producing country. Yet frequently these nations may be far from the stage where their products can compete in world markets.

MONOCULTURE

Many underdeveloped countries throughout the world, but particularly in Latin America, suffer from monoculture—dependence on a single export produced and sold according to the dictates of an external and often erratic market. Examples are Cuba—sugar, Colombia and Brazil—coffee, Chile—copper, Bolivia— tin, and Venezuela—petroleum.

When all the lands included in what today is known as Latin America were colonies, the mother countries were interested in them as sources of industrial raw materials and exotic foods and as markets for manufactured products. For many years all were forbidden to engage in manufacturing. The essentials of the system continued even after the nations gained their independence. Even today, the economies in most are subject in considerable measure to external domination and control, since they are primarily producers and exporters of raw materials and foodstuffs and importers of manufactured products. Obviously, they are vulnerable to changing international economic conditions.

FREE WORLD AND COMMUNIST COMPETITION

There is intense competition between the Free World and the Communist bloc of nations to win the allegiance, or even the neutrality, of the uncommitted nations, which are mostly the underdeveloped ones. About one third of the world's people are to be found in the Free World, another third in the Communist bloc, and still another third in the so-called neutral bloc. Since most of the uncommitted peoples dwell in South and Southeast Asia, this is the part of the world where the competition is keenest. India particularly is the target.

The Free World is infinitely wealthier than the Communist bloc (Fig. 1-10). With 10 per cent of the world population, it possibly possesses 80 per cent of the wealth. In 1960 about 4 billion dollars went to underdeveloped lands from the United States and nine other capital-exporting countries, compared with about 1 billion dollars from the Sino-Soviet bloc.

FOREIGN AID TO UNDERDEVELOPED LANDS

It has been pointed out that the basic problem in the world economic picture is the population explosion. Particularly is this true wherever there are too many people with respect to the natural-resources base; for this situation breeds poverty, poverty breeds hunger, and hunger breeds trouble. Every underdeveloped country on the globe needs capital for basic economic facilities—railways, highways, telecommunications, electric power, port works.

The United States government has tried to help the underdeveloped countries raise their levels of living. It has distributed billions of dollars through gifts and loans; yet there are more hungry people in the world today than when the program began. Significantly, the program has not made friends for the United States in many of the countries it has aided. Despite the billions dispersed in what Sir Winston Churchill called the greatest manifestation of national generosity in human history, the masses in the underdeveloped countries appear to know less and less about American institutions, national ideals, and underlying policies. Even the president of the World Bank has admitted publicly that economic assistance has been marred because in too many instances aid has been given too hastily, for the wrong motives or the wrong objects; and that in extreme cases, the aid was so poorly conceived that, instead of improving the economies of the receiving countries, it actually added to their already heavy burdens.

Lavish handouts are thus no passport to

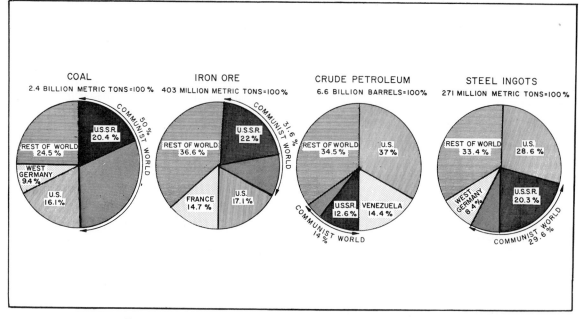

Fig. 1-10. *Free World vs. Communist bloc in crude oil, coal, iron ore, and steel ingots—the yardsticks of industrial and political power. The Communist bloc still is far behind the Free World in most of these sinews of power—coal being the exception. (After Elmer W. Pehrson.)*

friendship. In fact, aid has on occasion even aroused bitterness and outright enmity. In most instances, loans would be more satisfactory than grants. However, most underdeveloped countries do not offer attractive investment climates to private foreign investors. Moreover, such investment often is hedged in by legal and administrative restrictions, by nationalistic hostility, and by a number of risks —foreign-exchange problems, threats of expropriation that at times become confiscation, constantly increasing taxes, and demands for a larger share of the profits. Public loans in underdeveloped countries also face numerous other obstacles, including often an extended family system with its drain on resources, stifling of personal initiative, and certain systems of land tenure which inhibit saving and investment.

Unless there is the will to pursue sound policies within a country itself, outside aid, no matter how generous, can avail little. In short, there is no way to help those who will not help themselves. Yet the underdeveloped lands must be helped. No longer are the swarming peoples of Asia, Africa, and Latin America sunk, as in past centuries, in a passive acceptance of their lot. Some economists estimate that the needs of the underdeveloped countries will rise to 20 or 30 billion dollars a year during the next two decades, plus transfers of commodities—food, fertilizers, and manufactured goods—equivalent to another 20 to 30 billion dollars. These lands by themselves could not possibly raise more than 85 per cent of this amount from the sale of their own goods on the world market.

MAN'S USE OF MINERALS

That man's present economic progress depends upon his mineral heritage is general knowledge. From the Stone Age, through the Bronze, the Iron, and the Coal ages, to the Age of Light Metals, man has entered into a period of widespread use of *all* minerals. Because of the technological developments of the present century, it has been called the Electrical Age, the Age of Energy, the Chemical Age, the Aluminum Age, and the Atomic Age. *What is important is that each of these terms refers to the use of minerals.*

Although man has made greatest use of minerals since the Industrial Revolution, the past sixty-odd years have witnessed the most intense exploitation. The United States today consumes between 35 and 40 per cent of the Free World's output of basic minerals. No nation can draw so heavily on irreplaceable resources without ultimately using up many of them. Thus, the formerly abundant resources of the country have been much depleted by a century of rapid industrial expansion and the demands of two world wars. By 1960 the United States was self-supporting in only six of the fifteen basic minerals—coal, petroleum, iron ore, phosphate rock, potash, and sulfur. But even in these six, substantial imports were being made in petroleum and iron ore. This transition from a position of virtual self-sufficiency in minerals to that of the world's chief importer must be regarded as a major event in modern economic history.

The outlook for the nation would be grim if it had to depend exclusively upon its own mineral resources. Fortunately, the underdeveloped nations possess vast reserves, many of which still await development. The big question here, however, is political, not geological, geographical, or economic. In short, will the laws of the producing countries provide a favorable climate for the inflow of capital, equipment, technological know-how, and management skills?

MAN'S USE OF ENERGY

When ancient man wanted work done, he had to do it himself—utilizing his own muscles. Later he domesticated animals and still later enslaved human beings taken in armed conquest. Many of the high civilizations of the Near East and the Far East, as well as those of the New World, rested upon a pedestal of human slavery.

Even in the twentieth-century world in most underdeveloped lands, human muscle still out-performs the work done by inanimate energy. The developed parts of the world, however, are wholly different.

Man in developed countries harnesses and utilizes energy, the United States leading the world in this respect: with about 6 per cent of the world's population, it produces and consumes about 40 per cent of the world's mechanical energy. More than 90 per cent of all the work in the United States is accomplished with mechanical means. It is estimated that each American on the average uses about 3,400 kilowatt hours of electricity annually; *each has at his bidding twenty-four hours each day about 210 mechanical slaves.* Factory employees in the United States have at their command machinery with energy equivalent to 244 times their own muscle power, which is only $\frac{1}{20}$ horsepower.

Energy is extremely important in the economic life of the United States. This nation consumes almost 40 per cent of the world's oil production, 25 per cent of the coal production, and nearly 30 per cent of the harnessed water power; between 1940 and 1950 consumption of energy increased by 50 per cent, and by 1960 the nation consumed 25 per cent more than in 1950. Many competent scientists estimate that the world sources of the fossil fuels will be exhausted in the foreseeable future. Electric-power consumption is expected to double each fifty years during the next century. However, three major factors will determine energy use in the future: (1) the rate of increase in population, (2) the rate of improvement in per capita real income, and (3) progress in efficient utilization of energy. Energy requirements are apt to increase in the underdeveloped countries in the future.

Water power will be available for use as long as the sun continues to radiate energy. Yet a mere 17 per cent of the potential water-power resources of the world are developed. Even if all the world's streams could be put to most efficient use, which seems unlikely, the energy would satisfy only 3 to 15 per cent of the total energy requirements a century hence.

In the mind of the average man, the magic wand for meeting the power needs of the world's fast-increasing population is atomic energy, derived from uranium and thorium.

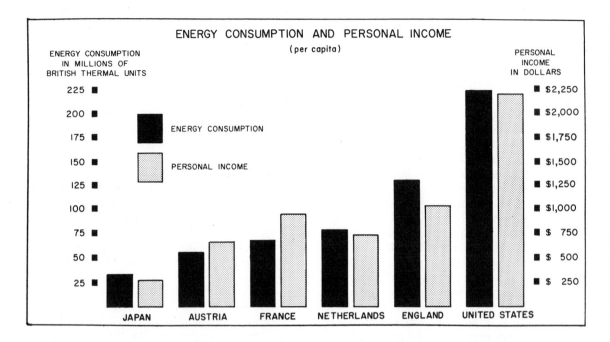

ENERGY CONSUMPTION AND PERSONAL INCOME
(per capita)

ENERGY CONSUMPTION IN MILLIONS OF BRITISH THERMAL UNITS

PERSONAL INCOME IN DOLLARS

■ ENERGY CONSUMPTION
□ PERSONAL INCOME

JAPAN   AUSTRIA   FRANCE   NETHERLANDS   ENGLAND   UNITED STATES

Fig. 1-11. Energy consumption and income for selected developed countries. (Courtesy of El Paso Natural Gas Company.)

The extent to which such power will be used, however, will depend on the relative cost and other advantages of nuclear power as compared with other means of producing electricity. Many technical difficulties lie athwart the path of economical utilization of atomic energy. If man can solve these problems, atomic power would be of inestimable value to the majority of the fuel-starved underdeveloped lands.

There is also the energy of the sun—energy that is available over the entire earth. However, sun power is potentially less useful in the lands with long, dark, polar winters and cloudy and foggy climates than in the dry, sunny ones. The amount of solar energy striking the land areas of the earth is far in excess of the amount needed to meet the energy needs of the world's population. The great handicap in utilizing it is the low intensity of this energy. However, the population explosion—particularly in the underdeveloped countries, which are largely without fuel; the determination of these lands to share in the better life; and the eventual exhaustion of the fossil fuels and ura-

nium are resulting in increased and intense research in the field of solar power.

A close relationship exists over the globe between energy and economic progress. Figure 1-11 shows that the United States and a number of other developed countries rank very high in energy consumption and in income per capita. In general, it may be said that developed countries rank high in both, underdeveloped ones very low.

OUR INTERDEPENDENT WORLD AND INTERNATIONAL TRADE

Not a single country on earth is or can be self-sustaining if it enjoys a high standard of living. From ancient times the leading nations —Phoenicia, Carthage, Greece; Spain, Portugal, Holland; Great Britain, Germany, the United States, Japan—have been great traders; and the two "heavyweight" powers today— the United States and the Soviet Union—must import scores of items, many of which are completely lacking inside their own boundaries. Almost half the trade of the United States is with underdeveloped countries, as is almost 70 per cent of Western Europe's. The unequal distribution of mineral wealth accounts for the large international trade in mineral raw materials.

Today the United States is the world's premier trading nation. In a recent year the total value of goods and services bought and sold by the United States was almost 47 billion dollars. The notion has prevailed for decades among a large segment of the American people that a country as rich in natural resources as the United States can support itself strictly from its own reserves of raw materials—that imports are unnecessary. Nothing could be further from the truth or potentially more dangerous. Although the United States accounts for almost half the world's heavy-industry output, it mines only a third of the world production of the fifteen basic minerals. In just two decades the United States shifted from virtual self-sufficiency in copper, lead, zinc, iron ore, and petroleum to very considerable dependence on foreign sources. The importation of products is not solely the result of the presence or absence of given commodities within countries; of very great importance, too, is the function of relative costs.

WESTERN EUROPE—AN EXAMPLE OF ECONOMIC STRENGTH

A common desire for a more secure economic future has prompted thirteen nations of Western Europe to form two regional economic groups: the "Inner Six" (European Common Market), created in 1957; and the "Outer Seven" (European Free Trade Association), created in 1959 to counter the effects of the unification of the Six. Within each group, tariffs and other trade barriers gradually were removed in order to stimulate more trade and mutual economic growth. By widening markets and increasing competition, the move toward freer trade within each group resulted in more efficient use of resources— each country concentrating on those goods that it could produce most economically.

Such strong trade areas, of course, meant more intense competition between the two groups and between foreign nations (particularly the United States) and both groups. Compared with the United States, the Six and the Seven in 1959 together had a 173 per cent greater trade volume: total United States international trade, exports and imports, amounted to 31.5 billion dollars; that for the Six, 49.5 billion dollars; and that for the Seven, 36.4 billion dollars.

The Common Market (often referred to as the European Economic Community) has become one of the fastest-growing economic units in the world. In 1960 its gross national product soared some 7 per cent, compared with the United States' 4½ per cent. It had become the world's largest importer of all types of goods and the second largest exporter of manufactured goods.

The rather spectacular success of the E.E.C. has prompted other nations, particularly those of the European Free Trade Association, to apply for membership. The most conspicuous of the recent applicants has been Great Britain; but by the middle of 1963, Ireland, Denmark, and Norway also had applied for full membership; Sweden, Switzerland, Austria, Spain, Turkey, and Cyprus had applied for associate membership; and Greece had been accepted as an associate member (Fig. 1-12). In addition, some eighteen "new" nations in Africa, most of them former colonies of France, are associated with the E.E.C.

The E.E.C. has made it clear that it will consider all applicants open-mindedly, but it is a truism of international political economy that major changes occur slowly and often with considerable difficulty. If Britain were to be accepted for membership, for example, it would mean disruption of many trading relationships between the United Kingdom and other nations of the Commonwealth. Consequently, Britain has attempted to secure certain concessions from the E.E.C. to soften the impact of this disruption. Such concessions were not readily forthcoming.

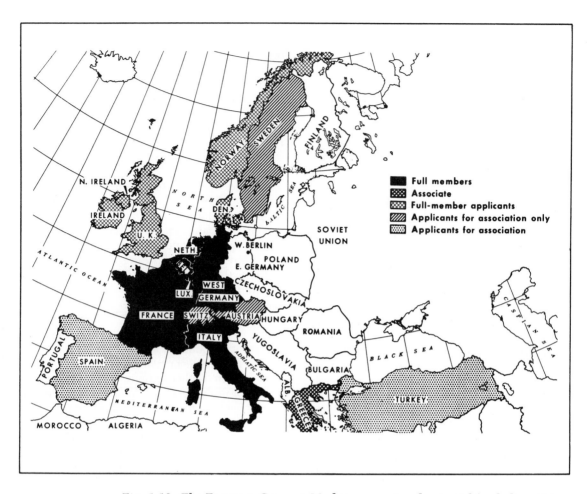

Fig. 1-12. The European Common Market—present and potential (excluding African and other associates). This Common Market (the original six full members) has been so successful in its economic and political achievements that even its most ardent proponents have been surprised. Western Europe's current unparalleled prosperity results primarily from the achievements of the Common Market. No longer does the idea of a united Europe appear as a utopian dream. (Courtesy of U.S. Department of Agriculture, Economic Research Service.)

In spite of a continuum of problems, however, the European Economic Community gives every indication of long-range prosperity. Its membership undoubtedly will grow, and closer economic association is likely to engender more intimate political affiliation as well. "Independence in interpendence" may or may not destroy nationalism, but it seems likely to provide the best guarantee of economic security and prosperity for the individual nations involved.

MAN AND THE CHALLENGE

Attention has been called to the fact that two thirds of the world's population still suffers from hunger, and life for them is burdensome, cruel, and short; and that all such peoples are currently insisting on sharing with those in the developed countries the things that constitute the better life. To the American, Australian, Canadian, and Western European workman, such grinding poverty seems remote and unreal; the problem among these developed peoples is *what* they eat, not *if* they eat. In fact, a major problem among several younger developed countries is agricultural overproduction.

Over the greater part of the habitable globe, a quiet revolution is taking place that is changing life everywhere. From simple tools man is turning to intricate power-driven machines, guided by hands and minds trained in wholly new skills. The American workman has benefited from the growth of science and technology as has no workman elsewhere on earth. His is the highest standard of living in the world. Can man in the underdeveloped lands improve his lot appreciably and in a short time? This is one of the most difficult of all questions to answer. The "Great Awakening" is indisputably a possibility, but whether it is a probability is uncertain. The authors believe the solution will depend largely on what those who inhabit the earth now do about the population problem. Mankind with respect to population, is not faced with immediate disaster. Further ahead, however, the outlook is far from attractive; some day the rise in human numbers must be curbed, and the sooner the better. Almost every underdeveloped country, if gauged with respect to its natural resources, is overpopulated. In possibly no underdeveloped country is agricultural production year in and year out keeping pace with the increase in population. Many are so poor that they cannot purchase what they need in commercial markets; they must have aid or loans with which to make such purchases from the surplus-producing nations. In almost none is the outlook bright. As long as 140,000 persons are added daily to the world's population, the goal sought by the "revolution of rising expectations" seems quite remote. As Sir Julian Huxley, British biologist, says:

We have to choose between two alternatives. One is that we undertake the conscious direction of the process of human evolution, including human reproduction. The other is that man will suck dry the resources of the planet, destroy the basis of civilization, and relapse into squalor and misery.[3]

[3] *New York Times*, November 20, 1959.

One of the main reasons little is being done about birth control on a worldwide scale is that our materialistic, optimistic philosophy maintains that a balance in population will come automatically—that technology can and will provide food, raiment, and shelter for any number of people and that urbanization and industrialization will reduce birth rates through some magical course. It is doubtful whether most underdeveloped countries, which already are caught in the population–natural-resources squeeze, can shift from an agrarian to an industrial society, for there are too many obstacles.

One final point: Although man has progressed fantastically, he has not really conquered nature. He cannot go his own way completely oblivious to nature; and the role of the natural environment in human affairs should not be minimized. The earth still is the source of all wealth; whether rubber comes from a tree or from coal, whether women's hosiery comes from the silkworm or the chemical laboratory, they and thousands of other products come from the earth. In the final analysis, capital becomes available only after wealth has been produced by the application of labor to land. And this interrelation between man and the earth as he attempts to make a living is the heart of economic geography.

ECONOMIC GEOGRAPHY— ITS SCOPE AND METHOD

The question of the futility or utility of man's economic and social advances is not fundamentally the question with which economic geography concerns itself. For economic geography deals primarily with the facts that underlie man's economic development and present dilemma.

So specialized has man's work become through the centuries that a social science known as economics has been developed to study the patterns of production and consumption of goods and services and other types of wealth the world over. Because of its emphasis on the processes, laws, and theories of production, marketing, and consumption, economics has tended to be an abstract science. The economist's particular concern is with the preferences of people. He relies on the geographer, as well as on the geologist, the engineer, and others, to advise him on the means available to give the people what they want.

Geography, by contrast with economics, is an interdisciplinary bridge, with foundations in both the social and physical sciences (Fig. 1-13). It studies the reciprocal relationships between man and his earthly environment. The geographer's aim is to develop an appreciation of the exceedingly complex interplay of natural and cultural forces and thus a better understanding of peoples and of regional differences.

Though economics and geography both deal in part with the same subject matter, they approach it from different points of view. Rather than being preponderantly concerned with theories and processes, the geographer studies, basically, present and potential areal differentiation of production, transportation, and consumption. Thus a separate social science—economic geography—has evolved, deriving its concepts largely from economics, its methodology largely from geography.

The scope of economic geography is clearly a very broad one. Importantly included in this discipline's methodology are (1) maps, the constant companions of the geographer, and (2) statistics, the trenchant tool of the economist.

No other social science demands so rich a symbolization of its facts in map form as does economic geography. Prerequisite to analyses are accurate descriptions. Maps are actually statements of facts and problems in economic geography; and their detail and revelation of the patterns of distribution, when studied with care and skill, can lead directly into the analytical phases of research.

Statistics, too, can be of substantial value if assiduously selected and studied. However, they should not be used "as a drunken man uses lampposts—for support rather than illumination."

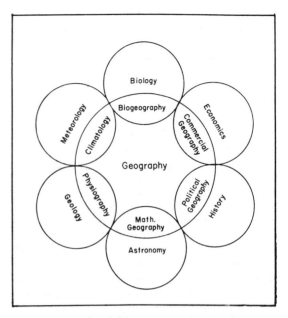

Fig. 1-13. The field of geography in relation to the physical and social sciences. The diagram stresses the fundamental concept that sciences overlap and that each specialized phase of geography is shared with some other science. Some geographers regard geography as a physical science, others as a social science. Possibly the only definition that all geographers would agree upon in essence is that "geography is the study of how much of what is where and why." (After N. M. Fenneman.)

The economic geographer tries to develop a practical comprehension, in time and space, of the relationship between the earth and man's economic life. He delineates the demonstrable features of commercial and industrial development and attempts to ascertain the factors which cause different forms of development to occur in different areas. What does the earth do, or what is it made to do, in providing man's material needs and catering to his desires? Economic geography serves as a guide to an evaluation of past and present commercial and industrial development in various areas. It offers useful bases for planning economic activities. It points the way to a reasonably accurate estimate of the probable future course of economic development as governed by geographical conditions.

SELECTED REFERENCES

Ballabow, M. B. "Putting the 'Economic' into Economic Geography," *Economic Geography*, 33:217-223, July 1957.

Bennett, M. K. "A World Map of Foodcrop Climates," *Food Research Institute Studies* (Stanford University), 1:284-295, November 1960.

Bogue, D. J., and C. L. Beale. *Economic Areas of the United States.* New York, Free Press of Glencoe, Inc., 1961.

Brown, Harrison. *The Challenge of Man's Future.* New York, Viking Press, 1956.

Guzman, L. E. "The Economic Geographer in Economic Development," *Professional Geographer*, 12:16-18, July 1960.

James, P. E., and C. F. Jones. *American Geography: Inventory and Prospect.* Syracuse, N. Y., Syracuse University Press, 1954.

Lukermann, F. "Toward a More Geographic Economic Geography," *Professional Geographer*, 10:2-10, July 1958.

McCarty, H. H. "An Approach to a Theory of Economic Geography," *Economic Geography*, 30:95-101, April 1954.

Osborn, Fairfield. *The Limits of the Earth.* Boston, Little, Brown and Co., 1953.

Shannon, Lyle W. *Underdeveloped Areas.* New York, Harper & Brothers, 1957.

Vogt, William. *People!* New York, Bartholomew House, Inc., 1961.

THE WORLD'S MINERAL

PART TWO::

AND ENERGY RESOURCES

CHAPTER TWO::

In the past, man the world over used his own muscles and those of certain domestic animals to supply energy. This situation is still surprisingly true over much of the earth—in many of the underdeveloped countries, which comprise about 75 per cent of the world's land and about 75 per cent of the world's total population. Later man made use of falling water; and quite recently (since the beginning of the Industrial Revolution), in the developed countries, he has adapted to his use petroleum, natural gas, and coal.

Americans use energy equivalent to about 9 tons of coal per capita each year. Europe and the Soviet Union consume less than 3 tons; Asia, about 100 pounds—except for Japan, which consumes about 1 ton of coal per capita. South America averages about 0.56 and Africa 0.26 tons of coal per capita. Of the energy produced in the United States in 1959, coal accounted for 23.5 per cent.

THE WORLD'S

KINDS OF COAL

All coal may be divided into three varieties on the basis of carbon content.

Lignite, often called brown coal, has the lowest carbon content and the highest water content, and is regarded by geologists and mineralogists as marking the transition to true coal. When exposed to air, it shrinks and crumbles; hence, in countries richly endowed with bituminous coal and lignite, the latter is commonly neglected, except perhaps for local use.

Bituminous, or soft coal (so called in the United States but known as hard coal in Europe), contains a higher percentage of carbon and less water and oxygen than lignite, and a considerable amount of gas. Bituminous coals are the most mined and most used; they are suitable for making steam, gas, and sometimes coke. Coke is essential in the manufacture of iron in blast furnaces (see pp. 176–177).

Anthracite, or hard coal, is high in pure-carbon content (92 to 95 per cent) and so low in volatile matter—oxygen and hydrogen—that it burns with almost no smoke. Among the nations of the world, only Communist China and the United States have appreciable deposits of anthracite. For many years anthracite was the preferred fuel in the United States; today it comprises only a small percentage of the amount of coal used in the nation.

KINDS OF MINES

Four types of coal mines—drift mines, surface mines, shaft mines, and slope mines—are shown in Figure 2-1. A close examination of these reveals the advantages and disadvantages of each. The type of mining followed depends upon the terrain and the geography of the area. Slope and drift mines are most

COAL

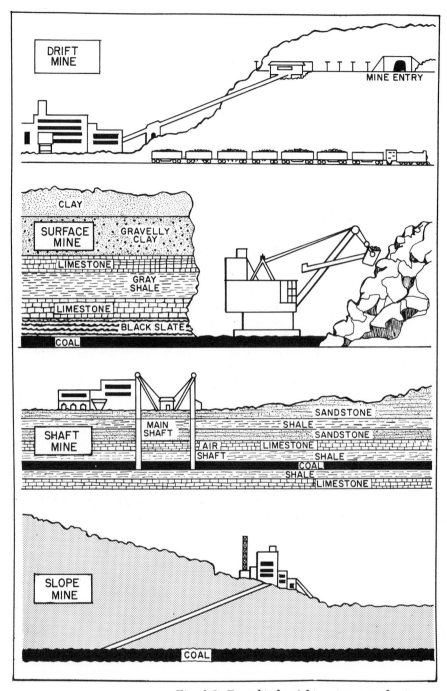

Fig. 2-1. Four kinds of bituminous coal mines. (Courtesy of National Coal Association.)

Fig. 2-2. "Big Paul," one of the largest shovels in existence for strip-mining operations. Standing 14 stories high and controlled by a single operator, it can lift 105 tons of overburden at a single bite. The coal is loaded by smaller shovels into trucks that carry 55 or more tons to a washing and preparation plant for the consumer. (Courtesy of National Coal Association.)

common in hill-country terrain with its innumerable valleys. Shaft and surface (strip) mines are found mostly in plains or on divides. Most of the world's mining is carried on underground.

The strip mine is a relatively recent development, dating back only to 1915. Strip mining, the process of removing an overburden of rock from an underlying mineral resource, is growing in importance because of its many advantages: (1) A large percentage of the coal (80 to nearly 100 per cent) is recoverable, compared with 40 to 60 per cent in underground mines. (2) Strip mines utilize larger units of machinery than underground mines (Fig. 2-2), resulting in a much larger daily output per miner (22 tons vs. 10 tons). (3) Danger is lessened, so that insurance rates are much lower. (4) Strip mines can handle coals that would not be economically feasible for

underground mines. Where the coal bed lies close to the surface, strip mining is usually the most economical method of recovery.

Auger mining, the newest form of coal mining, is an offshoot of strip mining. In many hilly areas considerable coal lies under an overburden too thick to permit economical recovery of the coal. Strip mining is impractical, for there is too much rock to remove; shaft mining also is impractical, because the ridges are not sufficiently large to justify expensive installations. The alternative is the coal auger (Fig. 2-3). Opportunities for auger mining are limited; but where it is possible, it is more economical of labor than any other type of mining.

WORLD DISTRIBUTION AND RESERVES

Coal is widely distributed over the earth (Fig. 2-4). The major deposits lie in the Northern Hemisphere, primarily between 35° and 50° north latitude. There is very little coal in the tropics, but a considerable amount in polar lands. The Russians, Norwegians, and Greenlanders all mine coal north of the Arctic Circle, and there are known deposits in Antarctica. In fact, Lawrence M. Gould (geologist and director of the United States I.G.U. Antarctic program, 1957-1958) has suggested that Antarctica may hold the largest coal deposits on earth.

The total estimated coal **reserves** of the world for 1960 are shown by continents and countries and by percentage of world total in Table 2-1 (p. 32).

WORLD PRODUCTION OF COAL

UNITED STATES

Three circumstances favor this nation above all others in coal production: (1) wide distribution in virtually every region (Fig. 2-5); (2) a great variety of coal types; and (3)

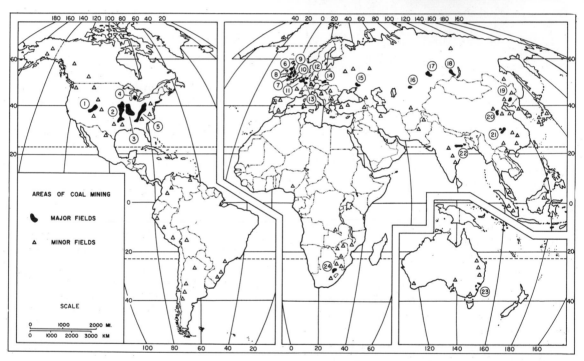

Fig. 2-3. Auger-mining machine boring into the "high wall" (hillside). The augers, 16 to 52 inches in diameter, bore horizontally into the seam for 200 feet or more. The loosened coal flows out of the hole along the auger to a conveyer, which loads it into trucks. (Courtesy of National Coal Association.)

1. Rocky Mountain	7. South Wales	13. Saar	19. Manchuria
2. Western Interior	8. Lancashire	14. Upper Silesia	20. Shensi-Shansi
3. Eastern Interior	9. Yorkshire-Derbyshire	15. Donbas	21. Szechwan
4. Northern Interior	10. Midlands	16. Karaganda	22. Bihar-Orissa
5. Appalachian	11. North France–Belgium	17. Kuzbas	23. New South Wales
6. Clyde	12. Ruhr	18. Irkutsk Basin	24. Transvaal

Fig. 2-4. World distribution and production of coal. Note that most of the coal is mined in the Northern Hemisphere (here, too, are most of the reserves). Richest continent is Asia, with over 45 per cent of world reserves; North America has about 38 per cent. All the Southern Hemisphere continents (Africa, Australia, and South America) combined possess slightly less than 3 per cent.

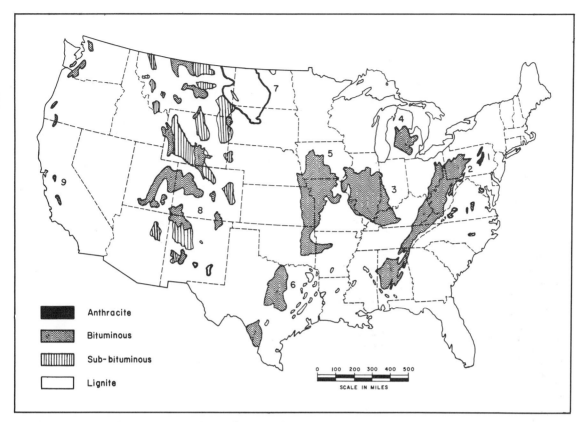

Fig. 2-5. Coal provinces in the United States: (1) Anthracite Basins, (2) Appalachian, (3) Eastern Interior, (4) Northern Interior, (5) Western Interior, (6) Southwestern Interior, (7) Great Plains, (8) Rocky Mountain, (9) Pacific Coast.

huge reserves—all joined together by the world's finest transport system. Still in the ground are an estimated 1,821 billion tons—about one third of the world's known reserves.

The country's energy requirements are expanding so rapidly that coal's future appears secure. The U. S. Bureau of Mines estimates that recoverable coal will provide the nation with more than 90 per cent of its future energy reservoir. Economically recoverable reserves of petroleum and natural gas are puny by comparison: recoverable oil from oil shale will provide only 7 per cent of the country's energy; and proved natural gas and proved petroleum will each provide about 1 per cent.

COAL PROVINCES

The Anthracite Basins. In eastern Pennsylvania occur five small synclines, or basins,

containing folded seams of anthracite scattered over 480 square miles. In 1960 the basins produced about 1 per cent of the nation's total energy consumption on a **BTU** basis. The anthracite industry is ailing—the result of the high cost of mining, which in turn is caused by the thin, broken, inclined seams on the one hand, and virtually obsolete methods of extraction on the other. Consequently, anthracite is being displaced in the domestic fuel markets (northeastern United States and southeastern Canada) by petroleum and natural gas, which are clean, convenient, easily transported, and reasonable in price.

The Appalachian Province. This province, extending from Pennsylvania to Alabama, is regarded as the greatest in the world. It possesses about 20 per cent of the nation's known

THE WORLD'S COAL :: 31

TABLE 2-1

ESTIMATED WORLD COAL RESERVES, 1960
(in millions of metric tons)

Country	Anthracite; bituminous and sub-bituminous coal	Lignite and brown coal	Total	Per cent Region total	Per cent World total
ASIA					
Soviet Union	998,000	202,000	1,200,000	52.4	25.9
China	1,011,000	600	1,011,600	44.1	21.8
India	62,427	508	62,935	2.8	1.4
Japan	9,897	258	10,155	.4	.2
Others	4,711	3,808	8,519	.3	.1
Total	2,086,035	207,174	2,293,209	100.0	49.4
NORTH AMERICA					
United States	1,099,906	405,970	1,505,876	94.1	32.4
Canada	62,472	24,450	86,926	5.6	1.9
Mexico	4,306	. . . . . .	4,306	.3	.1
Total	1,166,684	430,420	1,597,104	100.0	34.4
EUROPE					
Germany	224,300	62,000	286,300	47.5	6.2
United Kingdom	170,686	. . . . . .	170,686	28.3	3.7
Poland	80,000	18	80,018	13.3	1.7
Czechoslovakia	6,450	12,500	18,950	3.1	.4
France	12,288	430	12,718	2.1	.3
Belgium	5,988	. . . . .	5,988	1.0	.1
Netherlands	3,400	. . . . .	3,400	.6	.1
Others	2,622	22,154	24,776	4.1	.5
Total	505,734	97,102	602,836	100.0	13.0
AFRICA					
Republic of South Africa	68,000	. . . . . .	68,000	97.4	1.5
Others	1,650	200	1,850	2.6	. . . .
Total	69,650	200	69,850	100.0	1.5
AUSTRALASIA					
Australia	16,800	41,000	57,800	98.5	1.3
Others	99	785	884	1.5	. . . .
Total	16,899	41,785	58,684	100.0	1.3
SOUTH AND CENTRAL AMERICA					
Colombia	12,000	. . . . . .	12,000	63.6	0.3
Venezuela	3,068	0	3,068	16.2	. . . .
Others	3,556	254	3,810	20.2	. . . .
Total	18,624	254	18,878	100.0	0.4
World total	3,863,626	776,935	4,640,561	. . . .	100.0

SOURCE: National Coal Association, Washington, D. C.

reserves, the quality of the coal is high, and the deposits are accessible to major markets. A very considerable percentage is of coking quality. The mines of this province furnish about three fourths of the coal mined in the nation.

Structural conditions are favorable for low-cost mining. The beds are flat-lying or gently inclined and continuous over relatively large areas (Fig. 2-6). Streams have cut narrow valleys to such depths that one or more coal beds are exposed on the valley sides. Hence,

Fig. 2-6. Underground mining, which still accounts for about 70 per cent of the coal produced in the United States. (Courtesy of National Coal Association.)

both the development of mining by means of drifts and tunnels above the level of groundwater and the movement of coal by railway and/or river (Fig. 2-7) are facilitated. Virtually all the mines are mechanized, so that a large output per miner per hour is possible.

The Interior Province. This province includes four areas or fields: (1) the Eastern Interior in Illinois, Indiana, and Kentucky; (2) the Western Interior in Iowa, Missouri, Kansas, and Oklahoma; (3) the Southwestern Interior in Texas; and (4) the Northern Interior in Michigan. Of these, the Eastern Interior field produces the most and the best coal. The coal beds lie deeply buried near the center but are near the surface about the margins. Accordingly, most of the mines are located near the edges, and much coal is strip mined. Being of higher ash and sulfur content than much of the coal in the Appalachian Province, it is less desirable for making coke; but it is satisfactory for steam and domestic purposes under most conditions, and even competes with coal from the Appalachian Province for the industrial and urban markets of the Great Lakes region.

In the Western and Southwestern Interior fields the coals are deeply buried except along the eastern margin, where the deposits are worked. Since this coal is of inferior grade, the relatively small amount mined is for local consumption. The Northern Interior field is of little importance even locally because of the poor quality of the fuel and the ease and relatively low cost of procuring the superior coals of the Appalachian and Eastern Interior fields.

Great Plains, Rocky Mountain, Pacific Coast, and Alaska Provinces. Most of the coal in the Great Plains is of low quality. For example, that of Wyoming is mostly sub-bituminous, with only two thirds the heating value of good bituminous coal; North Dakota, which ranks second in coal reserves among all the American states, possesses only low-grade lignite; Montana, which is fourth, has mostly lignite. However, Colorado, which is third in reserves, has both bituminous and sub-bituminous coal.

The reserves of the Rocky Mountain Province are enormous, but actual production is small. Nonetheless, the coal has high local importance because of the great distance of the local market from the coal fields of the East and Middle West. Some of the coal is suitable for making coke.

The coals in the Pacific Coast area are relatively unimportant. Principal production is from scattered deposits in the Cascades between Tacoma and Ellensburg, Washington. The reserves are unimpressive. The coals are high in ash and costly to mine, the result of

Fig. 2-7. *Loaded coal cars near mine tipple in valley close to Fairmont, West Virginia. Nearly 80 per cent of all bituminous coal loaded at the mines moves by rail. (Courtesy of National Coal Association.)*

thin and steep-pitching seams. Even in the local market, the coal cannot compete with natural gas and hydropower in manufacturing, or with wood and natural gas for domestic heating; and it is no longer used as fuel by ships and railroads.

Considerable coal is known to exist in the state of Alaska (in the Matanuska, Bering River, and Arctic slope areas)—about 2 per cent of world reserves. However, the coal is of low quality; and since many of the beds are folded and faulted, mining is difficult and costly. Consequently, little coal has as yet been exploited. The only market outside Alaska is Japan, which has imported some coal from the Bering River area because of the comparatively low cost of transporting this coal to Japan.

PRINCIPAL USES

During the past two decades, the markets for coal in the United States have changed markedly. In the first place, the general demand for coal is by no means what it was in the 1940s, although it has risen to what it was in the 1930s. A major consumer of coal, the railroad industry, has shifted to petroleum; in 1959 railroads consumed less than 3 million tons of coal, in contrast to 132 million tons in 1944. On the other hand, the electric-power utilities have markedly increased their coal consumption (a 465 per cent increase); in 1959 the utilities consumed more than one third of all the coal mined in the United States. In turn, coal supplies more than two thirds of the electric-utility industry's power—mainly because coal is lower priced than the other forms of power. Furthermore, combustion techniques are improving: in 1920, 3 pounds of coal were needed to produce 1 kilowatt hour (**kwh**); today, only 0.94 pounds are needed.

Another large consumer of coal is the iron and steel industry, which converts coal into coke for reducing iron ore (for this purpose fixed carbon, coke, is required) and for many other purposes. In 1959, over 79 million tons of coal were transformed into coke. The cement industry is another large consumer of coal, and the aluminum industry increases its consumption annually as less hydroelectric power in large blocks and less natural gas become available.

TRANSPORTATION

Coal production must be synchronized to transportation, for large tonnages cannot be stored at the mines; and the average haul from mine to customer is about 300 miles. Thus, the movement of coal in a country as large as the United States poses a problem. Methods of shipment are changing radically. The amount moving by water and truck is increasing, since the cost is less.

Via Railway. The bulk of the coal is still moved by railway (Fig. 2-7). The railroads haul more tons of coal and receive more revenue from this resource than from any other single commodity. However, the railways are transporting less coal because of the high cost: to coal's mine price, rail freight adds 70 per cent, on the average.

Via Truck. About 12 per cent of the American bituminous coal loaded at the mines is shipped to market via motor truck. Because of the increasing capacity of trucks and the expanding highway system, truck transport is being more widely used. As would be expected, however, the truck is most useful on short hauls. Trucks also are employed to haul coal from mines to railway sidings or river docks for further shipment by train or barge.

Via Pipeline. Coal shipment by pipeline is new and spectacular. The pipeline constructed from Cadiz, Ohio, to Cleveland, a distance of

110 miles, is the first long-distance coal-transporting pipeline in the world. It carries approximately 1,200,000 tons of coal per year, effecting a saving of about 1 million dollars over conventional shipping methods.

To be transported by pipeline, the coal must be specially prepared. It is crushed and mixed with water to form a slurry, which is then pumped through the pipeline at a speed of 3 to 4 miles per hour. At the market end of the line, the coal is removed from the water, heated, and dried for use.

Via Wire. More and more coal is reaching consumer markets by wire in the form of electricity, which involves a minimum of surface transportation. Utilities are building many of their new plants on navigable waterways, sometimes near coal mines and sometimes near the markets for electricity.

Via Waterways. Towboat-propelled barges transport millions of tons of coal on rivers and canals. The Monongahela River handles nearly 30 million tons of coal by barge, and the Ohio handles about 25 million tons; much of this coal is destined for the by-product coke ovens in the Pittsburgh district. Because freight is so expensive an item in the coal business, many utilities, aluminum, and chemical companies have been moving to the banks of the more strategically located rivers. In addition, enormous amounts of coal, as much as 60 million tons, move over the Great Lakes via vessel to American and Canadian markets in the Upper Lake Region. The rates on coal *up* the lakes are only about half those on iron ore *down* the lakes—the coal functioning as return cargo (instead of **ballast**).

CANADA

As Table 2-1 shows, Canada has 1.9 per cent of the world's coal reserves. Two thirds of this amount is believed to exist as minable coal. Most of the coal (63 per cent) is bituminous, 9 per cent is sub-bituminous, and 28 per cent is lignite. The 31 per cent that is of medium-volatile bituminous quality is regarded as Canada's best because much of it is cokable. More than 90 per cent of Canada's coal is to be found in the West, over half in Alberta alone. Much occurs also in Saskatchewan and British Columbia; and a small amount is found in the Maritime Provinces, particularly in Nova Scotia (largely Cape Breton Island) and New Brunswick. Figure 2-4 shows the salient economic-geographic fact of Canada's coal situation: *the unfavorable location of the reserves with respect to the population— the cities and industrial centers of southern Ontario and the St. Lawrence Valley, the major markets for coal.* Because the great distance from Alberta to the major markets in Ontario and Quebec necessitates high transport charges, and the freezing of the St. Lawrence River in winter prevents year-round shipments from Nova Scotia to the same markets, Canada purchases much coal from the United States.

WESTERN AND CENTRAL EUROPE

In Europe the most important coal deposits extend in a broken belt from Great Britain through northern France into southern Russia (Fig. 2-4). Within it are the six major British coal fields; the important French-Belgian-Dutch fields; Germany's famous Ruhr and Saar Basins, and her intensively mined lignite fields near Cologne; Czechoslovakia's Bohemian fields; and the important Upper Silesian–Moravian field of southern Poland and Czechoslovakia. Few areas of equivalent size anywhere on earth possess greater power potential than this 300-by-1,200-mile belt.

Coal mining was important as early as the sixteenth century in England—much earlier than in the United States. As late as 1875, three fourths of the world's coal was mined in Europe; and in 1957 Europe ranked first in output among the continents, with two fifths of the world total. The continent still has impressive reserves (Table 2-1), but coal's contribution to the total supply of primary energy is contracting. Western Europe is currently in the throes of industrial conversion—the result of the large-scale shift in the use of energy (from solid to liquid fuel) and of the closing down of many pits because of deep seams and poor-quality coal.

GREAT BRITAIN

Great Britain has long been regarded as a country rich in coal and outstanding in production. It is today the world's fifth largest coal producer, and for decades during the nineteenth century it stood first.

The nation has been particularly fortunate in having coal fields near tidewater, in the interior, and near deposits of iron ore. Moreover, British coal has been of high quality— semianthracite and bituminous—excellent for all purposes.

British coal beds in general, however, present greater handicaps than do America's Appalachian beds. They are smaller; their seams are thinner (they average 4 feet, compared with 5.4 feet for the United States); they lie deeper; they dip at considerable angles, and are broken by a series of faults with such large offsets that each shaft serves but a limited area; the mine roof structure is difficult to control. The thicker and shallower seams are now largely exhausted. Hoisting coal, pumping out water, and forcing fresh air into deep mines are costly procedures and result in higher coal costs.

Labor, too, is a major factor in price, and price is vital in a world of intense competition. In the United States, the miner using highly mechanized equipment produces per mine-day more than five times the output of the British miner. Moreover, the American labor cost per net ton is less than half the British cost.

In 1946, following World War II, the British coal industry became nationalized. However, it still is plagued by many maladies, among which is stronger competition from the increasing use of petroleum.

Northumberland-Durham Field. This field, which ranks second in output among those of Britain, is eminently well located for making coke for supplying the requirements of much of the iron and steel industry of the northeastern coast. The coal also exports easily and is generally high in quality. For decades Newcastle, chief center of the field, has been synonymous with coal in the thinking of millions of people. However, the best seams there are near exhaustion, and the expression "carrying coals to Newcastle" may soon be an anachronism.

Clyde Field. The Scottish coal fields have long been famous, supplying much fuel for industry and export. They account for about one tenth of the total British output. Most of the fields, however, have thin seams and much faulting; and the coal, part of it at least, is below average in quality. For some years, the output from the Clyde field has been declining. Major causes of the decline are the decreased demand for coal abroad and the elimination of marginal mines following nationalization— the latter an economy move.

Lancashire Field. Though inland, this field has relatively easy access to tidewater through the ports of Liverpool and Manchester (the Manchester Ship Canal). The coal present here gave rise to important industrialization.

York-Derby-Notts (Yorkshire-Derbyshire) Field. This field, like its counterpart, the Lancashire field across the Pennine Mountains, has important coal deposits and manufacturing. Not only does it possess the largest reserves but it produces nearly half the total annual tonnage of the United Kingdom. It is served by Hull and other east-facing ports along the Humber estuary.

Midlands Field. Located near the southern end of the Pennine Mountains, the Midlands field—the famous "Black Country"—typifies England's inland coal fields. In this field the coal seams are deep, the coal is of rather low quality, and transportation costs are higher than for the other fields. Two important industrial centers, Birmingham and Manchester, owe their early growth to the coal deposits in this area.

South Wales Field. Coal has been mined in Wales since the thirteenth century. Near Cardiff are to be found some of the largest and best coal deposits in the United Kingdom. This field, which ranks second among British fields in reserves and third in output, is presently undergoing a thorough transformation:

many old mines are being abandoned, and new mines are coming into being. In the new mines, the most modern methods are being introduced to make possible the production of more coal with fewer men at less cost.

FRANCE AND BELGIUM

A major coal field extends in an almost unbroken belt across West-Central Europe from northwestern France across the Low Countries to the Ruhr of Germany. Largest producing fields in France are the Nord-Pas-de-Calais. The Lorraine fields, however, are experiencing the greatest increase in output—the result of a new technique for coking the coal. Prior to the 1950s, Lorraine coals yielded good coke only when mixed with 70 per cent coal from other fields possessing superior coal. The new technique has fostered modernization of mining, resulting in the highest yield per manshift, underground, in Europe. However, France still does not compare with West Germany in total output of coal.

France of necessity relies heavily upon imports—at least one third of her total coal requirements. French industry is said to depend absolutely on the importation of metallurgical coke from Germany. How serious underproduction of coal is in France may be realized when it is pointed out that of every dollar France got from the United States under the Marshall Plan, she spent 75 cents of it to import United States coal at very high prices. (Coal that cost $10 a ton in Pennsylvania sold for $22 a ton in Europe—including shipping costs.)

The coal fields of Belgium lie in the north and south of the country. In both areas, however, as a result of the high cost of mining (highest in Western Europe), production is falling. Production costs are high because these coal fields are among the oldest exploited in all Europe, and hence the easily accessible coal was mined long ago. Some of the world's most difficult mines to work are in southern Belgium, where the seams are thin and very deep; moreover, the structural complexities interrupt the continuity of the seams. Dozens of pits have been closed down, thousands of miners have been laid off, and coal output has been

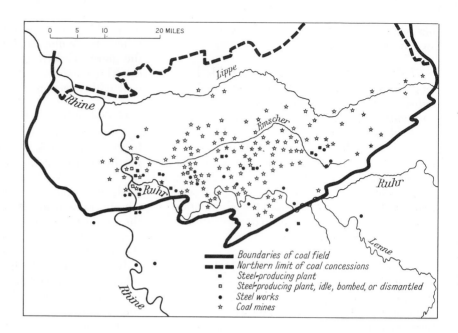

Fig. 2-8. The Ruhr—one of the world's leading coal-mining and iron- and steel-manufacturing regions. An enviable system of canals, railways, and highways interlaces the area. In 1960 the Ruhr turned out more than one fifth of all the steel manufactured in Europe. (Courtesy of American Geographical Society.)

The map legend reads:

Boundaries of coal field
Northern limit of coal concessions
Steel-producing plant
Steel-producing plant, idle, bombed, or dismantled
Steel works
Coal mines

drastically reduced. The fields of southern Belgium have the least promising future of all European coal areas.

GERMANY

Prewar Germany ranked among the world's leading nations both in reserves (Table 2-1) and production. Her dismemberment following World War II resulted in fragmentation of her coal reserves. West Germany retained the Ruhr; East Germany got the enormous lignite deposits of Saxony; and Poland and Czechoslovakia procured the Silesian field.

The German Federal Republic. West Germany possesses both bituminous coal and lignite, the best coal being located largely in the Ruhr and Saar Basins. The Ruhr, which ranks as one of the world's outstanding coal areas (Fig. 2-8), possesses three fourths of the total German output. Its proved reserves are estimated at 213.6 billion metric tons. Ruhr

mines are on the average the world's largest— a situation attributable to control of the industry by a small number of huge corporations and to geological conditions that favor large units. The coal is of excellent quality, and the Ruhr possesses the highest percentage of coking coal among the several fields of Europe.

The Ruhr contains several types of coal, ranging from semianthracite to high-volatile bituminous. The lowest seams, which reach the surface in the south, are anthracite. Above them in order lie coking, gas, and flame coals.

The exposed measures include an area about 10 miles wide and 40 miles long, extending east and west along the Ruhr River. They reach the surface along the valley of the Ruhr and dip northward beneath the North German Plain. The Ruhr beds are only gently folded and slightly faulted. The seams are both numerous and moderately thick. However, the top seams are becoming exhausted, which necessitates working at levels nearly 4,000 feet below the surface, where intense heat seriously interferes with operations.

Mining began along the southern edge but for more than a century has been spreading northward; as this northward spread has occurred, the mines have become progressively deeper. The oldest mines were in the Ruhr Valley, but the younger ones are in the valley of the Emscher and Lippe. There appears to be only one limitation to this northward expansion: increasing depth with consequent mounting cost of mining.

Prior to World War II, about 40 per cent of the coal mined in Germany was used within the Ruhr itself; about 30 per cent was sent to other parts of Germany; and about 30 per cent was exported, primarily to France, Italy, the Netherlands, Belgium, Luxembourg, Switzerland, and the Scandinavian countries—all with small or inadequate coal reserves.

Besides the deposits of coal in the Ruhr, there are large reserves and important production in the Saar and in the Aachen areas. The Saar was one of Germany's largest coal-producing areas prior to World War II. Actually this field is relatively small; also, the coal is highly volatile and does not alone make high-grade metallurgical coke.

In addition to the bituminous coal deposits and mines in the Ruhr and the Saar, enormous reserves of lignite are present in the Rhineland west of Cologne. The principal deposits extend from near Bonn and Cologne to Aachen in the west and to the Dutch border on the north. More and more brown coal is being mined and used in Germany because it is a cheap source of energy when used at the mine. Lignite in Germany is used largely for conversion into electrical energy, and the power stations have gone to the coal. Before World War II, nearly half of the total electricity generated in Germany was produced from lignite.

East Germany. East Germany possesses coal of low quality, largely unsuitable for coke manufacture. Much lignite, however, is mined in Saxony, where it is used primarily in thermal generating plants to produce electricity. Together with West Germany, East Germany produces half the lignite mined and the world.

POLAND

Following World War I, the German Upper Silesian coal field was divided among Germany, Czechoslovakia, and Poland, with Poland receiving the major share—78 per cent. After World War II, Poland took over all of Germany's portion. The result of these two allocations of territory is that Poland today ranks among Europe's leaders in coal, both in reserves (Table 2-1) and production. Annual output approaches 100 million tons. The principal fields, the Dombrawa and the Krakow, which are in eastern Upper Silesia, possess reserves ranking with those of the Ruhr. Coal seams 3 feet thick are numerous but some reach 30 feet; sporadically, two or more seams combine to form beds 50 to 60 feet thick. The mines are at depths of 1,300 to 2,600 feet, which obviously involves difficulties. At a time when the machinery being used was new, the output per man was the highest in Europe. This is no longer true, however, for most of the machinery being used today is prewar.

In addition to the bituminous coal, there is anthracite in the Walbrzych (Waldenburg) district and considerable lignite (possibly 40 million tons) scattered widely, but particularly just east of the Oder River and north, northwest, and northeast of Konin. The lignite has not as yet been exploited extensively because of the availability of bituminous coal.

SOVIET UNION

The Soviet Union claims to possess the largest reserves of coal on earth (Table 2-1). Figure 2-9 shows where Russia's coal is located. Unfortunately, although the reserves are huge and the distribution wide, most authorities regard the country's coal deposits as not well located, because more than 90 per cent of the total is in Asian U.S.S.R., whereas 75 per cent of the population and industry is in the European and Ural regions. These regions experience difficulty in meeting their fuel needs from their own areas, and they find it very costly to transport coal from the Kuznetsk and Karaganda basins.

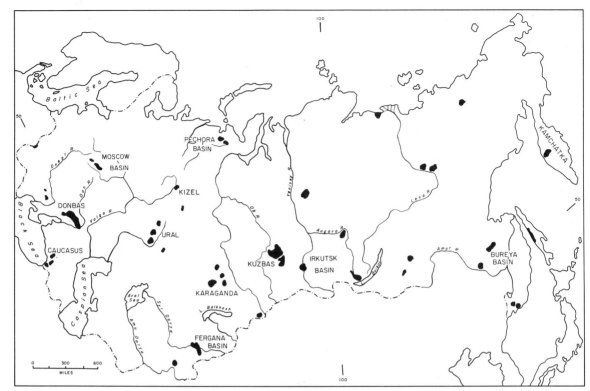

Fig. 2-9. Distribution of coal in the Soviet Union.

Russian coal production was formerly concentrated in the area north of the Black Sea. Now, however, coal is mined in such places as the Karaganda Basin in the Kazakh S.S.R., the Kuzbas (Kuznetsk Basin), and the Irkutsk Basin in Siberia, Volchansk in the Urals, the Pechora Basin in the North, and the Bureya Basin in the Amur region. During the decade 1960-1970, the principal sources of coal for the Soviet Union will be the Donbas, the Kuzbas, and Karaganda, at least as far as coal for metallurgical fuel is concerned.

In quality, the coal ranges from anthracite to bituminous and lignite. The biggest handicap appears to be the unsuitability of most of the coal for coking. Moreover, the best coals are poorly located with respect to iron ore and population centers.

DONETS BASIN (THE DONBAS)

The Donets Basin (whose name is usually shortened to Donbas) lies north of the Sea of

Azov. About half the coal is semianthracite but some is high-grade bituminous, suitable for coking. The Donbas is the best located of all the coal fields, both with respect to iron-ore deposits and markets for steel. Prior to World War II, this field contributed more coal than all the other fields combined. Though possessing a mere 5 per cent of the Soviet Union's reserves, it is the most fully exploited of all the Russian coal-producing areas and still leads in output. In annual production it nearly equals that of the state of Pennsylvania—about 100 million metric tons.

KUZNETSK BASIN (THE KUZBAS)

This area is Russia's largest coal field and its second most important producer. Among the strictly Siberian fields, it has the largest reserves and the best coal. Some seventeen seams of coal total more than 100 feet in thickness; many are up to 50 feet thick. Much of the coal lies so close to the surface it can be strip mined. In quality, the coal runs the whole gamut; but most of it appears to be high-grade bituminous coal, much of it cokable. In fact, it is the Soviet Union's best coking coal, low in sulfur with acceptable ash content. In the 1950s the Kuzbas was accounting for about 15 per cent of the national coal output.

Possibly the basin's most glaring disadvantage, from the point of view of the entire Soviet Union, is its remote location from important markets for coal. Both Chelyabinsk and Magnitogorsk, whose iron furnaces operate partially on Kuzbas coal, suffer by being 1,500 miles distant; for about 40 per cent of the coal is consumed in its own transport to market.

KARAGANDA

This coal field, in northern Kazakhstan, is the third most important coking-coal basin in the Soviet Union. Although coal was discovered there in 1833, the area did not become a major producer until 1932, when a railway was projected into it. Reserves are estimated at about 50 billion tons of bituminous coal. The harsh climate, however, affects the quality adversely: in summer it is contaminated with wind-blown desert sand, in winter it is frozen hard with ice and snow; and the coal, which is high in both ash and sulfur, presents problems in coke making. The field is only 700 miles from Magnitogorsk, contrasted with 1,500 miles for the Kuzbas—an advantage for Karaganda of 800 miles. This fact goes far to explain the field's importance, for its development has facilitated the production of a better coke through the mixing of its coal with that from the Kuzbas. However, even 700 miles means costly transport when it must be by rail. Accordingly, the Russians have been developing the Kizel Coal Basin on the western slope of the Urals. Kizel coal, however, is reported to be miserable for coking.

THE MOSCOW AND URAL BASINS

These two areas, though essentially producers of lignite, are nonetheless important because of their proximity to major markets. The reserves for the Moscow Basin are placed at 12.4 billion tons and for the Ural Basin at 7.6 billion tons.

EASTERN AND SOUTHEASTERN ASIA

Asia is rich in coal, ranking first among the continents in total reserves (Fig. 2-4 and Table 2-1).

CHINA

Coal is the most valuable mineral and the basic energy resource of Communist China. Although coal was mined there as early as 1100 B.C., the country still ranks very high among world nations in reserves—probably third.

China's coal, which is found in about thirty large fields, is located principally in the northwestern and northeastern parts of the country—in the Loess Highlands of Shansi, Shensi, Honan, and Kansu, and in Manchuria, Anhwei Province, Shantung, and Hopei, although fields are reported to be scattered over the entire country. Mainly because of transportation difficulties, the mining is widely dispersed, and the coal is mainly for local consumption.

For centuries the deposits were scarcely touched; before the days of the Communists, production never went above 62 million tons (1942); it soared to 130 million tons in 1957 and to 210 million tons in 1958. By 1959 Communist China had become the world's third largest producer of coal, exceeded only by the United States and the Soviet Union.

Most of the coal is bituminous, and seven of the thirty fields have impressive reserves of coking coal. China is said to have the most extensive anthracite deposits in the world, in the Shensi-Shansi area.

Manchuria is well endowed with coal, though estimates vary considerably. Much of the coal is high-grade bituminous, though less than 10 per cent is of coking quality. The beds are thick, continuous, and near the surface, with resultant low-cost mining. The two most famous mining centers are Fushun and Fuhsin. Fushun, lying about 20 miles east of Mukden, has modern mines, both underground and surface, and at the latter exploits the thickest-known bed of coal in the world—about 400 feet. Fuhsin, about 75 miles north of Chinhsien, has large coal reserves. Chief of the coking-coal areas is Pensihu, which is close to the larger metallurgical centers. Since Manchuria got a head start under the Japanese (1932-1945), it expectedly supplies a large part of China's current production.

INDIA

India is not generally regarded as one of the better-endowed countries in coal, but it does possess notable reserves (Table 2-1); and in quality of coal the country is surpassed only by the United States, the Soviet Union, China, West Germany, Canada, and Poland. Though some of the coal is lignite, much is bituminous, and some even is anthracite. Coal of some type is to be found in almost every province. The seams, which vary in thickness from 1 to 20 feet, lie in flat to gently sloping beds and can therefore be mined cheaply.

The largest deposits—more than 98 per cent and by far the best in quality—lie in the provinces of Bihar and Orissa, 100 to 200 miles northwest of Calcutta, which means that they are fairly accessible by rail and sea. Other deposits are to be found in Hyderabad, the Central Provinces, and the Punjab. The major better-grade coal fields extend in an arc from the great bend in the Ganges (where it crosses the boundary between Bihar and Bengal) westward and southward to the western edge of the Central Provinces, then sweeping back southeastward to the mouth of the Godavari River in Madras Presidency. Ninety-nine per cent of the good-quality coal is concentrated in several fields along the Damodar Valley of Bihar-Bengal.

India is characterized by an excessive number of mines, many too small in output and with too high overhead to permit much mechanization, decent mining conditions, or proper conservation measures. However, despite the fact that the output per miner is only about one eighth that in the United States, India's annual output now exceeds 40 million tons.

SOUTHERN HEMISPHERE LANDS

AUSTRALIA

Australia is believed to have the most valuable coal deposits in the Southern Hemisphere.

The coal is well distributed (there is some in every state); but New South Wales and Queensland have most of the bituminous, and Victoria has the lignite. These three states also have most of the people, cities, and industries.

The three leading fields are spaced approximately equidistant from Sydney. They are (1) the northern, near Newcastle (most important by far); (2) the western, near Lithgow; and (3) the southern, near Port Kembla. The coal in the northern and southern fields makes reasonably good coke.

Some of the world's thickest beds of bituminous coal and lignite have been found in Australia. Total annual production exceeds 30 million tons, 20 million tons of which are bituminous. Though strata vary from horizontal to steeply inclined, mining costs are not unusually high. Much of the coal can be strip mined. The Blair Athol mine in central Queensland, about 150 miles from the coast, exploits a seam 100 feet thick in what are reputed to be the largest-known deposits in the Southern Hemisphere. The coal is hard, low in ash, does not clinker, and is relatively smokeless.

Victoria's lignite deposits are in the Latrobe Valley, 100 miles east of Melbourne, and extend over an area of 50 square miles. Some 50 feet thick, they are covered by a soft overburden of clay and sand only 30 to 50 feet thick, and hence can be strip mined. The fuel is mostly used for generating electricity for the cities of Victoria.

AFRICA

With only 1.5 per cent of the world's coal reserves, Africa ranks among the poorest of the continents (Fig. 2-4). Most of the coal reserves are in South Africa, in Natal and the Transvaal. Some is found also in Orange Free State. Most African coal is noncoking; but that at Middleburg and Witbank (about 70 miles east of Pretoria and Johannesburg) and at Vereeniging (just south of Johannesburg) is suitable, yielding good metallurgical coke.

SOUTH AMERICA

Poorest of all the continents in coal is South America, with reserves estimated at a mere 0.3 per cent of the world total (Fig. 2-4 and

Table 2-1). Most seams are thin and badly broken, and contain coals of only medium quality. Though all classes of coal, from lignite to anthracite, are present, nowhere in South America is there a high-quality coking coal.

The coal is mostly in Colombia, Peru, and Chile. Argentina and Brazil, the leading South American nations politically, are very poor in coal. Not only are their reserves small, but none of their coals possess strong coking qualities. Chile leads in output; at Lota and Schwager, near Concepción, are mines that contribute 85 per cent of the total Chilean output. The Chilean mines are not mechanized, and the cost of mining is high—particularly since some of the operations are carried on beneath the Pacific Ocean. The coal does not make strong coke and accordingly is mixed with coal from the United States. High-quality American coal sells for about the same price as lower-quality domestic coal.

Colombia has the largest reserves in South America. Most of the coal lies in two areas: (1) northeast of Bogotá (the Paz del Río steelworks are here) and (2) in the valley of the Cauca near Cali. Peru ranks second in reserves, possessing coal ranging from bituminous to anthracite. The two principal producing areas are (1) Oyon, west of Cerro de Pasco in the Sierra, and (2) the Santa Valley, east of the port and steel center of Chimbote. Venezuela's coal reserves are small and of low quality.

WORLD OUTLOOK

We have seen that coal, a principal source of energy, is basic to world power. We have seen, too, that the United States and the Soviet Union enjoy commanding positions in coal.

Coal is largely responsible for the fact that some nations are industrialized and others are not. Particularly does this hold for the iron and steel industry, which is basic to present-day civilization. Coking coal is the "priceless ingredient" that determines in no small degree the locale of iron- and steelmaking. Coal may thus be regarded as the foundation on which the industrialization of such countries as the United States, the Soviet Union, the United Kingdom, and Germany were built.

Recently, coal has been losing out to other sources of energy, particularly to petroleum and natural gas. There are many factors responsible for coal's decline, among which high price and inconvenience are particularly important. Coal operators in developed countries have striven to compete, especially through complete mechanization. As a result, in 1959, output per miner in the United States increased to an average of 12.12 tons per day—almost three times what it was in 1924. Wages and fringe benefits have advanced with increased output per miner. Operators also ship more coal from mines via barge and truck.

Looking ahead to the year 2000 A.D., it is estimated that the world will be consuming energy at the rate of the equivalent of 25 to 37 billion tons of coal per annum. From what sources will so much energy come? Coal still will contribute an important proportion; petroleum and natural gas may be expected to be largely exhausted. Thus when we speak of conventional fuels in the long-range picture, we mean *coal*. However, by the year 2000, new sources of energy, solar and nuclear, undoubtedly will have to buttress coal. With the population explosion and the accompanying rise in the world level of living, the energy problem facing mankind will become increasingly complex.

SELECTED REFERENCES

Ayres, Eugene, and C. A. Scarlott. *Energy Sources: The Wealth of the World.* New York, McGraw-Hill Book Company, Inc., 1952.
Bituminous Coal Facts, 1962. Washington, D. C., National Coal Association, 1962.
Guernsey, Lee. "Outlook for Coal in the United States," *Focus,* 10:1-6, November 1959.
Hodgkins, J. A. *Soviet Power: Energy Resources, Production, and Potentials.* Englewood Cliffs, New Jersey, Prentice-Hall, Inc., 1961.
Miller, E. Willard. "World Patterns and Trends in Energy Consumption," *Journal of Geography,* 58:269-279, September 1959.

CHAPTER THREE::

Petroleum is today one of the principal sources of energy. It is currently the king of fuels. But important as petroleum's contribution to energy is, it has done much more. In the century since the famous Drake Well was brought in at Titusville, Pennsylvania (August 27, 1859), petroleum has changed the world. It has made possible modern industry; without it our machine civilization would grind to an abrupt stop, for oil has no satisfactory substitute as a lubricant. Moreover, petroleum is now converted into more than 5,000 products. It is the basis of the relatively new petro-chemical industry that today contributes synthetic rubbers, new clothing, new utensils from colored plastic, and new ways to produce better crops from chemical fertilizers and pesticides. Petroleum is as vital in wartime as in peacetime.

THE WORLD'S PETROLEUM

It is the lifeblood of military power. It propels most of the machines of war on the land, in the air, on the sea, and under the sea.

The national thirst for petroleum and natural gas grows apace. The United States is the largest consumer of energy the world has ever known, and more than two thirds of this energy is provided by oil and natural gas. In the past half-century, the demand for **crude oil** and other petroleum products increased 1,300 per cent. A recent study estimates that United States consumption of oil will continue to increase about 6 per cent per year. To date, energy use in the underdeveloped countries is at very low levels per capita—about one tenth of what it was in the United States in 1900.

Probably there is not a country on earth whose people are not better off because of petroleum. In some, such as the United States, the high standard of living depends in no small measure on oil. It is at the root of the vast mechanization that has completely transformed American agriculture and industry. It introduced the revolution in transportation by truck, diesel locomotive, and airplane. Most ships today are oil burners. And petroleum has redrawn the American map of population distribution—the trek to the suburbs.

In Venezuela, Kuwait, and Iraq, petroleum has been responsible for raising the standard of living. These governments set aside an appreciable proportion of the millions of dollars they get from oil to aid their people. The benefits are usually indirect. Venezuela, particularly, stands as an example of the unparalleled progress achievable by an oil-rich but other-

AND NATURAL GAS

Fig. 3-1. A seismograph party camp in part of the Rub' al-Khali (Great Sandy Desert) of south-central Saudi Arabia. In this enormous area, understandably called the "empty quarter," active dune sand may average 100 feet in thickness. Such a milieu presents a formidable challenge to man's carrying out any kind of work. (Courtesy of Aramco.)

wise underdeveloped country when a government spends wisely a considerable share of the oil revenue for public works.[1]

In the Middle East, which aside from petroleum is notably poor, the Arab masses feel that the monies from oil should be spent on the entire 40 million Arab people rather than solely for the benefit of the sheikdoms fortunate enough to have oil within their boundaries.

So important has oil become that companies scour the earth for it: no milieu is too inhospitable to keep oil geologists, petroleum engineers, geophysicists, drillers, and others from seeking oil, whether it be in polar lands, in muskeg terrain, in deserts, in mountains, in jungles, or even under some lakes, oceans, seas, and gulfs (Figs. 3-1 and 3-2).

[1] See Warren L. Baker, "Wise Use of Oil Income Gives Venezuela Bright Outlook," World Oil, 145:177-182, July 1957.

In a recent year (1956) the United States alone consumed 8.86 million **barrels** of oil per day. About 2 million barrels of the total are usually brought from foreign lands; the remainder is produced domestically.

ORIGIN AND LOCATION OF PETROLEUM

Scientists are not certain how petroleum was formed, but many believe that it consists of the remains of marine life, animal or plant or both. These remains were entombed in the briny muds of shallow sea floors at the edges of land masses. Such marine sediments cover a considerable fraction of the earth's surface. They are important geologically, however, only when they are concentrated into so-called "oil reservoirs" or **oil pools**. Actually there is no "oil pool" unless the position of the sedi-

Fig. 3-2. Oil wells in Lake Maracaibo, Venezuela. A basic pattern, designed for maximum conservation, spaces the wells in the lake on a 1,950-foot grid. Drilling techniques over the water have developed to the point where the lake crews can handle a well as efficiently and safely as land crews. Lake Maracaibo today ranks as one of the most prolific oil basins in the world. (Courtesy of Creole Petroleum Corporation.)

ments produces a **trap**. What oil men call a "pool" is really a buried layer of permeable rock (called the "reservoir rock") of varying thickness, which is saturated with oil and gas.

The form of this natural energy is complex and varies from pool to pool, but in general it is twofold: (1) hydrostatic pressure of water at the edges of the pool and underlying it; and (2) pressure of the compressed gas associated with the oil. When the drill penetrates an **oil sand**, thereby releasing the pressure, the gas expands and propels the oil to the surface.

Man now seeks oil wherever geological, economic, and political conditions warrant. However, more is being learned each year regarding the geology of oil. A. I. Levorsen, for example, believes that petroleum will be won from geologically older rocks than is presently the case.[2]

Reserves and producing fields are unevenly distributed over the earth. Figure 3-3 shows that the world's chief oil sources are centered in two areas: (1) the Middle East extending

northward into the Soviet Union and (2) the Western Hemisphere—western Canada southward through western United States and south into northern and western South America. Much of the world's oil is located in out-of-the-way and often even in almost inaccessible areas: man's task is to get it from where it is found to where it can be used.

Despite the development of geology, engineering, geophysics, geochemistry, and micropaleontology, and despite the invention of much helpful scientific equipment, man never knows for certain when he drills that he will strike oil. In fact, only one out of every nine exploratory wells (**wildcats**) produces oil or gas, and only one in five does so even in known oil-bearing territory. About one well in forty-eight proves economically profitable. For this reason oil companies must have enormous financial resources. Moreover, the cost of wells continues to soar: the average cost of each of the approximately 50,000 oil wells drilled in the United States in a recent year was $50,000; and the world's deepest well (in Pecos County, Texas), drilled to a depth of 25,340 feet, cost approximately 3 million dollars. Cost per well

[2] A. I. Levorsen, "Where Will Tomorrow's Oil Be Found?" World Oil, 140:76-81, April 1955.

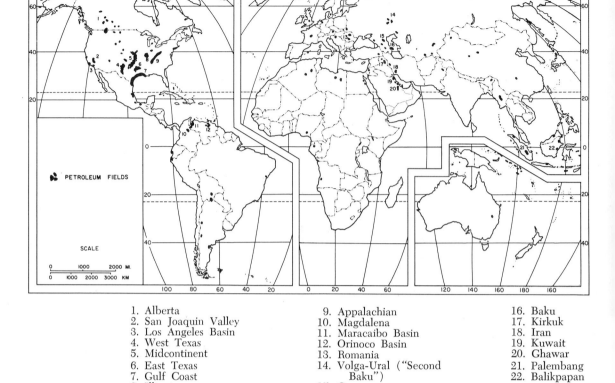

1. Alberta	9. Appalachian	16. Baku
2. San Joaquin Valley	10. Magdalena	17. Kirkuk
3. Los Angeles Basin	11. Maracaibo Basin	18. Iran
4. West Texas	12. Orinoco Basin	19. Kuwait
5. Midcontinent	13. Romania	20. Ghawar
6. East Texas	14. Volga-Ural ("Second	21. Palembang
7. Gulf Coast	Baku")	22. Balikpapan
8. Illinois	15. Grozny	

Fig. 3-3. World oil-producing areas. The richness of North America and of Asia, and to a lesser extent of South America, and the poverty of Australia and of Africa are emphasized. In 1960, exclusive of the Soviet Union, 43 countries were producing oil in some volume. Fifteen of these were net exporters and together accounted for roughly 50 per cent of the Free World output.

varies with the underlying geology, the climate, terrain, location, cost of labor and material, and output or yield per well.

Since the cost of developing oil fields today runs into billions of dollars, the present trend is for several companies to operate jointly in order to spread the risk; thus, four of America's strongest oil companies own Aramco. Joint operation is evident also in Venezuela, Bolivia, Libya, and Iran.

After a pool has yielded most of the oil recoverable by current methods and costs (only about 30 per cent is recovered, though this percentage can be doubled with good techniques of pressure maintenance under pool control),

operations are discontinued. Sometimes a "second crop" of oil is "reaped" by water-flooding or repressuring with gas.

Because of the speed with which oil fields become depleted, additional sources must continually be sought; and thousands of new wells are drilled annually. Nearly all the areas that are easily and economically exploitable have now been developed. Companies today must not only go far afield to seek oil but must employ new and more costly methods to win it.

The United States is a high-cost producer of crude oil, a barrel in 1959 costing $0.75 contrasted with $0.41 for Venezuela, $0.19 for the Middle East, and $0.75 for the Far East.

WORLD RESERVES

The ultimate petroleum reserves of the earth can be only conjectured. The term "proved reserves" is invariably employed when figures are given. It refers to the *known* stores of underground oil that can be produced under present engineering methods and price conditions. When the initial well in a new field is brought in, engineers are able to assign the pool a figure of probable production, a figure that is constantly revised as more wells are drilled and the limits of the field are determined.

Estimates of the total world oil reserves (proved in 1,000 barrels) are shown in Table 3-1. The Middle East alone is credited with more than three fifths of the total proved petroleum reserves of the world.

WORLD PRODUCTION

Since 1859 the United States has led all nations in petroleum production. For decades it contributed more than 60 per cent of the world output. Though still the leading producer, it now contributes only about 40 per cent. For many years Venezuela ranked second and the Soviet Union third, but in 1959 the Soviet Union moved into second place.

UNITED STATES

With about 12 per cent of the proved oil reserves of the earth, the United States produces roughly 40 per cent of its oil. More than 574,500 wells had been drilled by the end of 1959, and about 46,000 more are drilled each year. Average daily output per well is small (12½ barrels), and in only 12 per cent of the wells does the oil flow without pumping; 40 per cent are **stripper wells**, which produce less than one barrel per day. Some of the best areas, based on present knowledge, are offshore in Louisiana and California. Economics will govern the exploitation of these areas, where operation costs run two to ten times those on land.

TABLE 3-1

PETROLEUM RESERVES, CONTINENTS AND MAJOR COUNTRIES, 1960
(in 1,000 barrels)

Area	Amount	Percentage
EUROPE	2,820,741	1
Romania	903,532	*
SOVIET UNION	24,000,000	9
ASIA	172,499,800	65
Kuwait	60,000,000	23
Saudi Arabia	51,000,000	19
Iraq	24,000,000	9
Iran	22,000,000	8
Indonesia	8,200,000	3
AFRICA	8,374,000	3
Algeria	4,600,000	2
NORTH AMERICA	37,749,753	14
United States	31,613,211	12
Canada	3,678,542	1
Mexico	2,458,000	*
SOUTH AMERICA	20,405,698	8
Venezuela	17,353,558	7
Colombia	625,000	*
WORLD	266,249,992	100

* Less than 1 per cent.

SOURCE: *World Oil*, August 1961, p. 76.

OIL PROVINCES

For presentation here, oil deposits are grouped into so-called **oil provinces** in the United States (Fig. 3-4).

Appalachian Province. Southwestern New York, southwestern Pennsylvania, southeastern Ohio, adjacent parts of West Virginia, and Kentucky comprise the Appalachian Province, which cradled the American oil industry. This province has been declining steadily in importance and today yields only about 1 per cent of the national output. Yield per well averages only one-half barrel per day.

Southeastern Illinois–Southwestern Indiana Province. This province possesses many small producing fields and one very important one—that in southeastern Illinois. Deeper drilling in the late 1930s rejuvenated the area, which presently contributes 4 to 5 per cent of the national output.

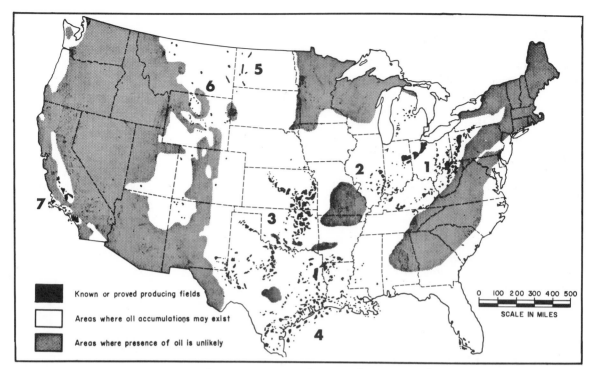

Fig. 3-4. Petroleum situation in the United States. Producing provinces are (1) Appalachian, (2) Illinoian, (3) Midcontinent, (4) Gulf Coast, (5) Northern Great Plains, (6) Rocky Mountain, and (7) Southern California.

Midcontinent Province. The hundreds of fields, large and small, comprising this large province make it the most productive oil region in the nation and possibly in the world. It includes one·of the greatest concentrations of oil and gas pools on earth. Within its boundaries are portions of such oil-producing states as Texas, Oklahoma, Arkansas, and Louisiana. It has 50 per cent of the proved reserves of the nation and accounts for 59 per cent of the national output. Although it has been producing for more than fifty years, it still is the major source of United States oil. New discoveries and new areas are constantly being brought in, indicating that the maximum output may not yet have been reached. The Midcontinent Province is unique in contributing oils with a **paraffin base,** with an **asphalt base**, and with a mixed paraffin-asphalt base; some of the oils are heavy, others light.

Located between the Midcontinent and Gulf Coast Provinces, but essentially separate from both, is an exceedingly productive petrolifer-ous area in eastern Texas, southwestern Arkansas, and ·northwestern Louisiana. The outstanding field in the area is the East Texas field, which has yielded nearly four times as much oil as the second most productive field in North America. Its discovery well was brought in in 1930, and more than 3,000 additional wells were completed during its first year of operation. Rapid and wasteful production brought about the establishment of conservation laws that have been of great value to controlled development of petroleum in subsequently discovered fields. Even today, the East Texas field yields more oil each year than any other field on the continent.

Gulf Coast Province. This province, including particularly parts of Louisiana, Mississippi, and Texas, but also portions of Alabama and Florida, now ranks second in national output, contributing some 22 per cent of the total. The fields comprising this province are advantageously located with respect to ports on the

Gulf of Mexico and to refineries, and they have spawned the world's outstanding petrochemical industry.

These fields, many associated with salt domes, are scattered along the Gulf Coastal Plain (Fig. 3-4). Much of the oil has a heavy asphalt base and is better suited for fuel oil, bunker oil, and lubricants than for gasoline.

Some of the best oil areas of North America are the so-called *tidelands*. This **continental shelf** is a continuation of the Gulf Coastal Plain into the sea to a depth of about 100 fathoms (600 feet), where it plunges abruptly into the oceanic depths. However, searching for oil in the ocean floor is considerably more expensive than on land. Drilling requires huge platforms, costing $500,000 to $1,500,000, to support the big rigs and withstand heavy seas and high winds—even occasional hurricanes. The proved reserves are enormous—up to 15 billion barrels (and 70 trillion cubic feet of gas), or one third those of the nation. The percentage of wells brought in is high, the success ratio ranging from 50 to 70 per cent. Most of this oil lies between Brownsville, Texas, and a point about 25 miles east of New Orleans, although most successful wells have been completed off the Louisiana coast.

The political aspect of the tidelands is important. For many years ownership, whether by the federal government or by individual states, was in doubt. Congress finally ceded to the states control and exploitation of offshore oil as far seaward as their historic boundaries. Obviously, determination of state boundaries in the Gulf of Mexico is difficult both legally and politically. However, in 1960 the United States Supreme Court established the federal government as the major lessor in the offshore Gulf area, and awarded the government title to lands 3 miles beyond the coasts of Louisiana, Mississippi and Alabama, and 10½ miles beyond those of Texas and Florida.

Williston Basin. This rather recently discovered source of oil is one of the most promising provinces in the nation. The discovery occurred in April 1951, at the Beaver Lodge Pool, North Dakota, after more than three decades of intermittent exploration. By 1952, many wells had been drilled; the general outline of the basin was established (118,500 square miles in the Dakotas, Montana, Saskatchewan, and Manitoba); and reserves of 2.5 million barrels were estimated. Unfortunately, the sparse population of the province necessitates marketing outside the area. If the province becomes a large producer, transport and marketing problems will have to be solved.

Rocky Mountain Province. This province, covering a huge area and including many fields, extends from the Canadian border southward into New Mexico. However, because of the restricted nearby market and the great distance to Eastern and Pacific Coast markets, it accounts for only about 3 per cent of the national annual output.

Scientists believe that the ultimate oil reserves are very large and that the area will grow in importance as it is more intensively explored, as the older and better-located areas decline, and as prices for crude oil become substantially higher. Exploratory work of the various structures is in an early stage. Wyoming particularly shows promise. Important recent developments in this province have taken place in the Four Corners country.

California. California has produced petroleum commercially since 1880. It still maintains some of the most productive fields in North America and accounts for about 16 per cent of total United States production, ranking it third in annual output among the American provinces. Moreover, its proved reserves, including those offshore, were estimated at 3,762 million barrels on January 1, 1960. California's big oil boom came, however, in 1921-1922, with the completion of three large fields at Huntington Beach, Long Beach, and Santa Fe Springs. From 1903 to 1915, California led all states in production. Ninety-six per cent of the state's petroleum is presently produced in the fourteen southernmost counties.

Despite substantial production (307.158 million barrels in 1959), California imports considerable petroleum, about 20 per cent of the total she refines. This results from the rapid growth in population; the large number of automobiles (California leads the nation); booming industrialization; and the heavy drain during World War II and the Korean War, when California supplied about 50 per cent of the military needs for petroleum products.

Alaska. Alaska promises to become an important producer of oil, but operators face difficult problems because both exploration and drilling are expensive and time-consuming. The climate and terrain necessitate costly outlays and advance preparations that greatly exceed anything encountered on land in continental United States. Transportation is also a problem; roads are largely lacking—but a pipeline has been built to Cook Inlet.

Thus far, oil has been found commercially in only a few places—on the Kenai Peninsula, near Cook Inlet, and in the Barrow area on the Arctic Ocean. A major problem, even if large reserves are discovered, will be to find markets —since the state is sparsely populated. Because Alaska's market is small, the bulk of the crude oil is being sold in Washington, Oregon, California, and Japan.

POSSIBLE OIL FUTURE OF THE UNITED STATES

No nation can continue decade after decade to produce almost one half of the world's oil without facing an ultimately discouraging future, for oil is a nonrenewable resource. In 1960 the United States possessed only about 12 per cent of the world's proved reserves of oil. Since petroleum is the lifeblood of our modern way of life, American oil companies have gone abroad in their search for oil (1) to assure the nation ample quantities of oil at all times; (2) to guarantee their own companies' future reserves; and (3) to supply the large markets in Western Europe, Eastern and Southern Asia, Africa, Australia, and Latin America. In 1955, United States interests controlled 68 per cent of the world's crude petroleum output.

Another source of oil within the country itself is secondary recovery of oil left in the ground during primary production. Ultimately

several billion barrels of petroleum can be recovered this way, but obviously the cost is greater than by conventional methods of exploitation.

CANADA

Since 1947, when Alberta's famous well at Leduc (Fig. 3-3) was brought in, Canada has grown steadily in stature as a producer of petroleum. Until 1947, domestic sources supplied less than 10 per cent of the nation's requirements; today they supply more than 70 per cent. Subsequently, other large pools— which extend into Saskatchewan, Manitoba, and British Columbia—were found. From the Rocky Mountains to the Canadian Shield and from the Arctic Ocean to the United States–Canadian border (geologically on both sides of the border) is a vast sedimentary basin, much of which is petroliferous. In western Canada alone, there are more than 280 producing fields with 15,000 successful wells. Although Canada produces only about 3 per cent of the world's oil, geologists are highly optimistic regarding the country's future.

Canada, however, faces problems. The oil fields are not located where most of the people live nor where the largest markets for petroleum products are found. Although Canada does operate more than 6,000 miles of oil pipelines, oil from remote, landlocked Alberta— which accounts for about 95 per cent of the country's total output—cannot be transported to Montreal or Vancouver at a price competitive with oil from overseas.

LATIN AMERICA

MEXICO

Mexico was once the second largest oil producer in the world. However, following government expropriation of the holdings of American, British, and Dutch companies in 1938, the Mexican industry declined. It is a government monopoly, though United States capital on a comparatively small scale is sharing in exploration.

There are several producing regions near the Gulf of Mexico (Fig. 3-3). Development from 1910 to 1919 was marked by sensational discoveries of new pools and persistently high yields of old ones. Discoveries since 1922 have been unimportant in comparison with the decline of old pools.

Almost 92 per cent of Mexico's total consumption of energy comes from oil and gas, the largest percentage for any country in the world.

VENEZUELA

Venezuela was for many years the world's second largest producer of petroleum; only the United States surpassed it. In 1959, it was displaced by the Soviet Union. However, the country still produces more than 85 per cent of the oil contributed by the entire South American continent; and, because of huge production and a small home market, it is the world's largest exporter of petroleum. Most Venezuelan oil is marketed in the Western Hemisphere, the United States being the principal customer—generally taking about one third of the total exports. The bulk of the remainder is distributed throughout Latin America and Northwest Europe. Some is exported also to Canada.

Venezuela accounts for about 14 per cent of world production and has about 7 per cent of world reserves (Table 3-1). Daily output exceeded 3 million barrels in 1962. Sixty per cent of this oil is medium and light crude, and these grades find their principal outlets in Western Hemisphere refineries outside the United States. About 37 per cent of the total output consists of heavy crude, mainly used as heavy fuel oil. This oil complements the crude oil of the United States.

Petroleum has done much for Venezuela: it is the economic lifeblood of the country, having transformed the national economy from that of a typical underdeveloped Latin American country to one of the soundest in the world. Venezuela has a policy based on the slogan *sembrar el petroleo* ("sowing the oil") —meaning that oil revenues are employed to help Venezuela. Seventy per cent of the government's income emanates from oil, and as much as 40 per cent generally goes to strengthen the country's economy. For years Venezuela was in the best financial condition of any nation in Latin America. Yet with petroleum comprising more than 90 per cent of the exports by value, Venezuela is virtually a one-product country and hence is subject to the vicissitudes of such an economy.

There are three oil regions in Venezuela— the Maracaibo Basin, the Orinoco Basin, and the Apure Basin (Fig. 3-5). Most important is the Maracaibo Basin, geologically one of nature's most favored areas for oil.

The Maracaibo Basin. This basin is a broad structural trough, lying between two branches of the Venezuelan Andes. Petroleum is being won from both sides of Lake Maracaibo. On its steamy shores many of the major oil companies of the world are operating. Wells have been drilled beneath the lake, and oil derricks extend as far out as 15 miles from shore. From the east side of the lake (over a distance of 65 miles), however, almost 73 per cent of total Venezuelan production comes. Reserves for the basin are estimated at about 8 billion barrels, but these increase annually as new discoveries are made.

There are several thousand wells in the lake itself; at the bottom of the lake, pipelines aggregating more than 1,000 miles carry oil to "flow stations" on the shore and then into storage tanks of 1,000 and 1,500 barrels capacity. From these tanks the oil is piped to larger tanks having capacities up to 150,000 barrels. Here the government determines volume and grade. The oil is then pumped or transported in tankers to refineries on the Paraguaná Peninsula, 145 miles distant, or shipped to the islands of Curaçao and Aruba in the Netherlands Antilles, some 30 miles from the coast.

About 45 per cent of the wells in the lake produce by natural flow, since the gas pressure is sufficient to force the oil to the surface; for the remaining 55 per cent, pumping must be resorted to. Recently, repressuring stations have been placed out in the lake to send natural gas, formerly wasted, back into the ground.

Formerly only shallow draft tankers drawing 13 feet could transit the lake because of the Maracaibo Sand Bar. But a deep-sea canal, 14 miles long, now enables large ocean tankers to go into and out of the lake.

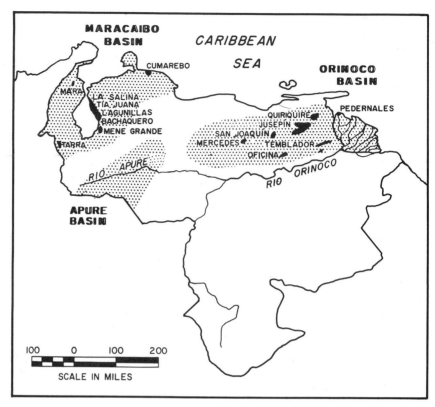

Fig. 3-5. *The three great sedimentary basins of Venezuela. The Lake Maracaibo Basin is by far the most important producer in the country. (Courtesy of Creole Petroleum Corporation.)*

Orinoco Basin Fields. Second richest producing oil fields in Venezuela are to be found in Anzoátegui and Monagas states. In 1958 there were 3,800 active wells in the basin with a daily output of 730,894 barrels. Principal fields are Quiriquire, Jusepín, and Oficina; but there are many less famous ones (Fig. 3-5).

Oil is pumped from the fields through four main pipelines to Puerto La Cruz (Anzoátegui) and one to Caripito (Monagas) for refining and shipping.

The Apure Basin. This basin, in the states of Apure, Barinas, and Portuguesa, does not as yet have impressive commercial production; in 1960 it contributed only about 2 per cent of the national total. However, a pipeline connects the fields with Puerto Cabello.

COLOMBIA

Colombia is believed to have rather large petroleum resources, but the country has not yet lived up to the high hopes held for it. New discoveries have been disappointing. Production in 1960 was about 56 million barrels.

The principal field, as well as the oldest and largest, is the Infantas–La Cira, in the Middle Magdalena Valley (Fig. 3-3). A refinery meeting domestic needs operates at Barranca-Bermeja on the river and is connected by pipeline with Cartagena on the coast and with Bogotá and Medellin in the Andes. A pipeline also connects this field with the port of Coveñas on the Caribbean, from which crude oil is exported.

A second producing field is the Catatumbo in the Barco Concession bordering on Venezuela. Development here languished until 1938, when a pipeline was completed over a branch of the Andes to the coast. Approximately half of Colombia's oil is exported.

PERU

Peru produces oil on both sides of the Andes, though most commercial production has occurred in the extreme north along the Pacific Ocean near Talara.

Several thousand barrels of oil are also produced daily in the Aguas Calientes Concessions (Ganso Azul) along the Pachitea River in the Upper Amazon region. Output here is limited, however, because the small population means a restricted market; most of the output is sent by barge to Manaus, Brazil, for refining and the balance to the national refinery in Iquitos.

BOLIVIA

Bolivia has potential oil land on the east side of the Andes extending from Peru to Argentina (Fig. 3-3). Developments may prove this area to be one of the most productive in all South America. At present the Camiri Field in the southeast outranks all others in importance. Development and output in Bolivia have been retarded for the following reasons: (1) The reserves lie in a sparsely inhabited, largely undeveloped area. (2) The country lacks the financial resources and technical skill to exploit the oil properly. (3) Until very recently foreign oil companies were unwilling to enter the country, which, in the 1930s, confiscated foreign concessions and placed oil wells and other installations under a state-controlled oil corporation; however, in 1954 Bolivia passed the Petroleum Code, which offers strong guarantees to foreign oil companies investing capital within the country.

Oil appears to offer the only possibility for strengthening the country's weakened economy; but oil development requires heavy investment of capital, specialized technical skills, stable political conditions, and a favorable investment climate. Bolivia has been woefully weak in the last two.

ARGENTINA

Even though it ranks thirteenth among the countries of the world in proved reserves (Table 3-1), until recently Argentina was unimpressive in the world of petroleum—mainly because (1) the entire industry was state-owned, and the state carried out all exploratory and development work; and (2) there was a dearth of capital. Violent oil nationalism is of long standing in Argentina, and it has steadfastly refused to allow any foreign companies to explore or drill. Under *Yacimientos Petroliferos Fiscales*, Argentina produced only about 100,000 barrels of oil a day but consumed 300,000 barrels. The imported 200,000 barrels cost the country some 350 million dollars annually and were a heavy drain on foreign exchange.

In 1958 the country was on the verge of bankruptcy and in desperation solicited foreign capital to aid the state monopoly in service and development. Drilling took place immediately from Tierra del Fuego to the Bolivian border; within seventeen months production was up 30 per cent; and by 1961 Argentina was meeting virtually her entire petroleum requirements.

The fields are in four areas: (1) near Salta in the extreme northwest; (2) near Mendoza, only a few miles from the Andes; (3) the Neuquén area in the Territory of Neuquén; and (4) around Comodoro Rivadavia (Fig. 3-3) in Patagonia's Chubut Territory (by far the most important).

EUROPE

Relative to its population, world importance, and consumption (about 17 per cent of the world output), Europe has been poor in petroleum production. It has about 1 per cent of the world's known reserves (Table 3-1) and accounts for some 3 per cent of the world output. Of the five great powers in Europe at the outbreak of World War II—Great Britain, France, Germany, Italy, and the Soviet Union—only the last named was a major oil producer.

Europe's petroleum record is unimpressive because the broken and disturbed rock structures that characterize much of the western and southern portions make them unpromising for discovery of extensive petroliferous areas. There are, however, a number of sedimentary basins, which represent potential producing areas. In some of these basins—in Alsace, southwestern France, northern Italy, northwestern Germany, eastern Netherlands, the Vienna Basin of Austria, and southern and middle England—small oil and gas fields already have been found.

Though exploration has been particularly active since 1950, Europe still must depend upon non-European sources for more than 90 per cent of its oil requirements. Most comes from the Middle East, though increasing amounts are moving from North Africa. Should Middle Eastern oil for any reason be denied Western Europe, as occurred during the Suez crisis, Europe's economy would be struck a body blow. Since Western Europe has been only superficially explored, its proved and potential reserves are imperfectly known; but some oil geologists believe that the area could supply as much as 50 per cent of its needs. Of the total European production, Eastern Europe (including the Soviet Union) provides much the larger share: 1,888,582,852 barrels compared with Western Europe's 97,501,920 barrels (1960).

ROMANIA

Next to the Soviet Union, Romania has been Europe's leading producer of petroleum. Several fields on the plains east of the Carpathian Mountains, most famous of which is the Ploesti area (Fig. 3-3) north of Bucharest, supplied almost all the country's oil and much of the needs of Central Europe prior to World War II. During and following 1941, Romania provided more than half of Germany's crude-oil requirements. The Ploesti area was first attacked from the air in August 1943, and a year later Ploesti's production had been so reduced as to cripple Germany's fighting forces. By April 1945, the German oil industry had been so devastated that the end was not far off. Germany's utter ruin demonstrated that, deprived of ample oil supplies, no nation can survive a protracted modern

war. Today the Ploesti fields supply only about one third of the total Romanian output.

SOVIET UNION

The Soviet Union,[3] by reason of its enormous size and the great extent of its sedimentary formations, holds considerable promise of becoming the richest of all nations in petroleum. Its ultimate oil reserves may amount to one third of the world's total. Its produceable reserves are estimated to comprise about 9 per cent of the world's proved reserves (Table 3-1). By 1959 the Soviet Union, which had been displaced by Venezuela, regained second place though Venezuela's capacity still was greater. Production exceeded one billion barrels in 1960. Soviet planners depend upon petroleum rather than upon coal, water power, or atomic energy to meet their power needs.[4] The share of oil and gas (mostly oil) in the fuel balance will increase from 33 per cent in 1957 to 67 per cent in 1972. At present, however, Russia is 65 per cent a coal economy.

The geography of oil in the Soviet Union has changed greatly. Prior to World War II, about 90 per cent of the total output was from the Caucasus fields (near Baku, and at Grozny, and Maikop). By 1950, the proportion had fallen to one half; and by 1960, to less than a quarter. Today the relatively new Volga-Ural area (formerly known as the "Second Baku") dominates, supplying more than two thirds of the total output. The whole of

[3] Russia's claims of oil reserves, fields, and production tend to be viewed with prejudice and distrust in the countries comprising the Free World. Yet these claims of the Russian government should not be discounted without direct evidence to the contrary, despite the fact that many claims have proved to be greatly exaggerated. Complete systematic reports on the Russian petroleum industry are lacking. Various Free World agencies are engaged in getting information out of the Soviet Union and assembling it painstakingly. Only against a background of world politics, economics, and geography can the Russian oil industry be viewed adequately.

[4] M. Brenner, "Problems of Oil in the Long Range Development of U.S.S.R. National Economy," *Current Digest of the Soviet Press*, 10:3-7, 39, July 9, 1958.

Soviet Asia contributes only about 7 per cent of the total.

Until the past several years the Soviet Union did not engage importantly in the world of oil-export business. Oil, however, offers the Soviet Union one of its most potent weapons for economic and political penetration of Free World countries. The move, coming at a time when there is a surplus of oil seeking an outlet from Venezuela, North Africa, and the Middle East, threatens the price stability of petroleum and its products in world markets.

Figure 3-3 shows the location of the Russian petroleum regions and fields. The pattern is impressive: most of the production comes from west of the Urals. The principal fields are in two major groups—the Volga-Ural and the Caucasus.

Volga-Ural Region. The discovery of this huge oil basin between 1930 and 1940, when the fields in the Caucasus definitely were declining, was a milestone in the history of Russian oil. The region, about the size of Spain, lies some 1,000 miles east of Moscow, in a rough quadrangle formed by the cities of Kirov and Perm in the north and Saratov and Orenburg in the south. The Ural Mountains now form the eastern border, the Volga River the western; but ultimately the area will reach farther west.

Three oil centers stand out in the Volga-Ural field—Perm, Ufa, and Kuibyshev. In 1959 the fields produced about 75 per cent of the country's total output of 2.65 million barrels per day. The oil is of high quality.

Baku's decline as the center of oil activities has all but eliminated the water transport of oil, which previously moved over the Caspian Sea, the Volga River, and canals to Moscow and Leningrad. Movement is now by pipeline. Russia's longest pipeline carries crude oil from the Volga River to Lake Baikal—a distance of 2,315 miles.

Caucasus Region. The fields comprising this region are located near Baku, on the west side of the Caspian Sea, and at Grozny and Maikop, north and south of the Caucasus Mountains. The area near Baku is the oldest in the Soviet Union, several fields having produced uninterruptedly since the 1870s. Because the oil deposits are concentrated in a very narrow space, there being up to 22 successive producing horizons, Baku has occupied an outstanding position among the oil-producing areas of the world. However, Baku is located a great distance from all the principal markets, and, in addition, its production is falling rapidly. Although during the middle 1950s an effort was made to maintain output by extensive repressuring, deeper drilling, and extensions over Caspian Sea waters, this oil cost three times as much as in 1946.

The Grozny and Maikop areas, along with Baku, have been declining in output for many years.

Sakhalin. No important proved oil reserves are known to exist in the huge area lying between the Volga-Ural oil field and the Pacific Ocean. However, on Sakhalin Island (Fig. 3-3) are deposits currently yielding an estimated 1.2 million tons per year. The oil fields lie mostly north of the 40th parallel. The importance of this production cannot be exaggerated, for without it the armed forces, industry, and shipping would have to depend either upon imports or upon European Russia.

ASIA

The petroleum reserves of Asia are put at about 65 per cent of the world total. However, the Middle East alone claims the bulk of the proved world reserves—about 60 per cent (Fig. 3-3).

THE MIDDLE EAST

The Middle East, possibly the best example of the fact that petroleum is seldom found where it is needed, produces about 5½ million barrels per day—approximately a quarter of the world output.

During the past two decades Middle Eastern oil has largely displaced Western Hemisphere oil in European and Asian markets. The region ships 4 to 5 million barrels of oil daily, most of it to Western Europe. Europe's economic growth is predicated upon a vast expansion of energy, and oil is counted upon to provide more than half that energy. However, Western Europe is capable of producing less than one eighth of its own daily requirements. The Middle East was formerly regarded as possessing the only reserves large enough to care for Europe's increasing demands, although the recent discoveries and production in Algeria and Libya are changing this picture considerably.

Though fabulously rich in petroleum, the Middle East is an otherwise poor area, without the capital or technical ability to develop its oil. Development is in the hands of foreign corporations operating under concessions that provide 50-50 terms (although Japanese and Italian companies are reported to be operating under 75-25 agreements, 75 per cent going to the country with the oil). Investments in Middle Eastern oil have a nominal value of approximately 3 billion dollars; United States companies control about 57 per cent of the output, British companies about 28 per cent, and British-Dutch companies about 8 per cent.

The region is unique because of the great size of the oil pools within a small area and the enormous yields per well. Wells flow naturally by gas or water drive. Some gas is returned both to increase oil output and to conserve the gas itself, though two thirds is believed to be lost. Nowhere else in the world is petroleum produced at such low cost. Production could be increased very appreciably with the addition of only a small number of wells.

The major oil fields are to be found in the sedimentary basin in the half-dozen countries around the upper end of the Persian Gulf. Exploration, however, involves many problems: much of the region is extremely rugged, and part is covered by migrating sand dunes. Some of the largest sand stretches in the world are in Saudi Arabia, where conditions are particularly trying to foreigners. Here workers experience difficulty working in out-of-door temperatures of 125°F to 130°F; at these temperatures metal becomes so hot the men must bury their tools temporarily in the sand before using them. Driving trucks in the deep sand

presents a problem, met only by employing vehicles with four-wheel drive and special tires of very low pressure (an idea obtained from the camel's super-padded foot). Moreover, men and materials have had to be transported thousands of miles and new communities had to be built on the hot, desolate desert.

Iran. British interests were long entrenched here; in 1904, a pioneering British crew drilled the Middle East's first well, near the present Iran-Iraq border, about 400 miles north of the Persian Gulf. The Anglo-Iranian Oil Company formerly exploited almost all Iran's oil. The principal fields (Fig. 3-6) are the Masjid-i-Sulaiman and the Haft Kel, in southwestern Iran. Crude oil is piped to the port of Bandar Mashar; and oil for refining is piped to Abadan, an island in the Shatt-al-Arab River. The Masjid-i-Sulaiman field has yielded more than a billion barrels of crude oil, ranking it close to East Texas, Lagunillas (Venezuela), and Baku (U.S.S.R.) in total output. Currently this field is surpassed by the Haft Kel in daily output. Iranian proved reserves are shown in Table 3-1.

In 1951, Iran, convinced that the petroleum resources were not bringing adequate financial return to the country, nationalized the industry. Prior to nationalization, it was producing about 243 million barrels of oil per year and was operating the world's largest refinery at Abadan. Expropriation proved disastrous and brought the oil industry to a virtual standstill. Finally, in 1953, with a new government, the oil problem was settled; in 1954, a consortium of eight international oil companies was formed, and large-scale production was resumed. Once more Iran ranks among the world leaders in oil output. New reserves have been developed and new areas opened for exploration.

Iraq. Following World War I foreign interests (British, Dutch, French, and American) acquired oil concessions in Iraq. Iraq's proved reserves are large (Table 3-1). The oil fields lie in the northern part of the country and are an extension of the deposits of southwestern Iran (Fig. 3-6).

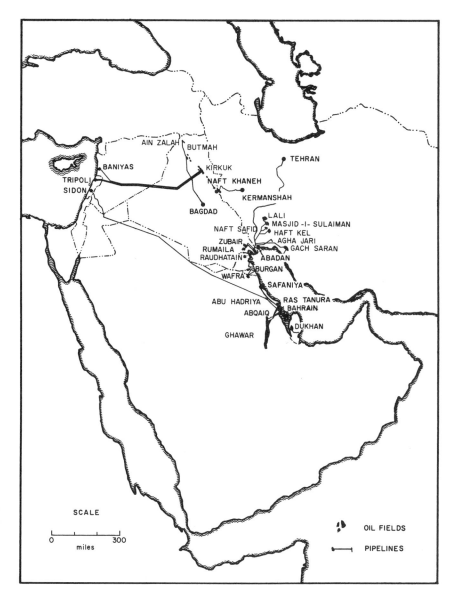

Fig. 3-6. Major Middle Eastern oil fields and pipelines. The "center of gravity" of world oil has shifted to this region. Note that pipelines move in two directions: (1) to the Persian Gulf and (2) to the Mediterranean.

Most famous field is the Kirkuk in the north. A new field—the Zubair, discovered in 1949—lies near the head of the Persian Gulf. A double pipeline was constructed from Kirkuk to Baniyas in Syria and to Tripoli in Lebanon on the Mediterranean, and from Zubair to the port of Fao at the mouth of the Shatt-al-Arab.

Production averages about 354.5 million barrels, which gives Iraq sixth place among the world's oil-producing countries. Royalties average about 200 million dollars per annum.

Kuwait. Before oil was discovered here, this tiny sheikdom of sand desert—situated at the head of the Persian Gulf (Fig. 3-6)—was known only for pearl fishing and international smuggling. Now, with an output of 594.2 million barrels in 1960, Kuwait ranks fourth among the oil-producing nations of the world. Though only about 100 miles across at its widest point, it possesses the world's largest proved oil reserves (Table 3-1). South of Kuwait is a so-called Neutral Zone, which also yields oil.

Kuwait, acre for acre, is regarded as the world's most valuable piece of real estate. The annual royalties amount to 260 to 400 million dollars. Much of the oil money has gone into new schools, welfare services for the poor, roads, waterworks, and many other benefits for the population of about 200,000 people.

Saudi Arabia. The oil industry in Saudi Arabia dates only from 1932, when oil was discovered. Today the country ranks second in proved reserves and fifth in production. Proved reserves are believed to be about one fifth of the total world reserves (Table 3-1); production in 1960 was 456.45 million barrels.

The principal producing areas, located and named in Figure 3-6, mostly are part of a single very large field stretching 140 miles—the Ghawar field. All production is confined to the eastern part of the country, on or relatively near the Persian Gulf.

Drilling has begun in the offshore area of the Persian Gulf, in what is said to be the largest offshore field in the world. This immense continental shelf is covered by 30 to 45 feet of water and extends nearly 600 miles from Kuwait in the north to beyond the Trucial coast in the south. Estimated reserves are the largest of any offshore field in the world. The oil is heavy and high in fuel content, just the opposite of the gasoline-rich crude of the onshore wells.

Saudi Arabia is well served by pipelines, which extend from the fields to ports and refineries. There is a great concentration of pipelines from the southwest and northwest on the sand spit that juts out into the Persian Gulf near Ras Tanura. The most important pipe-

line, however, is TAP-line, which extends 753 miles—from Aramco's tank farm at Qaisumah to its marine terminal at the ancient port of Sidon, Lebanon—and saves a 3,200-mile tanker voyage around Arabia. TAP-line has a daily capacity of 460,000 barrels but, because of excess capacity and an oversupply of tankers, is actually moving about 300,000 barrels.

INDONESIA

Although oil interests have searched intensively for petroleum in Eastern and Southern Asia, the Sumatra discoveries are the only ones of major consequence as yet. These deposits are more important because of their geographic and strategic location, near approximately half the world's population (the markets of oil-starved Eastern and Southern Asia), than because of the extent of the reserves and the annual output. Asia outside the Middle East can claim only about 4 per cent of the world oil reserves. Proved reserves for Indonesia are shown in Table 3-1.

Although the principal oil fields are in Sumatra, there is some production too in Borneo, Java, and Sarawak (Fig. 3-3). Sumatra's principal producing fields lie across the Strait of Malacca opposite Singapore. Virtually the entire output is consumed in the Far East.

NORTH AFRICA

What may prove to be one of the world's major oil developments is taking place over an area of 2 million square miles in North Africa's Sahara Desert. It is too soon to know positively the force of the impact it will make on the world oil market; and the reserves shown in Table 3-1 should not be accepted at face value, because oil companies have as yet investigated only very superficially. However, North African oil has a sure market in the six Common Market countries and is certain to bring about some reshuffling of the oil trade routes of the world. If the oil fields prove to be as productive as all signs presently indicate they will be, Western Europe no longer will have to depend upon Middle East nationalists; North African oil can be moved easily to market, and its flow cannot be plugged by closing the Suez Canal or by blasting pipelines that go to the Mediterranean. However, the whole of North Africa is a potential powder keg that could adversely affect the oil business of the region. Moreover, this oil must be sought and won in the Sahara, one of the most forbidding landscapes on earth; man can win here only with the most modern equipment and methods and by working with nature as closely as possible.

ALGERIA

North Africa's first oil well was brought in by the French in 1956 near the Tunisian border. Later oil was struck at Hassi Messaoud, to the west. Exploratory efforts already assure large reserves.

In 1960 the two leading fields were at Hassi Messaoud and Edjele. Production at Hassi Messaoud in a proved area of about 800 square miles comes from a depth of about 11,-000 feet. Drilling costs are high, up to a million dollars per well; but output per well is high, from 16,000 to 45,000 barrels a day. It is not yet known how long such production can be maintained.

A 412-mile pipeline, costing 105 million dollars, has been built from Hassi Messaoud to Bougie on the Mediterranean; and another from Edjele to La Skhira in Tunisia on the Mediterranean. Harbor and terminal facilities have also been constructed.

The importance of Algerian oil to France can scarcely be exaggerated, for France has been importing roughly 182 million barrels of oil per year (550,000 barrels a day)—over 90 per cent of her total requirements and at a cost of 350 to 400 million dollars per year. It is too soon to know how France will fare in the oil picture now that Algeria is independent.

LIBYA

In 1959 Libya moved impressively onto the world oil map. A number of producing wells were brought in over a dozen widely separated areas by several different companies. By January 1960, exploration was in full swing. The principal reason for the intensive exploration is that the concessionaires had to return one fourth of their acreage to the Libyan gov-

ernment at the end of 1960; and they did not wish to surrender any part of their holdings without first exploring for oil. The concessionaires spent an estimated 150 to 200 million dollars in exploration between 1955 and 1960.

The principal field discovered, the Zelten, is an extensive one situated only about 100 miles from the Gulf of Sirte on the Mediterranean Sea (Fig. 3-3). The wells lie at only moderate depth—less than 6,000 feet. The first producing well—one of the most prolific in North Africa—flowed at a rate of 17,500 barrels a day. The cost of constructing pipelines is not so high nor the task so difficult as in many other major oil-producing areas. Yet the cost of a pipeline from Zelton to the Mediterranean was about 50 million dollars.

Finding markets for Libyan production will not be easy at a time when there is a world surplus of oil—about 5 million barrels daily in the late 1950s. However, Libyan oil enjoys one significant geographical advantage over Middle Eastern oil: it is closer to Europe, and it does not have to go through the Suez Canal. It is also closer to Europe than is Venezuelan oil.

AUSTRALIA

Petroleum in Australia is considered here not because of the extent of the reserves or the annual production but because oil geologists for more than half a century have steadfastly believed that petroleum is present in commercial quantity. Oilmen remain mystified by the fact that the first well drilled, in Western Australia near Exmouth Gulf, was successful but that every well drilled around it has been a **duster**. Every new scientific device for the detection of oil has been employed, and more than 35 million dollars has been invested. In 1961 a producing well was drilled at Moonie, Queensland, about 225 miles west of Brisbane. Nine more wells were drilled nearby during the succeeding year, and, remarkably, every one produced oil. It is, however, too early to assess the potentialities of the area. The main point is that foreign oil companies continue to believe that ultimately Australia will yield petroleum in commercial quantities.

Fig. 3-7. Part of huge petroleum refinery at Lake Charles, Louisiana, on the Calcasieu River, 29 miles from the Gulf of Mexico. This refinery works day and night throughout the year. Outlined in the glitter of thousands of lights on their steel frameworks, these catalytic cracking units rearrange the atoms of the petroleum molecule into components of innumerable products. (Courtesy of Cities Service Company, by Tony Linck.)

PETROLEUM REFINING

After crude oil is brought to the surface, it must be refined before it can be sold commercially. In its simplest form, refining consists of *distillation*. Modern refineries (Fig. 3-7) may manufacture as many as 2,000 different products, most of which were not even dreamed of twenty-five years ago. Refining is carried on by a bewildering variety of instruments, ranging from a simple pressure gauge to a multimillion-dollar electronic computer.

GEOGRAPHICAL DISTRIBUTION OF OIL REFINERIES

Petroleum refining is widely distributed over the earth (Fig. 3-8). Generally considered, there are three types of refineries: field, market, and seaboard.

FIELD REFINERIES

These refineries, situated at or very near the source of their crude oil, supply products to their own area and elsewhere. Field refineries tend to be small, though several large ones have been established in the Midcontinent Province. They generally lack pipeline and tanker facilities for efficient transport of their petroleum and must, therefore, locate close to the oil fields in order to obtain continuous supplies for operation. In numerous instances these refineries are short-lived, operating for just a few years, after which they are shut down and dismantled. A typical example of a field refinery is at Shelby, Montana.

SEABOARD REFINERIES

Seaboard refineries are large refineries located on navigable water and served by pipelines or tankers and barges, or both. Often sea-

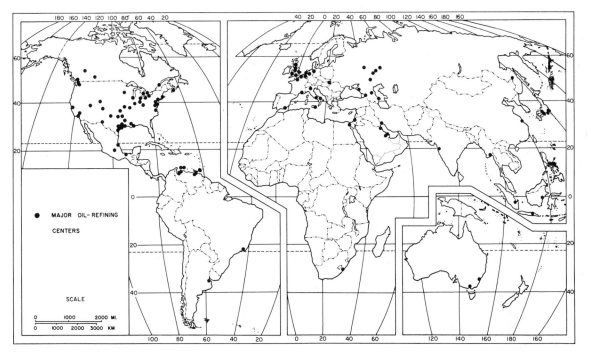

Fig. 3-8. *World petroleum refineries. Few economic world maps change as rapidly as the one of oil refineries. Nevertheless, the essential pattern remains quite constant. Note particularly the heavy concentration of refineries in Western Europe and in the United States.*

board-refinery locations are at intermediate trans-shipment points between crude-oil supplies and markets. Good examples are Abadan, Iran; Aruba and Curaçao, Dutch West Indies; and Ras Tanura, Saudi Arabia. Possibly the outstanding example of seaboard location is the United States Gulf Coast. From its refineries, products move by tanker or barge to domestic markets along the Gulf and East Coasts and along the Mississippi waterway, and by tanker to foreign markets.

MARKET REFINERIES

Refineries in this classification are large and are market oriented. They may or may not have significant oil reserves nearby. The refined products are primarily though not exclusively for local and nearby markets. Such refineries may be at seaboard locations near large cities and industrial complexes (for example, Philadelphia) or at inland points (for example, Chicago). Market refineries come

into being in order to reduce transport costs between the producing fields and the markets for petroleum products. The refineries are located as close to the potential markets as possible or where water transportation can be utilized to marketing centers.

Sometimes refineries of this class perform the functions of both the seaboard and market types. Thus, the Richmond refinery on San Francisco Bay not only supplies the important local market but reaches eastward for some distance, provides coast cities in Oregon and Washington, and ships to Alaska.

UNITED STATES REFINING

The refinery map changes constantly but the pattern does not, and this is what is significant. The importance of the United States with its 313 establishments out of a world total of 645 (January 1959) fairly leaps from the map. These American refineries account for more than half the total world output of refined-petroleum products. Although all but a few states have refineries, about 90 per cent of the total capacity is in ten states: Texas, California, Pennsylvania, New Jersey, Illinois, Indiana, Oklahoma, Massachusetts, Kansas, and Ohio. The notable concentration along the three seaboards indicates the influence of tanker and pipeline transportation on refinery location.

The *Gulf Coast*, with more than one third of the refining capacity of the nation, leads by far. Growth is associated with heavy crude production in the Gulf Coast and Midcontinent Provinces. In second place is the *Great Lakes–Midwest* area; with its large refineries between Buffalo and Kansas City, it accounts for about a quarter of the nation's refining. Chicago is the largest marketing and transshipment center in this area. The *East Coast*, stretching from New York to Philadelphia, is impressive. It serves not only the large domestic market but foreign markets as well. To some extent it has suffered by the expansion of facilities in the Gulf Coast. Until 1950 New York City was the largest oil-refining center in the nation. On the *Pacific Coast*, the metropolitan Los Angeles and the San Francisco Bay areas are outstanding. Los Angeles, with 10 per cent of the national refining capacity, exemplifies a location where an important oil-producing region, a large refined-products market, and an ocean and rail transport point all merge. The San Francisco Bay area receives Central Valley crude petroleum by pipeline and some California coastal oil along with imports by tanker from Venezuela, Sumatra, and the Middle East. *Rocky Mountain* refineries are mostly oriented to the nearby supply of crude oil, and their output does not exceed the regional demand for refined products. Any area, then, is satisfactory for refining as long as the immediate hinterland provides a sufficiently large market.

WESTERN EUROPEAN REFINING

Western Europe's refining industry is growing faster than that elsewhere in the Free World. More than 200,000 barrels of new capacity have been added since 1955, raising the total to 3.3 million barrels a day. Most Western European countries are sharing in the expansion. The circle of nations with refineries also is widening. Only three—Denmark, Luxembourg, and Switzerland—lack substantial capacity. Britain has the largest refinery output in Europe, closely followed by France. Italy, however, has the largest number of oil refineries and is most dependent on oil for energy.

Most of Western Europe's refineries fall into the market type, virtually no petroleum products being exported. Moreover, they tend to be large refineries, since these offer significant advantages in reducing processing costs where fluids and gases are handled.

OIL SHALE

When petroleum in pools either is exhausted or the cost of recovering that still in the ground in old oil fields becomes positively uneconomical, the oil shales offer a substitute source for petroleum. Since these resources can be measured with considerable accuracy, and since such deposits occur over extensive areas, the oil shales must be regarded as a future major source of liquid fuels. However, the real competitive position of oil shale will not be known until the first commercial plants go into operation. Development will come when the price of crude oil soars; a sufficiently high price for crude should permit the exploitation of oil shale on a competitive basis. For decades, fuel oil has been successfully recovered from shale in Northern Europe, China (Manchuria), and Japan. The countries with the most extensive oil-shale deposits are the United States, Australia, Canada, China (Manchuria), and the Soviet Union.

UNITED STATES

Oil shales, at least in part, are true greenish-black marine shales; but most, at least in the United States, are marlstone. They contain not petroleum but kerogen, which can be converted into liquid form as shale oil—which in turn can be catalytically hydrogenated under moderate heat and pressure, and processed by conventional oil-refining practices to yield the same products as petroleum.

Enormous deposits of oil shale are known to be present in the Rocky Mountains (particularly Utah, Colorado, and Wyoming), in the northern Appalachians, and on the margins of the Ozarks. By conservative estimates, these American sources are believed to contain a potential reserve of about 250 billion to 300 billion barrels, or a recoverable content about five times greater than the proved conventional oil reserves of the entire United States. Oilmen estimate that in Colorado, Utah, and Wyoming alone the deposits are sufficient to provide 2 million barrels of oil a day for 500 years. Less is known regarding the oil-shale reserves of other countries, but many scientists believe that American sources alone contain much more oil than the entire world has produced to date.

SOVIET UNION

With oil-shale reserves estimated at about 55 billion tons, the Soviet Union is one of the most important oil-shale regions on earth. The largest Russian deposits are in the northeastern corner of Estonia at Kokhtla-Yarve. Commercial production began there in 1918, when Estonia was an independent country. The oil-shale strata are on the average only 7 feet thick, but they cover an area of about 1,500 square miles. These deposits, estimated at 5 billion tons, might theoretically yield a billion tons of crude oil. Unexploited deposits are found in many areas.

ATHABASKA TAR SANDS

In western Canada, about 200 miles northeast of Edmonton, occur the Athabaska "tar sands," the world's largest surface show of petroleum. Estimates place the oil content of the tar sands at 100 billion barrels. However, this oil under present economic conditions is unavailable, for the bitumen-like crude will not flow; it must be mined. Moreover, because of high sulfur content and deficiency in hydrogen, refining (particularly into light products) is difficult. The tar sands thus present not only a great future source of oil but a technological and economic challenge.

NATURAL GAS

Natural gas—which is a mixture of hydrocarbons of the paraffin series, mainly methane (CH_4)—is generally but not always associated with petroleum, and is the ideal fuel. It is sootless and essentially odorless, and has twice the calorific value of manufactured gas. It is the most convenient and the most readily controllable of all fuels. It is also the cheapest source of energy for many purposes. Since production, transmission, and distribution require far fewer man-hours than coal and petroleum, salaries and wages are a relatively small item.

Most gas reserves were discovered during searches for petroleum, and about 35 per cent of all gas is obtained as a sideline to oil production. For many years natural gas was discarded as a nuisance and as a waste byproduct of petroleum, but it is now regarded as a precious source of energy, is saved, and sent to markets by pipeline.

Natural gas has two modes of occurrence: it is found by itself, in distinct gas reservoirs; and it is found with petroleum. Gas from oil wells, known as "wet" gas, is rich in volatile gasoline. It is run from well to gasoline plant, where the gasoline is extracted. Free gas, often known as "dry" gas, is usually ready to go directly into pipelines. About 30 per cent of all the gas produced in the United States comes from oil wells, and about 70 per cent is dry or nonassociated gas.

Although most petroleum-producing countries also possess natural gas, only the United States is at present a major producer, transporter, and consumer. Outside the United States there has been comparatively little exploitation and consumption of natural gas. Reserves for the entire world are estimated at about 7,500 trillion cubic feet of gas still untapped and as yet undiscovered in areas where they cannot currently be readily produced and transported. At least a fifth of the world reserves are believed to be in the United States.

UNITED STATES

As of 1960 only the United States used natural gas on a gigantic scale, it alone ac-

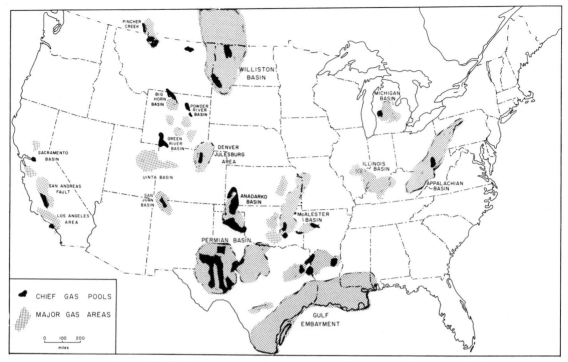

Fig. 3-9. *Major natural-gas provinces in the United States. A baffling paradox is that natural gas often is located in out-of-the-way and almost inaccessible places. Therefore, transporting it from where it is found to where it is wanted is a task of the first magnitude. (After map by American Gas Association.)*

counting for approximately 85 per cent of world consumption. In the past 50 years expansion of the natural-gas industry can be discussed only in superlatives: production increased 2,000 per cent. It has been gaining on coal since 1900 and is now moving up on petroleum. From less than 5 per cent a little more than 25 years ago, natural gas in 1959 supplied about 28 per cent of the total fuel energy needs of the nation.

The Southwest, plus Louisiana, possesses most of the natural gas. Texas and Louisiana jointly account for 68 per cent of the production and are credited with 67 per cent of the proved reserves. They, along with Oklahoma, Kansas, New Mexico, and California, account for 90 per cent of both output and reserves (Fig. 3-9).

The major uses of natural gas are for oilfield operations, house heating, water heating,

cooking, and generation of electricity; and in the manufacture of cement, clay products, aluminum, glass, and carbon black. It is employed also in oil refining. At least 40 per cent of all petrochemicals are derived from natural gas. New industrial uses being sought include evaporation processes for freshening sea water, smelting of iron ore, and construction of fuel cells powered by natural gas.

In the early 1920s consumption of natural gas was largely confined to areas close to the producing fields. The most important single development economically, has been the use in quantity, of large-diameter, high-pressure, seamless steel pipe capable of being welded together. When special pipe-laying machinery and scientific knowledge regarding the extent and life of the reserves became available, the building of long-distance transmission lines began. Improved conservation practice has made available large quantities of natural gas to the pipeline companies. At first natural gas was transported a few hundred miles, then distances up to 2,000 miles from the points of origin. Today major trunk pipelines extend into all but three states. All major producing areas are now connected with almost all important consuming areas. As of January 1, 1960, the United States had a network of natural-gas pipelines exceeding 654,000 miles —the nation's greatest privately owned land-transportation system.

In 1951 United States reserves of natural gas were estimated at about 262.6 trillion cubic feet, but many geologists predict that ultimate reserves will reach 400 to 600 trillion cubic feet—an amount that should last the nation 50 to 60 years irrespective of demands.

CANADA

Canada is reported to have reserves of about 21 trillion cubic feet (1955), three fourths of which is regarded as "dry" gas. This would last more than one hundred years at the present rate of consumption. Natural gas is by far the cheapest source of energy in Canada (only one third as costly as coal, which is next cheapest). But natural gas's share of the Canadian energy market, though rising rapidly, is little in excess of 6 per cent.

Even though Canadian consumption is rising and pipelines are being extended to the more populous and more industrialized areas, Canada still has huge surpluses of natural gas, which neighboring United States wishes to purchase. In April 1960, the Canadian National Energy Board and the federal government approved exportation to the United States of about 1 billion cubic feet of natural gas daily for a period of twenty-five years. Much of this supply is being sent by pipeline as far distant as California.

MEXICO

Mexico sends gas to Mexico City from the Poza Rica field; gas is also sent from Ciudad Pemex close to the Guatemalan border via a natural-gas pipeline that is more than 500 miles long and crosses marsh, plain, and mountain. A gas pipeline about 155 miles long serves the manufacturing city of Monterrey. Future projects will tie Mexico's natural gas fields in Reynosa, Poza Rica, and Tabasco to every major industrial city in the country. Mexico's gas is used for industrial purposes.

VENEZUELA

Venezuela is extremely rich in natural gas and accounts for about 10 per cent of the world output. A nationwide pipeline network is now under construction; and a new petrochemical industry at Morón in Carabobo State, 15 miles from Puerto Cabello, is based wholly upon natural gas.

Much gas is today injected under high pressure into producing oil reservoirs under Lake Maracaibo. The injected gas forces more oil out of the reservoir (one-third increase in ultimate recovery), and the gas itself is stored there for further use. Even so, nearly 70 per cent of the gas is flared into the atmosphere— wasted; in the past, as much as 85 per cent was flared.

ARGENTINA

A very long natural-gas pipeline reaches 1,100 miles across five Argentine provinces, connecting Comodoro Rivadavia on the south with Buenos Aires on the north. The line carries 250 million cubic feet of natural gas daily to the Pampa.

SOVIET UNION

The Soviet Union is extremely well endowed in natural gas, though as late as 1957 this source of energy was providing a mere 4 per cent of the total consumed. The most important and largest proved reserves are in the Bukhara-Khiva Depression. Russia is gearing more of its industrial fuel use to natural gas and has nearly tripled output since 1960.

WORLD OUTLOOK FOR PETROLEUM

Crude oil is today regarded as the world's most valuable single mineral product. No one knows how much petroleum there is in the world. Estimates of proved reserves, even of total reserves, have long been pessimistic. A common figure for the reserves of the world as a whole is an amount adequate to last for two hundred years at the present rate of consumption; for the United States alone, the figure is 25 to 50 years. Many experts in the industry, however, are far from gloomy. They point out the fallacy of the pessimistic group's arguments, calling attention to their misinterpretation of the oil industry's calculations of reserves, *proved reserves*—those available at any specific moment. Such estimates, they contend, are only an inventory of immediately available oil in the ground. Estimates by A. I.

Levorsen [5] showed proved reserves at 70 billion barrels and undiscovered reserves, on land and under the sea, at 1½ trillion barrels. He considers these estimates the best and most reasonable that can be made with man's present geological knowledge, *but he cautions against regarding them as final*. In any event, he envisages no petroleum shortage in the foreseeable future, for the world as a whole or for the two leading powers—the United States and the Soviet Union.

[5] A. I. Levorsen, "Estimates of Undiscovered Petroleum Reserves" in *Proceedings of the United Nations Scientific Conference on the Conservation and Utilization of Resources* (Lake Success, N. Y.: United Nations, Department of Economic Affairs, 1950), I:98, 99.

SELECTED REFERENCES

Hodgkins, J. A. *Soviet Power: Energy Resources, Production, and Potentials.* Englewood Cliffs, New Jersey, Prentice-Hall, Inc., 1961.

Knowles, Ruth Sheldon. *The Greatest Gamblers: The Epic of American Oil Exploration.* New York, McGraw-Hill Book Company, Inc., 1959.

Kostanick, H. L. "Oil in World Politics," *Current History,* 33:1-6, July 1957.

Melamid, A. "Geographical Distribution of Petroleum Refining Capacities," *Economic Geography,* 31:168-178, April 1955.

————————. "Geography of the World Petroleum Price Structure," *Economic Geography,* 38:283-298, October 1962.

Netschert, Bruce C. *The Future Supply of Oil and Gas.* Baltimore, Johns Hopkins Press, 1958.

Pratt, W. E., and Dorothy Good. *World Geography of Petroleum.* New York, American Geographical Society, 1950.

Skeet, T. H. H. "Past and Future: The Economic Impact of Oil," *Petroleum,* 23:373-376, October 1960.

Stockton, J. R., R. C. Henshaw, and R. W. Graves. *Economics of Natural Gas in Texas.* Bureau of Business Research, University of Texas, Austin, 1952.

CHAPTER FOUR ::

The world demand for energy is soaring to
dizzy heights and at an unparalleled rate.
The world's population today is estimated at
more than 3 billion, and the annual increase is
about 48 million. World population is expected to double each forty to fifty years.
With more people and a rising level of living,
consumption of energy is skyrocketing and
per capita use increasing.

From 1860 to 1954 man annually increased
by more than twenty-three times the amount
of commercially produced energy he used.
During this same period, world population
doubled, so that the amount of energy available to each person was about twelve times
greater. Unfortunately, these figures give only
an idealized picture of how much energy the
entire world uses, since countries vary in total
and per capita production and consumption.

THE WORLD'S SOLAR

Some countries lack the necessary resources for providing any sizable amount of energy; others, even though they have large potentialities, lack the technology and/or capital for developing them; still others, the industrialized ones, face the problem of rapid exhaustion of their conventional sources of energy. The average North American, for example, has about twenty times as much energy at his disposal as does the average Asian. The desire by all peoples for improved living will be a large factor in expanding the use of energy in the future.

It is believed that per capita energy requirements will continue to expand, at least doubling each twenty-five years in the United States and increasing even faster in other countries. The three major factors that will determine the rate of expansion in the future will be (1) the rate of increase in population, (2) the rate of improvement in real income per capita, and (3) the progress made in the efficient utilization of energy.

The life expectancy of the fossil fuels—coal, petroleum, and natural gas—is limited. Ultimate depletion, however, is a certainty. With their depletion, the only major potential sources of energy are water, wind, sun, and nuclear power. Even though man is developing hydro sites all over the world, many at great cost, hydropower today accounts for only 1 to 1.5 per cent of the total inanimate energy utilized by man, and the entire water-power potential of the earth economically capable of development comprises but a small part of the inanimate-energy needs of the world's peoples. Moreover, the development of any considerable amount of water power

AND NUCLEAR POWER

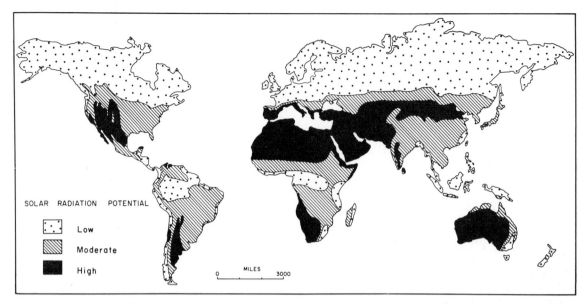

Fig. 4-1. Potential sun-power regions. A clear indication that the highest potential for solar power is obviously in the world's semiarid and arid lands—fortunately, in precisely the areas that for the most part are poor in conventional sources of fuel. (Courtesy of E. W. Miller.)

is restricted to relatively few regions of the earth.

In order to meet future energy requirements, therefore, untapped resources must be made available. The two great hopes for the future appear to be *solar* and *nuclear* power.

SOLAR POWER

In a single year the earth receives about 35,000 times as much energy from solar radiation as all its inhabitants currently consume. Most inhabited areas of the world receive ample solar energy to meet all of man's requirements.

Every hour the sun showers on the earth as much energy as can be obtained by burning 21 billion tons of coal. The average American home consumes only 5/100's as much energy in the form of electricity as its roof receives from the sun. . . . On a single day the land areas of the tropical and temperate zones are flooded with more energy from the sun than man has utilized in the form

of coal, oil, falling water, and muscle since he came out of the trees a million years ago.[1]

For all practical purposes, however, solar energy's use appears to be limited to areas between latitudes 20° to 45° north and 20° to 45° south. These are the lands least affected by cloud and water vapor. Latitude and cloud are the two most important factors determining total **insolation** at any particular time.

Figure 4-1 shows the location of the areas favored for sun-power development. In the United States, the Southwest stands out: thus, a single square foot of collective surface in southern Arizona receives nearly 730,000 **BTU** a year, compared with 440,000 for Maine or Oregon.

Sun power is needed immediately in the arid and semiarid lands of the earth for pumping water and for supplying the domestic and agricultural power needs of the people. If it could be produced cheaply, it might be employed for distilling sea water for irrigation—

[1] Waldemar Kaempffert, "Sun Power: 'The Time Has Come,'" *Think*, 22:14, January 1956.

one of the great hopes of mankind, since the dry lands cover approximately 20 per cent of the land surface of the globe. It could aid in operating solar cookers, solar refrigerators, solar engines, solar air-conditioning apparatus, and solar irrigation pumps. It could revolutionize human life almost as much as did the steam engine.

In some areas, solar power is already being used. For instance, in India in 1953 and 1954 solar cookers were mass-produced and offered for sale at a price of about $15. Few, however, were sold and their manufacture was discontinued. If they could be marketed for $5, it is believed the people could afford to purchase them. Their use would save valuable animal fertilizer from being used for fuel. Japan, which has a deficit of conventional fuels such as coal, petroleum, and natural gas, is not unexpectedly the first nation to make substantial use of sun radiation for supplying domestic energy. On an average the sun shines 2,000 hours per year, much more in the south than in the northeast. By far the most important application of solar energy is for heating water. In 1959 there were 200,000 solar water heaters in use. These heaters are filled with water and exposed to the sun on each clear day; by evening the 30 gallons of water have reached a temperature of 110°F to 120°F.

Solar power on any considerable scale now demands relatively large and costly power plants. A way must be found to store solar energy, mechanically or electrically, for subsequent use. Until large-scale solar-energy plants are fabricated, most use will be in situations where energy requirements are small and other forms of energy are not available. In addition, sun power is at present woefully inefficient, being rated at only 5 to 15 per cent efficiency, partly because solar energy cannot be converted directly into electrical energy but must first be converted into heat. Another handicap is sun power's low intensity of energy. Even when the sun is shining brightly, an area of 15 square feet is required to receive the heat equivalent of 1 kilowatt. For these reasons only an insignificant portion of the total solar energy available to mankind is utilized. In addition, one deterrent presently common to the development of electricity from all sources of energy is the limited distance electricity is transmittable economically —only about 300 miles from the power site. Often the source of energy is much farther away. Ultimately, however, physicists and electrical engineers may be expected to discover ways of transmitting electrical energy greater distances. Even now, the Russians claim that they can send electrical energy as far as 1,000 miles. If there is such a breakthrough, the exploitation of solar power will move forward rapidly.

NUCLEAR POWER

Although there has been much publicity about the use of nuclear fuels as an important source of energy, conventional fuels will be cheaper and more practical for at least a generation. There is evidence that nuclear power will make but a small contribution to the world's energy requirements until at least 1980. Industries and governments, however, are spending considerable time and money to solve some of the more difficult problems connected with the use of nuclear fuels—problems such as radioactivity, fission-product disposal, extremely bulky shielding, and high cost. More than a hundred reactors have now been constructed and are in operation, and a still larger number are being built or planned in various parts of the world.

The atom promises abundant power for the large areas of the world now lacking energy or facing future shortages; however, many millions of dollars must be expended to harness this energy. Being a new device, the nuclear reactor costs much more than do present-day conventional power plants. Also it is far more expensive to operate than a conventional coal- or oil-fired power plant. However, many engineers predict that nuclear power will become cheaper in the future, since advances in plant design and greater efficiency seem assured. Even if this were not so, there are many remote areas of the world where the costs of transporting conventional fuels make power derived from them so costly that they are practically ruled out. One might expect, therefore, that these high-cost power regions would be the first to benefit from nuclear energy. However, this is not so, for backward regions cannot afford such expensive plants. In short, where nuclear power is most needed, there is least ability to pay for it; where there is ability to pay, nuclear power cannot as yet compete with power developed from conventional energy sources.

DEVELOPMENT OF ATOMIC ENERGY

The key to nuclear power was found in the late 1930s through the discovery of the fission of uranium, in which the elementary particles, neutrons, caused the heavy nuclei of uranium to split into two high-speed fragments. These fragments were observed to throw out neutrons, which could be used to produce more fissions, so that a chain reaction was seen to be possible in principle. The energy released by one pound of uranium in the fission process is equivalent to the amount released in the combustion of 2.5 million pounds of coal.

Fission energy is produced when a large atom is split, yielding two smaller atoms. *Fusion* is the process whereby two light atoms are fused together to form a larger atom. In both cases, mass has been changed into energy. The source of fission energy is exhaustible. The fusion process, on the contrary, depends on light elements such as hydrogen. Since every molecule of water contains two atoms of hydrogen, the supply of fusion fuels is literally inexhaustible. To date, only the fission principle has been employed to produce practical reactors, and the fusion method is still in the experimental stage. It will be the fission reactor that will usher in the nuclear power age; but fusion reactors, which will follow, promise to make available unlimited power.

ATOMIC FUELS

As has been noted, uranium, like coal and petroleum, is exhaustible. This is an important fact, for though uranium is one of the more abundant elements in the earth's crust, it is not sufficiently concentrated for mining except in a relatively small number of places (Fig.

4-2). However, there is no shortage: the present estimate of total recoverable uranium and thorium is placed at about 1,700 Q of energy (one Q equals 1,000,000,000,000,000,000 BTU). This means that far more energy is available from atomic power than from coal, petroleum, natural gas, and oil shale combined.[2]

Between two thirds and three fourths of all known uranium deposits are in North America and Africa. Canada, the Republic of South Africa, the Congo, and the United States are the principal sources (Fig. 4-2). The Shinkolowbe mine near Elizabethville in the Congo is the world's largest producer of uranium ore.

India (Travancore State) and Brazil (Espírito Santo) are the leading producers of thorium ore. India has accounted for three quarters of the world's supply of this mineral to date.

WORLD DEVELOPMENT OF NUCLEAR POWER

UNITED STATES

Progress from 1946 to the present indicates that the first widespread application of atomic energy in the United States will be in the generation of electric power; that for some time this power will be more expensive than that generated from conventional fuels; but that it undoubtedly will become fully competitive in the future.

One of the world's first full-scale plants to generate power exclusively for civilian use was dedicated May 26, 1958, at Shippingport, Pennsylvania, near Pittsburgh. The nuclear part of the plant, constructed by Westinghouse Electric Corporation at a cost of 55 million dollars, generates enough power for a city of 100,000 people. Other commercial reactors are in either the operating or the planning stage. Three plants have been completed under the Atomic Energy Commission's Civilian Power Reactor Demonstration program.

The cost of electricity produced from nuclear energy for a time will exceed that of

[2] Elbert E. Miller, "Outlook for Uranium," *Focus*, 10:8, March 1960.

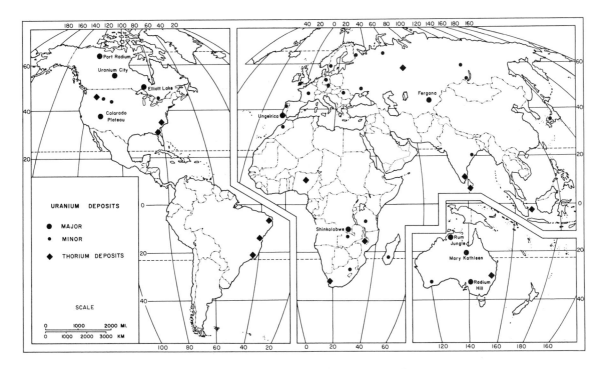

Fig. 4-2. World distribution of deposits of uranium and thorium, the two raw materials from which fissionable materials are extracted. Since many areas are still imperfectly explored, impressive new deposits are almost certain to be discovered.

electricity generated from coal, oil, gas, or falling water. According to recent estimates, the construction rate may be $300 or more per kilowatt of installed capacity, compared with about $150 per kilowatt for a coal- or oil-burning plant. Operating costs, beyond carrying charges on the original investment, also are high. The uranium fuel elements must be withdrawn from time to time and the unspent uranium separated from the newly created plutonium and from the radioactive "ash" of nuclear fire. Then the ash must be safely disposed of. These operations require skilled help and expensive equipment.

Electricity from atomic energy should reach a competitive level in the next 15 to 20 years—earliest in regions like New England, where present power costs are high. By 1975 perhaps as much as one tenth of the electricity used in the United States will be produced in atomic plants—new plants operated as additions to the existing electric power system, not as replacements for the older types of plants.

WESTERN EUROPE

Because of the critical fuel situation in the Western European countries, plans for the development of large-scale nuclear power plants are much more ambitious than in the United States. Western Europe is critically short of coal and petroleum, and therefore needs nuclear power as soon as technical progress and cost permit.

An important development is the formation of *Euratom*, a Western European atomic pool, that will make the six coal- and steel-producing countries an independent first-rank power in peaceful nuclear energy. Euratom's first major task will be the promotion—perhaps even eventual ownership—of a number of common installations.

Great Britain. The fuel situation in Britain is so critical that it imposes a degree of urgency in the development of atomic power. For generations the industrial economy rested upon plentiful supplies of cheaply produced coal now no longer available. With a decline in domestic coal output and a steady rise in energy requirements, the nation has become a net importer of fuels—both coal and petroleum, but particularly the latter.

The advent of nuclear power is, therefore, most timely for Great Britain. Its practical application on an industrial scale was first realized in 1956 with the opening of the full-scale nuclear power station at Calder Hall, which delivers 65,000 kilowatts. Since then several additional large plants have been constructed in other areas. By 1975 the British expect to produce from nuclear energy the equivalent of 40 million tons of coal annually, about 40 per cent of their electrical requirements.

France. The French government also is planning to generate large amounts of electricity from nuclear energy. A 40-megawatt (MW) plutonium reactor at Marcoule has been operating steadily since 1950, and work on other nuclear plants is progressing. Unlike the situation in the United Kingdom, nearly 100 per cent of France's available hydropower is now being utilized. France already is importing about 40 per cent of her energy in the form of petroleum and coal. Her problem, like England's, is to provide for the future a source of energy which, from the security and commercial points of view, does not depend heavily on foreign countries. By 1975 it is expected that nuclear energy will be producing about 30 per cent of France's total electric power.

Sweden. Sweden is faced with a serious long-term energy problem. Hydro currently provides more than 90 per cent of the total electricity generated from domestic energy sources. But this amount meets only one third of the country's needs. Energy consumption is rising about 7 per cent per annum, but hydro reserves are expected to meet future demand for only the next fifteen to twenty years. Moreover, much of the potential hydropower is situated at considerable distances from main load centers, necessitating long and costly transmission lines. Already two thirds of Sweden's total energy requirements are being imported, mainly in the form of oil. Sweden looks to nuclear power as the answer to her energy problems.

Italy. Italy expects to begin producing electric power from nuclear sources on a large scale by 1965. The average cost of conventional fuels in Italy is three times that in the United States; hence nuclear power provides a logical answer to her energy problem. To date, five companies own and operate nuclear power stations.

SOVIET UNION

Because the Russian economy is expanding at an unparalleled rate—both production of goods and plant capacity having doubled every five years since World War II—greater and greater demands are made on all sources of energy. Therefore, it is believed, the Soviet Union is developing considerable nuclear power despite large coal, petroleum, natural gas, and hydro resources.

However, the Soviet Union is less enthusiastic about atomic power than it was in 1955, when its objective was 2,500,000 kilowatts of atom electricity by 1960. It is now convinced that the "immediate potentialities of atomic power were oversold by the scientists." [3]

JAPAN

Nuclear power holds great promise for the future growth and development of manufacturing in fuel-poor Japan. The nation plans by 1975 to supply 50 per cent of her energy needs from atomic power. In November 1957, the Japan Atomic Power Research Institute set up at Tokai village in Ibaraki Prefecture a water-boiler type of research reactor, purchased from the United States. The institute also is planning to construct a research reactor, which will embody all the atomic knowledge now available to Japanese scientists.

[3] *New York Times,* November 8, 1959.

LIMITING FACTORS
AND OUTLOOK

In a meeting of the American Chemical Society, Dr. James B. Conant said:

The era of liquid fossil fuels is, by the close of the century, coming to an end, and the worry about future coal supplies is increasing. Atomic energy has *not proved* to be an expedient way of lengthening the period in which man taps the sources of energy stored in the earth's crust. *Solar energy, on the other hand, is by the end of the century the dominating factor in the production of industrial power.*[4]

Scientists in mounting numbers in many nations are attacking the difficult problems inherent in the development of sun and nuclear power. This research is of major importance, for, lacking harnessed energy, the civilized world, after it had utilized all the fossil fuels and burned all the wood, would once more lapse into the dark night of primitivism. Solar and nuclear power no longer pose a question of "if"; today it is "when."

[4] "Creating Tomorrow's Oil," *Fortune*, 44:149, November 1951.

SELECTED REFERENCES

"Conference on the Sun in the Service of Man," in *Proceedings of the American Academy of Arts and Sciences,* Vol. 79, No. 4, July 1951.

Isard, W., and V. Whitney. *Atomic Power, An Economic and Social Analysis.* New York, Blakiston, 1952.

Jones, Stephen B. "The Economic Geography of Atomic Power," *Economic Geography,* 27:268-274, July 1951.

Lansdell, Norman. *The Atom and the Energy Revolution.* New York, The Philosophical Library, 1958.

Miller, E. Willard. "World Patterns and Trends in Energy Consumption," *Journal of Geography,* 58:269-279, September 1959.

Nininger, Robert D. *Minerals for Atomic Energy.* New York, Van Nostrand Co., Inc., 1954.

CHAPTER FIVE::

Water ranks at or very near the top in any listing of the world's most essential, valuable, and precious minerals; for without it, there could be no life. Moreover, with the exception of air, water is our cheapest necessity. Most people think that, except for the arid and semi-arid lands, there is plenty of water. Actually, however, the need for fresh water almost everywhere grows faster than the supply. It has been characteristic throughout history that man often has chosen or has been forced to settle in areas where water was unsatisfactory in quantity, quality, or availability. As a result, he has had to use his ingenuity, imagination, and technical skills in developing a more harmonious relationship with his water supply, or else has been forced to relocate his abode. Water has greatly influenced the habits, mores, and legal code of mankind; and, as our population burgeons, fuller utilization and more thorough understanding of water resources become increasingly imperative.

THE WORLD'S

IRRIGATION

Irrigation, the act of applying water artificially.to soil to provide moisture for growing crops, has been practiced for millennia. In fact, some authorities claim that irrigation constituted the very foundation of civilization. According to archeologists, the earliest records of man show that civilization grew and prospered in lands along the banks of irrigation canals. Many lands throughout the world (Iraq, Egypt, India, Pakistan, China, Peru, and Bolivia, to mention but a few) possess irrigation systems that were established hundreds, even thousands, of years ago.[1] Entire

[1] W. C. Lowdermilk, *Conquest of the Land through 7,000 Years* (Washington, D. C.: Soil Conservation Service, U. S. Department of Agriculture), Agriculture Information Bulletin No. 99, August 1953, pp. 1-30.

civilizations both rose and fell on the success or failure of their irrigation projects.

In most countries the simplest and cheapest irrigation projects were developed first. Those that remain to be developed involve great engineering challenges and unusually large expenditures of capital. Only national governments can afford such outlays; and those in underdeveloped countries. in order to construct large irrigation projects, must obtain huge loans from the World Bank, the United States, the Soviet Union, Canada, and the countries of Western Europe.

At the present time, some 200 million acres of irrigated land are producing food—acres that, without irrigation, would be barren and unproductive. It is significant indeed that about half the earth's surface is arid or semiarid; among the inhabited continents, only Europe has no deserts (Table 5-1).

Vast dry areas of level to undulating land could become habitable and productive of

FRESH WATER

TABLE 5-1

LAND AREAS OF THE EARTH IN
RELATION TO PRECIPITATION

Climatic classification	Annual precipitation (in inches)	Per cent of land area
Arid	Less than 10	25
Semiarid	10-20	30
Subhumid	20-40	20
Humid	40-60	11
Humid-Wet	60-80	9
Very Wet	More than 80	5
	Total	100

SOURCE: G. D. Clyde, "Irrigation in the United States," American Society of Civil Engineers, *Transactions*, 118:312, 1953.

crops if man could solve the problem of making water available at reasonable cost. At present sufficient moisture for crop production falls on only about a quarter of the earth's land area, and irrigated land represents only about six tenths of 1 per cent of the world's land area; yet this small fraction supplies food and fibers for 15 to 20 per cent of the world's population.

In general, irrigation is required in regions where the mean annual precipitation is less than 15 inches. However, summer temperatures and seasonal distribution of precipitation also affect the need for irrigation. Both surface and groundwater are used for irrigation.

SURFACE WATER

A major use of surface water (rivers, creeks, lakes, and marshes) is for irrigation. Egypt, China, India, Pakistan, the United States, and Peru are but a few examples of countries that sustain large numbers of people through irrigation from rivers. Egypt's Nile irrigates millions of acres in a region receiving negligible rainfall; it prevents encroachment of the desert, and it largely sustains the 27 million people in the valley. The Nile is fed by water from huge lakes near the equator and from several rivers that flow down from the high-lands of Ethiopia. In western United States, great dams have been thrown across the largest rivers to form storage reservoirs for saving flood waters until they are needed for irrigating farmlands.[2]

GROUNDWATER

Groundwater is water that has soaked into the ground from rain, from snows and glaciers, and from streams. It is estimated that about one sixth of all rainfall soaks into the ground. This "soak-in" constitutes the major source of groundwater, and is also a permanent means of its replenishment. It occupies the cracks in rock, spaces between layers of rock and even between grains of rock, as in sandstone. The underground reservoirs contain this nation's hugest source of fresh water—far more than all its rivers, creeks, and lakes. Increasing amounts of groundwater obtained by pumping are used for irrigation (Fig. 5-1). So heavy is man's withdrawal of this valuable resource that the supplies in California's San Joaquin Valley, Arizona's Salt River Valley, and Texas's High Plains are being exhausted faster than they are being replenished by nature. California uses 40 per cent of all the groundwater utilized in the United States, and 60 per cent of the state's irrigation agriculture is sustained by groundwater.

IRRIGATION IN THE WORLD

Among the countries of the world, China, India, and the United States lead in the number of acres irrigated (Table 5-2). Brief presentations of irrigation (completed and projected) in three countries (India, Pakistan, and the United States) follow.

INDIA AND PAKISTAN

The subcontinent of India, along with China, leads all other countries in area under irrigation. Nowhere else on earth are so many millions of people dependent on irrigation for their food supply. Yet it is estimated that less

[2] The Hoover Dam and most other dams are multipurpose; they do not serve irrigation alone.

Fig. 5-1. Pumping water onto land in the American West. Underground water currently comprises a large part of the total water used in irrigation in the American West, and nearly all of it (except that from flowing wells) is pumped. In this photo a power unit is operating the pumps that are lifting water onto the land. (Courtesy of International Harvester Company.)

than 10 per cent of the runoff of the rivers is utilized. Most of the water employed for irrigation is surface water; little has been done as yet with groundwater.

Emphasis is placed here on the world's largest irrigation system: the Indus River system, which includes the 1,900-mile Indus and five tributaries—the Jhelum, Chenab, Ravi, Sutlej, and Beas. All the streams rise in the Himalaya Mountains and flow southwest to the Arabian Sea, but en route their waters are diverted by man to irrigate 30 million acres and support a population of 50 million.

In 1947 the partition of India split the Indus system, India gaining control of the headwaters of the six rivers and Pakistan getting 80 per cent of the irrigated basin, since all six flow into it. India claimed the right to divert Indus waters to increase her irrigable area; but Pakistan charged that this would ruin her granary, since two thirds of the irrigated area and 40 million of the 50 million people dependent on it dwell in Pakistan. On three occasions she threatened to go to war over the issue. In September 1960, however, the two countries signed a treaty for the division and development of Indus waters. Under it India receives the waters of the three eastern tributaries (Ravi, Beas, and Sutlej), and Pakistan gets the two western tributaries (Chenab and Jhelum) and the Indus itself. Both nations are constructing a series of works in a billion-dollar project being financed by grants and loans from the World Bank and six Western nations—the United States, Great Britain, Canada, Australia, New Zealand, and West Germany.

UNITED STATES

Irrigation by Anglo-Saxons in the United States began in July 1847, when Mormons at Salt Lake City put a half acre "under the ditch." The practice in the American West received a stimulus in 1901, when President Theodore Roosevelt, in his first message to

TABLE 5-2

COUNTRIES IRRIGATING MORE THAN
A MILLION ACRES ANNUALLY
(for one nonspecified year, 1950-1957)

Country	Acres
Communist China	78,977,500
India	54,897,500
United States	29,897,500
Soviet Union	25,825,000
Pakistan	23,765,000
Indonesia	12,725,000
Iraq	7,280,000
Japan	7,130,000
Egypt	6,525,000
Mexico	6,260,000
Sudan	6,022,500
Turkey	4,970,000
Spain	4,380,000
Iran	4,000,000
Argentina	3,750,000
Thailand	3,410,000
Chile	3,407,500
Peru	3,030,000
Philippines	2,182,500
Australia	1,640,000
Laos	1,625,000
Syria	1,147,500
Burma	1,350,000
Republic of South Africa	1,315,000
South Korea	1,290,000
Colombia	1,262,500
Nationalist China (Taiwan)	1,225,000

SOURCE: Based on *Production Yearbook*, Food and Agriculture Organization of the United Nations, Rome, 12:8-9, 1958.

Congress, urged that the federal government adopt some policy for reclamation of the arid lands on an extensive scale:

In the arid region it is water, not land, which measures production. The western half of the United States would sustain a population greater than that of our whole country today if the water that now runs to waste were saved and used for irrigation.[3]

The United States does not rank with India, Pakistan, and China in acreage devoted to irrigation; but it does have some 30 million acres (mostly in the West) under the ditch,

[3] Quoted without source by G. D. Clyde, "Irrigation in the United States," American Society of Civil Engineers, *Transactions*, 118:330, 1953.

and the largest single use of water is for irrigation—from 75 to 100 billion gallons per day, or approximately half of the fresh water used (Fig. 5-2).

A small but rapidly growing acreage in the East is also devoted to irrigation, but there the natural rainfall is usually ample to meet the needs of growing crops. However, as a result of dry periods, improved irrigation equipment (particularly, portable lightweight pipe and sprinklers), and the higher yields, supplemental irrigation is increasing. In the West, except for the Pacific Northwest, there could be little agriculture without irrigation.

The area presently under irrigation is reported to be about half the total possible irrigable land. The remaining portion undoubtedly will be reclaimed, but reclamation will require a huge financial outlay. The largest reservoirs, the longest canals, and the costliest tunnels and inverted siphons are yet to be constructed. Since dry lands become highly productive when irrigated, it is estimated that 1 acre of irrigated land is equivalent to 4 acres of non-irrigated, tillable (dry-farmed) land.

Much irrigation farming is high-cost farming. In addition to expensive water and improvements, irrigation farms must market their products mainly in the humid Middle West and East, where the same products are grown without irrigation and much closer to market. The irrigated areas in the subtropical part of the nation are an exception because they grow mostly noncompetitive crops. Many people fail to realize that most irrigated land is devoted not to specialty crops but to ordinary farm crops with modest income per acre.

California leads the nation in irrigation, with more than 7 million acres devoted to it. Some 68.5 per cent of all farms (about 84,500) are irrigated, and they require approximately 21 million **acre-feet** of water per annum. Moreover, 90 per cent of all the water consumed within the state is for irrigation. Yet only about one third of the land potentially available is being irrigated. For a third of a century irrigated acreage has increased by about 100,000 acres per annum.

Though irrigation is practiced in thirty-two of the fifty-eight counties of the state, it

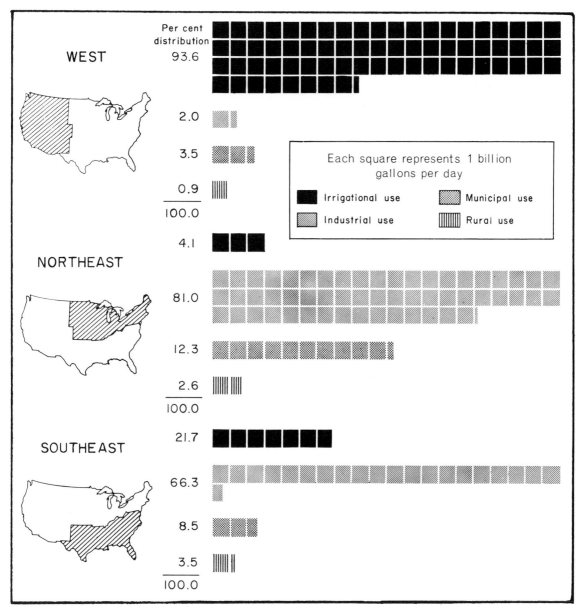

Fig. 5-2. Water consumption in the United States for irrigation, industry, municipal, and rural use. The chart points out the West's disproportionate use of its water for irrigation (93.6 per cent) and the Northeast's and Southeast's disproportionate share of theirs for industry (81.0 and 66.3 per cent, respectively). (From Stanford Research Institute and the Geographical Review, published by the American Geographical Society of New York.)

reaches its greatest prevalence in the San Joaquin Valley; but the Sacramento, Santa Clara, Salinas, and Imperial Valleys and the South Coastal Basin of Southern California are also important.

Both groundwater and surface water are used; but, except for the Imperial Valley and the extreme north in the state, groundwater is used the more heavily. The San Joaquin Valley groundwater reservoir provides water to the fields of that area equivalent to one fourth of all the water pumped from wells in the entire United States. Seventy per cent of the state's stream flow is to be found north of an east-west line drawn through Sacramento, but 77 per cent of the consumption is south of the line.

THE SILTATION PROBLEM

Erosion, transportation, and deposition of sediment are important in the control, use, and maintenance of water resources. Sediment deposited in reservoirs occupies space needed to store water for use for irrigation, power, domestic water supply, and recreation. Sedimentation plagues the irrigator in the arid lands where deforestation and overgrazing on steep slopes have resulted in soil erosion.

Where streams enter the reservoirs behind dams, their velocity is checked and their silt-carrying capacity is so greatly reduced that the sediment is dropped. Thus, in the reservoir behind Elephant Butte Dam on the Rio Grande some 18,000 acre-feet of silt are deposited annually. The reservoir lost 20 per cent of its capacity in a third of a century. More than 100,000 acre-feet of silt pass into Lake Mead behind Hoover Dam each year. This means that many huge reclamation projects in the West are in danger of ultimately having their reservoirs filled. Obviously, the need for reduction in siltation is imperative.

WATER POWER

Water power is man's oldest form of mechanical energy. The ancient Egyptians were among the first to find ways of putting water to work, using a crude water wheel, the noria. In early America, falling water was harnessed, and the grist mill became a most important community business. Since only a small amount of power was needed, low dams were built on small streams whose waters operated wheels for generating power.

The amount of power at a given site depends on the amount of fall or head, and on the amount of water the stream is carrying. A typical water-power development is found on a stream when nature provides favorable (though seldom ideal) conditions: (1) plenty of rainfall well distributed throughout the year; (2) relative freedom from floods, droughts, and severe freezes; (3) forests along the streams and lakes; (4) such geological conditions that a dam may be constructed to create, or aid in creating, a large pond or lake. To this natural endowment, man then adds accessories: penstocks for conducting water to hydraulic turbines in a powerhouse (Fig. 5-3); an electric generator and a tailrace to return the water to the stream after it has passed through the turbine and given up its power; and a means of conveying the electric energy to the place of its ultimate use—the market, which should be within 300 miles of the power site.

WORLD WATER POWER

The bulk of the world's *potential water power* is to be found in rugged areas receiving heavy, well-distributed precipitation. Thus, 85 per cent of the established potential power is in seven large areas—Middle Africa, Monsoon Asia, Siberia, tropical South America, Europe, the Pacific Northwest of North America, and the Great Lakes–St. Lawrence area (Table 5-3 and Fig. 5-4).

Most (possibly 90 per cent) of the world's *developed water power* is in or close to the populous industrialized areas—the countries touching on the North Atlantic Ocean; in fact, about 90 per cent of the world total is in five areas—Western Europe, the United States, Canada, Japan, and the Soviet Union. Thirty-seven per cent of the total is in Western Europe, where the demand is high; this is understandable considering the region's poverty in oil and natural gas, and even in coal—much of the best and most easily and cheaply exploited having been mined. France, Italy, Germany, Norway, and Switzerland have developed almost 100 per cent of their potential hydropower. North America has developed just over half of its potential (Table 5-3).

Space permits the presentation of developed water power in only a few countries or areas —Norway, Central Africa, the Soviet Union,

Fig. 5-3. Air view of John Hart station on the Campbell River, Vancouver Island. Water is being led gradually down pipes (penstocks) to the turbines, where it is shot through a nozzle against an impulse wheel; in the next fraction of a second, its force has become electric current. (Courtesy of British Columbia Power Commission.)

Canada, and the United States (the Pacific Northwest and the TVA).

NORWAY

Mountainous terrain, heavy precipitation (unfortunately mostly in the form of snow—resulting in minimum stream flow in winter, when the demand for electricity meets its peak), and almost complete lack of conventional fuels (coal, petroleum, and natural gas) have conspired to stimulate the development of water power in Norway. The country has developed more of its potential power than has any nation on earth, it has the highest per capita consumption of electricity in the world and the lowest cost per kilowatt hour, and electricity is available to more than 98 per cent of the total population. This is a notable accomplishment considering the topographical difficulties. It is believed that Norwegian water power will be competitive with atomic power even beyond the year 2000.

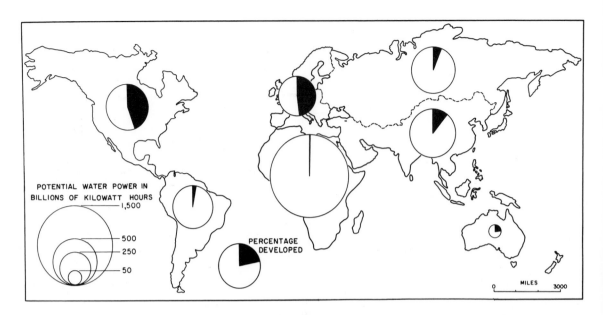

Fig. 5-4. *Potential and developed water power of the world by continents. Note particularly (1) the tremendous potential hydropower of Africa but the negligible portion developed to date (0.28 per cent), and (2) the much smaller reserves of potential power but the high proportion developed in the advanced nations.* (Courtesy of E. Willard Miller.)

Only 1 per cent of all the energy generated in Norway comes from thermal power plants.

TABLE 5-3

THE WORLD'S POTENTIAL AND DEVELOPED WATER POWER, 1952
(in thousands of horsepower)

Continent	Capacity of water-power plants	Potential water power, based on ordinary minimum flow	Per cent of developed power
Africa	715	250,000	0.28
Asia	14,392	156,000	9.22
Europe	48,516	64,000	75.80
North America	46,430	90,000	51.59
Oceania	1,778	23,000	7.73
South America	3,962	62,000	6.40
World (approximate)	115,793	645,000	17.95

SOURCE: B. E. Jones and L. L. Young, "Developed and Potential Water Power of the United States and Other Countries of the World," *Science,* 119:329, March 5, 1954.

CENTRAL AFRICA

The continent of Africa has two fifths of the world's potential water power. Central Africa —with its highlands, heavy rainfall well distributed throughout the year, and large lakes and forests—is the richest part. Until recently almost no water power had been developed; but the great revolution in mining and smelting, along with the scarcity of coal, petroleum, and natural gas in this part of the continent, stimulated the construction of several large dams.

The harnessing of the Zambezi in the Kariba Gorge forms one of the most imaginative schemes of the twentieth century. When completed, the dam—constructed at the border between the two Rhodesias, about 300 miles downstream from Victoria Falls—is expected to have an estimated annual output of 9,000 million **kilowatt hours.** Ultimately it will create a lake about 175 miles long and 40 miles wide in places, covering an area of 2,000 square miles—one of the world's largest reservoirs. The Zambezi has very wide seasonal variations, but the enormous reservoir will be capable of supplying plenty of storage water throughout the year for power generation. Kariba will provide power for Central Africa, particularly for the increasing demands in the great Northern Rhodesian Copper Belt.

However, the independence of numerous former colonies over the continent, with the resultant civil strife, augurs a reversion to tribal conditions and troubles, which may impede further large-scale development.[4]

SOVIET UNION

This enormous country is well endowed with potential water power (about 10 per cent that of the world), and there is also considerable development. However, as with many of Russia's resources, the water power is not well placed with respect to the principal population centers—the markets; 85 per cent is in Siberia on the great rivers, such as the Ob, Yenisei, and Lena.

Logically, most of the development up to now has taken place in the European or western parts of the country—on the Volkhov and Svir Rivers near Leningrad; on the Kola Peninsula; in the rugged, well-watered Caucasus Mountains; on the Dnieper at Zaporozhe; and at thirteen points on the Volga, Europe's greatest river. The plant at Kuibyshev is believed to be the largest of the Volga group, with a capacity of 2 million kilowatts, equal to that at Grand Coulee in the United States. However, it is in Siberia, at Bratsk, on the Angara River, about 200 miles north of the Trans-Siberian Railway, that the Soviet Union is constructing its and the world's largest hydroelectric complex. The 400-foot dam here will impound water in a reservoir 350 miles long, containing 145 million acre-feet of water, compared with 29 million acre-feet at Lake Mead behind Hoover Dam.

[4] Elspeth Huxley ("Africa's First Loyalty," *New York Times Magazine*, September 18, 1960, p. 14) says that colonialism was the glue that stuck the human units of Africa together into a shape recognizable on an atlas but that the glue is currently dissolving and many of the units are falling apart. The new nations are not nations as we understand the term.

CANADA

Except for the Prairie Provinces in the midwest, this large nation of innumerable lakes and rivers and much rugged terrain is well endowed with potential hydropower. In potential power, Canada ranks fifth among the world's nations, but she is more fortunate than some others because the water power is favorably located with respect to prospective markets. Canada ranks second only to the United States in total installed capacity, and second only to Norway in installation per 1,000 of the population.

From the standpoint of development, the Great Lakes–St. Lawrence area of Quebec and Ontario leads, with 70 per cent of the total—the result of numerous lake-fed streams with many falls and proximity to Canada's portion of the American Manufacturing Region.

UNITED STATES

The United States leads all nations in the total amount of water power developed—16.6 million kilowatts out of a potential of 95.5 million kilowatts. Actually, however, hydropower is the smallest contributor to this nation's over-all energy needs. Thus in 1959, on a **BTU** basis, petroleum contributed roughly 40 per cent, coal 24 per cent, dry natural gas 27 per cent, and hydro only 4 per cent of the total energy. Water power in just two American areas—the Pacific Northwest and the Tennessee Valley Authority—is discussed below.

The Pacific Northwest. The mountainous nature of this region, along with its heavy precipitation, gives the area a large hydroelectric potential. Unlike most other parts of the country, the Northwest is deficient in all three fossil fuels—coal, petroleum, and natural gas; but it does have 40 per cent of the undeveloped hydropower of the nation and about 25 per cent of the developed capacity.

Dams have been constructed at many points on the Columbia River and on Cascade Mountain streams near cities. Some authorities regard the Columbia as unrivaled among the world's rivers for development possibilities; for it carries a huge volume of water at all times, transports little silt, and has many fine dam sites. Already six of the world's greatest power developments on it—Grand Coulee, Chief Joseph, McNary, The Dalles, Bonneville, and John Day—are completed.

Tennessee Valley Authority.[5] The TVA, consisting of the Tennessee River and its tributaries and embracing an area of more than 40,000 square miles, lies in seven states. Since 1933, twenty dams and eight large steam-electric power stations have been constructed, each planned and placed with precision. The waterpower capacity is approximately 4 million kilowatts. At first, only hydropower was developed; currently, however, 75 per cent of TVA's power is steam-generated, and some students declare that the figure will ultimately reach 95 per cent. Congress, in creating the Authority, expressed the hope that electricity might be developed primarily "for the benefit of the people of [the region] as a whole and particularly for domestic and rural consumers to whom power can be economically made available." It accordingly established a rate of 50 per cent or less below rates then prevailing in the region.

Those who are critical of TVA point out that it pays no federal income or state taxes and low interest rates on money it uses. They declare that actually TVA power costs one third more than that from private utilities in the surrounding area. However, from the standpoint of properly coordinated conservation schemes, the transformation of the area has been little short of miraculous. It should be mentioned that though the TVA here has been treated only in relation to power, it is multi-purpose—soil conservation, navigation

[5] Few issues continue to be so hotly disputed as the TVA. People are either completely *for it* or completely *against it;* few see objectively both the good and the bad aspects. The student of economic geography is advised, however, to learn the facts on both sides so that he himself may decide where he stands. Excellent recent articles giving strong arguments pro and con are (1) "Progress of the Tennessee Valley Authority," *The Engineer,* Part I, 207:398-401, March 6, 1959, and Part II, 207:437-439, March 13, 1959, and (2) "Economist Scores TVA's Scope," *Electrical World,* 151:49-50, January 12, 1959.

improvement, flood alleviation, power production, industrialization, modern forestry, recreation.

INDUSTRIAL WATER

Manufacturing uses much water. However, in a country such as the United States, the use varies according to region (Fig. 5-2). Since most manufacturing takes place in humid areas, one might not expect water shortages. However, with the rapid increase in population, urbanization, and standard of living, the need for water is soaring to unprecedented heights. Obviously, different types of industries vary greatly in their water requirements. Thus, in the United States five industries—iron and steel (Fig. 5-5), chemicals, pulp and paper, and petroleum and coal—use about 80 per cent of the total; conversely, such industries as furniture, printing and publishing, tobacco, and garments have virtually no water requirements. The "water price" also is variable: 65,000 gallons to make a ton of finished steel, 100 gallons to make a pound of rayon, 770 gallons to refine one barrel of oil, 250 gallons to make a ton of sulfate wood pulp, 39,-000 gallons to make a ton of paper, 600 to 1,000 tons for each ton of coal burned in a steam-power plant.

Statistics dealing with the industrial withdrawal of water in the United States vary widely among authorities. However, according to the U.S. Department of Commerce, industrial withdrawal will have risen from 60 billion gallons daily in 1955 to more than 115 billion gallons in 1975. Most industrial water is *used* rather than *used up.* More than 75 per cent of it is used for cooling purposes; for the most part this water can be returned to its source without appreciable change in quality except for a rise in temperature.

DOMESTIC WATER

Wherever human beings dwell, they must have water for drinking, cooking, bathing, washing, and other uses. Daily consumption

Fig. 5-5. Aerial view of Inland Steel Company plant on the peninsula and near side of the Indiana Harbor Canal with Youngstown Sheet and Tube Company plant on the farther side. One of the largest industrial users of water is the iron and steel industry, and the Chicago-Gary district on the shore of Lake Michigan is reputed to be the most lavish user of all; it can be, for water is plentiful and cheap. (Photo by Chicago Aerial Industries, Inc., Courtesy of Inland Steel Company.)

of water per capita in underdeveloped countries is but a fraction of that in the United States (where it is about 143 gallons); even in Europe it rarely exceeds half the figures recorded in the United States for towns of identical size. This difference results from a higher standard of living, from the greater abundance of water in the United States, and from its relatively low cost (the average consumer in the United States probably pays less than 1 cent per day for his water).

In this chapter we are concerned principally with domestic water in developed lands and will emphasize the United States.

Despite the fact that the United States receives enough annual precipitation to cover its 3 million square miles to a depth of nearly 30 inches and consumes only 1½ inches, each passing year finds most parts of the country feeling the effects of water shortages. In 1953 more than 1,000 public water-supply systems restricted the use of water by part or all of their 24 million consumers. And in 1957, 47 states experienced some water shortage, so that 15 of every 100 persons in the nation were obliged to curtail their normal use of water.

RURAL AREAS

Rural homes in the United States get their water from individual dug and bored wells, though some in more backward areas depend on water from springs. Where pumps are employed, they are operated by hand, windmill, or small gasoline engine or electric motor.

Rural occupants of humid areas need be far less careful than those in semiarid and arid regions, where per capita daily consumption obviously must be restricted.

URBAN AREAS

Considering that the United States is today overwhelmingly urban and suburban and that per capita consumption of water is double what it was in 1900, it is easy to see what enormous problems face the gigantic cities. New York, for instance, uses more than 1 billion gallons of water daily—148 gallons per capita. Normally the city is assured ample water but not during droughts lasting through two successive years. Thus in 1949 one could find such statements as the following scattered throughout the *New York Times:* "Don't leave faucets or showers open when they are not actually being used. A drip can waste 15,000 gallons of water a year and a small steady leak can waste 1 million gallons a year."

Everywhere large cities are concerned about their water supply, and reach deeper and deeper into their hinterlands to acquire it. New York City has built reservoirs into the Catskills, 150 miles distant. San Francisco reaches back 200 miles into Yosemite National Park in the Sierra Nevada to get the 140 million gallons it uses daily. And fast-growing Los Angeles taps two sources that are more than 200 miles distant. It, more than any other part of California, stands to benefit from a bond issue passed in 1960, whereby water from the northern part of the state will be carried to the southern part.

It is estimated that 171 billion dollars of capital investment will be needed for additional water projects through 1975 to keep abreast of population growth, increasing standards of living, and industrial expansion in the United States. In the state of Texas, for instance, over a 50-year period, the population increased by 287 per cent, while *the use of water increased by 7,000 per cent.* The daily average intake for the United States by 1980 is estimated at 494 billion gallons.

CONVERSION OF SEA WATER

In water-short locales adjacent to oceans, domestic water must be hauled by ship or pro-

cured from sea water. There are several ways by which sea water can be converted—for example, by distillation, freezing, or chemical methods. The process is generally expensive; but crucial need in such areas relegates cost to a secondary consideration: water must be had at any price. Water-conversion projects have been developed at Kuwait on the Persian Gulf, at Aruba in the Caribbean, at Aden, and elsewhere.

The United States, as a result of growth in population and increasing industrialization, is showing much interest in water desalting; and the Department of the Interior is currently testing five of the best conversion methods on more than just a pilot-plant scale.

The importance of conversion of salt water becomes apparent when it is realized that 24 states have ocean coastlines and that they possess 65 per cent of the manufacturing and 55 per cent of the population. However, water desalting is soon to become widespread in areas contiguous to or underlying most of the fresh-water-short areas in the United States. In July 1952, the first Saline Water Act was passed; in September 1958, the Saline Water Demonstration Act was passed "to transfer experiments into production tests on a scale not possible of achievement otherwise." The cost of this water per 1,000 gallons has fallen from $5 to slightly more than $1. Under the federal government's research and development program, the city of San Diego is presently using more than a million gallons of freshened sea water daily. The cost exceeds $1 per 1,000 gallons, but it is expected that soon the price will drop to 50 cents or even less.

WORLD OUTLOOK

The foregoing pages have emphasized man's worldwide dependence on fresh water. But almost everywhere he is experiencing difficulties obtaining all he needs. Where nature yields too little or too much precipitation, man suffers; and he is impotent to do much about it. Great expenditures in technology and money are imperative to correct the situation. The one thing man cannot as yet do is control the weather.

The supplying of adequate water for mankind, which is doubling in numbers about every 40 years, promises to be one of the major problems facing nearly all governnments—problems that are three-pronged: economic, political, and social.

SELECTED REFERENCES

Behre, Charles H. "Our Most Important Mineral—Water," *Focus*, 7:1-6, January 1957.
Blake, Nelson M. *Water for the Cities*. Syracuse, N. Y., Syracuse University Press, 1956.
Frank, B., and A. Netboy. *Water, Land, and People*. New York, Alfred A. Knopf, 1950.
Huffman, Roy E. *Irrigation Development and Public Water Policy*. New York, The Ronald Press, 1953.
Jones, B. E., and L. L. Young. "Developed and Potential Water Power of the United States and Other Countries of the World," *Science*, 119:328-329, March 5, 1954.
"Water in the United States," *Focus*, 1:1-6, January 15, 1951.
Water: Yearbook of Agriculture, 1955. Washington, D. C., U.S. Department of Agriculture, 1955.
White, Gilbert F. *The Future of the Arid Lands*. Washington, D. C., American Association for the Advancement of Science, 1956, Publication No. 43.
—————————. "Industrial Water Use: A Review," *Geographical Review*, 50:412-430, July 1960.

CHAPTER SIX ::

Iron ore is one of the earth's most plentiful minerals, and from it is made steel, the most valuable and indispensable of all the metals. Steel is the key by which man produces and increases wealth. Its overwhelming importance rests largely upon its multifarious uses and its low price. Annual per capita consumption of steel in the United States is a staggering 1,232 pounds; in China it is about 18 pounds. Among the metals iron accounts for more than 90 per cent of the world tonnage, and there is no foreseeable time when it will not be the world's outstanding metal. At the present rate of consumption, the supply of iron ore available is sufficiently large to last the world for many centuries.

Although the ores of iron are widely distributed and almost every country possesses some, five nations—the United States, the U.S.S.R., France, the United Kingdom, and

THE WORLD'S IRON ORE

Sweden—produce about three fourths of the world's iron ore. Deposits vary greatly in size of reserves, in metallic content, and in accessibility.

Figure 6-1 shows the distribution of the world's major iron-ore deposits, and Table 6-1 shows the major reserves. Nearly 50 countries, with about 150 deposits, produce iron ore. Yet only a few of these ore bodies are of commercial value under present-day technology. Many, for one or more reasons, give no promise of ever becoming valuable.

ECONOMICS OF IRON MINING

The determining factors in the economics of iron mining in a specific area are:

1. Amount of ore.
2. Quality of ore.
3. Location of deposit with respect to coal and consuming markets.
4. Location of ore with respect to transportation facilities, mainly water transportation.

In any comparison of the quality of ore deposits, more than mere iron content must be considered. Such substances as phosphorus or sulfur, even when present in insignificant quantities, present obstacles to **reduction.** The quality of ore is so important that it sometimes retards the development of new discoveries and continues the utilization of deposits of known quality. Where ore of good quality lies close to the surface, as it does in the Mesabi Range (Minnesota), it can be mined cheaply by low-cost, open-pit methods. On the other hand, deep deposits are minable only by more costly shaft and tunnel methods.

AND FERROALLOY METALS

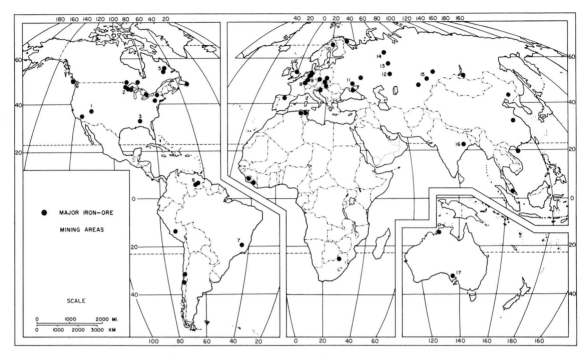

1. Iron Mountain
2. Lake Superior
3. Birmingham
4. Adirondacks
5. Quebec-Labrador
6. Cerro Bolívar
    and El Pao
7. Itabira
8. Lorraine
9. Luxembourg
10. Kiruna
11. Krivoi Rog
12. Magnitogorsk
13. Nizhny Tagil
14. Ivdel
15. Gornaya-Shoriya
16. Bihar-Orissa
17. Middleback Ranges

Fig. 6-1. Principal iron-ore-producing areas of the world. Although most countries possess iron ore, geographic, economic, political, and social conditions favorable for large-scale production exist concurrently in a relatively small number. Hence, commercial mining is much restricted.

The metallurgical industry requires so much fuel that iron-ore deposits are usually developed only when they are strategically located with respect to a supply of coal or are connected with markets by economical water transportation. The ores with the lowest net cost for making iron and steel will be the first to be exhausted. Thus the drain on the ore of the Lake Superior Region, which has supplied about 80 per cent of national requirements, began to show up at the close of World War II. Consequently, steel companies began importing high-grade ores. At the same time, mindful of the danger of relying on these distant sources of ore in times of emergency (Fig. 6-2), they began experimenting with the low-grade taconite ores in the Lake Superior

Region. They cooperated actively with the state of Minnesota in a costly research program to see whether these previously worthless rock deposits could be used for iron- and steelmaking.

KINDS OF ORE

The world's commercial iron ore falls into four major types—*magnetite, hematite, limonite,* and *siderite.*

Magnetite, a black ore with a green or brown cast, is a magnetic iron oxide that contains 72.4 per cent iron by weight. Often mag-

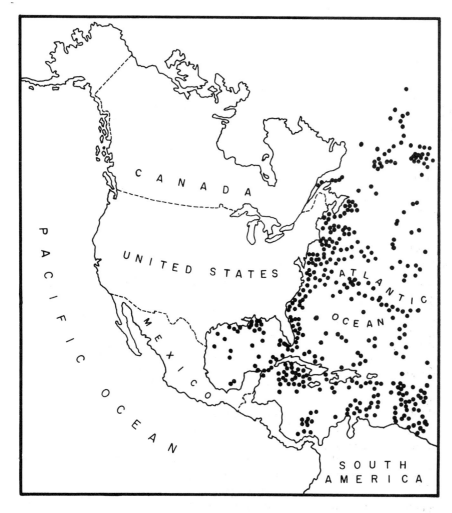

Fig. 6-2. Graveyard of merchant vessels during a six-month period of World War II, each dot representing the approximate position of a ship sent to the bottom by German submarines. Many of these ships were carrying minerals vital to the war effort. (After map in Mining World.)

netite is contaminated with other elements (sulfur, phosphorus, titanium), which limits its usefulness.

Hematite, the most common of the four, is reddish-brown and contains 70 per cent iron by weight.

Limonite, a brown ore, is abundant but makes up only a small percentage of all the ore mined. The common variety contains 59.5 per cent iron by weight.

Siderite is a grayish carbonate ore that contains 48.3 per cent iron by weight.

In nature, these iron ores are associated with objectionable impurities, which reduce the percentage of metallic iron. The high-grade ores obviously are in greatest demand, for the cost of treating ore of 30 per cent iron is more than double that of treating ore of 60 per cent iron.

THE WORLD'S IRON ORE AND FERROALLOY METALS::95

WORLD PRODUCTION

UNITED STATES

Iron ore in commercial deposits is concentrated in a few places in the United States. Reserves are shown in Table 6-1. This nation has led the world in production—at times mining almost as much as all the other countries combined.

TABLE 6-1

ESTIMATED MAJOR WORLD RESERVES
OF IRON ORE
(millions of long tons)

Region and country	Direct shipping ore	Ore needing beneficiation
NORTH AMERICA	12,055	71,700
United States	5,455	64,700
Canada	6,600	7,000
SOUTH AMERICA	23,708	36,600
Brazil	16,200	36,000
Venezuela	2,200	—
EUROPE	53,667	25,654
Soviet Union	33,757	23,984
France	8,350	—
United Kingdom	4,600	—
Sweden	2,400	—
AFRICA	9,459	—
ASIA AND OCEANIA	28,805	92,939
India	21,300	85,000
China	4,180	7,000
WORLD TOTAL (rounded)	128,000	227,000

SOURCE: U.S. Bureau of Mines, August 1962.

THE LAKE SUPERIOR REGION

The principal mining areas in the Lake Superior Region are shown in Figure 6-3. The region formerly supplied about 80 per cent of the nation's and 25 per cent of the world's iron ore. Four circumstances contributed to this production:

1. The huge reserves of high-grade hematite ore, well adapted to the American iron and steel industry.

2. The ease and economy of mining the ore.

3. The location of each range well above the lake port that serves it, so that loaded trains travel downgrade to the ports.

4. The excellent harbor and port facilities at the western end of Lake Superior.

These deposits do not lie in mountains as the word "ranges" suggests, but in elongated synclinal beds extending east and west between quartzite ridges. Formed during an ancient mountain-building period, they have been reduced by eons of erosion to mere residual ridges.

Outstanding among the six ranges comprising the region has been the Mesabi, whose ores lie relatively flat, with only a gentle slope from north to south across the range. To mine this ore, it is necessary only to strip off the surface cover to a depth of 10 to 150 feet and scoop up the ore with giant electric shovels. This method, known as *open-pit* (or *open-cut*) *mining*, is the fastest and most economical mining method known (only about one third as costly as underground mining).

The ore, which is mostly soft and crumbly, averages about 51 per cent after **beneficiation.** The near-to-the-surface, natural high-grade ore has now been largely mined. Most of the ore is carried to the surface by truck or railway, then to beneficiating plants, and finally to docks, from which it is dropped into ore boats and transported to Lower Lake ports.

The Mesabi does have one major handicap: no ore can be mined in winter. Navigation ceases on the Great Lakes system: the St. Marys River and the Soo Canals are frozen. Hence, enough ore must be shipped during late spring, summer, and autumn to keep the blast furnaces in the Lower Lake area operating throughout the year.

The other five ranges combined are less important than the Mesabi. Their mines are mostly underground, except for Wisconsin's Menominee Range, some at great depths. On the Gogebic Range, some mines are nearly a mile below the surface. Underground mines operate throughout the year, but the ore must be stockpiled during the winter (very little ore moves to blast furnaces by rail).

Taconite Ores. Taconite ores are produced from the lean, hard, taconite rocks of Minnesota. (Similar ores from the jasper formation are known as "jaspers" in Michigan and Wisconsin.)

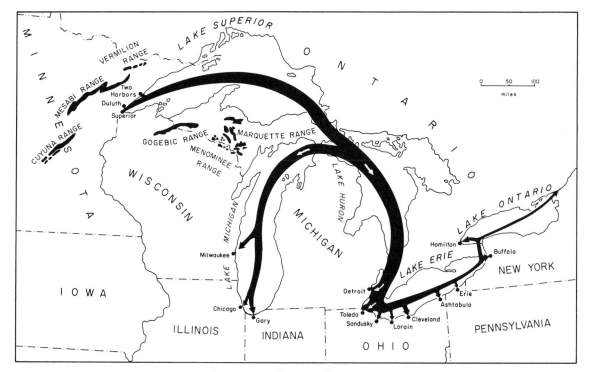

Fig. 6-3. *Distribution of iron-ore deposits in the United States.*

There are billions of tons of taconite in the Lake Superior Region, but the ore averages only about 25 per cent iron and exists mostly in a nonmagnetic form that is expensive to handle commercially. Until recently, this low iron content and the difficulty of handling it made exploitation impractical and uneconomic. Taconite is one of the hardest, toughest rocks known—three times as hard as limestone, twice as hard as granite. Moreover, the iron is scattered through it in tiny particles. The problem has been to separate those particles of iron from the rock and bundle them together into pellets that can be charged into the blast furnace. The pellets contain a higher proportion of iron than the natural ore, and they are moisture-free; hence there is considerable saving in shipping costs.

To get 1 ton of pellets, averaging 63 per cent iron, 3 tons of taconite must be drilled, blasted, mined, transported, ground fine, separated, rolled into balls, and baked (Fig. 6-4). The pellets, which are about the size of a marble, are very hard and can withstand

rough handling as well as sustain the burden of the charge in the blast furnace.

Taconite is so hard that it causes great wear and costly maintenance of equipment. The tough **alloy steel** liners in cone crushers last only one sixth as long grinding taconite as they do grinding other hard ores; abrasion-resistant steel teeth on the shovel dippers (even though made of manganese steel) must be replaced each eight-hour shift, and many bulldozer blades must have thick-ribbed steel backs welded on them.

Taconite's contribution to the American iron and steel industry has increased notably since the middle 1950s; thus in 1959, 20 million tons of the pellets moved down the Lakes, and an estimated 40 million tons will do so by 1970. In fifteen or twenty years taconite will provide a larger proportion of the charge to American blast furnaces than regular domestic ore.

Moving Lake Ore in the United States. An important and dramatic phase of the iron industry is the movement of ore 900 to 1,000

Fig. 6-4. Taconite pellets, containing about 63 per cent iron. The concentrated iron comprising the pellets is removed from material of such low grade it was once considered worthless. The tonnage of taconite pellets moving down the Great Lakes increases annually and is expected to reach 40 million tons by 1970. (Courtesy of Bethlehem Steel Corporation.)

miles from Upper to Lower Lake ports. Transportation is subject to weather conditions on the Great Lakes. During winter and early spring (December to March or April), the ships are immobilized; therefore, to ensure a continuous flow of steel products throughout the year, an almost fabulous tonnage of ore must be handled during the navigation season. The ore carriers start north on the first ribbon of open water, continuing as long as it is safe to do so. Occasionally, however, the carriers get frozen fast and have to be aided by ice-breakers.

The ore (not taconite) moves from the iron ranges to Upper Lake ports by rail. It is delivered to weighing and classification yards before continuing to Duluth, Superior, or Two Harbors. The mines are 60 to 100 miles from Duluth, and the trains coast much of the way. The railroad charge from mines to Upper Lake ports is more than that by lake freighter, which carries the ore ten times as far. Ore from Wisconsin and Michigan is shipped from Ashland, Marquette, and Escanaba.

In the Upper Lake ports, the docks jut out into Lake Superior like huge peninsulas rising 72 to 84 feet above water level. The trains move onto the docks and dump their ore into bins, from which it can be chuted by gravity into the hatches and holds of the lake carriers.

Once loaded, the vessel sails for one of the Lower Lake ports. As soon as it docks, the massive unloaders slide into position. With bucket-shaped shovels operating in batteries of four, they grasp and raise up to 30 tons of ore on every dip. So versatile and fast are the machines, and so skillful are the unloading operators, that the ore can be unloaded in from 3½ to 5 hours. Even faster time is made by self-unloaders. During the season of navigation, the vessel makes every effort to complete as many round trips as possible—the number varying from 23 to 30. The task is to accumulate enough ore at Lower Lake ports to keep the mills operating throughout the year.

New shipping facilities have been constructed for handling taconite from processing plants to ports. Processing plants are found at Virginia, Silver Bay, Iron Mountain, and Aurora, Minnesota; at Humboldt and Republic, Michigan; and at Copper Cliff, Ontario.

There are shipping facilities at Silver Bay, Taconite Harbor, and Marquette on Lake Superior and at Escanaba on Lake Michigan. The 2,200-foot-long docks at Taconite Harbor are equipped with shuttle-belt conveyers in place of chutes, an installation that considerably reduces the turn-around time of the ore boats.

BIRMINGHAM AREA

Although Alabama has four beds of minable ore, most of the production is from a single bed of hematite, which outcrops near Birmingham. This ore, which averages about 36 per cent iron, is so poor that high-grade Venezuelan ore (60 to 68 per cent) is mixed with it. This imported ore is shipped by rail from Mobile to Birmingham. However, Alabama ore contains about 15 per cent lime and hence is nearly **self-fluxing**. All mining, being underground, is expensive, and beneficiating costs are high. Reserves are estimated at 1.4 billion tons. Fortunately, the iron ore, coal, and limestone all lie in close proximity—reputedly closer than anywhere else on earth.

TEXAS

A relative newcomer among iron-mining areas is that near Daingerfield in northeastern Texas. Here open-pit mining yields the lowest commercial-grade iron ore in the nation (not including taconite)—ore running 19 to 25 per cent iron. The ores, mostly limonite, must be beneficiated up to an iron content of about 50 per cent before they are ready for blast-furnace use. Yet this ore is laid down at the Daingerfield blast furnaces at lower cost than is Lake Superior ore at any Lower Lake port.

NEW YORK STATE

Adirondack deposits of iron ore have been known and used since the days of the American Revolution. The ore, high-quality magnetite, is relatively free of impurities. Mining, however, is difficult: the rock is so hard that diamond drills must be used, and sometimes a shaft must be sunk as far as 1½ miles in order to reach a bed of ore. Although some of the ore is won from open pits, this production must be confined to the less cold months. The operations are on a large scale; and substantial quantities of ore are sent to furnaces in Buffalo, Bethlehem, Cleveland, and Pittsburgh.

EASTERN PENNSYLVANIA (READING)

Although eastern Pennsylvania is an old iron-mining and iron- and steelmaking area, large-scale iron-ore production dates only from 1958. The ore body, which consists of magnetite averaging 40 to 45 per cent iron, lies a mile below the surface. The ore is won by tunneling under the deposit to force the ore to cave into large funnel-shaped openings.

This mine possesses two great advantages: (1) it lies only 60 miles from the mills, and (2) the deposit is believed to have a life of at least half a century.

THE WEST

The iron-ore reserves of this region are not yet fully known because, until World War II, there was no significant demand for iron ore here. The region today accounts for about 7 per cent of the national total. The most important reserves are in Utah. Mining is carried on near Iron Mountain and Desert Mound by the open-pit method, and no beneficiation is required. This ore, which is magnetite and averages 50 to 53 per cent iron, is reduced in furnaces at Geneva near Provo. A productive mine at Eagle Mountain in San Bernardino County, California, supplies the blast furnaces at Fontana. The ore, hematite-magnetite, averages about 51 per cent iron but is upgraded to 60 per cent. Open-pit mining is employed.

CANADA

Whereas Canada had little stature in the world iron-ore picture at the outbreak of World War II, today she ranks quite high, particularly in reserves of high-grade ore (Table 6-1). She also ranks eighth in world output; and in the late 1960s it is expected that she will rank fourth or fifth.

Canada's deposits are in four areas: northeastern Newfoundland; various places in Ontario; on the Quebec-Labrador border; and British Columbia.

NEWFOUNDLAND (BELL ISLAND)

Here is one of the notable iron-ore reserves of the world and Canada's oldest operating iron mine. The ore, high-grade hematite averaging 52 to 54 per cent iron, extends for a considerable distance under the Atlantic Ocean. In all North America, this is the only deposit of commercial iron ore that can be and actually is being mined close to the ocean. In fact, miners are removing ore from underneath the Atlantic. The ore is found in three beds, one above the other but separated by thick layers of rock. These strata make possible the mining operation by forming a ceiling that protects the mine workings from the pounding sea.

The bulk of the ore is shipped to Nova Scotia and to Great Britain, West Germany, and other European countries. The recoverable ore is placed at 1.25 billion tons; potential reserves are estimated at 5 billion tons.

ONTARIO

In Ontario there are important deposits of iron ore. At Steep Rock (Fig. 6-1) northwest of Lake Superior is a major and unique deposit. Before mining could begin, Steep Rock Lake had to be drained, for the ore lay beneath the 130 feet of its waters. After the year required to drain the lake, large power shovels began scooping out enormous bites of red hematite ore having an iron content of 60 per cent. Open-pit mining is followed to a depth of 400 feet, and underground methods below that. Steep Rock makes Canada's fast-growing iron and steel industry less dependent upon United States sources of ore, and it provides the United States with strategically located ore.

Another source in Ontario is the Michipicoten area, whose ores are well situated for supplying the steel industry at Sault Ste. Marie.

Finally, 120 miles east of Toronto is the Marmora mine (taconite). About 20 million tons of overburden were stripped from the ore body over a period of three years. Some 500,-000 tons of pellets averaging 65 per cent iron now move to the port of Picton and thence via Lake Ontario and the Welland Canal to the large Bethlehem plant at Lackawanna, New York.

QUEBEC-LABRADOR

Few areas have moved from obscurity to renown so quickly as Labrador-Quebec through the recent discovery and development of rich and extensive iron-ore deposits (Fig. 6-1). Possibly the major deposit is the Ungava Trough on the Quebec-Labrador border—regarded as one of the great discoveries of all time. Several districts are being developed: (1) Schefferville (Knob Lake); (2) Wabash Lake; (3) Mount Reed–Mount Wright (150 miles north of Shelter Bay); and (4) the west coast of Ungava Bay.

The deposits occur as surface outcrops in ridges above the general level of the ground with little overburden. Proved ore reserves exceed 350 million tons, but further exploration will greatly expand this figure. A railway 360 miles long from the mines at Burnt Creek to the port of Sept Îles (Seven Islands) on the Gulf of St. Lawrence cost over $100,000 per mile. Additional railway mileage has been built to other mines in the Trough.

By 1960, Labrador-Quebec was shipping some 20 million tons of iron ore annually to Canadian and United States iron and steel mills, mainly to those located on the Lower Great Lakes.

BRITISH COLUMBIA

This area is the least important of the four, but it is expected to develop considerably over the next two decades. Production takes place at Quinsam Lake and Texada Island, the output going to Japan.

LATIN AMERICA

Several countries in Latin America have important iron-ore reserves and production (Fig. 6-1). According to some authorities, Latin America has from one fifth to one fourth of the world's commercial iron ore. Brazil has more than any other country in Latin America; but Chile, Colombia, Cuba, Peru, and Venezuela are also well endowed. Unfortunately, the bulk of the ore will have to be exported because the coal deposits are inadequate and of too poor quality to support a well-developed metallurgical industry. Ore is exported from Brazil, Chile, Peru, and Venezuela to the United States; from Brazil and Venezuela to Europe; and from Brazil and Peru to Japan. In 1959, of the 39.9 million tons of iron ore imported by the United States, 23 million tons came from Latin America—15.2 million tons from Venezuela alone.

MEXICO

Numerous iron-ore discoveries have been made in Mexico, but the country lacks the impressive reserves that characterize several other Latin American republics. The total reserves, however, appear to be adequate for the development and maintenance of Mexico's metallurgical industry for at least a century. The leading deposits (Fig. 6-1) are concentrated largely in five areas: (1) the North Pacific, (2) the North, (3) the Central Pacific, (4) the Center, and (5) the South. Because many of these deposits lie in isolated areas far from the supply of coking coal, they cannot be worked under present conditions.

CUBA

In Camaguey and Oriente provinces are impressive iron-ore deposits, but little mining has been carried on. The Daiquiri district supplies most of the ore, largely hematite but some magnetite. The ore averages about 55 per cent iron. To the north is the Mayari district, which yields brown ore—limonite, containing chromite and nickel, mainly for steel to be used for construction and ordnance.

PERU

Peru is a newcomer to the world's iron-ore map (Fig. 6-1). Total reserves are estimated at 740 million tons. At Marcona, 15 miles inland from the port of San Juan, is the nation's principal reserve and mine. The ore deposits consist of hematite and limonite in the upper levels and of magnetite in the lower ones.

The open-cut method of mining is employed, the overburden being drilled and blasted. Power shovels then scoop up the ore and load it into trucks, which deliver it to the port over a heavy-duty highway. The Marcona ore, averaging about 60 per cent iron, contains almost no moisture and is low in both phosphorus and sulfur. Destined largely for export, the ore is beneficiated to reduce shipping charges.

Acare in the same area is an important deposit of magnetite ore averaging 65 per cent iron. Although the reserves are small compared with those at Marcona, the mine shipped more than 1.5 million tons in 1960, compared with Marcona's 5.5 million.

CHILE

Chile has two iron-ore areas, both in the coastal belt—El Tofo and El Romeral (Fig. 6-1). For many years the El Tofo mine was the largest exporter of iron ore in all Latin America, but it is no longer important. The principal mine today is El Romeral, an open-cut installation north of La Serena. The ore is shipped by rail to a modern loading wharf on Guayacan Bay. El Romeral supplies all the iron-ore requirements of Chile's Huachipato iron- and steelworks and exports considerable ore to the United States.

BRAZIL

Brazil ranks among the world's leaders in iron-ore reserves (Table 6-1 and Fig. 6-1). Although the ore is widely distributed, the state of Minas Gerais leads by far. The reserves of Minas Gerais alone contain (1) 1½ billion tons of soft hematite ore containing 65 to 69 per cent iron; (2) 3½ billion tons of itabirite (taconite) ore with 50 to 60 per cent iron; and (3) 10 billion tons of iron-bearing material with an estimated 30 to 50 per cent iron.

Because of the unfavorable coking-coal situation, the bulk of the ore mined is exported to Northwest Europe, particularly to West Germany and the United Kingdom; to the United States; and to neighboring Argentina.

VENEZUELA

Following the heavy drain of World War II on the Lake Superior Region's high-grade ores, several American iron-mining and steel companies began explorations in Venezuela. Impressive discoveries have made Venezuela one of the world's leading producers and exporters of iron ore. Reserves are large (Table 6-1). Exports in 1959 were 16.9 million metric tons, of which 80 per cent went to the United States, 9 per cent to Great Britain, 8 per cent to Germany, and 3 per cent to Italy. Of the many discoveries (there are dozens of ore-crusted hills and mountains), only two have been developed—Cerro Bolívar and El Pao (Fig. 6-5).

Cerro Bolívar, a mountain of iron ore a mile wide, 4½ miles long, and 2,000 feet above the surrounding grasslands just north of the Guiana Highlands, is one of the most important iron-ore discoveries of all time. It lies 90 miles southwest of Puerto Ordaz, at the confluence of the Caroní and Orinoco Rivers, to

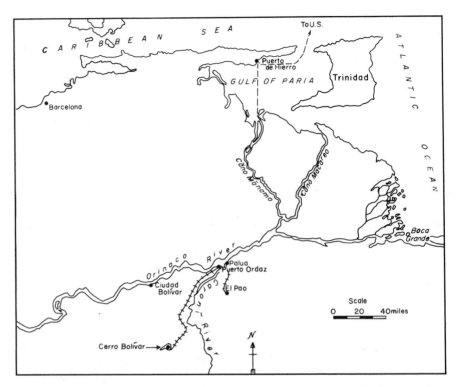

Fig. 6-5. The new iron-ore developments in Venezuela's Guayana region—Cerro Bolívar and El Pao. The exports from these mines make Venezuela the chief source of iron-ore imports (one third of the total ore used) of the United States. Total exports in 1960 to the United States, West Germany, Italy, Great Britain, the Netherlands, and Belgium amounted to 19.6 million metric tons. (Drawn by John Arrillaga.)

which the ore is sent by rail for loading into oceangoing vessels. This mountain, which is believed to contain 500 million tons of high-grade ore (63 to 68 per cent iron), lies in a region which geologists believe may well contain reserves up to 2 billion tons. The ore, a mixture of hematite, limonite, and magnetite, has an average thickness of 230 feet. The ore mined, except for the small amount used by the Venezuelan iron and steel industry, is exported to the United States, mainly to Morrisville, Pennsylvania, and Mobile, Alabama.

El Pao, a rich ore deposit and mine, lies on the east side of the Caroní some 30 miles southeast of its confluence with the Orinoco. The ore is hard, massive hematite, running 63

to 66 per cent iron, and can be used either in blast furnaces or open-hearth furnaces. The deposit being worked is a bowl-shaped formation about 2,600 feet long and 1,700 feet wide on top of a hill rising several hundred feet above the surrounding country. An overburden had to be removed prior to mining. The ore body itself varies from a few feet to about 400 feet in thickness. Mining proceeds by slicing off the top of the hill in benches. Eventually a pit will be excavated within the hill.

The ore is transported by rail to Palua, Bethlehem's port on the Orinoco (Fig. 6-5), whence it moves to Puerto de Hierro on the Gulf of Paria for stockpiling and delivery by ore carriers to Sparrows Point, Maryland.

EUROPE

Europe, particularly Western Europe, is richly endowed in minerals, including iron ore. Western Europe is a political aggregation in which no one nation possesses the raw materials or the mass market to rank alongside the United States or the Soviet Union. This disadvantage, however, has been largely offset by the formation of the European Economic Community and the European Free Trade Association. The countries represented possess enough iron ore to meet about half their needs; the rest they import. Domestic ore, except for Sweden's, is low grade; the high-grade ore is imported.

Figure 6-1 shows the major iron-ore reserves and producers in Western Europe: France, Sweden, Great Britain, West Germany, and Spain.

FRANCE

France, with the largest iron-ore deposits in continental Europe (Table 6-1), is the dominant producer in Western Europe (66 million tons in 1960). Although the ore is soft hematite averaging only 32 to 38 per cent iron, it is self-fluxing. Deposits lie in Lorraine, Normandy, and Brittany; however, 96 per cent of production comes from Lorraine, whose iron-ore area extends from Nancy to Longwy (a distance of about 60 miles) and covers about 450 square miles. Deposits are not continuous, but occur in four distinct districts: (1) Longwy; (2) Landres, Ottange, and Tucquegnieux; (3) Orne; and (4) Nancy. Most mines are underground, and in places mining is carried on at depths of more than 570 feet.

Approximately 60 per cent of French output of iron ore is consumed by the domestic iron and steel industry. The rest is exported to neighboring iron- and steel-producing countries—Belgium, West Germany, and Luxembourg.

Prior to 1952, Lorraine was burdened by transport discrimination and excess tariff charges on freight. The European Economic Community has abolished many of these charges. For a long time France has wanted to connect Lorraine iron ore and Ruhr coal by canal, and has finally accomplished this aim: the Moselle Canal, which reaches from Thionville to Coblenz, now joins the two areas.

SWEDEN

Although Sweden has iron-ore deposits in both its northern and central parts, the Kiruna and Gälivare districts in Lapland have put the nation on the commercial iron-ore map of the world (Fig. 6-1). The deposits are large and among the richest in the world—hard magnetite containing 60 to 70 per cent iron. Mining is both underground and open cut. The mine at Kiruna is the world's largest underground iron-ore operation. It is very highly mechanized: from 30 to 35 tons of ore per man-shift are procured, an amount only slightly less than that obtained from open-pit mines. Sweden's reserves are large (Table 6-1); at the present rate of production, the Swedish Lapland reserves have an estimated life of 500 years.

Most of the ore is exported, for Sweden has no coking coal; although she has ample hydro-electric power, furnaces so operated cannot compete with coke-charged blast furnaces. The exported ore goes to Belgium, Great Britain, Germany, the United States, and the Netherlands, through two small ports—Narvik, Norway, and Luleå, Sweden. Narvik, an ice-free port throughout the year, is devoted solely to the exportation of iron ore. Luleå, on the Lule River near the Gulf of Bothnia, is not accessible to vessels in winter.

The central Swedish deposits lie northeast of Lake Vanern. The country's best ore emanates from a small deposit at Grangesburg.

GREAT BRITAIN

The greater part of Britain's really high-grade iron ore has been used, and yet reserves still are sizable (Table 6-1). Particularly huge are the reserves of low-grade ore. British ores currently being mined contain about 30 per cent iron. Unfortunately, they are high in both phosphorus and sulfur, and must be mixed with higher-quality imported ore. British iron ore does, however, enjoy two important advantages: it is minable at low cost, and the deposits lie relatively near domestic supplies of coal. The chief source of domestic iron ore today is the English Lowland—more than half the output being from Northampton.

SPAIN

Spain has large reserves of iron ore near Bilbao. The ores mined, chiefly siderite and hematite containing 37 to 50 per cent iron, are utilized at home by a growing iron and steel industry and are exported primarily to the United Kingdom and West Germany.

Probably two thirds of the original deposits have been mined; and the beds of high-grade ore, especially in Viscaya, have been virtually exhausted. However, the reserves of direct-shipping ore still amount to about 1 billion tons. Mining is almost entirely from open pits, though there is some underground mining. Methods everywhere are antiquated.

LESSER EUROPEAN PRODUCERS

There is iron ore in Luxembourg, West Germany, Czechoslovakia, and Poland. Luxembourg, sharing in the Lorraine ore, produces about 6.5 million tons per annum, which gives her high rank in proportion to size. West Germany has iron-ore deposits totaling 1.5 billion tons in several areas—particularly in Lower Saxony, which accounts for more than half the annual domestic output of about 18 million tons. About 30 miles south of Bremen, there is considerable iron ore. Czechoslovakia, with rather small reserves of 230 million tons, nonetheless produces annually some 3 million tons; and Poland, with reserves of 370 million tons, produces about 2 million tons.

SOVIET UNION

The iron-ore reserves of the Soviet Union are enormous (Table 6-1). In fact, this gigantic country claims to have the world's largest reserves. Yet, like the United States, the Soviet Union is experiencing difficulty in meeting its requirements of rich ore. During World War II, the high-grade ores in the Urals were depleted at an alarming rate. Following the war, Soviet geologists engaged in a frantic search for new deposits of high-grade iron ore; and, though they announced a number of discoveries, all were considerably poorer in quality than the deposits they are intended to replace.

Deposits have been discovered in 71 places in 11 districts. Actual mining, however, is carried on in only about 30 of these 71. The distribution of Russian iron ore on the whole is unfavorable; in most instances, it lies far from the deposits of coking coal and from the major iron and steel centers (Fig. 6-6).

In 1960 there were only three major iron-mining areas—Krivoi Rog, Southern Urals, and Gornaya Shoriya; these account for roughly 94 per cent of the total output.

KRIVOI ROG

This district in the eastern Ukraine west of the Dnieper River is the best located in the entire U.S.S.R. With reserves of hematite, magnetite, and limonite of more than 2 billion metric tons running 48 to 64 per cent iron, Krivoi Rog provides the basic ore supply for the furnaces of the Ukraine; it also ships ore to the Moscow-Tula area and to satellite mills in Eastern Europe. However, the ore is high in phosphorus and pulverizes easily, which results in considerable losses in mining, transporting, and general handling.

So great has been the demand for high-grade ore that mining has been forced to great depths and into water-bearing strata. Hence, a point has been reached where open-pit magnetite taconites in European U.S.S.R. can compete with the underground mining of high-grade Krivoi Rog ores.

SOUTHERN URALS

Although iron ore is found and mined in other parts of the Urals, the south ranks highest both in reserves and production. The most important deposit, ranking second only to that of Krivoi Rog, is at Magnitogorsk. During World War II and the German occupation of Krivoi Rog, the Ural Mountain deposits supplied the country's wartime blast-furnace needs. These reserves today are placed at 300 million metric tons averaging about 50 to 54 per cent iron. Most of the ore is magnetite. Mining is by the open-pit method. The direct shipping grade of ore is now virtually depleted. Southern Urals iron ore not only is used in the great mills at Magnitogorsk but also comprises about 30 per cent of the mix in the iron and steel complex of Kuznetsk.

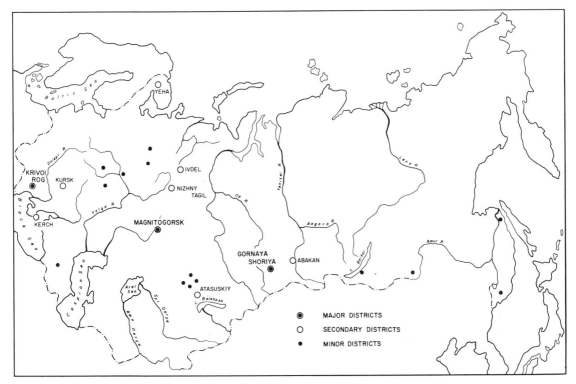

Fig. 6-6. Distribution of iron-ore deposits in the Soviet Union. The distribution is regarded by most Western authorities as unfavorable, since in most instances the ore is near neither the coking-coal deposits nor the major markets.

The highest-quality Magnitogorsk ore has been mined so assiduously that some authorities fear the better ore will be exhausted by 1978. However, large deposits of low-grade ore remain.

GORNAYA SHORIYA

This area lying south of Novokuznetsk is well located with respect to the Kuzbas steel-making complex. As early as 1947, about three fourths of the ore used in the Kuzbas was from this area, and today substantially all of it is. Formerly the ore was transported by rail some 1,500 miles, from the Southern Urals area to the Kuzbas. Coal went back in the same cars.

The usable ores are found in many deposits. The reserve is not large, nor is the quality of the ore high (32 to 54 per cent iron). The significance of the area and its deposits stems from its strategic location.

LESSER IRON-ORE DISTRICTS IN RUSSIA

The three leading districts contribute 94 per cent of the total output. Several others, which promise to grow in stature, lie in Kazakhstan and Western Siberia. Crude-ore output in Asiatic U.S.S.R. is expected to increase twentyfold by 1970 compared with 1955, whereas that in the Urals and European U.S.S.R. is expected to increase by only threefold and fourfold during the same period. Thus, a shift in the geography of Soviet iron-ore production appears in progress.

INDIA

In immensity of reserves and quality of ore, India is one of the world's best-endowed countries. Certainly it is best off of the nations in Asia (Table 6-1). India reserves exceed present reserves of comparable quality in the United States. It is this rich heritage that gives India its greatest natural advantage for the development of a major iron and steel industry. Most of the better ore is hematite that averages from 55 to 70 per cent iron.

The largest concentration of ore bodies is in the provinces of Bihar and Orissa, southwest of Calcutta. Ninety-eight per cent of the country's production of iron ore is here.

There are four large hematite deposits in central India; but they are not being exploited, largely because of their distance from currently operating iron and steel mills.

In 1956 India mined 4.83 million long tons of ore, which made her the world's seventh largest producer. The bulk of this ore was utilized in her own blast furnaces. More than a million tons of iron ore are exported annually to West Germany, Belgium, Czechoslovakia, and Japan, with Japan receiving the largest tonnage. Of the ore mined in 1956, only 10 per cent was below 55 per cent iron.

CHINA

Until recently, it was believed that China did not rank high among the nations in iron-ore reserves. In 1959, however, China was accorded ranking among the world's leaders (Table 6-1). Though the accuracy of the Chinese Communist statistics may be questioned, the reserves are indisputably immense.

Most of the ore discovered to date is of low quality, about 35 per cent iron, and hence requires concentration prior to reduction in the blast furnace.

Principal iron-ore reserves and mining centers are in Manchuria near Anshan and Penki. Other sources are Chahar, Hainan Island, Honan, Hupeh, Kansu in the Kilien Mountains, Kweichow, Paiyunopo in Inner Mongolia, Suiyuan, and in Wuhan.

Prior to World War II the bulk of the iron ore mined in China was exported, chiefly to Japan. Today the large tonnage produced annually is smelted mostly within the country.

The iron-ore picture is changing rapidly in China. More intensive geological field work is being carried on than at any time in the country's long history. Many impressive deposits of minerals, including iron ore, are not now exploitable because of transport deficiencies. But railroads are being built, more than

1,000 miles of track being added annually to the network.

FEDERATION OF MALAYSIA

This federation, despite rather small reserves, nonetheless ranks as the third largest producer of iron ore in Asia—following China and India. The mines are located primarily in the southeastern part of the Malay Peninsula (largest single mine is at Trengganu) and in the north—in the Ipoh area, state of Perak. All the ore is exported, Japan taking about 98 per cent, the Netherlands and Formosa the remaining 2 per cent. Exports fluctuate widely from year to year depending upon Japan's requirements.

THE PHILIPPINE REPUBLIC

The Philippine Republic has appreciable iron-ore reserves. Most ores, however, are laterites and are not regarded highly in the trade. The average metallic content is about 45 per cent iron, though some ores reach 54 to 67 per cent. About 1.5 million tons are mined annually, almost all of which following beneficiation is exported to Japan. Among the principal deposits are the Mati in Davao Province, Mindanao, and Sibuguey in Samar.

AFRICA

Africa is not expected to contribute greatly to the world's iron-ore picture (Fig. 6-1 and Table 6-1). However, since Africa has been only superficially explored geologically, generalizations regarding reserves are risky. Currently Algeria, Liberia, and South Africa are the most important producers; but Morocco, Egypt, Guinea, Gabon, the Rhodesias, Sierra Leone, and Mauritania also have commercial deposits, some of which are being worked. Liberia has at Bomi Hills, 42 miles inland from Monrovia, a deposit of about 30 to 40 million tons of possibly the highest-grade iron ore in the world. Averaging about 69 per cent iron, it can be charged directly into open-hearth furnaces. About a million tons of this ore are mined and exported annually to the United States. Liberia also has rich iron-ore deposits (60 to 70 per cent iron) in the Nimba Range, about 200 miles in from the coast, near the Liberia-Guinea border. Since in nature iron exists only in oxide form, a pure oxide has only 70 per cent iron. Hence this ore is about 100 per cent pure iron oxide. The reserve exceeds 200 million tons.

South Africa, although not outstanding in reserves, is reputed to have some 3.5 billion tons of direct-shipping ores. The ore, which is hematite and classed as medium to high grade, averages 40 to 60 per cent iron. Deposits have been discovered near Postmasburg, northern Cape Province; at Kuruman, near Newcastle, Natal; and at Pretoria and Thabazimbi in the Transvaal. Of the 2.25 million tons of ore mined annually, the bulk comes from the Thabazimbi mine, 150 miles by rail from Pretoria.

A reserve of about 120 million tons of direct-shipping ores is credited to Mauritania in Northwest Africa. The metallic content is reported to be 65 to 69 per cent iron. This resource is being exploited by a French-controlled international mining consortium. Before ore can be shipped, however, a 116-million-dollar railway will have to be built from the mine to Port-Etienne.

AUSTRALIA

Australia has considerable iron ore—both high grade and jasper. The principal deposits are in the Middleback Ranges of South Australia and at remote Cockatoo and Koolan islands in Yampi Sound of Western Australia (Fig. 6-1). Though these deposits lie far from the coal and the heart of the country's iron and steel industry, they are to all intents and purposes practically on tidewater. This ore is transported economically in large, specially constructed vessels to blast furnaces on the east coast—3,000-plus miles from Cockatoo Island and 1,350 miles from Whyalla, the shipping port for Middleback ore.

Suitable ore in adequate quantities for a modern iron and steel industry is conspicuously absent in New South Wales and Victoria. Large reserves of high-grade ore have been discovered on the west coast of Tasmania, but they are economically inaccessible at present. The deposits at Yampi Sound are very good and very extensive (about 100 million tons) and are being worked to conserve the more accessible deposits in South Australia, which has long been the chief source of iron ore for the Australian iron and steel industry. The ore being mined at Cockatoo Island averages about 60 per cent iron and is free from objectionable impurities; that in South Australia averages 60 to 63 per cent iron. All mining is by open pit.

As a conservation measure, a ban was placed on exports until 1961, when the government, having learned that reserves were adequate, permitted exportation. Most of the exported ore moves to Japan.

THE FERROALLOY METALS

Actually, the ferroalloys are manufactured products, so that it is perhaps misleading to speak of cobalt or nickel or chromium as a "ferroalloy." Rather, one should speak of them as "metals for making ferroalloys"; that is, they impart certain properties to steel that it would not have without them. Since, however, the term "ferroalloys" is in common parlance, it is employed in this chapter.

USES

Alloy steels are a response to engineering science's demand for steel that can do things that carbon steels cannot do. Scientists want steels that resist abrasion, fatigue, and shock; steels that resist corrosion and high temperatures; steels that allow for an increase in loads and speeds on machine tools and on machines which supply power to mills and factories.

When metals such as chromium, cobalt, manganese, molybdenum, nickel, tungsten, and vanadium are added in known quantities (generally less than 1 per cent) to plain carbon steel, the steel acquires new characteristics. Depending upon the materials added and the amount of each, the steel can be made stronger, tougher, more heat resistant, or more resistant to corrosion. Manganese is essential to the production of high-quality steel, 13 or 14 pounds going into every ton. Without columbium, chromium, cobalt, and tungsten, the special steel used in jet planes, tanks, guns, shells, and radar could not be made. Without nickel, certain kinds of steel would be unavail-

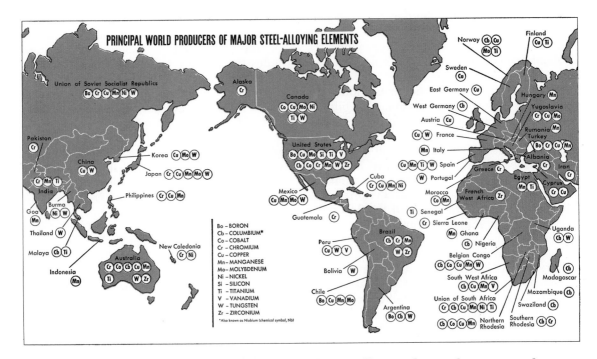

Fig. 6-7. Leading world sources of the ferroalloy metals. For the most part the major sources lie not in the great iron- and steelmaking nations but in the underdeveloped ones. The subtle economic and political implications of such ownership are thus evident. (Courtesy of American Iron and Steel Institute.)

able; and without cobalt, steels used in high-speed cutting tools, valves, drills, magnets, and jet engines could not be manufactured.

DISTRIBUTION

The ferroalloys, though widely distributed, do not exist in large reserves. Therefore, it is indeed fortunate that they are used in small quantities. Moreover, they are not equitably distributed politically. They are for the most part located in remote and thinly populated areas; few of them are found in the countries that lead in the manufacture of iron and steel. Not one of the modern industrial nations is an important producer of all or even most of the ferroalloys, and some of the world's leading steel-producing nations possess almost none (Fig. 6-7). For instance, although the United States is preeminent in steelmaking, it is forced to depend on foreign countries for the bulk of its ferroalloys. The United States, which produces only 1.6 per cent of the world total of such minerals, is the greatest market

for them, consuming about 35 per cent of the total output.

CHROMIUM

Chromium is one of the key metals; among the alloying agents, possibly only manganese is used in greater amount. Three fourths of the world's supply of chromite (the commercial ore of chromium) comes from five countries—South Africa, the Soviet Union, Turkey, Southern Rhodesia, and the Philippines. Turkey's deposits are believed to be the world's largest. Turkish ore is regarded as the world's highest-quality chromium and sells for the highest price. Cuba has been the only impressive source in the Western Hemisphere.

COBALT

Cobalt, like columbium and tungsten, is especially valuable in rendering steel capable of resisting high temperatures. Hence, cobalt steel is employed in the manufacture of jet engines and gas turbines. Because of its ability to retain a keen cutting edge at very high temperatures, it is also used in making high-speed tools. Moreover, because it improves the magnetic qualities in iron, it is useful in the electronics industry for producing permanent magnets. Cobalt also has atomic-power uses.

Substitutions are not feasible because of the sacrifice in performance and the necessity of using large proportions of other critical metals.

Five countries supply almost the entire world output of cobalt: the Congo (70 per cent), Canada, the United States, Northern Rhodesia, and Morocco.

COLUMBIUM

This additive metal is used to contribute to steel qualities of hardness and durability and particularly stability at high temperatures. It imparts superior creep resistance and fatigue strengthening to alloys employed in jet engines, gas turbines, rockets, and guided missiles.

Chief world source of columbium is Africa (the Congo, Mozambique, Nigeria, South Africa, and Uganda); smaller sources are South America (Bolivia, Brazil, and British Guiana), and Asia (Malaysia).

MANGANESE

This metal, the "work horse" of steelmaking, performs two functions: (1) it is used in the form of ore, for making pig iron, and (2) it is used in the form of ferromanganese and/or spiegel, for steelmaking. It is employed as a deoxidizer and desulfurizer (purifier) in producing all kinds of steel.

Normally five countries—the Soviet Union, India, Ghana, South Africa, and Brazil—account for more than 90 per cent of the world's output. The United States possesses large reserves of low-grade manganese, but almost none of high-grade manganese. Accordingly, it imports from India, South Africa, Brazil, and Cuba, and from the Congo and Chile.

A recent major source of manganese for the United States is Brazil, whose new development at Amapa has become one of the world's largest. A 122-mile-long standard-gauge railway was slashed through the rain forest, connecting the mine and docking facilities for ocean-going ore carriers, 13 miles upstream from Macapá on the Amazon.

MOLYBDENUM

About 90 per cent of the molybdenum output is employed to make hard tool steel. Some is used to increase resistance to chemical attack and to retain strength and dimension at high temperatures. For some purposes, it is substituted for other ferroalloy metals, conserving those ferroalloys that are used in smaller amounts or are rarer.

Molybdenum is regarded as the rarest of the common ferroalloys (it makes up only 0.001 per cent of the earth's crust). The United States yields more than 90 per cent of the world output of this metal. A deposit at Climax, Colorado, accounts for more than half the United States production. The bulk of the remaining United States output is a by-product of copper mining and smelting in Utah. Chile contributes about 10 per cent of the world output as a by-product of copper smelting. Communist China has recently become a medium-sized world producer.

NICKEL

Nickel is indispensable for the most important activities having to do with defense. It is readily alloyed with either ferrous or non-ferrous base metals. Nickel gives toughness to steel; in fact, it triples the strength of the iron that goes into steel. It also stiffens steel, making it more resistant to corrosion. For heat and corrosion applications, nickel has no satisfactory substitutes. Nickel is a major partner of chromium in the production of stainless steel. Its importance has so increased with the development of jet aircraft (some of whose parts operate at white heat), gas turbines, rockets, atomic energy, and electronics that fully one half of all alloys include nickel.

Although nickel-bearing deposits have been discovered in many parts of the world, actual mining is highly localized: Canada, the Soviet Union, New Caledonia, and Cuba together account for nine tenths of the world output. Nickel and molybdenum are the only two alloy metals that come predominantly from the

Western Hemisphere: Canada alone contributes about two thirds of the world output. Her two largest producing areas are Sudbury and Thompson. Sudbury has long been the world's largest nickel operation; but Thompson, 400 miles north of Winnipeg, was hacked out of the wilderness only in the late 1950s. The Soviet Union claims the largest reserves of nickel. She is mining nickel ore at Nickel, the former Finnish mining center. In the Oriente Province of Cuba are low-grade nickel-ore deposits that are costly to exploit.

TANTALITE

This ferroalloy metal, which is just beginning to play an important role in industry, retains its strength at white heat and accordingly is in great demand for making heat-resistant superalloys for jet aircraft and guided missiles. It is used also for chemical, electronic, and surgical equipment, and for cutting tools and dies. Tantalite is mined mainly in the Congo, Nigeria, Brazil, and Malaysia.

TUNGSTEN

Tungsten is used in steel for high-speed cutting tools that must retain hardness up to a red heat even for long periods of time. Tungsten, whose melting point is 6150°F, ranks second highest of all chemical elements; it is largely for this reason that tools of tungsten steel retain a tough cutting edge. Mainly because this metal can function at high temperatures, it alone is employed for filaments in electric light bulbs.

The principal ore of tungsten is wolframite, which averages only about 3 per cent tungsten and hence must be concentrated up to about 60 per cent metal for shipment to market.

For many years China led the world in output of tungsten—as late as 1949 accounting for one third of world production. Most of it came and still comes from Kiangsi Province opposite Formosa. Another producing area lies in Kwangtung Province near Kukong, about 90 miles north of Canton. Since the Communist victory in 1949, non-Communist lands have been combed in an effort to find new deposits; and some success has been achieved in the United States, South Korea, Bolivia,

Portugal, and Australia. United States deposits are small and costly to mine; hence, production takes place only under government support. In 1959 the last two independent tungsten mines closed down when federal funds became exhausted (there were 700 producing mines in 1956).

VANADIUM

This metal most closely resembles manganese in being a good deoxidizer and scavenger in the steelmaking process. As an alloy it, like tungsten, adds strength, durability, and hardness to steel. It also gives resiliency and resistance to shock and fatigue. Vanadium steel is used for making tools and automobile parts and gears. Two tenths of 1 per cent of vanadium increases the elasticity and tensile strength of mild steel by 50 per cent. Vanadium in combination with chromium produces a *tougher* steel than plain chromium steel, and a *harder* steel than plain vanadium steel. Associated with tungsten, vanadium is valuable for high-speed tool steel.

Vanadium is widely distributed, but commercial deposits are restricted to Northern Rhodesia, Peru, Southwest Africa, and the United States. The United States accounts for about 80 per cent of the total world output, but much of this is a by-product of the uranium industry in the Colorado Plateau of Colorado and Utah.

WORLD OUTLOOK

It has been pointed out that although iron-ore deposits are widely distributed, iron mining is not. This situation results from world economic and political conditions. Until recently the great steelmaking nations of North America and Western Europe, with few exceptions, could meet most of their own iron-ore needs. This is no longer the case. It sounds reassuring to say that America's iron-ore reserves amount to 65 billion tons. But of this amount only 4.5 billion tons are classed as direct-shipping ores and less than 2 billion tons are high grade (above 50 per cent iron). The rest is lower grade, some as low as 25 per cent iron. Supplementary supplies have been found in distant areas—largely, though not exclusively, in underdeveloped countries. These imports, which totaled almost 40 million tons in 1959 and accounted for more than one third of domestic requirements, are expected to increase in size in the future. A Canadian government mineral survey estimates that the United States steel industry may have to import as many as 100 million tons of iron ore annually by 1980. Foreign ore is both better and cheaper. In 1960, per-ton costs for shipping ore to East Coast ports of the United States were $3.75 from Brazil, $2.60 from Liberia, $3.25 from Peru, and $3.75 from our own Mesabi Range, despite the much longer distance the foreign ore moves.

Although most of the ore-rich underdeveloped nations want iron and steel industries of their own, the small scale of their present enterprises or even of those contemplated will allow large exports of iron ore for many years. Principal sources of ore for the highly indus-

trialized nations now and in the future appear to be Canada, Brazil, Chile, Liberia, Peru, Mauritania, India, Sweden, Venezuela, and Gabon. Thus, to secure ore for their iron and steel industries, the importing nations—the United States, the United Kingdom, West Germany, Belgium-Luxembourg, and Japan— must depend increasingly upon foreign sources to offset the impending scarcity of domestic reserves. But this brings to the fore the economic, fiscal, and political "climates" of the various underdeveloped countries. Particularly are the industrial nations concerned about the safety of their investments. One cannot but wonder whether the politicians in the underdeveloped nations will hearken to the economics and logistics of iron ore or be dominated completely by nationalism. Regardless, foreign policy of the developed nations must be aimed at winning and holding the good will of those lands where iron ore and other minerals originate.

SELECTED REFERENCES

Carlson, Lucile. "Luleå and Narvik: Swedish Ore Ports," *Journal of Geography*, 52:1-13, January 1953.
Fitzhugh, E. F. "Iron Ore at Bomi Hill, Liberia," *Economic Geology*, 48:431-436, September–October 1953.
"Iron Ore—U.S.S.R.," *Mineral Trade Notes* (U.S. Bureau of Mines), Part I, Vol. 45, September 1957; Part II, Vol. 45, October 1957.
Kohn, Clyde F., and Raymond E. Specht. "The Mining of Taconite, Lake Superior Iron Mining District," *Geographical Review*, 48:528-539, October 1958.
Mikami, Harry M. "World Iron-Ore Map," *Economic Geology*, 39:1-24, January–February 1944.
"Steel's Vitamins from the World Over," *U.S. Steel News*, 24:19-23, January 1959.

CHAPTER SEVEN::

The nonferrous metals [1] present a particularly interesting topic because their principal sources of output are the underdeveloped countries (Table 7-1), whereas the centers of consumption are limited largely to the developed ones. Moreover, the world's utilization of these metals has soared during the past

[1] The nonferrous metals fall into two principal categories: (1) those used alone or in combination with other nonferrous metals in ways in which their individual properties yield some well-defined advantages (copper, lead, zinc, tin, and aluminum) and (2) those employed for alloying with iron (in the production of special steels). In this chapter the authors depart somewhat from the above classification: aluminum is treated with magnesium in Chapter 8, "The World's Light Metals"; and the ferroalloy metals (chromium, cobalt, columbium, manganese, molybdenum, nickel, tungsten, and vanadium) are treated with iron ore in Chapter 6, "The World's Iron Ore and Ferroalloys."

THE WORLD'S

fifty years (Table 7-2). Although substitutions are possible and are increasing in importance, they are sometimes difficult and for many uses even impossible. Under present world conditions, the nonferrous group of metals—*copper, lead, zinc,* and *tin*—must be regarded as indispensable to twentieth-century civilization.

COPPER

Next to iron, copper is the most useful metal. Though used for millennia by man (prehistoric remains reveal copper tools, weapons, and ornaments), it did not really come into its own until the Age of Electricity. Copper is a good conductor of electricity, can be drawn into wire easily, and resists corrosion. More than half of all the copper used in the United States serves as a conductor for electricity. Copper can also be alloyed with ease.

MINING TECHNOLOGY

The ores of copper are generally more complex than those of iron and do not have so high a metallic content. Some of the large and experienced copper companies are mining ores containing only 1 to 3 per cent recoverable copper. In fact, much ore is being mined that contains less than 1 per cent copper. As late as 1880, ores containing less than 25 per cent copper could not be mined economically. However, mass-mining methods (such as those now employed at Bingham, Utah; at Globe, Arizona; at Chuquicamata, Chile; and elsewhere) have now so reduced production costs that the low-grade **porphyry** mines can be worked profitably. The profitable mining of lean deposits is indeed a tribute to the metal-

NONFERROUS METALS

TABLE 7-1

NONFERROUS METAL OUTPUT IN
UNDERDEVELOPED AREAS,* 1953
(in percentages of total world output)

Copper ore	51
Copper metal	43
Lead ore	41
Lead metal	27
Tin concentrates	96
Tin metal	38
Zinc ore	31
Zinc metal	6

* The underdeveloped areas include the countries of Africa, Asia (excluding Japan and mainland China), and Latin America, and the European nations of Finland and Yugoslavia.

SOURCE: *Non-ferrous Metals in Under-developed Countries* (New York: United Nations, Department of Economic and Social Affairs, 1956), p. 29.

TABLE 7-2

WORLD'S EXPANDING USE OF
NONFERROUS METALS
(in long tons)

Metal	1907	1957
Copper	709,671	3,412,000
Lead	981,100	2,405,000
Tin	104,549	268,000
Zinc	726,750	2,907,000

SOURCE: "Nonferrous Metallurgy 1908-1958," *Engineering*, 185:626, May 16, 1958.

TABLE 7-3

ESTIMATED PROVED WORLD
COPPER RESERVES, 1960
(millions of short tons)

Chile	46.0
United States	25.0
Northern Rhodesia	24.5
Congo (Katanga)	20.0
Peru	12.5
Canada	7.0
Yugoslavia	1.2
South Africa	1.1
Philippines	1.0
Australia	1.0
Communist countries	16.0

SOURCE: U.S. Bureau of Mines.

lurgists' skill and to the builders and inventors of earth-moving equipment.

WORLD DISTRIBUTION AND RESERVES

The estimated reserves of the world are shown for the leading nations in Table 7-3. Copper occurs as pure or **native copper** (but only in unimportant quantities); in the form of oxides, sulfides, carbonates, or silicates; and in chemical combination with other elements —that is, as porphyry deposits, deposits that are so large and so shaped that they can be mined to advantage by large-scale, low-cost methods.

Despite widespread occurrence of copper ore (Fig. 7-1), the bulk of it (90 per cent) is to be found in five areas in twenty-five mining districts: (1) western North America (Arizona, New Mexico, Montana, Nevada, Utah, and Sonora); (2) the Canadian Shield–Lake Superior Region; (3) the Andean districts of Peru and Chile; (4) Central Africa (Katanga and Northern Rhodesia); and (5) the Soviet Union, particularly Kazakhstan and the Urals.

WORLD PRODUCTION

Eighty per cent of the world's copper is mined in the countries listed above, but to produce the remaining 20 per cent requires the combined outputs of 25 other nations.

UNITED STATES

The United States leads the world in copper output, furnishing 30 to 35 per cent of the world's total in recent years. Production is stimulated by large reserves of low-grade ore; a high degree of inventiveness of the people; the presence of several large corporations with great technological skill and notable capital resources; a large home market for copper; and, until recently, little competition from abroad. The foremost mining states are Arizona, Utah, Montana, New Mexico, and Nevada, with Arizona as the leader. Reserves are shown in Table 7-3.

The country's first important source of copper was the Keeweenaw Peninsula of Mich-

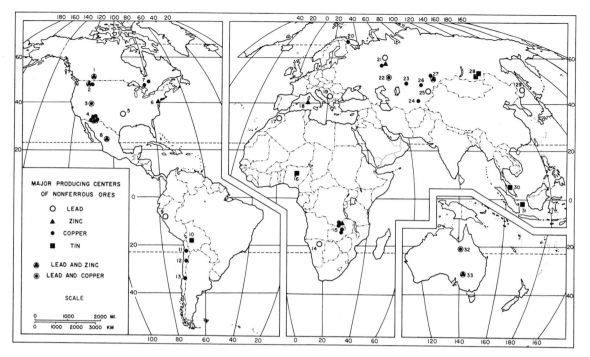

1. Kootenay	13. El Teniente	24. Almalyk
2. Coeur d'Alene, Butte	14. Tsumeb	25. Tekeli
3. Bingham	15. Katanga-Rhodesia	26. Kounradskiy
4. Arizona	16. Jos Plateau	27. Leninogorsk
5. Southeastern Missouri	17. Aouli	28. Khapcheranga-Olouyan-
6. Franklin Furnace	18. Sardinia	naya
7. Sudbury, Noranda-Rouyn	19. Zletovo	29. Tetyukhe
8. Chihuahua	20. Monchegorsk	30. Malaya
9. Cerro de Pasco	21. Central Urals	31. Bangka-Billiton
10. Potosi-Oruro	22. Mednogorsk	32. Mount Isa
11. Chuquicamata	23. Dzhezkazgan	33. Broken Hill
12. El Salvador		

Fig. 7-1. World distribution of nonferrous metals. Note particularly the richness of North America (except for tin), of South America, of Africa south of the equator, and of the Soviet Union. Europe by contrast is poor in these minerals.

igan, which began production soon after 1845. Its second important commercial producer was the Butte, Montana, area, which is reputed to have mined more copper than any other district in the world. From Berkeley Pit at the eastern end of the famous Butte Hill, open-pit methods are now turning out large tonnages of very low-grade ore, which for economic reasons could not be mined by conventional underground methods. This ore occurs beneath 250 feet of waste overburden, 2 tons of which must be removed for each ton of ore removed. *And more than 150 tons of ore must be hauled and processed before*

1 ton of copper can be produced.

The large hill at Butte is honeycombed with mine tunnels that have produced more than 2 billion dollars worth of copper and more than 3 billion dollars worth of zinc, manganese, lead, silver, gold, and copper (Fig. 7-2). Butte has been called the richest hill on earth. Today, however, as with all mining camps, there is concern for Butte's future because the higher-grade ore is nearing exhaustion. But with the recent discovery of 123 million tons of low-grade ore, Butte is assured a prominent place for many years on the world copper map.

THE WORLD'S NONFERROUS METALS :: 115

Fig. 7-2. Hill at Butte, Montana, honeycombed with mine tunnels. Butte ranks among the greatest copper centers of all time. (Courtesy of Anaconda Company.)

Other great copper-mining centers are Bisbee, Globe, Ajo, Morenci, and San Manuel, Arizona; Ely and Yerington, Nevada; and Bingham, Utah. In the 1950s Bisbee, an early-day mining camp, acquired new life as a result of the opening of a new project—Lavender Pit. Yerington, Nevada, has become the center of impressive copper operations, its craterlike pit going down into a mountain of copper ore nearly 2 miles square. Bingham, one of the world's largest and lowest-cost sources of copper, is probably the most interesting copper camp in the nation (Fig. 7-3). It is also the largest open-pit copper mine in North America. Located about 30 miles southwest of Salt Lake City, the mine consists of a pit that resembles a vast amphitheater carved out of a mountainside through the removal of more than 1½ billion tons of ore and waste rock; there are twenty-two levels on one side and fifteen on the opposite side. Because the ore is low in quality, containing only 0.82 per cent copper, large-scale mass-production mining methods had to be employed to operate on an economic basis. Over the years, however, as the pit annually went deeper, the cost of hauling ore out of the bottom and over the rim by railroad in-

creased sharply. Hence a tunnel more than 3 miles long was recently constructed from the bottom level of the pit to the outside rail line and marshaling yards at nearby Copperton.

CANADA

Canada now ranks in fourth place in reserves, if the Congo–Northern Rhodesia belt is regarded as one region (Table 7-3). Production takes place in four districts: (1) Sudbury, (2) Flin Flon, (3) Noranda-Rouyn, and (4) Britannia Beach (Fig. 7-1). Sudbury production is interesting because the copper is based on nickel-copper ores. This deposit, believed to contain about three fourths of Canada's known reserves of copper, accounts for more than half the output. The Noranda-Rouyn district of Quebec (near the Ontario border) ranks second, contributing roughly 20 per cent of production; the copper here is largely associated with gold mining. The Flin Flon district, which lies astride the Manitoba-Saskatchewan border, ranks third in output. The Britannia Beach deposits, near the head of Howe Sound, north of Vancouver, have not as yet become impressive producers.

Although most of the Canadian deposits are comparatively small, they are rich. Hence,

Fig. 7-3. Kennecott mine, Bingham, Utah. This mine is one of the world's largest, most interesting, and most profitable. Here a huge mountain of ore is being systematically torn down by blasting and with electric shovels. Note the many levels, each completely tracked and completely electrified. So immense are the mining operations that the trains look like toys. (Courtesy of Salt Lake Chamber of Commerce.)

they may be worked profitably even on a small scale. In 1954, a notable new strike—a copper-lead-zinc deposit in the Little River Lake area in northeastern New Brunswick, about 35 miles northwest of Newcastle—was announced. Scarcely a month passes without discovery somewhere in Canada of a new deposit or of plans for increased output from an existing mine.

SOUTH AMERICA

South America ranks as one of the world's leaders in copper, both in production and reserves. The copper belt extends along the west slope of the Andes in a series of major deposits from northern Peru to middle Chile.

Chile. Chile led the world in copper production until 1881; today it ranks second. If the Congo–Northern Rhodesia belt is regarded as one, then Chile ranks third. It still presumably possesses the world's largest reserves, about one third of the total (Table 7-3). Compared with the deposits in the United States and many other areas, Chile's ores are regarded as high grade.

Unfortunately, Chile does not have a well-diversified economy but is a victim of monoculture. Copper is Chile's lifeblood; more than 50 per cent of its foreign-exchange earnings are derived from this yellow metal. There can be little doubt that Chile will have serious economic ups and downs as long as her economic well-being is so intimately tied to cop-

per. The price, of course, is determined not by Chile but on the international market. Hence, every cent that copper rises or falls makes a difference of millions of dollars to Chile. Because of this great dependence on copper, the government has passed laws that irk foreign exploiters. For instance, the foreign producing companies (who furnish most of the capital for development of minerals) must pay a tax that is currently about 80 per cent—the highest such tax in the world. This kind of taxation obviously discourages investment and hampers expansion and new development.

Almost ninety per cent of the national output is from four large mines on the western flank of the Andes—Chuquicamata, El Teniente, El Salvador, and La Africana. Modern technology permits relatively inexpensive extraction, concentration, and smelting.

Chuquicamata is the world's largest-known copper deposit (estimated to have 1 billion tons). However, since neither the depth nor the horizontal extension of the ore body has been determined, the estimate is undoubtedly conservative. The ore assays about 2 per cent copper. The deposit lies close to the surface and is mined economically by the open-pit method. Moreover, the mine lies only 163 miles by rail from the port of Antofagasta. Until recently the ores mined were surface oxides; however—since the surface oxides are approaching exhaustion—copper sulfides, which lie underneath the oxidation zone, are

THE WORLD'S NONFERROUS METALS :: 117

now being worked. About 100,000 tons of ore are mined daily from which about 700 tons of copper are extracted.

El Teniente, situated high up in the Andes, slightly south of Santiago but only 30 miles from the Central Valley, is one of Chile's outstanding copper mines and the world's largest underground mine. It produces sulfides under extremely trying physical conditions; since workings, dwellings, transportation, smelter—in fact, everything connected with copper here is situated in a narrow canyon, the whole operation has necessarily had to conform strictly to exigencies of the site. The ore averages about 2.1 per cent copper, and the mine has yielded 10 billion pounds of copper.

El Salvador is the largest copper development to be inaugurated since World War II. It lies at an elevation of almost 8,000 feet on the west slope of the Andes some 18 miles north of the once famous Potrerillos mine, which in thirty-two years produced almost 2 million tons but is now exhausted. El Salvador's proved reserves are placed at 375 million tons of ore averaging 1.5 per cent copper. This project is one of the world's lowest-cost copper producers.

La Africana, a recent development on the west side of the Andes, lies about 11 miles from Santiago. The ore body, estimated at 2.5 million tons of sulfide ore, averages about 3.6 per cent copper. All the mining is carried on underground.

In addition to these large mines, there are many medium mining ventures and many small workings.

Peru. Peru has produced copper for four hundred years. Reserves are large (Table 7-3). For decades the name Cerro de Pasco was synonymous with copper. However, man's heavy drain on the ores year after year has finally taken its toll, and Cerro de Pasco is no longer outstanding. This venture should be remembered, however, as a remarkable development that flourished in a remote locale superimposed upon an almost feudal agricultural system, where it had to recruit and train a labor force from a population of Indians that was still living in the sixteenth century.

A recent Peruvian development is that at Toquepala in the southern Peruvian Andes, 114 miles inland from the port of Ilo. Here four American companies, operating jointly as the Southern Peru Copper Corporation, are developing one of the largest copper-mining operations in the world—a 230-million-dollar project. The ore body, lying at an elevation of 9,500 feet in the western Andes, has an estimated reserve of 400 million tons. With two similar ore bodies close by, it is expected that the three will ultimately yield about a billion tons of ore, averaging about 1 per cent copper. Before mining could actually begin, 130 million tons of overburden had to be stripped off. About 30,000 tons of ore are mined daily from open-pit operations.

AFRICA

Africa, with enormous reserves (Table 7-3), ranks second only to North America in world copper production. A copper belt 280 miles long and 50 miles wide, extending from Katanga in the Congo well into Northern Rhodesia, produces some 899,790 short tons of ore per year (1959).

The Katanga oxide ores average 6.5 per cent copper, and some attain a richness approaching 25 per cent. Northern Rhodesia's sulfide ores average about 3.5 per cent and are easier to smelt. Most of the Katanga ore is minable from open pits, whereas that from Northern Rhodesia is minable only deep underground. However, considering the entire African picture, underground mining predominates.

Principal obstacles to successful mining have long been the difficult transportation and the lack of coal for fuel. There are only two railways—one to Beira on the east coast of Mozambique, 1,600 miles from Katanga and 1,175 miles from Northern Rhodesia; and one to Benguela in Angola, on the west coast, 1,300 miles distant. The bulk of the production from Katanga moves to Benguela, and that from Northern Rhodesia moves to Beira. A newer rail project to the port of Lourenço Marques appears to be best for handling Rhodesia's copper.

Over many years, because of the shortage of

coal, hundreds of workers were needed to cut wood for the workings and smelters. In recent years, however, there has been much activity in the development of water power. The great hydroelectric-power development at Kariba on the Zambezi River, recently completed, should result in a 40 per cent expansion in the area's copper production.

SOVIET UNION

The Soviet Union has forged into fourth place among the world's copper producers. Ores are widespread throughout the great Russian realm; but the largest reserves and most productive mines are to be found in Kazakhstan, along the southeastern flank of the Urals, at the base of the Kola Peninsula, and in the Caucasus (Fig. 7-1). Most of the copper is mined from low-grade deposits in the Lake Balkhash area of central Kazakhstan, which is believed to possess 75 per cent of the known reserves. The Russian ore deposits are much like those in western United States. Official Soviet estimates of copper reserves give the nation one sixth of the world's known reserves (Table 7-3). The Russians claim to be first in the world in explored reserves. According to some reports, as many as six thousand field parties (some with as many as a thousand men), employing the most modern methods and tools, are seeking minerals wherever prospects justify. The principal weakness in the Soviet copper situation is that most of the ore lies far from present centers of population and manufacturing, and transport facilities between the two are woefully inadequate.

LEAD

Lead has been used by man since ancient times. In fact, its first use antedates recorded history. Lead receives frequent mention in the Bible; and it was used both by the Greeks and the Romans. Lead pipes were used in Rome, Pompeii, and elsewhere; and remains are still to be seen by travelers today in Italian museums. Since World War II, consumption of lead has reached unprecedented heights and shows no signs of leveling off.

PROPERTIES AND USES

Lead is soft and heavy. It is resistant to corrosion and to the action of most acids, and it is easily alloyed with other metals. It is, moreover, a poor conductor of electricity. These qualities, plus low cost, assure lead a heavy and consistent demand. The principal uses for lead have been in the manufacture of storage batteries, cable coverings, and white lead. It is also useful in the manufacture of ammunition, foil-bearing metal, and solder. In the United States, the largest user is the oil-refining industry. However, lead is finding new applications in some of the most modern industries—atomics, electronics, and thermoelectrics. The properties of lead are so unique and so useful to modern technology that research and market development promise to open up many new uses for it.

WORLD DISTRIBUTION AND RESERVES

Prior to World War II, lead was so widely distributed among the industrial nations or in their dependencies that there was not the mad scramble to acquire reserves that characterized so many other minerals. Today, however, few important industrial metals are in shorter supply than lead.

The principal world sources are shown in Figure 7-1. Most of the world's lead exists in combination with zinc or, sometimes, with copper, gold, antimony, molybdenum, or vanadium. Thus, lead mining relies not on lead deposits alone but upon those of kindred metals with which it exists. Few mines today produce only lead.

World reserves are estimated at 40 million tons—enough for about 20 years at the 1955 rate of consumption. These figures refer only to deposits capable of being mined, smelted, and delivered to market under present conditions.

WORLD PRODUCTION

The total world production of lead in 1960 was 2.56 million short tons. Australia had the largest output, followed by the Soviet Union, the United States, Mexico, and Canada. The majority of lead-producing countries are in

North America (Fig. 7-1). Though nearly all the industrialized countries comprising Western Europe produce some lead, the region as a whole is a deficit area. It is interesting to note that the world's consistently expanding requirements of lead are being met less and less by formerly major sources of supply and more and more by newly developed sources. Much of the demand, too, is being met from scrap.

UNITED STATES

The United States for decades led the world in production of lead. However, in 1957 the United States accounted for only 13 per cent of the world lead-ore output and for the first time since 1891 lost first rank. Steadily the high-grade ores containing lead have been depleted, so that the United States is now a high-cost producer. Accordingly, marginal or high-cost mines are forced to close whenever the government withdraws support; for they cannot compete with foreign lead, which is produced at much lower cost. Some operators, however, continue to mine lead because it would be more costly to shut down the mines unless all hope for a market upturn within a reasonable time were to be abandoned. The domestic lead industry, attributing most of its ills to imports, makes frequent appeals for tariff protection against the lower-cost imports. The government, however, cannot safely or politically isolate itself from the world market and from the world supply of a commodity for which 50 per cent of domestic requirements (and probably more in the future) must be supplied by foreign sources.

Most domestic lead is mined in Missouri and the northern Rockies. Southeastern Missouri, which has been producing since 1725, is currently the largest lead-mining area in the world (Fig. 7-1). The rather low metallic content of the ore in this area, however, necessitates large-scale operations. The largest single mine—at Flat River, Missouri, about 67 miles south of St. Louis—is operating at great depths.

The Coeur d'Alene district in Idaho is the largest producer in the West and second largest in the nation, yielding approximately one fourth or one fifth of the national output. This area gained stature in lead mining after the development and introduction of the selective-flotation process, which made possible the extraction of metals through their varying affinities to oils and chemicals. The Coeur d'Alene district is less strategically located than is the Missouri area with respect to the nation's principal markets for lead. Coeur d'Alene ores are associated with silver and zinc.

Utah contributes about 15 per cent of the national lead output. Lead-zinc mines are located in a number of centers, but much of the output is a by-product of the copper enterprise at Bingham.

More and more the United States is depending upon lead scrap. Since 1945, lead recovered annually from scrap has outstripped mine output by an average of 13 per cent.

CANADA

Canada ranks high among world producers of lead; reserves are believed to be adequate to yield up to 180,000 tons per year for at least twenty-five years. The nation contributes approximately 10 per cent of the world's annual output of lead. The Sullivan mine at Kimberley, British Columbia (Fig. 7-4), is Canada's largest producer. Located about 85 miles north of the boundary with Idaho, it lies in a huge ore body geologically similar to that at Coeur d'Alene. British Columbia alone accounts for approximately 95 per cent of the Canadian output.

MEXICO

Mexico has a long history as a lead producer. Most of the mines are in the states of Chihuahua, Zacatecas, and San Luis Potosí. At times Mexico attains second place in world output and is regularly the largest producer in Latin America. The ore is associated with both silver and zinc. Much of the output is from numerous small deposits, which are incessantly going into and out of production. In total they appear capable of maintaining past average production rates indefinitely. Most of the mines have been financed, at least in part, by United States capital.

Fig. 7-4. Blasthole diamond drilling at the lead-zinc mine at Kimberley, British Columbia. In this type of operation, more than a half-million tons of ore have been shattered in a single blast. The Sullivan lead-zinc mine, one of the world's largest, produces 2.5 million tons of ore annually. (Courtesy of Consolidated Mining and Smelting Company of Canada.)

AUSTRALIA

Australia has increased her output of lead so drastically that she now leads the world in annual output. The ore averages 11 to 17 per cent lead at Broken Hill and 7.5 to 9 per cent at Mount Isa. Broken Hill has long been famous as one of the world's greatest mining camps; nothing comparable to its ore body has ever been known heretofore in the history of lead. The outlook for Broken Hill "lode" (vein) is extremely hopeful in view of the high price of lead and the small deposits in the world.

Mount Isa, though its story begins in 1923, has become famous only in recent years. The temperature (which may reach or exceed 100°F for three months of the year), the aridity, and the vast distances from civilization all retarded development. Only when the state of Queensland constructed a 600-mile railroad at the seaport of Townsville did this mine attain real prominence. It is currently a highly mechanized, efficient, and profitable operation. The deposits of copper at Mount Isa lie adjacent to deposits of lead, zinc, and silver.

SOVIET UNION

The Soviet Union possesses large reserves of lead, and much ore is being mined. At present possibly three fourths of the lead production comes from the western Altai Mountains in northwestern Kazakhstan, Krasnoural'sk in the Urals, and the southern part of Western Siberia (Fig. 7-1). Another important district is the Kara-Tau mountain range, also in Kazakhstan. In 1960 the Soviet Union ranked second among world lead producers—trailing only Australia.

ZINC

In the discussion of lead, it was pointed out that the two metals lead and zinc (sometimes referred to as "twins") are in most areas found in combination. The same corporations usually are engaged in handling both metals—mining, milling, and concentrating, often even in smelting and refining. The important new zinc-lead deposits being developed are mainly producers of zinc and will not greatly change the lead picture. Zinc ores occur alone more frequently than do lead ores, and the deposits are usually larger and richer. Where the two metals occur together, the zinc content is usually in the higher ratio—two to one.

PROPERTIES AND USES

Zinc was used by the ancients with copper to make brass. It is still employed for this purpose, but its greatest use today is as a galvanizing material for protecting steel against atmospheric corrosion. The durability of galvanized steel depends upon the thickness of the zinc coating that adheres to the metal. Galvanized products consist of roofs, tanks, culverts, fence posts, wire, pipe, pans, and pails. About 40 per cent of all zinc used in the United States goes into galvanizing iron and steel. Other uses are in castings, battery cans, photoengraving sheets, the automotive industry, paints, and pharmaceuticals. Substitutes are available for almost every use of zinc, except as an alloy with copper for making brass. The automotive industry uses about 30 per cent of all the zinc consumed in the United States in base alloys for die-cast parts, for assemblies for pumps, and for carburetors.

WORLD DISTRIBUTION AND RESERVES

The world's leading zinc reserves closely duplicate those of lead (Fig. 7-1). The primary ores of zinc are frequently found in association with copper, gold, iron, lead, and silver.

Zinc is a relatively common metal. It is found on all continents and in many countries; but, as with many metallic minerals, only a relatively small number of countries —the United States, Canada, Mexico, Australia, the Soviet Union, and Poland—produce on a large scale. Lesser producers are Peru, Italy, Germany, the Congo, Spain, and Japan. *These same countries possess most of the known reserves,* which are put at about 70 million tons of recoverable ore. About 20 million tons of this reserve are in the United States.

WORLD PRODUCTION

Annual world output was 3.5 million tons in 1960, with the United States and Canada the leading producers.

UNITED STATES

For many years the United States led the world in output of zinc. In 1920, it accounted for 62 per cent of the world total; however, its mine output has been declining, so that in 1957 it contributed only 16 per cent of the world output. For many years the Tri-state district (Missouri, Kansas, and Oklahoma) ranked as the dominant producing area; but as the higher-grade ores became depleted, production declined. Thus, all producing mines in this once famous district were closed in 1958 and 1959. In recent years, Tennessee has been the leading zinc-mining state and currently stands second in output, followed by Idaho and New York. Arizona and Colorado also are important.

CANADA

Canada ranks second among world producers of zinc, with about 14 per cent of world output. The principal output is from the Sullivan and the Reeves-MacDonald mines at Kimberley in British Columbia, though there is considerable production at Flin Flon, at Buchans in Newfoundland, and in Quebec. Recently discovered but as yet scarcely touched zinc deposits are in the Yukon and Northwest Territories.

MEXICO

Mexico today ranks fourth in world output but first among the Latin American countries. Most of the deposits and the mines are lead-zinc. Principal mines are near Parral and the city of Chihuahua in the state of Chihuahua, near Fresnillo in the state of Zacatecas, and near Charcas in the state of San Luis Potosí.

EUROPE

Though European countries are minor producers, their output is nevertheless important because the deposits are close to a major market for zinc. Principal producers are West

Germany, Poland, Italy, Spain, and Yugoslavia, with the leading center in Upper Silesia (southwestern Poland).

AUSTRALIA

For decades Australia has been famous for its zinc production. In 1960 it ranked fourth in world output. It has the largest zinc reserves in the world—some 14 million tons. The leading mining centers are Broken Hill in New South Wales, Mount Isa in Queensland, and Rosebery in western Tasmania. All mining is underground. It is believed that the deposits at Broken Hill are capable of producing zinc at the present rate for a full century.

SOVIET UNION

Almost every statement made about lead in the Soviet Union holds for zinc. The two metals occur together in the same deposits; hence, the list of zinc mines is identical with that of lead mines. Russia in 1960 ranked third in world production, trailing the United States and Canada but standing first among European producers.

TIN

Tin, along with copper, was used by prehistoric man to make bronze. Unlike the other nonferrous metals, however, tin in commercial quantities is found in relatively few places. It is the rarest of the nonferrous metals presented in this chapter, for it makes up only 0.001 per cent of the earth's crust.

PROPERTIES AND USES

Tin is soft and malleable. It can be rolled into extremely thin sheets—to 2/10,000 inch in thickness. It is airtight and resists corrosion, and it makes excellent solder. Without tin, most electrical and electronic equipment would be useless tangles of disconnected wires. Tin is also valuable for bearing metal, and it is growing in importance in new alloys and chemical compounds essential to the automotive, aviation, and electrical industries.

Principal use for tin is as a coating for steel (tin plate), most of which is converted into "tin cans," which are 99 per cent steel and only 1 per cent tin. The United States utilizes about 42 per cent of the world tin consumption for tin plate, 60 per cent of which is used for making cans—mostly for food. The tin can as a food container is a response to industrialization and urbanization: city dwellers to a large extent "eat out of tin cans." The United States alone uses more than 22 billion cans a year. Tin's advantage for food containers is that it is nontoxic when in contact with food and hence prevents spoilage.

WORLD PRODUCTION

About three fourths of the world's tin is recovered from alluvial deposits of cassiterite (75 per cent tin). The remaining one fourth is won by hard-rock mining—by working lode deposits found in older rock.

The United States, long world-renowned for the wide variety of its minerals, lacks tin ore (although there is a small amount in Alaska). The International Tin Council—made up of the Congo, Bolivia, Indonesia, Malaysia, Nigeria, and Thailand (which accounts for 90 per cent of world production)—attempts to prop the price of tin on the London market. Study of the world tin map (Fig. 7-1) shows that production is confined to underdeveloped countries. Hence, the tin they produce is largely for export.

The leading tin-producing region of the world is Southeast Asia, which includes the southern part of the Malay Peninsula, the Indonesian islands of Bangka, Billiton, and Singkep, and parts of Thailand and China (Yunnan). Only four commercial tin areas lie outside Southeast Asia—Nigeria, the Congo, Bolivia, and the Soviet Union.

SOUTHEAST ASIA

Southeast Asia stands almost alone as a world source of tin, contributing 85 to 90 per cent of the annual world output. The Federation of Malaysia, with approximately 417 active mines in 1959 (the number fluctuates rather widely from year to year), leads all

Fig. 7-5. Chinese-owned hydraulic tin mine in Malaysia. Powerful jets of water cut and disintegrate the ground of the mine. A mixture of sand and clay, ore, and water collects at the bottom of the mine, whence it is all pumped to the head of a "flume." There the heavy tin is deposited, while the lighter sand and clay are carried away with the stream of water. (Courtesy of British Information Services.)

countries in production. The annual output of 52,000 long tons (1960) is significant, considering that Malaysian mines were virtually wrecked during World War II and that for several years afterward Communist guerrillas plagued the country, killing workers, cutting power lines, and destroying dredges.

Mining is of the placer type (the working of gravels), though there are some underground mines. Since tin is heavier than gravel, it is deposited in the deeper layers of alluvial deposits. Thus, an overabundance of sand and gravel must be removed before mining can begin. Two methods of winning tin are employed—dredging and hydraulic (Fig. 7-5). The former, used in 60 per cent of the mines, requires high capitalization and is chiefly in European hands; the latter, used in 40 per cent of the mines, requires far less capital and is chiefly in Chinese hands. In both cases, however, the labor supply is mainly Chinese. The most easily worked deposits are approaching exhaustion.

Indonesia has usually ranked second to Malaysia in world tin production but fell to third place in 1960. When the Dutch were still permitted to mine tin in Indonesia, they were the world's most efficient producers. Repeatedly they were the only members of the International Tin Council to fulfill their allotted share.

CHINA

Though tin is regarded as China's most important metal after iron ore, the country does not rank particularly high in reserves. The principal deposits are in Yunnan, though Kwangsi, Kiangsi, Kweichow, and Hunan in southwestern China also have deposits. Yunnan's reserves are placed at 1 million tons. Chief producing area is Kiochiu in southern Yunnan; output, however, is often handicapped by a limited water supply. China is important in the international tin picture because, being a Communist country, it trades primarily with other Communist nations. In 1960 China ranked second only to the Federation of Malaya in output. A considerable tonnage is exported annually to Russia, which re-exports some of it. In 1957, so much was re-exported that the Soviet Union was accused of **dumping**. The price fell, and a number of high-cost tin-producing countries (e.g., Bolivia) suffered severely.

AFRICA

The Congo and Nigeria are small producers of tin, contributing annually only about 10 to 15 per cent of the world output. Although the Congo is Africa's largest producer, Nigeria gained prominence in World War II, when the Malayan and Dutch East Indian deposits were taken over by the Japanese. The reserves, never large, are already beginning to run low. The most important mining area is that surrounding the city of Jos.

BOLIVIA

Among all the nations in the Western Hemisphere, only Bolivia produces tin commercially. In 1960 the country ranked fourth in world output. Bolivian deposits are widely distributed; though there were sixteen mines operating in 1959, the only three of importance were Catavi (largest), Colquiri, and Huanuuni.

Tin means everything to Bolivia. The economic life of few nations on earth is so inextricably enmeshed with a single product as is that of Bolivia with tin. Tin accounts for 71 to 78 per cent of the country's total exports based on value, and it contributes to the Bolivian treasury about 70 per cent of its total intake. Yet no region on earth prosecutes mining under greater physical handicaps. Most of the mines and their camps lie in the Cordillera Real at elevations of 11,000 to 16,000 feet. Often they lie high up on the sides of steep valley walls that are difficult to reach. The thin air all but excludes whites from performing hard physical labor; and although the Indians can live and work at these high altitudes, they are ill fed, ill clothed, and ill housed. Since they are frequently ill (there is much silicosis—the dust disease), they cannot be very efficient workers. A United Nations mission has reported, following a careful field survey, that work conditions are deplorable. There is little or almost no fuel. Hence, there is considerable hand preselection of ore (Fig. 7-6). The ore is not smelted in Bolivia, but concentrates (30 to 40 per cent tin) are exported to Europe, largely to Great Britain.

Not only are the Bolivian mines badly located but the ore is low-grade tin (0.9 to 2 per cent). It occurs in lodes that are often narrow—sometimes only an inch or so wide. The big job is to locate ore bodies of sufficient size and with ore of sufficiently high metallic content to permit profitable operation. Bolivian ores are complex and costly to mine, concentrate, and deliver to Chilean and Peruvian ports.

Bolivia is a marginal producer and positively cannot compete with the countries in Southeast Asia in an uncontrolled tin market. In 1952 the Bolivian government nationalized the entire mining industry, assuming control of the three big tin-mining properties. However, four years later the president openly admitted that nationalization had not been economically successful.

SOVIET UNION

Only in the past several years has the Soviet Union played a conspicuous role in world tin

Fig. 7-6. Hand preselection of tin ore at Potosí, Bolivia. Indian women remove as much earthy matter as possible. (Courtesy of M. Hochchild.)

production. The government recently announced officially that its tin output now exceeds that of the Federation of Malaysia. Yet in 1960, according to the United States Bureau of Mines, the Soviet Union ranked fifth in total world output.

Russian tin deposits lie in four widely separated areas: (1) in the Onon River Valley east of Lake Baikal, (2) near Verkhoyansk in northeastern Siberia, (3) near Tetyukhe on the Sea of Japan, about 200 miles north of Vladivostok, and (4) in the Peikhankai Depression in the Far East.

CONCENTRATION, SMELTING, AND REFINING

Nearly all of the nonferrous metals mined today are found in such complex form that the ores must be concentrated, smelted, and refined before they can be used for making secondary products (Fig. 7-7). We have noted that a large part of the nonferrous metals is mined in underdeveloped countries (Table 7-1). Much of the smelting and refining, as well as virtually all of the consumption, however, takes place in developed countries. Some of these countries, like Belgium, France, West Germany, and Japan (which rank very high

in the smelting of lead, for example), mine very little, whereas the United States ranks high both in mining and in smelting and refining.

However, an increasing amount of smelting is taking place in the underdeveloped producing lands for the following reasons: (1) They need badly to diversify their economies. (2) They want to increase their ability to earn foreign exchange. (3) They are developing hydropower, thereby having available a plentiful and reasonably low-cost supply of electrical energy. This is particularly true of Central Africa; the Union Minière, largest mining group in the Congo, operates four hydroelectric stations with a normal output of 2.5 billion kilowatt hours a year; and the Federation of Rhodesia and Nyasaland has recently gained access to the vast supply of energy at Kariba on the Zambezi River. (4) Occasionally—as in the Broken Hill area in Northern Rhodesia, where a lead smelter was erected—the rail haul is so great as to make economically impossible the outshipment of all but pure or almost pure metal. (5) Many nations engrossed in their revolution of rising expectations believe that industrialization more than anything else will enable them to achieve the better life.

Hence, those countries possessing deposits of nonferrous metals are insisting that a larger

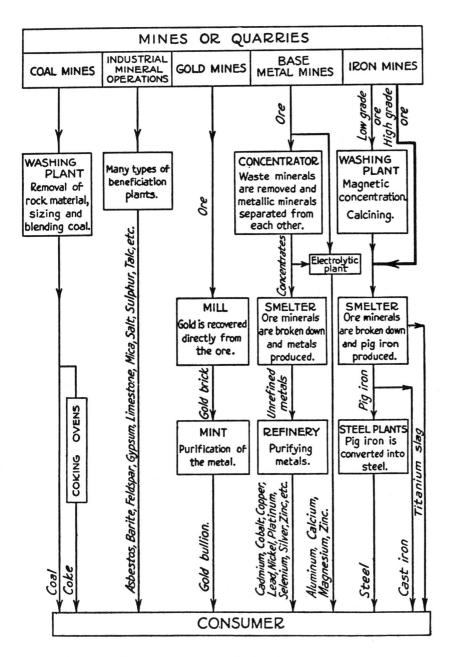

Fig. 7-7. What happens to a mineral after it leaves the mine or quarry and before it reaches the consumer. Reproduced (with modification) by permission from G. B. Langford, Out of the Earth (Toronto: University of Toronto Press, 1954), p. 90.

percentage be smelted and/or refined in their lands. And the United Nations has expressed the opinion that the mineral economies of these lands will gain if they process, at least partially, the ores they produce.

PROCESSING-MILL LOCATIONS

The selection of a processing-mill location is a splendid example of the application of economic-geographic principles. It also calls for keen engineering and technological skills and for appreciable expenditures of capital.

CONCENTRATION MILLS

Ores that contain only a small percentage of metal cannot be moved far from the mines because of the high cost of transporting so much waste material. Concentration consists of eliminating earthy material (gangue) preparatory to further treatment. As a result of improvement in processing techniques, the refuse of mining in the past—the old **tailing piles** and **slag dumps**—more and more become ore piles today. Thus, concentration mills are invariably placed near the mines they serve in order to lower transport costs on the product destined for the smelter (Fig. 7-8).

SMELTERS

The concentrates move to smelters, which remove impurities beyond the ability of the concentration mills. For copper, the concentrate is converted to a **matte**, which in turn is transformed into **blister copper**, which is 99 per cent pure.

When low-grade ores (3 per cent or less) are being treated, the smelter generally is so located as to draw ore and concentrates from several sources, since it must operate around the clock; a smelter can function profitably only on a large scale. The great smelter at El Paso, Texas, well exemplifies this principle. It derives its ores and concentrates not only from Arizona and New Mexico but also from Mexico and countries in Africa and South America. If high-grade ore is being mined, the ore may bypass the concentration mill and move directly to the smelter. In the United States most smelters are in the West

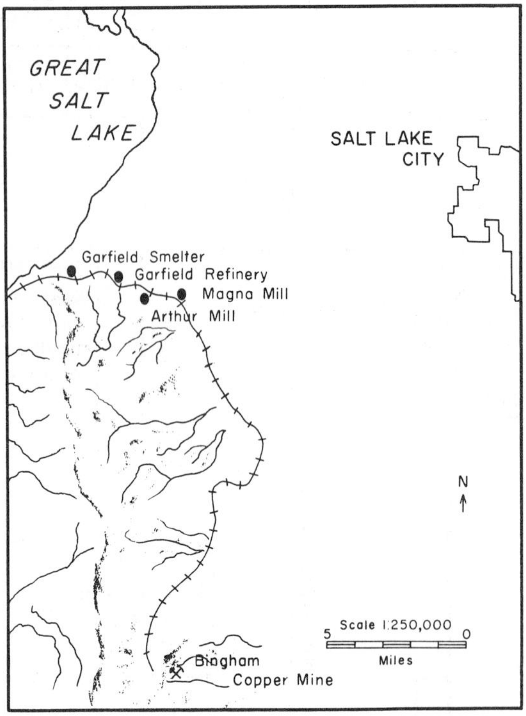

Fig. 7-8. Great copper complex—Salt Lake Valley, Utah. Note the railway (downhill) from Bingham to the concentration mills at Arthur and Magna and on to the smelter and refinery at Garfield. Here is to be observed one of the world's finest examples of the economic geography of plant location. (Drawn by John Arrillaga.)

and are so situated as to handle the output of nearby mines (Figs. 7-9 and 7-10). Though the United Kingdom mines very little tin today, it nevertheless ranks second among all nations in the smelting of tin, reducing most of the concentrates of Bolivia and Nigeria.

Sulfur has always been a by-product of copper smelting—the sulfur being discharged into the air as sulfur dioxide gas, which was harmful to natural vegetation and crops. As a result of the invention of the **Cottrell**, and its installation in most modern copper smelters, sulfur fumes are no longer a major threat to agriculture.

The distribution of world copper and zinc smelters (exclusive of those in North America) is shown in Figure 7-11; distribution of world lead and tin smelters is shown in Fig-

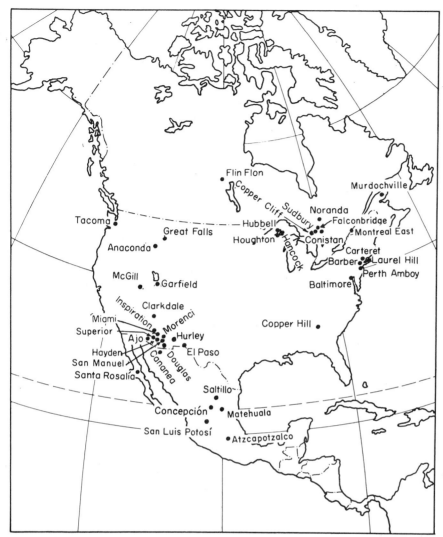

Fig. 7-9. Copper smelters in North America. In the United States the majority of the smelters are in the West; this is logical in view of the region's contribution of 92 per cent of the nation's total copper.

ure 7-12. For all the nonferrous metals, low-grade ores are concentrated as near the mines as possible, high-grade concentrates can stand a reasonably long haul to a smelter, and smelted metals are virtually footloose—they can travel almost any distance to a refinery.

REFINERIES

Refining is carried on for two reasons: (1) to purify the metal and (2) to remove the

silver, gold, antimony, lead, zinc, and other impurities that have very high value and can easily justify the cost of extraction.

Unlike concentration mills and smelters, which tend to be located close to their raw materials, electrolytic refineries generally are located on tidewater; in the United States, they are located mostly on the Atlantic Coast between New York City and Baltimore, but mainly in New Jersey. Smelted materials from

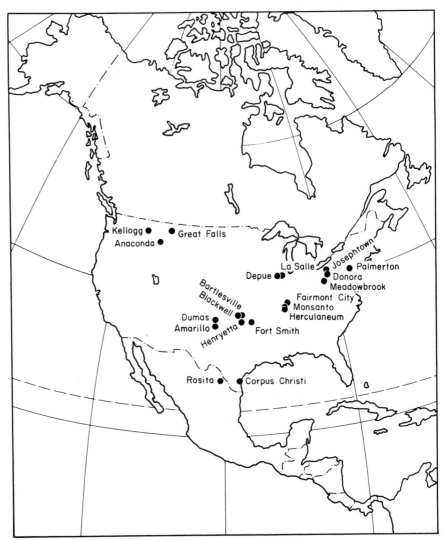

Fig. 7-10. Zinc smelters and refineries in North America. Note that all are in the United States and Mexico, and that they are widely scattered. Greatest concentration of smelting, however, is in Texas, Oklahoma, and Arkansas, since the West contributes 54 per cent of the nation's total zinc.

the American West and from South America and Africa focus here, and the refined metals move easily and economically by rail or truck to consuming mills in New England (chiefly Connecticut) and New Jersey or by ship to Northwestern Europe. There are a few refineries in the West. At times smelting and refining are carried on in the same location, as at Oroya, Peru (Fig. 7-13).

Refineries are fewer in number and larger in size than smelters because their operations are simpler and result in little additional cost of the finished product.

THE BINGHAM, MAGNA, ARTHUR, GARFIELD (UTAH) COMPLEX

Copper ore (averaging 8 pounds of metallic copper per ton) is sent from the famous mine

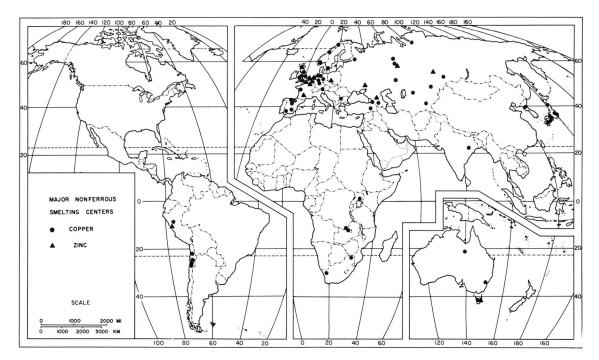

Fig. 7-11. *World copper and zinc smelters. (Those for North America are shown in Figs. 7-9 and 7-10.)*

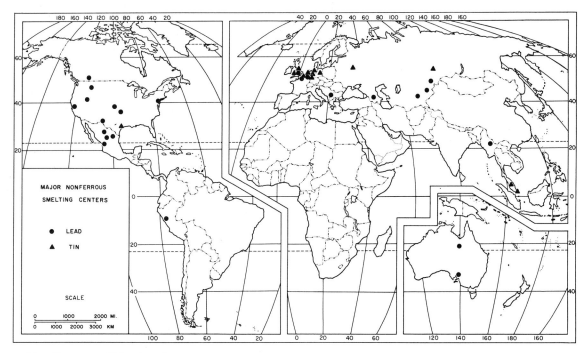

Fig. 7-12. *World lead and tin smelters.*

Fig. 7-13. Smelter and refinery at Oroya, Peru—highest in the world (12,200 feet). Cerro de Pasco mining and metallurgical operations embrace an area of 8,000 square miles in this portion of the Sierra, giving employment to a labor force of about 20,000. Many metals and compounds are produced here. The Andes are a formidable barrier, and level land here is extremely scarce. There is, however, an outstanding railway and highway, and water is supplied by the river. (Courtesy of Runcie-Graphs and of Grace Line.)

at Bingham some 17 miles northward to the concentration mills at Magna and Arthur, situated near the southern shore of the Great Salt Lake (Fig. 7-8). The concentrates move to Garfield, the world's largest copper smelter, for further treatment, and the resulting blister copper then travels to a nearby copper refinery.

This copper complex—mine to concentration mills to smelter to refinery—is one of the best examples of the application of industrial integration in the world. The smelter site was chosen because of its excellent transportation facilities, both railway and highway, its 35,-000 acres of largely alkaline land—almost valueless for agriculture, its adaptability for the economical handling of materials by gravity (the "hillside" type of layout permits reduced power requirements), and the fact that the prevailing winds harmlessly carry the fumes either over the Great Salt Lake or over the Oquirrh Mountains.

WORLD OUTLOOK

It is significant indeed that *consumption* of the four major nonferrous metals is confined

essentially to the industrial countries. In the years following World War II, more than 90 per cent of world consumption of copper, lead, zinc, and tin (not including that from the Communist bloc) has been accounted for by North America, Western Europe, and Eastern Asia (Japan)— more than 50 per cent by the United States alone. It is equally significant that these metals are being produced more and more in the underdeveloped lands. Such countries as the United States, Great Britain, Germany, and Japan have combed the land within their own boundaries and probably have discovered most of the largest and best nonferrous deposits revealed by surface outcrops. From now on, new deposits in these nations will be more difficult to find, lower in quality, and hence costly to process. The underdeveloped mineral-producing countries probably will consume only a small proportion of their output of nonferrous metals. The greater part of the output will continue to be exported.

Since the reserves of high-grade copper, lead, and zinc are being depleted rapidly, developed countries such as the United States will have to make proper provision to secure these resources beyond their own shores. This means, for instance, that United States foreign policy must be aimed at winning and holding the good will of specific underdeveloped countries—i.e., Bolivia, Chile, Peru, India, the Federation of Malaysia, and the Federation of Rhodesia and Nyasaland.

Dependence on foreign sources for nonferrous metals assumes mutual benefit by the resource country and the mining company or companies. Such dependence, however, has two major drawbacks: (1) a powerful enemy might cut supply lines, particularly with submarines; and (2) politically unstable underdeveloped countries may expropriate, confiscate, or so tax foreign companies as to force them out of production.[2] Over the entire underdeveloped world, economic nationalism is sweeping like a tidal wave. This means that the developed Free World countries, involved in the Cold War and fearful of political events in the underdeveloped countries, must maintain at home numerous marginal mines, which from a strictly economic standpoint ought to

close down. Such mines are able to operate only by subsidies or protectionist means.

Technology is helping the developed nations to meet their requirements, at least in part, by making workable many low-grade ores, particularly as prices for these metals rise. From 1910 to 1919 Arizona's copper ores yielded 48 pounds of copper per ton of ore; from 1920 to 1929, the yield had dropped to 35 pounds; from 1930 to 1939, to 32 pounds; from 1940 to 1944, to 21 pounds; and from 1944 to 1955, to 17 pounds. The ability to work such low-grade domestic ores is thus a form of insurance for the developed country —a vital guarantee to national security.

World reserves of the nonferrous metals are far from inexhaustible. In 1958 one world authority estimated that the world's copper reserves would last about 30 years, its lead 19 years, its zinc 23 years, and its tin 35 years.[3] These estimates may err, up or down, but the lesson they convey is incontrovertible: that man positively cannot consume over a considerable period of time great tonnages of these metals without experiencing shortages and increasingly high prices; hence, he must *learn to use these nonferrous metals with greater wisdom.*

---

[2] In the early 1950s, Chilean taxes (including hidden taxes) levied on the foreign-owned copper companies exceeded 80 per cent of net profits, thus constituting the highest tax imposed on the mining industry anywhere in the world. This high taxation led the American copper companies to increase their investments in marginal mines in the United States rather than in their Chilean holdings.

[3] Elmer W. Pehrson, *Man and Raw Materials,* An Edgar Marburg Lecture (Philadelphia, American Society for Testing Materials, 1958), p. 5.

SELECTED REFERENCES

Cotterill, Carl H. *Industrial Plant Location, Its Application to Zinc Smelting.* St. Louis, American Zinc, Lead and Smelting Company, 1951.

Franklin, James W. "Oxidized Copper: Where Do We Get Tomorrow's Copper?" *Engineering and Mining Journal,* Part I, 157:97-103, July 1956; Part II, 157:80-85, August 1956.

Hogan, Edward L. "The Panorama of Tin: Shifting Aspects of a Vital Metal," *Foreign Commerce Weekly,* 39:3-7, 46, June 12, 1950.

Miller, E. Willard. "Mineral Regionalism of the Canadian Shield," *Canadian Geographer,* No. 13, pp. 17-30, 1959.

Shea, William P. "Foreign Ore Reserves of Copper, Lead, and Zinc," *Engineering and Mining Journal,* 148:53-58, January 1947.

The Utah Copper Story (Fiftieth Anniversary). Salt Lake City, Kennecott Copper Corporation, 1954.

Van Nieukerken, J. M. "The Copper Industry," in Albert S. Carlson (ed.), *Economic Geography of Industrial Materials.* New York, Reinhold Publishing Corporation, 1956, pp. 166-197.

Ziegfeld, Robert L., and David M. Borcina. "Lead," in Albert S. Carlson (ed.), *Economic Geography of Industrial Materials.* New York, Reinhold Publishing Corporation, 1956, pp. 254-269.

CHAPTER EIGHT::

Mankind is on the threshold of a "Light-Metals Age." Until the sixteenth century, man worked with only seven metals: gold, silver, copper, tin, iron, lead, and mercury. In the following three centuries he added seven more: antimony, zinc, bismuth, arsenic, nickel, cobalt, and manganese (bismuth is not considered a metal by some mineralogists). In the 1900s, chromium and tungsten were added.

Since 1900, there has been an unprecedented revolution in man's use of light metals—aluminum, magnesium, titanium, and others. This revolution is creating new industries, in which the advanced nations of the world have been investing heavily. Not only have their companies built up complex corporate relationships, but they have gone far afield to ensure adequate supplies of raw materials—principally bauxite—the major sources of which are to be found in the underdeveloped countries.

THE WORLD'S

ALUMINUM

The history of aluminum in the market place is relatively short. Until Charles Martin Hall, in 1886, discovered and developed the electrolytic process of obtaining aluminum from bauxite, this light metal remained a laboratory oddity. Hall's discovery transformed aluminum into one of the world's most versatile and widely used metals. Each year witnesses a huge increase in output, mostly in the advanced industrial nations but to some extent also in the underdeveloped countries (e.g., British and Dutch Guiana and Brazil in South America; Ghana, Guinea, and the Congo in Africa; and Indonesia and China in Asia) that possess both bauxite deposits and hydroelectric power.

Aluminum constitutes approximately one twelfth of the earth's crust; however, it is not found free in nature but is always combined chemically with other elements. Bauxite, the principal ore from which it is extracted, contains aluminum hydroxide. Major steps involved in production of aluminum are threefold: (1) mining of bauxite, the principal ore; (2) removal of nonaluminous materials from the ore, and consequent production of alumina (aluminum oxide), a whitish powder; and (3) electrolytic reduction of alumina to metallic aluminum.

PROPERTIES AND USES OF ALUMINUM

For extensive commercial application, a metal must have certain properties that warrant its use in preference to other materials. Aluminum possesses many such properties. It is one of the lightest metals and is the only light metal produced in quantity. Because of its lightness, it has a potential use in practically every item that is pushed, pulled, or

LIGHT METALS

moved. Aluminum is strong in alloy form, it is ductile and can be shaped, it is resistant to atmospheric corrosion and attack by many chemicals, it has excellent conductivity for heat and electrical energy, and it reflects light and radiant heat. It is nonsparking, nonmagnetic, and nontoxic.

Major fields in which large quantities of aluminum are used include architectural and building construction, air and surface transportation, household appliances, cooking utensils, irrigation pipe, machinery and electrical appliances, containers, electrical wiring and cable, television antennae, awnings and venetian blinds, and foil. First on the list is building construction, which consumes about one fifth of the total supply. The use of aluminum panels for the exterior skin of multi-story buildings has been perhaps the most spectacular development in the building market since World War II.

Another large aluminum market is the transportation industry. About 70 per cent of all the van trailers made today use aluminum as the major structural component; and there is an increasing market for novel, lightweight railway passenger and freight cars; 2 million freight cars of all types—now mostly made of steel—move over American rails, and of this number more than 60,000 are retired annually. The cost of maintaining cars made of aluminum is considerably lower than that for steel cars.

Aircraft, especially military and naval, use more aluminum as they increase in size and speed. Another large, growing market for aluminum is the automotive industry. Since there is freight saving of 100 to 150 pounds in the average automobile (aluminum weighs only about one third as much as steel), aluminum's usage by the American automotive industry for passenger cars has climbed spectacularly from an average of 5 pounds per car in 1939 to 56 pounds in 1960.

At the consumer level, aluminum is increasingly favored for home appliances, furniture, wrapping, and packaging. These uses now exceed in importance the electrical-conduction field, formerly a leading aluminum outlet. At present, aluminum is the most economical electrical-conductor material; moreover, it has about 50 per cent more strength than an electrically equivalent copper cable and at the same time is 20 per cent lighter. Fewer poles per mile are used, too—10.8, contrasted with 14.9. In conductors and equipment for communications and electronics, the potential applications for aluminum are so great as to defy forecast.

BAUXITE (ALUMINUM ORE)

Bauxite, a claylike mineral low in silica and high in alumina, was first discovered in 1821 near the village of Les Baux in southern France. The word "bauxite" does not designate a specific mineral, but is a general term for a rock or a mixture of minerals with sufficiently high alumina content to be useful as an ore of aluminum.

Bauxite occurs in various forms. Some deposits may be hard as rock, others extremely soft. Those containing the highest percentages of alumina generally are found in warm tropical or subtropical locations, where bauxite is won from nonaluminous constituents by weathering and solution. Most bauxite deposits occur near the surface and are mined by the open-pit method, although some underground mining is done.

The bauxite ore comes out of the mines in vari-sized chunks mixed with gangue. As large a proportion as possible of the valueless materials is removed by washing and screening. Following washing, the ore is crushed to about the size of a walnut, washed again, and dried in rotary kilns. Traditionally, the ore then moves to alumina plants in distant lands. Factors that govern extraction are (1) size and purity of the deposits; (2) depth of overburden and thickness of the ore deposits; and (3) availability of transportation to an ocean port and to a reduction center. Although ores containing as little as 30-35 per cent of recoverable aluminum oxide are processed commercially, high-grade ores with 50 to 60 per cent aluminum oxide form the basis of the aluminum industry.

Because of the uncertainty of the labor, the generally unsatisfactory fuel situation, and tariff differentials in the underdeveloped mining countries, ores traditionally have moved directly from the mining areas to the industrial countries that process them and use the aluminum. However, this trend in some instances is being reversed; for the underdeveloped countries, which produce about two thirds of the world's bauxite (exclusive of the Soviet bloc), regard smelting as a major industry and are determined to have more than the 1 per cent of the world's total aluminum capacity they now have.

BAUXITE RESERVES

The world's known bauxite reserves exceed 5.5 billion long tons. The Western Hemisphere has 20 per cent of the total reserves; Western Europe and Africa, less than 10 per cent; the Soviet Union and her satellites (including China), about 10 per cent. The rest of Asia, the Pacific islands, and Australia have the remainder of the reserves. Consuming countries within each of these areas usually rely on bauxite producers in the same region, although in the future the Australian deposits will be used increasingly by American and Western European nations. The reserves by country are shown in Table 8-1.

TABLE 8-1

ESTIMATED MAJOR WORLD RESERVES OF BAUXITE, 1958

Continent or country	Millions of long tons	Per cent of total
Australia	2,000	40
Guinea	600	12
Jamaica	550	11
Hungary	250	5
Ghana	229	5
Surinam	200	4
Yugoslavia	128	3
Soviet Union	100	2
Greece	84	2
British Guiana	80	2
France	70	1
India	58	1
China	50	1
United States	50	1

SOURCE: William Goodwin, "Outlook for Aluminum," *Focus;* 11:3, January 1961.

Although bauxite is mined commercially in twenty-five countries, six of these—Jamaica, Surinam, the Soviet Union, the United States, France, and British Guiana—produce more than two thirds of the total world output (Fig. 8-1).

North America. About one third of the world's bauxite production (including that of islands in the Caribbean) is mined in North America. Only since 1952, however, when Jamaican deposits began to be exploited on a large scale, has this region's bauxite production become really significant. Chief areas of production are Jamaica and the United States.

Jamaica has surpassed Surinam as the world's leading source of bauxite (Fig. 8-2). A number of Anglo-American companies have invested many millions of dollars in their bauxite operations, the revenues from which are buttressing the island's economy, formerly dependent upon sugar, rum, and the resort business. The ore deposits vary in size from less than an acre to several acres; occasionally they are so close together that they form a continuous blanket for many miles. Mining and transportation conditions are highly favorable.

The *United States*, largest consumer of bauxite, mines only 10 to 12 per cent of the world's output, so that it has to import about 75 per cent of its supply, chiefly from Surinam, Jamaica, British Guiana, and Guinea. Virtually all domestic bauxite is mined in a 275-square-mile area southwest of Little Rock, Arkansas. This bauxite is of rather low quality —high in silica. Hence, some companies mix with it crude bauxite from Jamaica. Both open-pit and underground methods are followed, but the former accounts for 85 per cent of the total.

South America. Long the chief world source of bauxite, South America recently has been surpassed by both North America and Europe. Most of the commercial ore is mined in Surinam and British Guiana, which possess enormous reserves of bauxite (Table 8-1).

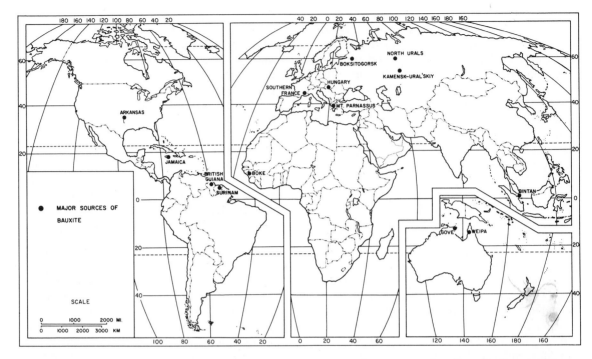

Fig. 8-1. Major world commercial bauxite deposits. Of the three leading nations in aluminum production (the United States, Canada, and the Soviet Union), note that only Canada possesses no bauxite whatsoever. Since it is anticipated that the world's aluminum requirements in 1972 will be four times as great as they were in 1955, a diligent search for new sources of bauxite is underway.

Surinam is the second largest producer of bauxite in the world. The deposits are in the north and accessible by the Surinam and Cottica Rivers and their tributaries. They are found in flat-lying or gently flexed layers near the surface of the coastal plain 20 to 80 miles inland from the Caribbean. Since they are more resistant than the enclosing clays and sands, they often cap the low hills, thereby greatly aiding man's search for ore in the dense vegetation of this rainy tropical land. Both surface and underground mining are used; but at some mines the near-surface bauxite deposits are now almost depleted, and mining is being forced into places having an overburden of 50 to 80 feet. The ore is crushed, washed, and dried before shipment to the United States, Canada, and Europe.

British Guiana, although not so large a producer as Surinam, nevertheless ranks sixth in world output. As with her near neighbor, the mines are located on the coastal plain, 60 to 80 miles inland from the Caribbean, along the north-flowing Demerara and Berbice Rivers. The ore bodies, flat-lying to undulating layers, are overlain by a 60-foot-thick overburden. The same methods of mining are used here as in Surinam, but the bulk of the ore exported is destined for Canada rather than for the United States.

Europe. Europe, with its large reserves of bauxite (Table 8-1), ranks second to North America in output among the continents. The deposits extend across Southern Europe from the Pyrenees eastward through France, Italy, Hungary, Yugoslavia, and Greece.

In *France,* the largest producer in Europe, bauxite is mined all the way from the department of Ariège in the Pyrenees eastward through the lower Rhone Valley into the department of Var, which contributes roughly three fourths of the total French output. France exports bauxite chiefly to West Germany and the United Kingdom.

Fig. 8-2. Open-pit mining of bauxite, Jamaica. This small island leads the world in production and is third in reserves. The overburden is less than 2 feet in thickness, and the ore ranges in thickness from a few inches to more than 100 feet. (Courtesy of Reynolds Metals Company.)

Yugoslavia, despite its large reserves (Table 8-1), is not outstanding in production—largely because of the upheavals of war, administrative weaknesses, and lack of modern machinery. Some mining is carried on, however, from the Istrian Peninsula in the north (on the Italian border) southward along the Dalmatian Coast. The bulk of the output is exported.

Hungary ranks third among European nations and seventh in world production, making it competitive with France for European leadership. The deposits being mined lie in four areas in the western part of the country, are thick, lie close to the surface, and are worked at low cost.

Greece ranks fourth among European and ninth among world producers of bauxite. The deposits are to be found in the hilly country north of the Gulf of Corinth, especially in the Mount Parnassus area.

The Soviet Union, with small reserves of high-grade bauxite, nonetheless is the second largest producer in Europe and the third largest in the world. The best reserves from the standpoint of quality extend along the eastern slope of the Ural Mountains to the 60th meridian—from north of Sverdlovsk to Orsk (Fig. 8-1) but particularly around Serov in the Central Urals and around Kamensk farther south. Low-grade deposits are scattered.

Asia. Compared with North America, South America, and Europe, Asia is a small producer of bauxite. In fact, the entire continent accounts for less than 4 per cent of the world output. *Indonesia* leads; Bintan Island, 80 miles south of Singapore, has the best-known deposits on the continent. *Malaysia*, where mining is carried on at Ramunia Bay in South Johore and at Sematan in Sarawak, is second.

India, despite total reserves estimated at about 250 million long tons and high-grade reserves approximating 58 million long tons, has to date possessed only a small mining industry with an annual output of less than 400,000 tons (1960). The deposits being mined lie in the provinces of Bihar, Bombay, and Madhya Pradesh.

China mines almost no bauxite. In fact, most of her reserves have been discovered only in the past fifteen years. She claims to have deposits in six districts, but little is known about them. Since almost no detailed geological field work has been carried on as yet, estimates of reserves are based on the flimsiest of geological generalizations. However, with an area somewhat exceeding that of the United States, China's mineral wealth must be considerable. Her bauxite and power, which form the basis of the aluminum industry, are regarded as strong both in reserves and in distribution. The main producing deposits are in Hunan, Kweichow, and Szechwan.

THE WORLD'S LIGHT METALS :: 139

Africa. Among the occupied continents, only Australia produces less bauxite than Africa. However, the reserves are larger than the reserves of North America and Asia (Table 8-1). Production was quickened considerably during the 1950s; and, unless the chaotic political conditions discourage both foreign capital and foreign technicians, the forward trend should continue during the 1960s. To date, most of the bauxite mined in Africa is destined for shipment abroad. However, an increasing amount of the ore is being converted into alumina and aluminum in the countries of origin.

So far, the principal development has been in *Guinea*, inland from the port of Conakry and on the offshore islands, especially Kassa Island. *Ghana* possesses large reserves of bauxite, which occur in a belt about 100 miles from the coast. The largest deposit is near Yenahin, 40 miles west of Kumask. However, the only deposits being mined are near Affoh, southwest of Kumasi. *Cameroon* also possesses bauxite; but as yet the reserves are far from known, and production, which is centered near Donala, is small. Finally, mineral-rich *Congo* has among its impressive list of minerals large deposits of bauxite, which were just beginning to be worked as the political explosion occurred in the summer of 1960.

Australia. In a few years Australia is likely to become the world's largest producer of bauxite. At Weipa, on the western shore of Cape York Peninsula, and at Gove, on the northeast tip of Arnhem Land, are large proved reserves of high-grade bauxite (50 per cent alumina), which are being developed for initial mining within a year.

WORLD TRADE IN BAUXITE

The pattern of trade in this mineral is interesting. Most of the countries possessing the largest-known reserves are underdeveloped and often have no capacity whatsoever (at best little capacity) for converting bauxite ore into alumina and particularly into aluminum. In many instances they lack (1) capital, (2) technological skill, (3) power (hydro, natural gas, coal), (4) transport facilities, (5) de-

pendable labor, (6) a market for aluminum, and (7) political stability to justify the risk of constructing the costly industrial complex. Conversely, the developed countries, which possess these requisites, lack the necessary reserves of bauxite, or have only very limited reserves. These complementary needs are the very foundation of foreign trade. Accordingly, international trade in this mineral is brisk. Jamaica, British Guiana, Surinam, Ghana, Indonesia, and Malaysia export virtually their entire production. Even Yugoslavia and France export large tonnages.

PLANT LOCATION—ALUMINA
AND ALUMINUM

The conversion of bauxite into alumina, and especially of alumina to aluminum, has always tended to concentrate in areas of relatively low-cost power. Until recently, such locales were for obvious reasons overwhelmingly in the developed industrialized nations. During the last half of the 1950s, however, there were numerous references to new alumina mills and aluminum reduction plants (smelters) in a number of underdeveloped countries, particularly in northern South America and in West Africa. In both areas are to be found the two main ingredients for successful reduction of aluminum—*huge reserves of bauxite and large sources of potential low-cost hydropower* (40 per cent of the world's potential water power is in Africa). A third favorable factor is proximity to deep water. Hence almost every aluminum company in the Free World has its corporate finger in one or more places in these two continents. But their interest to date has been principally in bauxite, which is produced by a much larger group than metallic aluminum.

MANUFACTURE OF ALUMINA

Alumina plants have generally been located in two kinds of places: (1) relatively near the bauxite mines, or (2) on navigable water either close to or far distant from the mines. In each instance, the purpose is to save on otherwise costly transportation, since about 2 tons of bauxite are required to make 1 ton of alumina.[1] Thus bauxite from the Guianas, after washing and drying (a process designed to decrease weight), is sent to Mobile, Alabama; to Burnside, Baton Rouge and Gramercy, Louisiana; and to La Quinta and Point Comfort, Texas. Ore from British Guiana destined for Canada is treated at Arvida, Quebec, whereas that mined in Jamaica but destined for reduction at Kitimat, British Columbia, is first converted into alumina on the island. Bauxite from Arkansas moves by rail to Bauxite and Hurricane Creek, Arkansas.

Most bauxite is mined by the big aluminum companies for their own use; therefore, when the mineral moves to alumina plants in developed countries, it is not only moving toward the ultimate market but to company plants.

MANUFACTURE OF ALUMINUM

The conversion of alumina into aluminum requires a great deal of power: to make 1 ton of aluminum metal requires 17,000 kilowatt hours of electric energy or 6.8 tons of coal. No other electrometallurgical operation consumes so much power. In the past the aluminum industry sought spots for its plants where large blocks of hydroelectric energy were available 24 hours a day, 365 days a year, *at low cost*. Often such spots were available only in remote areas where there was little competition for power. Even when the plants got cheap power, the cost factor in aluminum reduction averaged 16 per cent in contrast to 2.8 per cent for most industries.

In the United States, as the demand for water power soared during World War II and particularly during the Korean War, new aluminum works could no longer count on ade-

[1] Most of the large companies are experimenting with processes to produce alumina from common clay, and several have done so successfully in pilot plants. If this feat can be accomplished commercially, alumina mills—instead of being built on deep-water ports to reduce the cost of bringing the ore from distant sources—could place a complete aluminum plant on a single site where coal for electric power is cheap, and the shales (associated with most coal) could supply the alumina.

quate dependable blocks of hydropower at low cost. Hence, many new plants were located in Southern states such as Alabama, Louisiana, and Texas, where natural gas and lignite are abundant and cheap. As the demand for aluminum in the United States continued to soar (Table 8-2), new plants sprang

TABLE 8-2

MAJOR WORLD PRODUCTION OF
ALUMINUM, 1960
(in short tons)

United States	2,014,498
Canada	761,357
Soviet Union	745,000
France	259,263
West Germany	186,221
Norway	182,304
Japan	146,864
Italy	92,206
Austria	74,924
Hungary	54,564

SOURCE: *Mineral Trade Notes*, 53:7, August 1961.

up in the Ohio Valley, where coal could be delivered to them economically via barge. By 1960 approximately 40 per cent of the total primary aluminum output of the United States was from plants utilizing coal-based power.

The process of converting the concentrate alumina into aluminum consists of utilizing enormous quantities of electrical energy on a continuous basis to separate the metal from the oxygen. (It requires 8 to 9 kilowatt hours of electricity to make a single pound of aluminum.) Because the aluminum segment of the business is so important and demands so much low-cost power, alumina often moves thousands of miles by water (for instance, from Jamaica to Kitimat, Canada) or even by rail to low-cost power areas.

WORLD PRODUCTION OF ALUMINUM

The huge power requirements of the aluminum industry have made it imperative that the industry be located where power is developed, which is primarily in the industrialized countries—the United States, Canada, the Soviet Union, France, West Germany, Norway, Austria, Italy, and Japan.

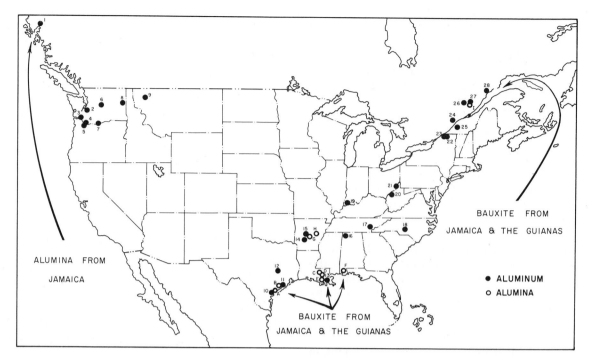

ALUMINA
A. La Quinta
B. Point Comfort
C. Baton Rouge
D. Burnside
E. Gramercy
F. Mobile
G. Bauxite
H. Hurricane Creek
I. Arvida

ALUMINUM
1. Kitimat
2. Tacoma
3. Longview
4. Vancouver
5. Troutdale
6. Wenatchee
7. The Dalles
8. Spokane
9. Columbia Falls
10. San Patricio
11. Point Comfort
12. Rockdale
13. Chalmette
14. Arkadelphia
15. Jones Mills
16. Listerhill
17. Alcoa
18. Badin
19. Evansville
20. Ravenswood
21. Clarington
22. Massena (Reynolds)
23. Massena (Alcoa)
24. Shawinigan Falls
25. Bauharnois
26. Isle Maligne
27. Arvida
28. Baie Comeau

Fig. 8-3. Alumina and aluminum plants in the United States and Canada. Note that the United States plants are located essentially in four areas—in the East, in the Pacific Northwest, along the Gulf Coast, and along the Ohio River—and that Canada's plants are on tributaries of the St. Lawrence River and on the Pacific Coast.

Three nations—the United States (45 per cent), Canada (15 per cent), and the Soviet Union (15 per cent)—together account for three quarters of the world output of aluminum. With 60 per cent of the total, North America leads overwhelmingly.

UNITED STATES

For many years (until World War II), the story of aluminum in the United States was the story of the Aluminum Company of America. This pioneer company had a virtual monopoly in the reduction of aluminum. Today, seven companies make primary aluminum, with plants scattered over the entire nation where energy is available (Fig. 8-3). Output grew from 164,000 tons in 1939 to more than 2 million tons in 1960.

The Pacific Northwest. The industry along the Columbia River got under way prior to Pearl Harbor to supply the needs of the boom-

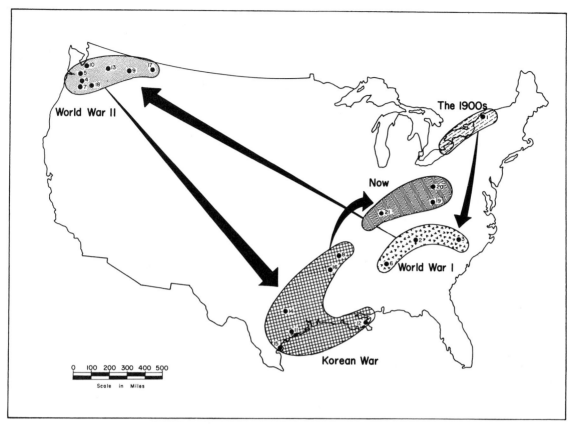

1. Massena, N. Y.
2. Alcoa, Tenn.
3. Badin, N. C.
4. Vancouver, Wash.
5. Longview, Wash.
6. Listerhill, Ala.
7. Troutdale, Ore.

8. Jones Mills, Ark.
9. Spokane, Wash.
10. Tacoma, Wash.
11. Point Comfort, Texas
12. Chalmette, La.
13. Wenatchee, Wash.
14. Rockdale, Texas

15. San Patricio, Texas
16. Arkadelphia, Ark.
17. Columbia Falls, Mont.
18. The Dalles, Ore.
19. Ravenswood, West Va.
20. Clarington, Ohio
21. Evansville, Ind.

Fig. 8-4. Migration of the aluminum industry in the United States. In the past, power costs were considered the most important factor in location, for they loomed high; now, however, power costs and freight costs (nearness to market) are getting increasing attention, for freight rates have been rising faster than power costs.

ing aircraft industry: In a way, however, the industry was war-nurtured and rose to prominence suddenly. Though no primary aluminum was produced until September of 1940, by 1944 the area was making 40 per cent of the national output. The Pacific Northwest has the largest hydroelectric potential in the United States. Hence in the beginning its low-cost power compensated for long rail hauls on alumina from the Gulf Coast and on aluminum to markets in the Middle West and

East. The area boasts the lowest firm power costs in the nation—2.1 mills per kilowatt hour, contrasted with 4 mills in Tennessee and the Gulf states, and 3.1 to 4.5 in the Ohio Valley. It was this differential that attracted the industry to the Northwest, permitting the Columbia River drainage basin to produce more than half of the nation's primary aluminum in 1949.

The raw material for these plants, alumina, is transported approximately 2,500 miles via

THE WORLD'S LIGHT METALS :: 143

boxcar from the Gulf Coast. One might expect the alumina to move via vessel, since both origin and destination are on water and since water transport is in most instances far cheaper than that by rail. However, railroads provide low rates in order to get the business.

Half or more of the aluminum manufactured in the Northwest is shipped some 2,500 miles to the American Manufacturing Region for fabrication. The Pacific Coast market, as of now, is of minor importance. Despite the distance of these plants from their sources of alumina and from their markets, they have been able to operate successfully. Since the Korean War, however, competition within the industry has been so keen and the logistics problem so complicated that the most recently constructed plants are closer to their market and power (coal) and receive their alumina by barge via the Mississippi and Ohio Rivers.

The South. The South has grown in stature in the manufacture of aluminum since World War II—the result primarily of hydroelectric-power shortages in the Pacific Northwest. The South's nine plants account for almost 60 per cent of the nation's primary aluminum output. This situation has resulted from a combination of circumstances: (1) the ease of receiving either bauxite or alumina, since almost all the former and even much of the latter come from the Caribbean area; (2) the presence of substantial water power, natural gas, and lignite; (3) proximity to needed raw materials such as lime and sodium carbonate; (4) the growing industrialization in the South; and (5) greater proximity than the Pacific Northwest to the American Manufacturing Belt, the major market for primary aluminum.

As has been pointed out, power is the most important location factor in the establishment of an aluminum plant, and in the past only hydroelectric power was considered cheap enough for smelting. Now, however, a number of plants (e.g., plants near Port Lavaca and Corpus Christi, Texas; at Jones Mills, Arkansas; and at Chalmette, Louisiana) use low-cost natural gas as fuel. The plant at Rockdale, Texas, uses lignite.

Finally, it is axiomatic that production is both simplified and made more efficient and economical if the plants of multi-process industries can be located near one another. This is no problem in the South.

The Ohio Valley. Figure 8-4 shows that the nomadic aluminum industry's last major move was to the Ohio Valley. A fundamental reason for this move is that some traditional economic-geographic assumptions have been discarded. The sole justification for locating reducing plants in remote regions was the availability of ample power at reasonable cost, which was believed to offset the larger transportation costs of raw materials in and of manufactured products out; recent developments make clear, however, that several other factors must be considered. Thus, after considering a total of one hundred sites, the Kaiser Aluminum and Chemical Corporation selected a 2,500-acre site on the Ohio River at Ravenswood, West Virginia, because it is near the center of the Midwestern and Eastern markets, especially for sheet and foil; furthermore, there were great advantages to be had for quick delivery by truck—one day to Cleveland and Cincinnati, and two days to Detroit and New York. The company, previously located in Washington, was thus able to reduce its transportation costs to Eastern and Midwestern markets by about 70 per cent. Other Ohio Valley plants are located at Evansville, Indiana (Aluminum Company of America) and Clarington, Ohio (Ormet Corporation).

All the Ohio River reduction works utilize coal. And because of more efficient coal mining and steam-plant design, power costs are constantly being reduced, though these costs are not yet so low as those of hydropower.

CANADA

Availability of low-cost power was the main factor in the establishment of Canada's aluminum industry, which uses wholly imported bauxite and alumina. Aluminium Limited, the parent company, operates forty-nine fully owned or affiliated companies in twenty-eight countries, and ranks among the most powerful in the world. Canada as a nation ranks second in world output of aluminum (Table 8-2), an interesting and impressive achievement considering that the country imports all of its raw material.

Rivers draining Quebec's Canadian Shield furnish power for smelting ores from British Guiana and Guinea. Quebec Province accounts for 65 per cent of Canada's aluminum pig.

The reduction works are located at Shawinigan Falls, La Tuque, and Beauharnois on the St. Maurice River, and at Arvida and Isle Maligne on the Saguenay. All plants in Canada capitalize on the enormous hydro potential. Thus Canada has installed more hydro capacity than any other nation.

Arvida. Arvida, which boasts the world's largest aluminum smelter, started in 1926. An alumina works was added in 1928. Arvida thus enjoys the distinction of being the first **integrated plant** located in North America. The Arvida area was able to benefit from three basic needs of the aluminum industry: (1) large amounts of uninterrupted low-cost power, (2) cheap transportation for handling inbound raw materials and outbound fabricated products, and (3) satisfactory labor.

Huge amounts of electricity are generated within the 30-mile stretch in which the raging Saguenay drops 330 feet between Lake St. John and tidewater. The Shipshaw Power Development, with a dam only a few miles distant from Arvida, has a developed 1.5 million horsepower, and a total installed capacity of 2 million horsepower in the valley.

Actually, Arvida is not on navigable water, the river-terminal facilities being at Port Alfred, 20 miles distant, with which it is connected by railway.

Kitimat. In Canada's far west, at Kitimat, in northern British Columbia, is to be found probably the greatest challenge to engineering science thus far encountered in setting up a fully integrated plant (Fig. 8-5). Here, as in all the other Canadian aluminum projects, low-cost hydropower was the principal location factor. The water for the power is pro-

cured by damming the Nechako River, which makes a reservoir or storage basin 150 miles long. A 10-mile tunnel was made to penetrate the Coast Mountains so that the water from the lakes can fall 2,600 feet to the hydroelectric plant located at Kemano in a cavern at sea level. Power lines then deliver the electricity over high-tension lines some 50 miles to Kitimat, at the head of a deepwater fiord, where there is enough flat land for the smelter and a town. The plant began operating in 1954. Its location shows how strong the pull of abundant low-cost hydropower is.[2] The plant draws alumina 5,600 miles from Jamaica and then ships the finished aluminum ingots 2,500 to 3,000 miles to manufacturers in eastern Canada and the United States.

SOVIET UNION

Although its industry dates only from 1932, the Soviet Union ranks third in aluminum output among all countries of the world (Table 8-2).

The Russian industry is located at widely dispersed points west of Lake Baikal—at Kandalaksha in the Kola Peninsula, at Volkhov near Leningrad, at Zaporozhe on the Dnieper River, at Yerevan north and east of the Black Sea, at Chirchik southeast of the Aral Sea, at Krasnoturinsk in the Northern Urals, and at Kamensk-Uralsky in the Southern Urals, at Kuznetsk in the Kuznetsk Basin, and at a recently built plant in Siberia on the power-rich Angara River northwest of Lake Baikal. Very large plants were recently constructed at Pavlodar on the Irtysh River in eastern Kazakhstan and near Shelekhovo on the Irkut River. Both these plants rank among the largest in the world.

The most authoritative sources state that between 50 and 60 per cent of the Soviet output comes from the two plants at Krasnoturinsk and Kamensk-Uralsky. Both draw bauxite from nearby sources and both use electricity obtained from steam plants.

[2] An increase of a tenth of a cent in the cost of a kilowatt hour would boost production costs $20 per ton.

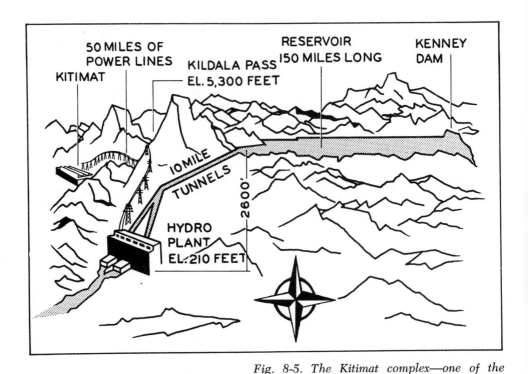

Fig. 8-5. The Kitimat complex—one of the world's outstanding aluminum-manufacturing areas. (Courtesy of Aluminium Limited.)

EUROPE

France. France is the fourth-ranking aluminum nation in the world, the second in Europe, and the first in Western Europe (Table 8-2). Fortunately, she has her own supply of bauxite (Table 8-1). In France, all reduction works are oriented with respect to sources of hydropower in the Alps and Pyrenees. This means that the industry is centered largely in the south, both east and west of the Rhone River (Alps and Pyrenees Mountains). Especially prominent is the Alpine department of Savoy with four plants. Most French plants, like most European plants, are small. That at St. Jean de Maurienne in Savoy is an exception, for it alone reduces 37 per cent of France's aluminum.

West Germany. West Germany, though it mines almost no bauxite, nonetheless ranks fifth among world producers of aluminum, third in Europe, and second in Western Europe. The industry is located in Bavaria, Westphalia, and the Rhineland. Three factors are responsible for West Germany's present high rank: (1) low-cost coal and lignite, (2) relative proximity to sources of European bauxite in France, Greece, and Yugoslavia (also imports from Indonesia and West Africa), and (3) the important market for primary aluminum.

Norway. Norway, like Canada and West Germany, has an impressive aluminum industry. Even though it mines no bauxite and does not have a large home market for aluminum, Norway ranks sixth; and within a few years, when present projects are completed, it is expected to become the largest producer in Western Europe.

The Norwegian industry exemplifies well the strong locational pull of low-cost water power. Moreover, this power is abundant and the output is reasonably constant—a factor of considerable importance in the aluminum industry. Finally, this power is available at tidewater—at excellent ports which, despite quite high latitude, are ice-free throughout the year.

Under these circumstances it is not surprising that Norway leads all nations in production of electricity per capita and in low cost per kilowatt hour.

The aluminum-reduction works are located along the coast at Stangfjord, north of Bergen; at Höyanger, on the Sognefjord; and at Haugvik in the north. The Norwegian industry manufactures aluminum from alumina imported principally from Canada and France. In addition, bauxite is imported, chiefly from France and Greece.

Italy. Italy mines bauxite, which it converts into alumina and then into aluminum. Though poor in facilities for the first task, Italy is well endowed with white coal (hydropower) for the second, ranking second among the European countries—exclusive of the Soviet Union—in developed water power. All the aluminum plants use hydroelectric power.

The Italian aluminum industry is to be found in two areas: central peninsular Italy and northern Italy (on the Po Plain and the slopes of the Alps). The central region has plants at Bussi on the Pescara River (a completely integrated unit) and at Aurilia, northwest of Rome. In the north, important works are to be found at Porto Marghera, near Venice, where both alumina and aluminum are turned out. This district, which relies upon the Istrian bauxite deposits, is one of the largest aluminum centers in Italy. Yet another important plant is located at Mori near the northern end of Lake Garda. It, too, makes both alumina and aluminum, using Istrian bauxite and hydropower from the Adige River. One of Italy's oldest reduction works is at Borgofranco, north of Turin; one of its newer reduction plants is at Bolzano, near the confluence of the Isarco and Adige Rivers.

ASIA

Japan. Japan is the leading aluminum producer in Asia, and it ranks seventh among world producers. Starting from an initial output of 19 tons in 1933, in five years the Japanese attained self-sufficiency at a production rate of 20,000 tons. Peak output of 150,000 tons was attained in 1943 to meet wartime demands.

Japan's aluminum industry is based on cheap hydroelectric power. The lack of suitable domestic ores and the consequent total reliance upon imports are the major problems facing the industry. Two thirds of the bauxite is brought from Bintan Island, Indonesia, the only large proved reserve of high-grade bauxite ore in the entire Far East.

The reduction works are scattered widely over the island of Honshu, both at seaboard sites and in interior points, principally at Niigata, Kitakta, Oomachi, and Kambara, and at Niihama on the Inland Sea coast of Shikoku.

THE UNDERDEVELOPED COUNTRIES

To date, little aluminum has been produced in underdeveloped countries. There is some output in Greece, Romania, Spain, Yugoslavia, India, China, Taiwan, Cameroon, Guinea, Ghana, the Congo, and Brazil; but their combined output averages less than 5 per cent of the world total. However, with nationalism sweeping over the underdeveloped lands, such countries are determined to industrialize. If they possess bauxite and potential hydropower, as do several in West Africa and South America, they insist on converting some of their bauxite and alumina at home. The present political unrest in much of Africa and Latin America, however, seems certain to delay any considerable development for many years; for companies dare not risk large amounts of capital only to have their properties expropriated. Hence, many plants scheduled for construction may not go beyond the blueprint stage.

MAGNESIUM

Lightness is the striking quality of magnesium, whose weight is only two thirds that of aluminum, less than one fourth that of iron, and only a fifth that of copper or nickel. In short, magnesium is the lightest of all structural metals and also possesses strength and machineability. It can be cast, rolled, drawn, spun, forged, blanked, and coined. The alloys are also resistant to corrosion.

Half of the magnesium consumed goes into commercial use—33 per cent into aircraft, 20 per cent into the aluminum industry, 10 per cent into machinery, and 37 per cent into miscellaneous uses. The automotive industry could use from 25,000 to 50,000 tons per annum, if the price could be reduced. American automobiles contain less than 1 pound of magnesium each on the average.

OCCURRENCE

Magnesium is the third most abundant of the engineering metals. It can be extracted from underground brines and sea water or from ores containing magnesium—chiefly brucite, dolomite, and magnesite.

The processing of sea water is by far the most important method of reduction. Immense mills employ this process at Freeport and Velasco, Texas. At Painesville, Ohio, underground brine is used. Silico-thermal plants are located at Canaan, Connecticut; Wingdale, New York; Manteca, California; and Spokane, Washington.

WORLD PRODUCTION

Currently in the entire world only twelve countries produce magnesium. However, only five of these are important, and only two, the Soviet Union and the United States, account for the bulk (Table 8-3).

TABLE 8-3

MAJOR WORLD PRODUCTION OF
MAGNESIUM METAL, 1960
(in short tons)

United States	40,070
Soviet Union	27,600
Norway	13,200
Canada	7,373
Italy	5,500

SOURCE: *Mineral Trade Notes*, 52:25, June 1961.

TITANIUM

Titanium, last of the triad of light metals presented here, has been known as a common element for well over 150 years; but the employment of metallic titanium as a *useful* metal dates only from 1948. Titanium has one very great advantage over aluminum and magnesium, both of which are lighter in weight: it holds its strength at temperatures as high as 800°F. But the metal has other valuable qualities: it performs better than stainless steel but is only half as heavy; it is six times stronger than aluminum, and nearly as rustproof as platinum; and it is extremely resistant to corrosion by salt water.

However, titanium owes its rise solely to the Cold War and to the aircraft industry's precise specifications. Its ability to hold its strength without much expansion at temperatures between 300°F and 800°F obviously gives it priority for use in the fabrication of air frames, rockets, turbojets, and ram-jet engines, where weight saving is at a premium and where temperatures to be withstood are so high as to discourage the use of alloys made with aluminum and magnesium. It is expected also that titanium alloys will be used commercially for high-speed fly-shuttles, for textile machinery in cotton mills, for high-speed cutting tools, and for pipes and tanks in food-processing plants.

Titanium mineral is abundant, being found as *ilmenite* (iron and titanium oxide combined) and *rutile* (a high-grade titanium oxide). Large deposits of either ilmenite or rutile have been found in Norway, Sweden, and Finland; in the Transvaal of South Africa; in the Ilmen Mountains (an extension of the Urals) in the Soviet Union; in the American states of New York, North Carolina, and Virginia; in the Allard Lake region 400 miles northeast of Quebec City, Canada; in Oaxaca in southwestern Mexico; and in Brazil. And extensive beach-sand concentrations are known in Australia (extending 50 miles on either side of the Queensland–New South Wales border), in Travancore, India, and elsewhere. The United States, India, Canada, and Norway currently account for more than 90 per cent of the world output. There is no foreseeable world shortage of titanium minerals.

WORLD OUTLOOK

The only thing that now appears certain in the outlook for the light metals is that their

TABLE 8-4

GROWTH OF ALUMINUM AND SELECTED
NONFERROUS METALS
(in long tons)

Metal	1907	1957
Aluminum	17,000	3,306,000
Copper	709,671	3,412,000
Lead	981,100	2,405,000
Tin	104,549	268,000
Zinc	726,750	2,907,000

SOURCE: "Non-ferrous Metallurgy 1908-1958," *Engineering*, 185:626, May 16, 1958.

use will continue to soar (Table 8-4). The trend is unmistakable as new major uses are found for them. Thus in 1960, steel consumption was increasing at a rate of 34 per cent, aluminum at a rate of 262 per cent. It is believed that aluminum output in the United States will increase from about 2 million tons today to 5 million tons in 1975.

The uncertainty in the aluminum picture has to do with international relations. It would seem that too many underdeveloped countries err in discouraging expansion of mineral exports, regarding industrialization as the sole magic wand that will bring to them higher levels of living.

Primary aluminum has become an international commodity whose raw material, bauxite, comes from all over the world, crossing many international boundaries. This circumstance makes lucid two things: (1) the aluminum industry does not lend itself to restrictive regional practices; and (2) in order to prosper, the industry requires world peace.

The other light metals are no less vital than aluminum, but present production is on a comparatively small scale. They are employed mostly for military uses as alloying agents. If they are to be produced in greater quantity and to be used commercially, they must be much reduced in price. Price reduction can come only with cheaper methods of extraction.

Only aluminum appears to be assured of large output now and in the near future. It alone has adequate raw materials and sufficiently low production costs to guarantee worldwide use. And only it among all light metals has become a *major* metal.

SELECTED REFERENCES

Brown, S. Earl. "The Ohio Valley Aluminum Industry," *Journal of Geography*, 61:241-251, September 1962.

Duncan, C. "The Aluminum Industry in Australia," *Geographical Review*, 51:21-46, January 1961.

Goodwin, William. "Outlook for Aluminum," *Focus*, 5:1-6, January 1961.

McGuire, B. J. "Aluminum—The Story of Fifty Years of Growth by the Canadian Industry," *Canadian Geographical Journal*, 43:144-163, October 1951.

President's Materials Policy Commission. *Resources for Freedom*. Washington, D. C., June 1952. Vol. 2, *Outlook for Key Commodities*, pp. 65-73 (aluminum), 73-75 (magnesium), 75-77 (titanium), 78-79 (zirconium).

Sutton, H. "The Future of Light Metals," in United Nations, Department of Economic Affairs, *Proceedings of the United Nations Scientific Conference on the Conservation and Utilization of Resources*. New York, 1951. Vol. II, *Mineral Resources*, pp. 246-252.

U.S. Bureau of Mines. *Mineral Facts and Problems*. Washington, D. C., 1956. Bulletin 556, pp. 17-35 (bauxite), 213-218 (columbium and tantalum), 471-492 (magnesium), 905-906 (titanium), 1005-1009 (zirconium).

CHAPTER NINE ::

The nonmetallic minerals,[1] other than fuels, are called in trade parlance "nonmetallics" or "industrial minerals." They include a wide array, and their manufactural ramifications are so numerous that it is difficult to classify them satisfactorily. Some authorities include nitrate, phosphate rock, and potash as nonmetallics. In this chapter, however, we are concerned only with building and ceramic materials and with minerals used in the chemical industries (except those entering into the manufacture of fertilizers). Nonmetallics such as nitrate, phosphate rock, and potash are presented in Chapter 12, "The World's Chemical Industries."

[1] Besides the nonmetallic minerals presented here, several others (e.g., asbestos, cryolite, graphite, mica, and quartz crystals) are widely used in our civilization. They are not presented here, however, because of space limitation.

THE WORLD'S

Because many of the nonmetallic minerals are abundant and low in cost, their economic significance is little realized or appreciated by the average person. It is not easy to believe, for instance, that the combined annual value of cement, clay, gravel, lime, sand, slate, and stone produced in the United States surpasses that of bauxite, copper, iron, lead, silver, and zinc. Fortunately, most of the nonmetallics are widely distributed over the globe —many in abundance.

DISTRIBUTION AND PRODUCTION OF NONMETALLIC MINERALS

Each continent has large areas of the different kinds of rocks. Hence, it would be futile to try to show on generalized world maps the sources of the various nonmetallic minerals because they are of too common occurrence. To a less extent the same holds for productivity, the heart of economic geography: in this instance, productivity is less dependent upon availability of resources than it is upon ingenuity and efficiency of the inhabitants of a given area in discovering and using such resources. At present, the advanced industrial nations are responsible for most of the world's output of nonmetallics (except in those rare instances where a given area or several areas possess *all or nearly all* of the deposits, or at least those of highest quality). Thus, the producing centers invariably cluster about major population centers.

The modes of occurrence of the nonmetallic minerals govern their extraction. Some—for instance, building stones such as sandstone, granite, and marble—are quarried; others—

NONMETALLIC MINERALS

for instance, sand or gravel—are scooped from lakes or streams by powerful electric shovels, or crushed to the desired size from rocks hauled to pulverizing mills. Sometimes underground mining is resorted to if all nearby surface deposits are depleted. The end cost of the commodity is definitely influenced by the mining method employed.

STONE

The more important stones utilized by man are *basalt, granite, limestone, marble, sandstone, and slate*. Limestone ranks first, accounting for about two thirds of the total tonnage. It is marketed in blocks of specified sizes or as crushed stone. Quarrying and preparation, because of the great weight of the stone, tend to be a local enterprise. Most building stones, therefore, are selected from the best varieties at hand on the basis of such qualities as beauty, ease of cutting and trimming, strength, resistance to weather, and freedom from stain-producing materials. However, certain demands, such as those for tombstones, monuments, public buildings, and statuary, transcend local supplies and hence create interstate or even international trade in building stone.

Because of Europe's dense population and restricted forests, quarrying is more important there (particularly in the Mediterranean lands —Greece, Italy, Spain—but even in Temperate Marine England, whose forests were removed long ago) than in the United States.

Certain stones decline in importance because of high price compared with competitive materials or because of change in fashion. Bedford (Indiana) limestone is used less today than in the past because of its high price; and Connecticut Valley sandstone ("brownstone"), which was so popular during the "Gay Nineties," is no longer of economic importance.

LIMESTONE

Limestone for construction is quarried in some twenty-nine American states, but it is important only in Indiana, Texas, Kansas, Wisconsin, and Missouri. Best known is the easily worked, attractive, and durable "Bedford limestone" from the Bedford-Bloomington district in Indiana.

Limestone is much used also in crushed form—as **ballast** for railroads, **flux** for blast furnaces, for cement, and in agriculture (Fig. 9-1). Thus, most developed industrial nations —the United States, the United Kingdom, West Germany, the Soviet Union, Japan—are large producers. But some underdeveloped nations (e.g., Egypt) have a considerable output.

SANDSTONE

Sandstone is no longer so popular for construction as formerly; but, at least in some areas, it finds many uses—as paving stone, breakwaters in ports, flagging for sidewalks, outdoor fireplaces, and abrasives. In the United States, Ohio, Pennsylvania, Tennessee, Maryland, and New York lead in output. The quarry at Amherst (near Cleveland, Ohio), known as the "Gray Canyon," is the world's largest sandstone quarry.

SLATE

Slate is **metamorphic rock** derived from clay or shale. It is characterized by almost perfect cleavage, so that it can be split readily into thick, smooth slabs. It is highly enduring to weather.

Slate has been used for centuries. Quarries in North Wales claim to have been in continuous production since the days of Queen Elizabeth I. Slate is used for roofing and for blackboards, billiard-table tops, baseboard, and wallboard. The leading states in production in the United States are Pennsylvania, Vermont, and New York.

GRANITE

Granite, an **igneous rock,** occurs in various colors—light gray, reddish, and brownish. Most varieties are capable of taking a high polish and of being readily shaped, and hence are in considerable demand for monuments and tombstones. Weighing 160 to 170 pounds per cubic foot, it is costly to transport except by water. Granite is to be found in nearly all mountainous areas. In the United States it is

Fig. 9-1. *World's largest limestone-producing plant. This quarry, located at Rogers City, Michigan, on Lake Huron, has an annual capacity of about 15 million tons per year in an 8½-month shipping season. At each side of the screen house are storage piles, one for open-hearth stone, a second for blast-furnace flux, and still others for finer stone used by the cement plants and chemical companies. (Courtesy of United States Steel Corporation.)*

produced chiefly in New England (Fig. 9-2) and the southern Appalachians, though Minnesota and Wisconsin also are important. It is quarried in Scotland, Norway, Sweden, and Finland, and in the Alps, Pyrenees, and Caucasus of Europe. Granite, though more costly than its substitutes (e.g., concrete, terra cotta, brick), will continue to be favored for large, dignified structures and particularly for memorial use.

MARBLE

This metamorphic rock, when quarried and shaped, is notable for its beauty. Marble is used for tombstones, monuments, and the foundations and lower floors (both interior and exterior) of large buildings, and for statuary. Its production (particularly if the stone is superior in quality) is important in areas close to navigable water and to large population centers, and where labor is cheap.

Among famous producing centers are Rutland, Vermont; Knoxville, Tennessee; and northern Georgia in the United States (which together account for 80 to 85 per cent of the national total). Of this group, Vermont is the leader, its principal quarry centers lying on the west flank of the Green Mountains. Al-

Fig. 9-2. Closeup of one of the world's most famous quarries—the Rock of Ages—at Barre, Vermont. Here quarrymen are freeing a three-block-long portion of granite, which will then be cut into smaller blocks. Since monumental granite is expensive, precision drilling is vital, and clean cuts are necessary. (Courtesy of Rock of Ages Corporation.)

most pure white to gray and pink marble is quarried. Tennessee marble, which varies from white to mottled maroon, finds wide use for floors and interiors of buildings. Georgia marble is used for exteriors of buildings.

Carrara, Italy, on the flanks of the Apennine Mountains, contributes desirable and beautiful marble for statues. For centuries its quarries have furnished the snow-white, uniformly fine-grained, flawless stone.

SAND AND GRAVEL

Because of their wide distribution, their extensive use, and their low cost (both production and selling price), sand and gravel rank first in tonnage of all minerals used by man. The United States' annual output reportedly approximates and often surpasses that of coal.

Both sand and gravel may be composed of materials from identical parent rock or from a mixture of many, but both result from nat-ural disintegration of rocks. The bulk of admixtures of gravel consists of the harder minerals, such as quartz, whereas sand consists chiefly of silica in the form of quartz particles.

Roughly, sand and gravel deposits may be classified into four groups, based on methods of formation: (1) *residual*, (2) *fluvial*, (3) *riverine* and *lake*, and (4) *glacial*.

Sand and gravel are used for concrete, railroad ballast, plaster, building sand, grinding and polishing sand, foundry sand, and railing sand (for keeping the wheels from slipping on the rails). About 90 per cent of all sand and gravel is utilized for construction and paving. Since these commodities have low value per unit of weight, the bulk of the product is marketed close by, and the business is highly decentralized into a very large number of small units, each caring for the demands of a restricted area.

The leading American states in production are California, Michigan, Ohio, Illinois, Wisconsin, Minnesota, Utah, New York, Texas, and Washington, in this order. These states as a group account for and consume more than half the total output of 1 billion tons. Large plants supply a disproportionate share of the total output.

Except for former glaciated areas, the leading sources are seashores, lake beaches, and river terraces. Sand and gravel are often dredged from river and lake bottoms. In areas where none of these sediments exists, limestone, sandstone, basalt, or other rocks are quarried, crushed, and screened to provide desirable (but more costly) substitutes. Unlike most other minerals, sand and gravel are renewable resources in that the processes that cause their accumulation are constantly at work.

GLASS

Glassmaking is an old industry. As an art, a handicraft, it was known to the Egyptians, Romans, Venetians, Dutch, French, and Belgians. But glassmaking is also a very new industry. Application of automatic methods, developed only since 1900, has made low-cost production a reality. Ninety-nine per cent of the glass manufactured in the United States (for window glass, bottles, light bulbs, and tubes) is machine-made; in many underdeveloped countries, however, glass still is produced by human labor.

Most glass is made from silica plus alkali and lime—soda or potash for lowering the melting point and lime for rendering the resulting product water-resistant. A superior fuel such as natural gas is extremely desirable because a high and uniform temperature must be maintained in order to melt the raw materials.

Glass can be made fragile or tough, transparent or opaque; it can pass heat or electricity, or it can stop both. Versatility makes glass a vital tool of modern industry. There are no substitutes for glass for some uses— light bulbs, windows, television tubes, eyeglasses, camera lenses, automobile windshields, thermometers, and hundreds of others.

LOCATION OF GLASS PLANTS

The glass industry arises only in places that are congenial for it. The chief location factors include the following:

1. Nearness to fuel—especially natural gas. Temperatures as high as 2867°F are required. In the manufacture of containers, fuel accounts for about one third of the total cost of production.

2. Ready access to raw materials. Glass sand is a heavy commodity of narrow specifications but of rather low value. *Fortunately, however, there are a considerable number of sources satisfactory for glassmaking close to market.*

3. Nearness to market. Because glass is fragile and bulky, freight rates on its shipment are substantially higher than on its chief ingredient, sand.

4. Efficient transportation.

5. Available labor. Before glassmaking became so highly mechanized, this factor was outstanding; it is now of but minor import.

WORLD GLASS PRODUCTION

UNITED STATES

Glassmaking was among the earliest colonial industries, particularly in Virginia, New York, Massachusetts, and Pennsylvania. Today it is concentrated largely in the northern Appalachian region—western Pennsylvania, northern West Virginia, eastern Ohio, and western New York.

The United States has the largest production of glass on earth. The industry employs more than 100,000 workers, and the value of its output exceeds 1.4 billion dollars. The types of glass are divided as follows:

1. *Flat glass* for windows, etc. There are only about 30 such plants, but they are mostly large; three fourths of this glass is made in the central part of the American Manufacturing Region (Pennsylvania, West Virginia, Ohio, and Indiana), where all the factors listed for plant location are highly favorable. Southern California, meeting all the require-

ments for location of the industry, has the only plant in the West.

2. *Glass containers.* These constitute 45 per cent of the total output. More than 60 per cent is accounted for by plants in the two states of Pennsylvania and Illinois.

3. *Other pressed and blown glass.* More than 80 per cent of the output is from the American Manufacturing Region.

Except for expected growth of the industry in California, it is unlikely that any major shifts will occur.

SELECTED COUNTRIES IN EUROPE AND ASIA

In Europe, glassmaking is very old, and for quality it has no peers. Unlike the American industry, that in Europe is little mechanized and much emphasis is placed on beauty and quality.

France. Glassmaking is widely distributed in France, and in those branches making products of quality and extraordinary beauty, France ranks very high. The French introduced a new spirit into the modern conception of glassmaking through the work of individual artists. French cut crystals and colored wares enjoy worldwide fame. Regionally, glassmaking is best developed in the coal fields of the north around Lille, with a second concentration of establishments in Lorraine, which utilizes glass sands from the Vosges Mountains. St. Louis is in the forefront of the entire glass industry, though it is most famous for crystal glass. Paris is the center of one of Europe's largest and best optical glass industries.

Belgium. Glassmaking, one of the traditional occupations of the Belgians, has long been concentrated in the provinces of Liège, Antwerp, and Hainaut. The country is not only one of the world leaders but it has one of the world's most modern industries. Though all types of glass are made, Belgium is world famous for window glass, which it has produced since the end of the sixteenth century. In fact, Belgium enjoyed almost a world monopoly on this branch of the industry until

1880. Much so-called "French plate glass" is really made in Belgium. This segment of the industry is situated in the Sambre Valley, especially in and around Charleroi. It is said that the world's largest window-glass furnace was constructed at Zeebrugge, a North Sea port, in 1958. Table glassware is manufactured mostly in plants in the province of Liège.

West Germany. An area as well endowed with coal and silica and as highly industrialized (particularly in the chemicals branches) as West Germany was certain to have an important glass industry and one of infinite diversity. The industry here ranks second in output only to that of the United States. It is centered in the Rhine-Ruhr district on the coal fields—Essen, Gelsenkirchen, and Düsseldorf. Cologne, on the Rhine, yet another center, is famous for the beauty of its glass.

Scientific and other specialized glass products are usually made in smaller plants employing a very few skilled workers—a fact accounting for the large number of small glassworks dotting the country. After the transfer of Jena to the Russian zone of occupation, optical works (for which Germany long held world leadership) were started in Swiesel, Bavaria; and since 1952 this phase of the business has been centered at Mainz.

Czechoslovakia. Bohemian glass and crystal have long enjoyed distinguished world reputations for beauty and quality. Both glass sand and coal are available. Outstanding are Telice-Sanoy in the Ersgebirge Valley in Bohemia, Yablonec, and Praha.

United Kingdom. English glass manufacture dates from the Middle Ages, production at first being for window glass for churches and dwellings. With the adoption of coal as a fuel, glassmaking, like nearly all English manufacturing, concentrated near the mines at Birmingham, Bristol, and Newcastle, where it has remained. London, as a result of the pull of the market factor, also ranks high; coal is delivered to it by vessel from Newcastle. Virtually every type of glass is made in the United Kingdom.

Soviet Union. The Soviet Union ranks high among the countries of the world in quantity and types of glass turned out. The country's enormous size, the imperfect transport system, and the difficulty of transporting glass (breakage), along with the long-pent-up demand of the people, account for the widespread distribution of glassworks. The five-year plans have created plants where fuel is abundant and cheap and where glass is in great demand, as in the Donbas (Konstantinovka). Glassmaking is particularly important in western Russia—in Leningrad, Vologda, Kalinin, Orel, and Smolensk—and in the central part—in Likeno and Dulevo. In Soviet Asia, glass is manufactured at Krasnoyarsk and Tomsk, and at Irkutsk and Ulan-Ude.

Japan. Japan makes glass—bottles, tubes, light bulbs, and sheet glass—by machine. But she also makes high-grade wares that require hand-blowing and are of exquisite design, finish, and polish. Currently, more than 70 per cent of the domestic demand is for sheet glass for construction. The chief centers are Tokyo, Osaka, Nagoya, Yokohama, Tobata, Moji, and Hiroshima. The Osaka-Kobe area accounts for about half the total output, Tokyo for one fourth.

CLAY

Clay is found in every country on the globe. It is composed of very fine particles of mineral substances; these substances become plastic when wet and can be molded into almost any shape. The leading industrial clays are (1) kaolin or china clay, (2) ball clay, (3) fire clay, (4) bentonite, (5) fuller's earth, and (6) miscellaneous clays.

Clays vary greatly in mineralogical composition and other properties, and the character of the raw materials determines the types of products that can be made. Clay may be used, among other things, as adobe, as brick or tile (which is hardened by burning), or as terra cotta, pottery, or porcelain. The manufacture of fired clay products is called "ceramics."

The clay industry is classified according to products: (1) refractory (fire bricks, crucibles, and retorts); (2) structural (brick, tile, and terra cotta); (3) domestic (vitrified brick, sinks, sewer pipe, chinaware, and pottery); and (4) electrical (insulators). The raw-material specifications are least exacting for structural brick, and most exacting for such articles as fine chinaware.

Common clay and shale are produced in forty-five of the fifty American states. In the northern states, operations are highly seasonal for two reasons: (1) open pits (except in Pennsylvania) yield most of the clay, and they are closed in winter; (2) the demand is seasonal. In the United States one of the most famous clay areas lies in the Lower Lake region—especially in the Allegheny Plateau. Eastern Ohio is a leading center in the manufacture of hollow tile, drain tile, and white ware.

CHINA CLAY

Kaolin, or china clay, is the aristocrat of clays. It is nearly pure clay and is comprised mainly of the mineral kaolinite. Such clay is an essential constituent in the bodies and glazes of china cups, saucers, and plates. Commercial deposits of kaolin are restricted to relatively few countries—the United Kingdom, Germany, Czechoslovakia, France, the United States, and China—with the largest of all in China. In quality, no clay anywhere else approaches that of the west of England—Cornwall and Devon. Few nations can match Britain's china industry in total output and quality of product; the name Wedgewood, for instance, is the hallmark of quality over the entire world. The industry centers in Stoke-on-Trent, its "six towns" accounting for three quarters of the total national output. Britain's clays for many years were, next to coal, her chief export based on tonnage (more than 1 million tons annually in 1913, 1925, and 1926). Despite clay's low value per unit of weight, England was able to export it because of the superior quality of the clay; the proximity of the quarries to ports, dominantly Fowey; and its suitability as return cargo: since most of the traffic across the North Atlantic is from west to east and thus American-bound bottoms cannot easily pick up homogeneous cargoes, many shipowners have been willing to let their vessels return with clay, even at a nominal freight rate, rather than return in **ballast**.

Leading American producing states are Georgia, South Carolina, North Carolina, Pennsylvania, Florida, Alabama, Illinois, Nevada, California, Utah, and Virginia. American clays are inferior to English clays; but, as a result of **beneficiation** and the American tariff, they supply the greater part of the market.

France's deposits of kaolin in Brittany supply the famous china industries of Limoges. Saxony in Germany supports one of the world's most famous china industries, particularly that of Dresden.

In the United States, pottery and china are made in many states. In quantity one area stands out above all others—the Uhrichsville-Canton-Akron (Ohio) area. The center of the pottery industry is East Liverpool; but Roseville, Crooksville, and Zanesville all are important.

BRICK

Most common clays, even though highly impure, are suitable for brick. When clays are fired to a temperature of redness or higher, they become rock hard. Man's use of them goes far back into antiquity. We know bricks were used in India at least 5,000 years ago; in Egypt they were used as early as 5000 to 3000 B.C. Bricks were in use throughout Europe by the seventeenth century, and kilns were quickly built by Europeans who came to the American colonies. The Hudson Valley was making bricks by 1792, and production spread westward so rapidly that by 1852 plants had been built as far west as California.

Today most nations of the world have brick-making industries, but the United States is the largest producer and consumer of bricks. Some 640 plants turn out about 6 billion ordinary building bricks annually. The industry is widely distributed because of the low unit value per weight of its product, availability of suitable clays, and the simple methods of production. Brick plants tend to be small and to locate near their markets. The Hudson River Valley near metropolitan New York is possibly the most important single area. Here are combined an enormous market and cheap transportation for raw materials, including coal, and for the delivery of bricks to market.

Eleven states—New York, Illinois, North Carolina, Pennsylvania, Ohio, Texas, Georgia, Alabama, Virginia, South Carolina, and California—make about 62 per cent of all the bricks manufactured in the United States.

TILE

Tile consists of a plate, or thin piece of fired clay, used for covering the roofs of buildings, and for floors, walls, drains, and furnace linings. Superior grades are frequently employed for ornamental work.

Tile, even more than brick, is costly to transport because it is low in value in proportion to bulk and because it is breakable. Hence tile-manufacturing plants are invariably located near markets. New York City alone has one third of all American-made tile—mostly for sewer pipe, flooring, and roof construction. Drain tile is used on level land in many rural areas of the American Midwest. Roofing tile is popular in the American Southwest, because of the prevalence of the Spanish style of architecture.

Important world centers of tile production are Asia Minor, for Persian floor tile; North Africa and Spain, for Moorish and Spanish roofing tile; the Netherlands, for Delft tile; Spain, for square tiles with painted figures or landscapes (used for wall wainscotings); Belgium, for many types of handmade wall tiles; Germany, for machine-pressed floor tiles; and the United States, for wall, roofing, and drain tiles.

CEMENT

As was noted, building stone is expensive because it must be quarried, cut into shape, and dressed. Moreover, the quarries frequently lie far from large markets. For the building of dams, masonry structures, sidewalks, airports, water and sewage systems, and larger buildings, it is both simpler and cheaper to use "man-made stone"—*cement*—which can be poured and molded into the desired shape. Since cement and concrete expand at the same rate as iron and steel, they are used around steel frameworks, and the resulting product is known as *reinforced concrete*.

MANUFACTURE AND USES OF CEMENT

Portland-cement concrete is so easy to use, so durable, and so cheap that it has become mankind's most common and necessary construction material. Few industries during the past half century have developed and grown as rapidly as cement making. Output in the United States rose from about 10 million barrels in 1900 to 334 million barrels in 1960, as a result of ever widening markets and simultaneous improvement of the product. Cement has gained increasing acceptance as a fireproofing building material, and as reinforced concrete it possesses sufficient strength to be used in constructing skyscrapers. The fast-growing motor-vehicle and aviation industries have generated a large demand for cement for constructing durable hard-surface highways and runways.

Standardization of the formula was one of the factors contributing to the decentralization of the industry. When raw materials were blended in proper proportions, it became possible to permit the manufacture of portland cement in various regions where the local demand was sufficient to justify the establishment of a mill. A market for 1½ to 2 million barrels a year is about the minimum to justify the capital expenditures required to erect a mill. Today there are 167 mills in the United States, with one or more in each of thirty-seven states (Fig. 9-3). The kilns' diet varies with location: it may be (1) cement rock and pure limestone, (2) limestone and clay or shale, (3) marl and clay, or (4) blast-furnace slag and limestone.

Cement making is a local industry. It is too costly to haul the product from one end of the nation to the other because cement is heavy and low in price. Moreover, delivery charges, irrespective of mode of transport, are based on weight, not on value of the product. About 15 per cent of the delivered price represents delivery cost. Under ordinary circumstances, shipping charges limit the market to a radius of about 100 miles from the mill. If the cement plant is located on a navigable waterway, the available market area is further extended by the possibility of cheap bulk or package shipment by barge or vessel.

WORLD CEMENT PRODUCTION

World production of cement has been growing at a rapid rate—threefold in the two decades from 1937 (482 million barrels) to 1957 (1,448 million barrels). In 1957 the United States contributed 21 per cent of the total, and the Soviet Union contributed 12.5 per cent.

The raw materials for making cement are so abundant and so widespread that the industry is to be found almost everywhere. Although some cement gets into international trade, its low value in proportion to weight, the desire of all nations to have their own industry, and the high water-damage coefficient in ocean shipping unite to restrict overseas shipments. Exceptions, in the form of **dumping**, do, however, occur.

UNITED STATES

In 1960 the United States produced about 334 million barrels of cement valued at more than 1 billion dollars. The industry in only three areas—the Great Lakes, Lehigh Valley, and Permanente, California—is presented here.

The Great Lakes Region. Nowhere in the cement industry is the factor of cheap water transportation with respect to raw materials and markets better illustrated than in the Great Lakes Region. Lakeside cement plants receive Michigan limestone, quarried on the Lake Huron side of the Lower Peninsula (Fig. 9-3) and delivered by lake vessel for less than $1 per ton. Usable local or nearby deposits of clay or shale are delivered by rail. Coal from the Appalachian and Eastern Interior Provinces is transported to the limestone at lake-

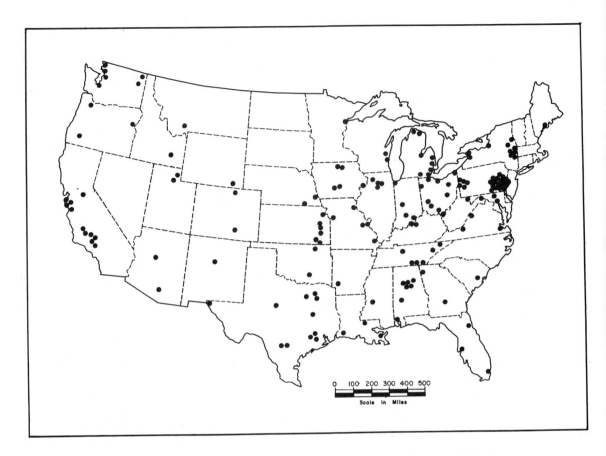

Fig. 9-3. *Distribution of cement plants in the United States. Each dot represents one plant. Though Pennsylvania's Lehigh Valley still is preeminent, the cement industry is widely dispersed—it is near its raw materials (limestone by all odds is the leading ingredient) and fuel and, particularly, near its market. Here is an industry distributed much as is the nation's population.*

side, partly by lake carrier and partly by rail. The supply of limestone and fuel also exerts great influence on cement-plant location.

Self-unloading vessels, carrying cement in bulk, haul their cargoes to large industrial centers strewn along the Great Lakes. The cement is stored in silos at the receiving ports and bagged for shipment by rail or truck to inland points.

The world's largest cement mill (capacity 12 million barrels per year) is believed to be at Alpena, Michigan. Its capacity is to be doubled. The largest cement plant ever constructed at one time was built at Dundee, Michigan, in the Detroit-Toledo corridor. There is presently danger of foreign compe-

tition via the St. Lawrence Seaway. Foreign labor costs are much lower than American costs.

The Lehigh Valley. The Lehigh Valley of northeastern Pennsylvania is America's oldest and the world's largest cement-producing region. Construction of the Lehigh Valley Railroad, requiring the blasting of deep cuts through the hills, exposed cement rock containing the essential ingredients—lime, silica, and alumina—for making natural cement; and the first mill was erected there in 1872. By 1900 this district manufactured nearly three fourths of the country's cement. Today the area's thirteen operating plants produce an-

Fig. 9-4. Cement plant at Permanente in the western foothills of the Santa Clara Valley near San Jose, California. In some years, this plant leads all United States plants in output. It has excellent-quality limestone at hand, ample and low-cost power, a large nearby market, and easy access to the port of Redwood City, whence cement may be shipped by water along the entire Pacific Coast. (Courtesy of Permanente Cement Company.)

nually about 50 million barrels of cement—15 per cent of the nation's total output.

The Lehigh district is favored not only by its large deposits of cement rock but also by cheap fuel and nearby markets along the Atlantic Seaboard.

Permanente, California. Henry Kaiser's Permanente Cement Company, located in the western foothills about 50 miles south of San Francisco, is one of the largest, most modern and efficient, and best-located cement plants in the world (Fig. 9-4). Limestone rock, the basic ingredient, is carried from the company's own quarry by conveyor belt to the producing plant, about a mile distant.

From twenty-seven storage silos, Permanente ships twelve different types of cement throughout Northern California by truck and rail, and to all parts of the globe by a fleet of Kaiser ships. Loading hoppers at the plant fill bulk trucks with 110 barrels of cement in less than ten minutes. Bulk cement moved by rail is loaded into cars from the storage silos. Cement for shipment by water carrier is transferred by bulk trucks to shoreside storage silos at Redwood City, a port on San Francisco Bay.

EURASIA

Although the industry is most common in industrialized countries in Eurasia, it is also found in nondeveloped ones. Immediately prior to World War II, the leading European countries in the manufacture of cement were Germany, Great Britain, the Soviet Union, Italy, France, and Belgium. Europe and the United States together normally produce about 80 per cent of the world output.

Soviet Union. Currently second in world output, the Soviet Union plans to rank first within a few years. The industry is centered in the Donets Basin, where a highly favorable combination exists: huge deposits of marl, good coal, and the best transport and market facilities in the country. The seat of the industry (seven plants in 1959) is the small town of Amvrosievka.

Japan. Japan has a sizable industry, ranking fourth in world output in 1960. Since the country is rich in widely scattered limestone deposits, its plants are well distributed throughout the four main islands, though Honshu has by far the largest number. Besides supplying its own market, Japan exports much cement throughout Eastern and Southeastern Asia.

Communist China. Communist China's cement industry, which ranked fifth among the nations of the world in 1960, is booming because so much of what the government contemplates accomplishing in the five-year plans depends on the growth and output of the vital cement industry. In 1959 there were thirty-two medium to large producing plants, scattered in various large cities and industrial centers—Canton, Nanking, Tangshan, Penki, Harbin, Lanchow, Livlienho, Peking, and Nanping, of which the last four were new. Eighteen more were under construction; one of these, a modern plant with a capacity of 14 million barrels per year, was completed in the early 1960s at Sian, Shensi Province, where extensive limestone deposits are present. Cement-making materials are plentiful, they are widely distributed, and they are of high quality.

LIME

Lime and limestone are not, as is generally believed, synonymous. Lime is calcium oxide (CaO), whereas limestone is lime carbonate ($CaCO_3$). Lime does not occur as such in the natural state but is man-made in kilns; limestone is calcined at a moderately high temperature to drive off the carbon dioxide (CO_2). Its manufacture is an ancient activity, many limestone outcrops in Europe still showing the quarries and lime pits of Roman or pre-Roman days. Lime was manufactured in the United States as early as 1661.

Lime has many uses, particularly in the chemical, building, and metallurgical industries. It is used by the building industry as an ingredient in making plaster, stucco, and mortar. It is employed in agriculture to correct acidity and soil **pH**, but its value along other lines is being pushed by scientists and agriculturists; for it aids soil organisms and nitrogen-fixing bacteria, promotes root development and moisture-holding ability of soil, and

improves soil structure and aeration. In short, lime on humid land soils helps crops help themselves.

Lime is produced in thirty-three of the American states, but Missouri and Pennsylvania contribute about 53 per cent of the total national output.

GYPSUM

Gypsum, a calcium sulfate compound, ranks near the top in importance among the nonmetallic minerals. Because of the growing popularity of prefabricated building materials, its consumption is soaring (three times now what it was in 1936). Moreover, gypsum enjoys versatility of use and low price. Thus, gypsum is used as plaster lath, wallboard, tile, stucco, and plaster of Paris, and as an ingredient in portland cement and fertilizer.

Gypsum deposits are widely distributed in the United States. Most of the larger ones lie west of the Mississippi River and hence are too far from major markets to be as yet commercial (gypsum is a low-value commodity). Transport costs loom large in the economics of gypsum. A gypsum-using plant should be as near the mine and important consuming markets as possible. Gypsum is present in many American states but is imported from conveniently located deposits in Canada (e.g., Hantsport, Nova Scotia) and Mexico. Principal gypsum-producing countries are the United Kingdom, Canada, Italy, Austria, and Japan.

SALT

Salt (sodium chloride or $NaCl$) is one of the more abundant commercial minerals, with at least 14,000 different uses. It is so abundant, widespread, and cheap that people in America, Europe, Australia, and New Zealand take it for granted, little realizing how precious an article it was to ancient mankind.

SOURCES OF SALT

Salt is recovered and used in both brine and solid form. The world oceans are an inex-

haustible source. However, economic geography and the requirements for chemical purity limit drastically the number of *commercial* sources. Salt is procured from (1) evaporation of sea water along desert coasts and on the lee sides of trade-wind islands; (2) extraction of brines from desert lakes or saline springs; and (3) the mining of separate beds or strata of rock salt which lie deep in the earth.

The two largest rock-salt mines in the world are operated at Retsof, New York, and Detroit, Michigan.[2] Rock salt may be mined by

shaft and tunnel (Fig. 9-5), or it may be extracted by drilling down to the salt deposit, to which water is sent via an outer casing, permitting the water to absorb the salt into a heavy brine, then forcing the brine to the surface by compressed air and evaporating it at the surface.

When sea water is used for producing salt, the water is passed through a series of evaporating ponds in which, by action of the sun and wind, it is evaporated to the point of saturation with respect to the sodium chloride. To obtain the maximum advantage of mechanical action, a single works should contain at least 1,000 acres of flat land. The south end of San Francisco Bay, California, has all necessary conditions, including a large market (Fig. 9-6).

[2] Every civilized person knows that Detroit is capital of the world's motor industry. Few, however, realize that it is also a salt city—that beneath Detroit exists a subcity of salt caverns and castle halls.

Fig. 9-6. Salt-evaporating ponds, San Francisco Bay, California. Through a system of dikes, sea water is collected into huge ponds, some as large as 800 acres. The sun and wind cause evaporation. But sea water contains, in addition to salt, a considerable amount of undesirable calcium sulfate. In the large evaporation ponds, the calcium sulfate is the first to crystallize and settle to the bottom. Meanwhile, the sea water is increased in salt content from 3 to 25 per cent. (Courtesy of Leslie Salt Company.)

WORLD SALT PRODUCTION

Almost all countries produce salt, but seven together contribute about 80 per cent of the world output: the United States, the Soviet Union, China, France, the United Kingdom, West Germany, and India. Of these, the United States leads by far, contributing about one third of the total.

UNITED STATES

In the United States, salt is mined or recovered in some ninety widely distributed facilities, chief of which are (1) the Northeast (which extends from central New York westward through Ohio into Michigan), (2) the midcontinent—chiefly in Kansas, (3) the Gulf Coast of Texas and Louisiana, (4) the Intermontane—at Great Salt Lake, and (5) San Francisco Bay in California. Every known method of extraction is employed somewhere in the nation. The chief use is in the manufacture of chemicals, with feeding livestock second, and household uses third.

COMMUNIST CHINA

Ranking second in the world as a salt producer, China uses most of her salt for food purposes; but industrial consumption for the making of chemicals is gradually increasing. Most of the salt is produced by evaporation of sea water in coastal provinces; the largest fields are situated in Hopeh and Liaoning. In addition, the inland areas of the northwest have numerous salt lakes; and salt wells are located in Szechwan, close to recently discovered oil and gas fields.

SOVIET UNION

The Soviet Union, which produces about 10 per cent of the world's supply of salt, obtains approximately half of it from rock salt and half from natural brines connected with the deposits. Lake Baskunchak on the Lower Volga, a leading producer, has a salt stratum 130 feet thick. The common salt deposits of the Solikamsk-Berezniki area on the Kama River were exploited as early as the fifteenth century. The development of new areas has led to new sources of salt. As is true of many Russian industries, poor transportation is a limiting factor.

SULFUR

Sulfur, one of man's most important non-metallic minerals, has a history that reaches far back into antiquity. Although an estimated 0.06 per cent of the weight of the earth's crust consists of sulfur, only an exceedingly small portion of it occurs in sufficient amount and concentration to justify mining. The principal potential sources are (1) native sulfur; (2) pyrites—a group term applied to various metallic sulfides, though its actual usage is largely limited in the sulfur industry to the iron sulfides; (3) metallic sulfide ores; and (4) the mineral fuels—coal and petroleum gases. Actually, however, most of the world's sulfur is produced only from native sulfur and pyrites. Around 1900, Herman Frasch developed a process, now known as the Frasch process, for mining native sulfur economically with hot water. Today the bulk of the world output consists of native sulfur, because of its much lower cost. However, under certain local conditions competitive materials are used within a few hundred miles of the source—e.g., acid recovered from gases at metallic sulfide smelters.

USES OF SULFUR

Sulfur has manifold uses—for instance, in the textile, fertilizer, paint, iron and steel, chemical, explosives, rubber, and insecticide and pesticide industries. The largest single user (more than one third of the total) is the chemical-fertilizer industry. Sulfur occupies a dominant position as a raw material mainly because it can be converted into sulfuric acid—a low-priced product having innumerable uses. More than three fourths of all the sulfur used in the United States is converted into sulfuric acid.

WORLD SULFUR PRODUCTION

Most of the world's sulfur is produced in a relatively small number of countries: the United States, Mexico, Italy, Japan, Argentina, and Chile.

UNITED STATES

The world's principal sulfur-mining region is coastal Texas and Louisiana. This area has a combination of characteristics favorable for sulfur mining: (1) enormous reserves; (2) high quality; (3) location near tidewater; (4) low cost of mining (Frasch process); (5) impervious strata above and below the sulfur deposits, which permit maintenance of the necessary water temperatures and pressure; and (6) abundant supply of petroleum and natural gas.

The United States contributes about 7 per cent of the total world production of pyrites and 90 per cent of the world output of native sulfur; it produces roughly about half the world total of all forms of sulfur.

When sulfur occurs in the caprock of salt domes, the Frasch process of exploitation is employed. Not all domes contain deposits of commercial value. In fact, few do. Thus, whereas more than two hundred salt domes are known in the United States, only about two dozen have been brought into production. The drilling for petroleum and natural gas in the tidelands of the Gulf of Mexico is adding to the number of known sulfur deposits.

The sulfur-bearing zone of a typical commercial sulfur deposit may be about 100 feet thick and contain about 20 per cent sulfur. The sulfur is mined easily and economically by melting with steam (Fig. 9-7). The molten sulfur then is either pumped into vats, where it cools, or moves via pipeline. The monolithic blocks are later attacked by power shovels, and the sulfur is loaded into railroad cars (Fig. 9-8).

MEXICO

Mexico today ranks second among world sulfur producers. Its deposits, located on the Isthmus of Tehuantepec, are similar geologically to those of Texas and Louisiana. American capital and technical skills are heavily invested.

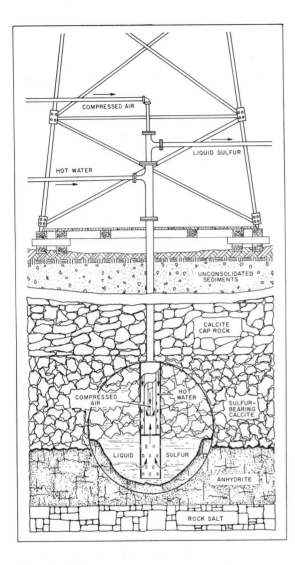

Fig. 9-7. How sulfur is removed from depths of 500 to 1,500 feet in Louisiana and Texas. Mining is relatively simple: since the melting point of sulfur is low (246°F), superheated water is used to melt it; and an air lift then brings it in molten form to the surface, where it is pumped into enormous vats to cool and solidify. (Courtesy of Texas Gulf Sulphur Company, Inc.)

Because taxes are low, and a day's wage only approximates the average hourly wage in the United States, Mexico has a substantial competitive advantage over the United States. Mexico's rapid rise in the sulfur world has resulted partially from the heavy production in the United States and the foreseeable exhaustion of its sulfur deposits. Mexico itself consumes less than 100,000 tons annually; but it produces more than 1 million tons, and it could supply 1.5 million tons should world demand and market permit. The bulk of the output is presently exported to the United States (60 per cent), France, the United Kingdom, and Australia.

JAPAN

Japan is the leading sulfur producer in the Far East and one of the foremost producers of pyrites in the world. The country is self-sufficient in sulfur and pyrites, with reserves of 36 million tons of sulfur and 120 million tons of pyrites. Chief centers of production are on the islands of Honshu and Shikoku.

ITALY

Italy ranks fourth among world producers. South-central Sicily is the major Italian source of native sulfur. The sulfur occurs in limestone deposits and is recovered by heating the rock material and then condensing the vapor.

SOVIET UNION

The annual production from about twenty sulfur mines is estimated at about 120,000 tons, compared with 8,000 tons prior to World War II. Among the sulfurous deposits are the iron and copper pyrites in the Urals and Central Asia. Important sulfur deposits occur in the Kara Kum Desert (250 miles east of the Caspian Sea), on the Kerch Peninsula, and in the Ferghana Valley, where they furnish the basis for a local chemical industry. Sulfur deposits have also been discovered in the Kurile Islands and in the Kamchatka Peninsula. A new deposit, up to 33 feet in thickness, is being mined by the open-cast (open-pit) method in the Drogobych area of the Ukraine.

Fig. 9-8. Vats of sulfur with the sides and ends (often of sheet metal) removed. Each vat is about 1,200 feet long, 175 wide, and 50 high. When filled, each vat contains about ½ million tons of sulfur. An increasing proportion of sulfur is currently being transported in liquid form. (Courtesy of Texas Gulf Sulphur Company, Inc.)

INDUSTRIAL DIAMONDS

Diamonds have been prized and sought by man since antiquity, but their use as an industrial raw material has come about only since their extraordinary utility as an abrasive became recognized and appreciated. As either the hardest or one of the two hardest substances known, the industrial diamond is an indispensable commercial mineral, being used for cutting tools, abrasive wheels, drills and boring heads, and glass cutters. Without the industrial diamond there would be no jet aircraft, guided missiles, tanks, or electronic equipment.

Industrial diamonds are produced almost entirely (99 per cent) in Africa (Congo, South Africa, Ghana, Angola, South West Africa) and South America (Brazil, British Guiana, and Venezuela). The largest single producer is the Congo with 72 per cent. In South America, the state of Bahía, Brazil, produces *carbonados* (black diamonds), the hardest and toughest variety of industrial diamond.

The Soviet Union was dependent on Africa for industrial diamonds until the 1950s, at which time it announced discovery of the stones in six districts in Yakutia. The principal district is the Mir, located between the Lena River and the Vilyuy River. Both open-pit and underground mining methods are used. Major deterrents to diamond mining in Yakutia are (1) complete lack of railroads and roads suitable for wheel traffic, (2) remoteness of the diamond-mining districts from navigable rivers, (3) only partial navigability of rivers (usable only at flood period), and (4) presence of **permafrost** (its thickness in the Mir **kimberlite pipe** is about 1,137 feet).

Industrial diamonds are procured from two types of deposits: pipes and **placers**. Ninety per cent of all African production and the entire output elsewhere is from placers (in South Africa only one pipe out of twenty or forty is a diamond ore). In the more productive districts of the Congo, the method of mining followed is to strip off the topsoil with bulldozers and wheel scrapers and then treat the diamond-bearing gravels in washing plants.

To meet industrial requirements, diamonds are employed in three main forms: (1) in rough, uncut, unpolished state; (2) in cut and polished state but with some particular shape; and (3) in the form of grit or powder called *bort,* which accumulates in all diamond-cutting centers.

More than three fourths of the bort and powder is consumed in making diamond grinding wheels for sharpening cemented carbide tools, rock drills, and wheels for cutting concrete and stone. Diamond bits are used for exploratory core drilling, quarrying, and drilling blast holes and oil wells.

Ever since 1797, when scientists learned that the diamond is elemental carbon, attempts have been made to produce synthetic diamonds. This presented a formidable challenge, for it meant duplication of natural conditions 240 miles below the earth's surface (a pressure of $1\frac{1}{2}$ million pounds per square inch and a temperature of $5000°F$). But man has succeeded in making synthetic diamonds, though they cost more than the natural stones.

SELECTED REFERENCES

Ladoo, R. B., and W. M. Myers. *Non-Metallic Minerals,* 2nd ed. New York, McGraw-Hill Book Company, Inc., 1951.

Lundy, W. T. "Known and Potential Sulphur Resources of the World," *Industrial and Engineering Chemistry,* 42:2199-2201, November 1950.

"1,100 Feet under Detroit," *Business Week,* January 6, 1951, pp. 38-39.

President's Materials Policy Commission. *Resources for Freedom.* Washington, D. C., June 1952. Vol. 2, *Outlook for Key Commodities.*

Rymarcewicz, H. "Cement Production in the Communist Countries" (map), *Pit and Quarry,* 51:98-101, April 1959.

U.S. Bureau of Mines. *Mineral Facts and Problems.* Washington, D. C., 1956, Bulletin 556.

Wang, K. P. "Rich Mineral Resources Spur Communist China's Bid for Industrial Power," *Mineral Trade Notes,* Supplement No. 59, 50:33-35 (nonmetals), March 1960.

THE WORLD'S

PART THREE : :

INDUSTRIES

CHAPTER TEN::

Steel is indispensable to modern civilization; its abundance, cheapness, and versatility of use are all-important. It is the cheapest and the most plentiful of the metals man uses. In twenty days, the steel industry can produce as much tonnage as the combined production of aluminum, magnesium, copper, lead, zinc, and tin in an entire year; and the price per pound is but a fraction of that of the others. Among the metals iron accounts for more than 90 per cent of the world tonnage, a situation that promises to continue far into the future.

A nation's steel capacity foretells to an amazing degree its destiny, for no other one item is so effective an index of a nation's ability to care for itself in both peace and war. Moreover, steel is a "seed industry"—one from which a long list of allied industries springs. Lacking steel, no country can aspire to become a "heavyweight" power. The fact that

THE WORLD'S IRON

at least 90 per cent of the steel capacity of the world is concentrated among a half-dozen nations is extremely significant in international relations.

EARLY DEVELOPMENT OF IRON

There is no conclusive evidence of when the first iron was extracted from iron ore, but it is known that the metal was used before the dawn of history. In recorded history, almost all ancient civilizations employed forms of iron for tools and weapons.

The first blast furnaces in most parts of the world, including England, China, and the United States, used charcoal for fuel. But as the drain on the forests outstripped natural growth, concern arose regarding the future supply of hardwood for shipbuilding and other purposes. In England, the close association of iron ore and coal led to experimentation in the substitution for charcoal of coal and later of coke. This new fuel also provided increased blast-furnace efficiency, and by 1865 England's annual output exceeded that of the rest of the world combined. In the United States, iron was first produced in colonial Virginia and Massachusetts. Since that time production has expanded rapidly, until today the United States leads all other nations in output of iron and steel.

FACTORS GOVERNING LOCATION

Three major factors govern the ideal location of plants for the production of iron and steel:

AND STEEL INDUSTRIES

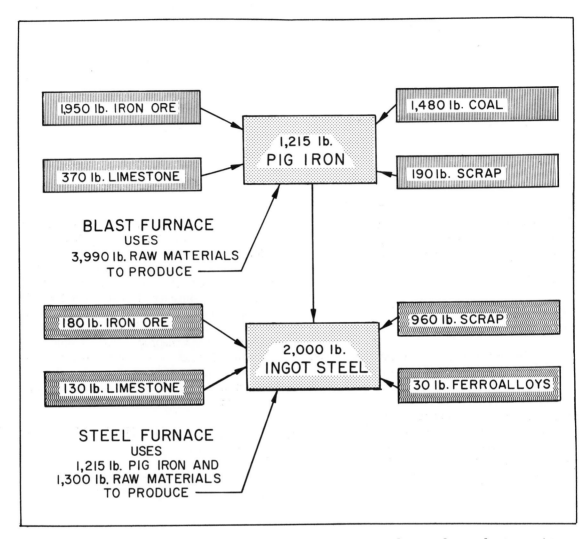

Fig. 10-1. A total of 5,290 pounds of raw materials is used to make 1 ton of ingot steel. (Courtesy of American Iron and Steel Institute.)

1. The cost of assembling raw materials.

2. The cost of converting raw materials into finished products.

3. The cost of transporting finished products to points of consumption. This factor, known as the *market factor*, is usually regarded as more important than either of the other two, but less important than the other two combined.

These same factors are of importance to almost every manufacturing operation, but they are particularly significant in the heavy indus-

tries such as iron and steel. Wherever any two of the three locative factors coincide in the same area, there an iron and steel area tends to spring up, provided only that the other be available at not too great a distance and that there be no special and insurmountable difficulties with respect to so-called minor locative factors.

ASSEMBLY OF RAW MATERIALS

In the United States about 3 net tons of raw materials ordinarily are used to make 1 ton of pig iron, and 5,290 pounds of raw materials are used to make 1 ton of ingot steel (Fig. 10-1). The assembling of ore, coke, and limestone is one of the most perplexing and expensive tasks confronting the industry; in fact, transportation is a major item in the total laid-down cost of steel.

COAL

In the United States, the metallurgical industry has from its inception felt the compelling influence of fuel—first charcoal, then anthracite, and now coke.

The iron and steel industry is frequently located in or reasonably near the coal fields, though there are important exceptions. The main reason for this (at least in the United States) appears to be that the largest markets for the greatest number of steel products are relatively near the coal fields.

IRON ORE

Since this industry requires greater quantities of iron ore than of coal,[1] one might expect coal to move to iron ore rather than vice versa. In the United States, however, the iron ore moves to the coal, mainly because secondary steel industries and principal steel markets are in or near coal fields: the Great Lakes penetrate interior North America for 1,700 miles and bring a wide area geographically and economically close to the mines of the Lake Superior area; also, the St. Lawrence River permits Labrador-Quebec iron ore and even ore from Venezuela, Brazil, Liberia, Peru, and Chile to reach ports and furnaces on the Lower Great Lakes. Hence, Upper Great Lakes and foreign iron ore moves to coal.

SCRAP

Scrap rivals iron ore as a raw material. More than 65 million tons have been used in a single year in American furnaces. If it were not for scrap (the usual furnace mixture or *charge* is half pig iron and half scrap), the reserves of coal, iron ore, and limestone would be short-lived indeed. Each ton of scrap used

[1] One ton of coking coal yields approximately 1,500 pounds of coke, and 1½ tons of coal make the coke needed to produce a ton of pig iron.

means a saving of 3½ to 4 tons of raw material—iron ore, coal, and limestone—from which comes 1 ton of pig iron.

Scrap metal originates wherever iron and steel are used. The biggest producers are the mills where the steel is made. Other sources are railroads, railroad equipment builders, automobile manufacturers, machine shops, shipyards, the oil industry, automobile graveyards, United States-owned equipment in foreign war theaters, and castoff items of city and farm families. In general, the profitable collection of scrap is limited to a distance of 300 miles from market.

LIMESTONE

Limestone is used as a **flux** to "draw" most of the alumina, manganese, sulfur, and other ingredients (except phosphorus) out of the molten iron. Fortunately, limestone is so widely distributed and is utilized in such small quantities in the furnace that *it never determines the location of the industry.*

THE MARKET FACTOR

In recent years markets have been the most impelling locative factor. Steel is used primarily to make machinery of all kinds, and the cardinal locative factor for machinery manufacture (because of the weight and bulk of most machines) is nearness to market. Freight rates play an important role. Hence, even if a plant assembles its raw materials economically, it will definitely be handicapped if obliged to ship its steel great distances.

MINOR FACTORS

In addition to the major factors, several minor ones contribute to the localization of the industry.

LABOR

Some students of iron and steel regard labor as a major location factor. It is true that the cost of labor accounts for 75 to 80 per cent of the costs involved in the entire production process; but since labor is mobile and wages are much the same throughout a given country, it can scarcely be considered a major location factor.

Often an old, well-established company, which started with what appeared to be an abundance of room, suddenly finds itself cramped. Unable or unwilling to purchase additional land at what it considers an inflated price, it migrates. In Pittsburgh, some of the steel companies, finding themselves hedged in by a river, steep hills, railroads, and neighboring plants, moved from the city, locating along the Ohio River—40 or more miles distant. In some suburbs, small towns, or rural areas, where land values are low, a company can afford to purchase several times as much land as it currently needs. This is the tendency today. Much land is needed in this industry because the work is done in single-story buildings.

WATER

Because the iron and steel industry uses large quantities of water, in most instances its mills are located on the shore of a lake or the bank of a river. In 1953 the iron and steel industry used an estimated 12 billion gallons of water daily.

The production of a ton of finished steel may, in an area with plenty of water, require as many as 65,000 gallons of water for cooling, washing gas, operating hydraulic machinery, and other purposes. Mills at Fontana, California, being situated on neither lake nor river, in an area with a desertic summer, must employ ingenious methods of conserving water. They do this by recooling and by recirculating the water forty or fifty times before it finally evaporates and has to be replaced. Instead of the 65,000 gallons used by the Chicago–Gary district, Fontana uses only 1,400 gallons.

IRON-ORE REDUCTION

Since iron, the most important of all the metals, is seldom found in a metallic condition in nature (except as meteorites), man obtains it by separating the metallic iron in the ore from the gangue or earthy material which constitutes the balance of the ore. To separate iron from gangue, he first **beneficiates** the ore and then reduces it in a blast furnace (Fig. 10-2).

THE BLAST FURNACE

The job of the blast furnace is to liberate iron from the ore. The furnace of today consists of a tall, cylindrical, brick-lined metal structure 90 to 100 feet high; powerful blowing engines to provide the blast; and four stoves for preheating the blast before it enters the furnace. Iron ore, coke, and limestone are dumped into the furnace at the top, and hot metal is tapped at the bottom. Heated dry air enters the furnace from the bottom, intensifying the heat of the burning coke and causing the iron in the ore to melt more quickly. The limestone serves as a flux and combines with some of the waste in the ore to become a fusible slag, which remains above the molten iron.

Blast furnaces are both expensive (a new blast-furnace complex with supporting coke ovens costs up to 50 million dollars) and inefficient. Currently, therefore, there is almost universal interest in by-passing the traditional blast furnace; that is, in producing iron without it. Almost every major steel manufacturer is conducting research along this line. At present, however, the blast furnace still does the job better than any other device.

COKE IN THE MANUFACTURE OF PIG IRON

In order to make pig iron, coal—one of the three raw materials—first must be converted into coke; that is, coal is heated in closed retorts, where the volatile matter is driven off as vapor, and the coke is left as hard lumps of almost pure carbon. Coke is the most satisfactory blast-furnace fuel because:

1. It is strong enough to sustain the heavy burden of 1,500 tons or more of the load in the furnace; a less hard fuel would be crushed.

2. It is porous, permitting the hot blast to permeate it freely.

3. It is almost pure carbon (88 per cent) and hence burns with little ash.

The discovery that coal, in the manufactured form of coke, could replace charcoal as

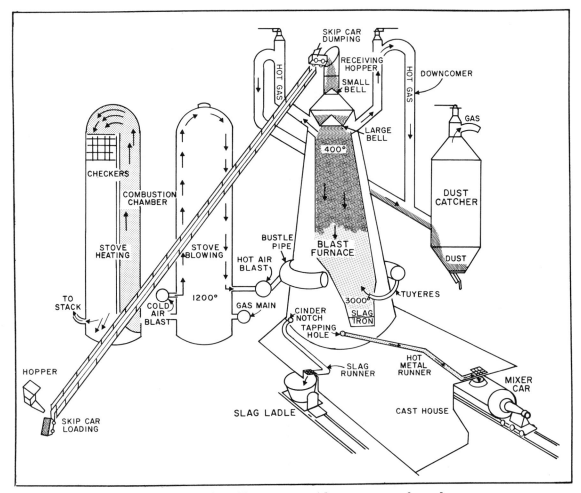

Fig. 10-2. Cross section of a modern blast furnace. The raw materials—coke, iron ore, and limestone—are charged into the furnace from the top, carried by cars on the skip hoist. As the cars charge the furnace, heat from the coke burning under forced draft reduces the ore to molten iron; the iron, being heavy, sinks to the bottom of the furnace, where it is drawn off at regular intervals and run into a mixer car. This molten iron is usually delivered immediately to furnaces for conversion into steel. Lighter impurities combine with the melting limestone and float as slag above. (Courtesy of Iron and Steel Institute.)

a fuel revolutionized the industry; for coking coal was abundant, efficient, and economical. However, an innovation in pig-iron production is the injection of coke-oven gas or natural gas in the air stream for reducing coke requirements, speeding ore reduction, and increasing iron output by as much as 10 per cent. Natural gas is considerably cheaper than coke in several metallurgical centers.

METHODS OF MAKING STEEL

Steel—which is really refined iron—is made in several ways, three of which are presented briefly: (1) in the Bessemer converter, (2) in the open-hearth furnace, and (3) in the electric furnace.

THE WORLD'S IRON AND STEEL INDUSTRIES::177

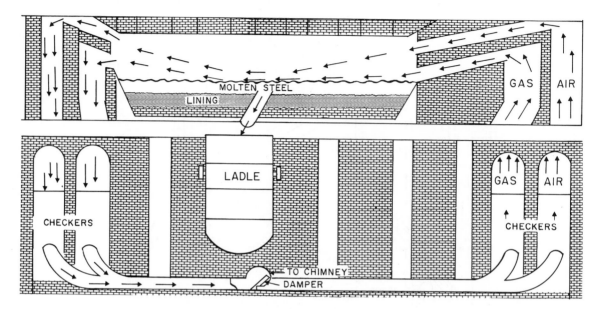

Fig. 10-3. *The open-hearth furnace, which accounts for about 90 per cent of the total United States output of steel. Molten iron is placed in the furnace with scrap steel and alloys, and exposed to gas flame. As the mixture "cooks," many impurities are burned out. (Courtesy of American Steel and Wire Company.)*

THE BESSEMER CONVERTER

The Bessemer converter, invented about 1855 simultaneously in Great Britain and in the United States, sharply reduced the cost of making steel. It is essentially a large, oval-shaped vessel, lined with refractory brick. Molten pig iron is charged into it, and perforations in the bottom of the vessel permit air to be blown through the metal to burn out the carbon and other impurities. At the end of the blow, the purified metal is poured into a ladle; and a measured amount of ferromanganese, carbon, or spiegeleisen is added to degasify the metal, which is then poured into molds for making ingots. The primary advantage of the Bessemer process is that it can produce steel *rapidly* and at *low cost*; however, partly because it can be used only by men who have a high degree of practical knowledge and skill, Bessemer steel comprises only about 2 per cent of the current American ingot tonnage.

Notable improvements have been made recently in the classical Bessemer method of making steel. The so-called L-D process, developed in Austria and based on top blowing with pure oxygen, accounted for more than 16 million of the world's 377 million tons of steel in 1960.

THE OPEN-HEARTH FURNACE

Most of the steel produced in the United States today (almost 90 per cent) is made in the open-hearth furnace (Fig. 10-3).

Pig iron (molten or cold) and scrap are fed into the furnace for melting down. Iron ore and limestone are added; and chemical reactions take place, during which the impurities are removed from the steel. The undesired elements are really burned out by a flame playing over the liquid metal. Some impurities accumulate as scum on the slag at the top of the melt. Various alloying agents, such as vanadium, molybdenum, nickel, tungsten, chromium, and manganese, are added in small amounts, depending upon the ultimate use to which the steel is to be put.

In this process, as compared with the Bessemer process, a greater variety of raw materials —including scrap and ores containing 1 and 2 per cent phosphorus—may be used. It is a costlier process than the Bessemer, and it requires much more time—eight to fifteen hours as opposed to ten or thirty minutes. But it has the advantage of making from 50 to 400 tons instead of 15 to 30, and it allows such close control of the reactions that the content is definitely known and the product may be warranted.

The open-hearth furnace is being improved and made more efficient by design and by use of oxygen through roof jets. The result is a substantial reduction in the time required to produce a "heat of steel" (five versus nine hours), reduced fuel consumption (less than half that required in non-oxygen practice), and increased ingot tonnages.

THE ELECTRIC FURNACE

The electric furnace has been used in the United States only since 1906. It is employed principally for the production of high-grade steels, mainly **alloy steels**. Stainless and heat-resisting steels—the so-called "aristocrats of steel"—are made exclusively in electric furnaces. The steel industry has been steadily expanding its electric-furnace capacity because of the increasing demand for high-grade steels. About 9 per cent of all the crude steel produced in the United States is made in electric furnaces.

WORLD IRON AND STEEL PRODUCTION

UNITED STATES

The United States is the world's leading producer and consumer of iron and steel (Table 10-1). Because of the high standard of living, the almost complete mechanization of its farms, the size and nature of its industries, and its highly mechanized transport, there is a very large home market for steel. The nation ranks first in per capita steelmaking capacity (Fig. 10-4) and in per capita steel consumption: 1,232 pounds (1956), compared with 847 pounds for the Soviet Union, in

TABLE 10-1

WORLD STEEL OUTPUT 1960

Country	Million Net Tons
United States	99.2
Soviet Union	71.7
West Germany	33.6
United Kingdom	27.1
Japan	22.4
China	20.2
France	18.9
Italy	9.0
Belgium	8.1
Czechoslovakia	7.7
Poland	7.0
Canada	6.1
Luxembourg	4.5
Australia	4.0
East Germany	4.0
Austria	3.4
India	3.4
Sweden	3.3

SOURCE: *Iron Age*, 187:224, January 5, 1961.

second place; 481 pounds for West Germany, in third place; and 20 pounds for India, in eighteenth place. The presence of abundant reserves of coal and iron ore, along with their high quality and favorable location with respect to each other and to major markets, has meant much to the nation.

America's iron and steel industry has been the most truly basic of the national industries; upon it and its products, at least in some degree, has rested nearly every other activity.

This industry in 1958 represented an aggregate investment of about 12.5 billion dollars and gave employment to approximately 420,-000 persons. It is an economic factor of importance in the more than 250 communities in which it operates.

Figure 10-5, showing the location of the iron and steel industry in the United States, indicates the wide distribution, though the greatest concentration (87 per cent of the capacity) is in the American Manufacturing Region (Fig. 10-6). Table 10-2 shows steel capacity of districts and centers presented, along with their increase in tons and by percentage from 1948 to 1959.

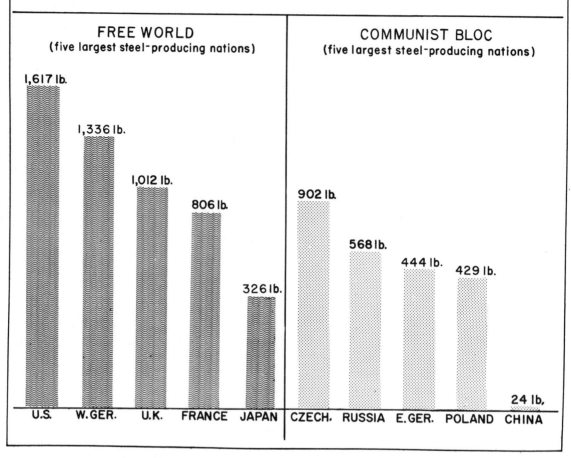

Fig. 10-4. *Better than words, these graphs show the progress of the two leading global ideologies—the Free World and the Communist bloc—and particularly of the leading countries—the United States and the Soviet Union. Figures are based on United Nations' steel-capacity figures and July 1958 population estimates. (Courtesy of American Iron and Steel Institute.)*

THE PITTSBURGH-YOUNGSTOWN AREA

This area vies with the Ruhr of Germany for preeminence in iron and steel manufacture. It includes (1) the Pittsburgh district, consisting of plants located in the valleys of the Ohio, Monongahela, and Allegheny Rivers, within 40 miles of their common center at Pittsburgh, and (2) the Youngstown or "Valley" district, comprising plants in the Shenango and Mahoning River Valleys, near

their junction in both Ohio and Pennsylvania —all within 30 miles of Youngstown. The center at Johnstown also may be included in this district.

Pittsburgh. Pittsburgh became the leading iron and steel center because of the following combination of advantages:

1. Momentum of an early start.
2. Access to local ores; later, when Lake

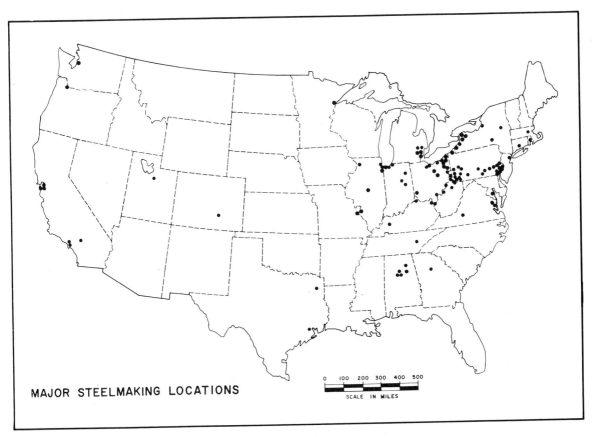

Fig. 10-5. Distribution of the iron and steel industry in the United States, 1960. Of the many points brought out on the map, the most vivid one is the great concentration of the industry in the American Manufacturing Region. (Based on data from Directory of Iron and Steel Works of the United States and Canada.)

MAJOR STEELMAKING LOCATIONS

0 100 200 300 400 500
SCALE IN MILES

Superior iron ore became available, it too was accessible via the Great Lakes.

3. Proximity and easy access to enormous reserves of high-grade coking coal.

4. Excellent river and railway transport facilities.

5. Large local, nearby, and distant markets —parts of all accessible by river barge.

6. A large water supply.

7. A huge pool of skilled, semiskilled, and unskilled labor.

8. The ability to compete on a nationwide basis as a result of **Pittsburgh Plus** and, later, the **multiple-basing-point system.**

Pittsburgh early became important because of its favorable geographic position, which facilitated the assembly of raw and partially worked materials. The industry first became integrated here, where Connellsville coke could be used with high-grade Lake Superior ore (local ore was used in the beginning).

Pittsburgh has maintained its position for more than a century. In the total raw-materials cost for making a ton of pig iron, Pittsburgh seems to have a slight advantage over some of the other districts using Lake ore (Table 10-3).[2] The further steel products

[2] Statistics of the type presented in Table 10-3 are difficult to obtain. Obviously they change from year to year. Their real value in economic geography is not so much their absolute timeliness as the comparative costs in the several districts. These will vary only slightly, if at all, from year to year, or even over a period of years.

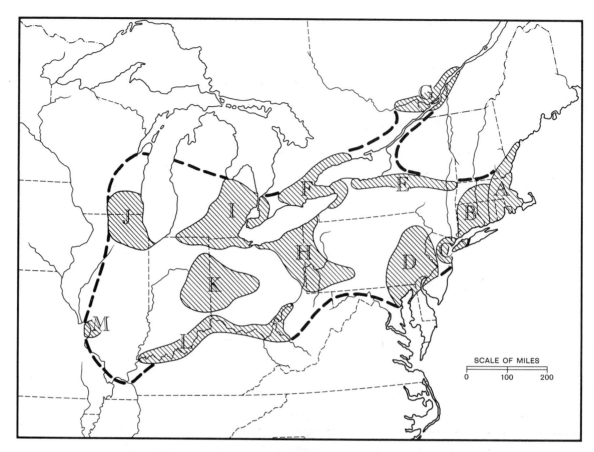

Fig. 10-6. *American Manufacturing Region. Principal manufacturing districts are (A) southeastern New England; (B) southwestern New England; (C) metropolitan New York; (D) Philadelphia-Baltimore district; (E) Central New York; (F) Niagara Frontier; (G) Middle St. Lawrence district; (H) Pittsburgh-Cleveland district; (I) southern Michigan automotive district; (J) Chicago-Milwaukee district; (K) Inland Ohio–Indiana; (L) Middle Ohio Valley; (M) St. Louis. (From C. Langdon White, Edwin J. Foscue, and Tom L. McKnight,* Regional Geography of Anglo-America, 1964, *published by permission of Prentice-Hall, Inc.)*

are processed, the more fuel is required and the greater becomes Pittsburgh's relative advantage over rival districts by reason of its cheap coal.

For several decades authorities prophesied that Chicago-Gary would displace Pittsburgh as the capital of the industry; and recently this happened. However, if the Pittsburgh-Youngstown district is considered as a unit, as it is by the American Iron and Steel Institute and which seems as fair as taking Chicago-Gary as a unit, then the Pittsburgh district still ranks first. Nevertheless, the center of gravity of the steel industry continues to shift steadily westward, and Pittsburgh *per se* is no longer the hub.

Youngstown. This is one of the nation's leading steel districts; its plants line the Mahoning River for approximately 10 miles. Nowhere else in North America is the local importance of this basic industry so great; more steel is turned out within Youngstown's city limits than in any other city in the world. Nonetheless, for a long time Youngstown has been slipping—a consequence largely of its *landlocked location.* Railroad transportation of both coal and iron ore is so expensive in

TABLE 10-2

STEEL CAPACITY FOR SELECTED DISTRICTS
OR CENTERS IN THE UNITED STATES

District or Center	Capacity (thousand net tons) 1948	1959	Percentage increase 1948-1959
Pittsburgh	14,734	18,345	24.5
Youngstown	8,932	11,155	24.9
Johnstown	1,924	2,425	26.0
Wheeling	336	336	0
Chicago	17,420	26,970	54.8
Cleveland	2,340	5,435	132.3
Lorain	1,884	2,648	40.6
Buffalo	4,131	7,200	74.3
Detroit	3,473	7,942	128.7
Duluth	690	973	41.0
Sparrows Point	4,746	8,382	76.6
Morrisville		2,687	new
Middletown	972	2,557	35.1
Birmingham	2,910	4,178	43.6
Houston	560	1,343	139.8
Pueblo	1,272	1,800	41.5
Geneva	1,283	2,300	79.3
Fontana	870	2,933	237.1

SOURCE: *Economic Geography*, 37:99-100, April 1961.

TABLE 10-3

RAW-MATERIALS COST FOR SELECTED DISTRICTS, 1950

	Ore			Coal			Stone			
	Lbs. per net ton pig iron	Cost of mining & benefi-ciation	Cost of trans-por-tation	Lbs. per net ton pig iron	Cost of mining & prepa-ration	Cost of trans-porta-tion	Lbs. per net ton pig iron	Cost of quarry-ing & prepa-ration	Cost of trans-porta-tion	Total raw-materials cost per net ton pig iron
Birmingham	5400	$8.97	$0.94	3700	$12.43	$0.74	500	$0.13	$0.16	$23.37
Chicago-Gary	4032	4.46	4.55	2350	7.14	5.02	1000	0.24	0.37	21.78
Duluth	4100	5.82	1.98	2460	6.82	4.55	1154	0.28	0.43	19.88
Fontana, Calif.	3255	2.19	2.29	2554	5.86	7.25	556	0.27	0.37	18.23
Geneva, Utah	3780	3.41	3.46	2880	6.12	3.28	918	0.23	0.40	16.90
Pittsburgh	4032	4.29	8.23	2485	7.16	0.78	1000	0.24	0.68	21.38
Sparrows Point	3580	3.39	6.90	2245	4.44	4.33	852	0.21	0.55	19.82

SOURCE: Marvin J. Barloon, "The Expansion of Blast Furnace Capacity,
1938-52," *Business History Review*, 28:17, March 1954.

comparison with water movement that distributing and assembling costs rise sharply as soon as these commodities are transferred to railroad cars. Youngstown long has unsuccessfully urged the United States government to link the Ohio River with Lake Erie by canalizing the Beaver, Mahoning, and Shenango Rivers, which would enable it to benefit from water transportation and compete more favorably with Pittsburgh and the Lower Lake districts.

Johnstown. Johnstown, in the maturely dissected Allegheny Plateau, lies about 60 miles east of Pittsburgh on the principal transport route to the Atlantic Coast. It is strategically situated at the confluence of two major tributaries of the Conemaugh River. Here the streams have cut through rich beds of bituminous coal, thereby stimulating coal mining and contributing to the development of the iron and steel industry. Some of the mines are so close that the coal goes by mine car directly to coke ovens adjacent to the steel plant. Paucity of level land has forced the city to grow up partly on valley floors and partly on the upland, but all the mills are located in the valley.

THE CHICAGO-GARY DISTRICT

This district is located at the foot of Lake Michigan, where major routes from the east and west converge. It was inevitable that a city so located would become a great transportation and industrial center.

Though iron and steel manufacture began as early as 1857, the industry amounted to little until the city became the world's leading rail center. The railways created an enormous demand for iron and steel.

Chicago's location is ideal for unloading iron ore from lake carrier to blast furnace. Coal is brought mainly from eastern Kentucky and West Virginia (Appalachian Province) but also from central and southern Illinois and adjacent Indiana (Eastern Interior Province). When the high-quality coal from the former is mixed with the lower-quality fuel from the latter, suitable coke can be produced. Limestone is obtained close by or from the state of Michigan.

The Chicago-Gary district differs from the Pittsburgh district in lying far from both its ore and coal; yet most authorities consider it the most scientifically located district in the Western Hemisphere; for here iron ore, coking coal, and flux meet the center of steel consumption. It is the best *balanced* of all districts as between production and consumption. Although not a single American steel center combines *all the ideal location factors,* this district undoubtedly comes closest to doing so.

Additional comment must be made regarding Gary, for it alone among the earlier metallurgical centers exemplifies *scientific planning.* In 1907 the United States Steel Corporation needed a new plant to serve the rapidly growing Midwestern market. What is now Gary was then an area of sand dunes and swamps. Its intermediate location between the northern Appalachian coal field and Lake Superior iron-ore deposits was nearly ideal. Its location with respect to markets was unsurpassed. Near enough to deal conveniently with Chicago's manufacturers, it was at the same time far enough away to escape high land values and high taxes. Labor was plentiful. Cold, clean water of good quality was available from Lake Michigan. The terrain was level, and there was plenty of room for industrial and residential expansion. Moreover, the soil was so sandy as to be unattractive for agriculture; hence, land in a huge tract was available at exceedingly low cost.

This district outranks all others in the world. Its capacity exceeds that of such whole countries as the United Kingdom and France. And recently it has grown more than twice as fast as the second and third largest American centers, Pittsburgh and Youngstown (Table 10-2).

OTHER LOWER LAKE CENTERS

Location on the Great Lakes brings these mills closer to the source of iron ore than location on the Ohio or Mahoning Rivers but places them farther from the sources of coking coal. However, they do have one major advantage: ore is unloaded from lake carriers directly at the blast furnaces, so that one extra handling of ore is eliminated.

For decades Buffalo and Cleveland have been the most important in the group. Buffalo has exceptional advantages as the terminus of many coal-carrying railways, it is on the New York State Barge Canal, and it obviously benefits from the St. Lawrence Seaway. Lake Superior iron ore delivered here costs no more than at sister cities on the lakes, and coal is cheaper than in some. Ample flat land on Lake Erie has been available, along with cheap water in desired quantities at low cost. Finally, its location between the Lower Lakes and the East Coast enables it to serve both large markets.

Cleveland, though less important as a rail center, is closer to the major coal fields and is the center of an important market area. For many years the Cuyahoga River, on which Cleveland's iron and steel industry is located, presented difficulties to shipping because of its tortuous course. In 1939, however, the city streamlined the lower course—an operation that consisted of cutting back nine of the worst bends, widening the channel at critical points, and removing and rebuilding several bridges so as to permit the largest freighters on the Great Lakes to navigate the river safely and with reasonable speed.[3]

Lorain, about 40 miles west of Cleveland, is geographically a part of the Cleveland area, sharing with it most of the advantages of location on Lake Erie. Although Cleveland possesses a larger local market, Lorain enjoys several advantages: the Black River, on which the mills are located, is superior in all respects to the Cuyahoga; there is more room for large plants; a cheaper water supply is available; and taxes are lower.

Detroit, one of the nation's two largest steel-consuming centers, possesses almost every economic-geographic advantage of other Great Lakes iron and steel centers. However, it did not assume its role as a major steel consumer until the twentieth century, and therefore new capacity in this area did not increase markedly until the decade 1948-1959 (Table 10-2). Iron and steel plants were established

[3] Some of the newest ore carriers are as much as 717 feet long, have a summer draft of 25½ feet, and a capacity of 22,500 tons.

in other areas before Detroit became a major steel consumer. The early trend in steelmaking, as already pointed out, was to locate near sources of raw materials. Today's trend, however, is toward producing steel nearer principal centers of consumption. Hence the growing importance of Detroit.

DULUTH—AN UPPER LAKE CENTER

The iron and steel industry at Duluth is presented here not because the city is a major producer or gives promise of becoming so, but because it is an unexcelled example of industrial locational maladjustment. Most North American iron and steel districts are located close to coal, and their iron ore is brought to them from a considerable distance. *At Duluth, however, the reverse occurs.* Duluth enjoys low assembly costs—the result chiefly of proximity to iron ore and of low rates on coal moving up the Great Lakes as return cargo on vessels whose primary function is to carry iron ore from Upper to Lower Lake ports. However, even in 1915, when the city's only iron and steel plant was built (largely as a result of political pressure), it was realized that remoteness from major markets would prevent this area from becoming a major iron and steel and industrial center. Only an increased demand for pipe from the oil-producing Williston Basin might stimulate production at Duluth.

NORTHEASTERN PENNSYLVANIA— MIDDLE ATLANTIC DISTRICT

The twin cities of Allentown and Bethlehem, sitting astride the Lehigh River, and Easton and Phillipsburgh, lying a few miles east of the confluence of the Delaware and Lehigh Rivers, are among the older iron and steel centers of the United States. Their advantages have been local iron ores, coal, and limestone; excellent transportation facilities; momentum of an early start; and nearness to the great market provided by the urban and industrial centers of the Atlantic Seaboard.

Sparrows Point. Sparrows Point has the distinction of being America's largest and most complete tidewater iron and steel center, as well as the world's largest steel plant. Most of the iron ore is brought from El Pao, Venezuela, directly to the blast furnaces at a much lower rate than domestic ores could be delivered. A special fleet of ore carriers, among the largest and fastest ships of their type, carry about 3 million tons of ore annually from Puerto de Hierro to Sparrows Point (and eastern Pennsylvania steel centers)—all operated by the Bethlehem Steel Corporation.

Coal from the Pocahontas, New River, and Fairmont fields in West Virginia and from the Clearfield and Westmoreland districts in Pennsylvania, and limestone from West Hanover, Pennsylvania, are easily and economically assembled. Moreover, shipments may be made to East Coast cities, the oil fields of the Gulf, the Pacific Coast, and to Europe or Latin America without resorting to any rail transportation. The water supply is less satisfactory, however, than that of many other districts; for the Patapsco River, on whose north shore Sparrows Point is located, is brackish and hence suitable only for some uses. Therefore, wells had to be resorted to—wells that later became contaminated. Since 1955 the plant has processed and used virtually the entire flow of sewage of the city of Baltimore—150 million gallons daily.

Morrisville, Pennsylvania. Where the Delaware River makes a big bend north of Philadelphia is one of the newest, most efficient, most scientifically located, and costliest (450 to 500 million dollars) **integrated plants** in the world. Never before was so complete an iron and steel plant constructed all at once. Scores of new ideas were introduced here for the first time.

Two principal factors prompted choice of the site: accessibility to large markets and availability of water-borne ore. Raw materials for the blast furnaces come from widely separated sources: coal from Pennsylvania and West Virginia, limestone from Pennsylvania, and iron ore from Venezuela (Cerro Bolívar). The iron ore comes all the way to the plant by vessel from Puerto Ordaz at the confluence of the Río Orinoco and Río Caroní.

HAMILTON-MIDDLETOWN DISTRICT

These two small, landlocked cities, lying 10 miles apart in Ohio's fertile Miami Valley, are unique among American metallurgical districts because the trend for more than a century has been toward concentrating metallurgical plants on navigable water in or near large cities. Hamilton and Middletown do not benefit from economical water transportation on incoming raw materials or on outgoing finished products. They do benefit, however, from having important patent rights, efficient plant operation, and more satisfied labor than is to be found in most other centers, and from concentrating on specific products ("Armco" drainage culverts, for example, are to be seen the world over).

THE SOUTH AND SOUTHWEST

The South for decades languished as a fabricator of iron and steel. However, the Cold War, mounting transport costs, availability of raw materials, increasing over-all industrialization, and growing markets have conspired to stimulate the industry in several Southern areas.

Alabama. Birmingham is the largest and most important iron and steel producer in the South. It is unique among American steel centers in being close to all three raw materials for the blast furnaces. About one fourth of the ore locally mined is **self-fluxing**, carrying 38 per cent iron oxide and 20 per cent lime. Rich ore is now being brought in from Venezuela to be mixed with local ore. Vast tonnages of fuel come from the Warrior coal field in the Cumberland Plateau.

The city is not on navigable water; but it is only 18 miles from Birmingport on the Black Warrior River, over whose waters a barge line operates. The two are connected by a short railroad which functions (as far as freight rates are concerned) as though the Black Warrior flows past the Birmingham mills. The district's big weakness in the past was a limited market, which offset its advantage in assembly costs by the expense of marketing north of the Ohio River. But since World War II, abolition of the multiple-basing-point system for pricing steel has given Birmingham's mills an advantage in the growing steel markets of the South.

Texas. Texas moved onto the nation's iron and steel map during World War II. The plant at Houston benefits from proximity to raw materials (though a portion of the iron ore comes from Durango, Mexico) and a large market—the productive oil fields of the Southwest. An integrated works at Daingerfield, 30 miles north of Longview, specializes in the production of steel pipe needed in the nearby oil and gas fields. This plant, within overnight trucking distance of the oil fields, thus has no competitors for pipe within a thousand miles. Daingerfield gets its coking coal and dolomite from southeastern Oklahoma and its iron ore from nearby in Texas. No raw material travels farther than 250 miles. Hence, its raw-materials cost per ton of pig iron is much lower than Houston's.

Considering the favorable raw-materials situation, the rapidly expanding market, and the military factor (national defense, which favors greater dispersion of the iron and steel industry), the future of Texas metallurgically would appear to be bright. However, strong Northern companies, in an effort to share the big Southern market, have established large steel-storage warehouses at geographically advantageous points in Texas.

THE WEST

For many years the West yearned for an iron and steel industry of its own, for it realized that steelmaking is basic in any program of industrialization. Especially was this true of the Pacific Coast, which did have a steel industry (based on scrap and imported cold pigs) but no iron industry. Hence, the West regarded itself as an economic stepchild of the East.

The heart of the American iron and steel industry was from the beginning, as has already been observed, centered in the East; and products could be sent easily and economically to the Pacific Coast via the Panama Canal from Sparrows Point, Birmingham, Pittsburgh, Chicago-Gary, and other centers.

This situation continued year in and year out. Then came World War II and the need for building great numbers of ships on the Pacific Coast. The water route via the Panama Canal was too dangerous because of the submarine menace. The railroads were straining under the terrific demands imposed on them by a two-ocean war. Iron and steel plants had to be built in the West, and they were: one at Geneva, Utah; the other at Fontana, California. In addition, there already existed an industry at Pueblo, Colorado (but it was *east* of the Rocky Mountains) and a small blast furnace south of Provo, Utah.

Pueblo. This Colorado piedmont city, located on the Arkansas River a few miles east of the Front Range of the Rockies, has the distinction of being the first in the West to have an iron and steel industry. The enterprise was linked with the building of the first section of the Denver and Rio Grande Railroad, which ran from Denver to Colorado Springs and Pueblo. In 1881 the blast furnace was "blown in," and in 1882 a Bessemer converter turned out the first steel to be made west of the Missouri River.

The company has large iron-ore deposits to the west and southwest of the city, but it also uses iron ore from southern Wyoming; and it has its own coal, limestone, and fluorspar properties in southern Colorado.

The Pueblo industry, of course, is small compared with several in the East, but it is exceedingly important to the Great Plains and Rocky Mountain regions.

Geneva. Close to the shore of Utah Lake, several miles from Provo and the Wasatch Mountains and about 40 miles south of Salt Lake City, the United States government built the first completely integrated iron and steel plant west of the Rockies—the first to assemble its own raw materials and fashion them into finished steel in a single plant. For its raw materials it reached 255 miles to the southwest for its iron ore, 120 miles to the southeast for its coal, and 35 miles south for its limestone.

This plant is believed to be as well located

as a Western inland plant can be; it has access to adequate transport facilities at minimum distances from the sources of iron ore, coal, limestone, and dolomite; and sufficient fresh water is available.

This plant is one of the most modern and efficient in the country. It enjoys the lowest raw-materials cost per net ton of pig iron in the country (Table 10-3). Geneva's biggest weakness is its distance from West Coast markets—850 to 1,100 miles.

Fontana. This plant is located about 50 miles east of Los Angeles. Originally the company wanted a tidewater location, but military security required an inland site.

Fontana gets its iron ore from the Eagle Mountain Mine, 176 miles distant; its coal from Utah, 807 miles away; and its limestone from quarries near the plant. Fontana is well served by railway and highway.

Its total raw-materials costs per ton of pig iron are higher than those of Geneva (Table 10-3); but Fontana is better off regarding market, since it is only 50 miles from Los Angeles, the leading industrial center in the West and a large consumer of steel. Steel destined for Los Angeles and other short hauls is carried in specially built trucks; that destined for distant markets moves by rail.

OUTLOOK FOR THE AMERICAN INDUSTRY

Fourteen of the fifty American states contain major steel-producing centers: each has a steelmaking capacity of at least 1.8 million net tons of ingots per year. There are few regions in the country that do not possess integrated plants. Yet 75 per cent of the national steel output is in the American Manufacturing Region. Since the iron and steel industry is not mobile, the map of its distribution is not likely to change fundamentally even in the future, for although the high-grade iron-ore deposits in the Lake Superior region are dwindling to dangerous proportions, billions of tons of taconite are available at competitive prices, and the new St. Lawrence Seaway enables foreign ore to reach the interior of the country by vessel during the months from April to December (Fig. 10-7). Thus, new

capacity will probably be added at existing centers. Another reason for this is the great cost of building wholly new mills—350 to 500 million dollars for an integrated plant.

Granting that the mills of other nations are equally modern and efficient and that their costs of assembling iron ore, coal, and limestone are roughly equivalent, the United States is definitely at a disadvantage in selling steel abroad—particularly because hourly wages of American steelworkers are consistently higher than those of steelworkers in other countries. Foreign producers can undersell United States mills by 20 to 30 per cent. Moreover, the St. Lawrence Seaway now permits foreign water-borne steel to invade the very heart of Anglo-America. Thus, unless there is some equalizer, foreign steel firms not only will force American steel out of most foreign markets but will gain an ever increasing proportion of the United States market itself. Can the United States meet this foreign challenge? It can do so only by (1) keeping future increases in hourly wages in tune with man-hour production efficiency, (2) increasing the protective tariff, or (3) replacing obsolete equipment with modern facilities: after World War II, many of the mills in countries of our allies, as well as our enemies, were rebuilt—at American expense—and equipped with the most modern machinery; by comparison with these mills, many in the United States are now obsolete.

CANADA

Canada's iron and steel industry is small compared with that of the United States, but the country ranks twelfth as a world producer (Table 10-1). Steel is the basal stone in the economic structure of the nation's manufacturing activities. Despite the importance of the industry, however, Canada does not meet all its own requirements and imports in excess of 2 million tons—most of it from the United States, but also from the United Kingdom, Belgium, France, West Germany, and Japan.

Iron and steel are manufactured mostly in three places: Sydney, Nova Scotia; Hamilton on the Ontario Peninsula; and Sault Ste. Marie, Ontario. New plants are scheduled for

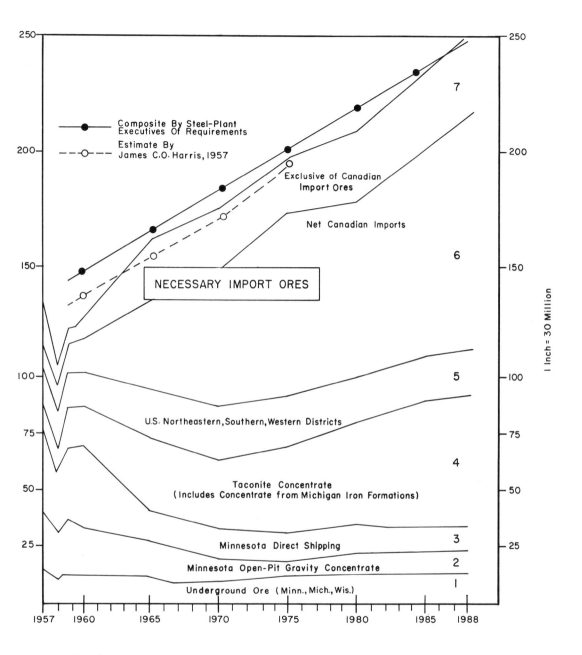

Fig. 10-7. *Where America's iron ore for its steel mills will come from, projected through 1988. The United States is becoming more and more dependent on (1) low-grade domestic ore (taconite), (2) Canadian ore, which is well located and of high quality, (3) other foreign ores. (Courtesy of* Mining Engineering.*)*

Contrecoeur, Quebec; Regina, Saskatchewan; and Kimberley, British Columbia.

NOVA SCOTIA

Sydney, center of the Nova Scotia industry, is a strategic locale for steelmaking for the following reasons: (1) It lies in the center of one of Canada's principal coal areas. (2) When the industry began, it had an abundance of land near the waterfront, well suited to the manufacture of iron and steel. (3) It has a commodious and well-protected harbor. (4) It is the eastern terminus of the Canadian National Railways System. (5) It can obtain Wabana ore cheaply from Bell Island, Newfoundland.

Despite low assembly costs and a tidewater location that facilitates the economical assembly of raw materials and the distribution of fabricated products, this plant accounts for less than 10 per cent of the total Canadian output. The tributary area is restricted industrially, which means that the nearby market is small. Steelmaking here has been hampered by a high United States protective tariff, which prevents exportation to the United States; by poor-quality coking coal; by ore high in silica and phosphorus; and by a scarcity of local scrap. Sydney is a good example of a center that persists because of **industrial inertia**.

ONTARIO PENINSULA

About 74 per cent of Canada's steel capacity is in the central part of the country—at Hamilton, Welland, and Port Colborne. This is Canada's best-located district because the principal market for steel lies in the vicinity of Hamilton, which enjoys a central location in the Canadian part of the American Manufacturing Region. The mills here differ from others in Canada in that they produce a greater variety of steel products. Both iron ore and coal are purchased from the United States, though ore from Quebec and Labrador is beginning to be used. Proximity to a large supply of cheap hydroelectric power enables the mills to make most of their steel in electric furnaces.

SAULT STE. MARIE

Despite low assembly costs—due to proximity to iron ore and low transportation rates on coal, via lake carrier—Sault Ste. Marie's location in a poor market area has kept the industry small. The mill does not, however, produce the same items as Hamilton. The long-run picture offers little hope of much ·growth.

UNITED KINGDOM

Although Great Britain is the fourth largest iron and steel producer in the world, it produces annually only about one fourth as much steel as the United States (Table 10-1). Of some three hundred companies, twenty-five account for 95 per cent of the steel. Most of the British industry was nationalized in 1949, but with the change of government, most of the companies have become denationalized.

Great Britain is particularly fortunate because its iron ore and coking coal are located near each other, and because a preponderant proportion of its facilities is on tidewater. The average haul for raw materials to works and for finished products to ports is 30 miles, compared with 150 for West Germany, 200 for France, and 80 for Belgium. Additional advantages have been superior harbors and ports, extremely skilled and competent labor, and excellent rail facilities.

PRINCIPAL DISTRICTS

The Midlands. In the Midlands district, comprising Birmingham and its satellite cities, the industry for many years has been based upon local coal and iron-ore deposits that are now becoming exhausted, precipitating a sharp decline in the area's importance.

Yorkshire. Like the Midlands, Yorkshire was early favored by domestic coal and iron ore but now has become less important, except for steelmaking based upon pig iron from Middlesbrough.

Middlesbrough. Here, iron ore and coal in close proximity along with navigable water (the lower Tees) initiated the industry. This district, now one of the country's most important, imports high-grade iron ore and ships steel by water to other parts of the United Kingdom and abroad.

South Wales. South Wales is currently the leader in production. The industry here has moved southward to the coast, principally to Cardiff and Swansea, where coal is close by and cheap imported ore is available.

The Scottish Lowlands. With depletion of the local coal measures, this area has turned from ironmaking to steel production based upon pig iron and scrap from local, domestic, and foreign sources.

CHANGES IN THE BRITISH INDUSTRY

In spite of Britain's early preeminence, other countries have passed her in output. Chief among the reasons for Britain's decline are the following:

1. She must depend upon foreign sources of ore for about 60 per cent of the pig iron manufactured.
2. Her coal supply is insufficient and expensive.
3. Her coke is of poor quality.
4. She has failed to keep equipment modernized. Whereas at the beginning of Britain's Industrial Revolution, and for decades afterward, the leaders in manufacturing were pioneers who knew their businesses from the ground up, many of the recent and present leaders have attained their positions less from ability than from family connections. Hence, until recently they were conservative and did not appreciably modernize their plants and machinery. Since 1946, however, the industry has been modernized, processes have become more efficient (e.g., integration of blast furnaces and steelworks), management techniques have been improved, and labor output has increased by 50 per cent.
5. Tight cartelized price policies. Cold-rolled sheets cost British automobile producers about twice what they cost American producers.

Today the United Kingdom ranks higher on all counts in the iron and steel industry than she has for decades. Since 1945, more than 2 billion dollars have been spent on development plans. Production has risen, costs have fallen, and quality of the steel is very high.

WESTERN CONTINENTAL EUROPE

Iron and steel long have been important in continental Europe. The industry has operated, however, under several major difficulties: (1) the uncertainty that must be present when frequent wars are fought, (2) shifting international boundaries, and (3) the vagaries of tariff making. In any appraisal of the European iron and steel industry, the first two of these unstable political factors in the equation of industrial development dare not be overlooked. Regarding the third, a European Economic Community (the "Inner Six") and a European Free Trade Association (the "Outer Seven") have been set up to eliminate the obstacles to trade between member countries and to form a mass market. Trade in iron and steel has been aided greatly within each group but particularly within the "Inner Six," which turns out about 48 per cent of the non-Communist European output of 116.4 million tons. By 1963 Great Britain and several other members of the "Outer Seven" had applied to join the "Six"—a move that could help all thirteen members economically, heal the growing rift between the two economic blocs, and strengthen over-all European unity.

GERMANY

Prior to and during World War II, Germany became the largest manufacturer of iron and steel in Europe, ranking second only to the United States in world production. This is significant considering that about 70 per cent of the iron-ore requirements had to be imported.

Germany's great growth metallurgically did not begin immediately after the Franco-Prussian War of 1870-1871, when she acquired the extensive iron-ore deposits of Lorraine. Hence, these deposits apparently were not a major motive for annexation of

Lorraine, since the high phosphorus content of the ores produced a brittle and very poor grade of steel. Not until after 1878—when two British amateur chemists, Thomas and Gilchrist, introduced a process for making good steel from this high-phosphorus ore—did the Lorraine deposits become really useful. The substitution of a limestone for an acid lining in the Bessemer converter neutralized the phosphorus. This new process gave Germany a large iron-ore reserve.[4]

By 1913 Germany was producing twice as much steel as England and four times more than France. Prior to World War I, more than 21 million tons of Lorraine ore and 7½ million tons of Luxembourg ore were used in German furnaces.

After Germany's defeat in 1918, with the subsequent Treaty of Versailles, her total iron production was cut in half and her steel capacity was reduced by one third. By 1922, however, the German industry had staged a comeback and was once again leading European production.

At that time, Germany's iron-ore deposits were scattered and low grade, so that large imports were necessary. In 1927 Sweden was shipping about 15 million tons of iron ore to Germany—ore averaging nearly 65 per cent iron, which met approximately three fifths of the German needs. Lorraine supplied from 2½ to 3 million tons averaging about 35 per cent iron, and Newfoundland contributed about 1 million tons.

Too heavy dependence upon these distant sources of ore led to the establishment in 1937 of the so-called Hermann Goering Works at Salzgitter. This locale was chosen because of its distance from the French border (out of convenient bomber range) and because of

proximity to extensive deposits of low-grade iron ore. Large-scale mining operations were begun, but the fall of France early in the war once again made the ores of Lorraine available and the low-grade German ores were neglected.

In 1960 West Germany ranked third in world steel production (Table 10-1) and anticipates an output of 43 million tons in 1970—an increase of about 10 million tons for the decade. Domestic iron-ore deposits can meet only a part of such enormous blast-furnace needs. Substantial ore imports are imperative—from France, Spain, Sweden, Canada, Venezuela, Brazil, Peru, Guinea and Sierra Leone.

The Ruhr. Germany's Ruhr is one of the world's outstanding concentrations of heavy industry (Fig. 10-8). It is a triangle—a mere spot on the map of Western Europe—extending from Wesel to Düsseldorf to Hamm and back to Wesel. Its base is only 35 miles wide, and its sides are 60 miles long; but within it is Europe's tightest concentration of industry. It has about one third of the country's industrial plants.

The Ruhr is served by a veritable labyrinth of railroads, canals, and navigable rivers; and freight moves cheaply in almost any direction. The Rhine, into which the Ruhr flows, is one of the world's busiest and best waterways and provides the German iron and steel industry with easy and economical access to the sea.

It is, however, the rich coal deposits that made the Ruhr so outstanding; without them there would have been no Ruhr as we envisage it. Prior to the outbreak of World War II, nearly 40 per cent of the coal mined in Germany was used within the Ruhr (see Fig. 2-8).

The Ruhr was badly bombed during the war, and destruction was thorough; but the centers of cities and towns, rather than their rims, received the great force of the bombs. Accordingly, the factories and mines largely escaped, and at the end of hostilities more than 75 per cent were in good shape. The Ruhr still is outstanding in coal production, and its iron and steel industries are currently booming.

---

[4] The Thomas process for removing carbon, silicon, manganese, some sulphur, *but particularly phosphorus,* from the iron by oxidation in conjunction with lime from limestone and dolomite must be regarded as one of the greatest inventions of all time. It permits a wide choice of iron ores. Though important to all of Europe, it was particularly important to Lorraine, permitting utilization of the "minette" ores (a term of contempt, implying worthlessness of the ore). The process is widely employed in Europe but not in the United States.

Fig. 10-8. *Concentration of industrial complex at Dortmund, one of the Ruhr's chief metallurgical centers. Nowhere on earth does steel dominate the cultural landscape more than here. (Copyright by Presse- und Informationsamt der Bundesregierung, Courtesy of German Tourist Information Office.)*

Most of the mills are situated on rivers and canals in order to facilitate the handling of imported ore and of domestic and imported coal. The water transport and the coal deposits together have been the key factors in the location of the mills.

The Saar. Another major steel district is the Saar, rich in coal and near the Minette iron-ore deposits of Lorraine. The 900-square-mile area is situated along the border between France and Germany. The market areas for Saar coal and steel have been determined chiefly by political and political-economic factors. The Saar has undeniably been a major factor dividing France and Germany: it has been craved by both, and following recent wars has regularly changed hands. In a plebiscite held in 1935, the Saarlanders voted overwhelmingly for incorporation into Germany. Linguistically and culturally they are German; but economically, their closest ties have been with France. Such political shifts

have hampered Saar steel production. Integration into the coal and steel community has reduced political tensions and improved the steel industry.

The Saar iron and steel industry utilizes its own and some German coal along with French iron ore, and the industry gives employment to one fourth of its approximately 1 million inhabitants. Agriculture is unimportant. The French believe that the Saar economy complements their economy much more than it does the German. About 40 per cent of Saar steel moves to France, compared with 3 per cent to Germany.

FRANCE

France has long made iron and steel, but the industry was not of the stature of those in the United States, Germany, or Great Britain. Though its metallurgical industry grew impressively from the end of World War I to the great economic depression following 1929, from then it began a steady period of decline.

THE WORLD'S IRON AND STEEL INDUSTRIES :: 193

During World War II, the industry, once again dominated by the Germans, stagnated. Plant facilities were old and depleted. France was no longer regarded as a major industrial power. In 1945, when Lorraine was returned to France, only 681,000 tons of steel were produced.

In 1947 the first Monnet Plan went into effect, and by the end of 1952 more than a billion dollars had been expended on the metallurgical industries—65 per cent directly on the iron and steel industries. Lorraine received 80 per cent of these funds.

Throughout the iron- and steelmaking areas, blast and steel furnaces have been increased in size but reduced in number. The result is that France today has the most modern steel-producing facilities in continental Europe. In recent years France's net finished steel exports have surpassed those of both Great Britain and West Germany. In fact, France ranks second in steel exports, and iron and steel comprise the nation's leading export. In 1960 France ranked as the third largest producer of steel in Europe and seventh in the world (Table 10-1).

The most important steelmaking area is the Lorraine Basin, which accounts for approximately three fourths of the French pig iron and steel output. Here coal moves to iron ore. Part of the coal is mined in Lorraine, the deposits being a prolongation of the Saar Basin into French territory, but much too is imported from West Germany.

Lorraine is not so outstanding as the Ruhr in steel output, partly because it lacks high-grade coal but partly also because it is served essentially by a network of land rather than water transportation. Consequently, Lorraine's assembly costs are high. For this reason France pressed for completion of the Moselle Canal from Thionville to Coblenz. This canal reduces the cost of sending a ton of Ruhr coal to Lorraine by 50 to 60 per cent; the cost of shipping a ton of rolled steel from Thionville to the world market via Rotterdam is reduced by 300 per cent. The canal also enables West Germany to get iron ore at lower cost than from any other foreign source. Blast furnaces and steel mills are located in or near Metz, Briey, Villerupt, Thionville, Hayange, Hagondange, Pompey, Neuves, Maisons, Sollae, Nancy, and Longwy. Most of the plants are integrated and modern.

A second metallurgical area is in the coal-producing portion of northern France—Sambre-Meuse, which receives iron ore from Normandy, Luxembourg, and Lorraine, or by sea. Its principal centers are Valenciennes, Denain, Anzin, Hautmont, and Jeumont. A third, less important, producing area has centers at St. Etienne, Firminy, Saint-Chamond, and Lyon.

BELGIUM-LUXEMBOURG

Together, these two small nations have a combined area only about the size of the American state of Maryland, but in iron and steel they rank very high. The two were joined in a Customs Union in 1922 to prevent tariff barriers from interfering with their trade. They are today members of the coal and steel community—the "Six."

Belgium has coal, and Luxembourg has iron ore (an extension of the Lorraine field); *yet about 70 per cent of the iron ore and 40 per cent of the coke consumed must be imported —the ore largely from Lorraine, the coking coal largely from West Germany.* The industry is located in the coal fields; the cost of assembling raw materials is low, the result of proximity to the Ruhr and Lorraine. It is still centralized in the south—in the valley of the Meuse, particularly in the province of Hainaut.

Since production ordinarily far outruns domestic consumption, exports play an important role. The Belgium-Luxembourg complex is a principal supplier of steel to the world market.

SWEDEN

Sweden is a small but important producer of steel. With one of the oldest iron industries in Europe, with one of the largest and reputedly the richest iron-ore deposits in Europe, and with a strategic location with respect to outstanding world steel markets, Sweden might be expected to be one of the giants in the metallurgical industry. However, poverty in coal has so far made that impossible. Until about 1931, most of its pig iron was made in charcoal blast furnaces, and half of it still is. Although charcoal is the purest of all metallurgical fuels, it is expensive; and the cutting of forests must be carefully controlled to ensure that depletion does not exceed natural growth. If scientists ultimately discover a means of making pig iron by by-passing the coke-using blast furnace or by employing hydroelectric power economically, Sweden might become a major source of iron and steel; for she is well endowed with water power. But until that day arrives, Sweden must, in what pig iron she manufactures, use charcoal and imported coke. In order to minimize the consumption of these costly fuels, Swedish metallurgists have made considerable progress in preparing burdens high in iron and low in silica that are easily reduced. The nation also imports considerable steel scrap.

Iron ore is mined commercially in two areas—central Sweden (low-phosphorus ore, on which the domestic industry is based), and Lapland (high-phosphorus ore, largely for export). The high-phosphorus ore is satisfactory for the Thomas process and hence is in demand in the Ruhr and in Britain. The principal Swedish works are to be found at Domnarvet, Norrbottens, Jarnverk, Fagersta, and Edsken.

ITALY

Italy is desperately poor in most minerals, particularly in those that enter into the manufacture of iron and steel. The country's full weakness in this respect was revealed in her early surrender during World War II. Yet, because of the importance of her secondary steel-using enterprises, Italy consumes much primary steel.

Italy is unique in having a relatively small iron industry but a rather impressive steel industry. Her coke ovens and blast furnaces operate largely on imported raw materials.[5] Her steel mills of necessity use much scrap and hydroelectric power. The many rivers in

[5] A United Nations study discloses that Italy is required to import 25 per cent of the iron ore, 25 per cent of the scrap, 90 per cent of the coal, and 100 per cent of the coke used in producing iron and steel.

the north—rivers whose sources are in glaciers and snow fields—provide abundant hydroelectric power, at least during the summer months. Italy fabricates mostly high-quality electric steel.

The industry, located in the north at Bagnoli, Corniguiano, Piombina, and Terni, turned out four times as much steel in 1956 as in 1947. Nearly all the mills are new.

EASTERN EUROPE

Before this region became enclosed by the Iron Curtain, it was overwhelmingly agricultural. In 1960 the entire group of satellites—Czechoslovakia, East Germany, Hungary, Poland, and Romania—had a steel output exceeding 16.5 million tons.

CZECHOSLOVAKIA

Czechoslovakia has long ranked as one of the world's most highly industrialized countries, and among its chief industries have been those engaged in making iron and steel (Table 10-1).

Most of the plants are integrated, and most are in Bohemia. The Silesian segment is growing in metallurgical stature. Its importance results from possession of the country's most productive coal field (three fourths of the nation's total) and of some iron ore. The leading centers are Bohumin, Kravina, Moravska, and Ostrava. The outstanding plant in the country, however, and one of the largest and costliest integrated plants in all Europe, is in Slovakia, a presently underdeveloped part of the country. Here near Kosice is the country's largest single industrial undertaking since the Communists took power in 1948. Costing approximately 750 million dollars and covering 5 square miles, this plant has an annual output of about 3.8 million tons of steel.

The iron ore for much of the output of the Czechoslovak mills is shipped from the mines of Krivoi Rog in the Russian Ukraine; but ores from Czestochowa, Poland, and from the Bohemian Basin also are utilized. In the new mill near Kosice, some iron ore is obtained from mines west of the city to make up for the amount not supplied by the Soviet Union.

Coking coal is supplied by large mines in the Ostrava district, a part of the Teschen coal field between Czechoslovakia and Poland.

POLAND

The most highly industrialized part of Poland is the area between the Oder-Niesse and Vistula (Wisla) Rivers. Part of this area formerly belonged to Germany. In this area of some 450 square miles is to be found 90 per cent of the Polish iron and steel industry.

The country's steel industry suffered much war damage; by 1945 it was virtually at a standstill. In 1960, however, Poland turned out 7 million tons of steel.

Plants lie on both banks of the Vistula River. The new plants (postwar construction) are located at Nova Huta, Warsaw, and Czestochowa. Largest and most fully integrated is the Lenin works at Nova Huta. Most of Poland's iron- and steelmaking facilities are, or soon will be, quite modern.

The coal for the furnaces is mined within the country; and, though Poland mines approximately 100 million tons annually, only a small percentage is suitable for making metallurgical coke.

About 80 per cent of the iron ore (52 per cent iron) used is brought in from the Soviet Union, and 20 per cent (36 to 38 per cent iron) is Polish ore.

SOVIET UNION

The Soviet Union is the second most important manufacturer of iron and steel in the world. In 1960 Russia turned out 71.7 million tons of steel, compared with 99.2 million tons for the United States (Table 10-1). (In 1960, of course, because of the recession, the United States was operating at an average for the year of probably 67 per cent capacity, whereas the Soviet Union was presumably operating at nearly full capacity.) The gap between steel production in the two countries has been narrowing each year (Soviet output more than tripled in the decade of the 1950s) because the government has assigned top priority to the industry. The Soviet Union now operates the world's largest steel company. Groups of American steelmen who have visited Soviet mills from time to time since World War II

invariably have reported favorably on the efficiency of Russian plants, some claiming that Soviet steelmakers are attaining results that vie with the best to be found in the American steel industry.

Both men and women work in the mills, women comprising approximately a third of the working force in the average plant. The cost of labor is about one fourth that in the United States.

Formerly, 75 per cent of all Russian iron and steel was manufactured in the Donets Basin, because the bulk of the known coal reserves were there and the area was well located with respect to population and markets. It was also served by the best transportation facilities in Russia.

The Russian industry today, however, looks different on the map (Fig. 10-9). It is far less concentrated, since many new sources of coking coal and of iron ore have been discovered —discoveries reflected in the establishment of new metallurgical centers extending all the way from European Russia to the Pacific Ocean. Possibly the geographical redistribution of the industry since the Revolution is even more significant than the phenomenal growth. Whereas in Tsarist Russia a line from the Ural Mountains to the Caspian Sea was practically the extent of the frontier of industry, the Soviet Union now has powerful centers of manufacturing in the Southern Urals, through Western Siberia, and in several areas even east of Lake Baikal.

DISTRIBUTION OF THE INDUSTRY

There are four major iron and steel districts, and many minor ones, in the Soviet Union. The four meriting attention here are (1) the Southern Ukraine, (2) the Central and Southern Urals, (3) the Moscow, and (4) the Kuznetsk.

Southern Ukraine. This, the oldest of the important iron and steel areas, has raw materials, transportation, labor, and markets. It is also in the part of Russia that was first influenced by the modern manufacturing practices of Western Europe. Prior to World War I, this area produced three fourths of Russia's pig iron; today it yields about half of the pig iron

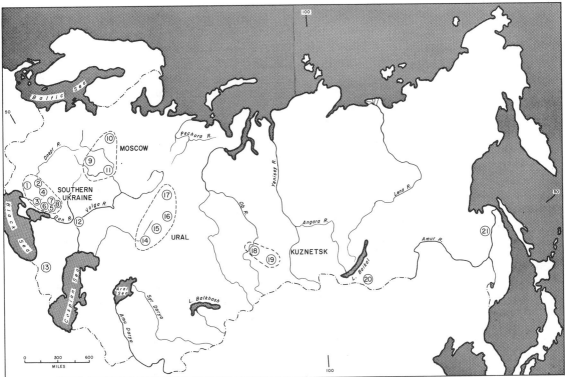

1. Krivoi Rog	8. Yenakryevo	15. Chelyabinsk
2. Dneprodzerzhinsk	9. Moscow	16. Sverdlovsk
3. Zaporozhye	10. Cherepovets	17. Nizhni Tagil
4. Dnepropetrovsk	11. Gorki	18. Novosibirsk
5. Donetsk	12. Volgograd	19. Kuznetsk
6. Zhdanov	13. Kramatorsk	20. Petrovsk-Zabaikalskiy
7. Makeyevka	14. Magnitogorsk	21. Komsomolsk

Fig. 10-9. Distribution of the iron and steel industry in the Soviet Union. Note that the industry is to be found in four main areas. Unfortunately, the raw materials are far less well located than in the United States; in fact, Russia's might be said to be in the wrong places. Hence, cross-haulage is the rule, not the exception.

and some two fifths of the steel. In this region, centers near the coal, such as Donetsk, Makeyevka, and Yenakryevo, help make the Donbas much like the Pittsburgh district and the Ruhr, whereas centers such as Krivoi Rog and Nikopol, near iron ore, resemble the centers at Lorraine in France and Duluth in the United States. There are centers, too (such as Zhdanov, Zaporozhye, Dnepropetrovsk, and Dneprodzerzhinsk), that are not located near coal or iron ore, but that lie between the coking coal of the Donbas and the iron ore of Krivoi Rog; these centers are similar to the important cities on the Great Lakes—Buffalo, Cleveland, Lorain.

The Southern Ukraine in Krivoi Rog has the richest iron-ore deposits in the entire Soviet Union—1.2 billion tons of red hematite ore with an iron content of 60 to 70 per cent iron. Even in recent years two thirds of the total ore mined has come from this area. The Donbas is rich in coal, all of it high grade, with reserves estimated in excess of 70 billion tons.

Central and Southern Urals. Long before Germany launched her attack against the Soviet Union in World War II, Russian leaders foresaw, as an essential of national defense, the need to shift a considerable part of their manufacturing to and beyond the Urals. The iron and steel industry already operating in the western part of the Soviet Union was to be maintained, but new capacity was to be developed in the east. Many plants and much equipment were transferred from the southern Ukraine when German troops invaded that area.

The first and by far the most important center in this area was the then new city of Magnitogorsk, lying in the valley of the Ural River. This was no slow evolution of iron and steel development; instead there was a sudden shift from small handicraft units to huge factories, from tiny charcoal furnaces to mammoth coke-fed blast furnaces. The iron and steel plants, which produced more than 12 million tons of steel in 1960, are among the largest in the world and comprise blast furnaces, open hearths, rolling mills, and coke ovens. Its blast furnaces, possibly the world's largest, are capable of yielding more than 2,000 tons of pig iron per day. Other important centers, in the Central Urals, are Nizhni Tagil, Chelyabinsk, and Sverdlovsk. Their blast furnaces, unlike those at Magnitogorsk, still rely almost exclusively on Kuzbas coal for coke. This area produces approximately one third of the iron and steel of the Soviet Union.

Moscow. In this market-oriented area, iron and steel manufacture occur in a belt extending northeast from Bryansk to Gorki. Iron and steel have been made in this area since the days of the Tsars, but the district is expected to decline in relative importance. Because the situation with respect to coal and iron ore is nowhere satisfactory, production is not so large as in more strategically located areas, and specialization is more highly developed.

Kuznetsk Basin. The iron and steel mills in this area were built during the first five-year plan. The coal reserves of the basin are estimated at 450 billion tons, which puts it next to the American Appalachian Province among rich coal areas of the world. This coal, which is concentrated in a small area of 10,000 square miles, is near the surface and is easily mined. The Kuzbas sustains six important coking-coal areas, whose output makes good-quality, low-sulfur coke.

The first Kuznetsk coal was utilized for reducing iron ore delivered to the area by rail from the Urals 1,500 miles away. On the return trip coal was taken to Magnitogorsk for conversion to coke there. Obviously, such long rail hauls were uneconomical,[6] particularly considering the inadequate and overcrowded condition of the railroad system, much of it single-track. Russian planners failed to appreciate the key role played by transportation in the regional location of iron and steel mills. Today, however, very little ore is hauled from Magnitogorsk, most of it being drawn from the Lower Angara deposits near Lake Baikal. Some ore, too, is obtained from Abakan west of Lake Baikal. The main center is Kuznetsk, which ranks second only to Magnitogorsk, but also included in the Kuznetsk district are Mazulskiy, Usa, Novosibirsk, Turochak, and Kamen.

Secondary Centers. Among the more important secondary centers of iron and steel production are Taishet near Lake Baikal, where a new integrated industry, producing 4.5 million tons annually, lies between coal and iron ore but is distant from major markets; Barnaul, where a new integrated plant utilizes iron ore from the Lisakousky deposits and coal from Karaganda and the Kuzbas; Krasnoyarsk, site of an open-pit iron mine, making possible low production costs, but distant from markets; and the Trans-Baikal centers of Petrovsk-Zabaikalskiy just east of Lake Baikal and Komsomolsk on the Amur River, both of which utilize poor-quality iron ore plus inexpensive hydroelectric power to produce electric steel.

OUTLOOK FOR THE RUSSIAN INDUSTRY

We have seen that the Soviet Union, realizing the importance of huge production of iron and steel to an industrial nation, has given the

[6] Here is one of the very best examples of poor industrial planning in the geography of iron and steel. Manufacturing costs in Ukraine plants were and still are lower than anywhere else in Russia. Hence, in order to make production costs at Magnitogorsk and Kuznetsk comparable with those in new plants in the Ukraine, the combine (the industry) in these two districts has to be subsidized by especially low freight rates. It is reported that both Magnitogorsk and Kuznetsk operate at a loss. See M. Gardner Clark, *The Economics of Soviet Steel* (Cambridge, Massachusetts: Harvard University Press, 1956), pp. 216-217.

green light to this industry. We have seen that slowly but nonetheless surely the Russians are narrowing the gap between their capacity and production and those of the United States. They plan to continue their steel expansion until they surpass the United States. In all probability, the Soviets will not be successful in this venture for some years, though ultimately it is to be expected that they will be. Soviet statisticians assert that the Soviet Union will catch up with the United States by 1970 and that by 1972 it will "surpass America."

Although the Soviet Union has not attempted to sell steel in foreign markets on any appreciable scale, there is no doubt that she could undersell all competitors in world markets, if she wishes to. This, of course, would mean ignoring cost and acting from political motives. Selling thus would really be **dumping**. With wages considerably lower than those of Britain and a fourth those in the United States, and with a somewhat comparable level of productivity, it is plain that Russia poses a potential problem to the steel-making nations of the Free World.

However, the Soviet Union has troubles. The country is enormous in size—two and a half times the size of the United States; and size is a problem of first magnitude, for the country has less than 100,000 miles of hard-surface roads and only about 75,000 miles of railway—about what the United States had in 1872. Also the resources of iron ore and coal, largely of poor grade, are for the most part in the wrong places. Accordingly, much inefficient and uneconomical cross-haulage is mandatory. Finally, the shortages of high-grade coking coal and iron ore must be regarded as serious limitations on expansion of this industry. The government can justify current expansion (3 or 4 million tons per annum) only in terms of economic autarky.

ASIA

Asia is on the threshold of its greatest economic development. The United Nations predicts that within a very few years Asia will have a steel capacity of 88 million tons, including Red China's forecast of 44 million tons. Other than the Soviet Union, the three countries that rank high in iron and steel manufacture are Japan, India, and China.

JAPAN

Until its defeat in 1945, Japan was the undisputed leader in the manufacture of iron and steel in the Far East. The industry, however, was of the "hothouse" variety, resulting in large measure from the national urge for industrial self-sufficiency on the part of the military. The government supported it in the form of (1) tariffs on imports, (2) government financing and low costs, and (3) preferential purchases by the army, navy, and government-owned railways. Thus, from the standpoint of economic geography Japan's iron and steel industry rested on a weak base. It was dependent on outside sources for 90 per cent of its iron ore (China, Malaya, and the Philippines) and for 30 per cent of its coking coal (Manchuria and North China). China, the prewar traditional source of coking coal, has been replaced largely by the United States, which also contributes more than 50 per cent of the scrap. Today's iron ore is provided mostly by Malaysia, India, and the Philippines, though lesser suppliers are Venezuela, Peru, and Brazil.

Despite the inadequacy of raw materials, Japan ranks as the fifth largest iron and steel producer (Table 10-1), and the outlook appears exceedingly bright. Nonetheless, Japan is a high-cost producer of iron and steel.

Iron and steel manufacturing is highly concentrated in several areas, mostly between Tokyo on the east and Nagasaki on the west, particularly around the Inland Sea (Fig. 10-10). Yawata, in northern Kyushu, has long been the outstanding single center of both Japan and all Asia. It produces more than half of Japan's total steel output. Additional capacity is to be found in (1) the Tokyo-Kawasaki-Yokohama district, (2) the Osaka-Kobe area, and (3) the Muroran district of southeastern Hokkaido. All the plants thus benefit from tidewater location—a situation attributable to overwhelming dependence on imported raw materials and on export markets for many fabricated steel products. Shipbuilding, too, is a heavy consumer of steel.

INDIA

Among the world's underdeveloped countries none is striving harder to industrialize than India, and among the various manu-

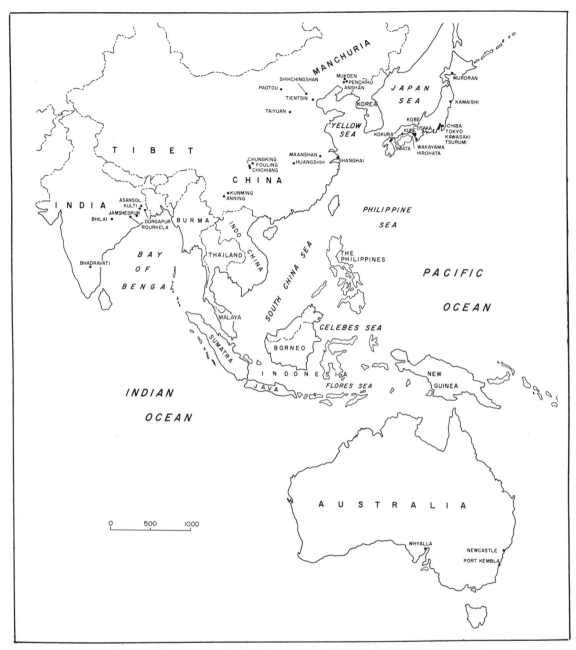

Fig. 10-10. Distribution of the iron and steel industry in Japan, China, India, and Australia. Note that in Japan the mills cluster around the Inland Sea; in China, still largely in Manchuria; in India, mostly in the Bihar-Bengal Heavy Industrial Belt; and in Australia, chiefly in New South Wales. (Drawn by John Arrillaga.)

factural projects none is being pushed more assiduously than that engaged in making iron and steel. Whereas at the end of World War II India's steel capacity was 1.5 to 2 million tons, today it exceeds 6 million tons. Then the great Tata mills at Jamshedpur were the principal producers; now there are altogether seven plants—three new and another recently altered and its capacity much increased. In 1960 Indian mills turned out 3.4 million tons.

Of the six major centers (Fig. 10-10), only the Bhadravati, 300 miles west of Madras, lies outside the so-called Bihar-Bengal Heavy Industrial Belt, which accounts for more than 95 per cent of India's current iron and steel output. Heaviest concentration of mills is in the Chota Nagpur area of Bihar. Bihar's heritage of minerals—coal, iron ore, manganese, and limestone—forms an excellent base for the metallurgical industry of the region. Also water in adequate amounts is present, and this natural resource has been a major factor in determining the locations of new plants. Though most of India's iron and steel mills are more raw-materials than market oriented, the market factor is favorable in most instances. The Bhilai and Rourkela plants were deliberately located in backward areas in order to encourage industrialization.

Three of the older districts, Jamshedpur, Asansol, and Kulti, all lie on the eastern fringe of the Chota Nagpur Plateau, northwest of Calcutta. And all three of the new districts—Bhilai, Rourkela, and Durgapur—are located there. These three new plants were built for the Indian government by industrial interests of foreign governments—Germany (Rourkela), Britain (Durgapur), and the Soviet Union (Bhilai).

Jamshedpur. This is India's oldest integrated iron and steel plant; unlike the three new ones, it is privately owned rather than government owned. It belongs to the famous house of Tata and has been successfully managed. During the interwar period, Jamshedpur became the largest single steel producer in the British Empire. It has a capacity today of about 1.1 million tons of steel ingots. Jamshedpur gets its iron ore from Mayurbhanj, 45 to 60 miles to the south, and from

Singhbhum, 80 miles to the southwest; its coal from the Jharia field, 110 miles to the north; its limestone from quarries at Gangpur, 110 miles to the southwest. Manganese and tungsten are available just a few miles from the plant. Jamshedpur has one of the best sites in India with respect to raw materials and water, and it is strategically located with respect to markets.

Asansol. Until the three new mills were constructed in the 1950s, the plant at Asansol ranked second only to that at Jamshedpur. Like most of the Chota Nagpur plants, Asansol is strategically situated with respect to raw materials and markets; the mills are in the Raniganj coal field.

Bhilai. The new works here are fully integrated and have a capacity of about 1 million tons of steel ingots per annum. This plant was financed and built by the Soviet Union. The interest rate on the 241-million-dollar cost is only 2½ per cent, principal and interest payable over a twelve-year period.

The iron ore for the plant runs 66 to 69 per cent metallic iron and is shipped from the Drug area, 52 miles distant. Coking coal is brought from the Jharia field 450 miles northeast of the plant. Coal not needed for conversion into coke is procured at Korba, about 100 miles to the northeast. Limestone is available some 15 or 20 miles north of the plant.

Rourkela. This plant, built with West German technical aid, also has a steel-ingot capacity of 1 million tons. It was completely financed by the Indian government. The plant's iron ore is delivered from the Iron Range, 35 miles distant; its coal comes from the Jharia field, 200 miles to the northwest; and its limestone is from quarries adjacent to the plant.

Durgapur. This plant, located in West Bengal about 98 miles northwest of Calcutta, was constructed under British guidance. The raw materials are obtained from approximately the same sources as those supplying the Asansol plant, which is only 26 miles distant. This plant is essentially raw-materials oriented, being in a central position with respect to both coal and iron ore.

The manufacture of iron and steel in China, viewed through Western eyes, was until the late 1950s unimpressive. Except for Manchuria, where the Japanese had built a large integrated plant at Anshan, there were only two blast furnaces: one at Hanyang near Hankow, the other at Yang Chuan in Shansi. *Their combined capacity was only 120 tons of pig iron per day.*

The Communists are trying desperately to industrialize their country, and they are determined to do so in just a few decades. At this time no one can say with assurance whether or not they will be successful. One of their principal professed goals is to overtake the United Kingdom in steel output by 1973. To some students of coal and iron ore and of iron and steel, this goal appears fantastic. Yet China ranks third among all nations in coal reserves and possibly fourth in iron-ore reserves. *And China is only now being intensively explored geologically.* Transportation, which is so fundamental for any nation's steel industry, still is poorly developed—total mileage of railways in operation is about 20,-500. Hard-surface roads are virtually nonexistent.

Production centers are shown in Figure 10-10. It is noteworthy that most of the capacity and production still are in Manchuria and were originally developed by the Japanese. The largest production by far (4.4 million tons of steel ingots and 3.3 million tons of pig iron in 1958) is at Anshan in Manchuria. Penchihu also is important. Though the Russians dismantled these works following World War II, the plant has been reconstructed. In this rebuilding, Russian metallurgical engineers supervised the work, employing the Soviet Union's latest achievements in technology. Anshan is well located—close to iron ore (78 miles), coal (85 miles), and limestone (14 miles)—and has good rail transportation. Weaknesses are (1) lack of facilities for economical assembly of raw materials and shipment of manufactured products by water, (2) the almost total lack of indigenous scrap for the open-hearth furnaces (this necessitates reliance upon pig iron), and (3) the remote and still inaccessible locations of most of the minerals. This plant stretches for more than 5 miles along the Chanchun Railway, and more than half the steel city's population is employed by this industry. As in the Soviet Union, women comprise a large part of the labor force. Anshan serves as a model for the industrialization of the rest of China.

Like all underdeveloped nations, China lacks capital; accordingly, construction of large, costly integrated steel plants is limited. Part of the capital may come from the Soviet Union; the rest must be squeezed out of the peasantry, which already lives on one of the world's leanest subsistence margins.

Despite the progress being made in heavy industry by China, the nation still must be regarded as underdeveloped—as a vast agrarian country experiencing increasing difficulty feeding itself. A regimented peasant populace is still doing by hand hundreds of tasks for which Western countries use machines.

AUSTRALIA

Recent Australian industrial expansion has been so great that manufacturing now sustains more people than agriculture and pastoralism, and the nation employs a larger percentage of its people in factories than does the United States. Australia no longer is dependent on overseas sources for its iron and steel.

The Australian iron and steel industry enjoys a virtual monopoly; all the iron and steel consumed within the country is also produced there. Most of the manufacturing (all branches of manufacturing, not just iron and steel) is concentrated in the southeast between Adelaide and Brisbane, for in this region dwell 85 per cent of Australia's 11 million people. Here also are most of the power and available raw materials.

The iron and steel industry is located chiefly in Port Kembla and Newcastle in New South Wales, and near Whyalla in South Australia (Fig. 10-10). Total production (Table 10-1), although small compared with the output of many countries or even a few individual American districts, is large in proportion to total population. A wide variety of products is made—the result of the nation's remoteness.

Most of the coal comes from within a radius of 25 miles of Newcastle and Port Kembla.

The limestone is quarried at Rapid Bay in South Australia and in Marulan, New South Wales; and dolomite is quarried at Ardrossan in South Australia. However, deposits of both are widespread through the country.

The iron ore is produced at two major sources: the Middleback Ranges, near Whyalla in South Australia; and remote Cockatoo and Koolan Islands in Yampi Sound, on the northwest coast of Western Australia.

Despite the rather limited domestic market (including that of New Zealand) and the great distance of the continent from leading foreign markets, major expansion has been taking place in recent years, and exports are substantial because of the low cost of production.

AFRICA

To date, only two countries on the African continent—Egypt and South Africa—have iron and steel industries; but only that of South Africa is important.

Although South Africa is a small producer of steel, the industry is extremely important to her. Each year since 1942 has witnessed a considerable increase in production tonnage with a corresponding reduction in dependence on other countries. South Africa appears to be bent on a program of complete self-sufficiency in steel.

The country is favored with extensive resources of high-quality iron ore and coal, which are conveniently located with respect to each other and to the principal market area. The government-financed plant, ISCOR (Iron and Steel Industrial Corporation, Ltd.) accounts for most of the country's output and meets about 72 per cent of its total needs. The company operates in two locations. The older plant, located at Pretoria, turned out its first ingots in 1934; the younger plant, at Vanderbijl Park in Vereeniging, about 30 miles south of Johannesburg, was established in 1947, mainly because the shortage of water at Pretoria threatened to limit expansion there. The two ISCOR mills derive their iron ore from mines at Thabazimbi (there is here a heavy-ore-beneficiating plant) and at Sishen; their coal from mines in the Transvaal and Natal; and their dolomite from Mooiplaas near Pre-

toria and from Glen Douglas near Henley-on-Klep (for the works at Vanderbijl Park). Both steel-producing areas are well located with respect to markets. The two works produce more than 70 per cent of South Africa's steel requirements. Another plant operates at Newcastle in Natal, but it accounts for only about 10 per cent of the national output.

LATIN AMERICA

In almost every country of Latin America—particularly in Brazil, Mexico, Peru, Colombia, Venezuela, Chile, and Argentina—there is an ardent and determined desire to industrialize and to become self-contained in iron and steel production. Yet the capacity for all the lands from the Río Grande to Cape Horn would not equal that in one of America's major districts. Brazil and Mexico currently account for about 85 per cent of the total Latin American output, but increasing production in Chile and Venezuela may lower this percentage.

BRAZIL

Brazil, with its large government-sponsored plant at Volta Redonda, ranks first among all Latin American nations in both iron and steel capacity and output. This integrated plant, which cost more than 100 million dollars, was constructed practically prefabricated in Cleveland, Ohio, and then sent to Brazil. The works have been expanded in capacity several times. Volta Redonda accounts for about 50 per cent of all the steel made in Brazil. In constructing this plant, the government aimed to stimulate infant steel-using industries. Prior to 1945 almost all domestic pig iron was made in small charcoal furnaces. Except for the plant at Volta Redonda, most of the works still use charcoal made from the fast-growing eucalyptus tree that is found in extensive stands in Minas Gerais. Because hydroelectric power is abundant and low in price, a number of electric furnaces also have been installed.

The vast iron-ore deposits of Brazil, estimated to contain 15 billion tons of ore averaging 50 per cent or more in iron content, are among the world's largest; they are mostly in the state of Minas Gerais.

Volta Redonda is located on the Central do Brasil Railway between Rio de Janeiro and

São Paulo, the two largest consuming centers. The cost of assembling raw materials is high,[7] especially for coal, which must be transported all the way from Santa Catarina (by rail to the port of Laguna), then by ship 500 miles to Angra dos Reis or Rio de Janeiro and again by rail to the plant. Every change in bulk obviously increases the cost of assembling the raw materials. However, domestic coal mines are not yet able to meet all requirements; in 1958, Volta Redonda consumed 705,000 tons of coal, of which 256,000 tons were from Brazil and 449,000 tons were from the United States. The mill was planned for progressive production, and two expansion programs (1956 and 1960) have already been carried out. A third plan is under study to increase annual production to 2 million tons.

It is probably too soon to state categorically whether or not the Volta Redonda location is a wholly satisfactory one. The problem was turned over to a technical commission, which studied the relationships of six places with respect to sources of raw materials, markets, existing means of transportation, and safety in time of war. At two of the locations, close to the Atlantic, assembly costs on raw materials would have been lower than at Volta Redonda. Because in time of war, tidewater plants are particularly vulnerable to attack Volta Redonda was favored as a location. Access to leading domestic markets also was an important consideration.

The site itself is advantageous—a level filled area 3 miles long and ½ mile wide on a bend in the Paraíba River; because of the elevation, 1,200 feet above sea level, the climate is less enervating than that characterizing so much of the tropics.

Most Brazilian mills are close to their iron ore, limestone, dolomite, and manganese. Two new mills have recently been built: one in the state of São Paulo near Santos, geared to meet the demands of São Paulo's growing automobile industry; the other at Ipatinga in the state of Minas Gerais, planned to supply extra-large plates for a new shipbuilding industry. Still

[7] According to "Letter from Brazil," *Fortune*, 35:210, February 1947: "There are no figures available but it is widely believed that one ton of imported steel costs less than one ton of coal delivered to Volta [Redonda]."

another integrated facility is under construction at Piacaguera.

MEXICO

The first modern iron and steel plant in Latin America was established by a group of American, French, and Italian promoters at Monterrey in 1900 and began production in 1903. A second major works was constructed at Monclova in the state of Coahuila in 1944. A plant making steel only was established in Mexico City half a century ago. Until 1941, Mexico was the largest producer of iron and steel in Latin America, but it is presently eclipsed by Brazil (1.4 million vs. 2.1 million tons of steel ingots in 1960). Both the Monterrey and the Monclova plants are integrated, and a third is on the way to partial integration. The two integrated plants are in the northern part of the country. The American company that is becoming partially integrated operates a small blast furnace and a steel plant at Piedras Negras, Coahuila, near the United States–Mexican border; a rolling mill at Lechería, near the Federal District; and two electric furnaces in Mexico City.

Unfortunately, in Mexico the raw materials are not well located with respect to one another, to transportation, or to the country's principal markets. Hence, the industry has grown against a background of handicaps. The largest coal deposits (and most of the coking coal) lie in the Sabinas Basin in the state of Coahuila, far from both the iron ore and the markets for steel. Most of the iron-ore deposits lie in inaccessible areas, which makes them presently unavailable. The largest commercial deposits are to be found west of Mexico City.

Mexico protects its iron and steel industry by high tariffs, tax exemptions, and financial support, including credit and the promotion of new enterprises. In spite of these aids, however, the country is unable to meet its steel requirements—there being an annual deficit of about 325,000 tons, including a number of products that cannot be made domestically.

CHILE

Chile today ranks second in production among South American steel-producing nations and third among the twenty Latin American countries, her output in 1960 exceeding 400,000 tons.

In 1950, Chile put into operation South America's second largest integrated iron and steel complex. The plant is well located at Huachipato on San Vicente Bay near Concepción. San Vicente Bay is sheltered and deep, and this is important since the iron ore must be delivered by vessel.

The cost of assembling iron ore, coal, and limestone at the blast furnaces is lower than in most Latin American plants. The iron ore comes primarily from El Romeral, 500 miles to the north; the domestic coal is close at hand (25 miles), at Lota and Schwager; fluxing limestone is obtained from deposits on Guarello Island just north of the Strait of Magellan about 900 miles distant from the plant; dolomite is quarried at El Maule 150 miles distant, but dolomite for the open-hearth furnaces is transported 4,000 miles from Uruguay. Hydroelectric power is obtained from a plant on the Laja River; transport by sea, railway, and highway is satisfactory; the water supply is good; and ample low-cost labor is available.

Like all other Latin American nations with iron and steel enterprises, Chile uses tariffs and other devices to protect the domestic industry. Nevertheless, it is believed that the Huachipato mill rests on a comparatively firm geographic and economic base and is an asset to Chile's economic development.

PERU

At Chimbote at the mouth of the Santa River is one of the best natural harbors along the northern two thirds of South America's west coast;· and here is located the national integrated steel plant of Peru. However, only about 60,000 tons of steel are made annually. The market is restricted by the country's small population, the biting poverty of the majority of the people, and the small per capita consumption of steel. Peru is still predominantly agricultural and pastoral.

Chimbote has several unique advantages as a metallurgical center; certainly it is the best location in Peru for making iron and steel. Large supplies of high-grade coal, as well as limestone and hydroelectric power, are available in the Santa Valley; and iron ore can be delivered economically by vessel from Marcona, 500 miles to the south. Finally, steel can be shipped economically by water to metropolitan Lima, the nation's largest market.

COLOMBIA

Next to Peru, Colombia has the smallest output of the Latin American countries with integrated iron and steel plants—about 100,-000 tons of ingots (1960). It is by no means certain that Colombia should have launched forth on an iron- and steelmaking program; the World Bank had strongly advised against it, suggesting that because of weaknesses in the location of the proposed plant and the restricted market, it would be better for the country to have a small steel industry at Barranquilla based wholly upon scrap. But the possibility of having an integrated steel industry of their own had fired the imaginations of nationalistic Colombians for many years, and the new plant was inaugurated in October of 1954.

The integrated works is located at Belencito, a village about 160 miles northeast of Bogotá in the department of Boyacá. Belencito is about 21 miles south of Paz del Río, the town that gave its name to the over-all enterprise. Within a radius of only 22 miles from the plant are found the basic materials for iron and steel production—iron ore, coal, limestone, and water. Thus from the standpoint of raw-materials-assembly cost, Belencito is a favorable location.

However, the plant is not in an industrial area, which means that the cost of distributing steel is high. In fact, the plant is quite remote from the more important industrial areas of the country. It is connected by a meter-gauge railway with Bogotá, some 156 miles distant; and to reach Medellín, transshipment to trucks is required. It is reported that the enterprise has not been a successful venture economically.

VENEZUELA

Motivated by the groundswell of nationalism that is continent-wide, Venezuela—not content to continue with the small scrap-fed mill in Caracas—was determined to have a national steel plant. Here, as elsewhere through South America, self-sufficiency is the key word behind the new industrial development.

Should Venezuela from the standpoint of economic geography have developed an integrated iron and steel industry? Venezuelans knew that they faced many formidable problems in developing a wholly new industry, but they did not realize just how formidable these would be. As in all other countries that have launched such programs, the cost of construction was underestimated.

Acting on studies extending over several years, Venezuela decided to locate the plant at San Tomé de Guayana, on the right bank of the Orinoco near its junction with the Caroní and about 9 miles west of the fast-growing new city Puerto Ordaz. Selection of the site was determined by (1) proximity to huge reserves of high-grade iron ore, to limestone, and to natural gas; (2) availability of unlimited, cheap hydroelectric power provided by the harnessing of the falls in the lower Caroní less than 10 miles from Puerto Ordaz; (3) navigability of the Orinoco by high-tonnage vessels; (4) extensive areas of unoccupied flat terrain for the plant and related industries; (5) plenty of water for cooling and other plant uses; and (6) ample labor. Venezuela, however, is poor in resources of coking coal, although this deficiency is partly overcome by the use of low-shaft electric reduction furnaces in making pig iron. These furnaces were chosen instead of conventional blast furnaces because of the poor coal situation. If and when necessary, United States coal could be brought as return cargo by ships carrying iron ore out.

Venezuela has one of the best markets for steel in Latin America. The standard of living is reasonably high, and the petroleum industry uses much steel, especially in the form of seamless tubing. High protective tariffs greatly aid the new mill. Finally, the iron and steel industry is giving Venezuela an opportunity to break the shackles of monoculture.

ARGENTINA

Under Juan Perón an effort was made to transform Argentina from an agricultural and pastoral land to an advanced industrial state. The country, then a small producer of iron and steel, was to have one of the most modern integrated works in Latin America. Such a mill had been an Argentine dream long before Perón came into power. However, after the dictator was forced to leave Argentina, his five-year-plan wilted.

In 1960, at San Nicolás on the Río Paraná upstream from Rosario, Argentina began operating one of the most modern and costly (280 million dollars) integrated iron and steel mills in all Latin America. Designed to produce about 1.8 million tons of steel per year, it has dock and other facilities for handling raw materials; and it makes coke, reduces iron ore, and produces steel. The plant is within 150 miles of 85 per cent of the Argentine steel market, much of which is accessible by water. The Pampa, of course, has the best rail facilities in all South America. It is estimated that the San Nicolás plant will be producing 1.5 million tons in two or three years.

However, from a strictly economic-geographic standpoint, Argentina does not have the suitable combination of conditions to justify a costly integrated iron and steel mill: the country completely lacks coking coal and even the iron-ore reserves are small, of poor quality, and badly located; the great potential hydroelectric-power resources of the Iguassú Falls are little developed and are too distant under present transmission conditions to be economically utilized.

WORLD OUTLOOK

The worldwide importance of iron and steel has been demonstrated. The 1960 output of 377 million tons of steel ingots is impressive; such a tonnage involves the use of quantities of raw materials—many of them assembled from the far corners of the earth. No country is absolutely self-sustaining in these raw materials, though the Soviet Union possibly comes closest. However, her iron ore and coal reserves lie far from one another and from the large steel-consuming markets.

The trend is for higher and higher output. Even the underdeveloped countries are now insisting on making their own steel. In 1960, fifty countries did make it; by 1965 it is estimated that seventy may be doing so. Yet just a few countries contribute the bulk of the entire world output (Table 10-1); in 1960 the United States (99.2 million tons) and the Soviet Union (71.7 million tons) together accounted for almost half of the world total.

Although the American steel industry is facing competition from foreign producers—particularly the Soviet Union—and from domestic aluminum, plastics, plywood, and prestressed concrete, this does not mean that the metallurgical dominance of the United States is going to be too seriously challenged during the next decade or two. On the contrary, the supplies of high-grade iron ore, coking coal, and ferroalloy metals available to the United States and its Free World allies assure an unmatched steelmaking potential.

Among the conditions to be anticipated in the future are better and cheaper methods of ore reduction. By the use of supplementary and less expensive fuels, coke savings are being effected, and the output of hot iron is being increased. Some iron and steel men hope that in the relatively near future electric smelting of iron ore may become economically justifiable. The emancipation of ironmaking

from a fuel supply (coking coal) would be so powerful a factor as to result in the redrawing of the iron and steel map of the entire world. It is claimed that the Norwegians even now make a ton of iron per year for a horsepower of electrical energy. However, alternatives to the blast furnace seem unlikely. Steel engineers at present see no serious rival to the orthodox blast furnace as the mass producer of the metal.[8]

Marked improvements have been made in the past century in this industry—especially in size, efficiency, organization, and quality of product. One of the principal achievements in recent years has been the development of alloy steels and the increased use of electric furnaces. The **oxygen process** in open-hearth furnaces is increasingly being used as a means of speeding up the steelmaking process and of appreciably increasing steel output.

The outstanding fact in the distribution pattern of iron and steel is its concentration around the North Atlantic Basin. This overall picture is expected to change very little, because the underlying factors are basic.

[8] "The Changing Face of Steelmaking," *Engineering*, 185:626, May 16, 1958.

SELECTED REFERENCES

Alexandersson, Gunnar. "Changes in the Location Pattern of the Anglo-American Steel Industry," *Economic Geography*, 37:95-114, April 1961.

Clark, M. Gardner. "Soviet Iron and Steel Industry: Recent Developments and Prospects," *Annals of the American Academy of Political and Social Science*, 303:50-61, January 1956.

Isard, Walter. "Some Locational Factors in the Iron and Steel Industry since the Early Nineteenth Century," *Journal of Political Economy*, 56:203-217, June 1948.

Kerr, Donald. "The Geography of the Canadian Iron and Steel Industry," *Economic Geography*, 35:151-163, April 1959.

Miller, E. Willard. "Lorraine: Metallurgical Center of France," *Mineral Industries* (Pennsylvania State University), 28:1-6, October 1958.

Parrish, John B. "Iron and Steel in the Balance of World Power," *Journal of Political Economy*, 64:369-388, October 1956.

Pounds, Norman J. G., and William N. Parker. *Coal and Steel in Western Europe*. Bloomington, Ind., Indiana University Press, 1957.

Rodgers, Allan. "Industrial Inertia—A Major Factor in the Location of the Steel Industry in the United States," *Geographical Review*, 42:56-66, January 1952.

————. "The Iron and Steel Industry of the Mahoning and Shenango Valleys," *Economic Geography*, 28:331-342, October 1952.

Shabad, Theodore. "China's Resources for Heavy Industry," *Focus*, 9:1-6, November 1958.

"Soviet Iron and Steel: The Drawbacks of the Wide Open Spaces," *Times Review of Industry*, 13 (N.S.):72-73, December 1959.

Sullivan, John D. "Iron and Steel: The Paley Report in Retrospect," *Mining Engineering*, 11:789-796, August 1959.

White, C. Langdon. *Is the West Making the Grade in the Steel Industry?* Stanford, Calif., Stanford University Graduate School of Business, 1956. Business Research Series, No. 8, pp. 1-24.

CHAPTER ELEVEN::

Machinery more than possibly anything else has altered our way of life. When our ancient prototype wanted work done, he had to do it himself. Later, he tamed animals and even enslaved other human beings through conquest to do his work. Civilizations of the past were based upon human slavery. Of course, twentieth-century civilization also is based upon slavery, but *not upon human slavery*. More than 95 per cent of the work performed in the United States, for example, is performed by mechanical slaves; each American has at his bidding some 284 slaves, in the form of 3,000 kilowatt hours of electricity per year.

MACHINE TOOLS

Machine tools are the machines used to make other machines. The manufacture of

THE WORLD'S METAL-

machine tools, therefore, is a very important branch of manufacture because all other mechanized industries depend upon it. Every product known to mankind today requires the use of machine tools. They make possible the production of interchangeable parts in great quantities and hence make possible mass production. Machine tools enabled the United States to evolve in a very short time from an agricultural country to an industrial one. Nations lacking such an industry are dangerously dependent on those that have it, and hence are vulnerable in time of war.

The machine-tool industry processes an intricate and complex set of products—hundreds of different types and sizes of lathes, drills, presses, planers, shapers, boring machines, threading machines, and many others. There are two types of machine tools: (1) special-purpose machines for performing a specific function on a rapid production basis and (2) general-purpose machines for performing multifarious operations.

The design and production of machine tools require much technical knowledge and skilled labor. Accordingly, machine tools are produced largely in countries regarded as maturely developed industrially (Table 11-1).

LOCATIONAL FACTORS

The principal location factors in the machine-tool industry are availability of skilled labor (the labor should be reasonably priced, for it represents at least 70 to 80 per cent of the total cost of making machine tools), presence of outstanding centers for training engineers and technicians, proximity to markets, and availability of raw materials.

FABRICATING INDUSTRIES

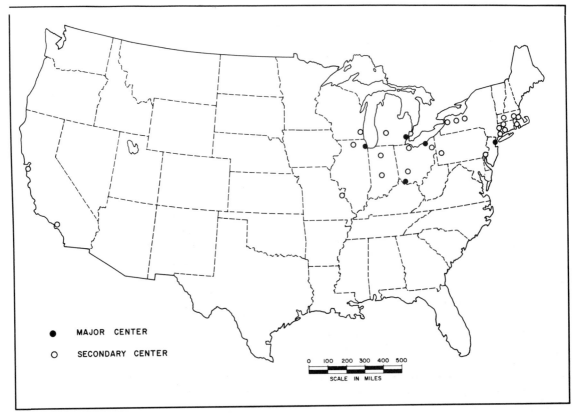

Fig. 11-1. Distribution of the machine-tool industry in the United States. The builders are scattered from New England to the Mississippi River. Almost none exists south of the Ohio River, and only one of substantial size is located on the West Coast. Note particularly New England, the Middle Atlantic states, and the Middle West. The plants shown here make the "master tools of industry." (Map based on data from National Machine Tool Builders' Association, from C. Langdon White and Edwin J. Foscue, Regional Geography of Anglo-America, 2nd ed., Prentice-Hall, Inc., 1954.)

TABLE 11-1

THE FREE WORLD'S MACHINE-TOOL
INDUSTRY

	Manufacturers	Persons employed
United States	500	115,000
West Germany	500	86,760
United Kingdom	480	51,030
France	180	20,100
Switzerland	150	12,000
Sweden	40	12,000
Italy	250	10,000
Belgium	37	3,000
Austria	60	2,300
Netherlands	32	1,600
Canada	9	848

SOURCE: "World Machine Tool Analysis for 1958," *Times Review of Industry*, 13:94, November 1959.

WORLD PRODUCTION

UNITED STATES

Plants producing machine tools in the United States are concentrated primarily north of the Ohio River and east of the Mississippi River (Fig. 11-1). There are seven major producing areas: (1) Chicago-Milwaukee, (2) Detroit-Toledo, (3) Cincinnati–Miami Valley, (4) Cleveland-Pittsburgh, (5) Buffalo-Rochester, (6) Metropolitan New York, and (7) Southern New England. The Lower Great Lakes area dominates with about 60 per cent of the total national output. Ohio, with twice as many companies as any other state, alone accounts for approximately one third of the national output. Its greatest asset is its pool of highly skilled labor.

There are about 500 manufacturers of machine tools in the United States. They are mostly medium sized to small; companies with less than 1,000 workers account for almost 75 per cent of the total United States machine-tool output. It has been intimated that the relatively small size of American plants, the lack of mass production, and the high wages paid, as contrasted with the greater efficiency and lower costs of plants in the Soviet Union, may result in America's losing its leadership in this industry.[1] Many American machine-tool builders, finding themselves unable to compete in the export market, whereas formerly they exported 25 per cent of their production, are now making tools overseas. Wages for skilled workers in West Germany are only 25 per cent of those in American machine-tool centers; even in the United Kingdom skilled labor is available at less than $1 per hour (contrasted with $2.72 in Chicago). Foreign machine tools are today invading the United States; in 1959 imported tools at United States prices accounted for 17½ per cent of United States machine-tool sales, and this despite a 15 per cent tariff.

SOVIET UNION

Prior to the revolution, Russia imported nearly all the machine tools it used. Today, however, the Soviet Union is believed to rank first in world output, exceeding the United States production about four to one. This eminence has been gained recently, for as late as 1955 the Soviet Union was reported to have only 56 per cent as many machine tools as the United States. The leading Soviet machine-tool-manufacturing centers are Chelyabinsk, Kharkov, Kiev, Moscow, Leningrad, Sverdlovsk, and Gorki.

[1] It is difficult for Americans to believe that the people who made mass production possible should operate the machine-tool plants on the job-shop principle of one-at-a-time production and repeated rehandling. However, there is a difference between those industries that turn out consumer goods by the hundreds of thousands and the machine-tool plants that turn out productive machines by the dozen or score; in the machine-tool industry, each machine tool is tailor-made.

WESTERN EUROPE

Nearly all the Western European countries make machine tools. Considered as a unit, Western Europe possibly leads the world in output.

West Germany. West Germany's machine-tool industry ranks third, and the country is also a major exporter. In fact, in the late 1950s, machine tools comprised 20 per cent of total German exports. German labor is highly skilled, hardworking, and reasonably priced compared with that in the United States. Tools comparable in quality and variety with those made in the United States sell abroad for only about a third as much. The German industry is probably the best equipped in the world.[2]

Production of machine tools in Germany is especially closely associated with the highly industrialized Ruhr. The principal manufacturing centers for machine tools are (1) Cologne-Essen-Düsseldorf, (2) Frankfurt, (3) Stuttgart, and (4) Berlin. In all, the outstanding locative factor is the availability of highly skilled workmen—workmen capable of operating machines requiring individual work.

United Kingdom. Despite its prestige as a pioneer (the foundations were laid here between about 1800 and 1887), by 1900 Britain had lost its leadership. Largely because of its failure to keep its plants modern, it now lags behind the Soviet Union, the United

[2] Hermann Heller, a prominent German machine-tool builder and president of the Hannover Fair, gives the following explanation of Germany's position: "The French, British, and Russians stripped our plants ruthlessly of all the machine tools and equipment that we had been operating for three shifts throughout the war. Meanwhile, as the old machine tools were going out the front door, brand-new ones, some purchased with U.S. dollars, were coming in the back. As a result, we have one of the best equipped machine-tool plants in the world today, with which we can produce at costs well below any competition. The French and British likewise have replaced their prewar equipment—with machine tools that we purchased fifteen years ago and operated seven days a week around the clock during seven years of war. It is not a bad way to lose a war." (From Dero A. Saunders, "What's Ahead for Machine Tools?" *Fortune*, 48:128, July 1953.)

States, and Germany in the manufacture of machine tools.

The quality of British machine tools is second to none, for emphasis has always been on quality. Among the principal centers are the Sheffield area (which accounts for about 75 per cent of the total), Birmingham, Coventry, Glasgow, London, and Manchester. Sheffield's predominance results from its proximity to coal and steelmaking facilities, to a large pool of highly skilled workers, and to a long-standing reputation for high-grade goods. The name "Sheffield" on a machine tool means what "sterling" does on a piece of silver.

Belgium. Belgium's machine-tool industry is world-famous. Its advantages are low production costs (as a result of comparatively low-priced labor), highly skilled workers, and machine tools of precision, high quality, and wide variety. With a limited home market, Belgium must export, and she is a formidable competitor. Liège and Namur are the leading centers.

France. With its skilled workers, France manufactures high-quality tools, but does not make enough to supply domestic requirements. The industry's 180 manufacturers are centered at Lille, St. Ouen, Mouseron, and Venissieux. France produces general-purpose tools.

Switzerland. Though poor in mineral resources and badly located for importing them, Switzerland nonetheless enjoys great assets in her highly skilled labor, advanced technology, and abundant and cheap hydroelectric power. (Switzerland ranks third among the countries of the world in per capita installation and in cost per kilowatt hour.) In the Swiss machine-tool industry, the labor factor represents 70 to 80 per cent of the final cost of the product. Almost every Swiss worker, urban dweller or farmer, is primarily a mechanic. The quality of Swiss machine tools is high. Plants are invariably small in size and in number of workers. Zurich is the principal center, but the industry is widely scattered. A sizable surplus (at least two

thirds) of all machine tools is available for export.

Italy. Italy has, in the north, a world-famous machine-tool industry. Nevertheless, Italy is not yet able to meet even all her own requirements. The principal centers are Milan, Bologna, Genoa, and Turin, whose major advantages are availability of skilled labor, high-quality steel, and abundant and low-cost hydroelectric power.

Sweden. Sweden enjoys an enviable reputation for the originality and high quality of her machine tools. She has great human resources, an abundance of hydroelectric power, and some of the world's highest-quality steel. Though the industry is highly decentralized, Göteborg and the cities and towns surrounding it lead; Bofors, Kopin, Sandviken, Stockholm, and Vasteras also are important centers. Swedish machine tools compete in all foreign markets because of their high quality and reasonable price.

EASTERN EUROPE AND ASIA

Czechoslovakia. Czechoslovakia's engineering industry has had a long and honored record. The country is the most highly industrialized and most skillfully managed of the nations behind the Iron Curtain. Czechoslovakia has one of the most highly skilled pools of labor in the world; it formerly served as the arsenal of the Austro-Hungarian Empire. Its machine tools rank among the best and are in great demand among the Communist lands. Principal centers are Pilsen, Czeskomoravska, Kolben-Danek (Praga), Strakonice, and Brno.

Japan. Japan is the only Far Eastern country with a modern machine-tool industry. Prior to World War II, there were more than 1,000 small Japanese factories in central Honshu turning out machine tools. In 1937, largely by government action, the small plants were consolidated into five large concerns, which accounted for about 90 per cent of the total output. In the beginning there was part-by-part copying of foreign machine tools. Invariably the machines were inferior, for the little plants lacked capital and competent technicians. Today Japan produces machine tools comparable with those made in the United States and Western Europe. Production is centered in the Tokyo-Yokohama, the Kobe-Osaka, and the Nagoya, Karatsu, and Niigata areas.

AGRICULTURAL IMPLEMENTS AND FARM TRACTORS

Since 1831, when Cyrus McCormick invented the reaper, farm implements have poured so profusely from the drawing boards of American inventors and manufacturers that almost every farm operation can be performed by a machine. These machines now enable the United States with fewer farmers to produce more food and fiber than at any time in its history. The American farmer making full use of these labor-saving machines produces four hundred times more food than he eats.

Conditions in the United States were just right for the development of the farm-implement industry: (1) huge areas of flat to undulating land with fertile soils; (2) cheap land (the best of it was available for as little as $2½ per acre); (3) relatively small farm population but costly labor; (4) growing markets in Northwestern Europe and eastern United States.

WORLD PRODUCTION OF FARM IMPLEMENTS

Nearly all the world's farm implements are invented, manufactured, and used in the developed countries and particularly those that are highly industrialized—the United States, Canada, Great Britain, West Germany, Australia, and the Soviet Union.

UNITED STATES

The American farm-implement industry produces essentially for the United States market. Instead of sending machines from Ameri-

can plants, American companies have manufacturing facilities in many of the nations of the world. Unlike so many other industries, whose number of companies and plants is diminishing, the agricultural-implement industry has more than 1,500 companies—twice the number it had in 1900. Besides the big, full-line companies, there are hundreds that construct highly specialized machines for regional markets.

The American implement industry had its inception along the Eastern Seaboard, but with the opening up of the Middle West the industry began to migrate westward via New York, Pennsylvania, and Ohio. Illinois ultimately became the leading producing state, and today about half the national output comes from there. Three fourths of all American farm implements are made in the so-called "Implement Belt" (Fig. 11-2).

The principal location factor underlying this industry is proximity to major agricultural areas, where transport facilities, ready access to steel production, and availability of farm markets are combined. For implements to be used in the Middle West there could be no better locations than Chicago, Detroit, Louisville, Milwaukee, Moline, Peoria, Racine, South Bend, and Indianapolis (Fig. 11-3). However, an announcement by the International Harvester Company in 1959 that it was discontinuing production of farm implements at its Chicago McCormick Works was of great interest to economic geographers; for Chicago had long been regarded as one of the most logical and low-cost locations for this industry. The reasons given for curtailing production in Chicago were the decrease in the number of farms in the United States, the decline of the export business, high cost of distribution of equipment, obsolescent buildings, and too much plant capacity.

California is selected for discussion here because it has an important place in the nation's agriculture and because it had to develop originality in manufacturing farm implements, since many of its problems and its crops differ from those of the East. Because California labor is so expensive, the farmer has to substitute machines for men in order

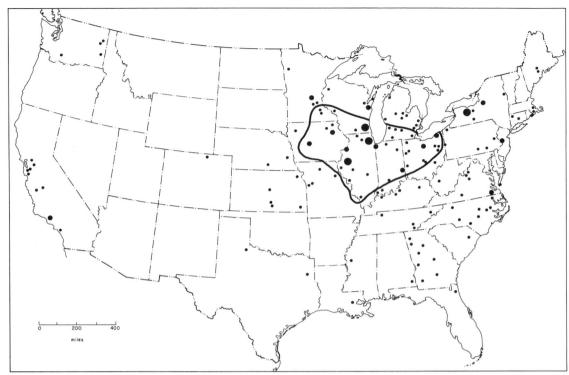

Fig. 11-2. Agricultural-implement plants in the United States. Though the industry is widely distributed, its heart is the so-called "Implement Belt" (outlined in black). This area is well located for assembling coal, natural gas, iron, steel, and equipment and for distributing the product to market—the major agricultural regions. (Based on data from Census of Manufactures.)

Fig. 11-3. International Harvester Company plant in Indianapolis. This facility produces motors for trucks, employing more than 3,000 workers. (Courtesy of International Harvester Company.)

to keep costs to a minimum. Emphasis is on the reduction and elimination of arduous hand and stoop labor. There is accordingly a machine to do virtually every task. Examples of farm machines developed in California are the crawler tractor (which pulls giant plows that turn a furrow 6 feet deep to bring to the surface flood or wind-buried topsoil), the combine, heavy-duty offset disk, deep tiller, subsoiler, special type of potato digger, sugarbeet harvester, seed harvester, pulverizer, bed shaper, crop and hay loader, land leveler, chisel, asparagus picker, grape harvester, improved cotton picker, and improved lettuce and tomato harvesters. Most of California's rice is seeded and most of its cotton defoliated from airplanes.

In California small agricultural-implement companies outnumber large ones. They manufacture items not produced by the large Eastern manufacturers—items that are specialized, expensive, and often custom-built.

The principal center is Stockton in the middle of the Central Valley; but Fresno, Bakersfield, and Sacramento, other valley cities, also are important. Los Angeles, San Diego, San Francisco, and San Jose also are impressive.

CANADA

With vast expanses of attractive farmland, a small agricultural population, and an enormous farm output, Canada logically has an outstanding agricultural-implement industry. Moreover, being highly nationalistic, Canada desires to manufacture as many as possible of her own goods, including agricultural implements. Her companies, particularly the larger ones, function precisely as do the larger ones in the United States. Her Massey-Ferguson Company, with branches in the United States, Europe, and elsewhere, is one of the oldest and largest in the world. It operates at Coventry the largest tractor plant in Europe.

Most of Canada's factories are concentrated in the Ontario Peninsula and in the St. Lawrence Lowland in Toronto, Brantford, and Woodstock. Ontario accounts for about 95 per cent of the total output. The plant locations are near the farmlands of Ontario and close to the primary iron and steel and machine-tool industries.

GREAT BRITAIN

The farm-implement industry is of long standing in Britain, many of the early machines having been invented and made there. Britain's advantages consist of an early start, availability of well-distributed iron and steel and machine-tool industries, and a pool of highly skilled workers. In the past the industry was based on the export market, inasmuch as agriculture was largely neglected until World War II. Now, however, Britain produces 70 to 80 per cent of her own food. The equipment used in growing the food crops is supplied mostly by British companies or Canadian and American companies operating in Great Britain.

The farm-implement industry is distributed throughout the south and east of England, the leading centers being Greater London, particularly Dagenham but also Gainsborough, Grantham, Hounslow, and Southampton, Coventry, Doncaster, Kilmarnock, Leeds, and Newark.

SOVIET UNION

Among the many claims being made by the Soviet Union is the assertion that its agriculture is today the world's most highly mechanized, and that it has correspondingly the largest agricultural-implement production. That farm operations in those areas of extensive production are highly mechanized is indeed true, but the bulk of Russian farm work still is performed by human labor rather than with machinery. Russia in farm mechanization is where the United States was more than 25 years ago.[3]

[3] R. V. Hanson, Editor of *Successful Farming*, returned from a trip to the USSR in October, 1959, and in addressing representatives of the farm machinery manufacturers stated: "... There was some beautiful, modern farm machinery on exhibition, but we saw not a single piece of it at work. The tractors we saw were 15 or 20 years behind American models today. It took three men to run a plow that one man would operate in America. The factories making farm machinery were usually dark and dingy...." (From "Soviet Agriculture Found Inefficient," *New York Times*, October 22, 1959.)

Nonetheless, the manufacture of agricultural implements is one of the most important industrial enterprises in the Soviet Union, output having increased more than fortyfold since the Revolution. The leading centers are at Zaporozhe in the Ukraine, Rostov in the North Caucasus (one of the largest and best equipped in the country), Saratov in the Volga region, and Lyubertsy near Moscow. A more recent development is Irkutsk—2,600 miles distant from Moscow.

WORLD PRODUCTION OF FARM TRACTORS

Most of the world's tractors are constructed in a dozen countries (Table 11-2).

TABLE 11-2

ESTIMATES OF WORLD TRACTOR PRODUCTION IN UNITS, 1958

Country	Production in units
United States	234,000
Great Britain	140,600
West Germany	118,900
France	83,000
Italy	15,000
Sweden	8,000
Austria	5,000
Argentina	4,500
Canada	4,200
Australia	2,000
Yugoslavia	2,000
World Total	617,200

SOURCE: "Traveling Tractors: Producers Spur Imports from Foreign Plants," *Wall Street Journal*, April 20, 1959. (No figures are available for the Soviet Union.)

UNITED STATES

Until 1934, when the tractor ushered in the technological revolution and drastically changed American agriculture, all machines were pulled by horses. The invention and later the almost universal adoption of the gasoline and diesel tractor caused the virtual elimination of the horse. By 1944, when the number of tractors was about half the number today, tractors were credited with saving farmers 1.7 billion man-hours.

The principal tractor-manufacturing centers are in the American Manufacturing Region—Chicago, Racine, Rockford, Detroit, Milwaukee, Moline, Peoria, and Louisville. The largest tractor factory in the world is in Louisville.

SOVIET UNION

The manufacture of tractors is the most important phase of the Russian agricultural-implement industry. The largest tractor plant in the country and one of the largest in the world is located at Chelyabinsk, which is situated at "the gates" of Western Siberia (a huge market) as well as near power and raw materials. Large tractor works also are to be found in Kharkov and Volgograd in the heart of important farming areas.

UNITED KINGDOM

Particularly since the outbreak of World War II the United Kingdom has been a leader in the manufacture of tractors. Production is restricted to a few plants at Coventry and Dagenham.

THE AUTOMOTIVE INDUSTRY

In little more than half a century the motor vehicle has completely changed the way of life and altered the distribution of population over many portions of the earth. The manufacture of motor vehicles is an assembly technique and involves standardized and interchangeable parts and mass production. The assembly line can turn out a finished car every minute. Twelve countries account for nearly the entire production: the United States, 48 per cent; West Germany, 14 per cent; the United Kingdom, 10 per cent; France, 8 per cent; Japan, 7 per cent; Italy, 5 per cent; the Soviet Union, 4 per cent; Canada, 3 per cent; and Australia, 1 per cent (Table 11-3). This distribution of world output illustrates the overwhelming weight of the market factor: only countries enjoying a high standard of living can have many motor vehicles. In the

TABLE 11-3

LEADING COUNTRIES IN MOTOR-VEHICLE PRODUCTION, 1961

	Passenger cars	Trucks	Buses	Total
United States	5,522,019	1,130,919	—	6,652,938
West Germany	1,751,889	387,360	8,548	2,147,797
United Kingdom	1,003,967	443,117	17,050	1,464,134
France	987,503	214,417	2,489	1,204,409
Japan	249,508	777,985 *	10,981	1,038,474
Italy	693,695	62,816	2,629	759,140
Soviet Union	148,800	405,600	—	554,400
Canada	327,979	62,918	—	390,897
Australia	182,464	49,187	—	231,651
Subtotal	10,867,824	3,534,319	41,697	14,443,840
World Total	11,390,629	3,779,893	57,723	15,228,245

* Includes 224,595 three-wheeled vehicles.

SOURCE: Based on Automobile Manufacturers Association, *Automobile Facts and Figures*, Detroit, 1962.

United States nearly three out of every four families own automobiles, and 14 per cent of all families own two or more cars. Sixty-six per cent of all the passenger cars in the world are used in the United States.

UNITED STATES

The United States is nearly as important in this industry as all the rest of the world combined. Conspiring to guarantee a huge market are the high per capita annual income, the incomparable highway system (over 3 million miles, two-thirds surfaced), the great amount of suburban living (the automobile made this possible), and the desire (largely created by advertising) to possess one or more cars.

The industry is concentrated primarily in the Lower Lake area (Fig. 11-4), where the following combination of conditions is highly favorable:

1. An early start by imaginative "pioneers" of the industry, such as Henry Ford and Ransom Olds.
2. Cheap water transportation for all raw materials needed for making iron and steel.
3. The Great Lakes and the new St. Lawrence Seaway for shipping parts and assembled cars.
4. Excellent railway and highway networks

for assembling raw materials and distributing assembled cars.
5. Ample room—flat land for the huge, sprawling plants.
6. Proximity to makers of parts.
7. A large pool of skilled, semiskilled, and unskilled labor.
8. A large market at hand.

Three companies (the "Big Three") account for 95 per cent of all automobiles and a good share of the trucks and buses. Survival in the field requires huge capital investment, customer and promotional acceptance, and high resale value. Consequently, casualties have been unusually high in the industry: of the many companies that manufactured 2,700 different makes, only six have survived.

Detroit is now the automotive-manufacturing center of the world (Fig. 11-5). During the early years of automobile manufacturing, however, operations were widely scattered: in eastern Massachusetts, northern New Jersey, the Hudson-Mohawk Valley, the Connecticut Valley, southeastern Pennsylvania, Cleveland, and Chicago. In 1909 the center of activity shifted to the Middle West. Detroit's supremacy came in 1914—the year the moving assembly line was perfected by the Ford Motor Company. Actually, Detroit had no economic-geographic advantages over Chicago, Milwaukee, Cleveland, or Buffalo as a center for automobile manufacture; and it became

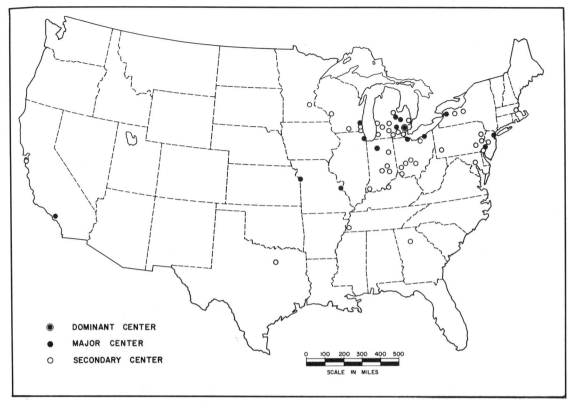

Fig. 11-4. Distribution of the automotive industry in the United States. Detroit is regarded as the heart of the industry; however, neighboring cities and towns in Michigan, Indiana, and Ohio also are important.

the automotive center largely through accident: it was the hub of a circle within which were located many of the pioneers of the business, notably Henry Ford. However, the choice of Detroit proved to be advantageous. In the first place, it is conveniently located for shipment of parts to assembly plants anywhere in the nation. Also the automotive industry had to be located centrally with respect to steel. Detroit is itself an important and growing iron and steel center; and, during the seven or eight months of the navigation season, it is accessible by water from the great steelmaking centers at South Chicago, Gary, Cleveland, Lorain, and Buffalo. Outstanding automotive-making centers besides Detroit are Flint, Lansing, Pontiac, Kenosha, South Bend, and Toledo.

Actually the automotive industry is decentralizing out of Detroit—decentralizing toward both sea coasts and even overseas to assembly plants located close to markets. The parts equivalent of ten automobiles can be put in a single boxcar that can hold only four assembled cars. There are at present more than 100 plants engaged in some phase of automobile assembly to better serve local markets. This does not mean, however, that Michigan-and Detroit are withering on the production vine; nearly all the qualifications that made this area the center of the industry in the beginning are still functioning.

Decentralization and the rise of the assembly plant result also from high labor costs in Detroit (which is particularly vulnerable to strikes and work stoppages because of the heavy concentration of the industry there), the strength of the unions, and the high cost of living in the Detroit area. Finally, the automotive industry appears to be fitting into a

Fig. 11-5. The Ford River Rouge plant, Dearborn, Michigan. This 2-square-mile industrial area includes blast furnaces, steel mill, foundries, pressed-steel operations, engine-producing facilities, final assembly, and other operations. (Courtesy of Ford Motor Company.)

traditional industrial pattern: in the early stages, there is much concentration, which is followed later by decentralization and dispersion.

Contrary to what many persons believe, the automotive industry is not a single industry; the automobile is an assembled product. As many as 5,000 factories may supply parts for a single automobile (in 1959 General Motors purchased items from 27,500 businesses —70 per cent of which employed fewer than one hundred persons). Factories making parts, but definitely a division of the industry, reach out a considerable distance from Detroit. Thus the symbol "Detroit" stretches out into a network of about 1,050 factories owned by about 850 companies with unnumbered hundreds of subcontractors and suppliers, in 1,-375 communities in 44 states.

CANADA

Canada, in eighth place, has an impressive automotive industry. On a per capita basis, its output roughly equals that of the United States. As in the United States, there is one major center, Windsor (Oshawa and Oakville also are important); but there are dozens of "automobile cities." Also as in the United States, the companies purchase most of their parts—sources being Chatham, Galt, Hamilton, Ingersoll, Kitchener, Merritton, Niagara Falls, Sarnia, St. Catharines, Stratford, and Wallaceburg. Windsor, across the river from Detroit, shares all the advantages of Detroit, except the large market. It also has branches of the big American companies. Windsor is the largest automotive center in the British Commonwealth. Since Canada's volume is comparatively low in this mass-production

Fig. 11-6. A night view of the great Volkswagen automotive works, Wolfsburg, near Hannover, Germany. The sturdy little automobile manufactured here outranks in volume all other foreign-car imports in the United States. (Courtesy of Presse- und Informationsamt, Federal Republic of Germany.)

enterprise, the Canadian automotive industry is protected by a high tariff (17½ per cent). It was this protection, plus British Commonwealth preferential tariffs, that caused United States companies to establish manufacturing plants in Canada.

UNITED KINGDOM

Though a small producer compared with the United States, the United Kingdom is the third largest manufacturer of cars in the world and is the second largest exporter of automotive vehicles. It builds the greatest number of trucks and buses in Europe. Production and exports each year reach record levels. More British people now own cars than at any previous time, and more roads are being constructed than at any time since the Roman occupation.

The industry is located in two major clusters: (1) the Birmingham-Coventry area and (2) the Greater London area. Coventry is the "Detroit" of Britain. Greater London's cars are mostly models assembled from parts that are largely manufactured elsewhere.

WEST GERMANY

West Germany, world's second largest automotive producer, is also Europe's principal manufacturer of automobiles. Its most famous make, the Volkswagen, produced at Wolfs-

burg near Hannover (Fig. 11-6), outstrips all other European makes in exports—57 per cent of Europe's total production. Its appeal results from reliability and economy. The Mercedes-Benz, made in Stuttgart, also is well regarded. Other important centers are Cologne, Frankfurt, and Kassel. In addition, several American companies manufacture small cars in Germany.

FRANCE

France, the world's fourth-ranking automotive manufacturer, has been attempting to overtake the United Kingdom and Germany. Present output is about five times greater than the output prior to World War II. Like the other European automobile manufacturers, France exports large numbers of small cars. Principal centers are Billancourt, Flins, and Poissy. The Renault plants at Flins and Billancourt are among the most automated factories in the world.

ITALY

Italy, the sixth largest manufacturer of automobiles, is known for the Fiat, which alone accounts for 90 per cent of the country's output of cars and 50 per cent of the trucks. Most of the Fiat plants are in Turin; the Mirafiori plant on the edge of the city is large and very modern, employing assembly-line methods.

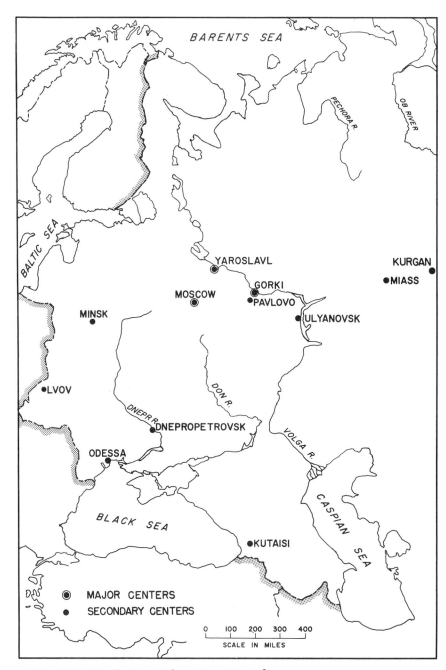

Fig. 11-7. Distribution of the automotive industry in the Soviet Union. The entire production is
in European Russia—from the Ural Mountains
westward. The Moscow area leads with plants
in Moscow, Gorki, and Yaroslavl.

Automobiles are made also in Milan and Bolzano.

SOVIET UNION

The Soviet Union today ranks seventh in world production of automobiles and trucks. The majority of the Russian output consists of trucks. The industry is concentrated in the Central Industrial Region (Fig. 11-7). Gorki—the Soviet "Detroit," with the largest automotive plants in Europe—has long been an important center in the construction of transport equipment and has many skilled workers. Moscow ranks second. These two cities together account for more than half of the national output.

The Soviet plants, unlike those in the United States, are self-contained units, with their own forging and casting shops, machine shops, and assembly shops. In addition, some plants make a number of their own machine tools and spare parts.

BRAZIL

Brazil is the principal South American country with a growing automotive industry. As a result of intense nationalism, all vehicles must be made with Brazilian raw materials and by Brazilian labor, and basic materials for the industry are difficult to procure. The industry in Brazil locates in areas of high population concentration and along highways, where automobiles operate best. Nearly all the plants are in São Paulo and en route to the Santos area, though a large transmission plant is in Valinhos, 45 miles northwest of São Paulo. Some plants are located along the São Paulo–Rio de Janeiro route.

JAPAN

Until recently Japan's role in the world's automotive industry was small. Prior to World War II, the automotive industry was the most backward of the Japanese heavy industries. However, today Japan is a major producer, with more than a million standard units pro-duced annually; a major achievement for an industry that had to be rebuilt from the rubble of World War II. More trucks than automobiles are made. The industry is concentrated in the Tokyo-Yokohama area.

ELECTRICAL EQUIPMENT

The electrical-manufacturing industry had its inception in the vision of a small number of pioneers; it grew because it supplied man with a means of lightening his work. It has had far-reaching effects on human existence. Today, motors are used in almost all industries.

Although the steam engine brought about an industrial revolution, it was limited by the distance the power could be transmitted. Electricity furnished the means of transmitting the engine's energy by wire over long distances. The result has been that in many countries every city, village, and hamlet, and even most farms have power at the turn of a switch. No longer is power chained to the coal mine and the steam engine.

ANGLO-AMERICA

In both the United States and Canada the greater part of the industry is located in the American Manufacturing Region, mainly because this area has raw materials, technological knowledge, skilled labor, efficient transportation, and other well-developed machinery industries, as well as a large market for the products. Schenectady, New York, and Pittsburgh, Pennsylvania, are world famous as the homes of General Electric and Westinghouse, producers of a whole gamut of things electrical. Large companies in the United States for many years had their plants in a single location, but recently they have decentralized in some instances into numerous localities. Few companies in any industry, for example, have plants so widely distributed as does General Electric. Research is a major aspect of this business; almost all companies, even the smaller ones, annually allocate large sums for scientific research.

A new branch of this industry is electronics, which has grown so rapidly that it now ranks fifth in size among all American industries, having done 16 billion dollars worth of business in 1960. This industry extends into every facet of the American economy; it is the very backbone of missiles and space satellites, office and factory automation, banking and insurance operation. It employs almost 2 million persons in jobs that did not exist about a decade ago. Though the enterprise consists of more than 3,700 firms, 50 account for three fourths of the dollar volume of the business.

One location factor of the electronics industry is particularly interesting: *scientific knowledge*. Plants tend to locate close to great universities—Massachusetts Institute of Technology and Harvard; California Institute of Technology and UCLA; Stanford and the University of California. By supplying highly trained research personnel, these institutions have spawned hubs of electronics, missile, and space industries. Pleasant climate also is a major factor in the location of the industry in California.

EUROPE

The electrical industry is particularly well developed in the United Kingdom, West Germany, and France; but it is important also in Belgium, Italy, the Netherlands, Sweden, and Switzerland. In all these nations the standard of living is high or reasonably so, technological knowledge and skilled labor are plentiful, and raw materials and markets are at hand. In the United Kingdom this industry is noteworthy in Birmingham, Greater London, and Manchester. British plants are internationally famous for heavy electrical machines, wires, and cables. In West Germany the principal centers are to be found in the Ruhr-Rhine region, in West Berlin, and in the provinces of Saxony and Bavaria. In East Germany, East Berlin perhaps ranks highest. The Soviet Union, with its extraordinary development of electric power, had to have a corresponding

expansion in the electrical industries. The outstanding centers are Leningrad, Bryansk, Ufa, Sverdlovsk, Kharkov, Tula, Ishevsk, and especially Moscow for motors, turbines, and electrical apparatus.

ASIA

In Asia, only Japan ranks high in the electrical-equipment industry. Industrial poverty in most of the fossil fuels, richness of water power, short distances for transmitting electricity, and a dense population with the highest standard of living for Asia have stimulated the electrical-equipment industry for the generation and transmission of power, light, and heat. Principal centers are Kobe, Osaka, and Tokyo.

MERCHANT SHIPBUILDING

Shipbuilding is custom construction; every ship is different and hence must be tailored to customer specifications. Mass-production methods have been tried but have not as yet proved successful. To make ships, a country or area must have technological knowledge, skilled and relatively low-cost labor, a long history of shipbuilding, an iron and steel industry of impressive dimensions, and numerous subsidiary industries for installing the thousands of machines, instruments, and fittings that go into a ship. A shipyard may be regarded as an assembly plant, to which various lines of manufacturing contribute— steam engines, turbines, furniture, pumps, etc., which are brought to the shipyard to fabricate into a ship.

The size of the modern ocean liner or tanker is almost beyond comprehension. The liner *United States* is 990 feet long and 101 feet wide, and can carry two thousand passengers and a crew of eleven hundred. It cost 72 million dollars to construct. Oil tankers are today huge and becoming bigger steadily. The Japanese build the largest tankers; one, the *Universe Apollo* (Fig. 11-8), is 950 feet long, 135 feet wide, 67.6 feet from bottom to main deck, has a draught of 48 feet when fully loaded, and cost about 15 million dollars.

Fig. 11-8. Huge oil tanker built in Japanese shipyard. Although a ship this size can transport oil at about half the cost of a 12,000-ton tanker, relatively few ports can accommodate it. Currently this tanker could not make a transit through either the Panama Canal or the Suez Canal. (Courtesy of Consulate General of Japan.)

LOCATION OF SHIPBUILDING

Production of merchant ships reflects a nation's concern for maritime trade. Any country or area that builds ships must benefit from a combination of favorable circumstances:

1. It must have a large, experienced, and low-cost labor supply. Labor accounts for about 35 per cent of the cost of a ship. A given yard employs thousands of workers, draftsmen, craftsmen, and engineers. Labor costs vary widely. The Society of Naval Architects and Marine Engineers gave these direct hourly wage rates for 1959: the United States, $2.71; Sweden, $1.06; the United Kingdom, $0.81; West Germany, $0.65; the Netherlands, $0.56; France, $0.51; Italy, $0.49; and Japan, $0.40.

2. It must either have at hand important iron and steel mills or have easy access to them. Materials comprise about 65 per cent of the total cost of ships, and among these steel makes up about 20 per cent for the hull and superstructure alone. Steel also is the principal ingredient in the main engines, auxiliary engines, and deck machinery.

3. It must have a climate that permits outdoor work for many days in the year.

4. It must have commodious harbors and ports.

WORLD PRODUCTION

The leading shipbuilding nations are mostly in Europe (Fig. 11-9). The only large producers outside Europe are Japan (Fig. 11-10) and the United States (Fig. 11-11), though some other countries do build ships.

JAPAN

Japan is today the premier shipbuilding nation of the world (Table 11-4). The country has long been important in this industry, but only since World War II has she moved into first place. In 1957 Japan set a peacetime construction record, accounting for 29 per cent of the total world output. She also led the world in oil-tanker construction, with 36 per cent. The Japanese are a hardworking and realistic people and are determined to adapt their economy to the changing times. Shipbuilding has been a major factor in restoring prosperity to Japan.

Japan's advantages for shipbuilding are (1) the world's biggest yards (and the trend is definitely toward larger vessels, particularly

Fig. 11-9. Principal shipbuilding centers of Europe. Western Europe constructs most of the world's ships.

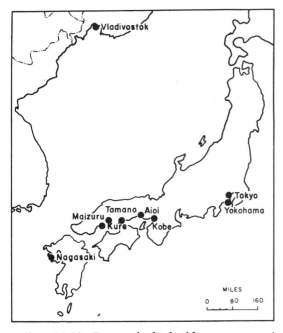

Fig. 11-10. Principal shipbuilding centers of Japan.

Fig. 11-11. Principal shipbuilding centers of the United States.

THE WORLD'S METAL-FABRICATING INDUSTRIES::225

TABLE 11-4

SHIP LAUNCHINGS FOR TEN LEADING SHIPBUILDING NATIONS, 1958

Country	1958 tons
Japan	2,066,669
West Germany	1,429,261
United Kingdom	1,401,980
Sweden	760,206
Italy	550,796
Netherlands	555,697
France	450,986
United States	732,381
Norway	259,020
Denmark	250,388

SOURCE: "Ship Launchings Reach High in '58," *New York Times,* February 22, 1959.

of oil tankers, (2) low cost of production—about 20 per cent below the European costs, (3) exceptionally attractive credit terms, (4) early deliveries, (5) high state of industrialization, (6) favorable exchange rates, (7) much skilled labor procurable at low wages (in 1957 the average monthly wage for Japanese shipbuilding workers was $50, but many earned an additional $12.50 to $17.50 a month in overtime), (8) ships built for delivery at fixed prices (whereas European yards make contracts with escalator clauses), (9) occasional government subsidization of ships for export, (10) a very large home market for ships as a result of the outstanding fishing and trading activities, (11) a relatively mild climate, and (12) numerous good harbors and ports.

The industry is concentrated in a number of centers: Kure, Kobe, Nagasaki, Tokyo, Maizuru, Taman, Aioi, Yokohama—mostly on the big island of Honshu (Fig. 11-10).

UNITED KINGDOM

For generations (until 1956, when Japan moved into first place) Britain led the world in shipbuilding, in keels laid, tonnage launched, and tonnage completed. Leadership stemmed from the availability of iron and steel produced at centers on tidewater, skilled labor at reasonable wages (cheaper than in continental Europe and the United States), an early start in the machine-tool industry, mild climate, adequate capital for financing, momentum of an early start, government aid and stimulation, and a large domestic market for ships as well as prestige in foreign markets. However, this nation has slumped into third place during the past several years (Table 11-4).

The numerous harbors and rivers along the drowned coast line provide many excellent sites for shipyards. Possibly only Japan is as well off in this respect. The British shipbuilding industry is located in several different areas; but the northeast coast of England centering on Tyneside, Sunderland, and Teeside leads, accounting for about 75 per cent of the total output. Farther south are London and Hull. Along the west coast of England, too, on the lower Mersey at Birkenhead and Barrow-in-Furness are impressive shipyards.

In Scotland the Clyde estuary below Glasgow, with twenty-two shipyards, is outstanding. There is also production in eastern Scotland at Dundee, Burnt Island, Leith, and Aberdeen. During the past seventy years, more ships were built along the 20 miles of river at Glasgow, Port Glasgow, and Greenrock than on any other river in the world. Important production also takes place at Belfast in Northern Ireland in the Lagan estuary, but the industry here is dependent on the Clyde area for its steel.

GERMANY

Possessing one of the world's outstanding primary iron and steel industries (as well as every type of industry using steel), skilled labor, technological leadership, and deepwater bays, and being a relatively poor country in natural resources, Germany logically should have a great shipbuilding industry. In 1958 West Germany ranked second. Her yards construct all types of ships—ore carriers, passenger-freighters, tankers. Principal shipyards are in Hamburg, Bremen, Kiel, Bremerhaven, Lübeck, and Emden.

SCANDINAVIAN COUNTRIES

The three great seafaring nations—Norway, Sweden, and Denmark—rank high in shipbuilding, despite their unimportance in heavy industry (iron and steel). Sweden is most important in the group and ranks fourth in world tonnage output. With lower construction costs than the United Kingdom, Sweden is a strong competitor. Chief centers are Göteborg, Uddevalla, and Malmö.

Shipbuilding is in many respects Denmark's most important industry. She ranks tenth in world output and exports more than half the ships constructed. Largest yards are at Copenhagen, but ships are constructed also at Nakskov, Odense, Elsinore, Aalborg, and Frederikshavn.

Norway, one of the world's great maritime nations, builds ships at Bergen, Oslo, and Stavanger, and ranks ninth in world tonnage output.

THE NETHERLANDS

Shipbuilding is the largest of the mechanical industries in the Netherlands. Almost every type of vessel is constructed. Chief centers are Rotterdam, Amsterdam, and Heusden.

FRANCE

France ranks seventh among world shipbuilding nations. Most of the raw materials and labor are readily available. The industry is widely dispersed, leading centers being Bordeaux, Le Trail, Dunkerque, Le Havre, Toulon, and Marseilles, with St. Nazaire as the outstanding one. France builds all kinds of vessels for her own use as well as for other nations. She has constructed a number of specially designed craft for the Soviet Union for use in areas of heavy ice. In one respect she is ahead of Great Britain: she can construct tankers of 100,000 tons deadweight. However, construction costs are high. The government subsidizes the industry on "prestige" grounds.

ITALY

Italy has long ranked among the ten top shipbuilding nations and now ranks fifth. She builds passenger-freighters and whaling vessels and tankers, and some of her craft rank among the world's finest. The industry is stimulated by a state subsidy amounting to 27 per cent of the cost of every ton of new shipping. Some of the shipyards are among the world's best, and many of the techniques (e.g., electric welding and the manufacture of aluminum alloy bodies) are unsurpassed. Principal yards are in the Genoa area; but Monfalcone, La Spezia (between Genoa and Leghorn), Palermo, and Trieste are also important.

UNITED STATES

Under ordinary conditions the United States does not rank high in shipbuilding (Table 11-4) because she cannot compete; it costs American shipyards twice as much to produce a dead-weight ton as it does Japan. In the United States approximately 80 per cent of the cost of building a large ship consists of wages for labor. Moreover, construction standards in American shipbuilding are very high, thereby adding further to the cost.

American shipbuilding has always been dependent upon the various aims of the United States government. As pointed out earlier, shipbuilding, except in time of war, is basically a job-shop type of operation, not a mass-production one. Hence, United States shipbuilders cannot mechanize to a high degree to offset their high wage costs. Accordingly, their construction costs run from one third to two thirds higher than those of competitors. American yards continue to make ships because of federal aid. In order to maintain American construction, which is important for reasons of national defense, the Merchant Marine Act of 1936 was passed. This act permits the government to subsidize the industry so that building costs are brought down to those in foreign countries. The Maritime Board, in calculating its construction subsidies, uses as its yardstick the costs of a "representative" shipbuilding nation; today it is Japan.

The chief shipbuilding areas are the Atlantic Coast, the Gulf Coast, the Great Lakes, and the Pacific Coast. The chief points are on New York Harbor, the Delaware River and Bay, and Chesapeake Bay (Fig. 11-11). The principal yards in the New York area are Staten Island, Brooklyn, and Kearney. The Delaware River is sometimes referred to as the "American Clyde." Its most important yards are in Philadelphia, Camden, Chester, and Wilmington.

Sparrows Point and Newport News are the two most important shipbuilding centers in the Chesapeake Bay–Hampton Roads area. They enjoy the advantages of nearness to steel, availability of skilled labor, proximity of supporting industries, and the presence of excellent harbors.

The Gulf Coast yards have risen in importance in the past several years. West Coast yards—at Los Angeles, San Diego, San Francisco, Portland, and Seattle—are hampered by higher wage costs and costlier steel, machinery, and equipment; hence, they cannot match either East Coast or Gulf Coast yards on cost. The Great Lakes shipyards at Manitowoc, River Rouge, and Toledo, except in time of war, specialize largely in lake carriers.

SOVIET UNION

Shipbuilding in Russia was never important in the past and is only now awakening after its long sleep. Particularly since World War II has it expanded—the result of enlarged merchant, fishing, and naval marines. However, compared with the United States, the United Kingdom, Norway, Liberia, and even Japan and West Germany, the Soviet Union still operates a relatively small fleet of ships of 1,000 gross tons and over.

Shipbuilding is widely distributed from the Baltic Sea to the Pacific and from the Arctic to the Black Sea. Seagoing vessels are constructed at Leningrad, Nicolayev, Riga, Sebastopol, Vladivostok, Komsomolsk, Kaliningrad, Odessa, and in a few other places. The industry is important, too, on many rivers—as, for example, at Predivinsk (north of Krasnoyarsk) on the Yenesei, in the vicinity of Chkalovsk on the shore of the Gorki Reservoir on the Volga, and at Rostov on the Don. These centers construct river boats and barges.

However, Soviet shipbuilding is not without its problems. For example, distribution among many ministries and organizations makes it difficult for Soviet planners to bring about much-needed specialization and cooperation. Also there is the detrimental effect of the long, cold winters on the building of ships. In the northern open-air yards, it is estimated that worker productivity drops 40 per cent during winter. There is even a labor law that forbids open-air work when the temperature falls to −13°F or lower.

POLAND

This industry not only supplies Poland with ships but also sells bottoms to Russia, Czechoslovakia, Indonesia, Egypt, and Brazil. It is centered in Gdansk and Stettin. Gdansk particularly benefits from being Poland's leading port and from nearby coal and steel.

AIRCRAFT

The American aircraft industry, regarded as the world's outstanding, was a relatively insignificant enterprise prior to World War II. In just two years it jumped from twentieth to fourth place. Aircraft manufacture is carried on only in the large, highly advanced, and wealthy countries of the world—particularly in those that have strong military forces; for the industry goes from feast to famine. In a recent year nearly 90 per cent of the total sales of United States companies was accounted for by the Air Force and the Navy. However, military production is highly uncertain over a period of years. With the unpredictability of the duration of the Cold War, the aircraft industry will probably persist, though it is developing more and more into a producer of missiles and space craft.

Commercial production consists of four separate and distinct parts: (1) *engines*, (2) *air frames*, (3) *propellers* (the future of this branch is seriously threatened by the jet), and (4) *instruments*. Only the engine and airframe segments are treated in this chapter.

ENGINES

During World War I the East dominated airplane production, though a large part of the engines were manufactured in Detroit. Today most of the airplane-engine factories are located in the East, principal centers being

Wood-Ridge, New Jersey; East Hartford; Farmingdale, Long Island; Trenton; Cincinnati; Indianapolis; and Muskegon, Michigan.

Among the most important location factors are local pride, skilled labor supply, access to markets, and **industrial inertia** (after once established). Not one of these factors, however, has exerted sufficient influence to cause concentration such as in the automotive industry.

There is little similarity between the manufacture of airplane engines and frames. Engines are made largely by machine, air frames largely by hand. The production of engines requires hundreds of separate and specialized skills; and five years, on the average, elapse to bring an engine to quantity production from the time design and engineering begin.

About half the dollar volume of engine producers' prime contracts goes to subcontractors and suppliers. Thus while the number of engine manufacturers is limited, the number of suppliers is legion. The Aircraft Industries Association estimates that some 50,000 different firms feed it.

AIR FRAMES

Automation and mass production are not important in the manufacture of air frames, primarily because of the restricted number of any one type and model sold and early obsolescence. Moreover, although a modified mass-production technique is followed, it appears that mass production will be delayed as long as designs change so rapidly.

LOCATION FACTORS

Only a few countries in the world can afford the luxury of an aircraft industry. The two leaders obviously are the United States and the Soviet Union. In the United States there is a complete lack of geographical centralization in this industry, allegedly because the leading companies to whom scientific location might presumably be important have not been dependent upon location for profit. The government has been these companies' largest source of business, and it insures against financial loss on any business and normally guar-

antees a profit. The government pays on a "cost-plus" basis.

The four most important location factors are climate, suitable terrain in large tracts, skilled labor (automation has not been able as yet to displace experienced men and women), and proximity to market. However, location factors are not the same for all countries. For example, in the Soviet Union resources, transportation, and established industrial metallurgy are the dominant location factors; thus because of the type of government, technicians and workers in large numbers could be forced to go to determined sites anywhere. Vent and Monier well state the situation when they say:

Location of aircraft production facilities in both the United States and the USSR has assumed definite locational patterns, each with its peculiar criteria for location. In the United States, it is dictated by climate, skilled labor pools, and basic economic conditions. In the Soviet Union, resources, transportation, and political considerations are more significant.[4]

Suitable Climate. Climate is the most important single location factor affecting the industry. Moreover, it is more important than in most industries. A mild climate is advantageous in four ways: (1) Good flying weather permits year-round flight testing of planes at almost any time. (2) Warm and relatively dry climate allows the storage of parts and equipment out of doors. (3) Mild temperatures reduce heating needs and consequently construction costs—important where hangars cover millions of square feet. (4) Work may be carried on out of doors throughout the year, a factor of special importance because the final assembly process requires a great amount of space owing to the huge wing span of modern planes. Such operations should, if possible, be carried on out of doors. Accordingly, much of the air-frame industry is to be found in California, Texas, Georgia, and Arizona.

[4] Herbert J. Vent and Robert B. Monier, "The Aircraft Industry in the United States and the USSR," *The Professional Geographer,* 10:7-8, May 1958.

Labor Supply. The availability of a large pool of skilled labor is another major location factor. Such skills take a long time to develop. However, skilled aircraft workers seem to be more mobile than workers in other industries.[5]

Level and Inexpensive Land in Large Tracts. Few industries demand so much room; not only are the buildings themselves enormous but there must be landing fields, hangars, storage space, parking areas for the automobiles of workers, and room for future expansion. And this land should be inexpensive. The need for room is apparent when it becomes known that one company has a mile-long, 200-foot-wide assembly line. The land should be level and free from obstructions for taking off and landing.

The Strategic Factor. In a world where destruction of industrial capacity by an enemy is possible in a matter of minutes, it appears that there is danger in having as vital an industry as the aircraft industry in only a few locations. Particularly have the Northeastern and Pacific Coast locations in the United States appeared vulnerable. At the beginning of World War II (1939), more than 80 per cent of the floor space devoted to air-frame production was concentrated on the Pacific and Atlantic coasts, two thirds of it in Southern California alone. The same proportion of engine-production facilities was located in the Northeast, as were all the propeller capacity and most of the instrument capacity. The government accordingly urged dispersal of fabricating facilities, and by 1944 much new integrated capacity had been constructed in the Middle West and the Southwest. This is doubtless the major reason for the rapid growth of aircraft manufacture in Texas and Kansas. Currently the four types of factories (air frame, engine, propeller, and instrument) are not found in any one area. Components must be gathered from widely scattered

[5] Tom L. McKnight, "Aircraft Manufacturing in Texas," *Southwestern Social Science Quarterly,* 38:44, June 1957.

sources throughout the nation for final assembly.

WORLD PRODUCTION OF AIR FRAMES

Principal producing countries are the United States, the Soviet Union, Great Britain, Canada, and France.

United States. The United States is by far the world's leading maker of planes. The airframe industry is located mostly west of the Mississippi River (Fig. 11-12). The principal centers for air-frame construction are Los Angeles and San Diego, Dallas and Fort Worth, Seattle, Baltimore, Buffalo, Wichita, and Atlanta. In San Diego and Wichita, 70 to 75 per cent of those employed by manufacturers are in the aircraft industry or its suppliers. In Los Angeles 222,700 people were employed in the various divisions of the industry in 1959; the aircraft industry accounts for about 30 per cent of manufacturing employment in the Los Angeles area. Los Angeles and San Diego together account for about one fourth of the entire employment of the American aircraft industry. Aircraft and now missile manufacturing, along with ancillary industries such as electronics and scientific instruments, comprise an industrial core.

The number of companies is small, but they operate on a gigantic scale. Douglas Aircraft, largest employer in Southern California, has four plants and employs about 60,000 persons; the Lockheed plant at Burbank has 32,500 employees.

Today Texas ranks second only to California. The industry, centered in the Fort Worth–Dallas area, employs 15 per cent of all workers engaged in the industry. The Texas plants are not raw-materials or market oriented. The chief locative factors were strategic location, suitable climate, and ample flat land at reasonable cost (Fig. 11-13).

The Seattle area is the home of the Boeing Aircraft Company, leader in the manufacture of heavy aircraft and long-range guided missiles. This company, founded in 1916, is the largest single employer in the Pacific Northwest; with 56,000 employees in 1957, its pay-

Fig. 11-12. *Distribution of the United States aircraft industry. Prior to World War II the industry was heavily concentrated in Los Angeles-San Diego, Seattle, Baltimore, and Buffalo. The industry today is highly dispersed. Important additional centers are Dallas-Fort Worth, Wichita, Kansas City, St. Louis, and Farmingdale and Bethpage (Long Island).*

roll constituted about a fourth of the total industrial payroll of the state—five times that of the aluminum and four times that of the pulp and paper industries. Although it undoubtedly plays too vital a role in total employment for the economic health of the state of Washington, the industry does complement the resource-based industries.

Boeing has remained in Seattle largely because of industrial inertia and because national dispersal of the aircraft and missile industry has been regarded as essential. However, it is not so good a location as Southern California; for it lacks a warm, sunny, dry climate and large tracts of flat land.

Soviet Union. Since the Soviet Union encompasses one seventh of the land surface of the globe and since its surface transport is as yet but modestly developed, its airways are extremely well developed. To move people into all parts of the country and to become ever more powerful militarily, the Soviet Union has had to build up an impressive aircraft industry. Major emphasis is on military planes. Moreover, the aircraft industry is government owned and operated.

The Soviet industry is located in four areas, making for effective economic-geographic distribution: (1) Moscow-Gorki; (2) Volga-Urals (Kazan, Votkinsk, Perm, Chelyabinsk); (3) the Southwest (Kiev, Rostov, Osipenko, Tambov); and (4) the Far East (Komsomolsk, Khabarousk). All these areas have important types of manufactures other than aircraft. Moreover, all were established centers of con-

Fig. 11-13. A large aircraft factory in Fort Worth, Texas, with its extensive acreage of outdoor maintenance area and parking lots. (Courtesy of Convair–Ft. Worth.)

siderable importance industrially—the reverse of the air-frame industry in the United States. During World War II, there was considerable dispersal of the industry to the interior—to the Urals and to the Far East. Much, however, remains in European Russia.

Great Britain. Britain has long been and still is a leader in the manufacture of aircraft. However, because of the financial strain of producing costly items that become obsolete almost as soon as they leave the plant, in 1957 the country withdrew from military-aircraft production and began concentrating upon missiles.

Despite the fact that Britain lacks weather conditions comparable with those of Southern California or even Texas, weather has been taken into consideration in locating the plants. The majority of them are in the south, principally in the Greater London area, at Hayes, Kingston, Luton, Hatfield, Dagenham, and Weybridge; a second area of importance lies to the south at Portsmouth and East Cove, and a third is in the Midlands at Coventry and Wolverhampton.

SELECTED REFERENCES

"Automotive Industry Is Key to Russian Mobilization Plans," *Automotive Industries*, 3:56-63, September 11, 1954.

Boas, C. W. "Locational Patterns of American Automobile Assembly Plants, 1895-1958," *Economic Geography*, 37:218-230, July 1961.

Clausen, Hugh. "British Machine Tool Industry," *Engineer*, 205:541, April 11, 1958.

Cunningham, William G. *The Aircraft Industry: A Study in Industrial Location.* Los Angeles, Lorrin L. Morrison, 1951.

Farm Equipment Institute. *Land of Plenty.* Chicago, 1959.

Fassett, F. G., Jr. (ed.) *The Shipbuilding Business in the United States of America*, 2 vols. New York, Society of Naval Architects and Marine Engineers, 1948.

Hurley, Neil P. "The Automotive Industry: A Study in Industrial Location," *Land Economics*, 35:1-14, February 1959.

Lonsdale, R. E., and John H. Thompson. "A Map of the USSR's Manufacturing," *Economic Geography*, 36:36-52, January 1960.

Pollard, Sidney. "The British and World Shipbuilding Costs, 1890-1914: A Study of Comparative Costs," *Journal of Economic History*, 17:426-443, September 1957.

Smith, A. J. Gibbs. "World Machine Tool Analysis for 1957," *Times Review of Industry*, 12:85, 87-88, November 1958.

White, C. Langdon, and Harold M. Forde. "The Unorthodox San Francisco Bay Area Electronics Industry," *Journal of Geography*, 59:251-258, September 1960.

CHAPTER TWELVE ::

Atoms are the building blocks of the chemical industries. The raw materials are substances of comparatively low value—substances such as air, brines from wells, coal, cornstalks, crude oil, natural gas, salt, soybeans, sulfur, and wood—which are torn down and rebuilt into numerous synthetic products of high utility. The chemical industries are unmatched in the variety of products they make—more than 10,000. Although these industries are not old, they have become so vital as to be among the most widespread of all industries. Certain branches are to be found in most countries of the earth, but the best development is expectably in the most technically advanced countries (Fig. 12-1).

Furthermore, the chemical industries are growing and developing rapidly. By 1970 three fifths of the sales of the American Chemical industries are expected to be accounted

THE WORLD'S

for by products not known to the public in 1960. In the United States it is estimated that fully one fifth of the employees in these industries are involved in research. Of their total research budgets (often as much as 1 billion dollars annually), the chemical industries spend as much as 14 per cent for basic research, whereas the expenditures of manufactures as a whole average 8 per cent. Chemical engineers, as the key men, convert chemical discoveries into profitable industrial processes. They are complemented by research chemists, who hybridize their science with the fields of metallurgy, zoology, and bacteriology, breaking down known combinations of molecules and rebuilding them into new combinations.

The United States is the giant of the chemical industries. In 1959 it had assets of 22.5 billion dollars—10 per cent of the total assets of all United States corporations; and it was using about one third of all the electrical energy going into industry.

AUTOMATION IN THE CHEMICAL INDUSTRY

No industry is so highly automated as the chemical, since a great many of the processes are readily adaptable to automation. Machines have been developed that can be fed with the basic raw materials in the form of powder or pellets, so that they produce finished products at a prodigiously fast rate. In one big plant, raw materials, catalysts, and diluting agents flow through a series of reactors under constant regulation from a central control house run by a single supervisor and a dozen men. Thus in 1958 the average investment per

CHEMICAL INDUSTRIES

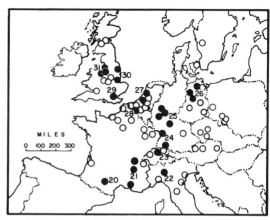

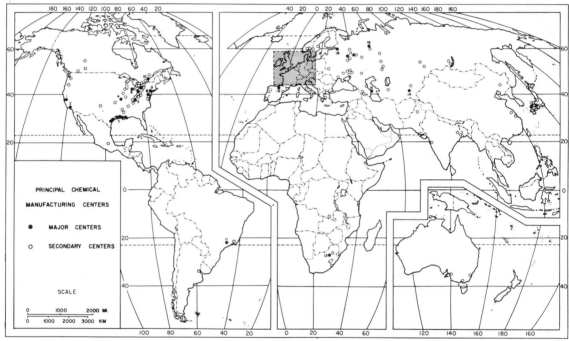

1. San Francisco	12. Johannesburg	24. Ludwigshafen, Meurthe-et-Moselle
2. Los Angeles	13. Osaka, Shimonoseki	25. Frankfurt, Cologne, Leverkusen, Ruhr
3. Corpus Christi, Freeport, Houston, Port Arthur, Lake Charles, New Orleans	14. Chirchik	
	15. Baku	26. Bitterfeld, Merseburg, Aschersleben
	16. Solikamsk	
4. St. Louis	17. Dzerzhinsk, Moscow	27. Amsterdam, Rotterdam
5. Charleston	18. Leningrad	28. Hainaut
6. Detroit	19. Santander	29. London
7. Cleveland, Niagara Falls	20. Haute Garonne	30. Middlesbrough, Humber
8. Philadelphia	21. Bouches du Rhône, Lyon, Isère	31. Merseyside, Winnington, Manchester
9. New York City	22. Milan	
10. Montreal	23. Basel	
11. São Paulo		

Fig. 12-1. Major world locations of the chemical industries. Note particularly the heavy concentration in the American East and Gulf Coast and in Western Europe, in contrast to the sprinkling in most of the Southern Hemisphere lands. Only highly developed countries can sustain such industrial complexes.

chemical worker was $2,577, compared with $981 for manufacturing as a whole. New processes and techniques occur so rapidly that some equipment is obsolescent before it has even paid for itself.

LOCATION FACTORS

It is impossible in a single chapter treating so many facets of the chemical industries to cover *all* the relevant aspects of plant location. Although the same factors for the most part underlie the location of all chemical plants, there are deviations from the pattern. Here, location is presented for (1) the industries as a whole, (2) the fertilizer branch, and (3) petrochemicals.

Before a site is selected and a detailed survey undertaken, plant specialists, either from the company itself or from a development agency, select the *general area*. This is done not by whim but by consideration of proximity to raw-material sources and to markets, since freight costs are of vital concern. These then determine the region where the plant can be operated most economically. The next step is to select the *specific plant site;* in the chemical industries, the site must meet a number of prerequisites: (1) acreage—seldom less than 500 acres for a sizable plant; (2) terrain—the site must not be exposed to floods; (3) purity of air; (4) proximity to a community—it should be outside corporate limits but not more than 10 miles from a community; (5) ample water of good quality (low in chlorides); (6) disposal of waste—a major problem for most plants in this industry; (7) access to transportation—it should be on a paved highway and on a main line or a spur of a railway (not more than 1 mile from main line); (8) ample electrical-power supply at all times—continuity, closeness of voltage, and frequency regulation. Energy at reasonable cost, too, is highly advantageous. Additional factors that should be favorable are the political and economic climates, high-quality trainable labor, fair taxes, and attractive living conditions for plant employees.

INDUSTRIAL CHEMICALS

The industrial chemicals (or the "heavy" chemicals, as they are more commonly called) make up a large and varied list of bulky products that are cheap per unit of weight. They include sulfuric acid, soda ash, caustic soda, chlorine, ammonia, nitric acid, and many others. The industries that make these substances turn them out in quantities not of several thousand pounds but of thousands, even millions, of tons. Even the value added by manufacture is small, since the processing involves relatively simple procedures—mostly moving, grinding, mixing, and separating huge amounts of solids, liquids, and gases. And in some instances a loss in weight occurs in manufacture. Hence, plants making heavy chemicals tend to locate near the raw materials. They also require much land, ample facilities for the disposal of waste, and sufficient remoteness to prevent acid fumes and other noxious substances from harming vegetation and man.

SULFURIC ACID

Sulfuric acid is the most vital of all industrial chemicals. A shortage puts an immediate brake on manufacturing generally, since this acid is used throughout the whole range of modern industry. Included in its long list of users are the drug and dye, leather-processing, oil-refining, paint, rayon, and fertilizer industries; it is even utilized for pickling steel. More than 12 million tons of sulfuric acid are used per annum in the United States, about 2½ to 3 million in the United Kingdom, and about 2 million in France. Viewed worldwide, possibly one fourth enters the fertilizer industry; one fifth, petroleum refining; one fifth, chemical making; and slightly more than one third, all other industries.

Prior to 1838 all sulfuric acid was made from brimstone, mostly from Sicilian sulfur. Today, however, it is generally made by roasting pyrites (iron sulfides) or by heating native sulfur. The sulfur dioxide gas that is given off is then oxidized into sulfur trioxide, which dissolves in water to form acid. Some sulfuric acid is produced as a by-product of lead and zinc smelting and from copper blast-furnace gases.

The manufacture of sulfuric acid generally takes place near the users (in short, it is market oriented) because it is low priced and because its handling creates problems.

Among all the countries of the world, the United States is the undisputed leader, accounting for about half the total output, followed in order by the Soviet Union, Japan, the United Kingdom, West Germany, Italy, and France. Principal centers for manufacture in the United States are in the fertilizer-making Southeast and the American Manufacturing Region.

SODA ASH

Soda ash is the most important of the alkalies; it is also the cheapest. It is used in large tonnages in making paper, soaps, and glass; in the manufacture of other chemicals; and in the refining of petroleum. In fact, soda ash is almost as important as sulfuric acid. The two raw materials for soda ash are common salt, which supplies the sodium, and limestone, which supplies the carbonate. Coal and coke provide the fuel.

The industry tends to locate near deposits of salt and limestone. Outstanding locales in the United States for manufacture are Detroit; Syracuse; Ohio's Lake Erie shore, particularly Painesville; Baton Rouge and Lake Charles, Louisiana; Saltville, Virginia; and "Chemical Valley," West Virginia. Although the United States is by far the largest producer, the Soviet Union, France, Italy, West Germany, and Japan also have substantial production.

CAUSTIC SODA

Caustic Soda (sodium hydroxide) is more commonly known and used as lye. It is employed in soap and paper making, in oil purification, in the treatment of textiles, and in the refining of petroleum.

The manufacture of caustic soda, commonly associated with the salt industry, tends to be raw-materials oriented but at the same time to be as near its markets as possible. Because of keen competition, location on navigable

water, as in Louisiana, is a distinct locational advantage. Plants are widely scattered.

The United States is far and away the world's largest producer; but the Soviet Union, West Germany, Japan, France, Canada, and Italy have impressive outputs. Manufacture in the United States is oriented toward raw materials and cheap water transportation—e.g., the salt deposits of Louisiana and the Intracoastal Waterway, the Mississippi River, and the Panama Canal.

AMMONIA

Ammonia is one of man's most used chemicals. Like nitric acid, it finds a large market in the fertilizer industry. Ammonia is made by combining enormous quantities of atmospheric nitrogen with hydrogen. Much of it is converted into ammonium sulfate, the most widely used nitrogenous fertilizer. Ammonia is also the starting point of most military explosives. Scarcely an industry is untouched by it.

Ammonia is produced by a number of systems. Among leading centers in the United States are Hopewell, Virginia; "Chemical Valley," West Virginia; Yazoo City, Mississippi; and Pittsburg, California. Presence of certain raw materials is an important location factor; thus cheap coal delivered by barge on the Kanawha River, natural gas, and a plentiful supply of water all contributed to the location of the industry in "Chemical Valley." In Europe very large operations are to be seen at Oppau and Merseburg in Germany and at Billingham, England. All industrial nations have large synthetic-ammonia enterprises.

NITRIC ACID

The basic ingredient of nitric acid is the element nitrogen, which constitutes about four fifths, by volume, of the earth's atmosphere. Its major use is in the manufacture of superphosphate fertilizer, dyes, drugs, and explosives. It is a vital ingredient for making every type of modern explosive; and in some areas—e.g., the United Kingdom, where it is more readily available—it replaces sulfuric acid in converting rock phosphate into phosphate fertilizer.

CHLORINE

Chlorine gas, a by-product of caustic soda manufacture, is made mainly from electrolysis of salt. Its original use as a raw material was for making bleaching powder, but today it has multitudinous uses—as an ingredient in detergent, dye, explosives, and plastics manufacture; as a disinfectant; in refrigeration; and as a water purifier.

Plants producing chlorine are essentially raw-materials oriented—located near deposits of underground salt. Location on navigable water is economically advantageous. One of the world's best locations for the industry is the area of salt deposits in Louisiana; here is raw material, fuel, and access to markets via the Atlantic Intracoastal Waterway (Eastern markets), the Mississippi-Ohio-Missouri-Illinois Rivers (Middle West), and the Panama Canal (Pacific Coast).

PLASTICS

Plastics, actually about a hundred years old, are regarded as comparatively new chemical products, possibly because their development began to skyrocket in the 1920s, when the infant but fast-growing radio industry provided a market for many new plastic products. Presently plastics are used in almost all world economies, and they exceed most of the non-ferrous and light metals (even aluminum) in annual tonnage. This widespread acceptance has generated a global trade of substantial volume. Plastics may be substituted for glass, wood, fibers, and even metals. The substitution of plastics for metals ultimately should prove particularly important, since most plastics are made either from very abundant or inexhaustible substances (proteins such as milk, soybeans, and dried blood; phenol compounds; lime; coal; and cellulose) and hence offer a means of prolonging the life of metals.

The United States leads in production, contributing annually about 35 per cent, followed by West Germany, the United Kingdom, Japan, France, and Italy.

CHARACTERISTICS

Plastics may be described as synthetic organic materials, which, through application of either pressure or heat or both, may be wrought into almost any shape desired. They run the gamut from solids so hard they must be turned on a lathe to liquids that can be sprayed onto a surface and left to harden. They may be made as firm as rock or as pliable as a sheet of rubber, thin or thick, in myriad shapes, translucent or opaque, and of every conceivable color. Moreover, they can be made resistant to acids, to moisture, and to many adverse weather conditions.

Among the most widely used are the polyethylene plastics, which possess such desirable qualities as toughness, flexibility, waxiness, and resistance to cold, heat, and moisture. These plastics are most commonly used in transparent containers for fresh fruits and vegetables and in "squeeze" bottles.

LOCATION OF THE PLASTICS INDUSTRY

The plastics industry is widely scattered. This is logical considering that most plastics are based upon low-cost, abundant, and widely distributed raw materials. Yet some of these materials are drawn from over much of the earth: casein from Argentina, Australia, and New Zealand; petroleum from Arabia, Indonesia, Venezuela, and the Soviet Union; and coffee, soybeans, and sugar cane from Brazil, China, and Cuba. In addition, the raw materials for the plastics industry include partly fabricated ones such as calcium carbide.

In the United States the greater part of the plastics industry is located in the American Manufacturing Region, particularly in Illinois (in the Chicago area), and in New England, New York, New Jersey, and eastern Pennsylvania. The South, too, is of growing importance, as are parts of the West—Southern California, the San Francisco Bay area, and Seattle. Everywhere the industry is disseminated in small units.

ORGANIC DYES

In 1856 W. H. Perkin of London succeeded in producing a purple dye from a coal-tar derivative known as aniline, thereby distinguishing himself as the founder of the coal-tar dye industry. Such dyes are used almost exclusively today. However, although England made the initial discovery and was the first to make use of the dye industrially, she lost the initiative; and Germany dominated for more than half a century. Many reasons have been advanced to explain how Germany so completely outstripped Britain: (1) Britain's patent laws allowed foreigners to patent processes in Britain without making any attempt actually to work them there. (2) Britain did not impose duties on dye imports into Britain, whereas British dyes were heavily taxed in Germany. (3) Germany had extensive research laboratories staffed by skilled scientists. (4) Germany had superb chemico-technical schools, which had been almost wholly supported by the state since 1870. (5) In Germany the teaching of organic chemistry was superior. (6) The Rhine River had proved eminently suitable as a connecting link between low-cost raw materials and the fabricating plants. (7) The Germans had a preeminent sales organization backed by technical-service departments.

German chemists ultimately produced so complete a range of colors of such high grade and at such low prices that other countries found it preferable to buy from Germany than to make their own. Output was concentrated in a relatively small number of very large establishments, which soon were welded into strong combines and later absorbed into the great chemical monopoly of I. G. Farben, which eventually sent its tentacles into so many countries that it became part of a giant international chemical cartel. The industry in Germany is raw-materials oriented and is located largely in the central part, where enormous deposits of salt and lignite are located. Among the leading centers are Leverkusen, Ludwigshafen, Leuna, and Hannover.

The United States dyestuffs industry, now the world's largest, dates primarily from World War I, when the government seized and held in custody some 4,500 German dye patents. American chemical manufacturers hastily assembled the best chemists available and ultimately succeeded in building an enviable dyestuffs industry. This segment of the chemical industries—located chiefly in response to raw materials, markets, and labor—is to be found in the east-central portion of the American Manufacturing Region.

England, France, Italy, and Japan today support dye industries that contribute more than nine tenths of their home consumption.

EXPLOSIVES

Explosives serve humanity for both war and peace. Most important are the amatols—mixtures of ammonium nitrate and trinitrotoluene (TNT). TNT is a widely used military explosive because of the simplicity and low cost of its manufacture. All high explosives are compounds of the element nitrogen—whose ultimate source is the air but is introduced in the form of nitric acid derived from synthetic ammonia.

Here, only the manufacture of explosives for peaceful uses (e.g., as a quick and easy means of moving and breaking up huge masses of rock, masonry, and soil) is presented. Many of the world's outstanding feats of civil engineering would have been impossible without blasting explosives—witness the Khyber Railway, the Simplon Tunnel, and the St. Lawrence Seaway in the rapids section. Mining is greatly simplified by use of blasting explosives.

In the United States the Middle Atlantic Seaboard leads, with more than half the annual national output. The Delaware River area, particularly the Wilmington district, is foremost; but the Newark Bay area also is outstanding. Here coastal marshes, extensive swamps, pine barrens, and other wastelands are utilized because of their isolation from populous urban-industrial communities. Since explosives are dangerous to manufacture and to ship, it is easier to assemble raw materials near markets than to transport the finished explosives considerable distances. Somewhat similar locations for the manufacture of explosives exist along the Pacific Coast and the Gulf Coast. The important Western mining industry provides a good market for explosives.

AGRICULTURAL CHEMICALS

The term agricultural chemicals includes a wide array of products that perform many functions, chief among which are enriching the soil and increasing the per-acre yield of the crops it sustains, controlling insect pests and diseases. Some examples are insecticides, fungicides, fumigants, plant growth regulators, weed killers, and fertilizers. Of this group only the last is presented here.

FERTILIZERS

Few industries are so vital to humanity as that making agricultural fertilizers. With the world's population doubling every forty years, frantic efforts are being made to keep the food supply abreast of burgeoning human numbers. In Japan, the United States, the Netherlands, West Germany, and several other countries, agricultural output has been skyrocketing as a result of increasing utilization of chemical fertilizers. Japan is reputed to use more commercial fertilizer than any nation— 200 pounds per cultivated acre, contrasted with 1 pound for India. But Japan gets a per-acre yield of rice four times that of India.

Fertilizer plants locate as near both raw materials and markets as possible. In the United States, the major raw materials are natural gas, phosphate rock, and sulfur. Natural gas is available almost anywhere because of the notable web of pipelines; sulfur and phosphate rock present no problem at plants on navigable water, but if they must move several hundred miles by rail, $11 is added to the cost of each ton of sulfur and $2 to $5 per ton of phosphate rock. However, in 1961 shipment of sulfur in liquid form was inaugurated, resulting in appreciable savings in transport costs.

In the manufacture of mixed fertilizers, the Atlantic Seaboard and the Gulf Seaboard lead, with plants on or near almost every port from Maine to Texas. A tidewater location favors the assembly of the bulky raw materials. Moreover, the South Atlantic and the Middle Atlantic states together comprise the nation's largest fertilizer market (about 40 per cent). Low-cost power is readily available, and manufactured fertilizer may be shipped easily and cheaply via water to widespread markets. Corn Belt fertilizer production has increased notably with extensive adoption there of high-yielding hybrid corn; some farms have increased their use of commercial fertilizers tenfold in a decade. The limited value of manufactured fertilizer per unit of weight, along with the large and expanding market, favors large-scale manufacture within the region.

The manufacture of fertilizer in Western Europe is of long standing, for the generally sandy soils require heavy fertilization in order to obtain satisfactory yields. The Soviet Union, Japan, India, and many other countries are today spending vast sums on fertilizer-manufacturing plants.

NITROGEN FERTILIZERS

World consumption of nitrogen fertilizers is supplied by four sources: (1) organic nitrogen (a small amount), (2) natural nitrate of sodium, (3) ammoniac fertilizers recovered in by-product coke ovens; (4) synthetic fertilizers obtained from atmospheric nitrogen.

Crop yields in lands of adequate rainfall are influenced more by soil nitrogen than by any other mineral element. Under natural conditions, nitrogen is not present in the soil but must be obtained from the air. Aside from legumes, which can take it from the air, natural sources are manures, composts, cottonseed meal, tobacco stems, fish refuse, slaughterhouse waste, and ammonium sulfate from gas plants and coke ovens. Only two sources, natural nitrate and synthetic nitrogen, are presented here.

Nitrate. Chile is the only country to have extensive deposits of mineral nitrate. In her

Atacama Desert, deposits (estimated at 160 million tons of nitrogen) lie in discontinuous beds in an area some 450 miles long. The minable areas are only 3 or 4 miles wide. The layers of *caliche* (the ore), some three feet below the surface, vary in richness from 5 to 70 per cent sodium nitrate. For many years Chile had a monopoly on this much-in-demand product, virtually living from nitrate (80 per cent of the value of her total exports). She was able to fix the world price, doing so without regard to actual producing costs; she also imposed a heavy export tax, which government officials considered would be a permanent source of revenue. In 1914, the German chemist Fritz Haber discovered a technique for producing nitrogen synthetically—by "fixing" it from the air. Overnight Chile's monopoly was broken. Today Chile exports less than 2 million tons; it supplies only about 3 per cent of the market, the synthetic branch contributing more than 70 per cent.

Synthetic Nitrogen. The technique for making nitrogen synthetically came as recently as 1914 in Germany, though the Norwegians claim ownership of a plant as early as 1905. The product is made in greatest amounts and most cheaply in countries rich in water power, for it is largely an electricity-hungry industry. In the electrolytic process, 14,000 to 18,000 kilowatt hours of power are required to produce 1 metric ton of pure nitrogen content. Aside from power, one of the two principal ingredients—the earth's air, four fifths of which is nitrogen—is free of cost; the other—limestone—is widely dispersed and low in cost.

World Production of Nitrogen Fertilizers. World production of nitrogen fertilizer has reached 10 million tons a year—a large figure, yet inadequate to meet the needs. Europe, including the Soviet Union, produces and uses more nitrogen than all the rest of the world combined. Its annual output is four times that of Asia, more than five times that of either North or South America, and fifteen times that of Africa.

Most of the fertilizers under this heading are obtained from phosphate rock, an exception being the by-product slags of iron and steel mills. Still other sources of phosphorus are barnyard manure and guano. Based on tonnage produced, phosphate rock is the dominant mineral-fertilizer product. The reserves of phosphate rock in the world are enormous (some 17 billion tons), but they are restricted to relatively few regions. The United States, North Africa, China, and the Soviet Union are credited with most of the reserves, smaller ones being found in Peru, Egypt, Spain, and the Pacific island of Nauru (Fig. 12-2).

The cost of phosphate rock at the mine is, on the average, low; but cost rises as the distance to the point of use increases—often three times that at the mine.

United States. The United States has such large reserves of phosphate rock (about 40 per cent of the world's known high-grade deposits) that they are expected to last for at least 2,000 years. Though the largest reserves are in the Far West, production there is restricted because of the limited regional market and because the nation's principal markets are too far away to be economically accessible; only rail transport is available, and it is expensive on such a low-cost raw material.

The deposits of Tennessee and Florida are, of course, better located with respect to markets. Florida, with more than a score of quarries in her northern and central portions, is the chief producing state, accounting normally for about 70 per cent of the United States total production and about 40 per cent of the world's. The deposits are worked by hydraulicking after large dragline excavators remove the overburden. In Tennessee, open-cut methods are employed; but the product is low grade. The combined reserves of the two states are expected to last about two hundred years.

Soviet Union. The Soviet Union contains very large phosphate deposits. Those in the Kola Peninsula at Kirovsk average about 83 per cent bone phosphate of lime and are

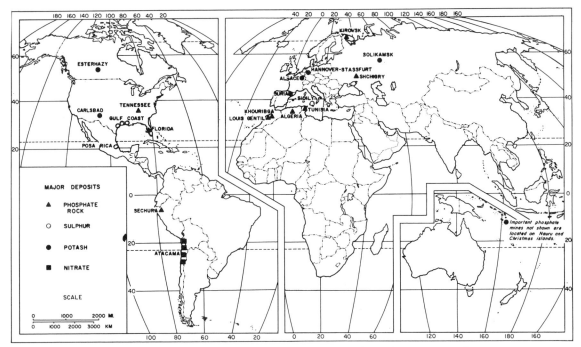

Fig. 12-2. *Distribution of the minerals from which commercial fertilizers are made. Few countries have any of these in commercial quantities or economically accessible, and not one possesses all four. Best off is the United States, with all but nitrate.*

estimated at 2 billion tons. Sedimentary deposits are to be found in central and southern Russia in the Gorki, Moscow, Central Black Earth, and Western Province areas, and in Asiatic Russia—particularly northern Kazakhstan. The greater part of the reserves, which are estimated at 5½ billion tons, are situated in the European part of Russia.

Peru. Important deposits of phosphate rock were discovered in the early 1960s in the Sechura Desert of northwestern Peru. The high-grade deposits are estimated to contain between 600 and 900 million tons. They are being developed by Peruvian, Canadian, Japanese, and United States interests; the largest company's concession covers 2 million acres.

POTASH FERTILIZERS

Potash fertilizers are obtained from a number of soluble salts in which potassium is present. Since potassium is so highly soluble, soils in humid lands (the **pedalfers**) are usually deficient in it.

Until relatively recent times, the principal sources of potash were wood ashes and burned kelp. Later, other sources—dust from blast furnaces and cement mills; certain minerals, such as alunite; and the brines of desert lakes—were developed. Major dependence now, however, is on potash deposits, which are known to be present and exploited in only a small number of countries—chiefly the United States, Canada, East and West Germany, France, Spain, and the Soviet Union (Fig. 12-2). Total world proved reserves are placed at 41 billion tons, an amount that should last approximately 5,000 years. Three countries—Canada, Germany, and the Soviet Union—possess the giant's share.

United States. The United States leads all nations in potash production, but it possesses only about 1 per cent of world reserves. Ninety per cent of production comes from one area—Eddy County (the Carlsbad area), New Mexico. Recovery is by the **room-and-pillar** method from mines about 1,000 feet deep.

The only other important producing area is Searles Lake in southeastern California, which supplies about 7 per cent of the domestic output. Here potash salts are extracted from brine in the crystalline salt mass. Unfortunately, both sources lie far from the principal domestic fertilizer markets, and transportation by rail is expensive.

Canada. Northeast of Esterhazy, Saskatchewan, lies the largest and possibly the richest reserve of potash in the world. It is reported that this deposit, comprising about 6.4 billion tons, could meet the earth's demands for 800 years.

Development has been fraught with problems: a 200-foot-thick layer of quicksand with water pressures up to 500 pounds per square inch was encountered, and it was a year before engineers found a way of sealing off the water. Output is increasing sharply, with the bulk going to the Far East—particularly Japan.

East and West Germany. Prior to World War I, Germany had a monopoly on potash. The several mining companies were members of an influential cartel which controlled all aspects of the business. The major deposits, located in six districts near Stassfurt in central and southern Germany, are associated with an extensive deposit of common salt. Reserves are estimated at 20 billion tons of potash. Major production takes place around Hannover, near Nordhausen in the Harz Mountains, and in the Werro-Fulda area near Vacha. The location is highly favorable for both the domestic market and the export market—only 155 to 186 miles from the port of Hamburg. The beds, lying at depths of 1,000 to 3,000 feet and varying from 6 to 120 feet in thickness, are mined by the shaft-tunnel method.

France (Alsace). Following World War I, Germany lost the potash deposits of Alsace, and her monopoly was broken. However, the two countries jointly created a Franco-German agreement for monopoly control. The reserves, placed at 200 million tons of potash, lie in the Rhine Valley about 25 miles north of the Franco-Swiss border. Principal development has been northwest of Mulhouse, though production there is diminishing.

Soviet Union. Potash has been found in several areas—particularly west of the Ural Mountains at Solikamsk, 217 miles from Perm on the Trans-Siberian Railway (reserves are placed at 15 billion tons of potash). The Soviet Union currently accounts for about 12 per cent of world production, but the country's status in both reserves and output is actually unknown.

THE PETROCHEMICAL INDUSTRY

Among the complex, overlapping fields that make up the chemical industries, one of the youngest and fastest growing is the petrochemical. Until the late 1950s it was largely a United States industry.

Between 1950 and 1959 the production of chemicals based upon petroleum and natural gas grew three times faster than the chemical industry as a whole. The industry is based on upgrading refinery products that were formerly of little value. Moreover, whereas refinery operations upgrade the value of petroleum by only about one third, petrochemical operations do so up to twelve times. Therefore, virtually all the oil companies have gone into the petrochemical business.

UNITED STATES

About 80 per cent of the petrochemical capacity in the United States is in the South, particularly along the Gulf Coast in a 700-mile strip between New Orleans on the east and Brownsville on the southwest, and reaching inland for about 100 miles. This represents the most concentrated distribution of this industry in the world. The industry is particularly centered in eight kernels of the major region: (1) New Orleans, (2) Baton Rouge, (3) Lake Charles, (4) Port Arthur–Beaumont, (5) Houston, (6) Freeport, (7) Corpus Christi, and (8) Brownsville. Major activity, however, is in the Houston and Port Arthur nodes; the Houston complex alone accounts for 20 to 30 per cent of the total capacity.

This area has certain unique advantages for the manufacture of petrochemicals:

1. It possesses 60 to 75 per cent of the nation's petroleum reserves and more than 36 per cent of its refining capacity.
2. It has a bountiful supply of natural gas, natural-gas liquids, and refinery gases for raw materials and low-cost fuel.
3. It has plenty of fresh water for industrial processes.
4. It can call upon a reservoir of trained manpower, including skilled labor, engineers of many kinds, and scientists. (Labor costs comprise a relatively small percentage of the manufacturing costs in this industry, however.)
5. It benefits from a complex system of pipelines.
6. It has the advantage of water transport to Eastern and to export markets.
7. It can dispose of chemical wastes in the Gulf of Mexico.
8. It lies close to and enjoys cheap transport costs on many raw materials—sulfur, salt, and lime (the last made from oyster shells).

The Middle West ranks second—the states of Ohio, Michigan, Indiana, Illinois, and Kentucky together accounting for about 16 per cent of the operating plants and 8 per cent of those under construction in 1959.

West Virginia, particularly "Chemical Valley," a 60-mile stretch along the Great Kanawha Valley from Gauley Bridge on the east to Nitro on the west, is highly favored for petrochemical manufacture and promises to become a particularly formidable competitor to all other areas. It possesses coal, natural gas, petroleum, salt, water, and hydropower. Transport is well developed.

The petrochemical industry on the Pacific Coast, particularly in California, is growing because of an important regional market; however, it currently purchases much crude oil and natural gas from the Southwest, Canada, and abroad. The state is too far distant to compete favorably in Eastern markets. The Northeast is important, with about 20 per cent of the operating plants. Its big disadvantage is high raw-materials costs; its big advantage is proximity to the substantial market.

EUROPE

Late in the 1950s, with the great increase in oil refining in Europe, the petrochemical industry got started and has since been one of the fastest growing of all the continent's manufactural enterprises. The creation of the Common Market (the Six) and the Free Trade Association (the Outer Seven) stimulated production, since *continental* rather than small regional markets now are available.

The newest branch of the industry in Europe is synthetic rubber, production of which jumped from 170,000 tons in 1956 to 300,000 tons in 1958. The principal producing countries are Great Britain, France, West Germany, Italy, and the Netherlands.

Great Britain boasts the world's second largest petrochemical industry. Capacity doubled between 1957 and 1959. Plants are located principally at Wilton, Partington, Shell Haven, Grangemouth, Fawley, and Avonmouth. One plant at Avonmouth covers more than 1,000 acres, and its construction cost in excess of 280 million dollars.

In 1960 France was expanding fastest in this industry, mainly because its natural-gas production was also expanding. Principal centers are Port Jerome, Gonfreville, and Lavera.

West Germany, as a result of war difficulties, got a late start in petrochemicals. However, it has expanded so rapidly that it is seriously contending for top rank among European nations. Principal centers are Cologne and Dormagen.

Italy's economic revival since World War II reached a peak in 1959—the best year economically in the country's long history. The nation ranks very high in the chemical industry, covering almost all phases, but is especially prominent in petrochemicals. Italy stands at the gateway of some of Europe's lowest-cost petroleum, has natural gas in the Po Valley, and possesses adequate water, good ports, and ample labor. The nation is therefore in an enviable position to benefit from the low cost of petrochemical manufacture. Principal centers are Mantova, Ravenna, Ferrara, and Azienda.

WORLD OUTLOOK

Few industries have the growth potential of the chemical industries, mainly because of the infinite variety of consumer goods they contribute. This industry is linked to almost all others and accordingly is sensitive to changes both in its own sphere and in the entire realm of manufacturing.

Two major trends are currently apparent:

1. Many American companies are establishing branches abroad, both in developed countries (in Western Europe, Japan, Australia) and in underdeveloped ones all over the world. This results largely from the economic revolution now under way, whereby nations as fully qualified as the United States are pitted against one another for the same markets. The quality of their products is often as high as the quality of United States products, and their costs are lower.

2. A rising percentage of chemical products sold in the United States bears the import label. Thus, in a recent year, United States production of some chemical products declined 14 per cent while imports rose 87 per cent.

As long as competition between nations is on an approximately equal footing, it acts as a spur to superior performance and is beneficial. But international competition is not on this common base today. Free and totalitarian ideologies collide; and the former, with its profit motive, cannot compete in neutral or any other markets. The United States experiences increasing difficulty competing with the Free World nations in Western Europe and in Asia, where wages are considerably lower. Wages, of course, are only one element in the cost of production, but so wide a differential makes their influence difficult to nullify if all other factors are equal. Until a few years ago, United States companies could overcome the low-wage differential with better equipment and production techniques; but this no longer is true. Hence, Americans are being rigorously shaken by the realization that nearly all their exports have not been rising sufficiently fast to offset the rise in imports.

Viewed worldwide, the chemical industries will undoubtedly expand as far into the future as can be seen; for such items as sulfuric acid, nitric acid, ammonia, alkali, fertilizers, plastics, and petrochemicals will be used increasingly as the world's population soars and demands ever higher levels of living.

In looking into the future, there is the matter, too, of new plant location. The trend in plant sites for many chemicals shows a change from almost exclusive raw-materials orientation to a high degree of market orientation. Some plants, nonetheless, are still raw-materials oriented, and some even display an interesting mix of market and raw-materials-oriented elements.

SELECTED REFERENCES

Alderfer, E. B., and H. E. Michl. *Economics of American Industry*. New York, McGraw-Hill Book Company, Inc., 1950, pp. 245-263.

Anderson, W. "What the World Fertilizer Situation Means to Future Farm Production," *Foreign Agriculture*, 21:9-11, 18, August 1957.

"The Chemical Century," *Fortune*, 41:69-76, 114-118, 121-122, March 1950.

Doan, L. I. "The Fabulous Chemical Industry," *Michigan Business Review*, 7:9-15, March 1955.

Hodgins, E. "Farming's Chemical Age," *Fortune*, 48:151-155, 202-216, November 1953.

Isard, W., and E. W. Schooler. *Location Factors in the Petrochemical Industry*. Washington, D. C., Office of Technical Services, U.S. Department of Commerce, July 1955.

Lamer, M. *The World Fertilizer Economy*. Stanford, Calif., Stanford University Press, 1957.

Williams, Trevor I. *The Chemical Industry, Past and Present*. Baltimore, Penguin Books, 1953.

CHAPTER THIRTEEN ::

Rubber [1] is today one of mankind's most essential, most vital raw materials. Valuable for many purposes, it is absolutely indispensable to transportation. Thus, more than two thirds of all the rubber consumed in the United States goes into transportation.

NATURAL RUBBER

Man's best source of natural rubber, the tree *Hevea brasiliensis,* is a native of the Amazon Basin. Nearly all of the world's supply of natural rubber (Fig. 13-1) comes from this source. Until 1876, this area was synony-

[1] Rubber might be presented under "forests" as a gathering enterprise, under "tropical plantation agriculture" as a crop, and under "manufacturing" as a type of industry. It seems appropriate in this textbook to present all phases of rubber in a single chapter.

THE WORLD'S

mous with rubber. That year, however, in the valley of the Rio Tapajos, an Englishman, Henry A. Wickham, collected 70,000 seeds of the tree; he smuggled the seeds to England, where they were planted in London's Kew Gardens. The 2,800 that germinated and survived were later sent to Southeast Asia—to Ceylon and to Perak in Malaya—where they were planted. Those that lived formed the basis for the 9 million acres of plantations and small native holdings there today.

In its emigration to Southeast Asia and to Western Africa, the tree has found conditions almost identical with those of its native habitat. The *Hevea* tree demands a tropical climate—temperatures ranging from 70°F to 90°F and a well-distributed rainfall of 70 to 100 inches. There must be no pronounced dry season; what is called the "dry season" in Amazonia might more appropriately be called a "less rainy season." The flow of latex falls off impressively if the rainfall drops below two or three inches per month. Dry periods occur more frequently in the Amazon Basin than they do in Southeast Asia, and this is one of several reasons why the latter is the preferred milieu. The tree also must have good underdrainage and protection from stagnant standing water. For this reason, it does not grow everywhere throughout the Amazon Basin but is largely confined to the well-drained benchlands and terraces that lie slightly above the level of the dank floodplains of the Amazon and its major tributaries. However, only about 10 per cent of the Amazon plain is subject to flood.

Soils are far less vital than climate and drainage, the tree doing well over a wide

RUBBER INDUSTRY

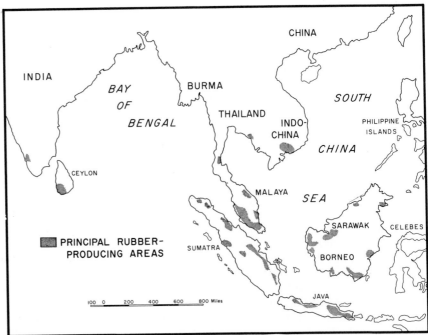

Fig. 13-1. Where more than nine tenths of the world's natural rubber is produced. Malaysia and Indonesia together contribute about three fourths of the entire world output. Here the enterprise is prosecuted under the most scientific and businesslike conditions. (Drawn by John Arrillaga.)

range of soils. Nonetheless, rubber does better on fertile than on infertile soils; over enormous areas favored climatically for rubber, trees do not grow because of infertile lateritic soil.

EXTRACTION OF LATEX

The rubber of commerce is procured from the milklike liquid latex, found in the thin layer of cells in the tree bark.

The tapper, who cares for 175 to 200 wild trees in the forest of Amazonia and for about 300 to 500 trees on a Southeast Asian or Liberian plantation, begins work very early in the morning. He first strips away from each tree a film of rubber latex, which sealed the wound after the previous tapping. He then makes a new cut in the thin rim of bark about one fifteenth of an inch from the lower edge of the earlier tapping cut, so as to start the latex flowing without injuring the tree (Fig. 13-2). The knife is especially designed, having a sharp blade that tapers into a hook. The tapper cuts only one third to one half way around the tree, depending upon the latter's size. At the bottom of the cut he inserts a galvanized iron spout, to which he attaches a cup. The rubber latex flows along the diagonal cut, emptying into the cup at a rate of about two drops per second. After three or four hours, or at about 9 or 10 A.M., the tapper returns to collect the latex, which must be gathered before noon in order to prevent spoilage. The contents of the cups are emptied into large buckets. The trees are retapped every other day by cutting at a fresh piece of bark.

The latex gathered by the plantation collector is taken directly to a central factory if the plantation is small or, if the plantation is large, to tank trucks which deliver the latex to a factory (Fig. 13-3). Here the latex is treated with formic acid and coagulated into a doughy white mass; this mass, known as coagulum, is rolled into sheets on power-driven mills and, after thorough drying, is baled for shipment.

Fig. 13-2. Closeup of tapping cut. The milklike latex "bleeds" from the cut and is led down to the cup attached to the trunk. (Courtesy of United States Rubber Company.)

In the Amazon forest, where mostly wild trees are tapped and where there is an average of only one *Hevea* tree to the acre, the *seringueiro* (rubber extractor) can collect from only 175 to 200 trees. He carries the latex he has collected to his camp; there, over a fire of palm nuts and palmwood, he coagulates the rubber by pouring the milklike latex on a flat-bladed paddle, which he turns gradually in the smoke. He continues the operation until a huge ball or biscuit of smoked rubber accumulates, whereupon he slits the ball to release the paddle. This is the ball or biscuit of rubber of commerce.

REGIONS OF NATURAL-RUBBER PRODUCTION

More than 95 per cent of the world's natural rubber is produced in Southeast Asia (Fig. 13-1)—75 per cent in the Federation of Malaysia and the Republic of Indonesia com-

bined. Malaysia derives about 48 per cent of its export proceeds from rubber, and Indonesia derives 44 per cent. Anything that adversely affects the world price of rubber shakes them to their very foundations. Thus, the current competition of American synthetic rubber threatens the economy of these two countries and their political stability as well.

FEDERATION OF MALAYSIA

The west coastal and piedmont zone of the Malay Peninsula accounts for about 40 per cent of the world's natural rubber. In 1960, Malaya led the world in natural-rubber output—moving ahead of Indonesia, who had held first place from 1949 to 1959. Approximately two thirds of the country's cultivated land is given over to rubber trees, which yield annually about 500,000 tons of natural rubber. Sixty-four per cent of the entire planted area in this country is devoted to rubber, and almost half of the total exports consist of it.

All the necessary conditions for successful rubber production are present: (1) Climate, soils, and topography are highly favorable. (2) The peninsular character of Malaya makes the area accessible by water transport. (3) Singapore occupies one of the most strategic sites of any port on earth. (4) There is an abundance of able, low-cost labor. (5) British capital, technical research, and direction are readily available.

About 42 per cent of the rubber acreage is worked by some 350,000 small farmers, mostly Chinese and Malayan, each of whom averages about 4 acres of trees.[2] The remaining 58 per cent is composed of large plantations ranging in size from about 100 acres to many thousands of acres. In recent years a marked shift has been taking place from the dominant Western-operated estate to the small holding, where often rubber is grown along with food crops—cassava, sweet potatoes, and bananas.

[2] A *small holding* is an area contiguous or noncontiguous, aggregating less than 100 acres, planted with rubber or set apart for the planting of rubber, and under a single legal ownership. It is convenient, however, to refer to an area of less than 25 acres as a *small holding* and one less than 100 acres as a *medium holding.*

Fig. 13-3. Loading latex, Southeast Asia. Latex is carried in pails to tank trucks for speedy delivery to a factory. (Courtesy of Natural Rubber Bureau.)

The large plantations produce more and better rubber than do the small holdings. In the marketing, about two thirds of the total moves as ribbed smoked sheet, about one fourth as crepes, and slightly less than one tenth as preserved latex.

This efficient industry became a shambles as a result of the long Japanese occupation during World War II, and much hard work and a huge amount of capital were required to restore productivity to its former proportions; however, the task was accomplished in three years' time.

INDONESIA

The Dutch, who ruled in Indonesia until 1950 (when Indonesia became a sovereign, independent state), had a great influence on the rubber industry: they originated bud grafting, whereby rubber growers no longer have to be dependent on nature through the planting of seeds. Buds from high-yielding trees are now grafted to the stumps of young seedlings, and the high-yielding characteristics of the mother tree are transmitted through her buds.

In Indonesia, as in Malaysia, small holdings have been increased notably. In Sumatra and Kalimantan (Borneo), small holdings produce more rubber than do the estates.

Indonesia's rubber industry suffered from the long Japanese occupation, police action, and civil strife. Accordingly, the estates lost about 345,000 acres of land, and by 1950 only half of them had resumed operations on 1.8 million acres. On the estates about 100 trees are planted to the acre, 30 of which ultimately are weeded out. Tapping begins when the trees are six years of age. Much rubber must be grown at high altitudes, since the lowlands must be devoted to food crops for the large and rapidly increasing population.[3]

AFRICA

The rubber industry in Africa came into being as a result of the Stevenson Plan. After World War I, the price of rubber fell to 14 cents per pound, a price that spelled ruin to the British owners on the Malay Peninsula. Accordingly, the British enacted a piece of legislation, the Stevenson Plan, to maintain prices by restricting exports. Each grower restricted his rubber exports to a certain per-

[3] See Stanley Levy, "Agriculture and Economic Development in Indonesia," *Economic Botany*, 11:22, January–March 1957.

centage of a standard production figure based on output for the year ending October 31, 1920. If the price rose above or fell below certain figures, exports were adjusted by 5 or 10 per cent, respectively. Under this plan the price of rubber advanced until in 1925 it reached $1.21 per pound. In 1921 British plantations controlled 75 per cent of the world's rubber, whereas the United States, which produced none, used about 75 per cent of world production. By the Stevenson scheme (1922-1928), the British gained a virtual monopoly on this fundamental product. Feeling in the United States ran high because of the price of rubber, and a number of manufacturers resolved to establish their own plantations. One of these, Harvey Firestone of the Firestone Tire and Rubber Company, selected some 2 million acres in Liberia. Today this holding, regarded as the largest plantation in the world, includes more than 80,000 planted acres and about 11 million rubber-producing trees. The annual output exceeds 75 million pounds of rubber handled by some 30,000 natives. The Goodrich Tire and Rubber Company also has large rubber plantings and impressive production in Liberia.

BRAZIL

Henry Ford, another of the original group, decided to circumvent the Stevenson Plan and produce his own rubber. After much careful preliminary work, in 1927 the Companhia Ford Industrial do Brasil purchased a tract of 2.5 million acres of land along the right bank of the Rio Tapajos about 135 miles upstream from its confluence with the Amazon. Here rubber trees were planted on a tract of some 8,400 acres at Fordlandia. Soon, however, Fordlandia became plagued by troubles: disease attacked the trees, soil erosion became critical, and the Tapajos proved to be poorly suited to transport during the so-called "dry season." Accordingly, in 1934, a portion of the concession was exchanged for a new site, Belterra, farther downstream and only 30 miles from the Amazon. Although not ideal for rubber production, it was superior in nearly all respects to Fordlandia. Little by little, the efficient Ford organization overcame

the technical difficulties involved in raising plantation rubber. Still the project was not successful. Finally, after spending about 20 million dollars, the company returned the plantation to the Brazilian government for a fraction of the total investment. Its reason for withdrawing was primarily a matter of labor. The Brazilian workers did not like the time-clock type of work; routine work simply was not for them. Yet, there is no other way to produce rubber efficiently. Furthermore, the high wages paid by the company, instead of providing an incentive to work, simply enabled the natives to work fewer days in the week. Finally, the over-all supply of labor was limited, for the population of the whole Amazon Basin is reputed to average less than one person to the square mile; it appeared to the company that with so marked a paucity of people the plantations could never count on enough workers to provide more than a fraction of the rubber that would be needed. As a result, Brazil, home of *Hevea brasiliensis*, today is unable to meet even the nation's own modest natural rubber requirements.

WILD RUBBER VS. PLANTATION RUBBER

In 1960 more than 95 per cent of the world's natural rubber came from plantations in Southeast Asia, another 2 per cent from plantations in Africa, and only 2 or 3 per cent from the forests of Amazonia. This situation is largely a matter of competition. Costs of production in Southeast Asia are but a fraction of those in Amazonia. Even the yield per tree is much higher—10 to 17 pounds, compared with 3 pounds. Moreover, one Asiatic worker attends up to 500 trees, whereas his South American counterpart handles 175 to 200. In the Amazon there is no supervision of tapping methods, no care of trees; in Southeast Asia trees get extensive care from scientists. At the Rubber Research Institute's headquarters in Kuala Lumpur, Federation of Malaysia, efforts are made to discover and promote ever better methods of growing and processing rubber; and the institute, through its field workers, helps hundreds of thousands of smallholders to improve their own rubber production. In the Amazon forest the workers are exposed to all the dangers and hardships of a remote, wild, and sparsely settled region. Moreover, they receive a very small return for their effort. Most are forced to supplement their small income from rubber by hunting and fishing and by engaging in subsistence shifting (**milpa**) agriculture. In Southeast Asia, plantation rubber workers are carefully housed, tended by doctors, and supplied a well-regulated diet. In Southeast Asia labor is abundant, skilled, used to routine tasks, and cheap; in Amazonia labor is scarce, quite incompetent (by comparison), and not so low in cost.

It is little wonder, then, that whereas Southeast Asia produced only 9 per cent of the world's rubber in 1910, the percentage had leaped to 60 by 1914, to 93 by 1924, and to 95 by 1960.

WORLD TRADE IN NATURAL RUBBER

Natural rubber, far from being a mere forest or plantation product, is one of the very important items in world trade. Its properties—elasticity, impermeability, softness, and electrical nonconductivity—have made it an essential industrial material. It enters into the manufacture of tires, industrial-rubber goods, sponge products, footwear, wire and cable insulation, and a host of other products.

World trade in rubber is largely from Southeast Asia and Central Africa to the United States and Western Europe, but also to the Soviet Union, Communist China, and Japan.

Although natural rubber encounters more and more competition from its synthetic rival, it nevertheless grows in world importance. The United States alone is expected to consume 3.3 million tons of rubber (natural and synthetic) by 1975—more than double the quantity used in 1958 and more than four times the amount consumed at the time of Pearl Harbor. Two conditions encourage continued use of natural rubber by the United States: (1) Many products made from it are superior to those made from synthetic rubber. (2) The economy and political stability of

Malaysia and Indonesia are so dependent upon rubber that a closing of the American market could mean ruin and might conceivably drive them to Communism. As long as the Cold War lasts, then, the United States will probably continue to purchase natural rubber, even if the cost is higher than that of the synthetic product and even if synthetic rubber should become superior to it in quality.

MANUFACTURE OF NATURAL RUBBER

Rubber products are not made in the areas that supply natural rubber; for, by and large, tropical peoples have not as yet taken kindly to steady and routine factory work. Moreover, their markets, made up essentially of poor people, are capable of absorbing only limited quantities of fabricated items. Hence, rubber goods are made (1) in countries that use them (a *single* American company manufactures 30,000 different items containing rubber), (2) in countries that employ power and machinery, and (3) in countries that possess hardworking, skilled, and dependable labor. In a number of Latin American countries, tires and tubes are manufactured by well-known American and European companies, whose plants are owned jointly with nationals.

Since the United States has 66 per cent of the world's automobiles and 45 per cent of the trucks, and since it has the world's highest standard of living, it is not surprising to learn that it consumes one half of the world's crude rubber. However, the rubber industry includes much more than automotive products. Rubber also yields shoe soles and heels, flooring, fan belts, hot-water bottles, shower curtains, upholstery, golf balls, rubber bands, and other items. The list is virtually endless. Its per capita consumption is about 20 pounds per annum, compared with about 1.5 pounds for the rest of the world. While raw rubber is received by Pacific Coast, Gulf Coast, and Atlantic Coast ports, New York normally is the recipient of almost three fourths of the nation's total imports.

PRINCIPAL MANUFACTURING CENTERS

To a whole generation of Americans, Akron and rubber were synonymous. Until recently the Akron metropolitan area manufactured half the nation's tires as well as a substantial part of all other rubber goods. Akron became the "tire city"—at first bicycle and carriage tires; later, tires for automobiles and trucks. It reached its rubber-employment peak in 1917-1918, when, with nearby Barberton, it employed 70,000 persons and was probably the most highly specialized city industrially in the country. This concentration was advantageous during the early days of rubber manufacture, for buyers and sellers could get together easily. Simultaneously rubber-machinery manufacturers became established there, so that spare parts were quickly available; and ideas could be tried out more easily and with greater understanding than would have been true had such companies been located 500 or 1,000 miles from Akron. Local concentration also assured a large pool of skilled labor. Proximity to Detroit, capital of the automobile industry, was a major factor; for, since rubber manufacture is essentially an assembly process, it is *market oriented*. The cost of shipping a given weight of finished product is about twice that for the same weight of crude rubber.

As Akron's rubber industry grew, labor unions became increasingly powerful, and the cost of labor soared. High labor costs led to more and more automation, which in turn led to strikes and ultimately to decentralization out of Akron (Fig. 13-4). Another decentralizing factor has been the need for greater economy in distribution. By plant purchase and by new construction, the big Akron rubber companies have extended into Alabama, California (second to Ohio in the manufacture of tires and inner tubes), Maryland, Mississippi, the New England states, and New York. The exodus from Akron is permanent. Nevertheless, Akron still is capital of the tire and tube industry, contributing about a third of the national output. Its chief assets are momentum of an early start, a large pool of skilled labor, and nearness to the nation's largest rubber markets—particularly the southern Michigan automotive cities.

Los Angeles, second most important rubber-manufacturing center, benefits from its importance as an automobile-assembly area, its

greater proximity than New York to Southeast Asia's rubber-producing centers (it costs about one tenth as much to lay down a pound of rubber in Los Angeles as in New York), a fast-growing market for rubber (California leads all states in the number of registered vehicles), ample skilled labor, and an impressive petrochemical industry for the manufacture of synthetic rubber.

Gadsden, Alabama, has gained stature as a rubber-manufacturing center in recent years. Natural rubber enters Alabama via the port of Mobile. There tires are made for Sears, Roebuck and Company, which is reported to have insisted that the fabricator, Goodyear Tire and Rubber Company, make the tires in a regional plant in the South.

Detroit ranks next to Akron in the manufacture of tires. This growth reflects a shift from Akron—a shift made in order to supply new cars more economically with the original set of tires.

SYNTHETIC RUBBER

The sudden sweep of the Japanese invasion forces into Southeast Asia in 1942 swallowed up nearly all the world's commercial natural-rubber production. What could a country such as the United States, which literally moves on rubber, do without it—particularly in time of war? Planes could not take off or land, supplies could not roll, troops would have to walk, guns and tanks would be immobilized. There was enough rubber stockpiled or en route from Asia to supply the national demand for possibly a year. Latin America, particularly Brazil, was urged to fill the critical need, but the entire Amazon Basin was able to send but a trickle—about 25,000 tons in 1943. The United States was desperate. For several years prior to the war, rubber companies in Akron had been carrying on research in synthetic rubber, but none was being produced commercially. In this crisis, the rubber companies agreed to pool talent, secrets, patents, facilities; the large chemical companies agreed to supply the key agents needed in making synthetic rubber, and the United States government agreed to con-

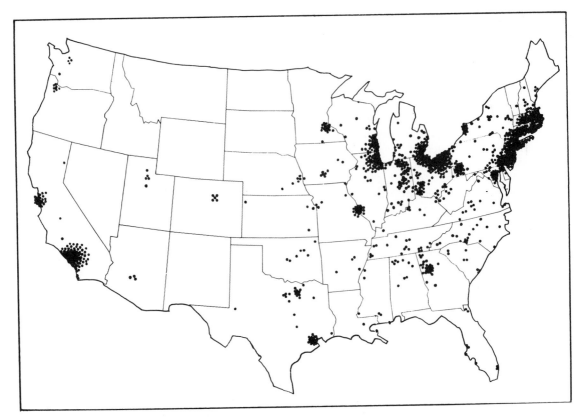

Fig. 13-4. Distribution of the rubber industry in the United States. This industry has changed since Pearl Harbor; for it now includes chemical companies and petroleum and natural-gas companies, as well as the traditional rubber companies. And it includes installations using natural and/or synthetic rubber. There are 1,881 rubber factories in the country. (Courtesy of Rubber Manufacturers Association, Inc.)

struct some 51 plants (Fig. 13-5) at a cost of about 750 million dollars. In 1942, a mere 3,600 tons were produced; in 1943, 200,000 tons; and in 1944, more than 800,000 tons. Production was still mounting when, in 1945, the war ended; and all the plants were sold at reduced prices to private companies. Present capacity is considerably in excess of 1 million tons.

QUALITY

Both synthetic and natural rubber have been used in the United States since the end of World War II, because each has been better suited than the other for specific services. Natural rubber is more elastic, has better heat-dissipating qualities, and wears better. Synthetic rubber is more resistant to

cracking in sunlight and to the deteriorating effects of ozone, withstands heat better, and is less soluble in oil. One of synthetic rubber's biggest advantages is its ability to be altered to fit specific needs.

QUANTITY

More synthetic than natural rubber is used today in the United States—almost 2 pounds of synthetic for every 1 pound of natural rubber (Table 13-1). The Communist bloc countries, particularly the Soviet Union and Czechoslovakia, are greatly increasing their production of synthetic rubber; and indications point to an output of 1.5 million tons by the late 1960s. During the decade 1960–1970, the output of natural rubber is expected to remain at about present levels, whereas that

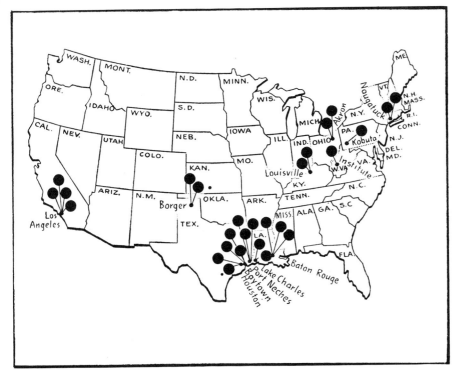

Fig. 13-5. Synthetic-rubber plants in the United
States. Note the heavy concentration in the Texas-
Louisiana Gulf Coast—heart of the world's petrochemical industry. These plants plus additional
ones under construction have given the United
States industry complete independence from natural rubber. Irrespective of political upheavals in
the rubber-producing areas of Southeast Asia, Liberia, and Latin America, the United States need
not be concerned regarding its supply of this important material. (Courtesy of Business Week.)

TABLE 13-1

UNITED STATES RUBBER CONSUMPTION
(in thousands of long tons)

Year	Total	Natural	Synthetic	Per cent synthetic to total
1949	989	575	414	41.9
1950	1,259	721	538	42.8
1951	1,213	454	759	62.6
1952	1,261	454	807	64.0
1953	1,338	553	785	58.6
1954	1,233	596	637	51.6
1955	1,530	635	895	58.5
1956	1,436	562	874	60.9
1957	1,465	539	926	63.2
1958	1,364	484	880	64.5

SOURCE: Rubber Manufacturers Association, New
York.

of synthetic rubber will increase appreciably.
Some students of the industry believe that
the world output of synthetic rubber will
more than double during the period 1960–
1970.

PRICE

In the United States, synthetic rubber has
been preferred for about one third of total
consumption, and natural rubber for another
one third. In the remaining one third, the
two types have been competitive; here price
has generally been the deciding factor. Synthetic rubber has been cheaper than natural
rubber in the United States for several years;
hence, its total share of the market has
climbed steadily. In addition, the price of the

synthetic product fluctuates very little (18.5 to 25 cents per pound), whereas that of natural rubber gyrates widely (from 3 cents to $1.25 per pound, and 20 cents to 60 cents a pound even in the past decade), so that synthetic rubber tends to be preferred.

Does the over-all success of synthetic rubber indicate that natural rubber is on the way out? At the moment, the answer is no. The growers in Southeast Asia have learned that scientific breeding of trees,[4] improved tapping methods, and careful replanting cycles for eliminating older and less productive trees can raise the yield per acre to 2,000 pounds and more a year, compared with 450 pounds in many areas today.

SYNTHETIC-RUBBER PLANTS IN THE UNITED STATES

The United States is by far the largest producer and consumer of synthetic rubber; it accounts for more than three fourths of world production outside the Iron Curtain. Since synthetic rubber is based almost exclusively on petroleum, the plants are oriented to it. At the very beginning (during World War II) the Gulf Coast, with its rich oil resources from Baton Rouge to Houston (Fig. 13-5), was chosen for the location of the major portion of the government-financed plants. This area's salient advantages are the presence there of (1) refining gases, which yield butylems and other chemicals; (2) petroleum, from which comes benzol and ethylene; (3) natural gas, major source of the carbon black used to reinforce rubber; (4) sulfur for vulcanizing; and (5) salt, lime, and clays, which have important uses in rubber synthesis. Butadiene (from oil companies) and styrene (from chemical companies) are the major

feedstocks for Buna-S rubber. Since it is uneconomical to ship butadiene great distances and since it is employed almost exclusively for making synthetic rubber, the feedstock plants usually form a part of the local industrial complex, consisting of the petroleum refinery, the butadiene plant, and the rubber-producing plant. The flow of materials is usually via pipeline. The styrene, used in smaller quantities than butadiene, is shipped to rubber-producing plants by tank car. The sixteen plants that make synthetic rubber in the Gulf Coast region are on or close to the Gulf and are located with respect to local oil refineries. The only Texas plant not located on water is that at Borger in the Panhandle.

Since latex rubber must be made close to its market, because the high water content (two thirds) discourages shipment to distant markets, this product is manufactured close to its local markets in the Middle West, the Northeast, and the West Coast. Los Angeles, center of the West Coast synthetic-rubber industry, makes latex and dry rubber as well as its own styrene and butadiene.

SYNTHETIC-RUBBER INDUSTRY OUTSIDE THE UNITED STATES

In 1957 Canada ranked second in production among all nations. More and more synthetic rubber is being manufactured in Europe —in Great Britain, France, Italy, West Germany. The Soviet Union and Czechoslovakia are greatly increasing their output and consumption. As yet the countries of Western Europe manufacture little compared with the United States, Canada, and the Soviet Union; but as a result of the burgeoning role of imported petroleum in the economic life of the various nations, the synthetic-rubber industry is growing rapidly. Appreciable increases in volume were recorded by France, the United Kingdom, and West Germany in the early 1960s; and in Asia, Japan's increase reached 94 per cent.

WORLD OUTLOOK

The only thing certain about the future of rubber is that the world will annually use

[4] Scientists noted that on their plantations (e.g., in Sumatra) 30 per cent of the trees were contributing 70 per cent of the total yield. They immediately embarked on a selection program, keeping individual-yield records. Buds from the outstanding mother trees were then grafted onto ordinary seedling rootstalks; thus, new families (or "clones") were formed, which were to become the high-yielding aristocratic families of the rubber world. Some families of trees are today yielding experimentally 3,000 pounds of rubber per acre. Often, these trees are only four or five generations removed from their wild jungle ancestors.

more of it. In the decade of the 1950s, consumption in the United States increased by 28 per cent, in Canada by 48 per cent, in France by 80 per cent, in Germany by 144 per cent, and in Japan by 183 per cent. World consumption is expected to increase 30 per cent by 1965.

Whether competition between natural and synthetic rubber will intensify, no one at the moment can say. All the big rubber companies, and many chemical, petroleum, and natural-gas companies, are attempting to improve the quality of their synthetic rubber. For a century, scientists have been trying to produce a "synthetic natural rubber"—one with a polymer structure and the physical properties of *Hevea* rubber. The Soviet Union claims to have made such a discovery, as have several American corporations. The Russians assert that they will soon replace most of their butadiene rubber with polyisoprene. United States companies are thus far holding back, because of (1) the high price of isoprene and the lack of producing facilities compared with large butadiene capacity, (2) the availability of ample natural rubber at reasonable prices, and (3) the expanding uses of present synthetic rubbers.

In the 1960s the continuance of natural-rubber production in Asia and Africa and continued access of the product to the United States, Canada, and the countries of Western Europe appeared assured. Available evidence seems to indicate that the American synthetic industry does not threaten the well-being of Southeast Asia's rubber growers. Their product continues to have a market of its own (Table 13-2); natural rubber still is superior for some purposes to any synthetic rubber presently available on the world market. In uses for which either natural or synthetic rubber may be employed, however, synthetic rubber, at least in the American market, appears to have an advantage. Natural-rubber producers in Malaysia and Indonesia are bending every effort to compete, by increasing efficiency and yields.

TABLE 13-2

WORLD CONSUMPTION OF RUBBER

Country	Pounds total rubber per capita	Pounds synthetic rubber per capita	Percentage synthetic
United States	19.2	12.1	63.2
Canada	11.6	6.3	53.8
Australia	11.4	3.5	31.1
Great Britain	10.4	2.5	24.0
France	9.4	2.5	27.0
West Germany	7.7	2.0	25.7
Netherlands	4.7	0.9	19.3
Argentina	4.2	0.5	12.1
Italy	3.6	0.9	23.8
Japan	3.5	0.3	9.1
Brazil	1.4	0.03	2.1
India	0.2	0.02	8.7

SOURCE: Charles F. Phillips, Jr., "The Competitive Potential of Synthetic Rubber," *Land Economics*, 36:331, November 1960.

SELECTED REFERENCES

Bauer, P. T. *The Rubber Industry: A Study in Competition and Monopoly.* Cambridge, Mass., Harvard University Press, 1948.

Broadway, Norman J., and Stephen Palinchak. "Synthetic 'Natural' Rubber—Technical Triumph," *Battelle Technical Review*, 8:3-10, December 1959.

Cramer, Robert E. "Outlook for Rubber," *Focus*, 6:1-6, November 1955.

Fisher, H. L. "Rubber," *Scientific American*, 195:32, 74-84, November 1956.

Grist, D. H. "The Plantation Rubber Industry," *World Crops*, 5:175-180, May 1953.

Phelps, D. M. *Rubber Developments in Latin America.* Ann Arbor, University of Michigan, Bureau of Business Research, 1957.

Phillips, Charles F., Jr. "The Competitive Potential of Synthetic Rubber," *Land Economics*, 36:322-332, November 1960.

Rippy, J. Fred. "Some Rubber-Planting Fiascos in Tropical America," *Inter-American Economic Affairs*, 10:3-24, Summer 1956.

Taylor, Wayne C. *The Firestone Operation in Liberia.* Washington, D. C., National Planning Association, 1956. Fifth Case Study in United States Business Performance Abroad.

CHAPTER FOURTEEN ::

When man began domesticating plants and animals, and thus assured a food supply for himself, he was able to stop his interminable roaming and to use his time, his energy, and his ingenuity for technical development; in short, he established the basis for a permanent civilization. It was then that the arts of spinning and weaving—the most ancient and universal manufacturing activities—were born.

Curiously enough, most of the natural fibers utilized for modern textiles are the very ones used in the far-distant past. As trade developed, first in India and around 1700 B.C. in Egypt, the explored world became acquainted with the world's great fabrics: Egypt offered linen; Mesopotamia, wool; India, cotton; China, silk. By the late 1600s Europe's textile industries were sufficiently advanced to stimulate spinners, weavers, fullers, and dyers to organize powerful craft guilds.

THE WORLD'S TEXTILE

TEXTILES

For many centuries the making of textiles was an important handicraft and household industry. Gradually the many and intricate processes involved in weaving, dyeing, and printing were improved; and finally machine fabrication changed this ages-old household art into both an art and a science. Yet in many places in the world textiles are still made entirely by hand.

Textile-mill products are divided into three broad classifications: (1) consumers' goods—products ready for sale to ultimate consumers (e.g., piece goods, sheets, blankets, rugs); (2) industrial goods—products (mostly woven fabrics) ready for uses by businesses outside the textile industry (e.g., ducks, twills, sateen, and some fine goods, to be incorporated directly into finished products like tents, sails, and upholsteries); and (3) cutters' goods—products (mainly finished fabrics) that comprise the principal materials used in manufacturing apparel and related products.

In contrast to most industries, the textile has not been notable for rapid improvements in machinery; for it is a mature industry whose basic processes never change—though, of course, they have been refined many times. Fundamentally, cloth is made today much as it was in the eighteenth century, when the spinning frame was invented. The spinning and weaving industry was the first to mechanize—and did so some decades prior to the use of electricity.

Yet, though there have been no truly revolutionary changes in textile machinery, there have been, especially during recent years, distinct improvements that have significantly altered the character of the industry. For

AND GARMENT INDUSTRIES

nearly every stage of manufacture, either a new machine has been developed or a traditional one improved. The chief aim of technical improvements has been to strengthen yarns and reduce breaks, so that a finer-quality product can be made and a single worker can handle more machines. But new weaving machines have not as yet made a pronounced impact; and the automatic loom remains the only widely accepted technical innovation in the industry. In a modern mill each worker can produce about 40 yards of cloth hourly.

Nagged by the desire to industrialize, the world's underdeveloped areas usually turn first to textile manufacture. In fact, a domestic textile industry for purposes of self-sufficiency is practically synonymous with a nation's infant industrialization. A contraction of the industry in several of the older manufacturing countries (e.g., the United Kingdom, continental European nations, and the United States) has followed in the wake of this expansion in less advanced areas (e.g., Asia, Latin America, Middle East, and Africa). The big consumers are turning into big producers. Those building up a modern industry have the advantage of modern equipment, which circumvents outdated production methods, largely nullifies the need for traditional skills, and can cope efficiently with the new man-made fibers. However, in some of the underdeveloped countries—where the textile industry is old, and large-scale industrialization is still largely a dream—adjustment to modernization is difficult, since alternative employment for a large labor force is wanting.

The older manufacturing areas, long complacent about foreign competition, must now discard their antiquated machinery and methods to compete in world markets and to combat ever higher labor costs. Modernization—which includes modern machinery, advanced managerial techniques, well-trained personnel, and improved work methods—is essential for all branches of the textile industry the world over. For competition becomes increasingly rough as world capacity continues to outpace textile trade; for example, since the early 1900s cotton-textile production has risen approximately 50 per cent, while the amount of goods entering international trade has dropped 40 per cent. High protective tariff walls and lower wages are, of course, additional safeguards against foreign competition, but in many instances are unfeasible.

Today more than forty countries have a substantial textile industry, but nine stand out: the United States, the Soviet Union, Communist China, Japan, India, the United Kingdom, West Germany, France, and Italy.

COTTON

The cotton-textile industry is unique in its geography: it is a widespread major industry, and it is usually the first to be developed when nations plunge into their industrial revolutions. The following causes underlie these two basic and closely related factors:

1. The processes of the machine industry are simple and, especially in coarse goods, similar to the familiar handicraft operations. Thus, areas lacking skilled industrial labor can develop the industry quite rapidly.

2. A comparatively small amount of capital is needed to set up a plant of economical size (particularly in comparison with the vast initial outlays required for the iron and steel or automotive industries).

3. The market for cotton yarn and cloth is extensive even in nonindustrial societies.

4. The locational pattern of the industry is little affected by the raw materials, even though their costs comprise the chief element in the total production cost.

5. The industry tends to expand in areas of low wages, since labor costs comprise the second most important element in the cost structure of the industry and show the widest variation both interregionally and internationally.

MANUFACTURING PROCESSES

In its transformation into cloth, cotton undergoes cleaning, ginning, lapping, carding, combing, and spinning—the processes that convert the raw fiber into yarn; next comes thread weaving (mostly performed on highly specialized power looms in big factories); and finally, bleaching, dyeing, printing, and finishing.

Although mills are increasingly being integrated, many continue to specialize in one of the three above stages. *Yarn mills* transform the baled raw cotton into yarn for sewing thread, tire cord, knitting, and electrical insulation. *Cloth mills* (the most numerous) process the raw cotton or the yarn through the weaving stage—producing the "gray goods." *Finishing plants* receive the woven cloth, which they wash, bleach, dye, print, fill, and calender, according to the kind of cloth required.

DEVELOPMENT OF THE MODERN INDUSTRY

The Industrial Revolution was punctuated by a number of high spots directly concerned with the manufacture of cotton and other textiles. Beginning in England around 1785, this cataclysmic changeover from hand tools to power-driven machines transformed a people with peasant occupations and local markets into an industrial society with global relations. Especially affected by the Industrial Revolution were the iron and textile industries; indeed, the latter literally transformed Lancashire. One invention invariably begets another, and so it was that a rapid series of inventions whirled the wheels of the revolution in England, producing the clumsy prototypes of today's complex textile machinery. John Kay contributed the *fly shuttle* in 1733; James Hargreaves, the *spinning jenny* in 1764; Richard Arkwright, the *spinning frame* in 1768; and Edmund Cartwright, the *water frame* or *throstle* in 1769. Then Samuel Crompton in 1774 invented the *spinning mule* —a combination of the jenny and throstle— which was best adapted to factories having considerable power available.

A new era of the cotton-textile industry was soon launched with the combination of the spinning machine, the weaving machine, and cheap cotton from the American South, topped by Eli Whitney's momentous invention of the cotton gin in 1793. England underwent a definite metamorphosis in the period 1785–1815, as handicraft industry in villages and on farms gave way to machine industry in cities. Lancashire became synonymous with cotton manufacture—relinquishing her posi-

tion only in 1932, when a flurry of difficulties besieged the industry.

The following conditions are invariably cited as favoring and stimulating the industry in the Lancashire area: (1) a previous textile industry, (2) soft water, (3) westerly winds providing the high humidity essential to prevent fuzzing and brittle threads in machine manufacturing, (4) location close to Liverpool—the nearest port to the United States, major source of raw cotton, (5) available water power, (6) forests to supply construction material for new machines, and (7) the presence of Flemish weavers. However, yet another factor must be added to penetrate the secret of concentration here: as the Industrial Revolution progressed, Lancashire's natural environment proved capable of meeting each new need; and, not the least important, there were men of vision to recognize and cope with these new needs. Water power was harnessed when machinery became available. Coal could be—and was—mined on the spot when steam took over. Chemical bleaching was developed with the aid of nearby Cheshire salt deposits and the plentiful supply of soft water. Construction of highway, railway, and canal transportation offered no great difficulties (the opening of the Manchester Canal in 1894 made Manchester an ocean port).

Although for more than a century Manchester was the focus of the industry, it was actually not the manufacturing center but rather the business and commercial nucleus. The surrounding villages became the spinning and weaving towns. The cotton-textile industry was ensconced within a 40-mile radius of Manchester—the strongest total agglomeration in the world.

Phenomenal growth is invariably accompanied by a high degree of specialization; the Lancashire area was no exception and soon had individual towns concentrating on single operations. By 1880, Britain—that is to say, Lancashire—had more than half of all the cotton spindles in the world. This proportion had been reduced to a third by 1913, and to a fifth by 1960. For many years sons tended to succeed their fathers, thus giving the area the added advantage of skill. However, complicated and highly efficient machinery has now nullified much of the need for trained labor. Air conditioning has minimized the advantage of atmospheric humidity. Likewise, electrical energy has largely obviated the need for water-power sites and a nearby coal supply. Yet Lancashire continues to manufacture roughly 90 per cent of Britain's cotton textiles, concentrating on high-quality fabrics to offset the competition of medium-grade goods.

Britain's advantages were so pronounced for so many years that foreign competition constituted a minor worry. Then other countries began industrializing by producing cheap, coarse cotton goods; they erected tariff walls to protect their fledgling industries and curtailed imports of the British product after World War I. But the British cotton-textile industry was developed chiefly to cater to foreign markets, for cotton manufacture more than any other British industry was—and remains—a matter of "export or die"; approximately 60 per cent of the output is designed for export. Britain's export supremacy persevered until 1932, when it was toppled as a result of (1) huge Japanese exports, (2) the emergence of strongly competing industries in China and India, both of which previously had been large markets for British textiles, and (3) the growing domestic cotton-textile industries in many other lands.

WORLD PRODUCTION

Until recently the cotton-textile industry, with few exceptions, tended to gravitate to industrialized countries far distant from the cotton-growing areas (Fig. 14-1). Now, however, nearly every nation, whether or not it is advanced industrially, either has a cotton-textile industry or is planning one.

United States. Paralleling the decline of Lancashire was the ascendancy of the United States as the world leader in cotton-textile production; it now accounts for about 25 per cent of the world total. The industry normally gives employment to more than a million workers. Abundant supplies of raw cotton, a large domestic market, and, until recently, a substantial export market all provided a firm foundation for the industry.

The nation's cotton-textile industry offers a valuable study in industrial location: since 1880, but especially since 1923, the great shift of the cotton mills from New England to the South has been dramatic in its economic, social, political, and psychological impact. By 1927 the South had overtaken New England in production.

Well aware of the importance of cotton manufacturing as a source of profit and employment in England, citizens in the American colonies and later in the United States envisaged a similar industry for their new nation. Prior to 1790 there was not great progress, for England guarded her textile machinery tenaciously: neither machines nor blueprints could be exported; it was illegal for skilled artisans to emigrate, and, if they did so, they suffered confiscation of property and loss of citizenship; the baggage of all English emigrants was searched for plans of machinery. However, in 1789, Samuel Slater, an apprentice to Richard Arkwright, was lured to America by a bounty offered for the introduction of Arkwright's patents into America. He thwarted British authorities by carrying the secrets of Arkwright's invention (and of Hargreave's and Crompton's machines) not in his baggage but in his head. He built from memory America's first cotton-spinning machinery and erected its first cotton mill at Pawtucket, Rhode Island, in 1790. Ten years later Slater's mill was surrounded by twenty-nine others.

Prior to 1830 spinning was the major operation, and the dominant source of power was falling water; hence, the mills located primarily along small, easily harnessed streams. When the power loom was developed, larger establishments, which engaged in both spinning and weaving, required additional power. Therefore, the "center of gravity" moved to large power sites along the Merrimack River and the rivers of Maine and eastern Connecticut. After 1850 steam power largely supplanted water power in some areas, and entirely in others. Most mills today utilize electric power.

A number of decided advantages, aside from an early start, propelled New England's

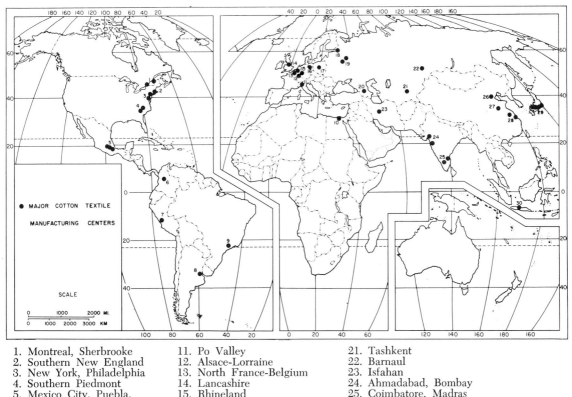

1. Montreal, Sherbrooke
2. Southern New England
3. New York, Philadelphia
4. Southern Piedmont
5. Mexico City, Puebla, Orizaba
6. Medellin
7. Lima
8. Buenos Aires
9. São Paulo
10. Alexandria
11. Po Valley
12. Alsace-Lorraine
13. North France-Belgium
14. Lancashire
15. Rhineland
16. Chemnitz
17. Lodz
18. Leningrad
19. Moscow-Ivanovo
20. Gori
21. Tashkent
22. Barnaul
23. Isfahan
24. Ahmadabad, Bombay
25. Coimbatore, Madras
26. Peking
27. Chengchow
28. Nanking, Shanghai
29. Southern Japan
30. Tegal

Fig. 14-1. The world's leading cotton-textile centers. Most of them are in the Northern Hemisphere—specifically, in the developed countries of North America, Europe, and Asia; but as one of the first industries in underdeveloped lands, cotton manufacture has become, particularly since 1900, widely dispersed. The cotton-textile industry is thus the most widespread of the major industries.

industry: (1) high humidity, which—by reducing the frictional electricity caused by rubbing the fibers during processing—retards tangling during spinning and reduces breakage during weaving; (2) water power; (3) soft, clean water, excellent for bleaching; (4) skilled labor working for low wages—the original labor force being gradually replaced by successive waves of European immigrants, each group poorer than the last; (5) ample capital available for investment—provided initially by merchants and seamen whose business had been cut off by wars, and later by

the whaling industry; and (6) location in the major market area and close to wholesale centers—the coastal cities of Boston, New York, and Philadelphia.

In every New England state except Vermont the cotton-textile industry is still important, but the two states of Rhode Island and Massachusetts have the majority of the mills and workers.

Though the entire textile industry for the past 60 years has been one of the slowest-growing industries in the nation, and at various times (e.g., in the 1950s) has suffered substantial losses, New England has been the hardest hit. Nevertheless, the billion-dollar enterprise still is one of the region's largest employers of labor. But, particularly since 1919, New England's economy has undergone an unnerving decline; whereas early in the 1900s the area accounted for approximately 80 per cent of the nation's cotton spindles, its proportion now is less than 10 per cent. At first, losses were only in coarse cotton goods, and New England complacently assumed that the South could not manufacture the quality yarns and cloth which brought the premium prices; but the Northern monopoly on finer cotton goods has been gradually dissolving.

Why was the decline so severe? Low labor productivity; the static nature of management; lack of enterprise; archaic organization; obsolescent plants and equipment; high cost factors such as labor, power, fuel, and taxes; subsidies in regions soliciting new industries; poor employee relations (improved only when it was too late to affect the bulk of the industry)—these are some of the reasons.

The cotton-manufacturing industry of the South, which has contributed so immeasurably to the economic growth of the region, actually had its beginnings forty years before the much-publicized "Cotton-Mill Campaign" of the early 1880s. In the depression of the 1840s, the Piedmont South, recognizing the advantages of its location and its cheap labor, established several mills, employing largely women and children and relying on Northerners for the operation of the plants. However, several disadvantages—among them inadequate transport facilities, marketing difficulties, and paucity of operating capital—hampered progress.

In 1880 the South was well launched on its cotton-textile industry. Relative political and economic stability, a railway network into the Piedmont, and a vigorous campaign to recruit Northern investment capital, machinery, and managerial talents incited a new surge of activity. The South, however, did not wait for Northern capital; Southern communities, within their limitations, supplied as much capital as they could—and thus contributed basically to the South's success. In contrast to

New England—where the capital of the rich built the cotton mill, and it was strictly a business—in the South the combined capital of many with meager means built the mill, and it was largely a social enterprise. Southerners were entreated to "take stock in the mills for the town's sake, for the South's sake, literally for God's sake."

Living conditions at the early mill villages were often deplorable beyond belief, but until 1900 the labor force was formed by the "hill people" who

came to the mills from their worn-out rented farms. They came from the spectre of five-cent cotton and from fields hungry for expensive fertilizer. They came from tables set with pellagra-breeding fare. They came from a countryside wretched and terrifying in its poverty, in the desolation of its gutted red clay hills. They came poor to the point of desperation, ragged and gaunt, uneducated, uncouth and awkward away from the background of hills and fields; uneasy and suspicious, bewildered and bitter . . . a farm people using the mills as an avenue of escape from the land that had failed them and for a bridge into the future.[1]

With a highly adequate labor supply as a foundation, the South exerted a magnetic attraction for mills through a number of advantages it enjoyed over the North:

1. The price differential plus longer working hours. Labor costs were lower: a large labor force was at hand, labor laws were far less stringent, labor unions were weak, high-priced skilled labor became less necessary with advanced technology. The wage differential historically has been cited as the most significant factor in the North-South movement; but following 1940, because of minimum-wage laws and pressures from high-wage industries, wage differences were much less marked.

2. Lower living costs. Most Southern mills are located in rural communities or in the outskirts of large cities. Also milder winters make for lower fuel bills. Moreover, longer frost-free seasons enable the workers, many of

[1] Glenn Gilman, *Human Relations in the Industrial Southeast* (Chapel Hill: The University of North Carolina Press, 1956), pp. 127, 128.

whom have come from the "hills," to grow some of their own produce.

3. Cheaper power—both coal and hydroelectric. Most of the Southern mills are some 400 miles closer than those of New England to coal deposits. In hydroelectric power the South was and still is definitely favored.

4. No archaic traditions to stymie cotton manufacturing. Scientific location of mills has been emphasized; plants are scattered rather than concentrated as in New England. More modern machinery is utilized, many of the mills starting operations with the latest equipment.

5. Subsidized housing—from the outset a universal characteristic of the Southern industry. Building could be carried on the year around, and both materials and labor for construction cost less in the Piedmont. Workers were given reduced rents in lieu of higher wages.

6. Lower taxes.

7. Since 1930, marked increase in mergers. Southern firms have acquired Northern plants and some of their machinery, with a resultant greater capacity for diversification and increased facilities for supplying, processing, and marketing goods.

The Piedmont, then, had on its side every advantage except two—experience and nearness to market; and New England evidently neglected her opportunities in both respects. Initially, the South with its largely unskilled labor force turned out only coarse goods and in ten years eclipsed New England in this branch, exporting a substantial quantity to China, South America, and Africa. After 1900 the mills entered the fine-goods field, aided considerably by mechanical humidifiers. Another significant development during the 1880-1910 period was the establishment of finishing mills. By 1929 the South's value of product was double that of the North. (It is not without reason that New England's contest with the South has been likened to England's with the rest of the world.) Today the South is the unchallenged center of the nation's cotton-textile industry, and the Piedmont is the throbbing heart of it. Among the outstanding centers are Anderson, Atlanta, Augusta, Charlotte,

Columbia, Columbus, Danville, Gastonia, Greensboro, Greenville, Macon, and Spartanburg (Fig. 14-2).

The industry is losing its "aged and inbred" label, for family ownership of mills is rapidly on its way out. But the mills have tended to remain small producing and employing units, although several of them may be owned by a single company.

Both the South and the North have been hard hit by textile slumps in the recent past—not only in cotton but in other fabrics. In the last forty years, textiles seem to have earned their way only when wartime shortages created unusual demands. Cotton manufacturers have been seriously concerned about the decrease in per capita consumption of cotton. This textile decline is in large part a result of foreign imports, which comprise so strong a threat that even the expected gain in the American textile market in the 1960s may be submerged by them. Though American manufacturers must purchase raw cotton at a fixed price, the federal government has sold American cotton abroad for 20 per cent less than in the United States. Foreign equipment is as good as that of the United States; wages are much lower (in Hong Kong, India, Pakistan, and Japan, hourly rates may be as low as 10 to 15 cents). These advantages, along with low import duties, enable foreign competitors to sell their textiles at prices that inflict a considerable loss on an American company. As Southern mills grow in economic power and political influence, they, together with Northern protectionists, no doubt will push for high-tariff legislation.

In order to combat the foreign textile deluge, the American industry is pressing research to develop new combinations of all fibers that foreign manufacturers cannot match; it is also stressing higher and more consistent standards of quality, adopting the most cost-saving and efficient machinery, and promoting more aggressively.

Soviet Union. Textiles comprise the basic industry that directly serves the needs of the Soviet people; and cotton manufacture is the

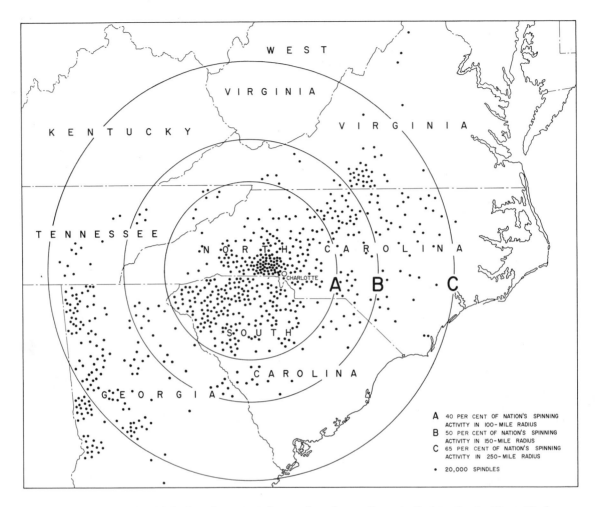

Fig. 14-2. Distribution of the textile industry (by spindles) in the Southern Piedmont. The heart of the industry is the Carolinas, and one of the most prominent single centers is Charlotte, North Carolina—the "textile capital of America." Within a 100-mile radius of Charlotte are more than 250 mills. Thus, the South launched forth on a new pattern —one of decentralized plants into smaller cities and towns.

principal branch of production, employing about half the total number of textile workers. Before the 1917 revolution, when heavy industry was woefully backward, textile manufacturing was the country's dominant large-scale industry.

Cotton manufacturing developed in the central region of European Russia—at Vladimir, Moscow, Yaroslavl, and Ivanovo—and in Leningrad. Raw-cotton production expanded into Central Asia to serve the industrial center when Russia was cut off from American cotton during the Civil War. Prior to the revolution half of the cotton used in Russian mills was imported—largely from the United States; and half came from Central Asia and Transcaucasia (today the Soviet Union claims self-sufficiency in raw-cotton production).

After the revolution the industry concentrated even more heavily in the industrial center: the Ivanovo Oblast became one of the densest textile areas in all Europe, though the

Moscow Oblast surpassed it in production. Since the 1920s the Russians have built cotton mills closer to their raw-material sources and consuming centers—e.g., Tashkent and Fergana in Uzbekistan; Ashkhabad in Turkmenistan; Barnaul in Western Siberia, Kirovabad in Azerbaidzhan, Leninakan in Armenia, and Kamyshin in the Volga region.

During World War II about one third of the spinning and almost a fourth of the weaving capacity was destroyed—some of it never to be restored. However, considerable restoration, coupled with brisk new developments, has been sufficiently rapid to outstrip the prewar rate of production, thanks in large part to revival of machine-building capacity. The industry has undergone such extensive decentralization that new plants are springing up in almost every Soviet republic, primarily to meet local needs. With the shift in the geography of the Soviet textile industry to outlying regions, the industrial center has tended to specialize in the higher-grade and technical fabrics.

Russia is far from filling domestic needs (per capita consumption of all textiles in the United States is estimated to be more than twice that in the Soviet Union). In 1959, with a view toward greatly increasing cotton-textile production during the seven-year plan (1958-1965), the Soviet Union signed a contract with a consortium of forty American textile-machinery companies to provide and install equipment for a huge new spinning and weaving plant at Kalinin. Within the next few years she hopes to install 4 million cotton spindles and 73,000 cotton looms. However, even with greatly increased capacity of Soviet cotton mills in the offing, the nation is not expected to make a drive for foreign markets until the distant future, when her domestic needs have been met.

Japan. Japan is today the world's leading exporter of cotton goods and the largest importer of American raw cotton (she grows no cotton). Cotton textiles, true to form, launched Japan's industrial revolution, the first cotton mill having been built in 1868. The industry really got under way after the turn of the century; but at the beginning of World War I, Japan was still importing substantial quantities of cotton cloth. When the war ended, Japan dominated the trade of China and thereafter the trade of the Netherlands East Indies, the Indian Ocean countries, and Africa—together comprising the greatest market in the world for cheap, coarse cotton goods. Japan developed machinery for spinning India's very short-staple cotton (which was in little demand elsewhere) and devised a process for blending it with Egypt's long-staple cotton. By the 1930s Japan's cotton goods were being offered the world around; and in 1934 Japan became the world's foremost exporter of cotton textiles.

Japan's phenomenal progress hinged on the ability of her mills to put out cotton goods at prices that other sellers could not match. This resulted from (1) almost continuous operation of mills and rapid amortization of equipment; (2) abundant cheap labor (a paternalistic system of training and maintaining mill staffs prevailed: children, usually girls, recruited from farm families worked for a fixed fee paid to their debt-ridden fathers); and (3) the introduction of the Toyoda automatic loom and of European machinery.

Japan's competitors quickly put a damper on her burgeoning trade; but neither restricted imports nor tariff barriers could upset her lead. In order to strengthen her position, in 1940 Japan consolidated the mills of seventy companies into ten strong combines.

Japan emerged from the shambles of World War II with her mills dismantled, her raw materials exhausted, and her trade smashed. Yet it took only eight years for her to rebuild the industry, regain her cotton-textile leadership, and become once again the world's largest importer of raw cotton.

Japan's cotton mills are to be found in the Kansai district of Honshu, with the greatest concentration around the city of Osaka. Twenty miles to the southwest on Osaka Bay is Kobe, the chief port of entry for Japan's raw-cotton imports.

Today Japan's spindles and looms are the most modern of any major manufacturing nation. Indeed, the industry is now actually hampered by its own notable efficiency, since textile-importing countries invariably try to supply their own demands, employing every technique from exchange controls to import quotas. Yet Japan must export half her production to keep plants operating. Her relative advantage in labor costs has been steadily declining as the Japanese standard of living rises and as other Asian nations press forward with industrialization.

India. The making of cotton textiles was the first and remains the foremost large-scale manufacturing industry in India. Although most of the production is consumed at home, India ranks second only to Japan as an exporter of cotton cloth, her major markets being those Asiatic countries where Indians have settled most densely.

In India output of yarn exceeds that of cloth, as is characteristic of lands where raw material is plentiful. Most of the yarn is coarse, because of the short- and coarse-staple cotton grown in India. Imported cotton from the United States and Egypt accounts for the increasing quantities of better-quality cloth.

The modern industry, built on ancient foundations, was really born with the establishment of a power-driven mill in Bombay in 1854. India's outstanding industrialist, Jamseti Tata, built his first cotton mill in 1869. In 1880, India provided the market for approximately half of Britain's machine-made cotton goods, which destroyed a substantial portion of India's cottage industries. The Indian industry developed slowly. However, later on, owing to the country's huge market, the availability of raw cotton, and the abundant and cheap supply of labor, the industry grew in stature.

Imports from Britain declined as India proceeded to build her own mills—with capital, machinery, and technologists supplied by Britain. Following World War I, Gandhi's nationalist policy (1921-1947) stressed handspun and handwoven cotton cloth and the boycott of English goods. Handloom weaving is still an important industry, being the largest and most widespread after agriculture; it gives employment to more than 10 million people and accounts for about one third of total cotton-textile production. Handwoven cloth maintains its popularity because a greater variety of patterns can be produced than on machine-woven cloth. Since partition, the industry has moved forward rapidly, and now is backed by more than 450 power-driven mills.

Bombay state turns out roughly 60 per cent of India's cotton textiles. Ahmedabad is the leading city, followed closely by Bombay. The state has always been the major center of production. Among Bombay's advantages were the following: (1) It was the leading port of export of raw cotton and therefore no special flow line of cotton had to be created when the domestic industry got under way. (2) It enjoyed cheap freight rates on imported mill equipment, particularly from England. (3) It was connected by railway with the interior sources of raw cotton and markets for piece goods. (4) It had a large supply of unskilled labor available in nearby coastal cities. (5) It possessed the climatic advantage of humidity for spinning the thread.

After 1921 the industry began to be dispersed into the interior, closer to the sources of raw cotton—largely because transportation and hydroelectric power became available farther inland, and labor costs were lower in less urbanized areas. The new mills of the interior have captured the markets for coarse goods in their own areas.

The Indian industry is handicapped by much obsolete machinery and hence is stymied by poor-quality products, high production costs, and the need for a very large labor force (34 times as many workers are employed in the handweaving industry as in a large modern mill). The greater use of automatic looms is regarded as essential if India hopes to compete, in quality and price, with other textile manufacturers in the export market. India, however, is proceeding cautiously with modernization, for she is faced with providing alternate employment for the many workers who would be displaced by the introduction of machinery.

China. Although cotton spinning and weaving was an ancient handicraft in China, the modern cotton-textile industry began only in 1890, when the first mill was built. In 1894, at the end of the Sino-Japanese War, the Treaty of Shimonoseki granted foreigners the right to set up factories in treaty ports. Great Britain, Germany, and the United States were quick to seize the opportunity, each constructing a cotton mill in Shanghai. However, development was slow until after World War I; for the industry was faced with many problems: (1) civil strife, (2) competition from Japanese mills, (3) inefficiency of management and labor, (4) labor strikes, (5) lack of capital, (6) poor-quality cotton, (7) slow and inadequate internal transportation, and (8) restricted buying power of the market.

In 1918 Shanghai had 80 per cent of the total spindleage and, before World War II, more than half the nation's spindles and looms. Standing at the mouth of the 750,000-square-mile Yangtze drainage basin, containing roughly one third of the nation's people, the city had a large and cheap labor supply and a huge market. In addition, after World War I it offered relative political security, access to imported raw cotton, foreign and domestic capital, and good transportation.

During the late 1920s and the 1930s the industry was decentralized to some extent (in the mid-1930s about half the spindles and looms were in Japanese-owned mills, about 5 per cent in British-owned ones). Communist China furthered decentralization by dismantling coastal mills and rebuilding them inland, closer to the raw-cotton sources. Mills operating with modern machinery have been built primarily in the important cotton-growing provinces of Hupeh, Honan, Shensi, and Sinkiang. The city of Tsingtao has become an important center, but the Shanghai-Nanking-Hangchow triangle continues to dominate the industry.

In Communist China's recent all-out trade offensive, cotton textiles have a highly prominent place and are exerting a resounding impact on the textile markets of the world. This sharp increase in exports was accomplished through a tripling of raw-cotton production in the decade 1948-1958, great expansion of the domestic textile industry, and strict rationing of domestic consumption. If China's present trend toward greater production and trade continues, the country may become a formidable competitor in world cotton-textile markets in the years ahead.

Great Britain. Although Britain still has more cotton spindles than any other nation (almost 20 per cent of the world total), she has now only the slightest edge over the United States. In production of yarn and of woven cotton fabrics she has slipped badly from first place—being eclipsed by the United States, the Soviet Union, China, India, and Japan. In 1957, cotton-cloth imports exceeded exports for the first time in 200 years (much of this cloth entered duty-free from Commonwealth members). This is not to say that the industry spent more on imports than on exports: the cloth brought in was largely unfinished; after being finished in British plants, it was re-exported at a profit. Yet although British spinners and weavers have suffered most from the flood of imports, even finishers are now becoming worried as the nations producing cheap cloth increasingly send out finished goods.

In addition to being plagued by export problems, especially since World War II, the British industry has been hamstrung by the obsolescence of many of its mills and much of their equipment, inefficient organization, and apathetic management. In early 1959 a third of Lancashire's spindles and a fourth of its looms were idle. Nevertheless, Lancashire's capacity continued to exceed demand. Its chief competitor, Hong Kong, was persuaded to give a three-year breathing space to Lancashire by restricting the quantity of exports. But the industry obviously required a complete reorganization in order to survive. In 1959 a scheme was designed to remove surplus capacity, to re-equip and modernize existing machinery, and to encourage installation of modern equipment.

Europe. As cotton spindleage and consumption spiraled downward in Britain, a concurrent increase took place on the European mainland, which now considerably surpasses Britain in both categories. Cotton textiles have long figured prominently among the industries of the continent, particularly in the major manufacturing area—West-Central Europe. The industry here was at the outset favored by (1) a large population which supplied cheap labor (working long hours) and a big home market, (2) numerous foreign markets (especially colonial possessions), (3) ample coal and water power, (4) abundant pure water, (5) an efficient transportation web of rivers, canals, and railways, (6) handy access to the sea, for importing raw cotton, and (7) the erection of high tariff walls.

The major cotton-manufacturing area extends from northeastern France (Lille is the leading center) through Belgium, the Netherlands, Germany, Poland, Czechoslovakia, Switzerland, and northern Italy. Raw cotton is imported primarily through Bremen, Dunkirk, Genoa, and Le Havre.

Many of these lands have a long history of textile manufacture, pre-dating the invention of machinery. Some of them turn out only coarse goods, while others make the finest of fabrics (the former use far more cotton per spindle than do the latter). Switzerland, France, Belgium, and West Germany are noted for their high-quality textiles and for such specialties as laces, ribbons, and hosiery. Italy, too, produces fine fabrics (chiefly in Milan and Venice) and, like Switzerland, makes ample use of her excellent water-power resources. The spinning and weaving mills are, for the most part, widely dispersed and small. About a third of the trade in cotton fabrics in Western Europe (including Great Britain) is intra-European.

In Eastern Europe, the industry is concentrated in Bohemia and western Moravia, in the southern portion of East Germany, and in "Little Manchester"—the Lódź area of Poland. The Eastern European industry elsewhere is widely scattered. Cotton goods enter foreign trade but little, some being exported to the Soviet Union in exchange for raw cotton.

In Western Europe mill modernization was the keynote during the 1950s. Progress was most marked in those countries where, after World War II, the industry almost had to start from scratch; wherever antiquated mills were demolished, new ones have risen—many with all new machines. The industry has been virtually revolutionized by the widespread rebuilding and replanning programs.

Brazil. Brazil's cotton-textile industry, which dates back to the colonial period, has had its share of ups and downs (the former occurring primarily during the two world wars). Today Brazil is self-sufficient in cotton textiles, is the overwhelming leader in their production among the Latin American nations, and normally exports substantial quantities.

Brazil's industry is well grounded, for the nation is one of the world's major raw-cotton producers. In addition, it has the largest population of any South American country; abundant water power favorably located with respect to raw-cotton sources, to labor supply, and to markets; a quite stimulating climate for the tropics; and an intense desire to industrialize. The major center of production and the leading industrial center of all Latin America is São Paulo.

Although Brazil ranks tenth in world spindleage, the industry has a basic need for modernization in order to compete more effectively in international trade. A partial solution appears likely as foreign firms—particularly Japanese and American—increasingly establish mills and textile-machinery factories in Brazil.

WOOL

The transformation of the fleece of sheep into fabric is one of the most ancient and fundamental of manufacturing processes. Peoples of high and middle latitudes early recognized the virtues of wool in their cold milieus: because of its long fibers covered with barbs, it could be spun easily into thread; it was light, yet durable; and its elasticity and scales produced a cloth that could preserve heat and absorb moisture. Wool was a necessity during the many centuries when cotton was still a luxury. Because of the firmly established traditional methods employed by subdivided crafts, as well as the greater complications involved in the manufacture of wool textiles, large-scale mechanization of wool manufacturing developed considerably later than that of cotton.

Wool, a highly variable fiber (there are about a thousand types, but less than one hundred grades meet normal trade needs), is sold primarily in the form of fleece wool clipped from the sheep (skin wool is taken from the skin of slaughtered animals) and preferably is bought "in the grease," since the grease retards felting. Arriving at the mill in a notably unalluring state (the grease is accompanied by much extraneous matter), the wool undergoes a cleansing process that shrinks its weight by one third or even up to two thirds (fine wool shrinks the most). It then must go through about a dozen processes before it can be spun.

All this requires much skilled labor and entails no little expense. Therefore, since most of the chief commercial wool-producing areas are sparsely populated and hence have a dearth of labor and a restricted market, it is small wonder that the modern wool industry —in contrast to cotton manufacturing—has not centered in the major wool-producing areas. Although these wool-producing areas— notably the belt of nomadic herding from the Mediterranean Basin to Central China, the grazing lands of the Andes, and the high plateau and mountain areas of the tropics— are slowly introducing mechanization into their wool manufacture, by far the largest portion of woolen cloth in these areas is made by hand in the ages-old manner. The wool-manufacturing industry, then, has centered in the advanced industrialized nations; the United States, the United Kingdom, Japan, France, West Germany, Italy, and Belgium import and manufacture about 75 per cent of the world's wool. The high value of wool enables it to stand the cost of long hauls to manufacturing centers; also it can be stored for a long time without deteriorating.

WORSTEDS AND WOOLENS

Historically, wool textiles have been divided into two main branches: the woolen—fabric made from short carded wool, and the worsted —fabric made from long combed wool. However, thanks to improvements in combing machinery, short carded wool can now be used in worsted manufacture. Worsteds have a tighter weave and harder finish than woolens. Loosely woven, rough-textured woolens are utilized largely for outer-wear purposes—e.g., overcoating and sportswear—but to some extent for suitings. Worsted mills, which carry on more complicated and specialized processes than woolen mills, are more concentrated in their location.

WORLD PRODUCTION

Europe and Asia. The groundwork for the modern wool industry was laid in medieval Europe—in the great manufacturing areas of the Low Countries and Florence. Flanders already exported cloth to Italy during the Roman occupation; by the twelfth century it had developed into a land of weavers and fullers, the industry reaching its apex in the early fourteenth century. But both the Low Countries and Florence depended on imported wool—mainly from England, whose Pennine Mountains provided excellent moorland for sheep—and this proved to be their downfall. Learning the art of wool-textile making from Flemish weavers and realizing that her high-quality wool was indispensable to the other countries, England proceeded to utilize the native supply and build up her own industry on a framework of abundant water power, easy access to coal, navigable waterways, soft clear water for scouring and dyeing, and ample capital for investment.

In the fifteenth century the wool manufacturers of the continent were eclipsed by those in England. For 700 years (from the twelfth to the nineteenth century) Britain's wool textiles constituted her foremost staple manufacture, and the industry was the first to undergo national control and uniform regulation. Contrary to the cotton-textile industry, which centered in one county, the wool industry was at first scattered throughout the realm, although three areas soon stood out—the west country, Yorkshire, and East Anglia. The Industrial Revolution had a profound effect on

Fig. 14-3. Night view of woolen mills in the Colne Valley, West Riding, Yorkshire, England. Woolen cloth has been woven here for at least six hundred years, and records suggest the possibility of its having existed for nearly twelve centuries. Such a night scene gives the viewer a far clearer picture of the importance of the woolen industry here than does a daytime scene. (Courtesy of British Information Services.)

the geography of the industry: Yorkshire took the helm and kept it (Fig. 14-3), not only because it had coal and iron in close proximity but, unlike the long-established seats, it was better able to adapt to the changed economic conditions created by the introduction of machines. However, western England and Scotland continue to turn out high-quality cloth. Leeds has become the trading, engineering, and clothing-manufacturing focus. The United Kingdom continues to lead the world in output of woven woolen fabrics.

Northeastern France, West Germany, northern Italy, Belgium, and the Netherlands today have important wool-manufacturing industries.

France is famous for its soft woven fabrics—the product of shorter-staple wool—which are utilized chiefly in women's apparel. The old Germany developed a substantial woolen industry in Silesia, Saxony, and Westphalia—on the coal fields; today West Germany's centers are Wuppertal (east of the Rhine) and München-Gladbach (west of the Rhine), which combine coal for power with good transportation facilities. Czechoslovakia, Bulgaria, Austria, and Switzerland are sizable producers, too.

Prior to the 1917 revolution, Russia's woolen industry was outstanding in Moscow and Leningrad, whose mills turned out fine cloth, and in the Black Earth Center and Central Volga region, which produced coarse cloth. In the Soviet period, particularly since World War II, mills have been constructed nearer to the raw-material sources (e.g., Kharkov and Kremenchug in the Ukraine, Kutaisi and Tbilisi in Georgia, and Semipalatinsk in Kazakhstan).

Japan ranks sixth in world production of wool yarns and fabrics, although, as with cotton, she must import all her raw material (about 80 per cent of the wool comes from Australia). There has been a fairly strong domestic demand for woolen fabrics in response to the desire for Western-style clothes, which feature wool as an important component. But Japan, living on trade as she does, has managed increasingly to export her woolens and worsteds, particularly to the United States. By 1960, Japan's subsidized, staple, mass-produced worsted cloth had so endangered the American industry that stiff tariffs were imposed on such goods.

United States. From the outset the American woolen industry differed from the cotton-textile industry: it began in the home, not in the factory; and it was (and still is) more widely scattered. Farmers manufactured woolen cloth from their own raw materials. As was true of cotton cloth, Britain used every possible means to stifle woolen manufacture in the colonies—by prohibiting importations of sheep into America and by forbidding exportation of colonial-made cloth; but her efforts were largely in vain.

Two circumstances stimulated native manufacture: (1) the War of 1812, which interrupted trade between Britain and America, and (2) high protective tariffs in 1816 and 1824. New England logically became the production center, by virtue of its textile tradition, damp climate, proximity to markets, adequate water power, pure soft water, ample capital, and accessibility to textile machinery. Wool manufacturing became identified with such cities as Providence and Woonsocket in Rhode Island, and Lawrence, Lowell, and Holyoke in Massachusetts. Cities and towns in New York, New Jersey, and Pennsylvania

also importantly entered the field. Boston, an excellent central market, became the capital of the wool trade.

In recent years the established wool-textile areas of the North (between Maryland and Maine) have undergone the same frustrating and seemingly relentless decline that has typified the cotton-textile industry—largely through the migration of mills to the South. The displacement of the wool-textile industry lagged considerably behind that of cotton, but the trend is accelerating.

Most of the standard wool products are turned out in very modern plants on the Piedmont. The Piedmont's woolen and worsted industry has expanded mainly because Northeastern firms have been building branch plants in the South rather than at home—largely for the same economic reasons that apply to cotton manufacturing. Yet, although the development of wool manufacture in the South has been impressive, New England continues to hold on to the major portion of the industry.

Interregional competition is being perilously paralleled by international competition, particularly from Japan, Great Britain, and Italy. In 1960 the United States was impelled to impose new tariffs to curb the rising tide of foreign imports of woolens. The industry is further vexed by the growing competition of man-made fibers (a problem being solved to some extent by blending with other fibers: some weavers of fine worsteds and woolens are adding as much as 15 per cent nylon to provide strength and abrasion resistance) and by the growing demand for lighter-weight fabrics.

The Southern Hemisphere. The great sheep lands of Argentina, Uruguay, Australia, and New Zealand export most of their wool. However, they have enough wool-manufacturing enterprises to be self-sustaining except in fabrics of fine quality, which they import chiefly from the United Kingdom.

LINEN

The ancient culture of flax for fiber and the manufacture of linen can be traced as far back as 1200 B.C. Though flax had grown wild from time immemorial, the Egyptians were the first to cultivate it and to recognize its usefulness. They early gained great proficiency in linen weaving and used exquisite fabric for their sanctuaries and sepulchers.

As civilization spread, linen manufacture sprang up in many other areas. With the crumbling of the Roman Empire, linen manufacture underwent a protracted eclipse until the tenth century, when the Flemings (literally "weavers")—the first people in Western Europe to make weaving their livelihood—brought it back. By medieval times, fine linen had become a symbol of refinement in most of Western Europe. Bruges became the linen capital of the world during the early Middle Ages. By the seventeenth century, the Dutch, without any flax of their own, had pushed linen manufacture so strongly that their commerce in the textile was larger than that of all the rest of Europe. However, religious persecutions in the Low Countries had already driven out thousands of skilled linen weavers, who settled permanently in England and Ireland.

In Ireland, where the industry was of great antiquity (its origins are obscure), linen manufacture got fairly well under way in the thirteenth century. Ultimately, Northern Ireland became the leading linen-manufacturing region of the world. Belfast, with 75 per cent of the mills within a 30-mile radius, controls the industry even more forcibly than Manchester does the cotton-textile industry.

Northern Ireland's advantages are several: (1) the early introduction of mechanized equipment; (2) a mild humid climate, which is not only stimulating but also highly favorable to the making of quality linen from the rather intractable fiber; (3) absence of a competitive textile industry; (4) a large supply of cheap, efficient labor—wives and daughters of men employed in shipbuilding and other heavy industries; (5) ample sources of pure soft water; (6) unsurpassed skill in bleaching, dyeing, and finishing processes; and (7) high quality of products. Actually Ireland herself provides neither the source of the raw material nor the market for the manufactured product. The fiber for the industry is imported from the Low Countries and Eastern Europe; the market for the manufactured product is foreign.

Today Northern Europe, from Northern Ireland to eastern European Russia, is the world's foremost flax-growing and linen-manufacturing region. The Flanders lowland of France and Belgium enjoys an enviable reputation for its fine linens, Lille and Ghent being the outstanding centers of production. Other concentrations are Germany's Westphalia and Czechoslovakia's Bohemian Basin.

The flax and linen industry of Russia is of long standing, the oldest centers being in European Russia. But in tsarist days flax mills were inadequate in number and uneven in distribution. Under the Soviets, the area in flax has been doubled, and the manufacture of linen has soared. The primary treatment of flax, formerly performed in farm households, has been relegated to an extensive network of new mills; and flax combines have been constructed in the old flax-growing areas as well as in new ones. Vyazniki, Kostroma, Smolensk, Vitebsk, and Tallnin are leading linen-milling cities in European Russia, the region that forms the base of the Soviet linen industry.

SILK

Silk has been a luxury-apparel fabric since olden times and stands in a class by itself to this day. Because of its costliness, it has been relentlessly buffeted by waves of wars and depressions and new, lower-cost, man-made fibers. Its demand, especially in lower-quality goods, was considerably curtailed between the two world wars when lower-cost rayon ("artificial silk") underwent such a remarkable development that it pushed silk completely out of the limelight.

EASTERN ASIA

In Japan, China, and Korea, where most of the world's raw silk is produced and where silk fabrics have had wider use than anywhere else in the world, the art of reeling and weaving silk is an ancient one. By far the greater portion of the silk fabrics—from the cheapest to the most costly—is still woven on hand looms in these lands where an abundant supply of cheap labor is available. Exports of superior-quality silk goods fell off badly in modern times, owing largely to the tariffs levied by the importing countries, who preferred to import the raw silk (which is of low bulk and high value and therefore can stand the transportation costs) and do their own manufacturing. Thus, more than 75 per cent of the machine manufacture of silk takes place far from silk's Oriental homeland.

Japan, which accounts for about 80 per cent of the raw silk in world markets (most of it goes to the United States), manufactures silk fabrics in the central and southern parts of the country. Reeling, formerly a home industry, is performed in factories known as filatures, most of which are located in central Honshu, particularly around Okaya and Nagoya. Weaving, a separate process, centers on the west coast around Fukui, Kanazawa, and Niigata, in the Kyoto area, and in Gumma and Tochigi west of the Kwanto Plain. In some of these areas, government curtailment of silk production has forced the manufacturers to change over to other textiles, particularly synthetics and woolens, in order to escape bankruptcy.

In China, the homeland of silk manufacture, the industry centers in the traditional sericulture areas—the valleys of the Si-Kiang and the lower Yangtze-Kiang. China supplies approximately 5 per cent of the world's raw-silk exports.

WESTERN EUROPE

When silk manufacture spread to Europe, it logically located in areas of raw-silk production and a large supply of cheap and skilled female labor; frequently these factors were complemented by ample coal and water power and large domestic markets. Foremost silk-manufacturing nation during the nineteenth century was France. Lyons became the center of the industry. It is situated in the Rhone Valley, a raw-silk-producing area and a major European thoroughfare; and it benefits from a good labor supply and from water power. By supplementing its native silk supply with imports from Italy, the Far East, and the Levant, Lyons manufacturers, aided by the locally invented Jacquard loom, turned out brocades of superior quality and great beauty, which were in high demand in nearby Paris, the world's fashion center.

Although the industry has been diffused to numerous towns in southeastern France, Lyons endures as one of the two leading markets and distributing points for European raw silk. The other center is northern Italy's Milan, which is first among the many cities and towns in the Po Basin and Alpine piedmont with silk mills. Zurich in Switzerland and Krefeld and Wuppertal in Germany are other outstanding silk centers, whose production has made Lyons look to its laurels. Today Europe accounts for approximately 30 per cent of the world's modern silk-manufacturing industry.

UNITED STATES

The United States, which produces no raw silk whatsoever, has a silk-manufacturing industry that commands three fifths of the world supply of raw silk; for Americans, with their high standard of living, provide a substantial market for luxury apparel. American silk manufacture in the beginning was a parasitic industry, for it tended to locate in surplus-labor areas where women were willing to perform the relatively light work for low wages. Paterson, New Jersey, was the first important center because of (1) a large reservoir of female workers whose husbands and fathers worked in the metal trades; (2) proximity to New York City, the center of women's fashions (roughly half of all the world's silk textiles are used within a 100-mile radius of the city); and (3) abundant water power—Paterson stands near the falls of the Passaic River. Gradually, similar labor advantages prompted the industry to shift to Pennsylvania's anthracite-coal cities of Scranton and Wilkes-Barre and to the cement centers of Allentown and Easton. New England and the southern Piedmont, too, garnered a sizable share of the industry.

After the 1930s the American silk industry went into a marked decline: the depression curtailed consumption of this luxury item, and silk companies turned to filament rayon yarns; moreover, World War II cut off silk supplies from Asia, and war needs consumed what was available; and, finally, competition from the rising tide of synthetic fibers nearly eliminated silk manufacturing as a separate industry.

JUTE

For many years jute has been in great demand the world over for bagging and baling agricultural and other commodities and as a raw material in the manufacture of rugs, carpets, and twines. Each year, United States industry and agriculture alone normally use more than 850 million yards of burlap and 100 million yards of jute carpet backing. More perishable than either cotton or flax, jute has been a cheaper fiber and, being also more easily spun, has replaced hemp for numerous uses.

Hand spinning of jute was practiced in India for centuries prior to British occupation. In the early 1800s the British East India Company perfected the cultivation of the "golden fiber" near Calcutta (jute is often called "Calcutta hemp") and introduced the English to its uses as a textile. Under the British, West Bengal developed the jute-processing industry into nearly a world monopoly.

Almost all the world's jute formerly was grown in India in the Ganges-Brahmaputra Delta. With partition, India got the mills, Pakistan the raw-jute acreage. Each country then attempted to rectify this situation. Pakistan now has a number of mills, and India today meets four fifths of its raw-jute requirements. Most of the jute mills, however, still are in India in a 60-mile riparian zone of the Hooghly River in and around Calcutta. Pakistan's mills are in the river ports of East Pakistan.

Most of the loomage outside India-Pakistan is in Europe, to a large extent in Dundee, Scotland. In India the more than 100 mills give employment to some 300,000 workers, and at least 5 million agricultural laborers are dependent on them.

MAN-MADE TEXTILE FIBERS

In only a few decades man-made fibers, the products of man's endless search for newer and better ways to do and make things, have emerged as redoubtable competitors in the textile realm, which was dominated for so many centuries by the natural fibers. The man-made fibers still account for little more than 20 per cent of all fibers used for textiles, but they have increased far more rapidly in production than have other branches of the industry and have demonstrated a spectacular ability to invade the textile market, offering seemingly limitless possibilities in apparel, household, and industrial textile materials. In the United States the synthetic-textile industry has grown so remarkably and steadily that, except for agriculture, it is now the largest single customer for the chemical industry.

LOCATION OF SYNTHETIC-FIBER PLANTS

All major manufacturers of man-made fibers carefully select the sites for their plants to secure the most economical and efficient operation. First, their plant specialists choose the general area, giving primary consideration to proximity to raw-material sources and to markets. They next select the specific plant site, considering such factors as terrain; purity of air; distance from a community; ample water of the desired quality, temperature, and price; disposal of waste; transport facilities (railway, highway, river, lake, canal); reliability of electric power supply; political climate; fairness of taxes; and type of labor (Fig. 14-4). A major decision involves the respective pull capacities of raw-materials areas and of fiber-market areas. Transport cost is apt to be the determining factor. If transport costs of raw materials are substantially less than those on finished products, the plant will give them priority.

RAYON

In his efforts to make imitation silk, man came up with a fiber that almost put silk out of business and stimulated the development of a host of synthetic fibers, with which it now finds itself in strong competition. By

Fig. 14-4. Acrilan acrylic-fiber plant of Chemstrand Corporation at Decatur, Alabama, on the Tennessee River. A synthetic-fiber plant of this type must operate on a 24-hour, seven-day-week schedule. Since the industry uses 12,300 gallons of water per 100 pounds of staple fiber produced, a river site is highly desirable—especially so if the river is navigable; for coal and certain other raw materials can then be barged to the plant. (Courtesy of Chemstrand Corporation.)

simulating the method by which the caterpillar makes silk, the chemist converts chemically treated wood pulp or cotton linters (most frequently the former) into a liquid "spinning solution," extrudes it through the tiny holes of a spinnerette, and solidifies it in a coagulating acid bath into an extremely fine continuous filament (sometimes as many as 150 filaments twisted together are needed to produce one thread).

Because rayon is a creation of the chemical laboratory, its foremost producers are logically the world's most highly industrialized nations and those with successful textile industries. Four countries—the United States, Japan, West Germany, and the United Kingdom—account for more than half the world output. The primary locational factor is proximity to an abundant supply of fresh water (from 150 to 200 gallons of water are needed to produce 1 pound of viscose rayon; 1 pound of acetate requires almost six times that amount).

In the United States production takes place predominantly in a crescent-shaped area from southern New Hampshire to Georgia, with a westward extension into Ohio. Since the rayon industry, like the other man-made-fiber enterprises, is an offspring of the chemical and textile industries, it was inevitably drawn to the South; here the chemical plants could supply the raw materials, the textile mills could convert the fiber into fabrics, and the parallel growth of these allied enterprises was soundly based on availability of ample supplies of labor, water, raw materials, power, and fuel, complemented by good transport

facilities. Thus, more than half of the plants have been set up in the South, with the greatest concentration in Virginia and Tennessee.

Japan accounts for approximately 30 per cent of the world's rayon production. In contrast to her cotton- and wool-textile industries, Japan is able to produce the bulk of the raw materials for rayon manufacture at home. Primarily because of her exceptionally low labor costs (labor comprises one third of the total cost of manufacture), Japan early was able to undersell all other producers and became the world's leading rayon exporter by 1937 (a position lost to West Germany and Italy after the war but regained in recent years). Production takes place in about thirty large modern plants lining the north side of the Inland Sea from Yamaguchi to Kyoto. Weaving, a separate process, is carried on in the established silk areas.

Before World War I, development of rayon staple fiber had its strongest boost in Germany, where new processes for the manufacture of sulfite and sulfate pulp from poplar birch trees were introduced for rayon production. Germany now ranks third in world rayon output.

The long-term prospects of rayon exporters are destined to be affected by the establishment of rayon plants in the traditional markets, for rayon manufacture is increasing in importance over much of the world—a trend prompted by wartime shortages. European nations (including the Soviet Union) continue to rank high; but Australia, New Zealand,

South Africa, Egypt, India, and a number of the Latin American republics have burgeoning rayon industries.

Nylon is the most famous and widely produced of the "miracle fibers." Its high tensile strength, elasticity, quick-drying properties, light weight, and resistance to wrinkling, moisture, and abrasion made nylon an instantaneous success.

Popularly described as being made of coal, water, and air, nylon is the result of a complicated manufacturing process involving the conversion of carbon from coal, nitrogen and oxygen from air, and hydrogen from water into a viscous fluid, which undergoes several treatments before filaments can be amassed and wound in a process called melt spinning. Nylon for textile use comes in three main forms: (1) multifilament—for dresses, upholstery, and tire cord; (2) monofilament—for very sheer hosiery; and (3) staple (short wavy strand)—for sweaters and socks.

In the United States particularly, nylon has virtually eliminated silk and rayon in the hosiery industry and has been making rapid inroads in apparel and household-fabric manufacture. Indeed, its success was so outstanding from the outset that it served as a stimulus to the lively development of an increasingly bewildering array of other synthetic fibers. So diverse are the components of the synthetic fibers that as many as thirty different chemicals may be needed just to make a man's shirt.

The United States is the world leader in production of noncellulosic man-made fibers, which account for approximately 10 per cent of the nation's textile fibers. On a world basis, the United States produces about 60 per cent of the noncellulosic fibers; Japan, 10 per cent; the United Kingdom, 8 per cent; France and West Germany, 5 per cent each; and the Soviet Union and Italy, 4 per cent each. However, noncellulosics account for only about a fifth of man-made-fiber production, the cellulosics (rayon and acetate) still being by far the most important commercially.

With each new man-made fiber created, the natural fibers face a greater competitive threat; yet, at the same time, the synthetic fibers, in blending with the natural fibers, can help them maintain their popularity by imparting to them the very qualities for which synthetics have become so rightly famed.

GARMENT MANUFACTURE

For many centuries garment manufacture was a household industry—and it still is in many parts of the world. But several centuries ago in other areas, dressmaking, tailoring, and allied occupations became small-shop enterprises and remained so until the late 1800s. Then garment making in industrially advanced countries began its routinized, mechanized life in the factory. By and large, peoples of the industrialized nations are today clothed by the ready-to-wear industry. The mechanization of the industry and the heights of style and quality have been especially notable in the United States, where good clothes are made at reasonable prices with an amazingly small amount of human labor. Therefore, the American segment of the industry is here elaborated upon.

DEVELOPMENT OF
THE AMERICAN INDUSTRY

The transfer of garment making from the home to the shop started around 1825 with the production of ready-to-wear men's work clothing either for seamen or for slaves in the South. With the growth of population, a demand was created by still others—notably bachelors who had no one at home to make their clothes and forty-niners en route to California during the Gold Rush. There was not a sufficient supply of second-hand clothes available; hence the second-hand dealers proceeded to have clothing made. Gradually workers were assembled in groups. In 1846, with the invention of Elias Howe's modern sewing machine; and in the 1850s, when Isaac Singer and others improved upon Howe's invention, volume production really got under way in urban areas. The Civil War, with its demand for factory-made uniforms, gave the industry further impetus. The women's clothing industry was developed by retail and wholesale dealers who located chiefly in large cities, especially New York. The introduction of mechanized cutting tools in the 1870s greatly simplified the garment worker's task and increased output.

Of notable importance in the development of the industry was a series of pogroms from 1848 onward in Europe, particularly Austria and Germany, which caused a mass exodus of Jewish people to the United States. Many of these immigrants had been in the garment business in Germany, which at the time was the world center of the women's tailoring industry. These people established new enterprises in the United States, employing primarily immigrant German and Irish women.

Then still another exodus assured New York's dominance in the women's apparel industry. In 1881 there occurred a great movement of peoples from Eastern Europe—from Russia (including at that time Poland), from Austria-Hungary, and from Romania. This westward movement stemmed not only from political persecution but also from the economic force of the "call to industrial America." Nearly all these immigrants arrived by way of New York City, many of them staying at their port of debarkation. Since in Europe tailoring had been a Jewish occupation, many of the newcomers were already skilled in the craft and logically entered the garment-making trades. Those without skills, without funds, and without knowledge of English found it easiest to settle among their own kind who continued to observe Old World customs.

As more and more workers squeezed into the industry, working conditions became more and more appalling, especially in the contractor shops crowded into tenement buildings. These were the "sweatshops," where immoderately long hours, bare-subsistence wages, and unsanitary surroundings were routine. Even when contractors became small manufacturers, unsavory working conditions continued; not until unionization rose in the early 1900s did the sweatshop go into eclipse.

In the 1890s incoming shiploads of Italian immigrants, many of whom also turned to the garment industry for employment, further swelled New York's capacity for apparel production (at least 1½ million European immigrants arrived between 1880 and 1910). By 1900 Italian workers comprised 15 per cent of the industry's employees in New York. Other large cities, such as Chicago and Cleveland, drew many Poles, Bohemians, Russians, and Syrians into their industries. But New York outstripped all its rivals in garment manufacture, thanks to the coincidence of the arrival of the immigrants, the rapid development of industrialization and urbanization of America, and the soaring demand for ready-to-wear apparel.

NEW YORK CITY—THE WORLD'S GARMENT CAPITAL

The making of garments is New York's most important industry. The city accounts for approximately 35 per cent (some 300,000 workers) of total employment in the nation's apparel industry, 45 per cent of its output, and 65 per cent of the sales of all women's and children's garments (though a good deal of actual production takes place elsewhere). Yet this gigantic industry is encompassed within a remarkably small (200 acres) area— Manhattan's famed Garment Center, roughly bounded by 34th and 40th Streets and by 6th and 9th Avenues.

In this humanity-clogged, incredibly congested area, the most concentrated industry in the world is located (Fig. 14-5). Thousands of manufacturers occupy approximately 170 buildings. In their shops an annual 4 billion dollars worth of suits, coats, dresses, undergarments, millinery, furs, and other garments are cut, shaped, pressed, and packed (Fig. 14-6). The concentration of apparel firms has led to concentration of ancillary businesses: e.g., the design, display, and sale of textiles; cloth shrinking; textile banking; trucking; model agencies; thread and trimming suppliers; belt manufacturers; and machinery-repair shops. Such activities in and around the Garment Center contribute strongly to keeping the apparel firms in the city. (Of

Fig. 14-5. A street scene in New York City's most congested area—the Garment District—which has made New York the world's leading fashion headquarters. This is an area of bulky buildings, bolts of fabrics, racks of dresses, sewing machines, drawing boards, showrooms, trucks moving at a snail's pace, and people in a hurry. (Courtesy of The New York Times.)

course, the Garment Center is not the only scene of action; various types of garments are manufactured at many points in the New York Metropolitan region, which takes in twenty-two counties, including nine in New Jersey and one in Connecticut.)

Garment manufacture can be conducted in limited space and with a comparatively small initial investment. In the first place, the industry lends itself to a division of labor; although more persons are employed in New York's garment trade than in Detroit's automotive industry, the shops are usually small, employing from thirty to forty workers—not many more than the average shop had a century ago. Moreover, unlike the typical manufacturing enterprise—which turns out large quantities of standard products, using highly specialized equipment in huge plants sprawled over great stretches of land—fashion demands hand-to-mouth buying, rapid delivery, short distribution channels, adaptable machinery, and proximity to markets. Capital

requirements generally tend to be relatively low because a firm can use contractors rather than engage in production itself. Only small and relatively inexpensive equipment is required. The human factor is still of utmost importance, for style and fashion in apparel making dictate that it remain basically a handicraft enterprise tooled by power machinery. The ease of entry into the industry, however, is naturally accompanied by a high mortality rate.

Despite the small physical investment and the rapid turnover of firms, both of which would suggest ease of movement, the location of the apparel industry has until very recently shown a marked geographical stability. New York has had two strong advantages: nearness to markets and an abundant labor supply. The city has an unequaled market outlet for a metropolitan population of more than 16 million persons. Moreover, a fourth of the nation's population resides within a 250-mile radius, and seven of the ten largest cities in

Fig. 14-6. Sewing department of a dress plant, New York—a typical garment factory of today. Gone are the sweatshops of the past. Machine sewing of a garment is divided into several operations. Only a core of skilled operators is needed for the more intricate work, most of the employees doing the more routine operations, which require little training. (Courtesy of Burton Berinsky, for ILGWU "Justice.")

America and the two most populous cities of Canada lie within a two-day drive of the city. Seasonality in women's apparel forces firms to locate in an area having ample reserves of skilled labor available on short notice. Moreover, within New York's nucleus of garment manufacture, materials in various stages of production can be transferred to different contractors and suppliers with such rapidity that frequent and sudden changes in style can be coped with.

The influence of fashion—more conspicuous in women's clothing than in men's, in outer wear than in undergarments, and in the higher-priced lines than in the lower—is felt throughout the entire garment industry. The more fashion oriented a garment is, the more likely it is to be produced in New York or a smaller fashion center like Dallas or Los Angeles. Normally, the moment a new style makes a "hit" at a high price, manufacturers of lower-priced goods start copying it (style pirating is commonplace), using less skilled workers and cheaper fabrics. The need for keeping up with the latest in fashion thus demands that a firm locate its headquarters near other producers of fashion merchandise. New York thus serves as the fashion center of America; here buyers from all over the nation converge to compare the output of competing sellers, and they save money by concentrating all their purchasing in one center.

In addition to its many other qualifications as a fashion center, New York (like its European counterparts—the cities of Paris, London, Vienna, Rome, and Berlin) is the headquarters of an elegant society, which patterns the tastes in clothes. Moreover, it is a resort city which draws women who will boldly wear the newest styles; a leading art center, with outstanding museums and more schools of art and designing than any other city; and, as America's publication capital, the fountainhead of the nation's fashion magazines.

Yet despite its unique labor pool, its unequaled external economies, and its unparalleled mingling and communicating facilities, New York no longer holds the commanding position in women's and children's apparel that it once held, though it remains the greatest source of these garments anywhere in the world. Its decline has been in its share of national *production* (its fashion leadership and proportion of sales remain unweakened). Production has undergone more rapid growth outside of Manhattan—in Brooklyn, in outlying counties, in Pennsylvania, New England, the South, and the Far West. The reasons for this shift in production are several:

1. New York suffered a cost disadvantage —most of all the labor-cost differential—in the production of standardized, inexpensive garments (the supply and cost of labor are the most important factors in determining the industry's location). Separation of sewing from merchandising enabled the entrepreneurs to establish production wherever costs were lowest. Since New York is a relatively high-cost labor area, production tended to move to lower-cost labor districts, especially those with surplus labor.

2. The decade of the 1950s was marked by a changing pattern of life and a westward movement that brought about a "revolution in clothes." The spectacular development of suburbs and the growth of cities in the climatically warmer West fostered a more casual way of living; hence, informal, lightweight sportswear largely replaced dresses, suits, and coats—a trend which was a blow to New York's producers of higher-priced garments.

3. The switch to new synthetic and cheaper fabrics adversely affected the New York industry, for manufacturers could not easily shift to the less expensive fabrics without lowering the prices of their merchandise in order to compete. Even by entering the lower-priced field, they were unable to match wage costs in competing areas on the outside.

4. Employers searched for lower-cost areas, where they would be freer from control of the unions with their demands for expensive concessions.

5. Hand in hand with interregional competition was international low-wage competition, particularly emanating from Japan, Hong Kong, and Puerto Rico, although imports consisted chiefly of inexpensive goods.

6. A decline in the older ethnic groups that had provided the core of the labor reserve necessitated the employment of another labor force willing to work at the lower rungs of the occupational ladder. In the 1930s the Negroes, and in the 1940s the Puerto Ricans, provided the new manpower (or rather, womanpower). But these workers, unlike the earlier immigrants, were largely unskilled and therefore worked primarily in the more standardized branches, so that a shortage of skilled operators, especially in sewing, developed.

7. Concomitant with being pulled to lower-wage areas, production is being pushed out by scarcity of manufacturing loft space. The growth of section work has made the normal 2,000 to 4,000 square feet per establishment far too cramped a space. Suitable space is not available even at the high rents that prevail in New York; annual rentals are $5,000 more than in New Jersey, almost $7,000 more than in Pennsylvania.

8. Fast transportation by truck now links the low-wage, low-rent areas with Manhattan. And as new highways are constructed and air freight is increasingly utilized, the distance between the jobbers and the contractors can be feasibly lengthened.

9. Favorable "tax climates" (particularly in Puerto Rico) and such inducements as free buildings and special financial aid (especially in the American South) have additionally lured production elsewhere.

10. When durable goods are plentiful and per capita income increases, expenditure for clothing tends to decrease. This decrease has been evident since the early 1950s; in particular there has been a decline in the purchase

of formal wear. Clothes as a symbol of status have given way to washers, television sets, Jaguars, and other durable goods.

All these forces of dispersal will undoubtedly continue to challenge New York's dominance in apparel production. Yet,

one can foresee, assuming no global catastrophes, that the Garment Center, far from becoming a ghost town, will continue as a teeming place of drawing boards and showrooms and trucks and perhaps helicopters or whatever features will characterize the urban life of the future. Buyers still will flock there from all parts of the country. Entrepreneurs still will pursue the "hot number" that may make them rich, and if they fail, they will bide their time and try again. The American woman, revisiting New York in the 1980's, will find Manhattan Island still supreme in the design and merchandising of her clothing.[2]

OTHER AMERICAN CENTERS

Though no other sales center is even a tenth as important as New York, increased decentralization of the industry has been notable—each outside center catering largely to specialty merchandise, which New York cannot produce in quantity.

As early as 1860, Boston ranked second to New York but presently is surpassed also by Philadelphia, Chicago, Baltimore, Rochester, Cleveland, and Cincinnati. All of these cities specialize in men's clothing, but only Rochester is noted for high-quality men's suits, overcoats, and topcoats.

St. Louis is a center for "junior-miss" clothes and half-size dresses; here the garment industry coordinates its design rooms with the art schools and colleges of the city. Kansas City is noted for its production-line methods, and Milwaukee and Minneapolis have made significant strides in the ready-to-wear field. Dallas and Phoenix have gained prominence as producers of moderately priced sports apparel. Miami specializes in garments that cater

to the special markets created by local seasonal patterns different from New York's.

However, New York's greatest competitor is located on the other side of the continent. Los Angeles–Hollywood and, to a lesser extent, San Francisco pose a growing threat to New York's dominance, particularly in the sportswear line. Although factory manufacturing dates back to the 1850s, only in the past several decades has California enjoyed a meteoric rise in the-garment industry. The products of Los Angeles manufacturers cover nearly the whole field of apparel; sportswear and bathing suits, the dominant lines, are sold not only throughout the nation but also abroad. This emphasis is a direct response to the California way of life: the mild climate has stimulated out-of-doors activities; and California's colorful, lightweight clothing is geared to casualness, utility, and comfort. Not the least important influence on the West's apparel industry is a certain lack of conservatism evidenced by California's soaring population; since nearly everyone in California has come from somewhere else, many of the restrictions of the previous environment are discarded in this new and distinctive climatic and social milieu.

Hollywood, where some of the leading motion-picture designers operate shops, has become a fashion center of considerable prominence. The magic label "Made in Hollywood," complemented by zealous chambers of commerce extolling the glories of California, has assured the state a permanent place on the apparel map of the world.

The state's one big disadvantage has been distance from major competing textile centers and dress manufacturers. However, air freight, which enables New York to have "the right style in the right place at the right time," is likewise more and more of a boost to California's industry.

OLD-WORLD CENTERS

Europe's larger cities have thriving clothing industries. However, because of the large supply of cheap and efficient labor, there is far less emphasis on machine-made garments.

[2] Roy B. Helfgott, "Women's and Children's Apparel," in Max Hall, ed., *Made in New York: Case Studies in Metropolitan Manufacturing* (Cambridge, Mass.: Harvard University Press, 1959), p. 134.

Paris has long been, and in most opinions remains, the world's fashion capital; for it is a French tradition that "frivolity, taken seriously, can be an art." About sixty *couture* establishments of various sizes employ 6,000 people and indirectly give work to as many as 200,000 more. Machines are a rarity in Paris apparel firms; no other city can match Paris in its wide array of craftsmanship (60 per cent of French women still make their own dresses or have them custom-made). A seamstress spends almost as many years as does a physician in learning her calling; yet she earns less than an unskilled worker in an automobile plant—all because she worships quality. The vast cost differential between Paris and New York indicates that Paris's prestige was built not just on creative genius but on the woeful living conditions of thousands of skilled laborers.

Although Paris still holds the title of fashion's mecca, the city's apparel industry is undergoing a pronounced change. The exclusive shop is slowly giving way. Big mass merchants, who also flock to other European fashion centers, visit the fashion houses not to buy outright but to acquire possession of a model for a few months, during which time they reproduce it (the fees for this right are a large source of income for the fashion houses). In addition to legitimate, cheap reproduction of expensive models, there is the menace of style pirating, which is estimated to cost the French fashion industry between 10 and 12 million dollars annually. Mass production, whether legal or illegal, may spell peril to the French industry, which is based on the production of luxurious apparel for the extravagant few.

WORLD OUTLOOK

Paris is said to remain the world's "only authoritative source for fashion inspiration," but New York City has unequivocally become the world's fashion distribution center. American designers have not only demonstrated their own fashion talents but have shown a remarkable ability to adapt Parisian, Italian, or other continental styles to the needs of the huge American market. America's, particularly New York's, claim to fame resides in its rapid production techniques, which can duplicate hundreds upon thousands of quality units in any given season—an operation that cannot be matched anywhere on the globe. Paris's preeminence is further threatened by the rise of Italian fashion centers.

In a chaotic world where there is an ever more insistent demand for higher living standards and where population soars to fearful heights, the garment industry, with fashion at its core, promises to assume an even greater role. At this time, only the American method of production can assure an abundance. With intensified attention directed at the arts of fabric design and garment manufacture, the United States may in time become the unchallenged leader in all phases of the industry.

SELECTED REFERENCES

Blicksilver, Jack. *Cotton Manufacturing in the Southeast—An Historical Analysis.* Atlanta, Georgia State College of Business Administration, July 1959. Studies in Business and Economics, Bulletin No. 5.

Crawford, M. D. C. *The Ways of Fashion.* New York, Fairchild Publishing Co., 1948.

Gilman, Glenn. *Human Relations in the Industrial Southeast: A Study of the Textile Industry.* Chapel Hill, The University of North Carolina Press, 1956.

Harris, Seymour E. *New England Textiles and the New England Economy.* Report to the Conference of New England Governors, February 1956.

Hornbeck, Bernice M. *Cotton and Chemical Fibers: Competition in Japan.* Washington, D. C., Foreign Agricultural Service, U.S. Department of Agriculture, July 1957. Foreign Agriculture Report No. 97.

Kirk, William. "The Cotton and Jute Industries of India: A Study in Concentration and Dispersal," *Scottish Geographical Magazine,* 72:38-52, April 1956.

Kisch, Herbert. "Textile Industries in Silesia and Rhineland," *Journal of Economic History,* 19:541-569, December 1959.

Mitchell, N. M. "The Textile Industry," in Albert S. Carlson (ed.), *Economic Geography of Industrial Materials.* New York, Reinhold Publishing Corporation, 1956, pp. 366-391.

Rodgers, Allan. "The Changing Geography of the Lancashire Cotton Industry," *Economic Geography,* 38:299-314, October 1962.

CHAPTER FIFTEEN ::

Innumerable enterprises could be presented under this topic. The size and scope of this book, however, restrict the number of such industries to be treated. Therefore, only a few typical food-processing industries are presented: flour milling, meat packing, cheese and butter making, sugar refining, canning, and quick freezing.

At one time in the United States (between 1850 and 1930), farmers met nearly all of their own food requirements; they canned, dried, salted, pickled, and smoked their products. Nearly all families lived on farms, and transportation was restricted by poor roads and horse-drawn vehicles. There were only a few cities, and they were not large. Today the picture has changed: 92 per cent of the American people live in urban centers, only 8 per cent on farms. These millions of people in cities must have delivered to them all kinds of foods; and more and more of these

THE WORLD'S FOOD-

foods are processed (60 per cent of all agricultural produce reaches market via commercial processing plants). Moreover, the housewife no longer processes much produce herself: fruits and vegetables are canned and quick frozen in special factories close to the growing fields; meat is prepared in packing plants, flour in flour mills; sugar is refined in large, modern plants; and butter, cheese, and other dairy products are made in factories. Even bread is no longer baked in the home.

The United States is well represented by food-processing industries. To achieve high rank in these enterprises, a nation must have capital, technology, a population with purchasing power, rapid and efficient transportation, and refrigeration. Food processing nationally ranks as the third largest industry, being surpassed only by machinery and transportation equipment. It employs one tenth of all American factory workers.

The greater part of the world—the underdeveloped lands—has almost no industries of this type; even such advanced lands as the Soviet Union, Japan, and Western Europe trail far behind the United States. Nonetheless, as they become more and more urbanized, they find it necessary to engage increasingly in those industries that prepare food. The Soviet Union is a case in point. Historically, the vast majority of the Russian people lived on the land; in 1913, the figure for those living in cities and towns stood at only 18 per cent. By 1939, about 30 per cent lived in urban centers, and by 1960 the figure had risen to nearly 50 per cent.

FLOUR MILLING

Flour milling is carried on in every country that grows wheat and in some that do not

PROCESSING INDUSTRIES

grow it. Usually the mills are located in larger cities well served by transport facilities. But although the milling of flour is widely distributed, the bulk of the output comes from a small number of areas—an indication that a few very large companies operate on a huge scale. Such companies can procure every type of wheat in the quantities needed. They can thus standardize the quality of their flour and maintain it year after year—hence the term *patent flour*. Flour milling today is so efficient—particularly in the United States— that a small labor force can turn out more than 30 billion pounds of flour annually.

UNITED STATES

Flour, made from soft wheat, was originally prepared in small grist mills wherever there were people. Tens of thousands of small mills sprang up. The mills, situated on streams, were operated by water power. Since transportation was poorly developed, the market was local. Following the Revolutionary War, Baltimore and Richmond dominated the industry for a considerable time. But the Middle West was being settled, and wheat production sprang up wherever there were settlers. Hence, a new group of flour-manufacturing centers came into being—Rochester, Niagara Falls, Springfield (Ohio), Chicago, Milwaukee, St. Louis, Hutchinson, and Minneapolis.

By 1870, St. Louis ranked first in flour production, but soon afterward Minneapolis took the lead. The wheat grown in the hinterland of Minneapolis, however, was hard wheat, not soft wheat; and, because of its flinty particles and their friction with the buhrstones, it made a dark, unpleasant-tasting flour. Such flour, accordingly, had to be sold at considerable disadvantage in the East (the Minneapolis millers frequently labeled their flour barrels "Made in St. Louis"). Even the hard wheat from which the flour was ground sold for about 20 cents a bushel below soft winter wheat. The Minneapolis millers solved this problem by inducing Hungarians, whose mills had much earlier encountered the same problem, to immigrate to Minneapolis, and introduce the roller-milling process there.

The principal advantages enjoyed by Minneapolis for making flour were (1) water

power at the Falls of St. Anthony on the Mississippi River and (2) location near the edge of the Spring-Wheat Belt (see Chapter 16, pp. 316-318). In 1930, Minneapolis lost first place to Buffalo, which later lost it to Kansas City. Thus, there have been notable shifts in the geographic center of the flour-milling industry since early in the nineteenth century— the result of shifts in wheat-growing areas and types of wheat produced, changes in population distribution, technological advances in milling processes, and changes in freight rates. The three traditional milling centers—Minneapolis, Buffalo, and Kansas City—are still the leaders.

Buffalo's principal advantages are the following: (1) It benefits from cheap water transportation on the Great Lakes in the grain trade of both the United States and Canada. (2) It is advantageously situated with respect to the large consuming centers of the East. (3) It enjoys low power costs. (4) It is served by almost unsurpassed rail and truck transportation. (5) It has benefited from the **milling-in-bond** privilege for Canadian wheat. (6) It enjoys almost unexcelled storage facilities—54 million bushels supplemented in winter by moored ships capable of storing 23 million additional bushels (Fig. 15-1). Since all grades of wheat reach Buffalo, the mills can select the best qualities in any amounts.

Kansas City's principal advantage for flour milling is its nearness to the Hard Red Winter-Wheat Belt—now the leading source of domestic wheat for flour. Since 1900 the production of hard winter wheat has been increasing, whereas that of hard spring wheat has been declining. Kansas leads the states in flour milling, its forty-three plants accounting for about 14 per cent of all flour milled in the nation.

In the West the leading milling centers are Ogden and Salt Lake City; Spokane, and Seattle; Portland; and San Francisco, Sacramento, Los Angeles, and Vallejo.

CANADA

Canada, one of the leading wheat-growing nations of the world, obviously is also an important miller of wheat. Small mills, doing a local business, are scattered throughout the

Fig. 15-1. Flour mills, elevators, and lake carriers, Buffalo harbor, New York. These mills and elevators rank among the giants. They are extremely efficient and operate at low cost per bushel of grain. In winter, millions of bushels of wheat are stored in the vessels, which are immobilized for five months or more. (Fitzgerald Airphoto. Courtesy of Fitzgerald Studios, Buffalo, New York.)

wheat-growing areas; but, as in the United States, they find it increasingly difficult to compete with the large, strategically located mills situated along the rail-water wheat routes to and on the seaboard. Among the provinces Ontario leads, with 34 per cent of the mills and 48 per cent of the capacity; Quebec ranks second in number of mills, but in capacity Saskatchewan is second. The southern Ontario peninsula and the St. Lawrence Lowland have the principal concentrations of mills; they benefit from cheap and abundant hydroelectric power, large market, and efficient transportation. Canada's largest flour-milling centers are Montreal, St. John, and Vancouver, all important ocean ports; Goderich, Fort William, Midland, and Toronto, all important lake ports; and Winnipeg, Kenora, Saskatoon, Regina, Moose Jaw, and Brandon, all important rail centers.

WESTERN AND CENTRAL EUROPE

Wheat has long been milled in Europe; but for generations, except in Hungary, small mills were the rule. Large tidewater mills had to await a combination of suitable conditions:

1. The rise of industrial cities.
2. Adoption of labor-saving machinery.

3. The evolution of the great subhumid and semiarid lands into surplus wheat regions.
4. Rapid and relatively cheap transportation by land and water. Once great railway and steamship systems were developed, Europe could tap the lower-cost wheat-growing lands anywhere on earth.

HUNGARY

Although its mills do not rank in size or output with those in the United Kingdom or France, Hungary is important because the modern system of milling—the steel-roller process, which ultimately completely redrew the world map of flour milling—was invented in 1820 in Budapest, then the world's leading milling center. During its years of leadership, Hungary received the top prices for its flour —the world's best. At that time Hungarian wheats were believed to have no peers. Today Hungary grows chiefly common-grade wheat, which in character of kernel ranges from soft to hard, but is mostly soft or semihard.

UNITED KINGDOM

The United Kingdom, premier wheat-import market of the world, is the recipient of about 40 per cent of the total world movement of this grain. Although Britain grows nearly one-fifth of the wheat it consumes, the soft wheat has poor baking quality for bread, since it is low in **gluten.** Hence, most of it is utilized for poultry feed.

The milling industry, therefore, is based almost exclusively upon *imported strong, hard wheat.* About two thirds of the flour is manufactured by four companies. Because of such pronounced concentration, the companies have bargaining advantages in the purchase of wheat and can operate their mills on a more nearly full-time basis and on a cheaper unit-cost-of-production basis. The large mills, completely modern, are strategically located either in ports or on waterways connected with ports—Liverpool (including the nearby Mersey-side towns), London, Hull, Cardiff, Edinburgh, Glasgow, Bristol, Newcastle, and Belfast.

FRANCE

Although France is a surplus producer of wheat, she imports some hard wheat for mixing with her own soft wheat in the milling process. However, the government does protect the French farmer against imports by having a high import tax on wheat and by stipulating the percentage of imported wheat (at times only 3 or 4 per cent) that millers may use. Principal milling centers are Le Havre, Marseille, Toulouse, and Metropolitan Paris.

SOVIET UNION

The Soviet Union boasts one of the largest milling industries in the world. The mills are both large and small. The 100,000 small ones —scattered through the country but particularly in the Ukraine and the steppe region— remain important, largely because of the poor condition of the roads in rural areas and because of the unpretentious taste of the peasantry. These mills use rye for most of their flour. The large, modern commercial mills, located to supply city populations, are generally in grain-surplus areas and at railroad junctions.

The oldest commercial milling area is that south of Moscow, but it is today less important than the Volga or Ukraine areas. The mills on the Volga are not only the country's largest but are the best located, being at the intersection of the railways with the Volga waterway. Such mills draw grain from the entire Volga Basin and from the trans-Volga and Ural areas—even from Siberia. The leading centers here are Gorki, Rybinsk, Saratov, and Kuibyshev. Next in importance is the Ukraine, with Kiev, Nikolayev, and other centers.

The Soviet government has constructed many new commercial mills in the area east of the Urals, the area neglected by the tsarist government. This policy is a part of the determination of the government to distribute industrial plants where they are needed. A few such examples are Karaganda in Soviet Asia, Blagoveshchensk on a branch of the Trans-Siberian Railway, and Krasnodar on the Kuban River.

MEAT PACKING

Meat packing involves all the stages from the dressing of the animal to the shipping of the finished product to retailers. This industry, not widely scattered over the earth, is particularly important in Western Europe, the United States, Canada, Argentina, Australia, and New Zealand but is relatively unimportant in Asia, Africa, and most of Latin America.

UNITED STATES

The American meat-packing industry is first among the food industries in dollar volume of business. The cash receipts from farm marketings in 1956 were more than 8 billion dollars; the quantity, nearly 42 billion pounds. Ninety per cent of the total consists equally of beef and pork.

The high standard of living in the United States ensures large meat consumption. In 1960 the consumption of meat per capita was 162 pounds.

In the United States, about two thirds of the animals are raised west of the Mississippi River, whereas more than two thirds of the American people (and hence most of the market for meat) live east of it. Thus, the livestock or meat or both must move considerable distances. On the average, meat travels an estimated 1,000 miles from point of production to point of consumption. Such distances demand an efficient and well-organized system of marketing and distribution.

Before getting into the meat-packing industry, the student should know where the majority of the various meat animals are raised and slaughtered (Tables 15-1 and 15-2). Three fifths of the nation's live-weight production in 1960 came from the North-Central states with their many livestock farms and feedlots. The association of cattle and sheep with pasture and forage production and of hogs with corn is evident. The Great Plains and the Corn Belt have a disproportionate share of the nation's beef cattle; the North-Central states, of the country's hogs; and the West, including Texas, of its sheep and lambs.

To a large extent, the meat-packing industry keeps close to the great livestock areas in order to avoid heavy freight charges on the non-meat parts of the animals [1] and to prevent the animals from losing weight en route to slaughtering centers. Many animals from the Intermontane, Rocky Mountain, and Great Plains regions move east to feeders, though large numbers go directly to slaughter. The latter, animals of low quality, bring low prices.

Obviously in the beginning, slaughtering was nothing more than local butchering. Since meat is so perishable, it could not be shipped fresh without spoilage. In 1870 the invention of the refrigerator car completely revolutionized the meat business. Today there are more than 3,200 slaughtering plants—some large, some small, many at stages in between. However, only plants with an output of 300,000 pounds or more live weight annually are included in this number.

Soon after 1850, Chicago became the world's leading slaughtering and meat-packing center. Strategic location in the heart of the new agricultural region, along with focal location in the rapidly growing rail network of the nation, assured it a place of major importance. Chicago, too, was home to three of the "Big Four" packers—Swift, Armour, and Wilson (the fourth was Cudahy, recently replaced by John Morrell). However, there was not just Chicago. The rapid industrialization and urbanization of the East, the amazing development of the livestock industry in the Middle West and Southwest, and the extension of railways into these regions encouraged the development of large livestock markets and packing plants at all major rail centers by the time of World War II.

THE CORN BELT

Most of the leading meat-packing centers of the United States lie in the Western Corn Belt—East St. Louis, Kansas City, Omaha, Ottumwa, Sioux City, St. Joseph, and South

---

[1] From a 1,000-pound steer, only 600 pounds consist of meat; the remaining 400 pounds consist of hides, hoofs, inedible fats, etc. A 240-pound hog dresses down to only 150 pounds of edible pork products.

TABLE 15-1

RANK OF STATES IN LIVE WEIGHT OF FARM PRODUCTION OF MEAT ANIMALS, 1960
(in millions of pounds)

Rank	Cattle and calves State	Production	Sheep and lambs State	Production	Hogs State	Production
1	Texas	2,714	Texas	190	Iowa	4,328
2	Iowa	2,444	California	115	Illinois	2,640
3	Nebraska	1,634	Wyoming	109	Indiana	1,692
4	Kansas	1,468	Colorado	107	Minnesota	1,343
5	Illinois	1,407	Iowa	105	Missouri	1,331
6	California	1,389	South Dakota	98	Ohio	889
7	Minnesota	1,368	Idaho	90	Nebraska	861
8	Missouri	1,260	Montana	88	Wisconsin	709
9	South Dakota	1,161	Minnesota	75	South Dakota	558
10	Oklahoma	1,107	Utah	63	Kentucky	445

SOURCE: *The Livestock and Meat Situation*, U.S.D.A., May 1961, Table 1006.

St. Paul. The industry has recently been characterized by notable shifts. Since the shipping of live animals is costly and there is considerable loss of weight, beef abattoirs are being located near the feedlots in the Western ranch country, and hog abattoirs are being located in the Corn Belt, to reduce the distance that live animals need be transported. In brief, the plants are moving closer to the livestock centers, and meat rather than livestock is being transported to consuming centers. The trend is being furthered by the development and widespread use of the truck, which has enabled farmers and feeders to sell their livestock to markets located close to home; today 75 per cent of all livestock travels at least part way by motor vehicle. Ninety per cent of all livestock today arrives at stockyards by truck. Packers, too, are utilizing the truck. Formerly they operated large numbers of railside branch houses, from which they sold and delivered meat to thousands of small meat and grocery stores. Now, however, more than 80 per cent of all United States meat is moved by truck. In short, the packing industry is no longer tied to the railroads.

At Kansas City stockyards, which may be regarded as typical, trucks account for 65 per cent of the total movements of cattle, 38 per cent of the calves, 93 per cent of the hogs, and 25 per cent of the sheep and lambs (1960). Seventy per cent of the meat is said to be de-

TABLE 15-2

RANK OF STATES IN COMMERCIAL SLAUGHTER OF LIVESTOCK, 1960
(in thousands of head)

Rank	Cattle State	Slaughter	Calves State	Slaughter	Hogs State	Slaughter	Sheep and Lambs State	Slaughter
1	Iowa	2,499.0	Wisconsin	1,132.5	Iowa	14,455.0	California	2,443.0
2	California	2,476.0	New York	911.0	Minnesota	5,428.0	Colorado	1,498.0
3	Nebraska	2,137.0	Texas	859.5	Indiana	5,024.0	Iowa	1,481.0
4	Texas	1,491.5	Pennsylvania	668.0	Illinois	5,003.0	Texas	1,284.0
5	Illinois	1,442.0	California	481.5	Ohio	4,558.0	New Jersey	1,197.5
6	Minnesota	1,424.0	Michigan	423.0	Nebraska	4,044.0	Nebraska	1,080.5
7	Ohio	1,186.0	Illinois	404.0	Missouri	3,879.0	Minnesota	1,073.5
8	Kansas	1,167.0	Iowa	389.8	Wisconsin	3,441.0	Michigan	724.5
9	Missouri	1,103.5	New England	388.7	Kansas	2,866.0	New York	646.0
10	Colorado	1,046.0	New Jersey	330.4	Pennsylvania	2,725.0	Missouri	596.5

SOURCE: *The Livestock and Meat Situation*, U.S.D.A., May 1961, Table 1003.

livered by truck, as compared with 30 per cent by rail. Delivery by truck is both cheaper and faster than by rail. Moreover, there is far less shrinkage.

The packers must be efficient, for their actual profit is so small as to have little effect on the retail price of meat. In fact, in 1957 profits after taxes averaged only 0.6 cents out of each sales dollar—one of the very lowest for any type of industry. In 1958, despite colossal sales, Armour had earnings of 0.3 cents on the dollar.

Other recent changes have come about. Largely because of high-cost transportation, many big-city terminal markets have been abandoned for. decentralized packing operations. Trucking, as mentioned earlier, has taken over much of the shipping formerly done by railroads. Smaller one-story buildings are everywhere replacing the less efficient multi-storied buildings of the past. Automation, too, has been widely adopted in the plants. Likewise, methods of distribution are changing. The big chain stores pre-package most of their meat, and they purchase and sell more and more of the total amount consumed.

CALIFORNIA

The California market is exerting an increasingly important effect on the Western livestock and meat-packing industries. Formerly the predominant movement of cattle and sheep from the West was eastward, the animals moving as feeder stock for fattening and ultimate consumption in the East. Today the greater part of the livestock and the meat produced in the West gravitates to California to help provide meat for the state's rapidly growing population. About 80 per cent of the pork, 60 per cent of the beef, and 40 per cent of the lamb consumed in California must be brought into the state.

California, with about 107 establishments, accounts for 35 to 40 per cent of the total meat packed in the West, even including Texas. The majority of the plants are in Los Angeles (largest by far), San Francisco, and San Diego, though a number of cities in the Central Valley also have plants.

THE SOUTH

The South has emerged recently as an important slaughtering and meat-packing region. The shift to grassland beef production (since acreage controls have enforced alternative uses of land formerly devoted to cotton), along with the rising level of income, has stimulated markedly the demand for meat.

In the South, slaughterhouses and packing plants exemplify a trend in plant location: plants locate somewhere between the market for meat and the area where the animals are raised. Instead of shipping their livestock into the Corn Belt to be fattened for processing, only to have them shipped back in the form of dressed meat, they now eliminate the back haul. Local plants are based partly on new feeding operations. Though the industry is to be found throughout the South, it is particularly important in Florida, Georgia, North Carolina, Tennessee, and Texas. Leading centers are Chattanooga, Knoxville, Memphis, and Nashville, Tennessee; Ocala, Florida; Lake Charles and New Orleans, Louisiana; Birmingham and Montgomery, Alabama; Pine Bluff and Fort Smith, Arkansas; Louisville, Kentucky; Richmond, Virginia; and Dallas, Fort Worth, and San Antonio, Texas.

SOME TYPICAL EXAMPLES OF
THE INDUSTRY

Chicago. Once the indisputable capital of the meat-packing industry, Chicago has steadily declined in recent years. In the early 1930s Chicago accounted for about 15 per cent of all hogs and cattle killed at federally inspected stations. By 1954 it handled only 6 per cent of the hogs slaughtered and 8 per cent of the cattle. And today—because they operated there at heavy loss—Swift, Armour, and Wilson carry on no slaughtering operations whatsoever in Chicago.

A key reason for Chicago's decline is that farmers increasingly send their animals to plants that are closer to the producing areas, so that transportation and labor costs are lower. In addition, the old multi-storied plants constructed in Chicago around the turn of the century are today obsolete and too large; and it is more profitable to construct new and smaller plants in better-located centers than to remodel in Chicago. Assembly-line techniques of new, single-story plants are replacing the top-to-bottom material flow of the earlier plants.

Omaha. In 1955, Omaha moved ahead of Chicago as the nation's and the world's largest livestock market and meat-packing center. Here, throughout any night, truck after truck backs up to unloading chutes to discharge loads of cattle, hogs, and sheep. In addition to the "Big Four," fifteen independent packers purchase livestock here. These local packers take most of the animals, but livestock from the Omaha yards are sent to packers in 215 other cities. Buyers from the packing houses purchase the number and grade of animals needed.

Omaha's prestige has been earned, its advantages being its strategic location in the principal stock-raising and stock-feeding part of the nation, outstanding rail facilities, and convenient access by hard-surface roads from all directions. In short, *Omaha exemplifies the principle of industrial location of plants moving closer to the livestock-producing areas in order to transport meat rather than live animals to consuming centers.*

New York City. Slaughtering in New York City is presented because the principle so strongly stressed for the location of slaughtering does not hold here. New York ranks high because of its huge orthodox Jewish population, which requires that its meat come from plants where the animals are slaughtered and flesh prepared under the close supervision of a rabbi or some representative of the religion. The preparation of the meat is thus a religious rite. After slaughter each animal is given a careful physical examination, particular attention being given to lungs and stomachs; only healthy animals are accepted. Such cuts (cattle and sheep only, since Jewish people do not eat pork) are usually sold within 72 hours after slaughter. Nearly all the cattle thus slaughtered are raised in southwest Virginia and West Virginia and fattened in Lancaster County, Pennsylvania.

CANADA

Since Canadians have much the same background and high standard of living as Americans, and since the southern part, where most of the 18 million Canadians live, is similar to the adjacent parts of the United States, slaughtering and meat packing are expectably important. The enterprise ranks seventh among all Canadian industries. Meat packing is to be found particularly in the long narrow belt that extends from Calgary on the west to Montreal on the east. Thus the pattern is almost identical with that in the United States. Although there are both large and small plants, the leading centers are Calgary, Winnipeg, Toronto, Peterborough, and Montreal.

ARGENTINA

Argentina occupies a very high place in the meat-packing industry. It ranks first as an exporter of beef (contributing three fourths of the world's total) and third (following New Zealand and Australia) in the exportation of mutton and lamb (one fifth of the world's total). Beef has been Argentina's major export, representing nearly 300 million dollars in foreign exchange each year. The Argentinians themselves are among the world's largest fresh-meat eaters: they consume 67 to 75 per cent of the entire slaughter, and consumption averages about 175 pounds per capita—fourth highest in the world. However, in the late 1950s, home consumption had to be curtailed because of the dangerous financial situation in the country; more beef had to be exported, and the prices of choice beefsteaks went up in one year from the usual 15 cents a pound to 50 cents.

The meat-packing plants (*frigorificos*), particularly those operated by foreign companies, are huge and modern. They are located in Buenos Aires, Rosario, and La Plata. They handle *chillers* and *freezers*, terms that apply both to the quality of the cattle and to the temperature maintained in shipment to Europe (the destination of the exports): 29°F to 30°F for chillers, 0°F to 10°F for freezers. Chillers are superior to freezers, which normally are shipped to the continent of Europe or are converted into canned beef. Exports consist of two thirds chilled and one third frozen. Since chilled beef is perishable, regulations require that it be shipped not more than seven days after the animal's slaughter.

In addition to the Pampa *frigorificos*, a number of small packing plants are scattered throughout the region and throughout the irrigated oases; also mutton-freezing plants are to be found in the port cities of sheep-producing Patagonia.

BRAZIL AND URUGUAY

These two countries possess important meat-packing industries. They supply all their own requirements but also have a surplus for export. Favoring factors are the large numbers of livestock (Brazil, for example, ranks fourth among the nations of the world in numbers of both cattle and swine), constant improvement in animals, numerous port cities, proximity of the stock-raising areas to tidewater, and adequate transport facilities. Plants are modern. East-central Brazil, where large United States packers early established themselves, is particularly important. Leading centers are São Paulo, Barretos, Cruziero, and Santos in the state of São Paulo; and Pelotas, Rio Grande, and Livramento in the state of Rio Grande do Sul. In Uruguay meat packing is the dominant food-processing industry. Montevideo, leading packing center, has three large *frigorificos;* and Fray Bentos and Paysandú, on the Río Uruguay, one each.

It is interesting to note that Uruguay has the highest per capita consumption of meat in the world—259 pounds (1960).

EUROPE

Europe, exclusive of the Soviet Union, produces one third of the world's meat and imports four fifths of all the beef and virtually all the mutton (95 per cent) that gets into world trade. The meat-packing industry is about of the same importance in Europe as in the United States, but it is different. The countries are small and densely populated. The livestock and people occupy the same general areas. Since corn is unimportant, European animals are not fed unlimited quantities of it, as they are in the American Corn Belt; consequently, they are not overfat and are of better quality. Moreover, most European families do not own a refrigerator, a deep freeze, or an automobile. For these and other reasons, meat moves only short distances; and the slaughter plants, small and more scattered, cater essentially to the local area. Many of these plants are municipally operated.

Although Britain has one of the most important slaughtering and meat-packing industries in Europe, the dense urban-industrial population necessitates very large imports. Principal source is Argentina. The United Kingdom in 1960 ranked eighth in per capita consumption of meat—132 pounds.

SOVIET UNION

In the Soviet Union, modern meat packing is an innovation since the Revolution. It now functions as a combine with numerous large plants, but they are neither so large nor so efficient as those in the United States. Russia reportedly produces slightly more than 10 per cent of the world's meat, but annual per capita consumption is only about 55 pounds. In 1959, meat production was still less than half that of the United States.

The Russian slaughtering and meat-packing industry is widely distributed: outstanding in European Russia are Moscow, Leningrad, Bryansk, Baku, Leninakan, Kirov, Kurgan, Petropavlovsk, Kuibyshev, Sverdlovsk, Ivanovo, Voronezh, Poltava, and Dnepropetrovsk; in the eastern part of the country (east of the Caspian Sea and Ural Mountains) Ashkhabad, Duyashambe, Semipalatinsk, Tashkent, Novosibirsk, Irkutsk, Ulan-Ude, and Khabarovsk lead.

The Soviet industry, especially in larger cities in areas where the rearing of livestock is important, is located at or near focal points on the transport systems. The aim is to have each meat-packing center supply its own tributary area. Specific examples of this principle are Irkutsk, Krasnoyarsk, Ulan-Ude, and Semipalatinsk.

AUSTRALIA AND NEW ZEALAND

These two commonwealths, with their large cattle and sheep populations, small human populations, great distances from principal world meat-import markets (New Zealand lies 13,000 miles from Great Britain), their favored political position in the Sterling Bloc, and Anglo-Saxon tradition and high standard of living, support an important slaughtering and meat-packing industry. Of Australia's seventy-odd packing plants, forty-two are in southeastern Australia, the rest in Queensland and Western Australia—in short, close to market and ports and not far from the raising grounds. Although beef and mutton and lamb all are handled and exported, the latter leads. There are fourteen sheep for every man, woman, and child.

Traditionally, exports have gone to Great Britain. In 1959, however, the United States became Australia's premier market. Exports to the West Coast of the United States soared to such heights in 1959 that California stockmen protested loudly, pointing out the much lower production costs. In a typical week, 2 million pounds of boneless beef and 100,000 pounds of boneless veal entered California from Australia and New Zealand. The California Cattlemen's Association reported that, in 1959, 10 per cent of the meat consumed in the three Pacific Coast states was imported.

Although Australia's per capita consumption of meat ranks among the highest in the world, the small population and the huge production of meat leave a large surplus—about a fifth—for export.

The principal export abattoirs are located in the large cities (Sydney, Melbourne, Adelaide, and Brisbane), and in the medium-sized ports of Queensland (as Townsville and Rockhampton).

In the late 1950s, New Zealand began stepping up exports of fresh, frozen, and boneless beef and veal, the amount reaching 91,000 tons in 1958. Most of this tonnage consisted of boneless meat. Seventy-six per cent of the shipments went to the United States. New Zealand plants are modern and efficient.

DAIRY INDUSTRIES

In all areas where butter and cheese are made, the distribution of the industry coincides with that of dairy cattle.

CHEESES

Cheeses, of which there are more than 400 kinds, consist of a concentration of certain constituents of milk fat, casein (a nitrogen compound), and salts. Being easily stored and shipped, cheese can be and is sent great distances. There are two commercial types—*natural* and *processed*. Natural cheese is produced from milk or cream, though mostly from whole milk. Processed cheese, made by combining natural cheeses with seasoning, is heated, pasteurized, and packaged; *it is never sold in bulk*.

In Europe, cheese factories are invariably small and are located in milk-producing areas, whereas in the United States most are large, being units of huge firms with nationwide affiliations.

EUROPE

As a result of differences in temperature, soil, water, types of animals kept, and processing recipes and methods, Europe produces numerous varieties of cheese—many intimately associated with specific areas. Among the most famous are the Edam and Gouda cheeses of the Netherlands, Limburger of Belgium, Swiss of Switzerland, Camembert and Roquefort of France, Gorgonzola and Parmesan of Italy, Bleu of Denmark, and Cheddar of England. Europe accounts for about two thirds of the world's total cheese output. Principal producers are France, Italy, West Germany, the Netherlands, Denmark, and the Soviet Union. The Russian output has increased more than 500 per cent since World War II, giving it sixth rank among all nations. European cheese is frequently held for several years before being sold. Handling demands much labor and considerable investment capital. Consumption of cheese in Europe is very high.

The famous cheese Roquefort is presented here to bring out the conditions underlying production of one of the world's tastiest and most famous cheeses. The village of Roquefort lies in southern France in a limestone area that is dry, sunny, and warm.

Roquefort, made from sheep's milk, is a highly flavored, blue-molded cheese. It is made only during the period from January to the end of June. The milk is first brought to a desired temperature and rennet added. Within two hours it curdles. After draining, it is poured into molds containing small amounts of *penicillium Roqueforti*. After resting for a few days, the cheese is placed in a salting room in a limestone chamber, where conditions are ideal for fermentation. The aging takes a minimum of four months.

UNITED STATES

Milk-processing plants locate close to sources of raw materials if weight loss during processing is appreciable. The greater the distance from major markets, the more an area goes in for dairy products—those with a high value per unit of weight—rather than for fluid milk. Theoretically the American Dairy Region is zoned with respect to large urban markets: (1) market milk in the zone immediately adjacent to the city; (2) condensed-milk factories in the zone outward; (3) cheese factories still farther removed; and (4) creameries farthest out of all. About 75 per cent of all American cheese is made in the North-Central states—North and South Dakota, Nebraska, Kansas, Minnesota, Iowa, Missouri, Michigan, Wisconsin, Illinois, Indiana, Ohio, and Kentucky.

In the United States, cheese is mass-produced and, while still relatively young, sold mainly as processed cheese. Although the quantity manufactured is steadily increasing, the number of factories is declining, production being concentrated more and more in large plants. Because of improvements in transportation and because of more complete use of plant capacity, the number of processing plants has dropped. Among the principal cheeses processed is American Cheddar, used when the natural cheese is very young.

FOREIGN TRADE IN CHEESE

The European countries, with the experience of generations, large production, and low labor costs, have considerable surplus for export. Europe accounts for about 60 per cent of the 800 million pounds that get into international trade annually.

Cheese is the most important dairy product imported into the United States. Many of these cheeses are made only in certain countries and would be unavailable to American consumers unless imported. During the past decade the United States has imposed import quotas on cheese as part of its dairy price-support program (Section 22 of the Basic Farm Law, which permits restriction of imports if they hamper the domestic price support). These quotas have been extremely unpopular in the Netherlands, Denmark, Switzerland, and Canada. Quotas were raised (doubled on Netherlands cheeses) in 1960. Cheeses made from sheep's and goat's milk are exempted, since they are noncompetitive.

BUTTER

Butter, the solidified fat of milk, is obtained by churning. In the United States about one fourth of the total milk output is converted into butter. Per capita consumption of butter has declined—slowly from 1934 to 1943, precipitously from 1943 to 1953; since then it has followed a fairly stable course. Competition with margarine, which costs only about half as much, accounted for much of the decline.

UNITED STATES

The principal butter-making area extends from New York and Pennsylvania to Minnesota and Iowa. The three states of Minnesota, Iowa, and Wisconsin (the so-called *Tri-State Butter Region*) account for 50 per cent of the nation's butter output. Creameries, like cheese factories, are getting bigger as the total number declines. Particularly is this trend noticeable in Minnesota, which makes 20 per cent of the butter. Improved roads today enable fast-moving trucks to assemble milk and cream from quite an extensive area.

DENMARK

Butter is the principal dairy product of Denmark, a famous dairy country. Danish butter, which has a worldwide reputation for flavor and keeping qualities, is packaged in tin cans and sold all over the world. However, gradual reductions in sales are occurring, largely because of agricultural protectionist policies in former important customer nations. Experiencing difficulty in making a reasonable profit,

Denmark is turning toward sale of industrial products.

NEW ZEALAND

North Island is largely devoted to dairying. The importance of the industry, the small population of New Zealand, and the great distance to Northwestern Europe together have conspired to make New Zealand the world's foremost exporter of butter.

SUGAR REFINING

Sugar refining involves the refining of two agricultural commodities—the cane of the tropics and subtropics, the beet of the subtropics and mid-latitudes.

CANE REFINING

Cane refining is carried on in two stages. The cane stalks as delivered from the growing fields to the sugar mill are converted first into raw sugar, which is about 96 per cent sucrose but contains some impurities, is brown in color, and is in need of further refining. This first step must be carried on near the cane fields because cane is seasonally produced, is bulky in relation to value, and is highly perishable. This raw sugar is then sent in jute or other fiber bags (or in bulk, as in Hawaii and Puerto Rico) to ports, whence it is shipped to a strategically located large-scale refinery.

Sugar is refined mostly, though not exclusively, in the region of consumption (in the cyclonic or so-called "temperate" zone) rather than in the region of production. The mills of exporting lands ship raw sugar for the following reasons: (1) Refined sugar should be moved and sold as quickly after manufacture as possible. (2) If sugar were refined in the tropics, it would absorb moisture en route to middle-latitude markets and become lumpy or caked. (3) The complete fabricating process in a single factory would require large capital outlay, much skilled labor, and ample fuel. In the infancy of the industry these requirements were lacking in most of the lands that produce cane sugar. (4) The consuming na-

tion invariably wants to carry on the refining —it gives employment to many persons.

Middle-latitude refineries are enormous in size, and many draw their raw sugar from divers parts of the world. All lie at seaports where the raw sugar can be unloaded without trans-shipment (Fig. 15-2). They operate around the clock, process up to 6 million pounds daily, and do it efficiently, economically, and cheaply.

Since the refining process adds little value to the sugar, refineries must operate on a large scale; for only through volume can profits compensate for the necessary capital investment.

The large refinery at Crockett, California— the only American cane refinery west of the 100th meridian—is a nonprofit growers' joint-marketing agency completely owned by the sugar producers of Hawaii—twenty-eight plantations.

Although India may be the largest world producer of sugar cane, less than half is believed to be refined. Large numbers of primitive mills produce *gur*, a product of 60 to 70 per cent purity. *Gur* has been consumed in quantities, mainly because defecants of animal origin, which had to be used in refining, were avoided because of religious prejudices of the Hindus.

BEET-SUGAR REFINING

The processing of beet sugar, because of the nature of the extractive methods, is an integrated operation at a factory located within the beet-growing areas. Each factory completely processes the beet, making the sugar in a straight-line, continuous procedure—from beet to refined sugar. Mills generally operate only about 120 days a year.

Because beets must move rapidly from farm to factory, the number of factories is large— far more so than with cane refineries. The scale of operation is much smaller than in cane refining—largely because the beets originate over a wide area, and transport costs (rail or truck) are so high that the factories must be near the beet fields. Another factor that necessitates locating the refineries in the beet-

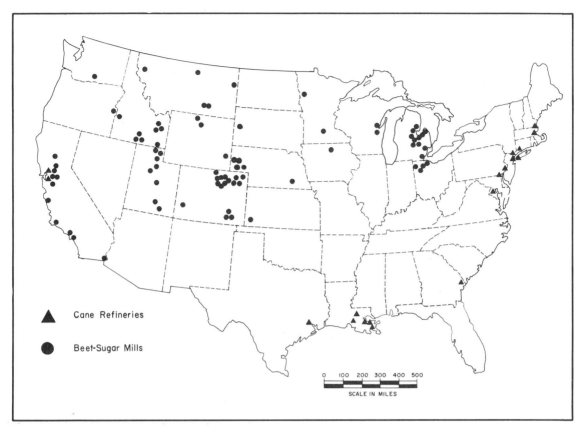

Fig. 15-2. Sugar refineries in the United States. Cane refineries are located at ports where they handle imported raw sugar (except for Crockett, California, which refines Hawaiian raw sugar, and the lower South, where home-grown cane is processed). Cane refineries are on the waterfront, where they can receive raw sugar and fuel by vessel or barge. They also are well located with respect to the domestic market, since they are near the principal population agglomerations and are well served by transportation facilities. About half the sugar imports are refined around New York City. Beet refineries either are small and widely scattered or are very large and located at strategic points. Almost invariably they are to be found close to the source of beets.

growing area is that only about one sixth of the weight of the beet is extractable sugar, the rest being waste and by-products.

Europe is distinguished as the world's leading continent for sugar-beet production and beet-sugar refining. The factories, as in the United States, are located primarily in the beet-growing areas. In Belgium they are scattered south of Ghent and west of Mons and between Brussels and Liége. In France they are to be found mostly in Picardy along the canalized Oise River and in Alsace; in Germany they are in the Magdeburg area and in

Saxony; in Czechoslovakia they are in every large town in the Danube Lowland, Morava Valley, and Labe-Ohve Valley, and in the Polaby area of Bohemia; and in Poland they are located mainly around Posen. In Russia, which ranks first in sugar-beet production, the principal beet-sugar refineries are situated in the beet-growing areas near the Volga, in Bashkiria, the Caucasus, Kazakhstan, Kirghizia, Western Siberia, and the Far East. Among the leading centers are Agara, Bekovo, Cherkassy, Dzhambul, Kant, Kiev, Kursk, Poltava, Sumy, and Vinnitsa.

VEGETABLE AND FRUIT CANNING

Food canning is based on man's desire to consume certain foods beyond the season when they would normally be edible in the fresh form. Canning has been possible because of three technological advancements: (1) the ability to make tin cans cheaply, (2) the development of the pressure cooker, and (3) the perfection of machines to perform every operation automatically—to clean, sort, cut, peel, stem, core, halve, pit, cube, dice, pack, weigh, seal, cook, and label the cans.

Food canning has come with (1) the decline of the home garden, (2) the widespread employment of married women outside the home, and (3) the increase in apartment living. Also, the high standard of living enjoyed particularly by Americans has created a desire for a greater variety of foods, a desire easily met by this industry. How integral a part of American life the tin can has become is apparent from the 100 million food-containing cans opened daily.

Although some food canning is carried on in most countries, the bulk of it is done in the industrialized ones—the United States (70 per cent of the world total), Canada, the countries of Western Europe, Australia, and the Republic of South Africa.

LOCATION OF CANNERIES

The selection of a location for a cannery is a complex problem and involves a thorough knowledge of economic geography. The first requirement is an adequate and dependable supply of fruits or vegetables—preferably within a 30-mile radius of the cannery. The second requirement is transportation: raw materials must move rapidly from grower to processor to ensure quality of product; moreover, transport costs may be the determining factor between profit and loss. Labor is also important. Canning is largely a seasonal industry (six weeks to eight months if the plant processes several products) and demands a pool of potential workers, mostly women, interested only in seasonal employment. High

school and college students in large numbers are hired during their summer vacations. Hence, rural communities, villages, and small towns are preferable to large cities as cannery sites.

Sewage and waste disposal are major problems and must be properly investigated before a cannery is built. Ample water of suitable type is essential for cleaning the raw product and for steam, brine, and syrup. Fuel and power in adequate volume and at low cost should be available. Finally, tax rates must be carefully considered.

UNITED STATES

CALIFORNIA

California is the greatest food-processing center on earth. Its annual pack amounts to nearly one third of the total for the United States—roughly 220 million cases. Canning is California's leading peacetime industry, the 250 canneries being supplied by some 700 square miles of land devoted to fruits and vegetables (Fig. 15-3). California accounts for about half of the total national tonnage of processed fruits. It also accounts for about 36 per cent of the nation's processed vegetables.

The San Francisco Bay area, with seventy-five canneries, leads. The principal fruits canned are apricots, peaches, and pears. The principal vegetables canned are asparagus and tomatoes, but spinach and beans (green and wax) are also important.

The operations of one of California's largest canneries, in Sunnyvale, south of San Francisco, begin in a big way with apricots (also green beans) in July, when it employs 1,100 persons. About August 1, the plant starts packing fruit cocktails (the season lasts about sixty days and involves peaches, pears, cherries, grapes, and pineapples). At the same time, the plant begins packing fruit salad (apricots, pineapples, peaches, pears, and cherries). This period lasts about thirty working days. The plant also quick freezes vegetables (spinach, Brussels sprouts, lima beans, green beans,

Fig. 15-3. Typical California cannery, at Kingsburg, about 20 miles southeast of Fresno. The lugs of fruit, delivered by truck, are piled for almost immediate use by the cannery. The majority of the canneries are not large. (Courtesy of California Packing Corporation.)

cauliflower, peas, and broccoli), the period lasting from fall until the end of the year.

EASTERN UNITED STATES

The Atlantic Coastal Plain, including New York City and Baltimore, is one of the world's leading vegetable-canning areas. Most (90 per cent) of the tomatoes, sweet corn, and peas produced in Maryland are sold to some four hundred canneries. Delaware and New Jersey are peppered with canneries.

Part of the Agricultural Interior ranks high in canning: Indiana, Illinois, and Ohio in tomatoes; Minnesota, Indiana, and Illinois in sweet corn (Fig. 15-4); Wisconsin in green peas, green beans, and cabbage for sauerkraut. Of the ten leading American canning states (based on number of establishments), five— New York, Indiana, Wisconsin, Illinois, and Ohio—lie in this region.

FLORIDA AND FROZEN ORANGE JUICE

An interesting phase of canning is that of frozen orange juice. In 1959-1960 about 60 per cent of the entire orange crop (about 80 to 85 million gallons) went into the frozen concentrate. By far the greater part of this

juice is packed in Florida; California is unable to compete. To understand this apparent anomaly, it is essential to distinguish California navels from Valencias and from Florida oranges. Navel oranges are bought to eat fresh; they are not well adapted for juice manufacture. Even though California Valencias are well suited for juice products, two thirds of this crop still is marketed fresh. Florida produces more than twice as many oranges as does California, but her fruit has less appeal as fresh fruit. Florida oranges provide fine juice; moreover, consumer acceptance of frozen concentrate has shown fantastic growth (about one third of all frozen food products by value is estimated to be orange concentrate). The shift from fresh oranges to frozen orange juice has come about because frozen orange juice is less expensive, more readily available (its storability permits sales throughout the year), and more convenient.

HAWAII

Hawaii, with 77,000 acres in pineapples and nine large canneries, processes most of the world's quality pineapple (three fourths of its total pack)—in a normal year some 12 million cases. As a state, it enjoys freedom from com-

Fig. 15-4. Harvesting sweet corn in northern Illinois. Hydraulically controlled hoppers dump sweet corn into field trucks for immediate delivery to cannery. In this area, which is a part of the Corn Belt, the sweet corn matures very rapidly. Hence, it must be harvested at virtually the precise moment it reaches the ideal stage for canning, and be delivered to the factory for immediate processing. There can be no delay in picking, in getting the product to the cannery, and in processing. (Courtesy of Del Monte Foods.)

petition in the huge mainland market, which absorbs about 95 per cent of the output.

FISH CANNING

The canning of fish is widespread—about 1 million tons of fish and shellfish being canned annually. On a tonnage basis, herring, tuna, and Pacific salmon lead. The United States outranks all other nations in the canning of fish products; but Japan, Canada, Norway, Denmark, Great Britain, France, Portugal, Spain, and Peru all make notable contributions.

SALMON

The principal salmon-canning areas are in the states of Alaska, Washington, and Ore-

gon—with Alaska accounting for about 90 per cent. Canneries are built at catching points beside the mouths of various streams from Northern California to the Bering Sea. They are supplied by craft fishing in inlets and the open sea with purse seines or troll lines (see Chapter 27, pp. 558-559). Japan also cans salmon, much of it in factory ships, using the fish caught by catcher boats. Consumption of canned fish in Japan, negligible before World War II, is growing rapidly.

As the season arrives for the salmon to begin spawning, the fish approach the mainland in enormous numbers. Within a matter of several weeks, hundreds of thousands of pounds of salmon are caught and delivered to the canneries, where they are cleaned, canned, boxed, and shipped to markets.

This is presumed to be the most highly mechanized of all the branches of fish canning. The fish are untouched by human hands: the so-called "iron chink" cuts off the heads, tails, and fins, then slits and cleans the fish.

TUNA

Tuna are canned primarily in the United States, Japan, Western Europe, and Peru. The San Diego area is the largest center in the world. The fishing boats, which are very costly (as much as $250,000 each), are capable of going as far south as Peru and Chile. Latin American waters supply about half the total catch. Tuna also is canned in Los Angeles, San Francisco, and Astoria (Oregon). France and Spain have large tuna fisheries and canning industries. Tuna caught by Japanese fishermen in many parts of the world's oceans are frequently processed—canned or frozen—on factory ships. The present trend has resulted from international restrictions on off-shore operations of Japanese shipping vessels.

SARDINES

Sardines (mostly small herrings, pilchards, and sprats) comprise the highest tonnage of the world's canned fish. The West European countries catch and can enormous quantities. The true sardine is caught only in the Bay of Biscay and the Mediterranean Sea. Portugal is the leading sardine-canning nation.

Americans, too, catch and can "sardines" on both the East and West Coasts. Eastport (Maine) is the leading canning center on the Atlantic Coast, Monterey (California) on the Pacific Coast. In Monterey, however, canning has sharply declined with the near-exhaustion of the "sardine" fisheries since the 1945-1946 fishing season.

QUICK FREEZING

The quick-frozen-food industry is the youngest member of the food-processing family. It differs from the older methods of freezing in that the foods are subjected to an extremely low temperature, which results in almost instantaneous freezing. Frozen foods retain their natural flavor because the process prevents the formation of ice crystals, which rupture the cellular structure and cause a loss of natural juices when the food is thawed out for eating. Actually, frozen foods are days fresher than the fresh produce the housewife purchases at the market, since foods are quick frozen when they have reached the correct degree of ripeness, tenderness, and color—a period that often lasts but a few hours. The chief function of quick freezing is to arrest the three processes that destroy fruits and vegetables—*oxidation*, *dessication* (drying out), and *ripening*.

The most advantageously located quick-freezing plants are those that can draw on a wide variety of products from close at hand. Because the raw materials to be quick frozen are extremely perishable, the processing plants must be located as close as possible to the fruits or vegetables to be handled. The maximum distance they can be transported is 50 miles, but most fruits and vegetables move no more than 25 to 30 miles. If possible, the plant should start with asparagus in the spring and pack products that mature in successive steps so as to operate over a three- to nine-month period: for example, asparagus, berries and other fruits, peas, beans, and corn; then the late crops—spinach, broccoli, and Brussels sprouts. Only in California and Florida does the season of operation extend over so long a period. On the other hand, the frozen foods of these states meet competition from frozen foods produced in Midwestern or Eastern areas closer to heavy consuming centers.

As in canning, California leads in volume of frozen-food production, contributing more than 60 per cent of the total United States frozen pack of vegetables and deciduous fruits. The greatest concentration of freezer plants in California is in the Santa Clara, Pajaro, and Salinas Valleys; next in importance is the area bounded on the north by Orland and on the south by Sanger in the Central

Valley, where Fresno, Modesto, and Sacramento are particularly outstanding. The south coastal area from San Luis Obispo to Los Angeles—particularly Los Angeles, Anaheim, and Santa Barbara—is also notable.

In the Pacific Northwest there is a major freezing area, whose greatest concentration of plants is to be found along Puget Sound and in the irrigated areas around Ellensburg, Grandview, Prosser, and Walla Walla in Washington and in the Willamette Valley of Oregon.

In the East, southern New Jersey (near Bridgeton) is particularly outstanding in quick freezing. Farming in the area is engineered on a clockwork schedule to ensure an even flow of vegetable planting and harvesting. The famous Seabrook Farms (really a farm-factory) turn out annually more than 100 million pounds of frozen fruits and vege-tables. About 50 per cent of the produce handled is grown on their own land, 35 per cent is purchased from 1,000 independent farms within 50 miles of the plant, and 15 per cent is bought in specialized areas—Long Island and the Eastern Shore of Delmarva.

This industry is not widespread throughout the world, for special sub-zero transport units and freezer compartments in stores and homes necessitate high cost of the products. However, the increase in the number of working women, more automobiles, growing prosperity, and the ever growing number of supermarkets are stimulating the consumption of frozen foods. In Europe the number of stores with frozen-food cabinets is rising rapidly. In 1961, it is reported, there were nearly 75,-000 in Britain, 10,000 in Switzerland, 12,000 in the Netherlands, 8,000 in Denmark, and 1,800 in Belgium.

SELECTED REFERENCES

Alderfer, E. B., and H. E. Michl. "The Sugar Industry," in *Economics of American Industry,* 3rd ed. New York, McGraw-Hill Book Company, Inc., 1957, pp. 530-552.

Blanck, F. C. "Food and Agriculture," in Albert S. Carlson (ed.), *Economic Geography of Industrial Materials.* New York, Reinhold Publishing Corporation, 1956, pp. 436-470.

Brown, Nona. "A Bushel of Wheat: Farm to Table," *New York Times,* October 9, 1955.

Gortner, Willis A., Frederick S. Erdman, and Nancy K. Masterman. *Principles of Food Freezing.* New York, John Wiley & Sons, Inc., 1948, pp. 3-95.

Panschar, William G. *Baking in America,* 2 vols. Evanston, Illinois, Northwestern University Press, 1956.

Paul, Allen B., and Lorenzo B. Mann. "Processing: What Our Grandparents Did Not Have," in *Marketing; Yearbook of Agriculture, 1954.* Washington, D. C., U.S. Department of Agriculture, 1954, pp. 120-127.

"Shift in Meat Packing," *Business Conditions* (Federal Reserve Bank of Chicago), November 1959, pp. 4-10.

Storck, John, and Walter D. Teague. *Flour for Man's Bread.* Minneapolis, University of Minnesota Press, 1952.

Trelogan, Harry C., *et al.* "Dairy Industry," in Albert S. Carlson (ed.), *Economic Geography of Industrial Materials.* New York, Reinhold Publishing Corporation, 1956, pp. 421-435.

White, C. Langdon. "Food Preparation Industries," in C. M. Zierer (ed.), *California and the Southwest.* New York, John Wiley & Sons, Inc., 1956, pp. 251-261.

THE WORLD'S

PART FOUR::

FOOD CROPS

CHAPTER SIXTEEN::

Cereals play the dominant role in the diet of the world's more than 3 billion inhabitants. Ninety-seven per cent of all food consumed by human beings, measured in calories, is supplied by cereals. Cereals provide man with most of his energy food. They are important also from the standpoint of the percentage of the world's cropland they occupy—*nearly one half*. It seems entirely accurate to say that the cereal grains comprise the most important group of cultivated plants on earth.

The cereals are many, but all fall into two types: (1) the *small grains*—wheat, rice, rye, oats, and barley; and (2) the *coarse grains*—corn, millets, and the grain sorghums. All, however, are grasses.

Only two of the cereals—wheat and rye—are regarded as true bread grains. The others used for food for man and feed for livestock contain too little **gluten** to be well suited to bread making.

THE WORLD'S

GEOGRAPHICAL
SPECIALIZATION
IN GRAINS

Grains are for the most part quite universal in their distribution. There are few countries in the world that do not grow some wheat. Corn, too, is widely distributed. Some rice is grown on every continent with the exception of Antarctica. And rye, barley, and oats are widely distributed, as are the grain sorghums. Nevertheless, all the cereals have definite points of optimal performance, and hence there are *major regions of production*. Thus, about 94 per cent of the world's rice is confined to Monsoon Asia, 60 per cent of the corn to North America, and 95 per cent of the rye to Europe—mostly Northern Europe. *In this book each cereal is presented only with respect to optimal conditions of growth and areas of maximum importance. Marginal areas are bypassed.*

The relative importance of each cereal in a specific area in the world depends upon a number of factors: (1) physical—climate, soils, terrain, drainage, size of area; and (2) human—food-yielding or feed-yielding capacity, consumer preference or prejudice, purchasing power, level of living, governmental policy, and world market price. The ranking of the grains in international trade, based on tonnage, is wheat, corn, rice, barley, and oats *or* rye.

THE SMALL GRAINS

WHEAT

Wheat is regarded as one of the world's two principal small grains. It is the Caucasian's favorite cereal—the result of tradition and

CEREALS

TABLE 16-1

WHEAT: ACREAGE, YIELD PER ACRE, AND PRODUCTION IN SPECIFIED COUNTRIES, 1960

Continent and country	Acreage (1,000 acres)	Yield per acre (bushels)	Production (1,000 bushels)
NORTH AMERICA			
Canada	23,198	21.1	489,624
United States	52,643	25.9	1,363,443
EUROPE			
Western Europe			
Belgium	498	56.5	28,150
France	10,776	37.1	400,000
West Germany	3,429	53.0	181,750
Italy	11,300	22.1	250,000
Spain	10,378	12.7	132,000
United Kingdom	2,114	51.6	109,000
Eastern Europe			
Hungary	2,598	25.0	65,000
Romania	7,383 ††	19.9 ††	147,000
Yugoslavia	5,090	25.8	131,170
SOVIET UNION	148,500	11.4	1,700,000
ASIA °			
India	31,508	11.5	363,400
Pakistan	12,193	11.9	144,700
Turkey	16,000 †	15.0 †	260,000
AFRICA			
Algeria	4,725	11.6	55,000
Egypt	1,512	36.4	55,000
Morocco	4,057	9.1	37,000
South Africa	3,156 ††	8.6 ††	28,200
SOUTH AMERICA			
Argentina	10,818 ††	19.9 ††	160,000
Chile	2,110	19.1	40,400
AUSTRALIA	12,857	20.2	260,000
Estimated World Total	488,840	16.7	8,180,000

° Figures for Communist China unavailable.
† 1958.
†† 1959.

SOURCE: "World Summaries: Crops and Livestock," *Foreign Crops and Markets,* Foreign Agricultural Service, U.S.D.A., March 30, 1961, pp. 16-17.

climate. World wheat production exceeds world rice production, but it is believed that more of the world's people eat rice than wheat. In 1960 8.3 billion bushels of wheat were produced (Table 16-1).

LOCATION OF WHEAT CROPS

Figure 16-1 shows where the world's wheat is grown. Wheat is the most widely grown of the major cereals, being found as far north as 60° north in the Northern Hemisphere and

as far south as 40° south in the Southern Hemisphere. Within these outward limits, the crop is most highly concentrated within two broad latitudinal belts—30° and 55° north and 30° and 40° south. The cold limit of wheat production is about 57°F average temperature for the three warmest months. The hot, wet tropics and subtropics are unimportant for wheat. Since wheat is a grass, it does best if the period of formative growth is cool and moist.

Although some wheat is grown on rugged land, the crop does best on flat or undulating

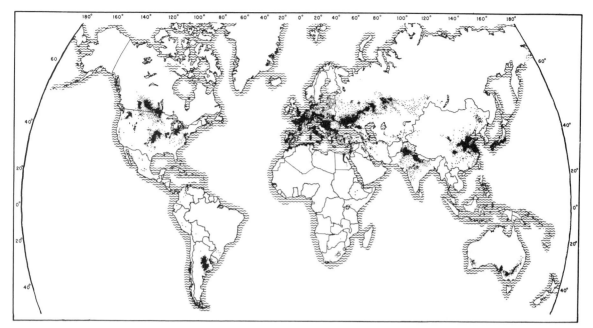

Fig. 16-1. *World wheat production, with dots at the approximate location where the wheat is actually grown. Most of the wheat is grown in those areas of the world having either middle-latitude or subtropical (Mediterranean type) climate. The tropics, except where altitude results in more moderate temperatures, are insignificant in actual output. Nor is wheat important in subpolar regions. Beyond the areas of important production shown here, there do not appear to be available any new wheat lands of appreciable extent. Note that about 90 per cent of the wheat is grown in the Northern Hemisphere, only about 10 per cent in the Southern Hemisphere. (Courtesy of U.S. Department of Agriculture.)*

land. Moreover, unlike rye and oats, wheat requires fertile soils. If soils are not naturally fertile, generous applications of commercial fertilizer must be used. Throughout the world, very little wheat is grown on sandy, gravelly, or peaty soils or on heavy clay soils in cool climates.

Wheat is grown on almost 500 million acres of land, or about 1 per cent of the total land area of the earth (Fig. 16-2 and Table 16-1). Though this amount seems small, it exceeds that of any other crop grown by man and is double the acreage of the two runners-up— rice and corn. Man continually enlarges the wheat-growing area through persistent, patient, and scientific work; he breeds drought- and frost-resistant varieties, and he fights insects and diseases that attack the crop. It is believed that about 5 million square miles or one tenth of the land surface of the world can be used for wheat.

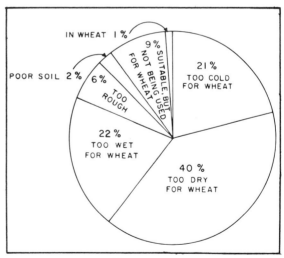

Fig. 16-2. *Earth's land area and its ability to sustain wheat. About 1 per cent of the land is sown in wheat, and only about 10 per cent (under present conditions) of the earth's surface is available for wheat. (After O. E. Baker.)*

THE WORLD'S CEREALS :: 313

In any discussion of the geography of wheat, one should note that the crop falls into two categories: *winter wheat* and *spring wheat;* also *hard wheat* and *soft wheat.*

Winter Wheat. This variety comprises the great bulk, at least 75 per cent, of the world's acreage and is grown universally when physical conditions permit. Only four wheat-producing countries of the world allocate less than 90 per cent of their total wheat acreage to winter wheat. Winter wheat is sown in the fall and harvested in late spring or early summer. It thrives in the mild, rainy winter of the Mediterranean Subtropical climate and lies dormant under a blanket of snow in the Humid Continental with Long Summers and in the Dry Continental climates.

Spring Wheat. Spring wheat, which is planted in the spring and harvested in late autumn, prevails in areas where winters are extremely severe, and where the snow cover is inadequate or sometimes lacking altogether, so that winter wheat would be killed. Only a few major wheat areas—e.g., the Columbia Plateau of the United States and North China —grow both winter and spring wheat. All told, only about one fourth of the world's wheat is of the spring variety.

Hard and Soft Wheats. The major difference between hard and soft wheat is in the gluten content: hard wheat has a great deal; soft wheat has little. Hard wheat makes a strong bread flour that absorbs more water and yields more loaves of bread per 100 pounds of flour. The loaf is large and light in weight. A miller is willing to pay a substantial premium for these qualities. Soft wheat makes a weak bread flour (the loaf is small and heavy), but is well suited for flour for making hot rolls, crackers, biscuits, and pastries. Countries that eat white bread but grow soft wheat, as does France, import some hard wheat for mixing with the soft domestic cereal.

THE WORLD'S MAJOR WHEAT REGIONS

Slightly more than one third of the world's wheat acreage lies in Asia; somewhat less than one third in Europe; not quite a quarter in Anglo-America; and about one eighth in Africa, Australia, and South America combined.

The world's commercial wheat production is concentrated in twelve belts or agricultural regions:

1. The Columbia Plateau.
2. Spring-Wheat Belt of the northern Great Plains (Canada and the United States).
3. Hard Winter-Wheat Belt of the southern Great Plains.
4. Soft Winter-Wheat Belt of the Middle West and adjacent Ontario.
5. The Pampa of Argentina.
6. Northwest Europe.
7. The Mediterranean Basin.
8. The Danubian Plain and Southern Russia.
9. Spring-Wheat Region of Central Russia (including Siberia).
10. North China (including southern Manchuria).
11. Northwestern India and adjacent Pakistan.
12. Southeastern Australia.

The Columbia Plateau. This region is important from many aspects: (1) it produces both winter and spring wheat; (2) nearly all of the crop is **dry-farmed;** (3) the area is essentially a one-crop region; (4) the bulk of the output is not used within the region or even within the United States; and (5) it accounts for approximately 8 per cent of the national wheat acreage.

In the semiarid Columbia Plateau, the population is small, the ranches are large, and all kinds of machines are employed—tractors, gangplows, disks, weeders, and combines (Fig. 16-3). When these large power units are utilized, one man can do the work of three.

The region produces both winter and spring wheat, but each is grown where the physical conditions are best suited to it. Some spring wheat is grown in the winter-wheat area when a dry autumn has prevented the germination of winter wheat or when the snowfall is so light and winter temperatures are so low that the planted winter wheat has been killed.

Then spring wheat is sown if there is certain to be adequate moisture for germination. Winter wheat is preferred, however, because it yields about 50 per cent more than spring wheat and it better equalizes the **seasonal distribution of labor.** Some wheat is grown under irrigation around the margins of the Columbia Plateau wheat belt; yields from irrigation are reputed to be the highest in the United States.

The popular wheats grown—common and club, both white in color—suffer extensively from **lodging,** so that varieties able to stand erect on fertile soil with heavy nitrogen fertilization are needed. Experiments along this line are being tested with semidwarf Japanese-American blends.

The area is nearly all in slope (Fig. 16-3)— the general effect being that of sand-dune topography. The soil—some loessial, some lacustrine, some alluvial, and some glaciofluvial—is all transported. The climate is Dry Continental—the semiarid phase: winters are cloudy and relatively mild, with considerable rain or snow—although severe cold waves are not uncommon; summer days are generally clear and warm, but nights are cool. The precipitation ranges from about 12 inches on the western margin to 25 inches along the eastern border next to the mountains.

Soil (sheet) erosion has been very bad here in the past, for too much land was kept in summer fallow and too much stubble was burned, thereby exhausting the soil-binding humus. Now the stubble is disked to a depth of about 7 inches. A relatively recent innovation is **strip cropping.** When strip cropping is combined with the use of ammonium nitrate and some sulfate, it is possible to grow a crop annually rather than every other year or two years in three.

Since the bulk of the wheat grown in the Columbia Plateau is soft and starchy, the price is lower than for hard wheat. Nor is this wheat in great demand in the United States. Hence, a large part of the crop is exported to Northwest Europe and the Far East (particularly to Japan but also to India and Pakistan).

The American Great Plains. The Great Plains of Canada and the United States comprise one of the world's leading wheat regions. The three Prairie Provinces of Canada account for virtually the entire Canadian wheat crop, and the nine American Great Plains states account for at least 70 per cent of the nation's wheat acreage.

Wheat production falls into two distinct regions—the Hard Spring-Wheat Belt and the Hard Red Winter-Wheat Belt (Figs. 16-4 and 16-5). They are not contiguous; between them is a belt ill suited to wheat, mostly because of sandy soils and sloping terrain.

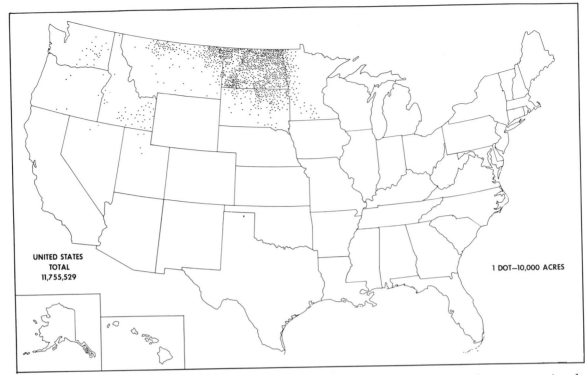

Fig. 16-4. Spring wheat in the United States. The Spring-Wheat Region (partly across the border in the three Prairie Provinces of Canada) is in the two Dakotas, western Minnesota, and northeastern Montana. The densest areas of wheat production are in the subhumid and semiarid portions of the Great Plains. (Courtesy of Bureau of the Census.)

From time to time wheat production in the Great Plains is affected by drought conditions. Heaviest damage from drought is in the twenty-county area in southwest Kansas, southeast Colorado, and the Oklahoma and Texas panhandles. However, the effects are felt, in greater or lesser degree, from the southernmost edge of the Great Plains in south Texas to the forested reaches of central Saskatchewan. There is a geographic axiom that steppe climates are risky for agriculture.

Northern Great Plains (Spring-Wheat Belt). This belt extends from the Red River Valley of Minnesota westward and northwestward to the Canadian Rockies and includes parts of Minnesota, North and South Dakota, and Montana in the United States, and parts of Manitoba, Saskatchewan, and Alberta in Can-

ada. This belt is limited on the north by a short frostless season and by infertile soils, and on the west by the Rocky Mountains.

Lying almost wholly within the Humid Continental with Medium Summers climatic realm, this belt is characterized by a frostless season of about four months and by a precipitation of 12 to 22 inches, most of which falls during the growth of the crop. The relatively cool summers enable the rainfall to go farther because of the reduced rate of evaporation. Summer days are long—16 to 18 hours.

Much of the terrain is level (Fig. 16-6)—the basin of old Lake Agassiz being so smooth and flat that artificial drainage is necessary in many places. To the west the surface is rolling. Soils, black and dark gray in color (prairie and chernozem), are fertile and productive. At about the 18-inch isohyet, the prairie and steppe overlap.

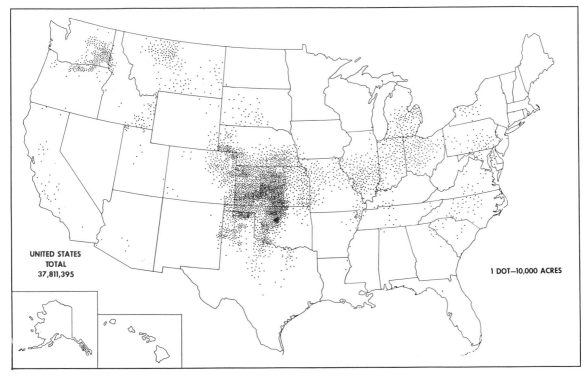

UNITED STATES
TOTAL
37,811,395

1 DOT—10,000 ACRES

Fig. 16-5. *Distribution of winter-wheat production in the United States. The winter-wheat "belt" of the southern Great Plains is particularly conspicuous. Important, too, are the Columbia Plateau and the Corn Belt. (Courtesy of Bureau of the Census.)*

The spring wheat grown here accounts for about 90 per cent of the total wheat acreage of Canada and about 30 per cent of that of the United States. Some **durum wheat** is grown here also.

Spring wheat grown here is hard, Canadian No. 1 being regarded as the world's best in strength and flavor. It also provides a higher flour yield than that of competing regions, a bushel outweighing by several pounds a bushel from the American segment of the region. In the southern portions of the Spring-Wheat Belt there is an increasing tendency to grow cold-resistant varieties of winter wheat.

Throughout the entire belt, farms are large and becoming larger, and they are highly mechanized. They are larger in Canada than in the United States. Nearly all the wheat is harvested with huge, fast-operating, and efficient combines. Many farmers own their combines, but many outfits still move northward

with the harvest season [1] as did the old threshing-machine outfits several decades ago.

Since the population is relatively small, the bulk of the wheat moves out of the area—to American and European markets. Canada, for example, exports regularly about four fifths of its total output. Most of the crop is trucked to primary elevators for storage, grading, and marketing. It then moves by rail to ports on the Great Lakes and by vessel to Europe or the American Atlantic ports. Some goes only as far as Buffalo, where it is milled. Substantial quantities, particularly from Alberta, move by rail to Vancouver and Prince Rupert, and thence to Europe via the Panama Canal; some even goes via rail to Fort Churchill on

[1] Harvesting, which begins in southern Texas in May, rolls northward, reaching the Dakotas and Montana in August and the Prairie Provinces well into September.

Fig. 16-6. Segment of an enormous field of wheat on the flat land of North Dakota. On these huge farms, every operation is performed by labor-saving equipment. (U.S. Department of Agriculture photograph.)

Hudson Bay and then by vessel to Northwest Europe.

This belt has been producing such enormous surpluses that foreign markets have not been able to absorb all the crop. Country and terminal elevators are choked, and the governments handle emergency storage. In 1960 the United States government owned outright, from all wheat-growing areas, over 1 billion bushels. The surpluses result primarily from the increasing use of commercial fertilizers, insecticides, and pesticides; greater employment of farm machinery (it may be used day and night and hence minimize losses resulting from bad weather) ; and crop improvement (rust-proof varieties).

The Middle and Southern Great Plains (Winter-Wheat Belt). This area, which grows hard winter wheat, is much smaller in size than that devoted to the production of spring wheat. Nevertheless, it ranks as one of the world's outstanding wheat regions, accounting for about 45 per cent of the total United States acreage in wheat. Kansas, which symbolizes wheat, alone produces more of this crop than either Argentina or Australia.

The area is characterized by smooth to gently rolling terrain and by extremely fertile soils—largely chernozems, chestnut browns, and chocolate-brown silt loams. No other American agricultural region, outside the Corn Belt, has so large a percentage of its land (80 per cent) suitable for crops. Chief handicap is the climatic variability, particularly the rainfall, which varies from about 12 inches in the west to about 25 inches in the east. Danger from killing frost is also a problem in spring after the wheat has come into head.

Blowing of soil is a major problem. According to some authorities, man has adjusted badly to the dry conditions in this region, much of which should have remained in grass. During the 1930s, tens of thousands of farm families had to leave the region, the majority going to California. Whole fields took flight; in many places the soil was blown off to the **plow sole.** The solution of this drought problem and of soil blowing rests largely with man: he must learn to work with nature, or he will fail and ultimately be driven from the land. This region of great climatic fluctuation and agricultural risk should be carefully studied by experts in the light of the mass of climatological data gathered by the United States Weather Bureau.

The wheat crop is harvested with large combines; sometimes on the largest farms one may see eight to thirty combines harvesting a 15,000-acre wheat field. They move relentlessly under the drying sun by day, and even at night if rain threatens. During good years the crop is tremendous. The *New York Times* said during the height of the 1959 harvest in Kansas: "Wheat today is more than a crop, more than the golden grain from which comes 'the staff of life.' Wheat is a symbol of a farm abundance that has become a major political-economic problem." [2]

No longer is this a one-crop region. Considerable corn is grown along the eastern portion for fodder, not for grain; much alfalfa is planted, and an extensive acreage of grain sorghums is growing in rotation with wheat.

A major wheat problem exists here as in all the other major growing regions. The government has a wheat-acreage allotment of 55 million acres, which is broken down by states and counties. Each farmer receives an allotment. When the allotment of 55 million acres was

worked out in 1938, it was based on average yields of that time and on the acreage needed to supply the domestic and export markets plus a reserve. However, as a result of expanded use of commercial fertilizer, there was a marked increase in yield per acre—14.5 bushels in 1937-1941, 17.3 bushels in 1953, 19.8 bushels in 1955, 27 bushels in 1958. Consequently, another government "brake"—the Soil Bank, paying farmers for making idle their surplus-producing acres—went into operation in 1956. About the only wheat moving abroad is that involved in subsidized sales and welfare programs. No solution is in sight, despite the millions of dollars being spent in an effort to balance production and consumption.

Soft Winter-Wheat Belt (American Middle West and Adjacent Ontario). Wheat in Anglo-America is not restricted to the subhumid and semiarid lands. It is grown also in the humid East, north of the Cotton Belt, where it is an important crop.

Throughout the region wheat is produced on a much smaller scale than in the regions to the west. Although the fields are small, mechanized equipment (including baby combines) is employed. Yields are high because the farmers use high-production seed, and government acreage allotments have discouraged growing wheat on any but the most productive land.

Although yields are high—40 to 60 and even more bushels per acre—the climate is far from ideal. Wheat should have a cool, moist growing season and a dry, sunny ripening period. Frequently, the winters here are too cold and lack sufficient snow to protect the plants from winter killing. If there is too much alternate freezing and thawing in late winter and early spring, the expansion and resultant lifting of the topsoil by freezing and the contraction of the thaw may gradually pull the wheat plants out of the ground. Finally, summers are often too rainy (and hot) for wheat during the ripening period. Accordingly, wheat is not the preferred crop that it is in the three regions already presented. Corn takes precedence, and wheat is grown mostly

[2] "Harvesting a 'Headache,'" *New York Times Magazine,* July 19, 1959, p. 6.

for use as flour for baking other than for bread (quick breads, pastries, and crackers), for feeding livestock, and for the purpose of equalizing the seasonal distribution of labor.

The entire Canadian production of winter wheat is in this region (southern Ontario), but winter wheat constitutes only 5 per cent of the total Canadian crop. This wheat cannot compete either in Canada or abroad with the high-quality Canadian spring wheat.

The Pampa of Argentina. Argentina usually is one of the four leading wheat exporters of the world, and in some years it ranks second only to Canada in the volume exported. For this reason there is a tendency to regard Argentina as one of the largest producers—when, as a matter of fact, it is one of the least important of the twelve major wheat regions, both in acreage and total output (Fig. 16-1).

Wheat in Argentina is largely confined to a relatively small area—a crescent that extends from Bahía Blanca to Santa Fé and has an over-all length of about 600 miles between the horns and a width of about 360 miles. The area is bounded on the west by the 18-inch isohyet; on the east by too much rain at harvest time and by poor drainage; on the north by increasing temperatures and humidity, a combination hostile to wheat; and on the south by aridity. Frost is never a threat, but drought and locusts are. In the 1950s Argentina at one stage was forced to import wheat because of drought. The land is flat as a floor, and the prairie soils are among the world's most fertile. Fortunately, almost the entire wheat-growing area lies within 150 miles of the principal exporting ports. Both winter and spring wheat are grown, but winter wheat is the more important; it is seeded in the autumn (March–May) and harvested in early to middle summer (December–January). But distribution between winter and spring wheat in Argentina is not definite. Argentina's wheat is both soft (80 per cent) and hard (20 per cent). The hard wheat is grown in the southern (drier) section.

The sparse agricultural population (less than ten working people to the square mile) plus the flat land, the large farms, and the

long, dry harvest season encourage the use of large agricultural equipment.

Generally wheat production is associated with the raising of beef cattle and the growing of alfalfa. The Argentine *estancieros* are interested primarily in cattle, not wheat; it is the tenant laborers who grow the crops. About 60 per cent of all wheat farms are tenant-operated. Highest yields, where the average is 17 to 20 bushels per acre, are procured in an area southwest of Rosario; lowest average yields of 6 to 9 bushels are in the dry southwest part of the crescent, west of Bahía Blanca. Wheat is crowded out of the best areas (that is, those that could yield highest) by corn, which yields twice as much as wheat and brings about the same price per bushel to the grower.

Although the number of country elevators has been increasing, there still is a great shortage. Accordingly, much wheat continues to be stored in bags at railway stations. The sacks are piled for storage in sheds and warehouses at the railway stations, most of which have from one to six galvanized sheet-steel sheds.

Northwest Europe. Since Northwest Europe is the recipient of the bulk of the world's exported wheat, and since it is not generally conceded to have a highly favorable combination of physical conditions for wheat, it might appear to be unimportant in wheat production; actually, however, it is one of the outstanding wheat regions in the world. The European continent as a whole is the most important wheat-producing area on earth (Fig. 16-1). Each nation not only grows wheat but tries to grow as much of it as possible. The best growing conditions and the highest yields are procured in the area lying west of the 20th meridian and between the 44° and 60° parallels (Table 16-1). High yields result mostly from the assiduous use of chemical fertilizers and manure.

The climate in Northwestern Europe is the Temperate Marine: rainfall averages about 30 inches, with a winter maximum; summers are cool (July average is about 65°F)—so cool, in fact, as to delay harvesting until middle or late summer; and winters are mild (January temperatures average about 36°F). The **growing season** is long—180 to 240 days.

For the most part, the terrain favors wheat production, and the gray-brown podzolic soils are among the best of all soils formed under a forest cover (though they are not really comparable with the black chernozems, the chestnut, and the chocolate-colored soils of subhumid and semiarid climates). The dense population, the small farms, and, in some areas, their fragmentation keep operations small, not permitting the use of the most efficient means of handling, and making for high production costs.

Since the wheat is soft, all the countries, even if they have a surplus, import some hard wheat (known as "corrective wheat") for mixing with their own. However, since they are high-cost producers and experience difficulty competing with foreign wheats even in their own markets, they must have high protective tariffs.

The Mediterranean Basin. As Figure 16-1 and Table 16-1 show, wheat is a very important crop throughout the peripheral portion of the Mediterranean Basin. The climate is highly favorable for winter wheat: winters are mild and rainy; summers are bright, sunny, and hot. The rough terrain of the area, however, restricts the percentage of tillable land. Nowhere else on earth does an outstanding producer of wheat utilize mountain slopes to so great an extent as Italy does: about one fourth of the crop is grown on land classed as mountains, one half on hill land, and only a fourth on plains. However, yields are highest on the Po Plain of the north. In the mountains, use is made of every spot of fertile valley; and considerable wheat is grown even on terraces.

Italy ranks first among the producing countries in this great basin. It is not often realized that Italy grows more wheat than Argentina. Wheat is Italy's basic crop. In recent years, however, there has been a large surplus of soft wheat; in 1956-1957 the country was trying to find markets for about a million tons of soft wheat. The surplus is the result of improved yields from more scientific production and of a change in eating habits: the Italians are eating more pasta products, made from durum wheat, and less bread, made from soft wheat.

Wheat is also an important crop in Spain and Algeria. It is grown widely throughout Spain, but the bulk of the crop is produced on the interior plateau—the Meseta. In Algeria, wheat is grown as far south as the 14-inch isohyet. Durum is the principal type produced up to an elevation of about 1,000 feet.

The Danubian Plain and Southern Russia. The Danubian Basin and the Crimea and Caucasus of Russia comprise one of the world's leading wheat-growing areas (Fig. 16-1). Here are to be found a desirable combination of favorable factors: a continental climate whose winters are cold and whose summers are hot; an annual precipitation varying from about 25 inches in the west to about 15 inches in the east; land that is largely plain; and soils, many loessial, that are fertile. The principal wheat-growing area in Hungary is a black-soil plain (western part of the chernozem and chestnut soil belts), which is hot and relatively dry during the ripening and harvesting period and is similar to the Hard Red Winter-Wheat Belt of the United States. Conversely, two conditions are unfavorable: frequent summer droughts, with consequent reduced yields; and the presence in Hungary of some sizable sandy areas.

In the nineteenth century, prior to the emergence of hard wheat in North America, Hungarian "strong wheats" (high in protein) were regarded as the world's best, and Hungarian milled flour commanded the top price in world markets. During the early twentieth century the introduction of high-yielding varieties with poor baking quality somewhat damaged the reputation of Hungarian wheat. It ranges from soft to hard, but the bulk is soft or semihard. Some spring wheat, probably about 2 per cent, also is grown.

The situation in Romania somewhat resembles that in Hungary. The best wheat areas lie in Moldavia between the Carpathian foothills and the Prut River. Many of the soils —particularly the chernozem, chestnut-brown, and chocolate-colored soils—favor wheat culture. Much of the wheat land in the Walachian Plain suffers from inadequate and poor seasonal distribution of rainfall.

Southern Russia (the Ukraine and North Caucasus areas) as far north as 50°, shows very heavy production of winter wheat with some growing as far as 58° to 60° north. Winters here are suitable for fall-sown wheat, and there is adequate snow to protect the crop from being winter killed. Today, as a result of advances in plant breeding, wheat is grown much farther north than was possible in the past.

North of the chernozem soils are the forest soils, largely **podsols**, which are poorly suited to wheat, particularly spring wheat, since it is more exacting in its soil requirements than winter wheat, preferring a well-drained loamy soil, neutral in reaction. Podsols are noted for their high acidity, low organic content, and poor drainage.

There is no sharp line separating the Russian Winter-Wheat and Spring-Wheat Regions, but northeast of Rostov spring wheat assumes preeminence. The two areas together make up the largest wheat region in the world (Fig. 16-1). Physical conditions are similar to those in the Anglo-American Hard Winter-Wheat and Spring-Wheat Belts. The terrain in the Ukraine is essentially flat, and the predominant black chernozem soils are fertile. It is climate, however, that plays the limiting role even in southern Russia. The growing season is short—only 151 days at Kharkov, in the same latitude as southern Minnesota. The growing season northward, from Leningrad to Moscow, is 110 to 130 days. In the non-chernozem belt, the winters are so severe and often the snow cover is so uneven and unreliable as to necessitate the planting of spring wheat. Precipitation in the non-chernozem zone averages about 20 inches. Hence, north of it both winter and spring wheat are grown. Although the amount of each fluctuates from year to year, in most years spring wheat comprises far more acreage than winter wheat— 70 to 90 per cent. Much of the region is deficient in moisture; drought has always plagued Russian agriculture with low yields

and recurring crop failures; thus famine is not alien to Russia.

These hazards are reflected in the low per-acre yield—about 12 bushels, compared with 37 in France and 26 in the United States. The enormous wheat acreage in the Soviet Union is obviously a limiting factor in making comparisons, as is the lack of incentives among the collectivized Russian peasantry. One way per-acre yields can be raised is by increasing the use of fertilizers—especially in the northern part of the region, where inferior podsol soils account for roughly one fourth of the tillable land available for crops. Fertilizer consumption was planned to increase about threefold between 1958 and 1965, a result of recent important discoveries of phosphate and potash deposits in the Soviet Union.

Russian wheat, whether in this Winter-Wheat Region or in the Spring-Wheat Region presented next, is grown on a large scale on collective and state farms.

The Russian Spring-Wheat Region. This region, the world's largest wheat-growing area, reaches from the lower Volga near Duyashambe northeastward to the Ural Mountains and beyond (Fig. 16-1). About 90 per cent of Europe's spring-wheat acreage is here. However, over much of the region north and east of the Caspian Sea, not more than 5 per cent of the land is arable, and nowhere over sizable tracts does the percentage exceed 20.

In this region, which is bounded by the 60° July isotherm on the north and the 10-inch isohyet on the south, nearly all of Russia's spring wheat is produced. Much of the region is semiarid steppe. Winters are severe, and over most of the region the growing season is relatively short—120 to 150 days.

A very considerable part of the region, too, is subject to summer drought by an extension from the south and east of the desert climate of Central Asia and from the southeast of the Mediterranean summer climate. Thus, lack of rainfall limits wheat output more than any other factor. Another climatic hazard is the threat of early frost, particularly if spring comes late or delays occur in sowing or harvesting. Because of these hazards, plus the fact that much of this region lies in the center of Eurasia, average yields tend to be low—near 7½ bushels per acre.

The level to gently rolling terrain favors mechanization and large-scale farming. The soils, largely the famous black chernozems and the chestnut-browns, extend in a narrow wedge into Siberia and northern Kazakhstan. Prior to World War II, this famous soil belt comprised roughly three fourths of the estimated tillable acreage available for crops.

Durum wheat is grown in considerable quantity, particularly along the southern margin of the Spring-Wheat Region, because it yields a flour well suited to quality bread.

So badly does the Soviet Union need wheat that in the 1930s—as the fertile chernozem soils became fully occupied—production was pushed northward into the non-chernozem (podsolic) soils (without impressive results). In the 1950s, wheat was introduced on a very large scale in the "new lands" of Kazakhstan, where results were far better—15.6 million tons in 1958. Since this program is being carried out in a risky zone, where drought is an ever present threat, unstable yields and frequent crop failures must be anticipated. Despite the glowing reports of success by the Russian press, Soviet figures must be viewed with considerable restraint.

Russia, once the world wheat granary and largest exporter, has not been a major factor in foreign trade for several decades. In Russia, foreign trade is a matter of government decision rather than of economic forces in a free market. However, the major factor in the decline of wheat exports has been the lag of production behind the growth of population—particularly the urban population, which the government is responsible for feeding.

Winter- and Spring-Wheat Region of North China (Including Manchuria). North China ranks as one of the major wheat-producing regions of the world. In fact, North China has a wheat acreage believed to be as large as that of the United States. Wheat is China's second most important crop and, on the basis of acreage alone, exceeds rice in importance. North China grows both winter and spring wheat. Nearly all the crop is graded as soft and is characterized by low gluten content and a high percentage of moisture. The people of North China are wheat and millet-kaoliang eaters, *not* rice eaters. Wheat and rice are not grown in the same areas. Wheat is grown mostly between the two great rivers—the Hwang Ho and the Yangtze-Kiang.

In this wheat region the rainfall is scanty (the average is about 24 inches) and unreliable, but summer is the season of maximum fall; long droughts or summer floods often bring crop failure, hardship, and even famine. The growing season is about 240 days in length. The terrain varies from hill country to mountains and plains, but the portion in plain is small. The soils are alluvial and loessial. The Hwai Ho comprises the boundary between the noncalcareous soils to the south and the generally calcareous soils to the north. The best soils for wheat are those receiving limited precipitation. Where winter wheat can be grown, the crop is planted in October and harvested in May or June. The same land is then planted in a summer crop—millet or kaoliang.

Methods are **intensive** by Western standards. Little machinery is employed. Yields are low—14 to 16 bushels per acre. Since little attention is given to seed selection, the quality of the wheat is poor. And the antiquated methods of threshing make almost certain the inclusion of much dirt and chaff. Though most of the crop is planted in pure stands, a considerable part of that grown in the Yangtze Delta and in the Szechwan Basin is interplanted with legumes—peas, beans, and rape seed.

In the Manchurian segment, the climate is more typically continental (same latitude as the Dakotas). Winters are long and bitterly cold; summers are short and generally very hot—temperatures of 103.5°F have been recorded. The growing season is 125 to 140 days in length. The precipitation averages 23 to 27 inches in the better areas, with approximately 60 to 80 per cent falling in June, July, and August—height of the growing season. This area cannot be regarded as entirely favorable for wheat.

THE WORLD'S CEREALS : : 323

The preferred wheat land is that lying between the mountain ranges, where the soils are quite fertile. Yields run 10 to 16 bushels per acre. However, little attention is given to seed selection, and the quality of the grain is poor—low in gluten and high in moisture. Almost the entire crop is soft spring wheat.

Northwestern India and Adjacent Pakistan. India and Pakistan together comprise an outstanding wheat-growing region (they rank fourth in acreage and fifth in world production). The most important part is the Punjab, which is reported to account for nearly a third of the total acreage (Fig. 16-1). In the Punjab and the Sind, wheat is irrigated; accordingly, the harvests are dependable and the yields reliable. The second most important wheat-growing area lies in the black regur soils of the northwestern Deccan Plateau. Although the precipitation averages only 20 to 40 inches, it is concentrated during the brief summer season; and the soils are extremely retentive of moisture. But where wheat must depend upon the light autumn rains of the fickle winter monsoon, production is uncertain. The semihard winter wheat grown here is harvested in the hot, dry early spring, just before the summer monsoon bursts. Most of the land given over to wheat is favorable from the standpoint of terrain, since the crop is planted in the wide valleys of the Indus and Ganges Rivers.

Yields in India average among the lowest of the twelve major wheat regions—about 12 bushels per acre; and one of the lowest average yields for a given area is the 3.4 bushels registered for the province of Hyderabad. Low productivity has plagued Indian farmers for generations. The use of chemical fertilizers has been traditionally negligible; even the manure of the 200 million cattle is used largely for fuel rather than for fertilizer.

The Indian subcontinent formerly exported wheat, but virtually none has been exported in recent years; in fact, the countries are now large importers.

Winter-Wheat Region of Australia. Although Australia's is one of the smaller of the twelve major wheat regions of the world, and although it accounts for only about 5 per cent of world production, its international significance is great because it is one of the four major exporters. Wheat is Australia's most important single crop; it occupies approximately one half of all the land in crops. The total wheat acreage, however, occupies but a fraction (less than 1 per cent) of the country's area. Broadly speaking, the wheat belt is a broken strip of country (between the desert and the mountains) extending southward from southern Queensland into New South Wales and across the northwest of Victoria into South Australia (Fig. 16-1); a smaller wheat belt lies in Western Australia inland from Perth.

The Australian crop is grown in the drier inland districts, where the rainfall is 25 inches or less. However, more important than the amount of moisture is the time when it falls—April and May and again in September and October. The wheat region does suffer from the vagaries of climate; thus in 1957, when a prolonged and severe drought cut the crop by 75 per cent, wheat had to be imported in large amounts. Normally, however, production greatly exceeds domestic requirements, so that about two thirds of the output is available for export. Only about one third of the area is in wheat at one time, the rest either being in **fallow** or not under cultivation at all. This means that Australian wheat is dry-farmed wheat.

Most of the terrain on which wheat is grown is level to gently rolling, for the slopes of the mountains descend to almost level plains.

Australia's wheat lands benefit from proximity to tidewater—few parts lie more than 100 miles from an ocean port. On the deficit side, Australia lies far from the world's major markets in Western Europe. However, the area is quite well located with respect to the growing wheat markets of India, Pakistan, Communist China, Japan, and the Philippines.

All the wheat is winter wheat and until recently was classed as soft to semihard. However, a new variety developed in South Australia is reported to have a higher protein content and good baking qualities. Because of the heat and aridity, particularly at the end of the growing season, per-acre yields are low —about 20 bushels—lower than in Argentina, Canada, and the United States (Table 16-1).

Since farms are large—400 to 1,200 acres— and since farm labor is scarce and expensive and land relatively cheap, much labor-saving farm equipment, specially adapted to Australian conditions, is utilized.

WHEAT IN INTERNATIONAL TRADE

No cereal enters foreign trade to so great an extent as wheat. Exports are more than double those prior to World War II. Northwest Europe is the market for the bulk of the world's surplus crop, receiving much of the surpluses from the United States, Canada, Argentina, and Australia. Before the war, Canada led the world in exports; today the United States does. Argentina and Australia with relatively small populations are obviously large exporters.

An important postwar development in wheat marketing, has been the adoption of the International Wheat Agreement of August 1, 1949, with forty-two importing and six exporting countries as members. The agreement was designed to bring about a reasonably orderly marketing procedure in the best interests of both surplus and deficient countries. Unfortunately, not all countries joined—not even the United Kingdom, one of the world's largest importers. Nevertheless, the agreement did include 90 per cent of the world's wheat trade. That there is need for such an agreement seems to indicate world overproduction of wheat.

RICE

The two leading cereals of the world used directly as food by man are wheat and rice. Wheat is the preferential grain of much of the Western world, whereas rice is the preferred grain of the Orient.

LOCATION OF RICE CROPS

Figure 16-7 shows where rice is grown over the earth. The overwhelming weight of the Orient is immediately apparent. Hence most of the discussion on rice in this book has to do with the crop in Monsoon Asia; only sec-

ondary consideration is given to Italy, Spain, Brazil, Peru, and the United States. China, India, Japan, and Indonesia are the principal producing countries.

Rice is adapted to the growing conditions in hot, wet climates, and it keeps well in storage for a longer time than does any other cereal. Yet it is more at home in the subtropics than in the tropics, for the periodicity of photosynthesis encourages higher yields. Methods of production vary from country to country according to the amount of rainfall, type of soil, and kind of terrain.

Rice fields almost never receive rainfall with sufficient regularity and in adequate amount to enable the farmer to plant and mature a satisfactory crop. In Thailand, for example, rice needs about 70 inches of water to yield a good crop; but the actual rainfall totals about 60 inches. Accordingly, if wet-land rice is to be grown successfully, the rainfall everywhere must be supplemented. So heavy are the plant's water demands that some authorities on rice question the wisdom of growing the crop in desert areas such as Egypt, West Pakistan, and Peru.

Rice requires level land because several inches of water must cover the field until the grain is ripe. The soils should be reasonably fertile and should be underlain by impervious clay. On the other hand, rice does not require particularly fertile soils because very little plant food is removed in the growing of the crop; only the grain is taken by man.

Generally speaking, rice is seeded in two different ways: by transplanting and by broadcasting. When transplanted, the seed is first sowed in a seedbed until the sprouted seedling is of sufficient size for setting in the rice field. While the young plants in the seedbed are growing, the fields are plowed and harrowed several times and then placed under 2 to 4 inches of water (Fig. 16-8). The seedlings are then transplanted to the paddy. When sown broadcast, the seed may be put on irrigated or unirrigated land. On the latter it is known as **upland rice**, which is of lower quality than **paddy rice**.

Throughout most of Monsoon Asia, rice is harvested with a sickle or hand knife. It is

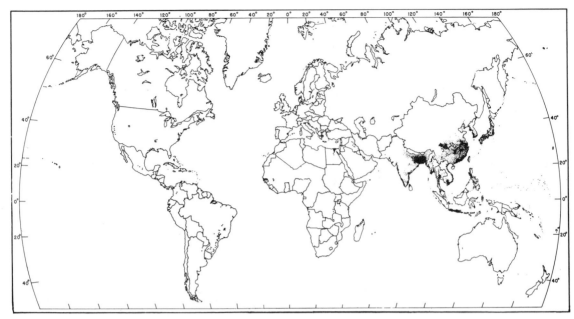

Fig. 16-7. World rice production. In Monsoon Asia the words rice and food are synonymous. Heavy rice concentration is to be seen in the valleys and deltas of all major rivers. The favorable climate, soil, and terrain are not the sole explanation of rice's importance here. The crop could be grown in nearly all tropical and subtropical lands having sufficient rainfall or adequate water for irrigation. This region's rank stems in large part, therefore, from the numbers and abilities of its hardworking people. (Courtesy of U.S. Department of Agriculture.)

then placed in bunches on sheets of grass matting or on clean baked soil and threshed by workers, who tread on it with their feet. If animals are owned, they may be used to trample the rough rice. The threshed rice is often winnowed, so that the wind carries away the chaff, while the heavier grain falls into a basket. Some small mechanized equipment has recently been developed for small paddies by the Japanese. Only in the more advanced countries and in those with much land and small populations are reapers, binders, and combines used—particularly in the United States, Brazil, and Mexico.

In considering the geography of rice, it is worth noting that even though the crop meets the dominant food requirements of about half the world's population, less is known scientifically about it than about any other major crop. A challenging problem is the great number of varieties—at least 7,000. And a rice that does well in one country does not necessarily do so in another. Other reasons for limited knowledge are that rice for the most part is a subsistence crop remaining on the farms where grown, and that the majority of the larger rice-growing nations are among the more backward countries in scientific agriculture. Steps are now being taken in Monsoon Asia to assemble more scientific information about this crop: eight Asiatic countries—India, Pakistan, Burma, Ceylon, Indonesia, Thailand, Malaysia, and the Philippine Republic —recently joined in a United Nations program for improving rice, particularly yields.

RICE PRODUCTION TODAY

More land is being made available for rice in Southeast and East Asia, improved strains of the cereal are being developed and grown here and there, and far more commercial fertilizer is being used than ever before; however, rice production still is not keeping pace with the increase in population.

Fig. 16-8. Planting rice in paddy field, Japan. The planting period is the busiest time of the year for the Japanese rice farmer. The men with oxen have prepared the fields; women are removing the rice seedlings from the seedbeds preparatory to planting them shoot by shoot. (Courtesy of Consulate General of Japan.)

Rice yields are highly variable; but in general they are highest in those rice-growing lands farthest from the equator, where the additional sunlight of longer days promotes plant growth (Table 16-2).

About 94 per cent of the world's entire rice crop is consumed in Asia, three fourths of it in China, India, and Japan. Asiatics on the average consume 300 to 400 pounds of rice annually, whereas Americans consume only 6 pounds. Unfortunately, the large rice-eating populations consume white or polished rice, which is low in vitamin content. All of rice-eating Asia suffers considerably from beriberi and related disorders.

ASIA

The importance of rice to Monsoon Asia's enormous population cannot be exaggerated.

Rice not only reflects the social and economic pattern of life for the agricultural masses of Monsoon Asia, but it is also the symbol of their hopes. Rice is the peasant farmer's means of subsistence, his first need and principal possession, his medium of exchange, and standard of value.[3]

Any disruption in the crop, no matter how slight, leads to hardship, economic disaster, and possible famine, since the people live very close to starvation. There is no sizable reserve for emergencies.

China. China ranks first among all countries in rice production; in fact, it is not unlikely that she produces more rice than all the rest of the world combined.

[3] M. K. Bennett and V. D. Wickizer, *Rice in Monsoon Asia,* Food Research Institute, Stanford University, California, 1941, p. 312.

TABLE 16-2

AVERAGE YIELDS PER ACRE OF ROUGH RICE, 1960-1961

Country	Pounds
Burma	1,494
China, Communist	2,353
Indochina	
Cambodia	941
Laos	747
Viet-Nam	1,325
India	1,353
Korea	2,488
Japan	4,348
Indonesia	1,541
Philippines	1,007
Thailand	1,174
Mexico	1,781
United States	3,411
Brazil	1,479
Peru	3,529
Italy	4,291
Spain	5,084
Egypt	4,469
Australia	5,200
World	1,720

SOURCE: "World Summaries: Crops and Livestock," *Foreign Crops and Markets*, Foreign Agricultural Service, U.S.D.A., June 29, 1961, pp. 6-7.

The rice-growing region in China—that is, the part where rice is the dominant crop—lies between 23° and 33° north latitude (Fig. 16-7). The northern limit is determined by both climate (the 32° isotherm for January and the 30-inch isohyet of annual precipitation) and soil (the southern limit of limey soils that are too porous to retain enough water for rice). Heaviest acreage and production are to be found in the lower valleys and deltas of the Yangtze-Kiang and the Si-Kiang.

The following physical conditions favor rice growing here: (1) the level terrain; (2) the Humid Subtropical climate, with its hot summers and somewhat mild winters, high humidity, and annual precipitation of 38 to 60 inches; (3) ample supplementary water supply during the entire growing season; and (4) heavy clay soils, with relatively impervious subsoils. Despite these favorable factors, the amount of farmland is limited: only 11 per cent of all China is arable; most of the rest is too rough, too cold, or too dry for agricultural use. This point is particularly significant in

a country of 700 million inhabitants, increasing by about 15 million persons a year. Moreover, for generations China has been regarded as the poorest nation in Asia from the standpoint of diet—averaging only 1,830 calories per capita per day.

On the human side, it may be said that China is following the Soviet Union in collectivizing agriculture (by 1960, 96 per cent of all Chinese peasant households had been forced into collectives). The rice crop is grown with a lavish use of manpower: 750 manhours of labor are employed to produce a single acre of rice, compared with 25 in the United States. Although some progress is being made in better selection of seed, somewhat wider use of fertilizers and pesticides, and control of plant diseases, methods and equipment still are antiquated by Western standards. The really crucial question is not how much per-acre yields of rice can be raised but whether production can outdistance population.

India-Pakistan. These two countries rank second in importance only to China among rice-growing lands. Principal producing areas include the lower Ganges–Brahmaputra Valleys and the coastal lowlands, deltas, and valleys bordering the Deccan Plateau (Fig. 16-7). In these areas the climate is mostly Monsoon Tropical, being characterized by a distinct rainy season and a distinct dry season. In the rice-growing lands the rainfall is about 50 inches or more, except in irrigated areas such as the lower Indus. In the Ganges–Brahmaputra Delta, the Rainy Tropical climate prevails; here there is rain every month in the year, though the amount is small in November, December, and January.

Because of poverty of soil, imperfect drainage, poor cultural methods, fragmentation of farms, limited use of machinery, and neglect of manure and commercial fertilizers, rice yields in India are low (Table 16-2). The bulk of the rice crop is consumed domestically, and a huge importation is necessary.

Japan. Although Japan ranks well below China and India in rice acreage and produc-

Fig. 16-9. Growing rice on terraces, Japan. With 75 per cent of Japan's area mountainous and only 16 per cent arable, and with a population exceeding 92 million, the Japanese must grow quantities of rice. On the best lands, rice yields of 75 bushels per acre are procured, and the national average is 41 bushels. Only densely populated countries with cheap labor can afford to grow rice on terraced land like this. (Courtesy of Consulate General of Japan.)

tion, it has made much fuller use of its rice lands through scientific methods. It is significant that Japan feeds more than four persons from each acre. The yield per acre is by far the highest in Asia—double that of Burma and Thailand and triple that of India (Table 16-2). On the best rice-producing lands, yields exceeding 75 bushels per acre are common. The crop is grown on all level floodplains, deltas, and even on mountainsides (Fig. 16-9). So great is the pressure of population that every square foot of potential rice land is pressed into use. Fifty-five per cent of the land under cultivation is in wet (paddy) rice. In parts of the islands two crops of rice are grown on the same field annually, and in extremely favored parts three crops are grown—so that heavy fertilization is required. The Japanese claim to be the world's leader in the intensive use of fertilizer, each farmer averaging annually 221 pounds per acre.

Physical conditions—particularly the heavy rain, with maximum fall in summer, and the hot summer temperatures—are highly favorable for rice production. Furthermore, unlike most rice farmers of the rest of Asia, the Japanese are literate; they read farm bulletins, get weather forecasts and market reports from their radios, and employ modern scientific methods. Accordingly, they have pushed rice production as far north as northeastern Honshu and even Hokkaido, where climatic conditions are less favorable than in the lands to the south.

High-yielding strains of seed (mostly hybrids) are used, and nearly the entire crop (except the upland varieties) is transplanted. Weak rice plants are removed from the seedbed. The seed is treated with hot water and chemicals to reduce losses from seed-borne disease. Hence the per-acre yields in 1961 were 13 per cent higher than in 1950. Japan's output of rice has risen almost to the place where imports are no longer necessary.

In transplanting, the rice shoots are set out in north-south rows to give them the maximum amount of sunlight; and they are set 4 or 5 inches apart in rows 1½ to 2 feet apart to facilitate hand weeding and cultivation. The paddy fields get four weedings per season. One hundred days later, the rice is ready for harvesting.

Much labor is employed in producing Japan's annual crop of rice. However, partly as a result of American postwar occupation and the wide adoption of machinery for every

THE WORLD'S CEREALS : : 329

Fig. 16-10. Javanese rice growers laboring on rice terraces near Bandung, Java. Torrential rains are frequent in summer (note clouds). (Courtesy of Indonesian Consulate.)

possible task, the Japanese are currently utilizing more mechanized equipment in their rice fields than at any time in the nation's history.

Indonesia. After China, India-Pakistan, and Japan, Indonesia is the largest producer of rice. Much of the total crop is grown in densely populated Java (Fig. 16-10). Farms average only about 2 acres in size. Yet on this mountainous island, two thirds of the area is under cultivation. After the rice is harvested, the fields are prepared again for a second crop or, if the water supply is limited, for a dry-land crop—maize (corn), sweet potatoes, or peanuts. Little land is in permanent rice fields outside of Java and Sumatra. Elsewhere a shifting (slash-and-burn) type of cultivation, known as "ladang," is followed. The big problem faced by Indonesia is how to produce enough food (rice) to care for the large and rapidly growing population of 82 millions when the rice output already is 11 per cent below domestic needs.

The Rice-Bowl Countries. Burma, the former Indochina, and Thailand comprise the so-called Rice Bowl of Monsoon Asia (Fig. 16-7): since their populations are much sparser than those of China, India, and Japan, they have long supplied the extra rice that the densely populated countries need. Before the outbreak of World War II, these three nations not only made up the rice deficits of India, British Malaya, Ceylon, China, the Netherlands Indies, and the Philippines, but they supplied in addition about 60 per cent of the rice requirements of Europe. They even exported impressive amounts of rice to Latin America, especially to the Caribbean countries, and to Africa. The importance of rice here is apparent from the fact that 71 per cent of the cultivated land in Burma is devoted to rice, as is 90 per cent of that in Thailand.

Korea. Rice dominates the agriculture of Korea, the crop being grown wherever the land is good enough to permit; hence about 30 per cent of the total crop area is in rice.

Rice attains greatest importance in the plains of the south (Fig. 16-7). Much of the country is too mountainous, and in the north the winters are too long and cold for sustaining a rice economy. Formerly Korea exported rice to Japan, but now the country is a deficit area.

Philippine Republic. Rice is the basic crop of the Philippines, about half the cultivated area being devoted to it. Eighty per cent of the crop is paddy rice; only 20 per cent, upland rice. Three fourths of the population eats rice, but domestic output is inadequate to meet the needs. Hence, some rice is imported from the Rice-Bowl countries. Nearly all the crop is grown on the west side of the mountains in Luzon, including the central plain (40 per cent of the total rice crop), where the southwest monsoon brings copious summer rains. The eastern mountain slopes of Luzon, Samar, Leyte, and most of Mindanao receive rain throughout the year; and although some rice is grown there, they are not outstanding in output. Where irrigation water is available, two crops are grown in the same fields annually. Most famous rice terraces in the world are those built by the Ifugaos in the mountains of Luzon.

United States. The United States is a small rice producer (it contributes about 1 per cent of the world crop). However, since at times it ranks among the top three nations in exports, and since its methods of production differ so markedly from those in Monsoon Asia (rice is grown **extensively** in the United States, **intensively** in the Far East), some discussion of it seems warranted.

Rice growing in the United States is highly localized. Commercially only three areas merit attention (Fig. 16-7): (1) the Coastal Prairie of Louisana and Texas (accounting for about 55 per cent of the domestic crop); (2) the Grand Prairie of Arkansas (about 20 per cent); and (3) the Sacramento Valley of California (about 25 per cent). All three areas have extensive plains with fertile soils, mostly silt loams, clay loams, or silty clays. The rice lands in each area are fertilized and rotated. Sometimes fields are rested every third year. In Arkansas, instead of allowing a field to lie fallow, farmers dump catfish and buffalo fish into the flooded fields. Yields in such fields always are higher because the fish have eaten harmful weeds and deposited rich waste. The subsoils in the rice-growing areas are heavy and slowly permeable, a quality that is essential if 3 to 9 inches of water are to be retained on the soil until just before harvest. Such heavy soils are of only limited value for other crops.

California's climate is the Mediterranean Subtropical (precipitation about 16 inches); that in the South is the Humid Subtropical (precipitation 34 to 58 inches). In neither is there sufficient rainfall to meet the heavy water requirements of the rice plant. However, there is ample water for irrigation: from wells in Arkansas, from rivers and bayous in Louisiana and Texas, and from streams in California. The growing season is long—about 286 days in the Coastal Prairie and about 155 days in the Sacramento Valley. Summers are extremely hot.

The relatively sparse population in all American areas allowed the rice growers to purchase huge holdings, which are essential where large mechanized equipment, particularly the self-propelled harvester, is to be used. In California the rice seed is sown from aircraft. The advantages of this method of seeding are that it is fast, slightly less seed is required, and less attention need be given the seedbed. Airplanes also are employed for putting on all kinds of chemicals—fertilizer, weed killers, insecticides.

California rice differs from that in the South —the result of climate. California grows only short and medium grain, whereas the South produces long-grained rice. Consumers in this country prefer the long-grained variety, apparently because it was the first to be grown and marketed here. Therefore, since very little California rice is eaten in the domestic market (except by the Japanese population in California), most California rice is exported.

FOREIGN TRADE IN RICE

The quantity of rice that gets into international trade is small—generally 5 to 10 per cent of total world output. More than 90 per cent emanates from Burma, Thailand, and the United States. Among the large producers in Monsoon Asia, only Burma and Thailand grow enough rice to feed their own populations and to export impressive quantities. Hence the "Rice Bowl" has great political as well as economic significance. India, Pakistan, Ceylon, China, and Indonesia purchase most of the surplus rice, because their populations are large and growing so rapidly that they positively cannot meet their own rice requirements.

Foreign trade in rice is subject to many restrictions: government monopolies, government-to-government trade agreements, barter agreements, export-import controls, subsidies, import duties, currency controls, preferential tariffs, and rebates. The United States is one of the very few rice-growing nations whose rice trade is not restricted.

RYE

Rye is a bread grain and like wheat possesses gluten, which gives the dough great elasticity as the yeast ferments; gas bubbles form in the dough, making it rise and increase in volume. However, dough made solely from rye flour makes a loaf of bread generally regarded as inferior to one made solely from hard-wheat flour. Rye bread, nonetheless, is consumed daily by millions of people, principally because it is low in price and because rye does better than wheat in the lands where it is the major cereal. However, the production and consumption of rye are declining over the world. Heavy consumption today is restricted to the area north of the 50th parallel, extending from the North Sea, across Europe and Asia, to the Sea of Okhotsk.

LOCATION OF RYE CROPS

Figure 16-11 shows that rye is essentially a European crop, that continent accounting for about 96 per cent of the world's total output. The Rye Belt in Europe lies north of the Wheat Belt; this means that rye can be produced where soil and climate conditions are not quite good enough for wheat. While some rye is grown on the fertile soils of Central

Russia and the northern Great Plains of America, the bulk of the crop is produced on poor sandy and heath soils. Without rye in such areas, the human populations there would be materially reduced.

Winter hardiness with a minimum loss is one of the superior characteristics of rye—one that makes the crop a godsend in climates too cool for wheat. When sown in autumn, rye will grow in areas where winter temperatures drop to —40°F and where even the mean winter temperature is about zero. Thus in Europe rye is grown as far north as the 67th parallel (Fig. 16-11). The moisture requirements are less exacting than are those of wheat—usually the amount of precipitation averaging from 20 to 30 inches, with the maximum falling in summer.

As far as soil is concerned, rye is the least demanding of all the small grains, withstanding considerable acidity or alkalinity, exhausted soils, peaty soils, sandy soils, and moors. The crop's tolerance for sandy soil goes far to explain its widespread distribution over Northern Europe. Finally, rye suffers less from damage by insect pests and diseases than does wheat.

EUROPE

Figure 16-11 shows that three countries—Germany, Poland, and Russia—produce most of the rye grown on the continent and in the world; in fact, they account for 95 per cent of the world output (the Soviet Union alone contributing 51 per cent). Most of the Russian crop is grown in the taiga on the strongly leached, acid, non-chernozem soils—soils poorly adapted to wheat. The cool summers also favor rye.

Poland generally ranks next to the Soviet Union in rye production, accounting for about 16 per cent of the world output. Germany contributes about 12 per cent of the world's rye. In Poland and Germany, as in Russia, rye is grown where climatic and soil conditions do not favor wheat.

ANGLO-AMERICA

Rye is not an outstanding crop in Anglo-America. However, prior to World War I,

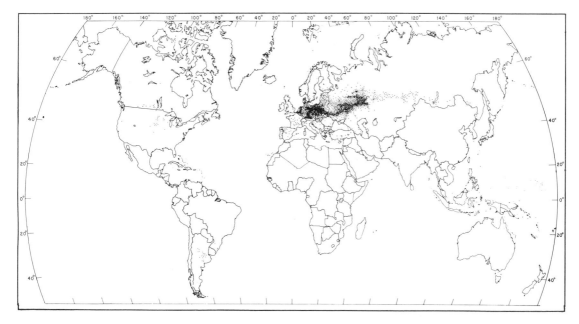

Fig. 16-11. World rye production. Rye is hardy—it can stand cold, cloudy, wet weather and infertile soils. It is, accordingly, a major crop in the northern marginal agricultural lands of Germany, Poland, and Russia. About 95 per cent of the world crop is grown in Europe. (Courtesy of U.S. Department of Agriculture.)

some rye was grown—mainly on the sandy soils of Michigan, Wisconsin, and Minnesota, and on the depleted soils of Pennsylvania, New Jersey, and eastern New York. Today the crop is confined largely to the northern Great Plains (both the United States and Canada), where—because winter wheat is excluded and because rye supplies feed in seasons when spring-sown crops do badly—it fits into the system of farming.

RYE IN INTERNATIONAL TRADE

Rye is a "stay-at-home" cereal, only 2 to 4 per cent of the total crop getting into international trade. Trade in rye is restricted largely to Europe itself, the chief exporters generally being the Soviet Union, Poland, and Czechoslovakia. The importers are entirely within Europe, mainly Germany, the Scandinavian countries, Finland, the Danubian nations, the Netherlands, and Belgium.

BARLEY

Barley is an important world crop, though less so than wheat, rye, rice, or even corn.

It is grown primarily for feed, though in Mediterranean climates a considerable amount is grown for malting. Barley comes into its own in areas where the rearing of livestock is important but where temperatures are too cool for corn to mature (for grain). Barley and oats are competitors: barley is preferred in places where it outyields oats; if it does not, oats is preferred. In areas where all the bread grains do poorly, barley is consumed by man as his chief cereal. In addition, barley is used in making soup, porridge, baby foods, beer, ale, and whiskey.

LOCATION OF BARLEY CROPS

Figure 16-12 shows where the world's barley is grown. This cereal resembles wheat in its distribution; *however, barley has a wider climatic range than wheat. In fact, its ecological range is wider than that of any other small grain; because of its low warmth requirement, barley can mature in a shorter period than any other small grain.* This quality enables barley to extend farthest north (in Finland beyond the Arctic Circle) and (be-

THE WORLD'S CEREALS :: 333

Fig. 16-12. World barley production. Heaviest concentration is in Europe and adjacent North Africa. Russia is the leader in both acreage and production. Almost three fourths of the world's barley is grown in Europe and the Near East. It surpasses all other small grains in resisting dry heat. It is mostly fall-sown on desert margins; spring-sown in the cooler, moister areas. In the last decade, world barley production has soared. (Courtesy of U.S. Department of Agriculture.)

cause of its rare ability to mature in the short rainy period of the desert margin) slightly farther into hot, dry regions such as North Africa. Moreover, barley can be grown at the highest elevations of all cereals, with the one exception of quinoa.[4] Barley is grown up to 10,000 feet in Tibet.

Barley's moisture demands are less than are those of wheat and oats. The fact that barley can mature in a short season has given it a reputation for being drought-resistant—a reputation hardly accurate. *Barley is a drought-escaping, not a drought-resisting crop.*

Barley can endure high temperatures if the area is dry, but a combination of great heat and high humidity is as fatal to barley as it is to wheat. Hence barley is absent from the wet tropics.

[4] Quinoa, the grain that grows highest in the Andes, was sacred to the Incas. It is grown on virtually every farm in the Bolivian Altiplano. It produces a crop when all other cereals fail.

Barley needs fertile soils even more than does wheat. The crop cannot thrive on poor sandy soils as can rye. It also demands good drainage. Hence, it is ill suited to heavy clay soils in humid regions. Nor does barley do well in acid soils; its aversion to such soils helps to account for its importance in Mediterranean lands.

IMPORTANCE TO EUROPE

Prior to World War II, about 72 per cent of the world's barley acreage was in Europe. The crop extends across the entire continent from the North Sea and the Baltic Sea to the Black Sea and the Mediterranean Sea, and eastward to the Ural Mountains of Russia and to Iran. Approximately 72 per cent of world acreage and production is in Europe and the Middle East, Russia being the most important individual country.

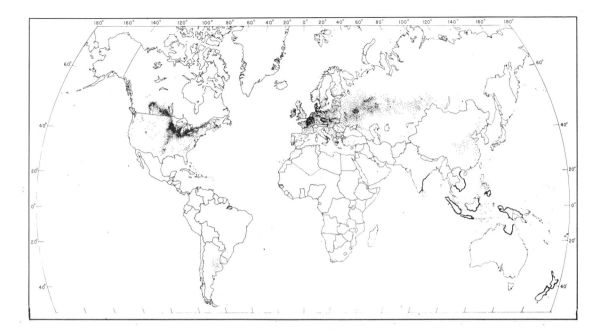

Fig. 16-13. World oat production. This crop is largely confined to the Northern Hemisphere and to higher middle latitudes. It is nowhere important in the tropics. It does well in areas having cool, wet summers; when oats are grown in hotter areas, as in the American Cotton and Corn Belts, they may serve as a hay crop or as a rotation (cover) crop as well as for grain. Europe accounts for about two thirds of the world crop. (Courtesy of U.S. Department of Agriculture.)

ASIA AND THE AMERICAS

Next to the Soviet Union, China is the leading producer, the lands north of the Yangtze-Kiang being particularly important. The middle and upper portions of the Ganges Valley also produce much barley. The United States and Canada in the northern Great Plains employ barley in the rotation system. Barley in Latin America is produced only in Argentina.

OATS

Oats are universally regarded as a feed for livestock, but in a few areas a considerable amount is consumed by human beings.[5] Oats are also grown in many areas (e.g., the American South) as a grain pasture and a

[5] In Dr. Samuel Johnson's famous dictionary, oats were defined as "food for men in Scotland, horses in England," to which the Scots replied "and England is noted for the excellence of its horses, Scotland for the excellence of its men."

grain hay, in which case they are a winter crop. Oats are relatively high in fat, mineral matter, and protein, and are therefore highly valued as feed for breeding stock and young animals. However, because oats are so bulky and so low in value per unit of volume, the crop is usually fed to livestock on the very farms on which it is grown. Almost no oats get into international trade.

Figure 16-13, showing world distribution of oats, emphasizes the fact that the crop is confined mostly to the Northern Hemisphere and is primarily a European crop. Actually, few oats are produced elsewhere. Whenever grown for grain, oats are a spring-sown crop. They are most at home in cool, moist regions and thrive particularly in cool, marine climates. When they are grown in continental climates—e.g., the United States, Canada, and the Soviet Union—the yield per acre drops. Virtually no oats are produced in the drier cultivated portions of the world.

THE WORLD'S CEREALS : : 335

Since oats demand a longer frostless season than barley, the crop is not grown so far north nor at such high elevations in the tropics and subtropics. Oats can yield better on poorer soils than wheat and barley, though an adequate amount of nitrogen is essential for satisfactory yields. The non-chernozem soils of the Soviet Union—the so-called "poor forest soils" that are badly leached, low in humus, and moderately to strongly acid—are much utilized for oats. If soils are too fertile, however, as they often are in the American Corn Belt, the crop tends to lodge. Though oats have long been an important crop in this region,[6] it is not because of favorable physical conditions: summers are definitely too hot and moist. The high rank of oats as a crop here results from several factors: (1) oats help to equalize the seasonal distribution of labor; (2) the fields need not be plowed, since oats follow corn (this saves much labor); (3) the crop is harvested while corn is maturing and after one crop of hay has been harvested; and (4) oats are excellent feed for livestock (and the Corn Belt is regarded as the world's leading commercial livestock region).

THE COARSE GRAINS

Among the coarse grains, corn ranks first. Few people realize how important corn is even in a country like the United States, where almost all cereals are grown. Yet corn is the leading crop in both acreage and production. The grain sorghums and millet are important particularly in those parts of the earth where a cereal is needed and climate is too hot and dry for corn.

CORN (MAIZE)

Corn or maize is the one cereal domesticated in the New World and unknown elsewhere on earth until the Age of Discovery. No one

[6] Oats occupy a less important role in the Corn Belt agricultural system than they did when horses supplied the power for most of the farm work. Horses and mules declined from 23.285 million in 1924 to 3.5 million in 1958. However, yield per acre of oats rose considerably during this same interim.

knows exactly where it was domesticated, but it was somewhere south of the Rio Grande (scientists have suggested particularly Colombia, Mexico, Paraguay, or Peru). In one respect maize is unique among the nine cereals presented in this chapter: *it cannot be grown without man*. It alone among all the so-called "grasses" has its seeds neatly arranged on a sheathed cob. Its biological helplessness is thus inherent in the manner it produces its seeds and the difficulty with which they may be dispersed. Despite this weakness, corn is regarded as America's greatest single contribution to the food supply of the world.

Except in parts of the Americas where Indians have been eating corn for centuries, so that it is an established item in their diet, the crop is associated with peoples having a low standard of living—the corn-growing areas of Asia, Africa, and Latin America. Except for these areas, little corn is consumed directly by man; most corn serves as feed for livestock.

LOCATION OF CORN CROPS

Figure 16-14 shows the major corn-growing lands of the earth. Though corn is quite important over much of the tropical and subtropical zones, its greatest concentration is in the intermediate zone and in one type of climate—the Humid Continental with Long Summers. However, in the United States it is an important crop also in the Humid Subtropical climate of the South; in the Humid Continental with Medium Summers, it is grown mostly for ensilage. As a result of plant breeding, the crop's geographic range is expanding; more corn is being grown in California's Mediterranean Subtropical climate and even in the deserts of the West (under irrigation, of course). The Pueblo Indians of the Southwest have grown corn for centuries.

Corn does best where the growing season is six months in length with average temperatures of 75°F and night temperatures exceeding 58°F. The crop also has heavy water requirements—25 to 50 inches, with a summer maximum of 7 or more inches. Although corn can be grown on almost all kinds of terrain, it does best on level or gently rolling land,

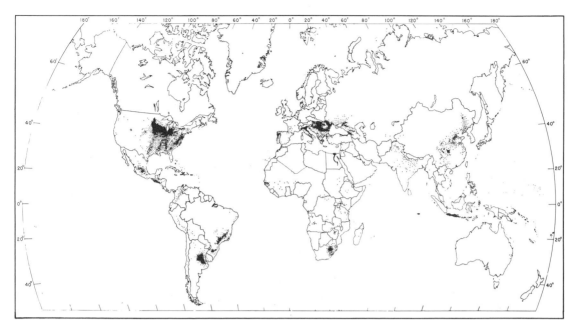

Fig. 16-14. *World production of corn. The crop is grown in many countries, in many types of climate, on many kinds of terrain and soils, but avoids the cold lands and the dry lands. The United States is responsible for about three fifths of the world crop. In Europe corn is grown south of 50° north latitude; in the United States, south of 45° north. (Courtesy of U.S. Department of Agriculture.)*

since soil erosion is much less than on steep hillsides or mountainsides. Corn requires fertile soils; best of all are the prairie soils, which are deep and heavy (with a medium to fine texture) and store water well. However, corn is grown in many parts of the world where conditions are by no means ideal; thus, in some places the stalks attain a height of only 2 feet and will mature in 60 to 70 days; in other places, the stalks grow 20 feet tall and require 300 to 340 days to mature.

HYBRID CORN

For centuries, only open-pollinated corn was grown. In the 1930s, Americans developed hybrid corn, which has revolutionized production not only in the United States but throughout the world. In fact, commercial production of hybrid corn increased yields by 500 million bushels without increasing acreage.

In open-pollinated varieties, the pollen from the tassel falls to the silk at the end of the ear or pollen from adjacent rows is blown to the silks; each plant thus includes both a male tassel from which pollen is shed and female silks that receive the pollen. Hybrid corn is produced artificially by man by crossing two inbred strains. New hybrid seed must be purchased each year from the breeding nurseries. The increased yield exceeds the cost of the seed plus the additional soil fertilizer required to produce the larger yield. Hybrids, which now account for 95 per cent of the corn grown in the American Corn Belt, mature earlier, yield more grain, and are more resistant to insects, diseases, and drought.

The large yields have resulted from the new variety of corn and from the heavy use of commercial fertilizer, which has caused such a technological revolution that people today speak of the "fertilizer fantasy." High yields are essential for profits; many farmers merely break even with a corn yield of 40 to 50 bushels per acre. Hence the average American farmer in 1958 spent approximately nine times as much for fertilizer as did the average farmer in 1940. Intensive use of commercial fertilizer has all but eliminated crop rotations

THE WORLD'S CEREALS : : 337

Fig. 16-15. Two-row corn picker operated by one man in large field. Until this machine was first built, about 1928, corn had to be harvested by hand— a grueling and costly operation in point of labor. The machine shown here can pick up to 20 acres of corn per day. It removes the shucks and elevates the ears to the wagon at the rear. The corn is then ready to be cribbed. (Courtesy of International Harvester Company.)

in the Corn Belt; some of the more progressive farmers today regard crop rotation as obsolete. Corn is now grown year after year on the same land.

UNITED STATES

The most famous corn-growing area on earth is the American Corn Belt, which O. E. Baker called "the heart of American agriculture and the most important agricultural region in the world for its size." A special combination of natural environmental conditions favor corn here: (1) level to undulating land (excellent for employing large-scale farm implements); (2) fertile soils (young geologically, not leached to any extent—also partly prairie soils); (3) hot days and hot nights over a period of three months (during this period temperatures often exceed for days and even weeks any ever recorded in the Rainy Tropics); (4) a growing season of 140 to 180 days; (5) rainfall of 18 to 20 inches at the western or dry-land border and up to 40 inches in the eastern Corn Belt; and (6) summer rainfall of the thundershower type (a bright sun and high temperatures follow the rain of short duration—an ideal growing condition for corn). Every farm operation in the Corn Belt involves the employment of costly labor-saving machinery (Fig. 16-15); it is not unusual for a Corn Belt farm to have an investment of $50,000 to $75,000 in such equip-

ment. Thus, the farmer can care for his crop at precisely the time it needs attention.

The husked ears are stored in ventilated cribs to prevent rotting or firing; the cribs must be rat- and mouse-proof. It is estimated that about two thirds of the crop is fed to livestock and poultry; much of this corn never leaves the farms on which it is produced. An exception is the corn (possibly one third of the total crop) shipped to Chicago-Decatur, Peoria-Pekin, Omaha, and Cedar Rapids for industrial purposes—for conversion into starches, dextrose, syrups, oil, feedstuffs, and whiskey.

MEXICO

Although Mexico is not one of the largest world producers of corn as far as acreage and output are concerned, in no other country on earth does corn mean so much to the people. As Mexico's most important crop and food, it meets about half the food (calorie) requirements. Three times more corn is consumed than wheat, although wheat consumption is increasing. Corn is grown in every state and from sea level to elevations up to 10,000 feet. It occupies about half the total cropland harvested, compared with one fourth in the United States. Much of the crop is grown on small subsistence-type farms; in the poorest areas, the basic diet consists almost entirely of corn.

Principal growing region is the Central Plateau, where the land between the mountain ranges is relatively level and the rainfall heavier—30 to 35 inches, falling mostly in summer. However, the crop cannot be regarded as reliable; drought and frost frequently reduce the anticipated crop. Yield per acre is low—about 10 bushels. Hybrid corn has been introduced in recent years. However, changes come slowly among Indian peons, who have grown corn in the same manner for centuries. Where corn is grown on *ejidos* of the Central Plateau, the farmers are being requested to plant on the same day an acre of their native corn adjacent to an acre of hybrid corn and to fertilize one half of each plot. This experiment invariably demonstrates the superiority of the hybrid strain and the benefit to be derived from fertilizer.

ARGENTINA

Argentina's corn belt comprises only a part of the Humid Pampa. Corn reaches greatest importance around Rosario. In fact, beyond the limits of the Rosario district, a notable decline in yield occurs, indicating a relatively small area really well suited to corn growing —that is, where soils are fertile and well drained, temperatures hot in summer and mild in winter, and rainfall ample (28 inches on the west and 38 inches on the east). Droughts occur from time to time. The Argentine Corn Belt is only about one tenth the size of its United States counterpart, but it is easily accessible to tidewater. Rosario is accessible to ocean ships.

Unlike the situation in the United States, where the bulk of the crop is fed to livestock, in Argentina 60 to 80 per cent is exported— principally to Western Europe. The corn also differs from that of the United States, being white and yellow flint varieties rather than dent varieties. The smaller kernels and sweeter taste make it preferred by European poultry raisers, and it absorbs much less moisture in ocean travel.

SOUTHEASTERN EUROPE

Europe is not outstanding in corn production, but that which it does produce is grown largely in the southeast—Hungary, northern Italy, Yugoslavia, Romania, and the southern part of the Soviet Union. This distribution results largely from the temperature factor: Northwestern Europe is too cool for corn to ripen. The main disadvantages in Southeast Europe are droughts and too little rainfall in summer. The Danube Basin is the most important part of this region, accounting for more than half the total crop.

The low level of living among the masses of people in these countries necessitates that much corn be used for human consumption (in Romania it is the principal foodstuff). Much, too, is fed to livestock, and prior to World War II large amounts were exported to Northwestern Europe.

SOVIET UNION

In the past, corn has not been a particularly important crop in the Soviet Union. Recent Soviet policy, however, has been bent upon expanding corn production at the expense of small grains. Actually, with the knowledge we now have, the Soviet Union appears not well suited for extensive growing of corn: the isotherms and isohyets run parallel to each other, but they increase in opposite directions; thus, areas that are warm enough for corn are generally too dry, and areas that are sufficiently moist are too cool. Possibly 90 per cent of the area in which corn planting is today being pushed by the Soviet government is too cool or too dry or both for high yields of corn. Introduction of hybrid corn and increased fertilization have not resulted in as high yields as in the United States. It is believed that the Russians will harvest their crop in the roasting-ear stage and will dehydrate the corn—a method employed on some of the most progressive farms in Iowa and Illinois today. Principal reason for Russian interest in corn is to increase the output of livestock for meat.

CHINA AND MANCHURIA

Corn is an extremely important crop in the eastern portions of the country (from southern Manchuria across the Great Plains of the Hwang-Ho and into the hill country of southern China). This area is too dry for rice. In the Manchurian segment, corn is grown only in the most favored spots; in the less favored areas, it yields to kaoliang and millet.

Corn, a summer crop, ranks about seventh in production among all Chinese crops. Generally it is consumed by those who are too poor to eat rice, the preferred food crop.

AFRICA

Corn is grown in all parts of Africa favorable to it. Roughly half the crop is grown north of the equator, and half south of it. South Africa alone normally accounts for about one third of the total crop; Egypt accounts for about 25 per cent. In both countries, however, corn is the staple in the diet of the natives. Three to four times as much corn is grown in South Africa as wheat. In the high plateau the climate is warm, and the rainfall varies from 25 to 40 inches, most of it falling in summer.

CORN IN INTERNATIONAL TRADE

Despite the enormous size of the world's annual corn crop, surprisingly little of the actual harvest (usually less than 10 per cent) enters foreign trade. Most corn is consumed on the farms where it is grown, or at least within the countries where it is grown; since the bulk of the crop in most countries (with the major exception of Argentina) is consumed locally as feed for livestock or as food for man, it is most economical to use it near the point of production. Also corn has relatively low value per unit of weight and hence does not lend itself to shipment to distant markets as do wheat and rice. Finally, dent corn does not ship well—it sweats. Despite all this, because of the enormous size of the world crop, even the tiny percentage exported makes corn one of the three most important grains in world trade.

Normally, Argentina exports from two thirds to three fourths of its annual production. Three major factors are responsible for so heavy a proportion of the crop's being exported: (1) proximity of the corn-growing area to ocean transportation, (2) the widespread use within the Pampa of alfalfa rather

than corn for cattle feed, and (3) popularity of the hard flint variety, which keeps and transports easily and whose small kernels are excellently suited to poultry feeding.

The bulk of the corn entering international trade moves to the heavy livestock-feeding areas in Europe, principally the United Kingdom, the Netherlands, France, Belgium, Germany, and Denmark, all of which are corn-deficit areas.

THE GRAIN SORGHUMS

Though not so widely distributed as wheat, rice, and corn, the grain sorghums are of outstanding importance in many of the hot, dry lands of the earth. In parts of the Old World, the grain sorghums have for centuries been regarded as a crop of stability, serving as a staple food as well as a desirable feed. Of the many kinds of grain sorghums, only kafir corn, milo, and feterita (mostly African varieties) and kaoling and durra (Asiatic varieties) are considered here.

An upsurge of production in many parts of the world in recent years has brought grain sorghums to a place of prominence among the cereals. Considering the world as a whole, grain sorghums are produced in greater quantity than any other cereals except rice and wheat. The grain sorghums have been widely adopted as a basic food crop among the poorer people of Africa and Asia. In addition, however, production in Europe and North America has increased notably, although most of the output is used for stock feed or as an industrial raw material. In the United States, for example, grain sorghums now are the third-ranking cereal in quantity of production, exceeded by wheat and corn.

LOCATION OF GRAIN SORGHUMS

Grain sorghums are grown in hot, dry areas (Fig. 16-16). No other grain crop is so tolerant of aridity. Morover, the grain sorghums can be grown on soil so sandy as to be wholly unsuitable for the small grains; accordingly, in areas where both wheat and the grain sorghums can be grown, the grain sorghums get the light soils, wheat the heavy ones. How-

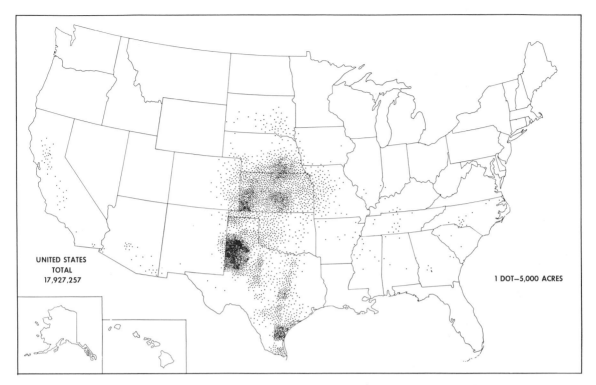

Fig. 16-16. United States grain-sorghum production. Texas and Kansas are the leading producers by far. (Courtesy of Bureau of the Census.)

UNITED STATES
TOTAL
17,927,257

1 DOT—5,000 ACRES

ever, all varieties are not equally drought- and cold-resistant; the dwarf types generally withstand dry conditions better than the tall, leafy types. Thus, in the United States the dwarf milo reaches farther west than the tall kafir, but the latter reaches farther east.

NORTH CHINA (INCLUDING MANCHURIA)

Kaoliang, which is grown mostly north of the Yangtze-Kiang, is unique among the sorghums in that it is more resistant to cold than all the others. Here the crop not only withstands the drought and poor soils so generally characteristic of areas that grow grain sorghums, but even withstands the cold. Kaoliang is grown for grain, but its usefulness does not stop here; for the stalks are used for fuel, fodder, roof thatching, dike building, fence construction, and for coarse mats and baskets. Even the leaves are fed to livestock. Kaoliang is less important in the Manchurian portion of China than in the past, for it experiences difficulty competing with the soybean, a major crop in southern Manchuria.

INDIA

In India this outstanding crop is represented by jowar, durra, or orcholum (depending on the part of the country involved). It is grown mainly in areas not suited to wheat or rice. The drought-resistant character of sorghums is reflected in the crop's pronounced absence from the wet lands—for example, the Malabar Coast and the Ganges-Brahmaputra Delta. Rather, it is concentrated on the Deccan Plateau on the leeward side of the Western Ghats. In acreage, the grain sorghums rank second only to rice. The crop is the principal food and feed in the Deccan.

AFRICA

The grain sorghums are one of Africa's principal crops, being grown mostly by the

THE WORLD'S CEREALS::341

native population; to date, Europeans have paid surprisingly little attention to the sorghums. The crop is produced mostly north of the equator, between the Sahara and the rain forest, though considerable acreage is to be seen also in North Africa (particularly in Egypt) and in Eastern and Southern Africa. In Africa the grain sorghums appear to be best suited to the savanna climates. Kafir corn, known also as guinea corn, is indigenous to Africa and is the most widespread crop on the continent.

UNITED STATES

For several decades (since the 1880s) the grain sorghums have been of considerable importance in the southern Great Plains, where the climate is too dry for corn and where the raising of livestock is important. Production has been stimulated by dust-bowl conditions since the 1930s. The crop, currently planted over much diverted wheat acreage in the southern Great Plains, has greatly stimulated beef-cattle production. In the late 1950s and early 1960s, however, the sorghums became of very great importance also in the Corn Belt (Fig. 16-16).

The grain sorghums obviously are better suited to the Dust Bowl than any other cereal.[7] No other crop has contributed so much to the establishment of a sound agriculture in the southern Great Plains as the grain sorghums. The crop is being extended into Nebraska, South Dakota, and Colorado—but for forage, not grain.

The recent development of hybrids has revolutionized the growth of this crop in the United States, for hybrids have increased yields 20 to 25 per cent (Fig. 16-17). In 1957, only seven years after the breeding technique was perfected, one third of the acreage was in hybrids; today the percentage exceeds 90. *In 1957 more grain sorghums than wheat were grown in Kansas.* The grain sorghums are becoming increasingly important in the Corn

[7] At first, African varieties did not do well in the southern Great Plains because the plants required too long a growing season; the African habitat has no killing frost. Shortly, American plant breeders developed sorghums well suited to the area.

Fig. 16-17. *A field of grain sorghums in western Texas. (Courtesy of Texas A & M College.)*

Belt, mainly because of the greater frequency of droughts; the development of dwarf strains that can be harvested mechanically (until quite recently a big obstacle to large-scale production was the irregularity of the stalks, which required hand harvesting); and the Federal Soil Bank, whereby prices for the grain sorghums have been supported without acreage restrictions.

The development of combine types of sorghums has made them competitive with both wheat and corn, particularly in the western third of the state of Kansas (Fig. 16-18).

MILLET

Like the grain sorghums, the millets are grains of hot, dry lands and of poor peoples. In fact, millet is known as a "poor man's cereal." So similar are the requirements of these two crops that if maps of the two were superimposed one upon the other, they would coincide remarkably well.

LOCATION OF MILLET

There is no satisfactory world map of millet because the statistical records of the principal millet-growing countries (all are underde-

Fig. 16-18. *Harvesting grain sorghum with combines in Kansas. This innovation in grain-sorghum production has aided in revolutionizing the extension and output of this crop. (Courtesy of Kansas Industrial Development Commission.)*

veloped) are unreliable. Hence, the authors make no effort to map the distribution of this crop. However, the principal producing countries are well known—China, India, Pakistan, Korea, the savanna lands of Africa north of the equator, the Balkans, and the southern part of the Soviet Union.

Millet's ability to mature in a short season (some varieties in sixty to ninety days) is an advantage. If rains come too late for preferred crops, millet can serve as a catch crop. Being very susceptible to frost, the millets have not as yet strayed far from the tropics and subtropics: they are high-temperature-loving plants. One of their strong points is their efficient use of water.

Millets are also tolerant of poor soils—more so even than the grain sorghums. In fact, some millets are grown in soils so poor that not a single one of the other cereals could be grown on them.

NORTH CHINA

North China, including Manchuria, accounts for about one third of the world millet crop; here millet, along with kaoliang and wheat, is a staple food. It is grown in the poorer agricultural areas—those where the soils are infertile, the precipitation low, and the growing season short. It tends to replace kaoliang in areas of higher elevation.

INDIA AND PAKISTAN

Millet (called "ragi" and "bajra") is a major crop, since much of the soil is too poor and the climate too dry for growing other crops; it is the food of the mass of the population, which is very poor. It tends to yield some kind of a crop even when the monsoon brings little rain—although, of course, if the monsoon fails completely, crop failure is inevitable and famine threatens. Principal areas for concentration of millet are the Deccan Plateau, particularly the lee side of the Western Ghats; Rajputana; and in the south in Madras and Mysore, where millet occupies two thirds of the planted acreage.

AFRICA

The growing of millet is widely scattered over the continent of Africa; invariably it is grown under antiquated conditions. The outstanding areas are the savannas: Chad around Lake Chad, East Africa, and northern Nigeria.

SOVIET UNION

The Soviet Union is the only country in Europe that has an impressive acreage in millet, but it is also the only country in Europe that has a considerable desert area. Most of the crop, produced north and east of the Black and Caspian Seas, is used for human food, mainly in the form of porridge and flat bread.

SELECTED REFERENCES

Anderson, E. "Millet Provides Food for Millions," *Foreign Agriculture*, 12:235-239, November 1948.

Carter, George. "The Origin of Maize," *Geographical Review*, 41:338-340, April 1951.

Farnsworth, Helen C. "Imbalance in the World Wheat Economy," *Journal of Political Economy*, 66:1-23, February 1958.

Findlay, W. M. *Oats: Their Cultivation and Use from Ancient Times to the Present Day*. Edinburgh, Oliver and Boyd, 1956.

Jackson, W. A. D. "Durum Wheat and the Expansion of Dry Farming in the Soviet Union," *Annals of the Association of American Geographers*, 46:405-410, December 1956.

Karper, R. E., and J. R. Quinby. "Sorghum—Its Production, Utilization and Breeding," *Economic Botany*, 1:355-371, October-December 1947.

Mangelsdorf, P. C. "The Mystery of Corn," *Scientific American*, 183:20-24, July 1950.

Milner, Reid T. "Future Utilization of Cereal Crops," *Economic Botany*, 12:54-61, January-March 1957.

Olson, E. T. "The Soviet New Lands—Destiny or Dust?," *Foreign Agriculture*, 25:4-6, February 1961.

Rivenburgh, D. V. "Is There a Wonder Method of Rice Culture?" (Japan), *Foreign Agriculture*, 20:13-14, October 1956.

Schaben, L. J. "Rye—A Source of Daily Bread," *Foreign Agriculture*, 12:163-168, August 1948.

Shands, H. L., and A. D. Dickson. "Barley—Botany, Production, Harvesting, Processing, Utilization and Economics," *Economic Botany*, 7:3-26, January-March 1953.

Weatherwax, P. "The History of Corn," *Scientific Monthly*, 71:50-60, July 1950.

Weaver, John C. "Barley in the United States: A Historical Sketch," *Geographical Review*, 33:56-73, January 1943.

Wickizer, V. D., and M. K. Bennett. *The Rice Economy of Monsoon Asia*. Stanford University, California, Food Research Institute, 1941.

Wissler, C. "Corn and Early American Civilization," *Natural History*, 54:56-65, February 1945.

CHAPTER SEVENTEEN ::

The part of Asia that was the earliest home of man was also the earliest home of many of the fruits grown today. As man began ranging over the earth, he took along with him his food plants. When he reached the Mediterranean region, he achieved a precocious agricultural development by adjusting commendably to the varied geographic conditions he found there—subtropical lands with summer droughts and mild winters, a prevailing mountain terrain, and intermittently fertile soils. The monsoon fruits brought from the Orient were planted, improved, and perfected in the garden spots of the Mediterranean—narrow valleys spreading out into deltaic flats. Fruit-growing became a notable part of the civilizations of the Greeks, Egyptians, and Romans; and even the Dark Ages were not able to obliterate the refined agricultural and horticultural practices contributed by these an-

THE WORLD'S

cients. With the advance of civilization, the nutritive qualities of fruits and nuts were increasingly recognized; and further painstaking selection and hybridization gradually produced our present-day varieties.

The growing of fruits and nuts is a specialized agricultural activity that requires intensive land use. Most fruit holdings are small; family orchards usually do not exceed 20 acres; commercial plantings rarely exceed 100 acres. Although capital and labor requirements average three times more per acre than for mixed farming, the value of output is usually three to five times greater.

Since the early 1900s, the world fruit industry has undergone one of the most remarkable expansions in modern agriculture, contributing notably to the health and wealth of many peoples. Improved transportation, particularly in the United States and Western Europe, has substantially influenced this growth, making increasingly available a wide range of tropical, subtropical, and mid-latitude fruits. The United States has become the leading producer in the world fruit market by virtue of its (1) varied climates, (2) abundant arable land, (3) advanced agricultural techniques, (4) development and widespread use of agricultural machinery, (5) excellent refrigerated storage facilities and transportation, (6) progressive development of processing techniques, and (7) high purchasing power. However, America's share of world production and trade in fresh fruit has declined considerably since prior to World War II.

Since the turn of the century, California, outstanding both for its salubrious physical conditions and for its agricultural research and technology, has become the greatest fruit-growing region not only in the United States

FRUITS AND NUTS

but in the world. Fruits and nuts account for 20 per cent of California's harvested acreage.

In this chapter only a few fruits and nuts are treated, the intent being to describe only those of high commercial value rather than those of subsistence value.

TROPICAL FRUITS

THE BANANA

As rice is to many Asians and wheat to many Europeans and North Americans, so the banana is to many peoples of tropical lands—it is a staff of life. High in carbohydrates, and with some proteins and fats, bananas have a food value (calories in relation to weight) three times that of wheat. The banana's gastronomic versatility is such that it may be used raw, cooked, or dried, and made into oil, flour, and wine. The fruit is never out of season, being harvested every day of the year.

Undoubtedly the banana is the most familiar and important of all the commercial tropical fruits. Until its introduction into the United States in the early part of the nineteenth century, this fruit, because of its highly perishable nature, was scarcely regarded as a potential international-trade commodity. But in its history of conquest over time, space, disease, and weather, it has garnered for itself a remarkable record not only as a food but as a product that indirectly has prompted revolutions, shaken governments, developed higher living standards, eradicated disease, and made men wealthy.

CHARACTERISTICS OF THE BANANA PLANT

The banana, contrary to what many people think, is not a tree but a gigantic plant, containing 85 per cent water; it has neither a woody stem nor woody roots nor a taproot. Its pseudotrunk—a dense mass of overlapping leaf-sheafs—about a year after planting attains a diameter of 9 to 16 inches and a height of 15 to 30 feet. On the rootstalk or "rhizome," large buds or "eyes" develop, which produce the flower stalk that pushes up through the hollow pseudotrunk. A towering crown, formed by huge leaves 8 to 12 feet long and

2 feet or more wide, protects the plant's development.

From twelve to fourteen months after the rhizome or "bit" has been set out, the plant grows to its full size and bears one "stem" or bunch of fruit weighing 50 to 100 pounds. A stem may carry from six to fifteen clusters or "hands," each of which has from ten to twenty "fingers" (bananas). After it has borne its fruit, the plant is cut down and permitted to rot and thus fertilize the ground. Suckers develop at the base of the plant; only the healthiest one is allowed to grow and serve as the new plant.

Not only the characteristics of the banana itself but also the distance between field and market demands that it be harvested unripe. If tree-ripened, the fruit becomes dry and insipid; and its skin, which is a naturally germ-proof wrapper, may split, admitting insects and dirt.

LOCATION OF BANANA CROPS

Possibly the world's oldest cultivated crop (it has been cultivated so long that it can no longer be propagated by seed), the banana can grow in practically every warm region on earth. Spreading from its original home in humid tropical India or Malaya, it attained considerable importance in all early civilizations and eventually girdled the tropical world, reaching the West Indies in 1500 A.D.

The story of the development of commercial banana production is not one of mere chance, for the exacting requirements of the banana plant and the pressure of economic and political conditions preclude any willy-nilly approach to large-scale cultivation. The vicissitudes of weather, disease, insect invasions, soil depletion, and politics have caused a frequent shift of leadership in exports. In the past, the high perishability of the fruit and proximity to the United States market enabled the Caribbean countries to dominate world trade. From the 1870s (when banana exporting began) until 1926, the world's leading shipper was Jamaica, closely followed by the Central American countries, by Cuba, and by Colombia. Then the lead vacillated until after 1951, when dominance was transferred to Ecuador, which by 1955 handled 20 per cent of the world trade. Ecuador today remains unchallenged as the leading exporter (Table 17-1).

TABLE 17-1

WORLD BANANA EXPORTS, 1961

Country	Thousand stems	Per cent of total
Ecuador	44,451	24
Honduras	23,836	13
Costa Rica	12,898	7
Panama	11,992	7
Brazil	11,000	6
Colombia	9,982	5
Guatemala	8,450	5
Canary Islands	8,300	5
Jamaica	6,140	3
Martinique	6,074	3
Dominican Republic	5,906	3
Guadeloupe	5,395	3

SOURCE: Based on *Foreign Crops and Markets* (U.S.D.A.), August 30, 1962, p. 6.

Stringent physical conditions limit commercial banana production to well-located Rainy Tropical and Monsoon Tropical lowlands or piedmont plains. The fussy banana plant requires 75 to 200 inches of rainfall distributed throughout the year (although the fruit is grown in regions with short droughts where irrigation supplements the rainfall), uniformly high temperatures—between 55°F and 105°F, and a maximum of sunshine. The land must be low lying but well drained. Rigid soil requirements are demanded by this thirsty yet water-sensitive plant: to prevent waterlogging around the roots, the clay content must not exceed 40 per cent; depth should be sufficient for adequate drainage; nutritive elements, especially nitrogen, must be plentiful; and lime content should be sufficiently high to prevent the diseases that acid soils expedite.

But even if all these requirements are met in a large area, banana production cannot be economically feasible if hurricanes or even moderate winds are a potential threat; mature banana bunches are so heavy and the plants so weak that a 25-mile wind can knock them down. In addition, infectious diseases spread so rapidly that banana cultivation must often be discontinued. Hence, in order to guarantee a constant supply, many different producing areas are requisite.

ECONOMICS OF BANANA GROWING

The return realized from exports by banana producers is exceptionally high in comparison with any other agricultural pursuit that they may follow. The banana is one of the few tropical food crops that has such a high and valuable yield (from 125 to 400 bunches per acre) as to warrant the large and ever increasing capital investment (from 20 million to 25 million dollars initially for 20,000 producing acres) needed for its large-scale production and marketing. Understandably, in economically immature areas, growing bananas to provide a constant supply for export has long been dependent on a large-scale integrated organization, predominantly financed and controlled by foreign companies. Such an enterprise can (1) meet the unusually heavy capital necessary for establishing and maintaining extensive banana acreage; (2) provide the safety insurance of other large growing areas should disease, floods, or blowdowns (calculated to cause losses of about 25 per cent in the total annual production of a large enterprise) force successive shifts in cultivation; and (3) cope with the high expenses, split-second timing, and intricate logistics of distribution demanded by one of the most perishable of the world's major trade commodities.

A typical modern banana plantation is divided into individual banana farms of up to 1,000 acres, each having its own operating and living facilities. But in some banana-growing areas (e.g., in Jamaica, Costa Rica, and especially in Ecuador) the economics of production have increasingly favored small holdings over large holdings. Most of the new banana farms in Ecuador comprise 10 to 30 acres, and foreign-owned large plantations are estimated to grow less than 15 per cent of the total exportable banana crop. The economic conditions contributing to this trend in Ecuador have been (1) the increased European market demand, (2) abandonment of many of the older banana areas in Middle America,

(3) high fruit prices, (4) cheap agricultural credit, (5) readily available shipping at low cost, (6) removal of export taxes on the fruit, (7) a brisk road-building program financed in large part by the United States and the International Bank, and (8) the decline of cacao as a money crop. In addition, bananas make an outstanding pioneer crop wherever adequate transportation is available, for no other crop on newly cleared land can so easily and quickly provide a cash return once production has been established.

THE CARIBBEAN BANANA INDUSTRY

The Caribbean region has long dominated the commercial banana industry. The crop here is produced and transported most economically under the large plantation-corporation system. The United Fruit Company, organized in 1899, dominated this type of development and, until recently, encountered little competition. Years of experience in planning, organizing, and experimentation made the company an outstanding example of international investment based on agriculture—one that received more than a fair share of praise and condemnation.

The United Fruit Company is rich in assets and problems. It is the world's biggest producer, carrier, importer, and distributor of bananas, and the largest private landowner, corporate employer, and single business in Costa Rica, Honduras, and Guatemala. However, its traditional dominance in the industry has changed in recent years. Although it is still often regarded as a monstrous monopolizer (it is known as El Pulpo, the octopus), its position in the major markets has undergone severe alterations: formerly supplying 75 per cent of all bananas consumed in the United States and 66 per cent of those in Europe, it now supplies only 57 and 6 per cent, respectively.

By furnishing the capital and technological requirements for six major banana-producing lands—Colombia, Costa Rica, Ecuador, Guatemala, Honduras, and Panama—the United Fruit Company, in addition to contributing to economic progress, has made vast new lands habitable and productive, introduced modern scientific techniques and equipment, and trained many thousands of local inhabitants. Moreover, the company provides scholarships for study in the United States and Canada for its employees' children; and it subsidizes the Pan-American School of Agriculture in Honduras, graduates of which are not permitted to enter the company's employ.

But development and diplomacy have not always gone hand in hand. The company's performance in the field of labor relations has often been seriously criticized, and it is still regarded in some quarters as the epitome of malevolent and greedy foreign exploitation. In its beginnings, the company was tardy in recognizing its public-relations responsibilities, which historical and other circumstances had rendered almost hopelessly complex; and in recent years, at the insistence of both the governments of the producing lands and of the United States, has been more successfully meeting its obligations of "good citizenship."

In 1954 the United States federal government filed an antitrust suit against the company. A final judgment, entered in 1958, assured that by 1970 the company would relinquish facilities that have enabled it to import about 9 million stems annually into the United States and that it would refrain from a variety of practices generally regarded as incompatible with healthy competition.

Selection and Preparation of the Land. Virgin tropical forest land is usually the site of a new plantation. Once a suitable area has been found, the problem of adequate transportation (including a shipping port) and the feasibility of securing laborers must be considered. If an area can meet these stiff tests, the land is purchased or leased from the government. As the plantation develops, a new community—actually a factory town—grows up, with schools, hospitals, golf courses, and various other niceties of civilization.

Planting. Stakes are set in rows 15 to 20 feet apart; and rhizomes, weighing from 10 to 15 pounds, are planted near the stakes in holes about 18 inches deep. Before the sprouts emerge above ground, the larger trees are

Fig. 17-1. Banana plantation near Tenguel, Ecuador. The stems of bananas as harvested are delivered to the tram line on the backs of pack mules. Here in a clearing the stems are stored under shade for several hours preparatory to being picked up by the tram railway for delivery to a main rail line, which then hauls the bananas to a port for shipment to mid-latitude markets. (Courtesy of Grace Line.)

felled, leaving an almost impenetrable jungle through which roads and rail lines must be constructed. Until the plants are large enough to shade the ground, weeds are removed at intervals of three to four months and then placed between the rows to rot.

On the Caribbean side of Central America, no irrigation is required, but on the Pacific side (as also in the Santa Marta district of Colombia and in a few areas of Ecuador), the banana lands are irrigated for a short time.

Harvesting and Loading. Twelve to fifteen months after planting, the harvest is on (only stems of certain maturity are cut each week in various sections of the plantation). The harvest crew usually consists of a cutter, a backer, and a mule man. The backer transports the bunches of bananas on his own back to gangs of mules or to well-padded, oxen-drawn carts or to a tram line if it is close by (Fig. 17-1). Under certain circumstances bananas are transported by aerial tramway. The fruit is then delivered to a main railway

line and moved to loading ports for export. From 40,000 to 80,000 stems can be loaded in twelve hours. The fruit is washed, disinfected, and usually sealed in transparent polyethylene bags, which protect against chilling, scarring, and shrinkage and also allow easy inspection. Some shippers are now boxing hands of bananas without their stems to avoid transport of unnecessary materials.

Transportation. The banana, being one of the most pampered of food commodities, requires the tenderest of care during transport. Since stored bananas give off heat, the refrigerating apparatus of ships and trains must maintain a temperature of about 57°F; the temperature is recorded hourly. At the most modern banana terminals, up to 8,000 stems of the fruit are handled per hour, each being given a swift roller-coaster ride from ship to truck or rail car. Received green by the wholesaler, bananas are ripened in three to ten days in special rooms at temperatures from 62°F to 68°F.

THE WORLD'S FRUITS AND NUTS::351

Changes in Production. In the heyday of Caribbean commercial banana production, the fruit grew in abundance almost anywhere on the virgin soils of the coast. Even when Panama fungus disease, a wilt disease, attacked the plantations in 1910, production did not waver; for more land was available, and, despite the necessity of constant costly moves, a fair margin of profit could be maintained. But by 1920 the disease had become a major menace. In the same year sigatoka leaf blight began to threaten the plantations and was largely responsible for the steady abandonment of older banana areas and the establishment of new ones. In the 1930s it was discovered that Bordeaux mixture (hydrated lime, copper sulfate, and large quantities of water) could arrest the disease, but it was costly and difficult to apply without a great deal of water.

Panama disease is even more destructive and hard to control; once it infests the soil, it remains virulent for years. Since it attacks only the Gros Michel—Big Mike—variety of banana, which accounts for the majority of bananas marketed in the United States, scientists have developed other, though poorer-quality bananas resistant to the disease.

By 1942, physical, economic, and political phenomena had combined to necessitate a complete shift of the United Fruit Company's Central American operations in the production, purchase, and exportation of bananas from the Caribbean Lowlands to the Pacific Lowlands.

In the brief period 1950-1954, Ecuador, previously a minor producer, capitalized on the disease situation in Central America and, bolstered by her own highly favorable natural and economic conditions for banana growing, shot into first place in world banana exports. The two main diseases that have so badly afflicted the older banana lands do not thrive as well in Ecuador; in most of the banana regions a heavy overcast provides sufficient shade to restrain the development of sigatoka.

The United Fruit Company plays a far less conspicuous role in Ecuador than in Central America; its total planted acreage accounts for scarcely 6 per cent in Ecuador.

WORLD TRADE IN BANANAS

World trade in bananas has in recent years expanded at the rate of 5 per cent annually. About 25 per cent of all bananas produced is exported. Approximately 80 per cent of this quantity originates in Middle America (including Mexico and the islands in the Caribbean), in Ecuador, Colombia, and Brazil; 20 per cent in Africa; 1 per cent in Formosa; and 1 per cent in Oceania.

Because of preponderant initial commercial production of bananas in Caribbean lands, since the turn of the century the best customer for the fruit has been the United States. However, increased production in South America and in Africa—together with improved transportation, refrigeration, and handling methods and more open and competitive marketing channels in Europe—has, particularly since World War II, greatly augmented demand for the product in Western Europe. The United States and Western Europe provide the markets for almost 90 per cent of banana exports.

THE PINEAPPLE

Known as the "king of fruits," the pineapple once was primarily a fruit for kings. In the last half century this former delicacy for dignitaries has turned into a commodity for commoners. The pineapple is grown chiefly for home consumption, only 10 per cent of total production entering international trade. Most of it is shipped in canned form (largely as juice) and finds its biggest markets in Anglo-America and Western Europe.

LOCATION OF PINEAPPLE CROPS

Northern South America, probably Brazil, is regarded as the pineapple's place of origin. It spread to many parts of the tropics, being carried by Spaniards and Portuguese to the Old World and thence thriving all over tropical Asia, Africa, and Polynesia. The Hawaiian Islands have until recently accounted for more than 75 per cent of the pineapples entering international trade.

The pineapple, an herbaceous perennial, can be grown even in semiarid areas; for though it is not tolerant of low temperatures, it requires approximately the same amount of precipitation as does a crop of corn and needs irrigation in areas of less rainfall. Usually Hawaiian pineapple fields are situated on interior uplands; the lowlands, with their high water tables, are ideal for sugar cane (which is Hawaii's leading crop); the two crops thus nicely complement each other in land use.

Soils, other than wet ones, are not a restrictive factor in cultivation, since fertilization is heavily practiced in commercial plantings. Hawaii's deep, rich clay soils—decomposed volcanic materials—are extremely congenial to pineapple cultivation, and yields may reach as high as 40 tons per acre under optimum conditions.

PLANTING AND HARVESTING

The pineapple is propagated by suckers, crowns, slips, or stumps set in rows. In eighteen to twenty months the first crop ripens and two suckers are retained, which yield in another twelve months. The peak harvest period extends from July through September, but the harvest season is sometimes prolonged by the use of plant hormones that speed up fruit maturation. The fields are kept in constant use.

THE HAWAIIAN PINEAPPLE INDUSTRY

Although the pineapple was introduced into Hawaii early in the nineteenth century, commercial production and canning did not begin until the turn of the twentieth century. By the 1930s its cultivation had proved so successful that it attracted mainland fruit-packing corporations to establish plantations on the islands. Lack of tariff barriers between Hawaii and the mainland (before statehood) was an outstanding factor in encouraging the growth of the industry.

More than 100 million dollars gross revenue annually is realized from the pineapple cultivation of approximately 73,000 acres in Hawaii. The island of Molokai produces more than a third of the state's pineapples. The fruit, which is Hawaii's second largest export, is grown on fourteen plantations owned and operated by nine corporations.

Intense mechanization is associated with the life cycle and distribution of the pineapple—the result of scientific planning for maximum yields and minimum expenditures and of the necessity to compensate for the scarcity and high cost of labor, which has always plagued the industry. Although the actual picking of the fruit is still done by manual labor, machines carry out the rest of the harvesting process (Fig. 17-2).

Although the history of the Hawaiian industry is a brief one, it represents an exceptionally high level of scientific and commercial development of horticulture. Australia, the Philippines, Formosa, and Malaysia have a locational advantage in penetrating the huge potential Asiatic market, but Hawaii's aggressive and efficient production and distribution methods assure her continued dominance in the near future. However, lower freight rates, cheap labor, government subsidies of various foreign competitors—especially Malaysia, Australia, South Africa, Mexico, and Formosa—are making strong inroads in Hawaii's share of the world market.

The industry has other problems: not only must it now pay a special 2 per cent "processing tax" on its gross income, but also its plantations are confronted with the withdrawal of the leased pineapple lands for other uses deemed of more value to the owners; moreover, stiffer competition is faced in the mainland, where other canned and frozen fruits and juices, plus inroads by foreign pineapples, are jeopardizing Hawaii's dominance.

THE DATE

One of the oldest of crops, the date can be traced back at least 5,000 years. Though probably a native of India or Arabia, it has long been domesticated throughout Southwest Asia and North Africa. This sugar-saturated fruit is often a staple food of desert peoples. More than a thousand varieties are grown, and the palms are extremely long-lived—some reach an age of 200 years.

The fruits are either picked one at a time, since a whole bunch does not ripen at once, or are artificially ripened off the tree. Usually the dates are dried before shipment. The date

Fig. 17-2. Harvesting pineapples near Wahiawa, Hawaii. The pineapple-harvesting machine uses a crew of sixteen men to harvest up to 22 tons of pineapple an hour. Pickers are seen placing the fruit on a conveyer belt, which runs along the 50-foot-long boom, stretching across ten rows of pineapple. The belt carries the fruit up an enclosed elevator to an overhead storage conveyer, from which it is dumped into a field truck, visible just ahead of the harvester. (Courtesy of Del Monte Foods.)

palm contributes substantially to oasis economy. It has more than 800 different uses, and the fruit even serves as money; the palm also indirectly encourages production of other crops by providing shade for smaller fruits and vegetables.

The best varieties demand long hot summer days and nights, mild winters, a rainless spring when the fruit is setting, and a rainless autumn when the fruit is ripening.

Most varieties begin to bear in their fourth year. When properly irrigated and fertilized, the palm may yield 100 pounds of fruit after the fifth to seventh year. For maximum yields, the palm demands abundant water (an average tree loses about 100 gallons of water a day through evaporation)—hence the Arab proverb which cautions that the palm have its "feet in water and its head in the fires of heaven."

The palms are amenable to a variety of soils —the clays of Iraq's Shatt-al-Arab, the sands of Algeria, and the sandy loams of Oman and of California's Coachella Valley.

Approximately one fifth of the total date production is exported, the majority of it in dry rather than fresh form. Iraq, Iran, Sudan, and Algeria account for 95 per cent of total world exports. Seventy-five per cent of the world's dates of commerce flourish in Iraq's Shatt-al-Arab, a tidally irrigated oasis 120 miles long and 1 to 2 miles wide. The environs of Baghdad and scattered oases further contribute to Iraq's heavy output.

Iran has about one third the production of Iraq, most of the cultivation being centered in the region adjacent to the Shatt-al-Arab and in the Minab district on the southern coast near Bandar Abbas. A large part of Sudan's agricultural wealth is based on an annual date crop grown chiefly along the Nile from El Damer to Wadi Halfa. Approximately 20 per cent of production enters world trade. Algeria, Tunisia, West Pakistan, and Saudi

Fig. 17-3. A sea of date palms surrounding the city of Qatif on the Persian Gulf in Saudi Arabia. Date palms are familiar sights in all the oases of the Arabian peninsula. Apparently the palm was at home in Arabia long before the dawn of history, and it was accorded religious honors because of its great importance in the food supply and because of the beverage made from its sap. Its status in nourishing the Arab peoples remains high to this day. (Courtesy of Arabian American Oil Company.)

Arabia (Fig. 17-3) grow dates primarily for home consumption.

Although dates were grown in California in the eighteenth century, commercial production in the United States did not start until the early 1900s, when California's Coachella Valley was found to have optimum conditions for the palm. The date gardens hold about fifty palms per acre, which begin to bear only after the tenth year. So carefully nurtured is the crop that from 250 to 350 pounds of dates are produced annually by each tree. Arizona's Salt River Valley is another producer of high-quality dates. However, the annual United States domestic production supplies less than 50 per cent of the nation's demands.

SUBTROPICAL FRUITS

THE CITRUS FRUITS

More than 3,000 years ago citrus fruits began to be domesticated from wild ancestors in warm, humid Eastern and Southern Asia. The citron, around 300 B.C., was the first to reach the Mediterranean Basin; the sour (bitter) or Seville orange slowly wended its way from India and Indochina through Persia and Palestine to land in North Africa and Southern Europe about 500 A.D.

Although citrus fruits are actually tropical plants, their commercial production has concentrated largely in subtropical regions (Fig. 17-4), many of which are climatically mar-

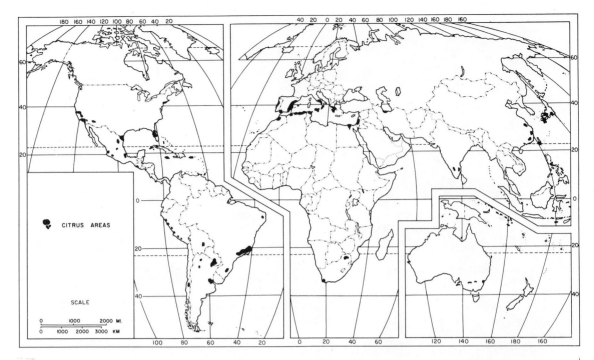

Fig. 17-4. World citrus-growing lands. Most of the commercial citrus is grown in the Northern Hemisphere, particularly in the United States (Florida, California, Arizona, and Texas) and in the countries along the periphery of the Mediterranean Sea. Brazil, South Africa, and Australia are the leading centers in the Southern Hemisphere.

ginal but are near the major markets; these fruits are bulky and perishable and hence expensive to import. There are at least a hundred species of *Citrus*, but only a few—the orange, grapefruit, lemon, and lime—are of commercial importance.

A belt between 35° north and 35° south latitudes provides most of the citrus fruits of commerce, and the finest fruits are often obtained at the cooler margins. At these poleward edges, where the trees are gently chilled by occasional, slight winter-night frosts, maximum development occurs. Semidormant at this time, the trees can tolerate temperatures as low as 28°F; if frost occurs earlier, before the trees have ended their annual growth, the fruit crop is endangered.

Because of temperature and moisture requirements, commercial cultivation is restricted to a few areas. The most favorable temperature range is approximately 55°F to 100°F; minimum rainfall demanded is 35

inches, or its equivalent in irrigation water. Any well-drained soils, other than exceptionally sandy ones, are compatible, since mineral and organic lacks can usually be overcome by fertilization, cover cropping, and mulching.

THE ORANGE

Topping the list of citrus fruits is the orange, which has the admirable and not universal attribute of a food that tastes good and at the same time is good for the health. Its popularity and its adaptability to subtropical regions have made it the most widely cultivated citrus fruit. Commercial production is especially notable on the warm and sunny edges of the subtropics, where irrigation is required; in warm and humid regions—i.e., Florida, Brazil, and Japan—the fruit usually flourishes without irrigation (Table 17-2).

More than one third of the oranges of commerce are produced in the United States, Florida and California accounting for about

TABLE 17-2

WORLD PRODUCTION OF ORANGES, 1961

Country	Million boxes	Per cent of total
United States	138.6	34
Spain	52.1	13
Japan	33.0	8
Italy	31.0	8
Brazil	25.0	6
Argentina	17.0	4
Morocco	14.2	4
Mexico	14.0	3
Israel	13.0	3
South Africa	12.0	3
Egypt	9.5	2
Algeria	8.0	2
Total world	403.4	100

SOURCE: Based on *Foreign Crops and Markets* (U.S.D.A.), June 28, 1962, pp. 27-29.

95 per cent of this total, Texas, Arizona, and Louisiana for the remainder.

Florida. In the early period of citrus production in this state, which today produces the bulk of the nation's oranges, cultivation was a haphazard affair, little attention being given to quality or to favorable locations. Jolted out of horticultural indifference by the "big freeze" of 1894-1895, which practically annihilated production, the growers began to locate groves in frost-protected areas and to develop a few standard varieties of higher quality. Three commercial areas stand out today: (1) the Central Ridge, where interior slopes provide air drainage and lakes temper the effect of cold north winds; (2) the west coast (especially around Tampa Bay), where the ocean modifies winter temperatures; and (3) the Indian River area along the east coast. Although oil heaters are sometimes used to control frost, most growers gamble on the occasional loss of a crop through frost rather than undergo the expense of buying and maintaining orchard heaters.

Several varieties with different ripening dates are cultivated in order to ensure a year-round supply. Most of the groves are small—10 to 25 acres; and whereas twenty to thirty years ago most farmers had their own packing houses, marketing today is in the hands of the Florida Citrus Exchange or individual large companies with centrally located packing houses.

Prior to World War II, almost all Florida oranges were marketed in fresh form. In postwar years there has been a dramatic shift to processed oranges in the form of canned and frozen juice. There is little competition in this field from California, which specializes in selling fresh fruit at premium prices. Cost of production is somewhat lower than in California, since labor and land are less expensive and irrigation usually is unnecessary.

Florida's flourishing citrus industry has been profitable in another respect: by utilizing the by-products, it has strengthened the state's booming cattle industry. Dehydrated citrus pulp provides a low-cost cattle feed, and citrus molasses has been found eminently successful for finishing and fattening the cattle.

California. In 1804, Jesuit missionaries planted the first oranges at San Gabriel Mission. But extensive commercial development did not begin until 1876, when the Southern Pacific Railroad completed connections with the East. Despite high prices, California oranges were in strong demand in Eastern markets, and frenzied planting and speculation were halted only in 1882-1883, when many growers—faced with drought, frost, and scale, together with the lack of a coherent marketing organization—gave up. By 1890, production had resumed on a stable basis and expansion was rapid.

The lands around Los Angeles, Riverside, Redlands, Corona, Orange, and Santa Ana traditionally have led in production—the robust, almost seedless Valencia thriving near the coast in the Los Angeles Basin, the seedless Washington navel (which comprises 70 per cent of Southern California's crop) prospering in the inland eastern section of the basin. But a spectacular shift in production has occurred in the past decade. An orange mecca is in the making in the southern part of the Central Valley, for urbanization and industry in the Los Angeles area have relentlessly forced production northward (simul-

Fig. 17-5. Beautiful, mature, heavy-laden navel orange trees in a Southern California grove. The groves are meticulously and scientifically cared for. About 65 per cent of the acreage of fruits and nuts in Southern California is in citrus. (Sunkist photo. Courtesy of Sunkist Growers.)

taneously stimulating many new plantings in Arizona). Higher temperatures in the Central Valley permit the fruit to ripen and be marketed earlier than in the older areas.

California oranges are painstakingly cultivated and harvested (Fig. 17-5). Every tree in the best orchards is of pedigreed stock, and seeds are often planted in beds heated by electric cables beneath the soil surface. In the rainless summer months, the groves are irrigated at three- to five-week intervals. Wherever possible, trees are planted on sloping alluvial fans in order to accommodate air drainage and thus lessen the frost hazard. In addition, wind machines or orchard heaters are frequently used to combat frost. At ten years of age, a grove is normally in full bearing; but, if the trees are properly tended, size and yield may increase for many years thereafter. Oranges are harvested throughout the year.

Most growers are members of a massive cooperative marketing organization, Sunkist Growers, Inc., which emphasizes research, advertises vigorously, demands high standards, and provides a marketing efficiency impossible to independent shippers.

The Mediterranean Basin. The orange is a highly important crop in the warm areas of the Mediterranean Basin; for good-quality, low-cost fruit can be produced in advantageous locations for export to the markets of Northwest Europe.

The major producer is Spain, whose principal export is citrus fruits, chiefly oranges, accounting on the average for one fourth of the country's total exports based on value. Western Germany provides the largest market. Small holdings (1 to 2 acres) are concentrated in the Valencia district; mechanization is nil.

Second in output is Italy, with groves centered on the southwest coast and on Sicily. Italy is unique in having the most northerly citrus areas in the world—latitudes 44° to 46°—at the foot of the Italian Alps along Lake Garda's shores and on the coast around Genoa.

A strong role in the economy of Israel is played by citrus fruits, especially oranges; most of the groves are located on the coastal plain, from Haifa in the north to the Gaza Strip. In recent years citrus fruits, including processed by-products, have accounted for approximately two fifths of the value of all Israeli exports. In Israel, as in Spain, there is a moderately good capacity for processing; but the modern plants languish as a result of inadequate supplies of fruit, since the fresh fruit brings higher prices.

Algeria and Morocco are becoming increasingly important in commercial orange production. France is the major outlet for the oranges, which are grown in Algeria (mainly in the environs of Oran and Algiers), and in Morocco on the Atlantic coastal plains.

Japan. In the Orient, only Japan is an important commercial grower; and the preponderant fruit produced is the mandarin orange (tangerine). Although cultivation is intensive, cheap labor and utilization of otherwise unarable land (as on the terraced hillsides of small Inland Sea islands, where each terrace can hold only one row of small trees) render production feasible. The south coast of Honshu—from Yokohama southwestward to the island of Kyushu—is the major area of production.

Latin America. Although all Latin American nations cultivate oranges, only Brazil, Argentina, and Mexico are commercially important.

Production in Brazil—on 50,000 to 60,000 acres—centers chiefly in the state of São Paulo and to a lesser extent in the states of Rio de Janeiro and Minas Gerais. At present, Brazil is not a major orange-exporting country.

Mexico, with major commercial acreage on the west coast in the states of Sonora, Sinaloa, Nayarit, and Jalisco, has been expanding orange production notably. However, inferior agricultural practices, with resultant low-quality fruit, limit exports.

South Africa. Long a producer of oranges, especially in the dry-summer subtropical area, South Africa has a marketing program that vies in efficiency with that of the United States. Approximately two thirds of the output is destined for export, primarily to Great Britain. Citrus ranks second only to wool in the nation's export trade.

Australia. Oranges are grown in five of the six Australian states, Tasmania being the lone exception. Production is mostly under irrigation and in areas of sandy soils. Principal areas of orange growing are in the irrigated districts of the Murray and Murrumbidgee Rivers and in the Gosford district on the coast north of Sydney. Most of the output is consumed in Australia; very little is exported.

THE GRAPEFRUIT

Brought to Florida from the West Indies in 1809, the grapefruit served as merely an ornamental tree until 1880. By 1905, production started to become impressive, and today the United States dominates world output. The nation accounts for more than 90 per cent of the total annual crop, with Florida producing the bulk. Texas has always ranked a close second, but production there has been marked by violent ups and downs. Grapefruit (and to a lesser extent, orange) production has centered in the lower Rio Grande area. This northerly limit for citrus cultivation has been harassed by freezes and droughts. However, extensive cultivation of the popular, high-quality pink grapefruit has helped to boost production and marketing.

Numerous other citrus countries grow some grapefruit, but Israel and South Africa are the only other exporters of note.

THE LEMON

From its probable birthplace in Cochin China, the lemon eventually reached the Canary Islands, whence it was brought to the New World by Columbus. Today more than half of the world's lemons are grown in California and Arizona. The frost-sensitive tree finds its best clime in the coastal areas of Southern California. Florida formerly was a lemon producer, but output has become negligible because the frost hazard has proved to be too formidable.

Almost half of California's and Arizona's output goes into concentrate for lemonade and concentrated lemon juice, which have the blessing of an expanding domestic and foreign market. By utilizing cull lemons, California has become an impressive producer of citric acid (which brings in a yearly profit of almost 7 million dollars), lemon oil, and pectin.

Ranking second in world production, Italy grows most of her lemons on the island of Sicily; lemons and oranges together normally account for more than two fifths of Sicily's export trade. The island's arid, rugged terrain demands intensive cultivation of the crop. The expression of oil from lemon rinds is an important Sicilian industry (800 to 1,100 lemons are needed to yield 1 pound of oil). Spain, Argentina, and Greece are the only other lemon producers of note.

THE LIME

The lime, one of the sourest fruits marketed, was domesticated in the East Indies; since it is extremely susceptible to cold, it therefore remains a distinctly tropical crop. It is grown primarily for juice, is a source of citric acid, and has long been used medicinally to prevent scurvy (although its vitamin-C content is actually only one fourth that of the orange or the grapefruit).

Mexico produces more than 50 per cent of total commercial world output; the West Indies and Florida supply about 25 per cent, and Egypt the remainder.

WORLD TRADE IN CITRUS FRUITS

Higher-quality fruit, expanded plantings, improved marketing facilities, progressive technology, rising level of living, and nutritional education have combined to almost triple world citrus production and consumption in the last three decades. Imports were sharply intensified in the 1950s in Canada, Scandinavia, and the countries in the European Economic Community. Consumption in the United States and in Latin America has increased 270 per cent, while that in the Mediterranean producing countries rose only by 50 per cent.

The major Mediterranean citrus lands and South Africa, though together accounting for less than 25 per cent of the total world output, each export more than half of their production (except Italy, which exports only a third), and their Western European markets absorb more than three fourths of world citrus exports.

The United States, the only major citrus area that provides fresh citrus fruit throughout the year, contributes more than 40 per cent of the world output; but only 11 per cent enters the world market. Yet in recent years citrus shipments have averaged more

than 30 million dollars annually—the highest of any United States fruit exports in value. Half of the American crop goes to Canada, supplying her with 90 per cent of her demand. The balance of United States exports, including a substantial portion in processed form, is shipped primarily to Europe. American shipments to European markets are normally heaviest between April and August, after the bulk of Mediterranean fruit has been marketed and before heavy exports arrive from the Southern Hemisphere, chiefly from South Africa.

It is expected that five Mediterranean lands —Algeria, Spain, Israel, Morocco, and Italy— together with South Africa will continue to supply the bulk of the fresh oranges and tangerines destined for foreign markets. But exportable supplies are likely to increase in other nations, particularly the United States and Brazil.

THE GRAPE

In mythology, in history, in literature, in use and abuse, the grape is unsurpassed among all the fruits of the earth. The cultivation of the vine and the march of civilization are inseparably linked.

The European or wine grape (*Vitis vinifera*), whose descendants today account for nine tenths of the world's wine, is believed to have originated at the southern end of the Caspian Sea, thence spreading through Asia and Europe. Egypt began grape cultivation 6,000 years ago; and from the Nile, the Tigris, and the Euphrates, the grape moved to Greece, to Rome, to all the fringes of the Mediterranean, and into the heart of Europe. The grape proved to be an inspiration not only to Europe's poets but also, if more prosaically, to Europe's economy. Wine became the staple mealtime beverage.

Eastern America had a profusion of native vines—forebears of the famous Concord, Delaware, Catawba, and Niagara grapes (hybrids of native species and the wine grape)—which moved Leif Ericson to bestow the name Vineland on the land. Vine cultivation was established by Cortez in Mexico two decades after the arrival of Columbus; and these vines, imported from Spain, eventually accompanied the Franciscans to Southern California, where in 1769 Father Junipero Serra planted the vinous colonizer that initiated California's vigorous viticulture. However, it took a half century for grape growing to become a commercial enterprise.

NATURAL ENVIRONMENT OF GRAPES

The European grape is a species that thrives in the Mediterranean Subtropical climate, for it requires a short rest period; a long, hot, dry summer (summer rains enhance the possibility of fungus); and a mild, moist winter. Therefore, few species are cultivated within 20 degrees of the equator. Freezing may destroy the vine, and a 150-day frost-free period is necessary. Untimely precipitation during ripening or harvesting (September to the north of the equator, March to the south of it) causes the grapes to rot. In eastern humid United States, varieties developed from native American grapes or hybridized with the *vinifera* can tolerate lower temperatures and more moisture, and are less susceptible to fungus diseases and insect pests.

A loose, well-drained soil is the most congenial to the grape; therefore, as Virgil put it, "Bacchus loves the hillsides." It is the type of soil that decides, in large measure, whether the grapes will produce a good wine: arid, gravelly hills rather than fertile plains bring forth the best wines, and a distance of just a few feet can make the difference between a good wine and a superb one.

KINDS OF GRAPES AND THEIR USES

Grapes are classified as wine, raisin, currant, table, juice, and canning varieties. Most grapes can be eaten dried or fresh. When crushed, the mature fruits of all grapes—of which there are about 8,000 varieties—ferment into wine, but only a few varieties result in high-quality wines. Approximately 80 per cent of the world's annual grape crop goes into wine. Through the ages, wine making has emerged as a science and an art, which, among its most dedicated practitioners, hovers precariously at the edge of mysticism.

Raisins are the sun-dried fruit obtained from wine grapes having a firm flesh and high sugar content. The sun literally makes raisins, boosting sugar content to about 20 per cent. The raisins of commerce are principally produced from two varieties—sultana (seedless) and muscats (seeded). Less than a dozen types of grapes are cultivated extensively for table use. *Currants*, a variety that has long been concentrated in Greece, are small, dried, seedless grapes.

WORLD GRAPE PRODUCTION

Grapes contribute approximately 60 per cent of the world's deciduous-fruit tonnage. Europe easily dominates world production; together with North Africa and Mediterranean Asia, it accounts for at least 80 per cent of the world crop. France, Italy, and Spain produce approximately three fifths of the world's wine; France, long the major grape and wine nation on earth, has recently been superseded by Italy in production. Portugal, Algeria, and Yugoslavia maintain a sturdy grape industry, while the United States, Argentina, and Chile lead in the Western Hemisphere. Soil and weather conditions, as well as dense populations offering much skilled labor for such an intensive industry, have made virtually all Mediterranean localities especially outstanding in viticulture.

In the Mediterranean lands, viticulture thrives on stony uplands and steep slopes, for the vine's deep taproot is a natural drought resister. The northern limits of commercial grape cultivation are determined by low summer temperatures, and the eastern limits by low winter temperatures and shorter summers. Viticulture thus extends from western coastal France near the mouth of the Loire River northeastward to about 53° north in Germany (Fig. 17-6) and as far east as the Polish border and Moldavia in Russia.

France. Most of France's grape crop is used for wine—an annual average of 1.6 billion gallons; and the nation exports two thirds of all the wines entering the world market. Wine grapes, yielding as high as 400 gallons of wine per acre, are widely grown in central and

Fig. 17-6. Grape culture in the Rhenish Palatinate, Germany. From this area, where the multi-terraced slopes are literally covered with vineyards, emanate the southernmost German Rhine wines for which Germany is so famous. Germany is notable far more for the quality than for the quantity of her wines; the supply is usually less than the demand, and the best bottles command exceedingly high prices. (Courtesy of German Tourist Information Office.)

southern France; but the area between the Pyrenees Mountains and the Rhone River contributes more than half the total production. As in other European wine lands, several regions, each renowned for a particular type of wine after generations of cultivation, are outstanding—e.g., Burgundy, Bordeaux, Champagne, Cognac (famous for its brandy, which is distilled wine). Since France exports only its finest wines, the French themselves drink only one tenth of the luxury wines, their intake (some 25 to 30 gallons per capita a year)

being largely comprised of *vin ordinaire*, much of which is imported from Algeria, Italy, Spain, and Portugal.

Since (1) Frenchmen regard water as eminently suitable for washing and little else (in at least 26,000 French villages water is undrinkable in any case), (2) wine is the cheapest beverage available, (3) workers often have been paid partly in wine, and (4) the livelihoods of 4 to 5 million Frenchmen are indirectly or directly dependent on wine, it is doubtful that France will easily yield her traditional supremacy as a wine-producing and wine-consuming nation.

Italy. Vying with France as the world's foremost grape and wine producer, Italy contributes more than one fifth of the world's total crop. Yields are lower than in France, though acreage—about 25 per cent of the cultivated land—is larger. Limestone hills and dry summers strongly favor viticulture, which is practiced all over the country—northern Italy providing almost half of the crop. Interculture —planting the vine in association with other crops—is a notable feature in the Italian agricultural landscape. Italy's wines, usually totaling more than 1 billion gallons annually, are not so greatly esteemed as those of some other countries; yet they manage to account for approximately 20 per cent of the value of Italian agricultural production.

Spain and Portugal. Spain (the world's third leading source of wine) and Portugal are both important wine producers and exporters. Viticulture is practiced almost throughout Spain; but the largest acreage and choicest grapes are to be found in the south, where Malaga, Alicante, and Jerez de la Frontera ("sherry" is a corrupted version of the name Jerez) produce particularly highly regarded wines. Spain's sherry is largely exported to the United States and Britain.

In northern Portugal's densely populated, intensively cultivated Douro Valley, viticulture has a prominent place on the well-exposed slopes. At the mouth of the Douro is Portugal's second port—Oporto—which since the eighteenth century has exported its prized "port" wine, mainly to Great Britain. Though Portugal's vineyard acreage is something less than half that of Spain, her exports sometimes exceed those of her peninsular partner.

Greece. Greece has the most diversified grape industry in Europe. She is the world's foremost producer and exporter of currants and is also noted for her raisin, wine, and table grapes. Currant production is centered in the Corinth section of the Peloponnesus. The Peloponnesus also produces sultanas, but the island of Crete contributes the bulk of the nation's sultanas on its coastal plain. Since raisins and dried currants are by far the world's main dried fruits, Greece has become the world's largest exporter of dried fruits, her chief market being Western Europe.

Turkey. Soil and climate favor viticulture over much of Turkey up to an altitude of 4,500 feet. Long outstanding as an exporter of sultana raisins, Turkey produces these grapes mainly in the Aegean Sea region. Yields are poor, from 1,000 to 3,000 pounds per acre (compared with an average 6,000 pounds in California), but total raisin production in the 1960s approached 90,000 tons.

North Africa. Although Morocco and Tunisia are substantial wine producers, it is Algeria that is outstanding (450 million gallons in 1959), its exports going almost entirely to France. Algerian viticulture is centered in the departments of Oran and Algiers. Since Moslems do not drink wine, North African wines are relabeled and exported under French, Italian, and Spanish flags.

Western United States. Robert Louis Stevenson once prophesied that California would become distinguished for its "bottled poetry," and his prediction has generously borne fruit: California's vineyards annually provide about 90 per cent of the national crop, and from them come some of the finest wines in the world. However, they account for only about 3 per cent of the world's wine grapes.

Some 20,000 farmers are engaged in viticulture, many of them working large holdings of several hundred acres (the largest is approximately 5,000 acres). Fresno in the San Joaquin Valley is the center of raisin production; the valley's sunny, rainless summers are ideal for natural drying. Here are grown all the raisins in the United States and normally more than in the rest of the world combined.

Wine-grape acreage, too, is large in the Central Valley (the San Joaquin Valley and the Sacramento Valley). In contrast to most European grape areas, the vineyards here are planted on relatively level land and are sometimes irrigated. The Sacramento Valley and the coastal valleys north and south of San Francisco Bay are second in wine-grape output; Southern California is the third producing area. Compensating for the encroachment of housing and industrial developments on the older vineyards, new wine-grape-growing areas are being established.

California is a wine-favored state because it not only reflects but in some ways improves upon the European climates and terrains. Because of rather stable climatic conditions and methods of production, uniform wines are produced year after year; the rare vintage year, which gives distinction to European wines, is therefore commonplace in California.

California has pioneered in the use of highly mechanized equipment in wine production. Crushing and pressing, which for centuries were carried out by laborers stamping on the grapes with their bare feet, is seldom practiced anywhere today; in California two mechanized operations perform the task. Through expensive and painstaking cultivation and processing, California wines now vie with the best European imports.

In the West, the only other producer of note is the dry, irrigated Yakima Valley of Washington.

Eastern United States. Wine-grape growing had its inception in the eastern United States when the Colonial Assembly in Jamestown offered a prize to anyone who could produce a palatable wine. For 200 years viticulturists tried and failed, because the roots of imported European vines were killed by fungi native to America. This viticultural misdirection was remedied only after hybrids between the native species and the European wine grape were developed; expansion thereafter was rapid and consistent. Today grape culture prospers mainly in New York, and continues through Pennsylvania and northern Ohio, and then jumps over to western Michigan. The Great Lakes, through their tempering influence, promote maturation of the grape on the leeward shores. Central New York's Finger Lake district benefits from similar environmental conditions together with air drainage.

Although California, with its 22,000 vineyards, contributes almost all United States wines, the East outranks it in production of champagne. New York particularly is outstanding, turning out annually some 720,000 gallons of premium champagne, in contrast to California's 660,000. The site of New York's champagne industry lies in the same isothermal line and benefits from similar soil and climatic conditions as does the heart of the French champagne industry, the Espernay district. Wineries in Ohio and in a few scattered spots around the nation contribute an additional 36,000 gallons of champagne each year.

South America. Several South American nations cultivate the vine for home use; only Argentina and Chile, however, are substantial commercial producers. Since the South American grape season is opposite that of North America, considerable trade in fresh grapes has developed, the export season to the United States being from February to June.

Surrounded by desert land, the Mendoza and San Juan districts of west-central Argentina, irrigated by streams running off the nearby Andes, produced enough wine grapes in 1959 to rank the nation fourth in world wine output. Mendoza utilizes its grapes almost exclusively for wine, while San Juan packs raisins and fresh table grapes in addition to wine.

In the Mediterranean portion of the Central Valley of Chile lies an area with a grape culture of long standing. The irrigated land produces large, sweet, juicy grapes, which yield a rich red wine in a class of its own. Domestic consumption is substantial (about 18 gallons per capita annually), as are wine exports.

Most South American wineries obtain more wine per ton of grapes than do United States producers; they add sugar and water—a practice prohibited in California. About 90 per cent of Argentine and Chilean grapes is crushed for wine.

South Africa. The wine industry of the Cape Province, established by the Dutch more than

300 years ago, today contributes notably to the nation's economy: it provides employment for 25,000 permanent workers and for an additional 20,000 migrant laborers during the two-month harvest period.

The valleys of the Hex River Mountains and Drakensberg Mountains have a subtropical climate and chalky soils similar to those of Spain and Portugal and, like those countries, produce high-quality sherries and ports. Although the extremely hot weather precludes production of the finest wines, South Africa has a large domestic consumption and an export market of more than twenty countries—Britain, Canada, and New Zealand being the main outlets.

Australia. Like Greece, Australia emphasizes raisins and currants rather than wine in her grape culture, although her wine output is not negligible. The outstanding areas of production are in the irrigated middle courses of the Murray River and the Murrumbidgee River (mostly drying varieties) and in the non-irrigated Barossa Valley, near Adelaide (wine and brandy varieties). Most of the dried-grape products are exported, particularly to the United Kingdom, Canada, and New Zealand. Wine exports (to New Zealand, various Pacific islands, and the United Kingdom) are increasingly significant.

THE PRUNE

Prunes are plums that have a firm flesh and high sugar content and are capable of being dried whole without fermentation at the pit. Since the fruit requires a fairly long season of clear, warm, dry weather, its commercial production is limited primarily to the Pacific Coast states in North America, and to Yugoslavia, France, and Italy in Europe.

UNITED STATES

The United States annually produces more than three fourths of the world crop, with California contributing the bulk. Three central-coast valleys—Santa Clara, Sonoma, and Napa—take first place in world prune output (most of the state's remaining prune acreage is located in the Sacramento Valley).

Lesser but important prune producers are three Pacific Northwest valleys—Umpqua and Willamette in Oregon and Walla Walla in Washington—which market most of their output in the fresh or canning trade; by contrast, the bulk of California's fruit is dried.

Largely as a result of increased demand for dried prunes, production in California expanded. Not only did the sunny climate produce the sweetest fruit, but the rainless summers were ideal for the sun-drying process. After 1918, when uncommon summer rains caused a 5-million-dollar loss, gas dehydration became the preferred system and is now used almost exclusively. Artificial drying provides a much more sanitary product in far less time (ten to fourteen hours compared with ten to twenty days), results in only slight weight loss, and requires less labor. Prune production in general, however, may well be short-lived, since orchards are being rapidly uprooted to make way for industrial and urban expansion.

YUGOSLAVIA

Although in some years Yugoslavia is a poor second to the United States in dried-prune output (about one eighth that of American production), she has the advantage of proximity to European markets and therefore looms as a strong competitor. Much of her production goes into the manufacture of a plum brandy called *slivovitz*. Production is concentrated in hilly to mountainous areas south of the Sava River and west of the Morava River, where the trees are planted on sloping valley walls and on plateaus.

THE FIG

The fig has been cultivated since antiquity. Believed to have originated either on the Anatolian Plateau or in southern Arabia, it spread throughout the Mediterranean area at an early date and today is grown in almost all subtropical lands.

Of the 600 to 800 varieties of figs extant, the most important commercially is the Smyrna fig. Turkey, Algeria, Greece, Italy, and Spain are outstanding producers and exporters, accounting for the bulk of total world output. A large portion of the supply is marketed in fresh form. Turkey is famed for its high-quality dried figs produced in the environs of Izmir (formerly Smyrna). Total fig exports, preponderantly in dried form, make up less than 1 per cent of the world fruit trade.

In the United States, California and Texas are the only important fig-growing states. In contrast to Mediterranean producers, one fourth to one third of the output is dried.

FRUITS OF THE MIDDLE LATITUDES

THE APPLE

First among the fresh deciduous fruits in world trade and extent of cultivation is the apple. Native to Southwestern Asia and Southeastern Europe, it has been grown for more than 3,000 years. Apples hybridize so readily that today there are 6,500 varieties. The hardy character and superior keeping qualities of the fruit have made it a familiar one in mild mid-latitude areas; it is not grown in the tropics, where it is barred by extreme heat conditions.

The Romans carried the apple throughout Europe, including Britain. In North America, the native species was found to be of little value; only nine years after the founding of the Massachusetts Bay colony, the Pilgrim Fathers planted the first European apple trees; by 1750 numerous apple orchards dotted the landscape. Apple seeds accompanied almost every family of settlers that pushed westward across the Appalachians; not infrequently the family orchards were planted before the ground was broken for homesteading. In the first half of the nineteenth century, John Chapman (who received the deserving sobriquet "Johnny Appleseed") traveled through Pennsylvania, Ohio, Indiana, and Illinois, planting and carefully nurturing apple trees. Through his efforts and his example, apples were prodigiously planted in all the favored areas of the East and slowly accompanied the settlers westward.

In the first half of the twentieth century, home orchards declined sharply as commercial apple production became concentrated in the several areas favored by environmental, marketing, and technological conditions.

LOCATION OF APPLE ORCHARDS

Apples adapt to a variety of climates and soils (a soil with a slight amount of lime gives the best yields). The fruit can be grown at latitudes as high as 65°, but its most favorable localities lie approximately from 30° to 60° north and south of the equator. Apples need considerable cold during their rest period (about forty days, with temperatures below 45°F for commercial production) but are subject to frost injury and demand a frost-free period of about one hundred days. In late summer and early autumn, ample sunshine is desirable to develop a pleasing color.

Precipitation of 20 to 40 inches, or its equivalent in irrigation water, and freedom from severe summer drought are requisite. Topography is generally more important than soil in the selection of orchard sites. Preferred locations are (1) sloping hillsides, which provide air drainage and allow the soils to be well drained (Fig. 17-7) and (2) the leeward sides of large water bodies, where winter conditions are somewhat moderated and, in addition, early blossoming in spring is delayed until the hazard of frost damage lessens.

WORLD APPLE PRODUCTION

Table 17-3 illustrates that regionally Western Europe is by far the greatest apple producer. France takes first place nationally, normally accounting for about 20 per cent of the world crop; the bulk of her output, emanating from Normandy and Brittany, is pressed for cider. The United States is a close national second, accounting for about one fifth of the world total.

Because of the high quality of North American apples and their interesting economic-geographic pattern, a brief discussion of their production is presented.

Apples are grown commercially in thirty-nine American states, but three—Washington, New York, and Virginia—lead in output,

Fig. 17-7. Apple-blossom time in the Shenandoah Valley of Virginia—one of the nation's most famous apple-growing areas. Hillside orchards benefit from air drainage as well as good soil drainage. (Courtesy of Norfolk and Western Railway.)

TABLE 17-3

WORLD APPLE PRODUCTION,* 1962

Country	1,000 bushels	Per cent of total
United States	121,400	21
Italy	101,300	17
West Germany	77,800	13
Japan	46,100	8
France *	37,500	6
United Kingdom	22,800	4
Switzerland	20,200	3
Argentina	20,100	3
Canada	18,100	3
Australia	14,400	2
Turkey	13,800	2
Austria	13,600	2

* Dessert and cooking apples only. In addition, a few countries have notable production of apples for cider; France, the only outstanding cider producer, produced 180.5 million bushels for this purpose in 1962.

SOURCE: Based on *World Agricultural Production and Trade* (U.S.D.A.), April 1963, p. 25.

Washington alone contributing one fourth to one third of the national total. Michigan, California, and Pennsylvania compete for fourth place. The Eastern states, of course, have the advantage of proximity to the largest metropolitan markets and account for about 50 per cent of the harvested crop. Canadian production, which is to be found principally in British Columbia (Fig. 17-8), Ontario, and Nova Scotia, amounts to one tenth that of the United States.

Nine important commercial apple districts are found in North America:

1. Nova Scotia's Annapolis-Cornwallis Valley, protected by a low mountain ridge from winds blowing across the Bay of Fundy.

2. New England, benefiting from air drainage of its hilly terrain; and western New York and southern Ontario, lying in the lee of Lakes Erie and Ontario, whose tempering influence expedites the fruit's maturation.

3. Appalachia—the piedmont of southern Pennsylvania, Virginia, and northern North Carolina. The Virginia Piedmont, fringing the Blue Ridge from the James River to the Rappahannock River, is particularly outstanding. Here are combined a cool climate with adequate sunshine and rain; fairly rich, deep soils retentive of moisture; and the benefits of air drainage.

4. The Shenandoah Valley—where natural and economic conditions have made the region famed for its apples; in the foremost area, "Apple Pie Ridge," an almost continuous series of apple orchards stretches from Frederick County, Virginia, to Berkeley County, West Virginia.

Fig. 17-8. Apple orchards on gently sloping land in the Kamloops Valley of British Columbia. (Courtesy of the Canadian National Film Board, Ottawa.)

5. Lower peninsular Michigan, lying in the lee of Lake Michigan with its highly favorable moderating effects.

6. The Ozark Plateau, where the rolling-hill country from northwestern Arkansas through southwestern Missouri makes it one of the few Southern areas congenial to apple production; lack of nearby markets is, however, a disadvantage.

7. The Rocky Mountain irrigated areas, where apples are grown largely for consumption in urban areas and mining towns within the region; some of the fruit is even shipped east.

8. The inland irrigated valleys east of the Cascades—Okanagan (British Columbia), Wenatchee and Yakima (Washington), and Hood (Oregon)—which vary in altitude from 300 to 1,000 feet. From these areas are sent out some of the most beautiful apples in the world; a large part of American apple exports (15 to 20 per cent of the commercial crop) is shipped from Washington ports.

9. The coastal valleys of California north and south of San Francisco, where there is air drainage and where the ample sunshine helps produce highly colored, highly marketable apples.

WORLD TRADE IN APPLES

International conditions and size of crop. combine to make foreign trade in apples fluctuate widely. However, the European producers maintain the bulk of importing and exporting. United States exports have greatly declined in recent years. Australia and Canada export approximately the same amount as does the United States.

THE PEAR

Like the apple, the pear is a native of Eurasia and was familiar to all ancient peoples. Today pears are second only to apples as the most important fresh deciduous fruit entering world trade, though amounting normally to less than one third of the apple's volume.

Less hardy than the apple, this fruit has a more limited range. It does best on heavy soils having good drainage and considerable humus, and prefers regions with a relatively equable climate. More than 80 per cent of United States production is concentrated in the irrigated, dry-summer valleys near the Pacific Coast.

Europe supplies about 75 per cent of world pear output: leading countries are France (where most of the pears are pressed into a cider called perry), West Germany, Italy, and Switzerland.

The United States is the only major producer outside Europe but is a relatively modest exporter. California is by far the largest supplier, accounting for about half the United States output; Oregon, Washington, and Utah each contribute a third to a fourth as much as California. In the East, Michigan is the only important producer.

Other pear lands of note, in approximate order of production, are Japan, Turkey, Argentina, and Australia, each having an output approximately equal to that of the state of Washington.

THE PEACH

Native to China, where it has been cultivated for thousands of years, the peach had entered the Mediterranean region by the time of Alexander the Great; it reached the New World in the sixteenth century, when it was brought to Florida by the Spaniards.

Less hardy and far more perishable than either the apple or the pear, the peach does best on sandy soils and cannot be grown at the colder margins except where local conditions—e.g., slopes extending to protected valleys or proximity to large bodies of water—can mitigate spring temperatures during blossoming or delay blossoming until the frost hazard is over.

Because they are extremely perishable and attain their highest quality when nearly ripe, fresh peaches lack the marketing advantages of the more hardy deciduous fruits, which are capable of standing long periods of storage and transportation. Therefore, in the United States more than a third of the tonnage is canned; and peaches have become the most popular canning fruit.

The United States contributes more than half of the world's peach output, California normally accounting for about half the nation's production. The state's Central Valley—especially the irrigated portions of the San Joaquin Valley and the Sacramento Valley—supplies the bulk, with most of the peaches

destined for canneries (about nine tenths of the nation's canned peaches emanate from California). Washington, Utah, and Oregon are the only other producers of note in the West.

In the eastern United States, South Carolina and Georgia are the major sources. Michigan (benefiting from the tempering influence of Lake Michigan) and Pennsylvania (with peach cultivation in its elevated portions) are the leading producers in the Midwest and East, contributing only slightly less tonnage than the two major Southern peach states. Chief importers of United States canned peaches are West Germany, the United Kingdom, and Canada.

In Europe, Italy's commercial plantings on the Mediterranean coast have made the nation the outstanding European producer. Italy's fresh peaches enjoy an ever growing market in Western Europe. France annually produces about a third to a half, and Spain a sixth, of Italy's volume.

In Argentina, Chile, and Japan, substantial quantities of high-quality peaches are grown mainly for domestic consumption. By contrast, both Australia and South Africa can most of their peaches and export a high proportion of them, primarily to the United Kingdom.

THE APRICOT

The apricot, native to Asia, was cultivated in China by 2000 B.C. and reached Europe by the first century. The fruit thrives on loamy soils in the same clime suitable to the peach, but it is even more sensitive to frost.

The United States normally accounts for one third to one sixth of world output, of which California yields approximately 90 per cent and Washington and Utah the remainder. About half the tonnage is canned, and much of the remainder is dried; possibly only a quarter is consumed fresh (and that mostly in the local markets), since the apricot, like the peach, spoils rapidly. Susceptibility both to late-spring frosts and to a snout beetle—*curculio*—drastically limits apricot cultivation in the eastern United States.

In Europe, Spain traditionally dominates the market, with Italy and France vying for second place. Australia and South Africa are substantial producers, both usually processing and exporting over half the output.

NUTS

Nuts are of great value not only nutritionally (they have a high protein and fat content and are rich in mineral elements) but also agriculturally (they can be grown quite readily on otherwise nonagricultural land, and need little if any cultivation). Although in the United States nuts have been regarded primarily as a confection, in other areas—particularly in the tropics, where meat is scarce—they are used as a staple food by thousands of people.

TROPICAL NUTS

THE BRAZIL NUT

The brazil-nut tree is a native rough-barked giant of South America's Amazon forest. Each tree bears from eighteen to twenty-four capsules having a hard bony covering and containing twelve to twenty-four seeds, which are the brazil nuts of commerce. High in fat content (65 to 75 per cent) and with some protein (17 per cent), they are an important native food, but production is highly dependent on foreign demand.

The tree is well distributed in the Amazon Basin as far inland as Bolivia and Peru. The trees are never cultivated and, unlike most tropical-forest species, usually occur in groups. Particularly outstanding in output is the Tocantins River Basin.

The collection and shipment of these nuts constitute a very important industry, for edible nuts are the most valuable single commodity exported from the Amazon Basin.

From Belém and Manaus each year a large proportion of the production (which ranges from 25,000 to 45,000 tons) is exported, chiefly to the United States and Europe.

THE CASHEW NUT

Native to Brazil, the cashew nut is today most extensively cultivated in tropical southwest India and Mozambique—less so from Mexico to Peru and Brazil, in the West Indies, in Florida, in Indonesia, and even in the Mediterranean area.

The state of Kerala provides 70 per cent of India's cashew exports, of which the United States takes the bulk. The Soviet Union has recently become an additional outlet. Mozambique's cashew industry is a particularly thriving one.

Difficulty in shelling has hampered commercial culture, but improved methods of handling the nut kernels have recently made this very rich nut more popular in Europe and the United States.

SUBTROPICAL NUTS

THE ENGLISH (PERSIAN) WALNUT

Native to Southwestern Asia (probably the Caucasus Mountains), the English walnut is now widely cultivated in most Mediterranean lands, in Asia (especially China), and in California and Oregon in the United States. The hardier varieties can tolerate temperatures as low as —10°F to —15°F. Since growth begins in early spring, less hardy varieties are endangered by frost. The trees are not widely cultivated outside of dry-summer areas because they are susceptible to fungi in more humid climates.

France and Italy are the major European contributors, with Turkey a poor third. In the United States the main producing areas are California's Central Valley and coastal valleys north and south of San Francisco Bay and Oregon's Willamette Valley. California, not only through its heavy output but also through its highly efficient marketing organization, easily dominates the United States market. American walnut production is often equal to that of the entire Mediterranean area. However, American walnuts are competitive in European markets only during years of a short crop abroad or a domestic surplus. Chief competitors at home and abroad are France, Italy, India, and Iran.

THE ALMOND

The almond, being the world's most popular nut, understandably has the largest volume in world trade. A native of the eastern Mediterranean region, the nut continues to be widely grown there and enjoys extensive cultivation throughout Mediterranean lands, in California, and even in Australia and South Africa.

Italy dominates world production, yielding 36 per cent of the world's crop. Spain ranks second and the United States third. Most of the balance is made up by Iran, Portugal, and Morocco. The United Kingdom, West Germany, and France, in order of rank, are the largest importers.

For quality, no other almonds in the world equal those of California. The almond was first brought to the state by the Franciscans; large-scale cultivation began in the late nineteenth century, and in the 1950s, thanks largely to improved varieties, output zoomed —a mammoth crop of 82,800 tons being produced in 1959. Six thousand farm families are dependent on some 110,000 acres of almonds in the state. Since almonds are not easy to grow and production costs run high, marketing has always been a problem because of far lower production costs abroad and the consequent challenge of foreign imports. This competition has been considerably subdued by the efficiency of the grower-owned Almond Growers Exchange, which has enabled California almonds to account for one fifth of the world's commercial kernel production, though only for approximately 10 per cent of the unshelled nuts.

THE PECAN

A native of southeastern United States and Mexico, the pecan was originally obtained from wild trees. However, its popularity in the past few decades has soared sufficiently to initiate extensive cultivation in the South—particularly Texas, Oklahoma, Georgia, and Louisiana; and new varieties are now to be found northward into Virginia, Indiana, and the upper Mississippi Valley. Pecans are unique in having a higher fat content—more than 70 per cent—than any other agricultural product. The trees are easy to grow, start to bear within three to four years, and their nuts

sell for a high price. Exports, however, are not large.

MIDDLE-LATITUDE NUTS

THE FILBERT

The thick-shelled, sweet-flavored filbert (or hazelnut) is an old-timer in Europe. Today Turkey's Black Sea region near the Russian border has made the nation the giant in filbert production, annually contributing about 60 per cent of the world output. Italy ranks second, with one fourth of the total; and Spain, in third place, accounts for about one tenth. West Germany and the United Kingdom are the largest importers. Because of its sensitivity to weather conditions, the size of filbert crops varies widely from year to year.

WORLD OUTLOOK

The outstanding producing nation in fresh and processed fruits generally has been the United States, but it now faces a number of problems in maintaining leadership.

Two important factors affect world trade in fruits and, to a lesser extent, nuts: (1) Weather conditions in any season may so affect supplies as to eliminate normal markets or create abnormal ones. (2) Consumer incomes may rise enough to establish new trade patterns—as, for example, has happened recently in Western Europe (which takes 43 per cent of United States fruit and nut exports) and Canada (which takes 41 per cent). Today the Soviet Union and Europe are generally net importers of dried and fresh fruits, while South America and Africa normally import only dried fruits in large quantities.

Trade opportunities for the United States are quite seriously impeded by import and exchange controls of foreign countries. For example, extremely rigid import controls are imposed on fresh apples and pears, for most European nations are substantial producers of these fruits and desire to assure a market for their domestic production; thus, only when domestic supplies become short are United States apples and pears permitted entry. Italy prohibits almost all imports of United States fruits; and only recently has France allowed imports of United States fruits. The continued development of "common markets" all over the world promises to create additional trade barriers.

For these reasons, the United States' share of world output and trade in fresh fruits has decreased notably since prewar years. Though contributing about one fifth of the world's fresh deciduous fruit crop, the nation has accounted for only about one tenth of its world trade. In the processed form of these fruits, the exports are, however, considerably higher.

Although the United States is the world's largest producer of dried fruits (about 40 per cent of the world's commercial pack and 25 per cent of the world's trade), its output has been downward in recent years. In addition, the major importing countries have decreased consumption. Moreover, high labor requirements increase competition, on a price basis, with other producing countries.

Foreign nuts are usually imported into the United States. Only in years of surplus American production do domestic nuts generally compete for foreign markets.

Normally, foreign competitors in fruits and nuts are far more dependent on their export markets than are United States producers, who export a much smaller share of their output. But as foreign supplies continually improve in quality and increase in quantity, and more serious attention is given to marketing problems, United States producers and marketers are becoming more and more concerned about their future foreign-trade opportunities in the fruit and nut realm.

SELECTED REFERENCES

Griffin, Paul F., and Ronald L. Chatham. "Population: A Challenge to California's Changing Citrus Industry," *Economic Geography*, 34:272-276, July 1958.

May, Stacy, and Galo Plaza. *The United Fruit Company in Latin America.* Washington, D. C., National Planning Association, 1958. Seventh Case Study in Series on U.S. Business Performance Abroad.

Minneman, P. G. "France and Its Wine," *Foreign Agriculture*, 25:9-10, August 1961.

Nixon, Roy M. "The Date Palm—'Tree of Life' in the Subtropical Deserts," *Economic Botany*, 5:274-301, July–September 1951.

Norbeck, Edward. *Pineapple Town: Hawaii.* Berkeley, University of California Press, 1959.

Olmstead, Clarence W. "American Orchard and Vineyard Regions," *Economic Geography*, 32:189-236, July 1956.

Parsons, James J. "Bananas in Ecuador: A New Chapter in the History of Tropical Agriculture," *Economic Geography*, 33:201-216, July 1957.

Schreiber, W. R. *The Amazon Brazil Nut Industry.* Washington, D. C., Foreign Agricultural Service, U. S. Department of Agriculture, June 1950. Foreign Agriculture Report No. 49.

CHAPTER EIGHTEEN::

Probably no group of crops ranks with vegetables in importance both in total tonnage produced and consumed. Some types of vegetables are grown in every type of climate save the Polar Icecap. However, on a world basis, most vegetables are grown for subsistence; in most underdeveloped lands—whether in the tropical, subtropical, mid-latitude, or polar zones—vegetables have low value per unit of bulk or weight; they are perishable; and transport and refrigeration facilities are inadequate. Hence, vegetables are grown commercially (traded and shipped) essentially in the developed countries—mostly Canada and the United States, the countries in Western Europe, and Japan. However, in many of the underdeveloped countries that are emerging into intermediate status, huge quantities of vegetables are carried on the backs of mules and donkeys (and even on the backs of human beings) or in trucks and on rivers to nearby markets.

THE WORLD'S

VEGETABLES GROWN
FOR SUBSISTENCE

The bulk of the vegetables grown worldwide are not grown for sale but essentially for subsistence. This is particularly true in the tropics and the subtropics.

TROPICAL AND SUBTROPICAL VEGETABLES

MANIOC [1]

This crop, the staple of the tropics, was first domesticated by Amerindians in South America. As the basic food crop in the rain forest, manioc was grown in both the bitter

[1] Called *manioc* or *mandioca* in Brazil, *yuca* in Spanish-speaking countries, and *cassava* elsewhere.

and sweet varieties, but particularly the latter. It extended northward from Brazil to Sinaloa in Mexico, southward to Argentina, and westward and northwestward to Peru and Colombia.

Sweet manioc was eaten as a vegetable after boiling or baking, and varieties low in prussic acid were even eaten raw. Today, however, although it is still eaten as a vegetable, possibly most manioc is eaten as a coarse meal.

The Portuguese colonists who settled along the coast of Brazil turned to manioc because wheat did not do well. Soon manioc became the principal food crop. The Portuguese via Brazil also introduced manioc into Africa— to their coastal stations from West Africa to Somalia. The crop is now grown throughout the tropical world, being of major importance over immense areas. However, in Africa it has become particularly important, both in total area given over to it (more than in the Americas and Asia combined) and as a com-

VEGETABLES

ponent in the diet. It has now been spread over the entire world tropics, where it is a food of primary importance. Wherever it is grown, it is used largely for subsistence and hence has not received as much attention as such export commodities as sugar cane, palm oil, and rubber.

Manioc is grown in both the forest and the savanna. It is planted at the onset of the major rainy season, harvested in the dry season. It is grown on a given plot of land for only a few years, four at the most; the cost of clearing with hoe, knife, and axe is high. In the forest, clearing is carried on to let in more sunlight to the ground and to remove weeds and undergrowth, which would compete with the crop. The small trees are cut down, whereas most of the larger ones are left standing. Just before the rains arrive, sections of manioc stem are planted in the burned-over area. If growing conditions are particularly favorable, the crop can be harvested in as short a period as six months. On savannas, matted roots of burned grass must be hoed out; the farmers avoid land covered with elephant-grass types. Manioc is tolerant of soil, can get along with almost complete neglect, and is virtually oblivious to drought and insect invasions. The fact that it is propagated by stem cuttings appeals to the natives; for farm work in the tropics is tedious and debilitating.

Manioc is a good crop for natives to grow because it yields a high tonnage per acre (up to 40 tons) and a high amount of calories per acre and per man-hour. In addition, being a root crop, it may be left in the ground until needed—an important quality in hot, humid lands, where food spoilage is rapid (manioc is famous throughout the tropics for its remarkable keeping qualities). Moreover, it is low in price and hence attractive in lands where consumer income is low.

THE SWEET POTATO

This yellowish-colored root plant (not a tuber) is widely grown throughout the tropics and subtropics. Like the root crop manioc, it is high in starch, vitamins, and minerals. In fact, it is one of the richest of all plant foods.

Though of tropical origin it is successfully grown over a wide range of climates—in the subtropics and, in a few instances, even in the middle latitudes.

Throughout the greater portion of the tropics, the sweet potato is strictly a subsistence crop, being planted in almost every garden patch and comprising an important part of the food supply of the families of the growers. Like manioc, sweet potatoes are dug and eaten as needed, not entering trade of any kind. The aggregate of such production is indisputably high.

If one part of the world may be called most important for this crop, it is Asia (China and Japan), where the sweet potato supplements, but by no means competes with, the great staple rice. Here the sweet potato occupies the light, sandy soils, those in which rice cannot be grown. It is often confined to uplands when there is no irrigation. The sweet potato was introduced into China in 1594 as a means of relieving the frequent famines. China is believed to produce eight times more sweet potatoes than the United States. The sweet potato is important, too, in many parts of Africa; in East Africa, it often serves as an emergency crop when grain does poorly or has been damaged by locusts, since it matures in about five months.

Sweet potatoes are grown in several parts of the United States, but particularly on sandy soils in the Humid Subtropical Gulf Coast region and as far northeast as Maryland, Delaware, and New Jersey. The crop from these states is marketed in the cities of the North.

THE YAM

The yam, not to be confused with the sweet potato and more characteristically tropical, is an orange- or orange-brown root and is primarily a source of carbohydrates. It supplies starch in the Rainy Tropics and Monsoon Tropics, where white potatoes will not grow. The crop has much the same natural environmental requirements as the sweet potato, and its range is similar—although yams take longer to mature (from eight to ten months). Actually, not much is known about the yam, historically, genetically, or distributionally. However, the crop has been grown in Southeast Asia, Melanesia, and Polynesia for centuries. The yam is widely grown among the tropical-forest tribes of South America, and is also grown in the United States, China, and Japan; but in all, it is less important than the sweet potato.

MIDDLE-LATITUDE VEGETABLES

Enormous quantities of vegetables are grown in the farm gardens of temperate North America, Europe, Asia, and Australia. In the United States alone, it is estimated that vegetables grown for farm use have a value exceeding 300 million dollars, compared with the 500-million-dollar farm value of those grown for sale. The typical American farm garden generally contains a great variety of vegetables handled as annuals—onions, beets, potatoes, radishes, lettuce, turnips, parsnips, sweet corn, tomatoes, beans, and peas. The amount of land used by each family is small indeed, but the vegetables are grown **intensively** and are heavily fertilized. Many retired farmers living in hamlets, villages, and towns maintain vegetable gardens.

COMMERCIAL PRODUCTION OF VEGETABLES

Vegetable production throughout the world is increasing, particularly in the developed countries, where the per capita annual wage is high (people can afford to purchase vegetables any time in the year) and where the people are educated and made highly aware of the bases of sound nutrition—so that, for instance, they are urged to eat more of the protective foods, one of which is green and yellow vegetables. Thus in the United States, the average annual per capita consumption of vegetables is 400 pounds.

To grow vegetables commercially, areas must be endowed with favorable climate or soil, or both, and have access to market. Climate, however, is regarded as the dominant factor in vegetable production. From 30 to 40 inches of rainfall or ample water for irriga-

tion, with 20 to 25 inches during the growing season, is a prerequisite in the middle latitudes, with more rainfall being required in the tropics and subtropics. The length of the growing season is no problem in the tropics, where winter never comes, and not much of a problem even in most parts of the subtropics; but it definitely is a factor in middle latitudes, where vegetables are a summer crop. Therefore, regions at high elevations and those far removed from the modifying and equalizing effects of large bodies of water generally are hazardous for vegetable production. As far as temperature is concerned, vegetables fall into three major classes:

1. Those that require a large amount of heat and a long growing season—manioc, sweet potatoes, yams.

2. Those that do best under intermediate temperatures and seasonal conditions—tomatoes, beans.

3. Those adapted to cool and short growing seasons—broccoli, turnips, cabbages; or those that thrive in warm climates but only during the cooler part of the year—lettuce.

Sandy to loamy soils, readily cultivated, responding well to fertilizers, and capable of warming up rapidly in spring are regarded as best for growing vegetables of high quality. Yet so much fertilizer is used in the major commercial vegetable-growing districts that soil is commonly regarded as little more than a medium through which the various crops are fed.

Access to market is important, too. No agricultural enterprise is more subject to the operation of economic laws than that of vegetable growing. Bulk vegetables of low cost, such as potatoes, cabbages, or cauliflower, can be transported only within limited distances before the packing and haulage costs equal their market value. Exotic artichokes and Brussels sprouts, however, may be shipped considerable distances.

MARKET GARDENING

Large quantities of vegetables are produced for sale by market gardeners, whose crops are grown in the environs of large cities. They do not specialize but grow a wide variety of vegetables, replanting as soon as one crop is harvested and repeating as long as the growing season lasts. They gather their vegetables in the late afternoon and early evening, prepare them for market later in the evening, and deliver them to city markets during the night. Land and labor invariably are expensive, but propinquity to market is the prime economic factor. All types of soils are employed, but possibly the preferred one is sandy loam. Thus, west of Cleveland, Ohio, the sandy loam soils on either side of the old ridge roads are preferable to the heavy clays of the old lake plain, since they favor earlier harvests. Warm soils bring into bearing successive crops, each a bit earlier than in ordinary nearby gardens. Lavish application of commercial fertilizers enriches the light soils, producing yields that are high in quality and quantity. The value of market-garden land is greater per acre than that devoted to any other type of farming. Most cities are literally ringed by market gardens.

The greenhouse is an important aspect of market gardening. In many areas vegetables are grown under glass. Two areas are presented here—that in the Netherlands and that near Cleveland, Ohio.

THE NETHERLANDS

In an area west of the road from The Hague to Rotterdam may be observed nearly one fifth of the world's market gardening under glass. Here some 900 acres in fruit and 6,000 in vegetables yield products valued annually at 85 million dollars. An additional 5,000 acres are under glass elsewhere throughout the Netherlands. The total in 1960 was 12,500 acres. Favoring this enterprise are the warming influence of the Gulf Stream, the type of soil, and the nearness to ports.

The leading vegetable crops are tomatoes, cucumbers, lettuce, and cauliflower; the principal fruits are grapes, peaches, strawberries, plums, and melons. The small, red, quality tomatoes are popular throughout Western Europe. Catch crops of flowers and lettuce assure year-round utilization of the houses.

Greenhouse gardening requires great skill, hard work, much capital, and adaptability to new methods. Besides supplying such large domestic markets as Amsterdam and Rotterdam, the gardens under glass send much produce to West Germany, the United Kingdom, and Sweden.

CLEVELAND, OHIO

Over a distance of 60 miles south and west of Cleveland are to be seen dozens of vegetable greenhouses (Fig. 18-1), covering about 400 acres—by far the largest concentration in the United States and third largest in the world. Several factors favor this industry:

1. Light, sandy soil that does not pack down when watered.

2. The modifying effect of Lake Erie (fewer extremes of outdoor temperature).

3. Greater elevation of the lake ridges; even though they are only 200 feet above the lake, there is a greater condensation of moisture and higher humidity.

4. Water of correct quality for irrigation.

5. Short distance to Cleveland and many other large cities; trucks can reach Cleveland in fifteen minutes, and railways can deliver the produce rapidly as far as Chicago on the west and New York on the east.

However, it was by accident that the business got started. One farmer experimented and was so successful financially that many of his neighbors decided to share in the business. As far as natural environmental conditions are concerned, other locales in the Lower Lake region are equally suitable for gardening under glass.

Although the cost of putting an acre under glass is high ($75,000, not including the land), and land, labor, heat, and fertilizer all are costly, nonetheless there are compensations: an acre in a greenhouse will grow four times as much as an acre out-of-doors. Each year 100 tons of vegetables are harvested from each acre under glass—a total of about 28,000 tons.

Tomatoes comprise about 80 per cent of the total crop, with lettuce accounting for 10

per cent, and water cress, cucumbers, endive, and radishes the remaining 10 per cent. The emphasis on tomatoes results from their being America's top vegetable. In an average spring and autumn, some 19,000 eight-pound baskets move to market from each acre—three fourths going outside the Cleveland area. Although the greenhouse growers must compete with Southern, Cuban, and Mexican growers, tomatoes from these other areas must be picked green for shipment to Northern markets, and hence they lack both the flavor and color of the glasshouse tomatoes.

Greenhouse owners must have a crop that grosses $35,000 an acre to make a fair profit, for the replacement cost of an acre of greenhouse alone is $100,000.

TRUCK FARMING

Truck farming differs from market gardening in a number of ways but mainly in the specialization of one or perhaps two, three, or four varieties of vegetables on land that is farther from consuming centers. Its advantages are climates and soils especially suited to the production of the crops grown, and cheaper land and labor; its comparative disadvantage is greater distance from markets and hence greater transport costs. Some truck-

farming areas produce two successive crops of different vegetables on the same field. Others, those in warm-winter areas, specialize in "out-of-season" vegetables and market their crop in winter or spring.

Only in Europe and North America is the urban population able to support truck farming. Major districts in Europe are (1) along the Channel Coast of Brittany and the Netherlands (for supplying the markets of Great Britain, West Germany, and northern France) and (2) the Rhone Valley—an almost continuous ribbon of truck farms. Oases in Algeria, Morocco, and Tunisia also supply appreciable quantities of early vegetables to the North European market.

In the United States there are many truck-farming areas, but only three are presented here: (1) the Middle Atlantic, (2) the South, and (3) California—the Sacramento-Stockton district, the Los Angeles area, and the Imperial Valley.

MIDDLE-ATLANTIC TRUCK FARMING

The Middle Atlantic truck-farming region extends roughly from Charleston, South Carolina, to Portland, Maine. It is more than 900 miles long and averages about 50 miles in width.

Truck farming here owes its existence primarily to three conditions: (1) sandy to loamy soils that warm up rapidly in the spring, are readily cultivated, respond well to fertilization, and produce vegetables of high quality; (2) a mild, semi-marine climate with a long **growing season**, so that vegetables can be marketed in the large urban centers one to three weeks in advance of the crops from inland districts of the same latitude; and (3) the chain of large cities that extends from Norfolk to Boston and provides the greatest market for vegetables in the world. Actually this area comprises a gigantic urban metropolis (Megalopolis) of 31 million persons. With about 2 per cent of the nation's land area, this truck-farming region contains about 20 per cent of its people.

Vegetable crops occupy but a small acreage. With a high value per acre, their aggregate worth far exceeds that of any other agricultural commodity. Although the acreage and intensity of vegetable production varies, the average area of truck crops per farm is 15 to 20 intensively cultivated acres. Crops are planted successively from early spring to late fall. Highest possible yields are attained by frequent cultivation and heavy fertilization. The use of supplementary irrigation through overhead sprinkling during dry periods ensures vegetables of the finest quality.

Because of its sandy soils and nearness to markets, New Jersey is an important producer of fresh vegetables; more than 70,000 acres are planted each year. The state leads in market production of sweet corn, peppers, asparagus, beets, eggplant, lima beans, and white potatoes.

One of the most intensive truck-farming areas in the United States is the district around Camden, New Jersey. The world's largest commercial truck-farm enterprise lies south of Camden at Seabrook; concerned with freezing vegetables, it alone accounts for almost 100 million pounds, or 15 per cent of the nation's annual frozen-foods output. Seabrook works more than 20,000 acres of farmland. One can drive for 45 miles in one direction and still be on Seabrook land. In addition, it contracts with about 1,100 other farmers for their produce. All told, it draws thirty different vegetables from some 54,000 acres. In peak

summer months, Seabrook employs approximately 3,500 workers, mostly migratory helpers from the South.

Seabrook is run on a production-line basis. From the day a seed is planted until the frozen vegetable is loaded into refrigerated trucks for shipment, each step is synchronized and carefully scheduled. Crops are harvested on specific days—sometimes even at a certain hour to prevent production bottlenecks. Through careful planning and crop scheduling, Seabrook is able to harvest and process over a period of about eight months. Spinach and kale, the first crops, begin to move to the freezing plant in late April or early May; and from then until mid-December, when broccoli and Brussels sprouts have been harvested and processed, vegetables in great variety and in an unending stream are grown, harvested, and frozen. Lima beans, peas, and spinach are the three leading crops based on volume; but corn, snap beans, asparagus, cauliflower, turnip greens, squash, and others rank very high.

Long Island, an important vegetable producer mainly for the New York market, has an extensive acreage devoted to truck farming. The white potato dominates, followed by sweet corn, cabbage, Brussels sprouts, cauliflower, beans, and tomatoes. By the middle of July, Long Island potatoes are being harvested and shipped to big cities along the Atlantic Coast to compete with early potatoes from Virginia and the Carolinas.

The Delaware-Maryland-Virginia area is noted for vegetables. Sweet corn, peas, tomatoes, lima beans, sweet potatoes, squash, cucumbers, and green beans are grown in large quantities. Rapid truck transit places the fresh vegetables from this area within reach of the large urban markets in just a few hours. In addition, nearby canneries and frozen-food plants process enormous quantities.

FLORIDA'S TRUCK-CROP PRODUCTION

Central and southern Florida grow more vegetables in the winter than any other place in the world. Huge truck farms raise as many as five crops in the season, which lasts from mid-October to June.

During a recent year, Florida's vegetable crops totaled over 158 million dollars at shipping points. This compares with 347 million dollars for citrus products. About 500,000 acres in the state are planted with citrus fruit; 398,-000 acres with truck crops; and 1,237,500 acres with field crops.

A great quantity of the state's vegetables is grown in the Glades area. Belle Glade and its neighbor, Pahokee, are the principal marketing towns in the Lake Okeechobee district. Other major markets in Florida are Homestead, Pompano Beach, Fort Pierce, and Sanford. The vegetables grown here include beans, cabbage, carrots, celery, chicory, collards, sweet corn, cucumbers, and eggplant.

The biggest truck farms in Florida total as many as 500 acres each. Here truck farming is highly mechanized. Large machines, on which about thirty persons can work at a time, harvest celery, prepare the stalks, and wash and pack them all in one fast operation. Large watering trucks irrigate the growing plants during the winter, usually the driest season in Florida. Although much of the work here is done mechanically, thousands of migrant farm laborers find employment in the fields during the fall, winter, and spring; for there is no break in the harvest season. When one crop is shipped to market, another is being planted.

Packing houses in Belle Glade and Pahokee grade, wash, pack, pre-cool, and ship fresh vegetables to all parts of the United States and Canada. The icing of loaded trucks is done with crushed ice. At the peak of the harvesting season, as many as 150 carloads a day are shipped out of this area.

CALIFORNIA'S TRUCK-CROP PRODUCTION

California produces 30 per cent of the nation's commercial vegetables for the fresh market—70 per cent of the nation's lettuce, 41 per cent of the carrots, 55 per cent of the celery, 25 per cent of the fresh market tomatoes, and virtually all of the nation's garlic,

artichokes, and Brussels sprouts. No other state raises so many different kinds of vegetables.

In dollar value and tonnage, tomatoes are California's leading vegetable crop; others of importance are asparagus, green lima beans, and snap beans. One third of the total fresh vegetables produced in California is consumed within the state. New York, Chicago, and Philadelphia are the three major terminal markets for California interstate vegetable shipments.

This state's vegetable industry is successful because climate and soil favor growth of a given crop to coincide with a profitable market. Rapid transportation, large-scale operations as a means of curbing production costs, and refrigeration justify cultivation of vegetables for distant markets.

Locally, environmental conditions are ideal for certain vegetables: the earliest vegetables —asparagus, carrots, cabbage, lettuce, and tomatoes—come from the practically frostless Imperial Valley; almost all the lima beans come from a plain near the Pacific Ocean in Ventura and Santa Barbara Counties; the celery for Eastern shipment is grown on peat lands in Orange County; cabbages and Brussels sprouts are from the Half Moon Bay littoral of San Mateo County; asparagus and tomatoes are from the Delta district near San Francisco Bay; artichokes are grown near Castroville and Carmel in Monterey County and Half Moon Bay in San Mateo County; winter lettuce comes from the Imperial Valley; and early-spring, summer, and late-fall lettuce is from the Salinas Valley (Fig. 18-2). Smaller areas of vegetable production are more scattered; but everywhere the local soil, exposure, and climate are primary considerations.

California is a leader in the vegetable-seed-growing industry, mainly because it has a relatively dry autumn, the period when the seed is harvested. Before the seed crops become available to farmers, the various strains of vegetables have had to be scientifically bred. The ultimate market gets attention: if the seed is to provide vegetables for the fresh market, the aim is to grow seed that matures over an extended period, so that a supply is available over much of the year; if, on the

Fig. 18-2. *Growing lettuce in the Salinas Valley, California, which accounts for 45 per cent of the national crop. Nowhere else in the United States does so small an agricultural area produce so large a percentage of a widely consumed commercial crop. No person can travel through this valley, with its enormous fields of lettuce, without realizing that production here is not only a science but an art. (Courtesy of Jack Bias, Grower-Shipper Vegetable Association.)*

contrary, it is to provide vegetables for freezer or cannery, the aim is to grow seed that will permit the entire crop to ripen simultaneously, so that the processor can both harvest and pack in a matter of just a few days.

LABOR AND MACHINERY IN VEGETABLE FARMING

In vegetable farming, the cost of labor has soared to such heights that farmers have been forced to buy or lease machines to do the work. In California, Mexican farm labor long provided a supplemental force (about 10 per cent of the total in 1959), but a dependable, even indispensable, force in many vegetable crops. But the unions, in organizing farm labor in California, obviously wished to halt the importation of the Mexican *bracero*. In 1963 the American Congress voted to prohibit the use of bracero labor. Many Californians who understand the seriousness of the labor shortage assert that it is impossible to get American labor. For this reason, machines are being invented and introduced to replace human beings. Single machines today do the job formerly done by whole crews of laborers. They harvest spinach, pick and shell beans, pick, top, and ready radishes for washing, dig potatoes and load them into waiting trucks, to mention but a few of their talents. In 1961, machines were developed for picking tomatoes and lettuce. The former, operated by about thirteen persons, do the work of sixty people picking by hand. They are regarded as the economic salvation of producers of California's largest canning crop, valued at 60 million dollars per annum to the growers. The lettuce harvester moves through the fields at ½ mile per hour; the cutters toss the heads into a hopper, where the lettuce is sealed in plastic bags. A conveyer belt then moves the bags to trucks, where they are crated for vacuum cooling and shipping. This machine reduces the cost of marketing lettuce by as much as 40 cents a crate.

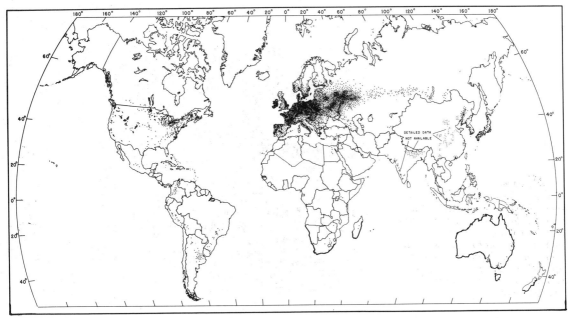

Fig. 18-3. *World potato production. Note the overwhelming concentration in Europe. All other parts of the world are insignificant by comparison. (Courtesy of U.S. Department of Agriculture.)*

GROWING OF CERTAIN SPECIFIC VEGETABLE CROPS

THE POTATO

The potato is by far the most important of all vegetable crops. First domesticated in South America, probably in the high intermontane valleys of Peru but also in south-central Chile near the coast, it was taken to Europe by the Spaniards and English toward the end of the sixteenth century. For more than 100 years following its introduction there, the potato was grown in the gardens of England and on the continent, more as a curiosity than as a food.

The potato, a tuber of the nightshade family, grows in almost any soil but finds most congenial conditions in a light, sandy, deep, mellow loam. The soil should be retentive of moisture but well drained and must not become waterlogged.

Climatically the potato is grown over a wide range—in the Northern Hemisphere from as

far north as Fairbanks, Alaska (with its growing season of 89 days), to Cuba (with its year-long growing season). Nevertheless, the potato—a hardy, short-season crop—thrives only in areas with cool, uniform temperatures and moderate rainfall. In the world's major potato-growing regions, the average total precipitation for the five-month period May–September varies from 6 to 15 inches. Heavy rainfall during the latter part of the growing season is harmful, favoring late blight and rot, and retarding harvesting of the crop in a satisfactory condition. Thus, in the United States the potato has reached its most successful culture in the northern tier of states (Maine to Minnesota), where the mean annual temperature is 40°F to 50°F and the July isotherm 70°F. The highest potato yields per acre are procured in those states where the annual temperature is below 45°F and where the mean of the warmest month is 65°F. The optimum temperature for potatoes (for tuber formation) is 59°F to 64°F.

Figure 18-3 shows where the world's 175 million tons of potatoes are grown.

THE WORLD'S VEGETABLES : : 383

Fig. 18-4. Harvesting potatoes, Aroostook County, Maine.
Once a laborious, backbreaking
task requiring gangs of field
hands, the potato harvest of today is a fast, highly mechanized
operation. (Courtesy of University of Maine Agricultural Extension Service.)

EUROPEAN POTATO PRODUCTION

Potatoes are to Europe what rice is to Asia
and corn to North America. Four countries—
the Soviet Union, West Germany, Poland, and
France—account for approximately two thirds
of the world output. Europe leads, too, in
annual consumption of potatoes in pounds per
capita per annum. For example, Western
European peoples consume two to four times
as many potatoes as do Americans (who average 142.7 pounds per capita annually): Belgium, 440; France, 400; Germany, 398; Denmark, 246; Great Britain, 210.

UNITED STATES POTATO PRODUCTION

The United States is a small producer of
potatoes compared with Europe. Yet some
potatoes are grown in every state of the Union:
Maine leads by far, producing about 17 per
cent of the total crop; California ranks second,
and Idaho third. Additional states in order
of output are New York, Pennsylvania, Colorado, North Dakota, Michigan, Minnesota,
Wisconsin, Oregon, and Washington. Potato
production in three areas only is presented
here.

Aroostook County, Maine. Aroostook County
is America's outstanding potato-growing area,

producing nearly one eighth of the national
crop and getting the highest per-acre yield
of any major American district. The county
combines a glacial soil of light silt loam,
a nearly level terrain, an abundant rainfall,
and a cool growing season. Today the business is highly mechanized (Fig. 18-4).

Both food and seed potatoes are grown.
Aroostook potatoes used for food are to be
found in markets as far west as Cleveland
and at times even Chicago. The seed potatoes
are in strong demand in the Middle Atlantic
truck-farming region and throughout the South
where potatoes are grown.

San Joaquin Valley, California. This valley,
particularly the Kern County portion, ranks
high in the production of early potatoes.
Hundreds of carloads are shipped out of the
valley each year. The crop is irrigated and,
95 to 100 days after planting, is dug. After
sacking, the potatoes are taken to sheds for
washing, grading, and final sacking, and then
to market under suitable refrigeration.

Idaho. Idaho, unique among potato-growing regions, is an exception to the statement
that potatoes have low value per unit of bulk

and weight, are perishable, and hence cannot be shipped great distances. Idaho potatoes are shipped into every part of the nation (irradiated to preserve them). Potato production is favored here by volcanic soil and by high altitude, hot days, and cool nights. Idaho's moist, mealy tuber is higher in starch than potatoes grown elsewhere. The "Idaho baker" is regarded as the world's tastiest baking potato. Consumption of Idaho potatoes has been increasing, whereas that of potatoes grown elsewhere in the nation has been declining. Great quantities of potatoes are dehydrated; this enables the product, which is high in value in proportion to weight, to stand transport charges to distant markets.

Since potatoes are grown on land valued at $600 to $800 per acre and under irrigation (also expensive), and since labor is high, production costs also are high. In order to slash such expenses, farmers are using more and more labor-saving equipment. Since most of the farms are small, much of the agricultural machinery is purchased cooperatively. More than three fourths of the potatoes as harvested are elevated from the digging machine into motor trucks as a means of saving the labor of picking up the potatoes by hand.

EXAMPLES OF VEGETABLE CROPS IN UNITED STATES

THE TOMATO

Tomatoes—which comprise one of America's most important vegetables, leading all others (except potatoes and sweet potatoes) in both acreage and value—are grown in every state in the United States. The principal areas are eastern Maryland, Delaware, and New Jersey —the greatest tomato-growing district in North America and probably in the world, western New York, western Ohio, central Indiana, southern Michigan, northwestern Illinois, and the Sacramento Valley of California. The commercial crop of early tomatoes is grown in Florida, the lower Rio Grande Valley, and Southern California. (They are grown unprotected all winter, but in California's desert valleys windbreak protection is in-

stalled on the north side of the rows with the approach of cold weather.)

This crop will not tolerate frost and is not grown where the season is less than four or six months from seed to harvested crop. Tomatoes do best where monthly mean temperatures are 70°F to 75°F; yet they will scald if exposed to a hot sun.

Tomatoes grown for canneries are harvested several times during the season (three or four times in California), and are carefully inspected before being hauled to the canneries, which may be as far as 100 miles distant.

LETTUCE

Lettuce is an outstanding commercial vegetable—particularly in the United States, where salads are popular. Lettuce is a cool-weather crop, and hence its growers adjust production accordingly. It is grown in all parts of the nation, but the tiny Salinas Valley of California —despite its remoteness from the large Eastern urban markets—accounts for about 45 per cent of the national commercial head-lettuce crop, the most popular type. Here is to be found a favorable combination of circumstances: a prevalence of summer fogs, which maintain a lower and more even temperature during the high-sun period, clay loams and sandy clay-loam soils, flat land, and ample underground and surface water for irrigation. The crop is planted on raised beds, which facilitate irrigation and drainage.

Because lettuce is perishable and is grown a great distance from Eastern markets, the business is necessarily speculative. The crop is received in distant markets six to ten days after it leaves Salinas. Salinas Valley lettuce must meet competition from Arizona, Texas, Colorado, Idaho, Oregon, and Washington at various times throughout its season, and from mid-June through September with Eastern market gardens for New York and New Jersey markets. Large shipments move by truck to San Francisco and Los Angeles.

The California winter crop of lettuce and about one fourth of the total annual output is grown in the Imperial Valley. This lettuce is consumed in December–March, when the fields in the Salinas Valley are unproductive.

WORLD TRADE IN FRESH VEGETABLES

Considering the enormous production of vegetables throughout the more densely inhabited portions of the earth, the proportion entering foreign trade is indeed small; but it is increasing. Denmark, Italy, the Netherlands, and Spain both export and import vegetables. Principal markets for exports in Europe are the United Kingdom and West Germany.

In North America there is considerable international trade in vegetables. The United States exports mostly to Canada (about 70 per cent) and imports mostly from Canada (50 per cent) and Mexico (36 per cent). United States imports of fresh vegetables come mostly in the winter months and cease just as soon as domestic producing areas begin to ship in volume. Imports of winter vegetables from Mexico's west coast consist of tomatoes, green corn, garlic, peppers, and squash. The last shipments pass through Nogales, Arizona, usually between June 16 and June 30 but occasionally as late as July 15. This part of Mexico, with the Culiacan Valley as the chief center, is outstanding in the growing of both ground and pole tomatoes and in a given year may have as many as 60,000 acres in tomatoes.

WORLD OUTLOOK

In most developed countries people eat more and more vegetables, especially those rich in vitamins A and C, calcium, riboflavin, and iron. In the United States the average use of tomatoes has doubled in the past fifty years; much more lettuce, too, is eaten. (Consumption of potatoes, on the contrary, declined 28 pounds per capita from 1943 to 1958—a situation attributable to the great concern of Americans over the matter of overweight caused by too many starchy products.) As a result of the work by WHO (World Health Organization), efforts are also being made to get the peoples in the underdeveloped lands to grow and consume more vegetables; for their diets are notoriously deficient in vitamins (particularly vitamin C) and several minerals.

It is interesting to note that the trend in vegetable production and consumption is up, whereas in area it is down. Better methods of cultivation, including particularly heavy fertilization, result in larger per-acre yields. Land given over to vegetables invariably is **intensively** tilled.

The tendency is to have each area that can do so grow its own vegetables; for the crop is costly to produce and to distribute, and—despite refrigeration of rail cars, trucks, commission houses, and markets—deterioration ever threatens. Moreover, the high proportion of water content means that vegetables occupy much space and pay heavy transport charges in proportion to their nutritive value.

All areas that specialize in commercial production of vegetables constantly face the threat of glutted markets, since it is easy to produce more fresh vegetables than markets can absorb. In 1955, transportation accounted for 8 cents of every retail vegetable dollar, up from 6 cents in 1945. When vegetables are sold at retail in a city closer to the source of supply, the proportion of the price made up by transportation is generally lower than for the same commodity sold at a longer distance from the point of supply. Thus, California lettuce carried a transportation charge of 23½ cents per retail dollar in Chicago (in 1955), contrasted with one of 33 cents for New York City.

The low value and perishability of most vegetables make their transportation to market a real challenge to growers. Hence, each area will attempt to supply its own nearby markets; however, subtropical areas such as California and the South, which produce vegetables in winter (the rest of the country's off season), are able to get their crops to more remote markets despite costly transport.

SELECTED REFERENCES

Baker, O. E. "Agricultural Regions of North America—Part VII, The Middle Atlantic Trucking Region," *Economic Geography*, 5:36-69, January 1929. (Though dated, this still is one of the best articles ever written on the subject.)

Fruits and Vegetables; Production, Trade and Policies in Europe. Rome, Food and Agriculture Organization of the United Nations, October 1952. Bulletin No. 23.

Griffin, Paul F., and C. Langdon White. "Lettuce Industry of the Salinas Valley," *Scientific Monthly,* 81:77-84, August 1955.

Hodge, W. H. "The Plant Resources of Peru," *Economic Botany*, 1:119-136, April-June 1947. (Though not restricted solely to vegetables, this excellent article gives much valuable information on all crops evolved in Peru, many of which were vegetables.)

Jones, William O. *Manioc in Africa.* Stanford, California, Stanford University Press, 1959.

King, W. C. "Gardening under Glass—A Prosperous Industry in the Netherlands," *Foreign Agriculture,* 26:12-13, November 1962.

Parker, C. O., and R. Royston. *Usual Dates of Planting and Harvesting Commercial Truck Crops for Fresh Market, by Seasonal Groups and States.* Washington, D. C., Bureau of Agricultural Economics, U.S. Department of Agriculture, July 1945.

Salaman, Redcliffe N. *The History and Social Influence of the Potato.* Cambridge, England, Cambridge University Press, 1949.

Smith, M. G. *The Mexican Winter-Vegetable Export Industry.* Foreign Agriculture Report No. 21, May 1947.

Thompson, H. C., and W. C. Kelly. *Vegetable Crops*, 5th ed. New York, McGraw-Hill Book Company, Inc., 1957.

CHAPTER NINETEEN::

Sugar was unknown to the peoples of the ancient world. Today it is regarded as a necessity, and it will be more so in the future. Per capita consumption varies widely among the countries of the earth. Thus, the United States and Australia have an annual per capita consumption of about 103 pounds, whereas China, India, and Pakistan have only about 2½ pounds. It is no exaggeration to say that global hunger for sugar is widespread. In recent years, however, consumption has been increasing markedly in underdeveloped countries.

Although sugar cane and sugar beets—the two sources of sugar—are produced in totally different world environments, they yield a commodity that is identical in chemical composition and reaction, dietetic effects, sweetening power, and food value. It is impossible to

THE WORLD'S

distinguish one from the other by appearance, taste, or analysis. Each is commonly substituted for the other. The role of the two crops in the economies of their respective growing areas is of particular interest and significance to economic geography. Whereas the sugar beet fits into a crop-rotation, diversification, and crop-and-livestock economy, sugar cane grows in areas that are highly specialized in monoculture and externally oriented both for markets and for in-shipments of the basic food supply. In only a few instances, as in Java, does cane enter into a crop rotation.

Sugar is the only major commercial product where real competition exists between the tropical zone and the middle latitudes, as shown by conditions in the United States, where both cane and beets are grown (Fig. 19-1).[1] From the sixteenth to the nineteenth century, the world relied wholly upon sugar cane from the tropics. The beet became a source of sugar when the British blockaded continental ports during the Napoleonic Wars. With the supply of sugar in France (and other European countries) exhausted, the price soared—averaging 30 cents per pound from 1807 to 1815. Napoleon therefore offered bounties and other aids for a substitute for cane. The beet ultimately became that crop. For a brief period following the Napoleonic Wars and the reopening of trade, the beet-sugar industry suffered; for it could not com-

[1] Occasionally, sugar cane and sugar beets are grown in adjacent fields, as at Malaga, Spain. But this situation represents the culture of the two crops at about their respective northern and southern limits.

SUGAR

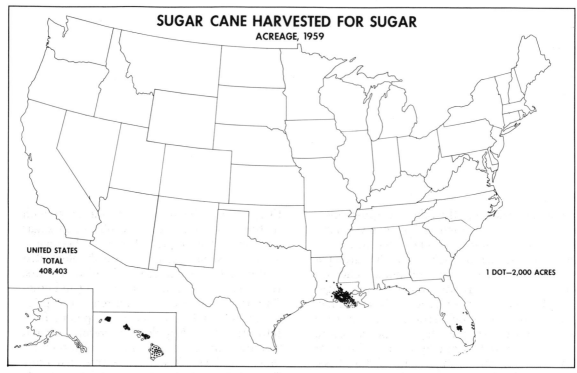

SUGAR CANE HARVESTED FOR SUGAR
ACREAGE, 1959

UNITED STATES
TOTAL
408,403

1 DOT—2,000 ACRES

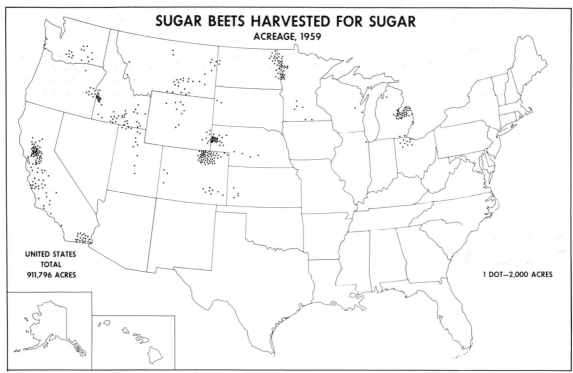

SUGAR BEETS HARVESTED FOR SUGAR
ACREAGE, 1959

UNITED STATES
TOTAL
911,796 ACRES

1 DOT—2,000 ACRES

Fig. 19-1. Distribution of sugar-cane and sugar-beet production in the United States. (Courtesy of Bureau of the Census.)

pete with the cheaper product from the American tropics. Before long, however, the development of higher sugar-yielding beets, improved processes, and protective tariffs revived the industry.

THE WORLD'S SUGAR-SURPLUS PROBLEM

The competition between the sugar cane and the sugar beet over the world has resulted in chronic overproduction. To the person unacquainted with the story of the world's sugar, it may seem paradoxical that there should be overproduction when there is world sugar hunger involving millions of people. The paradox arises from the fact that the deficit world consuming areas (the underdeveloped lands) have not been able to afford to purchase the sugar surpluses of the large producing areas.

POLITICS AND SUGAR

Economic nationalism has been for many years a fundamental cause of trouble in the international sugar situation. In short, almost every country is determined to supply the sugar for its own market, irrespective of cost (Table 19-1). So important is sugar to man

TABLE 19-1

COST OF SUGAR BY SELECTED COUNTRIES
(work time per 1 kg sugar, in minutes)

United States	8.8	Switzerland	28.7
Denmark	8.8	Chile	33.1
Australia	13.2	Finland	39.7
Canada	13.2	Czechoslovakia	48.5
Norway	17.6	France	59.5
Israel	17.6	Germany	59.5
Sweden	19.8	Italy	101.4
United Kingdom	22.0	Soviet Union	310.8

SOURCE: *Sugar*. Rome: Food and Agriculture Organization of the United Nations, September 1952. Commodity Series Bulletin No. 22, p. 43.

that politicians make provisions for needs both in time of war and in peace. Some governments (for example, that of Peru) regulate

sugar prices and producers, so that the poorest people may have sugar at low cost. United States government control has been called a government-sponsored cartel. Almost every country, however, by one means or another—tariff duties, excise taxes, regulations, controls, and subsidies—is responsible for variations in the retail and wholesale price of sugar.

SUGAR LEGISLATION

Beginning with the first tariff on sugar, that of 1789, the United States government has continued it through various sugar-quota acts of 1937, 1943, 1948, and 1953. The goal sought has been to control both domestic production and imports. Under the United States Sugar Act, Cuba was designated the largest single share in the American market—in excess of 3 million tons a year.

SUGAR CANE

Cane yields more sugar per acre than the beet and is produced at lower cost; accordingly, it supplies between 60 and 65 per cent of the world's sugar. When grown on tropical plantations, the crop is designed for the export market. Cane sugar entering the export trade comprises about one third of the total world output of sugar.

LOCATION OF SUGAR-CANE CROPS

Sugar cane is a member of the grass family and in some respects is not unlike corn in appearance. It has a wide distribution in the tropics and is even found in several subtropical areas—from as far north as latitude 32° north in Spain to as far south as latitude 37° south in New Zealand. An average annual temperature of 75°F to 85°F and a year-long **growing season** favor high yields. In general, sugar cane requires eleven to fifteen months—and in some places as many as twenty-four months—to produce maximum sugar content. The long growing season necessary for optimum production confines it in general to the tropics. In most cane-growing lands frost never comes; but it must be reckoned with in Argentina, India, Formosa, and Australia, which are partly outside the tropics, and in Louisiana, which is entirely so. When the crop is grown on the poleward margins of its growing region at the warm edge of the Humid Subtropical lands, the annual killing frost requires the cutting of immature cane, with resulting lower yields. Thus, Cuba's cane grows from ten to fifteen months or even longer; Louisiana's must be harvested after an eight-, nine-, or ten-month growing season. The crop also demands much sunshine and a bountiful supply of moisture (50 to 65 inches). Yields suffer, however, unless there is a pronounced dry period for maturation. Optimum conditions are most closely approximated in those areas in the Monsoon Tropical (wet and dry) climate where water for irrigation is available. In this type of climate the wet season allows seven to ten months of rapid growth, and the dry season brings on maturity and an increase in the sugar content. The dry season also facilitates harvesting.

Sugar cane grows in a variety of soils. It will even tolerate moderate acidity or alkalinity. Flat to rolling land is best, for in most commercial cane-growing areas large mechanized equipment is employed for many of the tasks. Such terrain also facilitates transport; since harvested cane is bulky and perishable, it must be delivered promptly to nearby mills. (Cuba has more than 150 mills or *centrales*.) Commercial cane growing has tended to localize on lowlands.

THE CANE-GROWING PROCESS

PLANTING

Sugar cane is planted by laying pieces of stalk from growing cane horizontally in a shallow furrow and covering them with soil. In some places the planting is done by hand, in others by machine. The first crop is harvested anywhere from seven or nine to twenty-four months following planting, depending on the milieu of the growing area. New shoots develop from the rootstock planted thus and form successive **ratoon** crops. However, each yields less. Following the first crop, sugar cane is harvested every twelve months, although

producing areas vary so greatly that there is no single pattern. The growing period varies from less than ten months in subtropical Louisiana to almost two years in Hawaii and Peru. Sugar cane throughout most of the tropics is a **perennial**, though in Java it is handled as an **annual**—the reason being that rice land is devoted only temporarily to sugar cane. It must be returned to growing rice immediately, in order to protect the essential food supply for the dense population (only a third or less of the land in any given community is devoted to sugar cane at any one time). Ratoon crops are not worthwhile under these conditions. In all subtropical cane-growing areas (for instance, Louisiana), there is always danger of frost, and hence the crop is invariably grown as an annual.

The height of sugar cane varies according to soil fertility, rainfall regimen, amount of cultivation, and the number of crops taken from the same ratoon. Fully mature cane usually averages 8 to 12 feet, though it sometimes attains a height of 20 feet.

Yields per acre and percentage of sugar content vary from nation to nation. The wide gap in yield per acre between countries results from a number of circumstances: (1) soil differences, (2) water availability, (3) temperature, (4) amount of fertilizer employed, (5) amount of labor used and its effectiveness, and (6) degree of reliance on ratoon crops, which successively decline in productivity.

HARVESTING

Sugar cane is harvested by cutting the stalks near the surface of the ground and cutting the tops and leaves, which contain no sucrose. In most parts of the cane-growing lands, these operations are performed manually; but in places where labor is scarce or costly or both (e.g., Australia, Hawaii, Louisiana, and Florida), mechanical harvesters are used. (It is reported that hand cutters prepare cane for milling better than mechanical harvesters.) In Australia, Hawaii, and Florida, where labor costs are very high, the cane fields are burned just before harvest—a procedure that saves labor, destroys the leaves, and does not injure

Fig. 19-2. Tractor-drawn carts being used in the more progressive cane-growing areas of Cuba to carry the stalks from field to railway. Note the rolling terrain, which typifies the Cuban cane landscape. (Courtesy of United Fruit Company.)

the cane if it is cut promptly. In Hawaii, bulldozers are used to push the tangled cane into bunches, which are picked up by giant grab forks and dumped into large truck-drawn trailers. The harvest period lasts at least five months in the Caribbean area; nine months in Natal, South Africa; and the year around in Hawaii and Peru.

PREPARATION INTO RAW SUGAR

The harvested cane is transported to nearby sugar mills for conversion into raw sugar and other products. Some plantations have all of the cane transported in ox-drawn or tractor-drawn carts; others use trucks, trams, or narrow-gauge railways (Fig. 19-2). From mills the raw sugar is shipped either in bulk or in jute bags to refineries in the countries of consumption.

MAJOR PRODUCING COUNTRIES

CUBA

Cuba has dominated the world in sugar cane production for about 75 years. She has been called the "world's sugar bowl" because her exports exceeded those of all other sugar producers, either cane or beet.[2] Sugar has

[2] Though still ranking first in exports, Cuba in the crop year 1958-1959 fell into second place as a producer—behind the Soviet Union.

overshadowed all other aspects of Cuba's economic life, so that the nation is frequently regarded as one of the world's most flagrant examples of monoculture. She depends almost entirely on sugar exports for her economic life. The great fields of green cane and the buildings of the *centrales* dominate the landscape over most of the island. In the central and eastern provinces, cane stretches as far as the eye can see. Sugar cane occupies a quarter of the entire territory and half the cultivated land, employs a fourth of the entire labor force, provides 25 per cent of the national income, and supplies 85 per cent of the exports by value (including, of course, rum, molasses, alcohol, and syrups).

Yields per acre are low because it does not pay to irrigate and fertilize heavily when land is cheap and when the bulk of the crop (prior to 1960) has been assured a market in the United States at a premium price—about 2 cents per pound above the world price. Despite rather backward methods of production, by and large Cuba experiences little competition on the world market.

Cuba also has been backward in her manner of exporting raw sugar—shipping in bags rather than in bulk. Cuban labor has resisted both field mechanization and bulk shipment.

Until the Castro revolution, most sugar was grown on large estates—the average *central* owned or controlled 40,000 acres. These

THE WORLD'S SUGAR : : 393

estates obviously held much timberland in reserve, land capable of being cleared for sugar. The system worked satisfactorily except during depressions, when great numbers of landless rural workers and scarcity of food created an explosive situation. Sugar has been called "the lifeblood of the nation and the fuel of the revolution."

By 1960 the landowners and the estates had vanished, and the cane fields had been turned into coöperatives controlled and supervised by the government. At this time no one can assess accurately the future of the Cuban sugar situation.

The United States since 1903 has given Cuba a preferential tariff. American interests, including refiners eager to be assured of an offshore supply of raw sugar, invested heavily in Cuba. (In 1924 at least two thirds of the 950 million dollars invested in Cuban sugar production was controlled by Americans, and the proportion did not change until Castro's expropriation in the late 1950s and early 1960s.) By the outbreak of World War I, Cuba had entirely displaced Java, the European beet-growing nations, and other foreign producers from the United States market. No foreign sources of sugar are so close to United States refiners as Cuba, and this was indisputably an advantage. As a result of Cuba's hostility against the United States and of her close relations with the Communist bloc, in July 1960 the President of the United States reduced by 95 per cent the amount of sugar that Cuba could send to the United States during the remainder of the year; and in 1961 the United States purchased no sugar from Cuba. The Cuban quota cut is not anticipated to be permanent. Expectably, the Soviet Union immediately agreed to purchase 1 million tons of sugar from Cuba, and China agreed to buy ½ million tons; but they pay the world price, and they remit in part by barter. The Soviet Union pays 3.25 cents per pound, compared with the 5.40 cents the United States had been remitting. Russia pays 20 per cent in dollars, the remainder in crude petroleum, machinery, and other products; China pays 20 per cent in sterling and the rest in Chinese merchandise and, in some years, the whole amount in merchandise.

BRAZIL

Brazil ranks third among all cane-producing countries and fourth in world sugar output (Table 19-2). The crop is grown on the fertile

TABLE 19-2

SUGAR PRODUCTION IN LEADING
PRODUCING COUNTRIES, 1962
(in thousands of short tons, raw value)

Soviet Union (beet)	7,300
Cuba (cane)	5,400
United States (cane and beet)	4,398
Brazil (cane)	4,094
India (cane)	3,775
France (beet)	1,878
Poland (beet)	1,807
Mexico (cane)	1,651
Philippines (cane)	1,642
West Germany (beet)	1,584
Australia (cane)	1,490
World Total	56,649

SOURCE: *Foreign Crops and Markets* (U.S.D.A.), June 28, 1962, pp. 10-11.

piedmont plains of northeastern Brazil and on the rolling plateau of east-central Brazil. Both regions are characterized by the Monsoon Tropical climate (the wet and dry) and by fertile soils. Recife's hinterland produces the bulk of the crop, but the coastal area between Vitória on the north and Rio de Janeiro on the south is also important.

The crop was introduced into Brazil in 1532 around Vicente; but the business languished and did not come into its own until grown in the northeast, where the Portuguese had capital to purchase Negro slaves, to clear the land, to plant the crop, and to build sugar mills. Little by little the plantation area was extended until it encompassed most of the good soils.

Despite rapid growth and large over-all output, Brazil grows sugar cane essentially, really exclusively, for the domestic market.

INDIA

India, believed to be the native home of sugar cane, is regarded as the leading country in acreage though not in total output or yield per acre. The crop is grown mostly in patches on small farms, there being no plantation industry. India's sugar is consumed at home.

The crop is grown throughout the country except in the dry northwest and the driest portions of the Deccan Plateau. Principal output stems from the Coromandel Coast in the vicinity of Madras and from the middle and upper Ganges Valley. Three fourths of the entire Indian crop is grown in the United Provinces, Bihar, Punjab, and Bengal.

India's per-acre yields are low—mainly because the soils have been used for long periods without proper fertilization; Hindus refuse to use **night soil**. The commercial-fertilizer industry is so new and so small that it affects only a small part of the total cane-growing lands.

Until three decades ago, India had no white-sugar industry but depended entirely upon *gur*, a hard mass of varying sweetness and stickiness. Even today gur comprises three fourths of the national sugar production.

REPUBLIC OF THE PHILIPPINES

The Philippine Republic ranks ninth among the sugar producers of the world (Table 19-2). However, sugar cane is not raised under the plantation system, as in Hawaii and Cuba. Rather, it is grown by individual farmers or planters who make contracts with a sugar mill to which they deliver their cane.

The cane is grown on the low plains of the western portions of the islands (a mountain core runs north and south through the archipelago, giving different climates to the east and west sides). The natural environment— Monsoon Tropical climate (wet and dry), fertile soils, location near tidewater—is favorable for sugar-cane growing. (Favorable also are such nonphysical factors as cheap labor, American capital, and tariff aid by the United States.) Some 50 inches of rain fall on the west sides of the islands between July and October, leaving only 20 inches to fall during the remainder of the year. Hence, sugar cane is irrigated for best results.

Fortunately for the Philippines, the United States in 1934 passed the Philippine Independence Act, which guarantees the nation a duty-free outlet in the United States of 800,-000 tons of raw sugar and 50,000 tons of refined sugar per annum. Rates will be increased gradually until 1974, when a full tariff will be levied on goods imported from the Philippines.

MEXICO

Mexico currently ranks eighth in world sugar output and fifth in production of sugar cane (Table 19-2). Both production and consumption are increasing significantly. The crop is grown on the coastal lowland from Tampico to Tehuantepec both on haciendas and on small farms. The rich soils, together with improved varieties of cane, favor heavy production.

AUSTRALIA

Australia ranks eleventh in world sugar output (Table 19-2). No area in the world is more committed to cane production than the Queensland coast, where the crop occupies as much as 99 per cent of all cultivated land. Nonetheless, Australia does limit cane production. Her own market is restricted in size; and the United Kingdom, by a system of certification of colonial imports, has killed any incentive to expand. The cane is grown in coastal valleys that thread through the relatively rough terrain.

Because of the nation's "White Australia Policy" (Orientals are prohibited), all the work is carried on by descendants of Europeans. Thus, the cost of labor and of sugar is high. This situation has encouraged the introduction of labor-saving equipment. The type of harvester used cuts 25 tons of cane per hour, enabling the grower to harvest his 1,000 tons of cane in about five days. There is much room for expansion of sugar-cane acreage in Australia; the availability of markets is the only major drawback. During the early 1960s Australian sugar was being imported into Japan and the United States in increasing quantity, and the over-all market outlook was bright.

UNITED STATES

Hawaii. Sugar is one of two major commercial crops in Hawaii, the other being pineapple. The two crops do not, however, compete for land (since pineapples are not irrigated). The crop is grown on plantations on the four main islands. The industry supports 50,000 people; the crop is grown on twenty-eight plantations, covering about 200,-000 acres of land, and is ground in twenty-seven mills. A few small farmers also grow cane. The plantations occupy two types of locations: (1) the rainy windward (northeastern) slopes and (2) the drier leeward sides. Irrigation is imperative on the dry sides. In fact, all fields are irrigated if they receive less than 90 inches of rainfall annually. About two thirds of Hawaii's sugar cane is grown under irrigation.

Cost of production in Hawaii is highest in the world because of the outlay for irrigation and expensive unionized labor. (Manpower at first had to be recruited at considerable expense from abroad—China, Portugal, Japan, the Philippines, Korea, Spain, and Puerto Rico.) Hawaiian conditions permit full-time use of plantation labor because planting, cultivating, and harvesting can go forward throughout the year. Twenty-two to twenty-four months are required for the cane to mature.

The cane, which is converted into raw sugar in local mills, is transported in bulk via large freighters to a refinery at Crockett, California, on San Francisco Bay. This refinery is owned by all the Hawaiian sugar-plantation companies. Annual production is about 1.1 million tons. Yields are highest in the world, and the companies have been leaders in sugar-cane research ($3.00 per ton of sugar spent for research).

Louisiana. The delta of the Mississippi has sustained a sugar-cane industry since 1751, when the Jesuits introduced the crop. The cane is grown on the natural levees of the Mississippi, Atchafalaya, Bayou Lafourche, Bayou Teche, and other waterways. In the early days of cane growing, the harvested cane was hauled to the mills by boat; but today, as elsewhere, trucks and railways are employed.

Since the area lies near the poleward limit of cane growth, spring and winter frosts set rigid limits, and the crop must be ready for harvest in less than ten months. Cane in Louisiana is a marginal crop and shows wide fluctuations in annual output. Acreage planted vacillates with sugar prices, and yield per acre varies substantially with threatening recurrences of early frosts. Thus, Louisiana's sugar industry is possible only because of tariff protection and federal aid in research and education.

The cane fields require both drainage and irrigation, drainage being effected by ditches that lead from the levee to the lower lands away from the river, to the deltaic swamps, which lie at much lower level than the levees (the Mississippi here stands *on* its floodplain, not *in* it). Irrigation water, when needed (which is only occasionally, since the area receives 50 to 60 inches of rain), is pumped from **bayou** or river to the cane fields. The crop is grown both on small and medium-sized holdings and on large plantations. The business is highly mechanized, a response to costly labor and the danger of frost, which puts an extra premium on speed. However, in planting, the cane is still placed in furrows by hand. When slavery was abolished, this area responded by being the first in the world to mechanize the harvest of standing cane. The harvested cane is converted to raw sugar in numerous mills and is refined also in the area.

Florida. The only other important cane-growing area in the United States is the recently drained portion of the Florida Everglades, near Lake Okeechobee. Natural environmental conditions for sugar cane here are superior to those in Louisiana; they are more like those in Cuba. Frosts are not heavy and occur only infrequently. Several crops may be produced from a single planting. Yield per acre is about twice that in Louisiana. It is believed that in time this area will become the nation's leading producer of sugar cane. Considerable expansion followed United States debarment of Cuban sugar.

Once one of the world's truly outstanding cane producers, Java currently is not listed among the world's leaders in total output and is mentioned here only because of an outstanding past. Only part of the explanation of Java's decline is attributable to the density of population—more than 50 million (compared with about 6 million for Cuba, which is about equal in size). To be sure, a large part of the land must be used for production of food crops, particularly **paddy rice**. Part of the explanation, however, is political: Java simply has not reassumed the status that she had before World War II. After the war, Java lost most of her Dutch agronomists and sugar specialists. Under Dutch tutelage, Java was equaled only by Hawaii in scientific cane production. Between the hundred years 1840–1940, Java increased the yield of sugar from 1.8 tons to 18 tons per hectare—partly the result of improved varieties, partly of improved milling facilities. Cane was grown scientifically and intensively in Java.

PERU

In some fifteen valleys of the dry coastal plain north of Lima, Peru grows much sugar cane under irrigation. Friable, alluvial, sandy loam soils generously fertilized by **guano**; high percentage of sunshine; and continuously high temperatures give the region almost ideal conditions for growing sugar cane. However, eighteen to twenty-two months are required for the crop to reach maturity. Because of the virtual lack of rain, cane is cut and ground throughout the year. Yield per acre is high. The crop is grown by tenants (many are Indians who come down from the Andes) who work for large corporations and by small planters on small parcels of land. The trend is toward larger holdings; one large corporation north of the sugar capital, Trujillo, owns land formerly held by sixty independent landowners.

THE SUGAR BEET

In nearly every important country, the production of sugar forms a part of the agricultural economy. Climate, of course, more than any other factor, determines which source of sugar, cane or beet, will be grown. We have noted already that sugar cane is restricted to the tropics and subtropics. The sugar beet, a cool-weather plant, is grown almost entirely in the Northern Hemisphere from latitude 32° north to about 60° north.

The sugar-beet industry is slightly more than 150 years old, dating from the time of the Napoleonic Wars. From the outset the beet industry had to be and was highly subsidized.

The sugar beet is an excellent crop for outstanding agricultural areas, those engaged in rational crop rotations. It requires deep plowing, careful cultivation of the soil, and ample use of fertilizers; and it contributes substantially toward higher yields of other crops in the rotation, particularly of grain. Moreover, the by-products of an average acre of sugar beets are equal in cattle-feeding value to the yield of an average acre of corn.

WORLD DISTRIBUTION OF SUGAR-BEET PRODUCTION

Sugar beets have exacting requirements both as to climate and soil; and, being a **clean-tilled crop**, they should be confined to level or at least gently rolling terrain. Climatically, beets are grown successfully in both marine and continental climates in middle latitudes and even in subtropical areas. The crop does particularly well within that zone lying between the summer isotherms of 67°F and 72°F. Beets do best in areas having warm but not hot summers; in the Northern Hemisphere, as the crop nears the close of its growing season, the sugar content is increased by a succession of bright, sunny September days and cool nights. The beet must grow in areas having more than 25 inches of rainfall, or water must be made available by irrigation. The growing season should be six months long. Wheat soils are regarded as best for sugar-beet cultivation. Deep loess soils, rich in humus and lime, characteristic of relatively dry regions, are highly favorable because they are easy to work and afford ideal facilities for penetration of the exceptionally long roots of the beet.

Fig. 19-3. Farm boy holding large, topped beet—one of millions in a huge pile awaiting processing outside an American beet-sugar factory. (Courtesy of Western Beet Sugar Producers, Inc.)

In appearance, the sugar beet is as white as a turnip and shaped somewhat like a parsnip (Fig. 19-3). The ideal factory beet weighs about 2 pounds.

Recent developments in planting, thinning, harvesting, storing, and processing have greatly increased the efficiency of production. The sugar beet formerly demanded much "down-on-your-knees" labor; however, in the United States, hand methods have yielded to mechanical means, so that in 1958 the entire crop was gathered by some 20,000 harvesters. These harvesters top, gage, cut, lift, and load the beets into trailers. Mechanization of the beet harvest has brought large savings in labor

requirements and costs (Fig. 19-4). In addition, through better plant breeding, scientists have been able to obtain larger sugar yields. In 1836, for example, 18 pounds of beets were required to make 1 pound of sugar; in 1882, 10 pounds; in 1924, 7; today less than 5 pounds.

WORLD PRODUCTION

Large-scale production of sugar beets is restricted to continental Europe and to the United States and Canada. The stronghold of the sugar beet is in Germany, Austria, Belgium, France, the Netherlands, Czechoslovakia, Hungary, Italy, Poland, and the Soviet Union. These nations have a fourfold reason for growing the beet: (1) They are far removed from the tropics, where sugar cane grows best. (2) They have the added incentive of more than 150 years of development, improvement, and investment in the beet. (3) Their labor costs are comparatively low. (4) There are no "big-money" crops to compete with sugar beets for the land. Because of duties, taxes, bounties, and transportation, the retail price of cane sugar in Central Europe is much higher than in America.

SOVIET UNION

The Soviet Union—where the growing of sugar beets is more than 150 years old—leads the world in both sugar-beet acreage and total output of sugar. The beet-sugar industry was from the outset highly subsidized. In 1959 output reached 6.5 million metric tons, compared with cane-growing Cuba's output of 5.9 million metric tons. The increase of 1959–1960 over 1950–1951 was 171 per cent.

The center of the beet-sugar industry has always been in the Ukraine, which has particularly favorable natural environmental conditions. There has been some expansion, however, into the irrigated areas of Soviet Central Asia and even into Siberia, as well as into the Baltic republics. Nonetheless, wide-scale expansion is limited by (1) insufficiently high temperatures on the north, (2) short duration of the growing season in the north and in Siberia, and (3) inadequate moisture. As is well known, the increasing continentality

Fig. 19-4. Thinning beets mechanically. This mechanical thinner cuts excess young plants from field, six rows at a time. Note that the revolving blades are so set as to skip sufficient plants to provide a good stand. In the past, blocking and thinning were done by individual workers; hence sugar-beet growing was called "down-on-your-knees labor" and was not popular with American farmers. (Courtesy of Western Beet Sugar Producers, Inc.)

of the climate from west to east reduces the effectiveness of the land for sugar beets; even the best of these areas are less favorable than the Ukraine and the central chernozem region. In spite of all statements to the contrary, the agricultural basis of sugar-beet production continues unsatisfactory; yield per acre remains low—about 6½ tons—and production still is uneconomical. The system of *collective* and *state* farms has not yet succeeded in mastering the organic processes of agriculture, particularly as far as rational crop rotations and animal husbandry are concerned.

As a result of better land distribution for this crop and of more widespread use of commercial fertilizers, however, the per-acre yield had risen considerably by 1960; yet the outlay of labor in minutes per kilogram of sugar in the Soviet Union is highest of all countries (Table 19-1).

UNITED STATES

Compared with the Soviet Union, the United States is a small producer of sugar beets. The crop, essentially a Western crop, is grown quite successfully in numerous irrigated valleys there. In the East, where the crop is not irrigated, only Michigan, Wisconsin, and Ohio are important. Some twenty-two states grow sugar beets, though more than half the total output comes from three—California, Colorado, and Idaho. All these states could produce far more beets and sugar than they do, but only with a guaranteed market. Their initial quota for 1960 was slightly over 2 million tons. Like the sugar-cane industries of Louisiana and Florida, the United States beet industry exists only by reason of a tariff.

California leads all states in the growing of sugar beets. The arid tropical Imperial Valley accounts for 23 per cent of the state's crop and 6 per cent of the nation's. Here the beets are planted in late summer and early fall, grown during the winter, and harvested in early summer. But the beet is grown in countless valleys throughout California.

In most parts of the state the industry is almost completely mechanized. The crop is thinned mechanically, and chemical weed killers have largely replaced hand hoeing. Thinning in this manner was not possible until the 1930s, when plant breeders succeeded in producing a seed ball that contains only one seed. With this seed, too, came the precision planter that permitted 2 to 6 pounds to do what formerly required 18 to 20. Yields are high, the Salinas Valley laying claim to the world record of 30 tons of sugar beets to the acre and a 16 per cent sugar content or better.

The sugar beet is a particularly satisfactory crop for the West, for this sparsely populated area must market in the East much of what it grows. Because transportation by rail is costly, the sugar beet thus is an ideal crop; for it can be shipped in the concentrated form of *refined* sugar.

WEST GERMANY

Sugar-beet cultivation is important in almost all parts of West Germany, which ranks first among European nations in total output (exclusive of the Soviet Union). Yields are quite high—about 12 tons to the acre—though much lower than in Italy, France, and the United States. The Lower Saxony and North Rhine–Westphalia districts lead, with sugar beets occupying more than 6 per cent of the arable land. No other crop has contributed so much to German eminence in agriculture. Production is favored by ample summer rainfall, cool but sunny maturing season, level terrain, and sandy loam soils of glacial and loessial origin. The large supply of labor at reasonable cost is an advantage, as is the large domestic market.

ITALY

Italy ranks among the world's leading producers of sugar beets, the crop being confined largely to the north—80 per cent to the delta of the Po River; the remaining 20 per cent is dispersed quite widely throughout the country. Beets grown in peninsular Italy are irrigated. In the north, where the highest yields are obtained, the crop is grown on recently drained marshland.

In the south, the beet is a winter crop, grown to avoid losses from summer heat. In the north, it is grown in summer; and summer temperatures are so high as to shorten the season, making the harvesting obligatory during August and September, before the leaves wilt. Because of the extremely hot and dry summers, even the Po Delta is not so well suited to the crop as are Europe's other great beet-growing areas. Nevertheless, Italy gets the highest yield per acre among major European beet producers.

FRANCE

France ranks sixth among world sugar producers and second among beet-growing nations (Table 19-2). Sugar-beet culture is confined chiefly to the north—the plains of Flanders, Picardy, Brie, Beauce, and also in Limoges and the Paris region. Two thirds of the entire output comes from six departments, in each of which sugar beets compose more than 10 per cent of the arable area. It is believed that sugar-beet cultivation in France has reached its natural limit. Eighty-five per cent of the total French sugar-beet acreage and most of the sugar factories are included in a compact area made up of just ten departments.

Beets are grown on a given field only once in five or six years. The excellent methods employed result in much higher yields per acre for the other crops entering the rotation. Seven leading sugar departments rank among France's largest users of commercial fertilizer.

THE LOW COUNTRIES

Belgium and the Netherlands lead all other European beet producers in the percentage of total arable land devoted to the crop. The production of the sugar beet is pursued vigorously and economically by the Dutch. Greatest concentration occurs on the west coast, where 13 per cent of the intensively cultivated marine clay soils are planted to beets. In Belgium, beet acreage comprises about 6 per cent of total arable land. More than 12 per cent of all Belgian farms cultivate sugar beets.

EASTERN EUROPE

Central Germany, comprising parts of both West and East Germany, possesses prize beet lands (on loessial soils) which make the region a surplus sugar producer. The North German Plain between Hannover (West Germany) and Leipzig (East Germany) is the heart of German beet culture. Magdeburg, the largest beet-manufacturing center, lies in the midst of fine beet fields in Germany's famous potash region. The Bohemian Basin of Czechoslovakia, prior to World War II, ranked with central Germany as one of the most progressive centers of European beet culture. The Prague district had the greatest intensity of beet-sugar production. Under Communist rule, mass parceling of large estates into small, poorly equipped farms—combined with a shortage of agricultural labor because of expulsion of national groups—has caused a decline in production.

Poland in acreage and total output ranks among Europe's leading sugar-beet nations, but in per-acre yield it is on a par with the Soviet Union and far behind the nations in Western Europe. The Polish beet area occupies the eastern end of the European Sugar-Beet Belt, which extends from northern France and the Low Countries to Galicia. Outstanding is the loessial region north of the Carpathian Mountains, with its highly calcareous soils. Although the climate obviously is more continental than that in Western Europe, thus requiring later planting of beets, the growing season is sufficiently long for the crop to reach maturity.

WORLD TRADE IN SUGAR

With a world output of 49 million metric tons, raw value (1959), and with the majority of cane producers dependent on foreign markets, foreign trade in sugar logically should be very important. Production of sugar is more artificially controlled than that of any other major crop. Twenty-one sugar-producing and consuming countries signed an International Sugar Agreement in London in 1937. In that year these countries represented 85 to 90 per cent of the world's production, 85 per cent of its consumption, and virtually all that entered world trade.

The primary objective [of the agreement] was to establish and maintain an orderly relationship between supply and demand for sugar on the world market in a manner equitable to both producers and consumers.[3]

Headquarters were established in London to administer the agreement. A new agreement was negotiated in 1953.

The foreign trade of the United States, an important world producer but also the world's largest importer, is interesting. The First Congress imposed a tariff on imported sugar as a source of revenue for the United States government. The Sugar Act of 1948 with subsequent amendments regulates all major foreign and domestic aspects of the sugar business. It set fixed quotas, which determine the amount of sugar that may be produced in the United

[3] *Sugar Facts and Figures, 1952* (Washington, D. C.: United States Cuban Sugar Council, 1952), p. 59.

States and imported: it assigned Cuba 96 per cent of the remaining consumption requirements and other foreign countries 4 per cent. It granted Cuba a 20 per cent lower duty than any other foreign country. Likewise, it granted the Philippines a period of preferential treatment.

The United States has experienced no difficulty making good the sugar exports recently denied Cuba. Many cane-producing countries, along with both the domestic cane and beet industries, have been eager to increase their quotas.

WORLD OUTLOOK

There is currently world sugar hunger. This does not stem from a dearth of land capable of producing sugar: Cuba alone could supply all the sugar needed by the world's 3 billion inhabitants at the present rate of consumption. As the level of living of peoples, particularly in the underdeveloped countries, rises, world consumption of sugar will continue to soar.

How can consumption be increased? Possibly the best way would be to reduce the high sugar excises that prevail in many nations. Attention has been called to the inequalities in per capita consumption—103 pounds in the United States and Australia; 2½ pounds in China, India, and Pakistan. However, the trend toward increasing consumption already is in evidence; the greatest increases in sugar consumption during the past decade and a half have occurred in the poorest parts of the world—the underdeveloped lands (except for Eastern and Southern Asia).

There has long been, there is now, and there almost certainly will be trouble in the sugar world: this is politically engendered. Sugar today is more than a commodity. It is a pawn in international diplomacy. For the most part, sugar-growing lands, certainly those that produce for the export market, are not prosperous lands. In those instances where the exporting regions do prosper, it is not so much because of the efficiency of their production methods as because of political decisions in the importing countries.

SELECTED REFERENCES

Cottrell, R. H. *Beet Sugar Economics*. Caldwell, Idaho, Caxton Printers, Ltd., 1952.

Fryer, D. W. "Recovery of the Sugar Industry in Indonesia," *Economic Geography*, 33:171-181, April 1957.

Griffin, Paul F. "Some Geographic Aspects of the California and Hawaiian Sugar Industry," *Journal of Geography*, 53:325-336, November 1954.

Myers, Lawrence. "The World Sugar Problem," *Foreign Agriculture*, 20:3-5, May 1956.

Nightingale, John E. "Transportation Trends Today in Selected Sugar-Plantation Areas," *Foreign Commerce Weekly*, 37:6ff, November 28, 1949.

The Silver Wedge—The Beet Sugar Story. Washington, D. C., United States Beet Sugar Association, 1959.

Simonett, D. C. "Sugar Production in North Queensland," *Economic Geography*, 30:223-235, July 1954.

Sitterson, J. C. *Sugar Country, the Cane Sugar Industry in the South, 1753-1950*. Lexington, University of Kentucky Press, 1953.

Szulc, Tad. "Cuba's Future Is Written in Sugar," *New York Times Magazine*, pp. 13, 30-31, July 24, 1960.

Timoshenko, V. P., and B. C. Swerling. *The World's Sugar: Progress and Policy*. Stanford, California, Food Research Institute Studies on Food, Agriculture, and World War II, No. 12, 1957.

CHAPTER TWENTY::

The three most important crops used by man as common nonalcoholic beverages are coffee, tea, and cacao (Fig. 20-1). Only the last is a food product. Moreover, cacao does not compete to any great extent as a beverage with coffee and tea. The real competition is between coffee and tea. Each has hundreds of millions of devotees; deprivation would cause considerable psychological hardship, though neither hunger nor famine. For this reason alone every effort is made to maintain trade in both items, even in time of war.

Coffee and tea are alike in several respects. They have no food value and accordingly are judged solely on flavor and aroma; the better grades grow on mountain slopes; about five years are required for the trees or shrubs to reach maturity; the crop is picked by hand. However, the two also have one important

THE WORLD'S

dissimilarity: coffee prices fluctuate sharply, whereas tea prices fluctuate hardly at all.

COFFEE

Although the tea industry is making a desperate effort to induce more Americans to drink tea, coffee is and undoubtedly will continue to be the favorite beverage. This is indicated by the American annual expenditure of 1.5 billion dollars for coffee and a mere 50 million dollars for tea. The American also drinks twice as much coffee today as he did in the 1890s and half again as much as he did in the 1920s. He has become the world's dominant coffee consumer. In short, the United States consumes more than 125 billion cups of coffee a year. The National Coffee Association estimates that 98 per cent of all American homes serve coffee.

Until World War I, Europe comprised the largest coffee market, totaling 55 per cent of world sales between 1909 and 1913 as against 38 per cent for the United States. Between 1935 and 1939, however, Europe's share had fallen to 42 per cent, whereas that of the United States had risen to 50 per cent.

Coffee has the greatest value of any tropical farm product entering world trade. In fact, it is the second most important commodity in world trade—second only to petroleum.

HISTORY

Coffee is a native of Ethiopia; at least it was first domesticated there. From Ethiopia, Arab traders carried the crop to the southwestern tip of the Arabian Peninsula, near

BEVERAGES

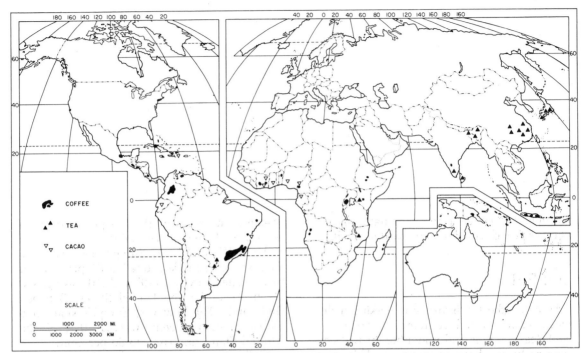

Fig. 20-1. *World producing areas—coffee, tea, and cacao. All three products are mostly tropical, though coffee does cross over the Tropic of Capricorn in Brazil as does tea over the Tropic of Cancer in India, China, and Japan. Cacao, however, does not get far from the equator.*

Mocha. It is believed that coffee was first cultivated here about 575 A.D. From Arabia, coffee ultimately spread into those lands where it is today important, though the Arabs attempted to prevent the growing of the bean in other countries.

COMMERCIAL CULTIVATION OF COFFEE

Coffee trees are grown from seeds planted in seed beds. Here the seedlings receive great care for about six months. Then they are removed to a nursery, where they remain for approximately a year and a half, at the end of which time they are about 18 inches tall. The healthiest seedlings are then transplanted in rows, both seedlings and rows being spaced about 12 feet apart.

Grown under natural conditions, the evergreen coffee tree would attain a height of 18 to 20 feet. To facilitate picking, however, the tree under commercial cultivation is kept pruned to a height of about 6 to 10 feet (Fig.

20-2), although in Brazil trees frequently attain heights of 15 feet.

A fragrant white flower yields a "cherry," composed of two seeds or beans, with their flat sides together. These "cherries," which grow in clusters along the stem at the base where the leaves branch, ripen into bright red and, finally, purplish berries.

PICKING AND PREPARATION FOR MARKET

The berries are picked when they are ripe; that is, during the dry season. Some coffee is being picked in one country or another right around the calendar. The harvest generally lasts from three to six months, depending upon the region. On the very large estates—particularly if there is inadequate labor to pick and repick only ripe berries—the green, semiripe, and ripe berries may be stripped simultaneously. This last operation, of course, results in a lower-quality coffee. Hand labor is employed exclusively in picking. No ma-

Fig. 20-2. Family picking coffee, Colombia. Note that the trees are pruned low to permit picking without using ladders, and that they are shaded from the equatorial sun by larger trees. (Courtesy of Federación Nacional de Cafeteros de Colombia.)

chine has yet been invented that is capable of selecting only ripe berries.

Obtaining an adequate supply of harvest hands is a basic problem of coffee growing in every region on the globe. A common practice is to operate with a skeleton crew of day-wage workers, and augment it with extra workers during the picking season. In some areas sharecroppers are employed. And in some coffee-growing countries, the wives and children of the workers assist in the harvest.

HARVESTING

In some countries—for example, Brazil—only one annual crop is harvested; but in others, like Colombia, there may be as many as four selective pickings. In Brazil, too, the branches are stripped directly onto the ground or on a cloth spread upon the ground.

Each tree yields approximately 2,000 cherries—an amount that supplies about 1 pound of coffee. This means that a family consuming one pound of coffee per week would require in a year's time the *complete harvest of 52 trees.*

Two methods—the *wet* and the *dry*—are employed in the handling of the freshly picked coffee. In the wet method, which is widely followed in countries where there is an abundance of water, the cherries, immediately following picking, are depulped, exposing a sticky substance that surrounds the parchment. The beans are then placed in thoroughly clean concrete tanks and left for twelve to fifteen hours. The beans are thoroughly washed. After draining, the beans are spread out for drying, in layers several inches deep —either in the open air, on cement, brick, or tile floors, or in buildings with removable roofs. Coffees so prepared are called "washed" coffees. During the drying process, the beans are frequently raked and turned so that evaporation will be uniform. Next the beans are hulled and threshed by machine, during which process the parchment is removed. Coffees prepared by the wet method are called "naturals"; they are mild, outstanding in aroma and flavor, and are regarded with special favor in world trade.

The dry method is employed where water is scarce. The berries, along with any foreign matter present, are passed through washing tanks, which separate the dry, ripe, and immature beans and thereby eliminate the impurities in a single process. The beans are then spread on the drying ground and exposed to the sun until they can be handled in machines. The drying period may last fifteen or twenty days. This method is followed particularly in Brazil.

Regardless of whether the wet or dry method is used, the beans are raked into piles each evening and covered with tarpaulin for protection against dew and possible rain. Also regardless of which method is employed, much labor and time are consumed. Hence it was encouraging when technicians in El Salvador developed a quick and efficient chemical method of removing the mucilage from the parchment—reducing the time previously involved (eight to thirty hours) to a few minutes.

VARIETIES AND GRADES OF COFFEE

In this book three varieties of coffee are mentioned: (1) *Coffea arabica*, regarded as the outstanding type, since it accounts for at least 90 per cent of present world output; (2) *Coffea robusta*, next most important; and (3) *Coffea liberica*. The last two are better suited to a more typically humid climate than is *Coffea arabica*. Latin America grows almost no coffee other than *arabica*. Africa accounts for most of the commercial output of *robusta*.

In addition, Latin American commercial coffees fall into two main grades, "Brazils" and "milds." Both grades are identified not only by the country in which they are cultivated but also by districts or states within the country or by ports from which the coffee is shipped. Elevation is also a significant factor in determining grade, quality, and distinctive flavor. These coffees are also classified as "soft" (sweet and mild), "strictly soft" (sweet and very mild), "hard" (harsh taste), or "Rio" (harsh and bitter). Brazilian coffee is generally strong and pungent; that from Colombia, Venezuela, Mexico, and Central America is mild. In Brazil, the "hard" coffees are associated with the Rio de Janeiro and Vitoria areas, the "soft" coffees with São Paulo. Brazil's soft coffees, being mild and rather sweet, are considered to be her best.

The coffees consumed in the United States are not the product of a single country but usually of two or more. The blending process achieves the particular flavor, aroma, and body for which various brands are known. Roasting is prosecuted in the country where the coffee is consumed. Each coffee roaster has one or more experts who carefully select the blend they think will be liked by the most people in the market for which the coffee is intended. (In Western Europe and in the American South, the roasted and ground roots of chicory, a salad plant, are added to coffee to impart a deeper color and a more lasting flavor and aroma; they are also sometimes used as a substitute for or adulteration of coffee.)

LOCATION OF COFFEE CROPS

Coffee is a tropical crop—the belt suitable for it extending from latitudes 28° north to 30° south latitude. Yet the best-quality coffee is grown at elevations of 3,000 to 6,000 feet. Though the crop can be and sometimes is grown on plains near sea level, *high-quality coffee has never been successfully grown in tropical plains*. Thus in Colombia no appreciable amount of coffee is grown below an altitude of 3,300 feet. Below this height Colombians do not believe the crop can be grown efficiently or a quality bean yielded. Both heat and cold are enemies of coffee trees.

Despite the wide range of the coffee plant, it is Latin America that is really impressive; for it contributes 83 to 89 per cent of the world's exportable coffee (and 95 per cent of that consumed in the United States).

Coffee is grown where there is an abundance of rain, but where there is a marked rhythm in its distribution; the tree produces its fruit during the wet season. Rapid growth is promoted by daytime temperatures in the 70s and 80s, along with plenty of rain. The fruit comes to maturity and is picked during the cool, dry season, when the temperatures are in the 50s and 60s, and when there is a high percentage of sunshine, all of which favor ripening, picking, and drying.

The crop thus finds its optimum growing conditions on tropical and subtropical plateaus where temperatures range from 60°F to 78°F, and where precipitation varies between 50 and 90 inches per year. A considerable cloud cover is desirable, for the tree does not thrive under the vertical tropical sun, except near the outer margins of the tropics. If no cloud cover is present, trees grown near the equator, in areas having a pronounced dry season, must be planted under shade of other trees or of the banana plant. The trees do best on slopes, where they benefit from good water and **air drainage** (the latter being significant only where there is danger of killing frost).

Soils, too, are important. The crop does best on loamy soils that are deep, well drained, neither strongly acid nor alkaline, and contain considerable humus. In Latin America the best coffee soils are derived from volcanic lavas and ashes. Coffee exhausts soils rapidly, and hence large quantities of nitrogen and potash must be added to them.

WORLD PRODUCTION OF COFFEE

LATIN AMERICA

Of the fourteen Latin American countries that grow coffee commercially, seven depend upon it as their major source of foreign exchange. Thus, for every cent-per-pound difference in the average price of green coffee, national income drops or rises by approximately 19 million dollars in Brazil and 7 million dollars in Colombia (these two furnish about three fourths of the world's export coffee). No wonder these countries suffer from financial chills and fevers. Coffee contributes about 85 per cent of El Salvador's total export receipts, 82 per cent of Colombia's, 72 per cent of Guatemala's, 70 per cent of Haiti's, and 66 per cent of Brazil's.

Brazil. Brazil leads the world in coffee production, supplying between 49 and 62 per cent of the exportable crop. Brazil became the leader in the early years of the nineteenth century—in Campinas. Coffee production spread out from there. Brazil accounted for about two thirds of the market from the 1880s until the 1930s, when overproduction and the world depression brought low prices. Brazil's response to these conditions was price supports and destruction of stocks, which cost her a gradual loss of markets; for her neighbors to the north, the producers of "mild" coffees, increased their output at Brazil's expense. Although Brazil has resorted to **valorization schemes** to support coffee prices, in the long run they have only compounded her problems.

Brazil's peak production occurred simultaneously with the great depression; prices tumbled more than 50 per cent, and thousands of Brazilian coffee growers went broke. In desperation the nation began to destroy coffee; in the decade prior to World War II, Brazil burned 68 million bags—28 per cent of her total output. Since that time Brazil has had her ups and downs with coffee. In the late 1950s and early 1960s there was again heavy overproduction, the result largely of spectacular increases in planting in the northern part of the state of Paraná.

Brazil's coffee-growing area, centering chiefly in the states of São Paulo, Minas Gerais, Paraná, Espírito Santo, and Rio de Janeiro, at one time comprised over 8 million acres with about 3 billion trees. However, continuous production of coffee (a row crop) induced severe soil erosion and considerable land abandonment, particularly in São Paulo. The total number of coffee trees is now down to 2.3 billion.

Brazil's coffee-growing region is near the outer margin of the tropics. As more and more land went out of coffee production in São Paulo, there was a move southward into the state of Paraná, where topography and soils are well suited to coffee but where there is danger from periodic killing frosts; in June of 1953 occurred the worst killing frost in Brazil's history, and the total output of coffee was reduced by one third. Another serious frost affected Paraná again in 1955. Many Paraná plantings have been abandoned because they were pushed too far south and hence were damaged by frost. The movement is once again toward the equator; but if there is no severe damage from killing frosts in Paraná over a period of several successive years, the coffee plantations will probably remain there.

Brazil's *terra roxa legitima* soils are regarded among the world's best for growing coffee; their porosity permits the roots of the trees to penetrate far into the ground. In São Paulo they occur in patches making up only about 7 per cent of the area. Though red in color, they should not be confused with the tropical laterites, which are basic in reaction, poor in humus, and rich in iron. The coffee soils, derived from basic eruptives under thick tropical-forest cover, are rich in iron oxide, show a neutral or acid reaction, and are relatively rich in humus. The color results chiefly from the parent rock.

Much of Brazil's coffee is grown on enormous estates called *fazendas*. *Fazendas* with a million or more trees are not uncommon. In fact, one *fazenda*—the country's largest—has 5.8 million bearing trees. It would be incorrect, however, to believe that such huge estates dominate the coffee picture in Brazil, for actually small estates do. Moreover, as a result of the breakup of older and larger estates, the number of small estates is increasing.

Despite the fact that Brazil is the leading coffee-growing nation, she has no monopoly on the product and hence cannot influence unduly the world price or control the entry of new producers. Accordingly, Brazil's share of the world market is being eroded. Obviously, then, her biggest problem is overproduction, consequent low prices, and reduced earnings. All three are serious when a country depends so heavily upon a single product for so large a part of its foreign earnings (60 to 70 per cent). In recent years there has been a surplus of 7 to 14 million bags per year— each bag weighing 132.2 pounds.

There appear to be but two possible solutions: (1) a shift from coffee to other crops and livestock (in 1960 there was considerable substitution by cotton), and (2) reduction of subsidies to inefficient producers. This latter would mean political suicide for the government that attempted it. Hence, it appears that overproduction will persist for several years at least. Time has shown that reduction in total output of coffee is one of the most difficult objectives to achieve. The basic problem, of course, is the impossibility of adjusting supply to demand, since coffee is not an annual.

In 1959 Brazil was maintaining a minimum export price; she did, however, permit the exportation of some coffee below this figure— coffee labeled as "off-grade" or inferior that was presumably destined for the instant-coffee market as a means of competing with Africa (see p. 412).

Colombia. Colombia ranks second only to Brazil in world output; but it leads all nations in production of "milds" (*café suave*). However, in output Colombia produces only one fifth or one sixth as much as Brazil. Colombia depends upon coffee for her economic life, the crop accounting for 87 per cent of the nation's dollar income. Coffee is so important that it affects the welfare of every man, woman, and child in the country.

Colombian coffee is mountain coffee, and most of the crop is grown in the interior of the country (Fig. 20-1), chiefly on both flanks of the Cordillera Central and to a lesser extent on the western slopes of the Cordillera Oriental and on the Sierra Nevada de Santa

Fig. 20-3. Transporting coffee, Colombia. Colombia's main technical problem in overland transport is the mountainous terrain: gradients are steep, curves sharp, and the roads narrow. Many roads are little more than trails. Coffee, grown on the mountainsides of interior Colombia, is probably the only crop that has high enough value per unit of weight to justify costly transport via muleback. (Courtesy of Federación Nacional de Cafeteros de Colombia.)

Marta. It is grown at an elevation of 3,000 to 6,500 feet, though most of the coffee *fincas* lie at elevations of 4,500 to 6,500 feet. In highland areas temperatures are moderated by altitude. Here also the rainfall is heavy—80 to 100 inches per annum, most of it falling in summer.

Unlike Brazil's coffee trees, which are freely exposed to the sunshine, those of Colombia, except where much cloud is present, are planted under the shade of trees of the legume family (guamo), poplar trees, or even the plantain, which has very large leaves and grows rapidly. Hence, Colombian coffee is known as "shade-grown" coffee.

The *fincas* are small compared with the *fazendas* in Brazil; 36 per cent of them have less than one hectare (2.471 acres) in productive plantings. Many of the trees are old and in need of replacement.

Trees are pruned to about 6 or 7 feet, which not only facilitates picking but increases the yield and produces uniformity of ripeness and flavor. Since the cherries do not all ripen simultaneously, only the fully ripe ones are picked; hence as many as four pickings are made before the crop is fully gathered.

Because Colombia's coffee is grown mostly in the interior mountainous area, it has a long and difficult trip to an ocean port. Sometimes bags of coffee are transported across deep valleys by aerial cable cars, often by muleback to a railway or a river (Fig. 20-3). About half the total coffee exported moves to ocean port via the Río Magdalena. Hence coffee, which has high value per unit of bulk or weight, is an excellent crop for Colombia. Once the crop is processed on the *fincas*, its high unit value makes its transport economical over considerable distances. Moreover, coffee can be stored for long periods without deterioration in quality. Accordingly, more bulky or perishable crops probably will not replace coffee to any extent in this interior region.

Colombian coffee, used primarily for blending with Brazilian coffee, is regarded as *quality coffee* and brings a premium price. In fact, the government even prohibits the sale of the lowest grades, known as "sweepings."

CENTRAL AMERICA, MEXICO, AND THE WEST INDIES

This entire region is famous both for the great quantity and the high quality of its coffees. Coffee dominates the economy of a number of the small republics, particularly El Salvador, Guatemala, and Costa Rica.

In Central America the coffee is produced in discontinuous and widely separated parts of the interior plateau and mountaintops facing the Pacific Ocean. Coffee is much less important on the mountains facing the Caribbean, for here the rainfall is heavy and is distributed throughout the year. Little El Salvador ranks fourth in world production, the crop being grown on mountain slopes of 1,500 to 5,000 feet on fertile soils of volcanic origin. The country is regarded as a one-crop country.

Mexico ranks third among Latin American countries in production. Principal states are Chiapas and Oaxaca along the Pacific Coast and Vera Cruz along the Gulf of Mexico. Mexico is the only Latin American coffee-growing country having a considerable amount of land suitable for expansion of coffee planting.

In the West Indies the growing of coffee is spasmodic, though nearly every important island grows some coffee. Jamaica is world-famous for its Blue Mountain coffee. Puerto Rico grows much coffee in the mountains of the western half of the island, the entire crop being grown under shade as protection from both intense sunlight and strong wind. Following World War I, Puerto Rico lost many of its former markets in Europe because of quotas, embargoes, increased tariffs, and a host of other trade restrictions that resulted from the wave of nationalism sweeping over the world.

AFRICA

African coffee is grown both in East Africa and West Africa; the largest stretch of new planting, oddly, has been in West Africa, *outside the ordinary coffee-producing areas*. Until 1939 a relatively insignificant producer of coffee, Africa more than doubled its share of the world crop from the prewar period to 1950. According to Jonasson,[1] this situation resulted primarily from the high prices attained by coffee grown in Latin America and by the suitability of cheaper African varieties of *robusta* for soluble or instant coffee. There has been a definite shift from brewed to powdered coffee in the United States. From an unimportant part of the United States market following World War II, instant coffee increased its sales to 17.2 per cent of total green-coffee sales in 1959, and by 1960 it accounted for one cup in every five consumed in the nation. This growth has resulted primarily from convenience and lower cost per cup.

ASIA

At one time Southeastern Asia ranked high among the lands producing coffee, the Dutch having established one of the first European-owned plantations in Java. Mocha (Arabia) and Java blended gave man one of the finest and most famous coffee blends ever attained. For years "Java" and "coffee" were synonymous. As late as World War II, the Netherlands East Indies ranked third in world production. They (now Indonesia) no longer have impressive exports of coffee. Ceylon and India, too, at one time were important in coffee production; in fact, the coffee stock introduced into both Brazil and Java was Indian. However, the dread coffee rust, an air-borne fungus disease, almost removed coffee from Ceylon and drastically decreased production in India.

[1] Olof Jonasson, "The Potential Areas of Coffee-Growing," *Geografska Annaler*, 40:98, 1958.

NEED FOR RESEARCH

Although the principal coffee-growing countries are engaged in impressive research projects, nonetheless coffee farmers continue to utilize the backward methods long in vogue. The improvements of the scientists have not as yet found their way into the actual farm practices of the growers. There is remarkably little mechanization, and harvesting and marketing methods are still crude.

Many coffee plantings in Brazil's state of São Paulo are in poor condition because of excessive age, poor care, and the predominance of low-yielding trees. Output per worker in one area in Brazil is what it was a hundred years ago. Yet costs of producing coffee, as of all commodities, have risen in every growing area.

A major problem, particularly in Latin America, is to develop strains of trees that combine the rust resistance of *robusta* coffees with the flavor and aroma properties of *arabica*.

Efforts are being made to control and conquer the coffee-bean borer (Brazil) and the amaga ant (Colombia), whose fantastically rapid rate of breeding constitutes a threat. It is estimated that coffee growers in the Western Hemisphere alone lose more than 400 million pounds of coffee annually to pests and diseases.

Another objective of researchers is to develop strains that will yield more coffee per tree than the single pound at present. That scientific coffee growing will pay has been proved by a new system introduced into São Paulo: (1) high-yielding trees; (2) their closer spacing; (3) intensive fertilization; and (4) soil and water conservation. These have resulted in yields per acre four or five times higher than those obtained on traditional plantings.

TRADE AND CONTROLS

Coffee has high value, is in great demand, and hence ranks high among commodities entering foreign trade. A very considerable number of countries depend overwhelmingly upon it for their economic life. Unfortunately for them, the price of coffee is extremely variable, its ups and downs resembling a stock market chart. These fluctuations result essentially from:

1. Small crops, which in turn result from killing frosts, floods, and severe droughts that occur in important growing areas.
2. Very large crops, owing to the lack of killing frosts, floods, and droughts.
3. Expanding world production, particularly notable in Africa.

Violent price fluctuations are extremely hard on individual growers and on the producing countries as well. During the decade 1930-1940, the surplus of coffee was so huge that prices fell to the lowest levels in the history of coffee commerce; *for ten years prices averaged less than 8 cents per pound.* At this time Brazil alone was producing more coffee than the entire world was consuming. Obviously, economic advancement in the producing countries came to a standstill. Often Europeans and North Americans ask why production is not adjusted downward. The answer is that this would be extremely difficult. Since coffee is not an annual like wheat or corn, production cannot be controlled from year to year. Once coffee trees attain an age of five years, they must continue to produce or the long-term investment is dissipated. Under such circumstances, a rise in coffee prices is not reflected in increasing output for several years, and a fall in price does not normally discourage output at once. There is no immediate remedy except destruction of the trees themselves.

In 1962 an International Coffee Conference was held in New York under the auspices of the United Nations with representatives from coffee-producing nations (Latin America, Asia, Africa, and Oceania) and from consuming countries. The purpose of the conference was to try to reconcile the varied interests of exporters and importers and to establish a universal coffee policy in the world. This would be accomplished by controls on both the production and price of coffee. It has been proved that the coffee problem cannot be solved unless such cooperation is achieved. To make such planning possible, a reasonably long-term agreement was imperative. Only a few of the producing countries refused to join; they declared that the export quotas assigned to them were too low.

It is significant that Brazil and, to a lesser degree, Colombia have been in an awkward position; that is, they control enough of the market to exert a strong influence on the price of coffee, but they are unable to prevent the entry of new producers into the field. Under the new agreement, Brazil alone would uproot as many as 2 billion coffee trees.

TEA

Tea ranks next to coffee in commercial importance as a table beverage. In number of persons drinking the two each day, however, tea outranks coffee; for the principal tea-growing-and-consuming lands are also the most densely populated ones, and the bulk of the tea is grown for subsistence. Orientals, Russians, and Britishers are the largest tea drinkers. Per capita consumption in Great Britain and the United States in 1960 was 10 pounds and 0.6 pounds, respectively.

COMMERCIAL CULTIVATION OF TEA

The tea plant, *Thea sinensis*, is an evergreen that begins to bear at three or four years of age and continues to do so for about thirty years. Left to itself, the tea tree would attain a height of 30 to 60 feet, but the bushes are kept pruned to a height of 3 to 5 feet to simplify picking the leaves and to force the bush to form a large plucking surface and many twigs, thereby yielding a greater quantity of leaves.

PICKING

Picking or plucking the leaves is a year-round task except in the colder areas of Japan and China, where the plants do not put out new leaves in winter. The manner of plucking the leaves affects the quality of tea. "Fine plucking" means picking only the bud and the two youngest leaves of the tea shoot (Fig. 20-4). "Coarse plucking" removes not only the two young leaves and the bud of the "fine plucking" but some of the larger leaves and

Fig. 20-4. Plucking the top two leaves and a bud of tea plant, Ceylon. This procedure is known as "fine" plucking as opposed to "medium" and "coarse" pluckings, which take more leaves. Fine plucking is customarily practiced, although it lowers the yield and thus tends to raise the cost of production; it is usually necessary when output must be curtailed. (Courtesy of Ceylon Tea Centre.)

even stems. Native pickers pluck the leaves directly into bamboo baskets. A tea plucker, using both hands, can pluck about 30,000 shoots a day. It requires about 3,200 shoots to make a pound of processed tea. After picking, the tea goes through a curing process.

LABOR

Since all tea is picked by hand and since the operation demands deft fingers and great skill, low-cost labor is a major requirement. Hence, Southern and Eastern Asia, where population swarms, is the most logical place to grow tea. Various attempts (some going back to 1800) were made in the United States to grow the crop; and though teas of excellent quality were produced for many years in South Carolina, the enterprise was uneconomical because of the high cost of labor. In the late 1950s, the experiment was terminated.

VARIETIES OF TEA

Although there are hundreds of varieties and blends of tea, they all fall into three principal divisions: (1) green or unfermented; (2) oolong or semifermented; and (3) black or fermented. *All three, however, can be processed from the leaves of the same plant.*

GREEN TEA

This tea, produced in China and Japan, is the type preferred by the people of these countries, by the Arabs of North Africa (where religious code forbids their drinking fermented tea), and by Americans of the older generation. It is made from unwithered, unfermented leaves. Since the tannin released by fermentation gives black tea its aroma, it is obvious that the green varieties, which are unfermented, have almost none. Green tea, however, has a distinctive flavor highly prized by those who drink it.

BLACK TEA

The leaves are placed in the sun to wither, a means of reducing moisture content. Rolling, either by hand or machine, breaks down the leaf cells, exposing the juices to the air. It is during the rolling process that chemical changes begin. As the tannin oxidizes, the essential oil is released, which gives black tea its characteristic flavor.

The leaves are then spread on trays for several hours for fermentation. Finally the leaves are fired in a hot, dry room, where they change to the familiar black tea of commerce.

OOLONG TEA

Oolong tea is processed much as is black tea, except that fermentation is stopped sooner, giving it some of the characteristics of both black and green tea.

LOCATION OF TEA CROPS

Tea, a tropical and subtropical plant, is grown where there is a sufficiently mild winter to prevent permanent damage to the shrub and where there is a sufficiently high rainfall to foster an abundant growth of young leaves. Accordingly, tea is grown over a rather wide latitudinal range, from the shores of the Black Sea (43° north latitude) to Natal in Africa (about 30° south latitude).

Soils and climate are the major physical factors in successful economic production. Although the shrub will grow on soils ranging from light sands to heavy clays, the soils should be deep, permeable, and acidic. In Java the young volcanic soils are highly favorable.

WORLD PRODUCTION

Tea production has been increasing rapidly. Prior to World War II, world production was about 991 million pounds per year. In 1956, the figure was 1,524 million pounds; and in 1959, 1,671 million pounds. So marked a rate of increase is too rapid for the consuming market to adjust to. This overproduction has resulted from (1) diminished consumption in Europe during the war years when tea was scarce, (2) present availability of cheap African *robusta* coffee, and (3) falling quality of tea (there is too much medium- and low-grade tea; high-grade tea is almost unavailable at any price).

Figure 20-1 shows where the world's tea is grown. Except for Africa, which is a small but growing producer, the crop is restricted mainly to Southern and Eastern Asia. A small amount is produced in the Soviet Union, in Turkey and Iran, and in three Latin American countries—Argentina, Brazil, and Peru. All in all, twenty-three countries grow tea, about half of them for the export market. Asia appears to be the original habitat of tea.

The conditions of the natural environment play an important role in determining where tea shall be grown; but even more important is a large labor supply that is skilled, experienced, and available at low wages. Additional factors are the long history of tea growing, the enormous size of the market for tea, and the availability of land in slope. Most tea

Fig. 20-5. *Women working in tea on slopes of island of Honshu, Japan. In mountainous Japan the pressure of population necessitates tea's being grown on slopes; the crop also needs good air and soil drainage. Japanese tea bushes are usually trimmed as is an ornamental hedge, and shears are used in harvesting; "scissor picking" increases by about ten times the output per worker but makes for less control over quality. (Courtesy of Consulate General of Japan.)*

land in Asia, for example, would make poor rice land.

CHINA

China leads in production of tea but has been unimportant in foreign trade, the bulk of the crop being consumed within the country. The principal producing area extends from the northern border of the Yangtze Valley southward to the drainage divide between it and the Si-Kiang (Fig. 20-1). Both green and black tea are produced. Everywhere the trees are grown on dry hill and mountain slopes at elevations of 1,000 to 3,000 feet.

JAPAN

Japan, which ranks fourth or fifth in world tea production (it is surpassed only by India, Indonesia, Ceylon, and China), grows both black and green tea, but the latter is the more important. Japan is said to consume at home three fourths of the output; there is only a small export.

The Japanese grow their tea on small patches of land (an acre or less) on terraced hillsides, south of 37° north latitude in central Honshu and southern Kyushu (Fig. 20-5). Commercial production is centered in the Shizuoka area, which normally accounts for about half of the national output and about 90 per cent of that exported. Tea is grown in sizable amounts also in other parts of the three southern islands. However, the amount of land given over to tea has been steadily declining. In 1892, 148,744 acres were planted to tea—the largest acreage ever recorded. In recent years the figure has been closer to 96,100 acres. Yield, however, has increased—the result of more scientific methods.

Most of the gardens are located on hill slopes and uplands between 500 and 1,500 feet elevation. They are also confined largely to the Pacific side of the country, where the winters are milder than on the west side. Water drainage must be adequate.

Tea picking in Japan is not around the clock, there being never more than three or four pickings per year. Quality of the leaves of the final picking is poor. In Japan the tea plant is pruned to produce a bushy growth (Fig. 20-5). Fertilizer (soybean cake, superphosphate, and potash) is generously utilized. For this reason production has increased even though acreage has declined considerably. To obtain leaves of high quality requires the liberal use of both organic and inorganic fertilizer.

Tea in Japan is grown more efficiently and more scientifically than in China, and the quality of the tea is better.

INDIA

India is the world's foremost commercial producer of tea. This importance stems essentially from British stimulation, for it was they who supplied both the capital and the principal market (they are acknowledged the world's leading non-Oriental tea drinkers). India's major tea-growing lands lie in the hilly margins of the Brahmaputra Valley in Assam. Here at Cachar and Dooars are present extremely favorable natural environmental conditions for growing the crop, as well as a large supply of labor. India has several other important tea-growing areas—the Nilgiri Hills, Anamallais, Travancore, and Darjeeling. Indian tea, grown on large estates mainly for export, is one of the country's few strictly plantation crops.

The future of tea in India is uncertain, for the rising tide of nationalism in the country (for example, the nationalization of foreign-owned tea plantations in the state of Kerala in the south) has shaken the confidence of many foreign investors. During the 1950s a number of British planters shifted their investments and operations to Ceylon and Africa. Yet in the late 1950s, tea was India's leading export based upon value.

CEYLON

Ceylon ranks next to India in commercial production of tea, and this crop is the island's leading commercial product and export. Tea represents 60 per cent of the total exports. More than any other country, Ceylon is favored for growing tea. Its southerly position assures warm winters; also, because of its insularity, it receives rain throughout the year (during Asia's rainy summer monsoon as well as its dry winter monsoon). **Flushing**, which continues throughout the year except at pruning time, permits plucking every week or ten days.

More than 570,000 acres are in tea, mostly in the south-central mountainous area (up to 6,000 feet), whose moderate temperatures, good drainage, and lessened humidity all are growing assets. On the large estates are employed more than half a million workers. Ceylon tea commands a higher price on the international market than Indian tea.

INDONESIA

Indonesia has been the third- or fourth-ranking commercial producer of tea in the world. The Dutch created tea plantations, whereas the natives maintained innumerable small holdings. Most of the tea is grown in western Java on the slopes of the mountains, where, at elevations exceeding 2,000 feet, the rainfall is abundant and is distributed over the greater part of the year. At elevations of less than 1,000 feet, tea does not produce leaves of high quality.

As in India and Ceylon, the future of tea growing is uncertain. The Dutch were expelled at the close of World War II. Will the industry languish under the Javanese? One thing is certain: production today is only about 70 per cent what it was prior to the outbreak of World War II.

SOVIET UNION

The Russians, like the British, are tea drinkers. A small tea industry has been established on the well-watered slopes of west Georgia where these face the Black Sea near Rize (Fig. 20-1). The bulk of the tea consumed by the large population is procured from Communist China.

AFRICA

Africa has been an important world factor in tea for only a few decades. Expansion has been aided by (1) the strong feeling of nationalism that characterizes the producing countries—Kenya, Mozambique (most important), Uganda, Tanganyika, Southern Rhodesia and Nyasaland, and the Congo; and (2) the fleeting confidence felt by investors in India, Ceylon, and Indonesia. African tea is produced as a plantation crop by white planters.

The tea is grown here as elsewhere in the wetter parts of the highlands. There was considerable planting following World War II, and those trees were coming into production during the late 1950s. Thus exports doubled between 1950 and 1960. The bulk of Africa's tea is exported to the United Kingdom, the Republic of South Africa, and Egypt. Despite this growth, Africa contributes a mere 5 per cent of the total world output.

WORLD TRADE IN TEA

Since overproduction characterizes commercial production of both coffee and tea, the two beverages are currently vying strongly for the same markets. About 1 billion pounds of tea enters foreign-trade channels each year; most of it emanates from India, Ceylon, and Indonesia. Approximately half the amount is destined for the United Kingdom, whose per capita annual consumption is about 10 pounds. Second largest importer is the United States, but it takes only about 10 per cent of the total. Major variation in United States trade has been the switch from green tea, which in 1940 represented 72 per cent of imports, to black tea, which now comprises 97 per cent. Other large tea importers are the several British Commonwealth countries, the Soviet Union, the nations comprising Northwest Europe (exclusive of the United Kingdom), and the Arab lands.

CACAO

Cacao, unlike coffee and tea, has nutritive value. The product was long used by the Amerindians of the tropical New World, of which it was native. Cortez introduced "chocolat" into Spain, whence its use spread rapidly over Europe.

The word "cacao" refers to the raw bean; "chocolate" designates the manufactured product (sweetened or unsweetened); and "cocoa" is the pulverized cacao bean from which part of the cacao butter has been removed.

COMMERCIAL CULTIVATION OF CACAO

When mature the cacao tree is between 15 and 25 feet high. It comes into bearing when about five years of age, into full production when ten to fifteen years of age, and maintains production for an additional twenty years, depending upon physical and human conditions. Flowering is profuse, but fruiting is scanty. Flowering occurs twice annually, and there are two harvesting periods. The fruits or pods mature about five months after the flowers have pollinated. The pods, from 5 to 10 inches long and 3 to 5 inches in diameter, are shaped somewhat like a cucumber. Unlike the tree fruits characteristic of middle latitudes, however, the cacao pods grow on the trunks and main branches, giving the tree an artificial appearance (Fig. 20-6). The pods vary in color from yellow-orange to reddish-purple. Each pod contains 30 to 45 almond-shaped beans or seeds which, when dried and fermented, are the cacao beans of commerce.

Cacao is grown on small native holdings and on plantations, depending on the country and on local conditions. Most cacao, how-

Fig. 20-6. Cacao tree with mature fruit. Note the novel manner in which the pods grow directly on the trunk and main branches. Each pod contains 30-45 seeds, which ultimately become the beans of commerce. A tree may reach a height of 30-40 feet in its natural forest environment, but it is customarily pruned to 15-25 feet in commercial cultivation. (Courtesy of U.S. Department of Agriculture.)

ever, is grown as a product of peasant agriculture. In Africa the cacao farms are of small size, irregular in pattern, and widely scattered. Trees, planted at random and given little or no care, are treated more as a forest product than as a crop to be nourished, guarded, and improved. Hence diseases and pests take a heavy toll.

The pods are cut with machetes. Those on the highest branches are cut with a curved knife blade fastened to the end of a long pole. Only the ripe pods are harvested. Yields range from 300 to 400 pounds of dry beans per acre.

The pods as cut from the tree are dropped into baskets and delivered to a spot where members of the family cut them in half with cutlasses or machetes. In some places the

workers open the pods by hitting them with stones or short wooden sticks or even by cracking two pods together. The beans are removed from the slimy white coatings by hand and fermented. Fermentation reduces the bitter taste and astringency of the beans and develops the essential oil that gives chocolate its characteristic aroma.

After fermenting, the beans are dried in the sun—sometimes on bamboo mats placed either on the ground or on bamboo trestles. In some areas drying houses are utilized. To obtain uniform and even coloring, the beans are turned many times during the day. With good weather, the drying process is accomplished in ten to fourteen days. Rain is detrimental and increases the degree of mold.

THE WORLD'S BEVERAGES: : 419

In West Africa the beans are moved from the villages to grading stations, being carried on the heads of natives who follow forest trails, or they may be sent down streams in dugouts. The graded beans are bagged and moved to seaports via rail, trail, or barge. They are then placed in large storage sheds for final inspection, weighing, and shipping.

PLANTATIONS

In Latin America (but not in Africa), most of the cacao is grown on plantations. Research and scientific production have resulted in better groves, superior trees, fewer insect pests and diseases, finer-quality beans, and higher yields. Costa Rica, for example, has developed disease-resistant trees with yields of 4,000 to 7,000 pounds per acre, compared with about 225 pounds per acre when they used old stock.

DISEASES

The cacao tree is victim of a number of ruinous diseases. Among these is pod rot, which attacks immature fruit and renders it useless. Although this disease is widespread, it can be controlled with copper compounds; but the cost is as yet too high to justify its use by small growers. The planting of resistant stock appears more promising. The disease is less menacing where there is a pronounced dry season—e.g., on the Pacific side of Central America. Another serious disease is witches'-broom—a cancerous growth that appears on the trunks of cacao trees. Witches'-broom almost ruined the cacao business of Ecuador. A virus disease called swollen-shoot complex also makes serious inroads into annual production. In Africa, particularly in Ghana and western Nigeria, capsids (insects that feed on pods and new shoots) menace the crop.

LOCATION OF CACAO CROPS

The cacao tree grows only in the tropics, from 20° north to 20° south latitude, reaching its best development nearest the equator (Fig. 20-1). Thus, the principal producers—the "Guinea Coast" of West Africa, Brazil, Ecuador, and Indonesia—all are so located; the less important producers—the West Indies (Haiti, Jamaica, Puerto Rico, the Dominican Republic), Venezuela, Mexico, Samoa, and the Malagasy Republic (Madagascar)—lie in the belt of the trades and must restrict their production to wind-sheltered valleys.

The cacao tree requires an average shade temperature of 80°F and an evenly distributed rainfall of between 60 to 150 inches; the humidity must be high the year around; strong winds must be absent, and the soils should be deep, warm, porous, and moist. The tree cannot grow in areas having a prolonged dry season or in areas where it would have to grow under the direct rays of the tropical sun.[2] Accordingly, cacao is planted under shade provided by larger trees. During the clearing process, certain tall trees are permitted to stand. The shade they provide is so dense that a photographer's light meter gives no reading whatsoever. The world is quite limited in areas where climate and soil combine to afford almost ideal conditions for the crop.

WORLD PRODUCTION

Many varieties of cacao are produced, but all may be grouped roughly into two types— "fine" and "ordinary." Venezuela, Ecuador, Costa Rica, Surinam, the West Indies, Ceylon, and Java are the principal producers of "fine" cacaos, but their combined output accounts for only about 10 to 15 per cent of the world total.

"Ordinary" cacaos, which account for 85 to 90 per cent of the world crop, emanate from the largest producers—the "Guinea Coast," Brazil, and the Dominican Republic.

THE GUINEA COAST REGION [3]

The outstanding producer both in this region and the world is Ghana, much of whose economy depends upon cacao. Half a million Ghanaians are directly concerned in cacao

[2] Scientists in Ghana are currently experimenting with growing cacao trees in sunlight.

[3] Throughout this presentation of cacao, the "Guinea Coast region" will include the entire Gulf of Guinea area—the Ivory Coast, Ghana, Nigeria, the Cameroons, Togo, Dahomey, and the islands of São Tomé, Príncipe, and Fernando Po.

farming, and the lives of all are influenced by the crop. Ghana produces about one third of the world crop, and cacao accounts for 60 to 75 per cent of its total exports.

Cacao was developed here as a supplement to subsistence farming, the first trees having been planted as late as 1890 following the ravages of the crop by disease in Latin America. Cacao is reported to be grown by more than 300,000 individual farmers, each of whom averages annually less than 1 ton of beans. The crop is grown on small native farms, averaging possibly about 15 acres each and widely scattered through the forest. The methods employed are backward, but the government expends considerable money and effort to educate the native growers (no Europeans or European capital is involved) in scientific methods. Several producing areas lie many miles (sometimes hundreds) from the coast. Some rivers are not navigable; railways and highways are not as yet well developed, but progress is being made in the building of roads.

The Guinea Coast region's rapid development following 1920 resulted from extraordinarily favorable physical conditions for growth of the tree, low labor and production costs, and comparative freedom from insect pests and diseases. Obviously the fact that wages are lower here than in Latin America gives the area a distinct competitive advantage: in 1959 the hired worker averaged 68 cents per day. By African standards, the owner of a cacao farm in Ghana is wealthy, earning five or six times the average per capita income for the whole country ($160 per year).

Further expansion in the Guinea Coast region appears improbable, for the present acreage seems up to the available labor supply, and diseases and pests are becoming a serious problem. Scientists are experimenting with commercial fertilizers and have achieved yields of 3,000 pounds per acre compared with the customary 200 to 300 pounds.

BRAZIL

Brazil, which contributes 16 to 20 per cent of the world's cacao, ranks second to the Guinea Coast region in world output. From the beginning of the seventeenth century down to 1890, the crop was confined largely to the Amazonian and Pará areas; but since 1890 the bulk of the crop (95 per cent) is grown in the Cacao Coast of Bahia. This area lies in a block at the foot of the Brazilian massif and is bordered on the east by a narrow coastal plain or by the South Atlantic Ocean. In latitude it extends from about 14° to 16° south. Here both climate and soils favor cacao; and, in the lands best suited pedologically, no other crop equals cacao in return per hour or per hectare. Moreover, there is available a cheap pool of labor.

The crop is grown on plantations—small, medium, and large. The Cocoa Institute regards the ideal cacao farm as one containing 123 to 185 acres of cultivated land, supplemented by a proportionate grazing area, forest reserve, and some diversified farming.

ECUADOR

Until 1916, Ecuador was the world's leading producer and exporter of cacao. Methods, however, were backward and careless, scientific advice was largely disregarded, and, as a result, two diseases—witches'-broom and monilia—almost destroyed the plantings.

Nonetheless, cacao still is an important crop of the *costa*, where it occupies roughly half the land devoted to commercial crops. Cacao is grown on both large and small plantations, particularly in the Guayas Basin, where it flourishes on the hot, humid, almost windless lowland. Through research, an effort is being made to find disease-resistant trees, and thus bring back production.

VENEZUELA

Venezuela is far more famous for the quality than for the quantity of its cacao. The crop is grown on plantations situated in the bottoms and on the lower slopes of the wet east-facing valleys of the Rio Tuy and the wetter north-facing slopes of the Coast Range overlooking the Caribbean in central and eastern Venezuela, where it has been raised for generations. Venezuela's crop, which is grown for export, ranks second only to coffee among the country's agricultural exports.

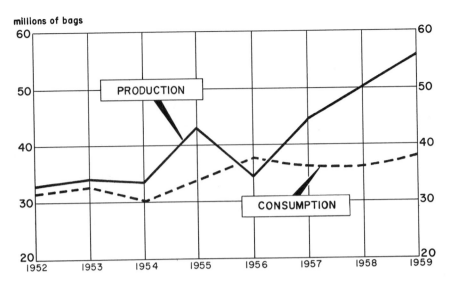

millions of bags

PRODUCTION

CONSUMPTION

Fig. 20-7. World supply and demand of coffee, 1952-1959. The supply far exceeds the demand. Great efforts have been made to increase coffee consumption in producing countries, in normal markets, and in new markets (e.g., the U.S.S.R. and Great Britain), but progress is slow at best. Consumption has inched up some as a result of price declines. (Adapted from The New York Times.)

COSTA RICA

Cacao is the oldest cash crop grown in Costa Rica, having been cultivated since 1650. In the early eighteenth century it so dominated the economy that the beans were accepted as authorized currency. The enterprise began to decline about 1747 and a century later had almost disappeared. But in 1914 cacao began to substitute for bananas on the Caribbean plain. Here physical conditions are favorable: soils are friable, deep, and well drained; rainfall is abundant; and hurricanes are unknown.

Much of the cacao is grown in the Limón area along the Caribbean coast, but there are also important plantings on the Pacific side. Yields are high, and the quality of the beans is good. Progress in part results from research by the American Institute of Agricultural Sciences at Turrialba.

THE DOMINICAN REPUBLIC

The Dominican Republic today ranks second to Brazil among the Latin American na-

tions in cacao production. The trees are grown throughout the republic although the principal areas are in the north and east. The crop is grown by small producers and the quality of the beans is "ordinary." About 95 per cent of the yield is exported, the bulk of it shipped to the United States.

WORLD TRADE

Roughly 2 billion pounds of cacao beans are produced and sold annually (only part of which is used in making chocolate and cocoa). About two thirds of these come from Africa, the rest from Latin America. A very small quantity, too, is contributed by Asia. Principal importers are the United States (which takes 25 to 30 per cent), the United Kingdom, France, the Netherlands, Germany, and Switzerland. New York City is the major cacao-trading center of the world, and the New York Cocoa Exchange regulates prices for the entire industry.

Cacao prices fluctuate widely; in fact, they are among the most unstable in the world. In a six-month period the price of cacao has been known to drop 25 per cent and more. When prices are depressed, the economies of the countries dependent on the crop suffer serious privations, even considering their meager living standards.

WORLD OUTLOOK FOR BEVERAGES

Underconsumption, in relation to overproduction, is the bane of all three beverage crops. The situation in coffee is shown in Figure 20-7. Since all are perennials, regulation of the annual crop is all but impossible. Invariably, artificial devices have proved to be no more than ephemeral panaceas. Moreover, the principal producing countries, all in the underdeveloped category, suffer because they rely too heavily upon coffee or tea or cacao for their foreign exchange. Monoculture is a great evil in all Latin American coffee-growing nations as it is in tea-growing Assam and Ceylon and in the cacao-growing Guinea Coast region. To diversify their economies, hundreds of thousands of workers would have to change their entire way of life. This would require time—and time is the one thing that lands with low levels of living and fast-growing populations believe they do not have. They insist on moving into the twentieth century now.

Finally, there is the specter of synthetic coffee, which threatens to make an appearance within a few years bringing economic dislocation to all the countries whose economies are geared to coffee. What this would mean to Brazil, Colombia, and El Salvador can hardly be overestimated.

SELECTED REFERENCES

Cheney, Ralph H. "The Biology and Economics of the Beverage Industry," *Economic Botany,* 1:243-275, July-September 1947.

Coffee in Latin America, Productivity Problems and Outlook: I. Colombia and El Salvador (E/CN 12/490). United Nations, 1958. Sales No. 58IIG4.

Dobbins, William F. "Tea—Enough Today, Too Much Tomorrow," *Foreign Agriculture,* 22:5-7, July 1958.

Gehr, James F. "Cacao—From Pod to Port," *Foreign Agriculture,* 19:108-111, 118, June 1955.

Hurt, L. C., and W. C. King. "Soluble Coffee—A Worldwide Industry," *Foreign Agriculture,* 25:8, 16, July 1961.

Jonasson, Olof. "Potential Areas of Cacao Cultivation in South America: A Review," *Economic Geography,* 27:90-93, January 1951.

King, W. C. "Coffee Harvest to Be Large," *Foreign Agriculture,* 24:3-4, 14, August 1960.

Stevens, R. L., and Paulo R. Brandão. "Diversification of the Economy of the Cacao Coast of Bahia, Brazil," *Economic Geography,* 37:231-253, July 1961.

"Tea Issue," *World Crops,* 6(5):175-208, 1954.

CHAPTER TWENTY-ONE::

Man's climb up the ladder of civilization has depended on the domestication of certain animals, and animal products today often rank as the most desired of human foods. The level of living of a nation is gauged more by per capita meat consumption than by possibly anything else.

In 1961, Uruguay, with 259 pounds per capita, overshadowed all other nations; next in line were New Zealand with 229; Australia, 226; Argentina, 175; the United States, 162; Canada, 142; Denmark and the United Kingdom, 132; France, 119; and West Germany, 112. In the Soviet Union consumption was 68 pounds per capita, while in Japan it was only 8.[1] Where the pressure of population precludes lands being utilized to any extent for

[1] "U.S. Eats Most Meat but Ranks Fifth per Person," *Foreign Agriculture*, 25:16, December 1961.

THE WORLD'S

feed and/or pasture (as in China) or where religious principles restrict the use of meat (as with beef in India and with swine in Muslim lands), populations tend to fall into the under-developed category.

Thus the world over, the raising of live-stock is a major phase of agriculture, and more land is devoted to it than to anything else; the tundra, steppe, savanna, and even parts of the prairie are used primarily for grazing, as are the deserts and mountains. Even a consider-able share of good farmland is given over to pasture and forage and feed crops for live-stock. In some farming areas animal enter-prises form the very basis of the agriculture; the Corn Belt of the United States has long produced mostly feed for livestock rather than food for man, and the Argentine Pampa must be regarded primarily as a beef-cattle region —alfalfa being by far the dominant crop.

However, use of land for growing feed is expensive. One acre sown to rice will support a whole family; but seven acres are needed to do so on animal products—meat or milk. Do-mestic animals convert only a fraction of the feed they consume into meat or milk.

The animals raised vary markedly in their requirements. Some are adapted to cold cli-mates, others to intermediate climates, and a few even to tropical climates. Some thrive on lands with poor vegetative cover, whereas others demand lush pastures and concentrated feed. Some require man's constant attention; others can graze on their own, being capable of defending themselves and their young against predators.

Domestic animals have received consider-able attention from man. By means of careful scientific breeding, he has actually altered ani-mal physiology, so that livestock better suited

ANIMAL INDUSTRIES

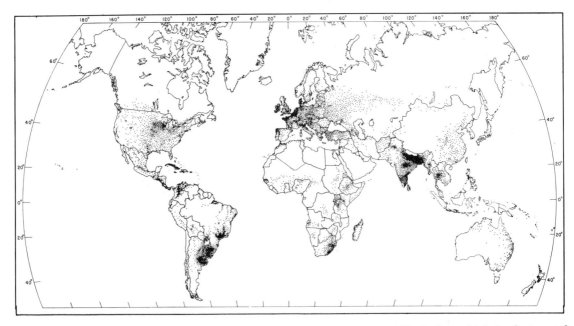

Fig. 21-1. World distribution of cattle. Note especially India, which leads in total number of cattle but whose enormous numbers result from the fact that the animal is regarded as sacred and hence is not slaughtered. (Courtesy of U.S. Department of Agriculture.)

to the various physical environments is produced. However, man needs optimum conditions in a given habitat if he is to raise superior animals. There is a vital and inseparable relation between climate, natural vegetation, and soil and the rearing of livestock. If vegetation is to produce protein generously, there must be enough precipitation for carbohydrate production and at the same time enough fertility in the soil for the biosynthetic conversion of this fuel food into protein as the growth-promoting food. This combination of proper climate and soil fertility is not universally found. It is to be encountered chiefly in limed areas or in those places where man manages the soil most scientifically.

CATTLE

Figure 21-1 shows the world distribution of cattle.[2] The main points to be noted from

[2] Cattle fall into two types: (1) European, which are found mainly in middle latitudes; and (2) zebu or Brahma, which are found mostly in the tropics.

study of the map are that cattle are largely excluded from the polar lands, the drier lands (*true deserts*), the higher and the more rugged mountainous areas, and usually from the hot, humid lands. Most of the world's cattle (used for meat and/or milk) are to be found in middle latitudes—Europe, the United States and adjacent southern Canada (Fig. 21-2), eastern South America (the Argentine Pampa, Uruguay, and southern Brazil), Australia, and New Zealand. However, in Australia, the northern *tropical* part (Queensland) is more important than the temperate southeast in cattle rearing.

BEEF CATTLE

EUROPE

Many of the choice beef breeds—the Shorthorn, Hereford, Aberdeen-Angus, Galloway, Red Poll, Devon, Sussex, and West Highland —were developed in the eighteenth century in Britain. British beef cattle are reared almost wholly for home consumption, and they meet nearly 60 per cent of the domestic demand

Fig. 21-2. Cattle roundup on a 54,000-acre ranch near Abbey, Saskatchewan, Canada. This enterprise, so little understood by the general public, has nonetheless had a great impact on the Anglo-American consciousness. Many of the animals born and grazed on the range ultimately find their way into the Corn Belt for fattening. (Courtesy of National Film Board of Canada.)

for beef. Cattle are most numerous in the western part of the country, though fattening takes place mainly in the Midlands and in the east. Cattle graze on pasture in summer but are stall-fed in winter.

On the continent the breeds are good but are less well known over the world than the British. The principal French breeds are the Charolais and the Parthenaise. French beef cattle are raised mostly in the northwest and in the central plateau—regions of large forage production but poorly adapted for wheat. Elsewhere on the continent great numbers of cattle are to be found, but the beef is produced in connection with dairying.

UNITED STATES

The United States ranks among the world's leaders in beef cattle and first in commercial production. Moreover, beef cattle are increasing at the expense of dairy cattle. The United States stands far above all other nations in the total output of beef, and possibly in quality of animals. The distribution of beef cattle results from availability of cheap range, pasture, hay, and other feed crops, such as corn. The greatest density is in the western Corn Belt, where both corn and hay are cheapest and most profitably utilized as fatteners for cattle. Moreover, the Corn Belt, which lies midway between the Western breeding grounds and the great Eastern consuming area, is today the principal beef-cattle slaughtering and meat-packing area of the nation. The Corn Belt is world famous both for breeding and feeding of beef cattle. Large numbers of feeders are brought into the region from the areas to the west.

Cattle are also important in the Great Plains, the Rockies, the Great Basin, and the Central Valley and numerous other valleys throughout the state of California. Over most of these

Fig. 21-3. Wyoming cattle being driven from lowland ranches to mountain pastures for summer grazing. (Courtesy of Union Pacific Railroad Company.)

areas, water and arable land are scarce, but there is a vast expanse of wild grass and shrubs that are best utilized by livestock (Fig. 21-3). Cattle, however, graze profitably on the better parts. Thus, the Great Plains (in both the United States and Canada) are particularly outstanding for cattle. Yet even here 'the drier years wreak havoc with the cattle business; there were fewer cattle on the ranges of western Texas in 1957 than at any time since cowboys drove cattle over the famed Chisholm Trail to Abilene.

California raises large numbers of beef cattle in valleys and low mountains, and brings in huge numbers of range-fed cattle from Colorado, Montana, Texas, and other Western states for fattening in commercial feedlots. On October 1, 1961, there were more than ¾ million head of beef in the 600-odd commercial feedlots that are distributed widely over the state. Some lots are capable of feeding as many as 10,000 head at one time.

Nationally, a rather recent development is the tendency to sell cattle directly from feedlot to chain stores and other large purchasers, thus bypassing the stockyards. It is estimated that chain stores purchase 25 to 35 per cent of their meat directly from packers.

In the southern Great Plains much land formerly given over to cotton is no longer available for this crop because of government controls. Accordingly, much of the acreage has been put into drought-resistant grain

sorghums, which are being fed to beef cattle. As a result, the southern Great Plains is rapidly becoming one of the nation's major areas for beef-cattle feeding and fattening, and grain sorghums sell here for about 10 per cent less than Midwestern corn. Corn, which traditionally is regarded as the great fattener, cannot be grown here because it requires much more moisture; and the range-cattle industry cannot survive on grass alone. Moreover, cottonseed meal and hulls are readily available as feed supplements.

Some of the animals from the Great Plains and the Rocky Mountain regions are shipped to farmers in the Corn Belt for fattening; increasing numbers, however, are being fattened in irrigated oases and slaughtered nearby. The place of slaughter today tends to move closer to the areas where the animals are produced. Very considerable numbers, too, are being shipped to California's Imperial Valley and Central Valley for fattening. Sugar-beet and citrus by-products encourage cattle feeding in these areas.

For a period of 400 years after Ponce de Leon landed a few head of cattle on Florida's Gulf Coast in 1521, cattle were commercially unimportant in the South. Pastures were poor, the cattle tick was widespread, and the animals were large and bony—not very good for meat. Moreover, little attention had been given to upbreeding them. However, during the period 1925-1937, amazing progress was made in the raising of beef cattle in the South. The cattle tick was eradicated,[3] new pasture grasses were successfully introduced, livestock was tailored to the climate, and man learned how to control pasture deficiencies in calcium, phosphorus, iron, copper, and cobalt; and permanent pastures became well established (a combination of native range pasture and improved pastures). A half century ago the South was devoted to the one-crop system of agriculture: cotton was king. Today one notes that large acreages have been shifted from cultivated crops to grass. Florida has more than 14 million acres of grazing land today. Most Southern cattle are slaughtered locally as grass-fat cattle.

Today outstanding pastures are in evidence over much of the South. Hay crops well suited to the region have been introduced, and new breeds of beef cattle have been developed by the crossing of Hereford and Aberdeen-Angus strains with Brahma cattle from India. The Santa Gertrudis, Charbray, Brangus, and Beefmaster all are new breeds that have been tailored for Southern conditions. The degree of progress may be seen in Florida: whereas it had only one purebred herd in 1903, it now has more than 600.

EASTERN SOUTH AMERICA

Northeastern Argentina (the Pampa), Uruguay, and southeastern Brazil comprise one of the world's most important beef-cattle regions (Fig. 21-1). Heart of it, of course, is the Pampa, a region about the size of the American states of Illinois, Iowa, and Missouri, flat as a floor and covered mostly with grass and alfalfa. It is a region of large estates, most of them comprising 6,000 to 12,000 acres, though many are larger. From an economic

[3] The federal government began a tick-eradication campaign in 1906 in some 985 counties (all were under federal quarantine) in fifteen Southern and Southwestern states—almost one fourth of the area of the nation. Southern cattle now move without any sanitary restrictions for tick fever. In 1956 there was only one strip of cattle country (that adjacent to the lower Río Grande in Texas) that was quarantined. Reinfestations continue to occur here as a result of Mexican cattle, which either stray or are smuggled across the border.

standpoint, the *estancieros*, owners of the large estates (*estancias*), are interested almost solely in cattle rather than in crops. This situation is unique, for the Pampa's climate and soil are among the world's best for agriculture. Since alfalfa is the principal crop, the *estancieros* rent a portion of their land to tenants for a period of four or five years, permitting them a share of the crops—wheat, corn, and flaxseed. The contracts, however, oblige the tenants to plant the land with alfalfa and move away after a specified number of years. The alfalfa fields then yield well for five to ten years with three cuttings per year, after which new tenants are obtained and the cycle is repeated.

The Pampa, which is primarily a land of pastures, produces prime beef at lower cost than any other region, or indeed any country, in the world—the result of mild climate, extensive systems of operation, low-priced labor, relatively inexpensive land, and low taxes.

Prior to 1877 Argentine cattle were *criollo* cattle, descendants of the scrub animals of the Colonial Period; they were virtually wild cattle that ran at will over the vast, unfenced range. In 1877 the first refrigerator ship made it possible to send frozen meat to Europe. But the discriminating taste of the British would not accept Argentine beef. Hence high-grade breeding stock was imported from Britain and carefully bred in fenced pastures. This transition occurred between 1880 and 1900. Also, since British cattle required better feed, a shift took place from a grazing enterprise based upon uncultivated pasture to an enterprise based upon cultivated alfalfa. The **carrying capacity** of these fine alfalfa pastures is one cow or steer for each 1½ to 2 acres. The Pampa is unique in one respect: despite its importance as a producer of corn, the beef cattle are fattened on native grass and alfalfa range, mostly the latter, without shelter or grain ration.

The principal breeds on the Pampa are the Shorthorn, which predominates on the better pastures, and the Hereford, which thrives in the less favorable areas—for example, in Entre Ríos. In addition, some Aberdeen-Angus are

Fig. 21-4. Brazilian cattle fair in Bahia. Brahma cattle have a high degree of heat resistance, are hardy, and can survive on poor and limited fare. Long-legged and bony, they seem unattractive to some people. They have proved to be well suited to hot, humid Tropical Brazil and are becoming extremely valuable for crossbreeding with European cattle. (Photo by Eric Hess, Courtesy of Panair do Brasil.)

raised in the cooler southwestern part of the Pampa.

Uruguay is regarded as a typical ranching nation; 83 per cent of the total national territory is used as pasture, on which the carrying capacity is high—roughly the same as for the Pampa. The neighboring grasslands of southern Brazil rank among the world's more important cattle lands (Fig. 21-1) and are the heart of the Brazilian cattle business (Fig. 21-4). It is not generally known that Brazil, with about 73 million head, is the world's third largest cattle-raising nation—after India and the United States. Some Brazilian experts maintain that the number of cattle could be quadrupled. The great size of the country with its many climates and vegetation forms would seem to lend credence to such an estimate.

AUSTRALIA AND NEW ZEALAND

Australia ranks among the leading beef-cattle-producing countries; but in actual numbers it is far below the United States, Canada, Argentina, and Northwestern Europe. The limiting factors have been (1) severe and frequent droughts; (2) great heat of the savanna lands in the monsoonal north, the principal beef-cattle region; (3) unfavorable grass growth; (4) poor transportation facilities in the cattle regions; (5) restricted domestic market for beef (even though three fourths of Australia's total meat production is consumed domestically, and even though per capita consumption is among the highest for any nation, there still remain some 376 million pounds of beef and veal for export); (6)

pests and diseases; and (7) great distance from the world's major markets.

Most of the beef cattle are to be found in the north, primarily in the Northern Territory and Queensland in what is known as the "Outback"—the lands inland from the coast (Fig. 21-1).

The average cattle station consists of about 2,000 square miles of land on which some 18,000 to 30,000 head of cattle graze. One station, Victoria River Downs, is about 13,000 square miles in extent and carries more than 100,000 cattle. Water is a problem. Highly fortunate stations may have permanent springs or reliable rivers, but most stations are dependent upon deep-drilled wells for bringing up highly mineralized water. The cattle are almost wild. Mobs of fat cattle are driven through difficult country over rough trails up to 200 miles. One cattle route, possibly the longest in the world, exceeds 1,000 miles; and there are many in the neighborhood of 800 miles. Walks over such long trails may require as many as 100 days and hence are costly in labor and in loss of weight by the animals. The cattle must be marketed as feeders and be fattened before they can be slaughtered.

The area has droughts that can kill a man in a day if he runs out of drinking water. Thousands of cattle die in some years. The 1958 drought, the worst in more than 50 years, turned much of the cattle land into a giant dust bowl. Tens of thousands of cattle died; it was a common sight to see them lie spent on the parched ground or wallow knee-deep in the mud by the waterholes as death drew closer.

Most Australian cattle are English breeds —Herefords, supplemented by Aberdeen-Angus; but efforts are being made to introduce breeds with Indian blood (zebu) for their better tolerance of heat, ticks, and coarse tropical forage. Some Santa Gertrudis stock is being imported from the American South.

Internal transportation is a major handicap; the practice of walking cattle to market, to have them arrive in such debilitated condition that they are sold as poor beef, is rapidly being replaced by truck transport. The mileage in hard-surfaced roads is negligible, but unpaved "beef roads" are being constructed with rapidity.

In New Zealand, beef cattle are really an adjunct of sheep farming, the cattle being used to control pasture growth and destroy undesirable vegetation.

THE TROPICS

Except for the humped cattle of India, the tropics have not been outstanding in cattle. In fact, tropical cattle have shown low productivity in both meat and milk. Tropical grasses and forage plants frequently are lacking in nutritive value. Lands experiencing long periods of scanty rainfall, particularly if they also experience a hot season, can hardly be expected to support important cattle enterprises. In the Rainy Tropics, the rainfall and temperature conspire to leach the soluble minerals and nitrogenous compounds from the soil, leaving the vegetation poorly suited for the nourishment of animals.

There is obviously a difference in the ability of animals to withstand tropical conditions. Cattle from cool Northwestern Europe do not thrive; zebu or Brahma cattle expectably show a greater heat tolerance. Their white color throws off a larger proportion of the intense solar heat than is true of deep-colored coats; their short hair permits greater elimination of body heat; and their deeply pigmented skin impedes the penetration of strong solar rays. The surest way to improve tropical livestock is to breed animals adapted to the environment, but such a program is necessarily slow. The present breeds of cattle found in the American tropics, for example, have not been highly selected either for meat or milk production. They are, however, eminently suited by heredity to withstand the rigors of the tropical environment. Thus the aim of the breeder is to combine in a single animal the qualities of adaptability and/or high milk production or desirable beef-type qualities.

Only one tropical area's beef-cattle enterprise is presented here—that of the South American Llanos. The Llanos are tropical grasslands in Colombia and Venezuela. During the rainy season the rivers swell tremendously, overflow their banks, and inundate ex-

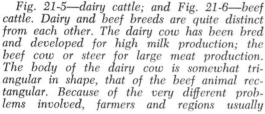

Fig. 21-5—dairy cattle; and Fig. 21-6—beef cattle. Dairy and beef breeds are quite distinct from each other. The dairy cow has been bred and developed for high milk production; the beef cow or steer for large meat production. The body of the dairy cow is somewhat triangular in shape, that of the beef animal rectangular. Because of the very different problems involved, farmers and regions usually specialize *in one type or the other. The dairy scene is in the famous dairy state of Wisconsin; on this farm of 267 acres, 63 are in hay, 100 in pasture. The total dairy herd consists of 80 purebred Guernseys. Note the big barn and the silo. The Aberdeen-Angus cow and calf are on pasture in Florida. (Courtesy of U.S. Department of Agriculture and of Gulf Power Company, Pensacola, Florida.)*

tensive areas along their lower reaches (estimated at more than one third of the entire Llanos). During the dry season, many of the rivers dry up into pools and swamps, and the grasslands literally burn up.

The Spaniards introduced European cattle into the region in 1548. The descendants of these cattle, today known as "native" or *criollo* cattle, have reverted to a semiwild state. They are small, long-horned, slow maturing, and varicolored. The *criollo* is an excellent foundation animal on which to build crossbred cattle (with the Brahma). In order to improve the Llanos herds, very considerable numbers of new American breeds—Santa Gertrudis, Charbray, Brangus, and Beefmaster—are being imported. All these breeds contain Brahma blood and hence endure well the high temperatures. Their rather oily hide offers greater defense against flies, ticks, and other parasites and pests, which are so very difficult to control in the tropics. All are good rustlers and do well even when the grass is dry and water scarce.

The Llanos have considerable potential for increased production of beef; also the demand

for meat in the cities to the north is great. Moreover, the keeping of cattle has been the most persistent and permanent enterprise in the region, having survived for four hundred years.

DAIRY CATTLE

Dairy breeds of cattle are distinct from beef breeds (Figs. 21-5 and 21-6): they do not have the blocky build; their shoulders and hips are narrow; and, viewed from above, the body is somewhat triangular; the stomach is full and the udder very large. Dairy animals demand much more care than beef cattle: they must be milked twice daily, and they are not adapted to range grazing. Moreover, they have been bred and developed for high milk production. Such cows do not produce milk until they are about two years old—beyond the age when most beef cattle are slaughtered.

DAIRY CATTLE AND NATURAL ENVIRONMENT

Dairy cattle are to be found in many climatic habitats. They really thrive, however, in middle latitudes—mainly in the Temperate

Marine (west coast) and Humid Continental climates. They must have good grass and hay forage. Moderate temperatures coupled with drizzly, long-drawn-out, and frequent rainfall produce excellent pastures with high carrying capacity. Low rate of evaporation is conducive to grasslands of high quality; "green pastures" are thus a notable feature of the preferred dairy landscape. In the Temperate Marine climate, dairy cattle can graze ten to twelve months per year. In parts of Ireland and New Zealand the grasses remain green throughout the year. Dairy cows should have at all times easy access to a large supply of good water; the average cow needs up to 40 gallons daily.

NORTHWEST EUROPE

Since Northwest Europe is famous for its pastures and for its breeding of fine dairy animals—and since the dense, urban, industrial populations afford an excellent market for fresh milk, butter, and cheese—one naturally expects dairy cattle to be numerous; and they are. Seventy per cent of the total milk produced in the United Kingdom is consumed as fluid milk. The reverse of the highly favorable conditions mentioned here for Northwest Europe is to be found in Mediterranean Europe, where dairy cows are indeed scarce (Fig. 21-1).

Western Britain is a land of meadows and pastures. The average dairy herd is larger than in Denmark and the Netherlands because the holdings are larger. The dairy herds are confined mainly to lowland locations.

In Denmark, farms average about 40 acres in size, 40 per cent of which is in pasture, 40 per cent in grain crops, and 15 per cent in forage crops. Red Danish cattle prevail in some areas, Holsteins in others. Danish farmers specialize in butter, with sidelines of bacon and eggs. The cream of several hundred farms is marketed at cooperative creameries, the skimmed milk being returned to the farms to be fed to swine and poultry. Most of the butter is exported to the United Kingdom and West Germany, whose growing nationalism, however, is affecting somewhat the marketing of the Danish product. The small size of the farms necessitates a large turnover of livestock products if the farmer is to make a living. Denmark has, accordingly, one of the world's most highly productive livestock enterprises.

In the Netherlands, cheese is the primary product. In the polders of the west and north, reclaimed from the sea, are lush pastures. Dairying here is one of the very few possible rural occupations; for the moist, heavy soils and the high **water table** are not well suited for the cultivation of most crops but make excellent pasture.

Switzerland's alpine meadows and her carefully bred herds are world famous. *Transhumance*, a part of dairying here, involves the seasonal movement of people and animals to parklike meadows at higher elevations in summer. Low wooden *chalets* house the cows, serve for storage of hay, and even function as cheese factories. Transhumance differs from pastoral nomadism in that only one or two members of the family accompany the animals in their vertical migration, the rest of the population remaining in their permanent homes. Cheese is made because it can stand the delay in transportation from mountain pasture to village better than any other milk product.

Dairy farming in Western Europe is so intense that the cattle of nearly all sections, despite the immense production of white potatoes (a large portion of which is fed to livestock), have to be supported in part by the importation of concentrated feeds from abroad —cottonseed, soybean, and flaxseed meals from the United States and flaxseed meal from Argentina.

UNITED STATES

Though dairy cattle are widely distributed over the United States, the principal dairy sections coincide with two types of climate— the Humid Continental with Medium Summers and the Temperate Marine. However, because of the large markets for fresh milk, there are very important dairy herds and outstanding output of milk in the Middle West (Humid Continental with Long Summers),

California (Mediterranean Subtropical), and even the Deep South (Humid Subtropical).

The nation's principal dairy region is in the North—in a formerly glaciated region characterized by undulating to rolling surface, countless marshes and swamps, and numerous perennial streams. Much of the land is too wet for tillage but is well suited to marsh hay or pasture. Much land, too, is left in pasture because of its stoniness, which would injure farm equipment and make farming hazardous. Many of the soils, particularly the **podosols,** are so poor that they are ill suited to crops but are satisfactory for pasture. The cool autumn temperatures also favor dairy cattle over crops.

All the cattle in this region are of European origin, but Holsteins are the most numerous and the most widely distributed. Not all farmers and dairies are satisfied with the Holstein, however; for although it gives the largest quantity of milk, the butterfat content is low. When a higher butterfat content is desired, the Jersey and Guernsey are the preferred animals.

Outside this main dairy region—that is, in the Corn Belt, the Deep South, and the southern half of California—the Jersey tends to replace the Holstein. When a Southerner speaks of a milk cow, he usually means a Jersey.

California, despite its desertic summers (except in the northwest), ranks high in dairying. Although Wisconsin, Minnesota, New York, Pennsylvania, and Iowa each have more cattle, California is fourth in the nation in total milk production. Indeed, Los Angeles County produces more milk than any other county in the nation. California cows produce 39 per cent more milk and 36 per cent more butterfat than do the nation's as a whole. Most California dairy cattle do not tread green grass pastures but feed in stalls.

Another important American dairy region is the Pacific Northwest, which meets the needs of the cities for market milk and provides a very large surplus for manufacture, particularly for evaporated milk. Dairying is favored here by abundant precipitation, cool temperatures, long **growing season,** and very good pastures.

CANADA

Canada's principal dairy belt has the same climate as the chief dairy region of the United States—the Humid Continental with Medium Summers. It differs, however, in having more land in hay and less in corn for silage. Since the winters are longer, more hay must be stored per farm. Whereas most milk from the American dairy region is used as fresh milk, most of Canada's goes into cheese and butter—the result of small urban population in relation to large milk output.

NEW ZEALAND

New Zealand is the only world-famous dairy country in the Southern Hemisphere. In the west-coast lowlands of North Island is one of the densest milk-cow populations on earth. Both North Island and South Island have outstanding pastures—*planted pastures*—on which year-round grazing is carried on. The mild marine climate makes housing of the animals unnecessary.

SHEEP

Sheep were native of rough uplands and high plateaus in the Old World. Their domesticated offspring are raised for milk and meat (mostly in the Northern Hemisphere) and for wool and meat (in the Southern Hemisphere) (Fig. 21-7).

Since sheep are among the oldest of the domesticated animals, it is natural that man should have developed many breeds. Some of these are wool breeds, some meat breeds, some dual-purpose breeds, and a few are even multiple-purpose breeds. (The wool breeds are presented on pages 492-495.)

The British are credited with having developed the mutton breeds—Shropshire, Southdown, Hampshire, Romney Marsh, Suffolk, Oxford, Cotswold, Cheviot, and Leicester. The French developed from the merino the Rambouillet, which is suitable either for mutton or wool; New Zealanders did the same with the Corriedale.

Sheep are raised in approximately sixty nations; but they are numerically outstanding

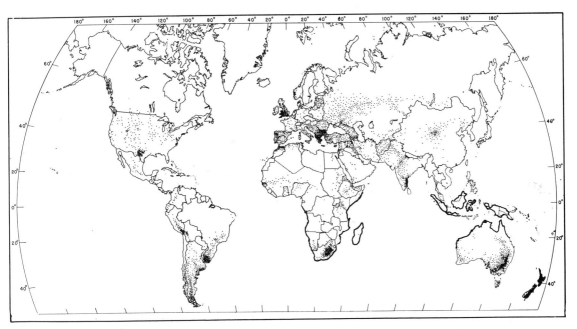

Fig. 21-7. *World distribution of sheep. Sheep over most of the world have been relegated to the less desirable milieus—mostly sparsely populated lands that are arid and semiarid, or bleak, or rugged. There are surprisingly few exceptions to this generalization; but parts of Britain, the Soviet Union, the Argentine Pampa, and Uruguay deviate from the pattern. (Courtesy of U.S. Department of Agriculture.)*

in India, the Middle East, the Mediterranean Basin, Great Britain, eastern Australia, New Zealand, South Africa, southern Argentina (Patagonia), and western United States (Fig. 21-7). In the first three areas, the sheep are multipurpose animals. Of the commercial lamb and mutton producers, Australia, New Zealand, the United States, the United Kingdom, and Argentina are the most important.

SHEEP AND NATURAL ENVIRONMENT

Sheep, like cattle but unlike swine, are grass eaters; but they have one advantage over cattle—they do well on poor range, even range where grass gives way to shrubs. They do well where aridity holds sway; they also graze steep and rugged lands far better than do cattle (Fig. 21-8). Sheep are raised as both range and farm animals. So adaptable are sheep that in many countries they have been pushed into the least desirable parts; thus few sheep strongholds remain in eastern United States. The choicer portions of the Argentine Pampa, too, have witnessed a

phenomenal shrinkage in sheep numbers. In both the United States and Argentina, sheep have been pushed into the drier and more rugged lands. However, the range of sheep is limited by water supply and by pasture; sheep need water at least every fourth day and in summer every other day. Forage farther than 15 miles from water is out of reach of sheep.

AUSTRALIA

Australia is the premier sheep nation of the world. It exceeds all nations in number of head—over 160 million in 1963—amounting to 17 per cent of the world total. Sheep comprise the foundation of the Australian economy. The country is climatically well suited to sheep, which are reared largely for wool. More than 75 per cent of Australia's sheep are merinos, a wool breed; and an additional 5 per cent are merino "comebacks" (with more than half merino blood). However, sufficient numbers of crossbreeds and dual-purpose breeds are kept to give Australia

Fig. 21-8. Navajo Indian girls herding sheep in the American Southwest. Since less than 1 per cent of the Navajo Reservation is suited to agriculture, the Navajos are essentially pastoralists. They were not pastoralists, however, until Coronado introduced sheep into the Southwest in 1540. The carrying capacity of this dry, badly overgrazed land is low. (Courtesy of Hal Rumel Studios.)

first place among countries of the world in sheep-meat production. The mutton breeds are raised mainly in the southeastern part of the country, and are usually slaughtered as fat lambs.

The sheep belt lies on the west side of the Great Dividing Range, forming a broad crescent that extends through the semiarid land from Queensland through New South Wales and Victoria into South Australia; another but less important belt is to be found in the western part of Western Australia. In Australia there is a close relationship between the distribution of merino sheep and of precipitation. Thus the merino belt is confined to the lands lying between the 10-inch and 30-inch rainfall lines, with the heaviest sheep population occupying those ranges between the 21- and the 23-inch isohyets. Here one sheep can be sustained on about 3 acres.

Australia's sheep graze in bands of several hundred to several thousand animals on good land on "stations," which are grazing establishments similar to ranches in the United States (Fig. 21-9). Fewer than fifty stations today carry in excess of 50,000 sheep each— the result largely of scarcity of labor. In the past some of the larger stations had as many as 500,000 head, but most of these have been broken up; many outfits today have no more than 500 head. To reach a station, one usually must travel many miles beyond the nearest railhead. Here one finds corrals for the sheep, a shearing shed, a well, a windmill, large tanks for storing water, a windbreak, and a neat white house with wide verandas and a metal roof.

The Australian sheep industry is plagued by pests. Dingoes, for example, prey on sheep; and single ranches are known to lose hundreds of sheep in a single year to them. Fences do help—fences hundreds of miles long, of dingo-proof mesh, 5¼ feet high and anchored in the ground at double thickness to prevent the animals from tunneling under them. Also the heavy bounty paid for the dingoes' scalps helps somewhat in reducing their numbers. The industry also must contend with rabbits and kangaroos, which compete with sheep for herbage.

NEW ZEALAND

From some points of view, New Zealand is the foremost sheep country in the world. The density of the sheep population per square mile and per head of human population is the heaviest in the world. And sheep account for about 50 per cent by value of New Zealand's total exports.

More than half the sheep are to be found in North Island, the area of greatest concentration being in the southeast. In South Island, it is again the eastern portion where sheep

Fig. 21-9. Merino sheep being mustered for shearing on a 40,000-acre sheep and cattle property in the southern tablelands of New South Wales, Australia. In the background is the Murrumbidgee River. The dark patches on the river flats are irrigated plots of alfalfa. Australia has more sheep than any other country on earth and ranks as the largest producer of wool. (Courtesy of Australian Information Bureau.)

are dominant. These are the drier portions of the islands, though heavy rainfall does not of itself preclude sheep from a given area. In South Island, grass was the predominant vegetation, whereas in North Island it was bracken fern or dense scrub. So unsuitable were the last two that sheep could not be raised in North Island until a technique was developed for converting the country to grassland. This was accomplished by burning and then sowing grass seed in the ashes. As both grass and fresh fern growth appeared, sheep were introduced to tramp out and eat the fern.

UNITED STATES

Though sheep are to be found in the majority of the American states (unimportant, obviously, in the hot, humid Deep South), they are most important in the West (80 per cent of the 28.3 million are west of the 100th meridian—the 20-inch isohyet), where they thrive in all but the driest parts of the desert of southwestern Arizona and southeastern California, and in the dense forests of northern Idaho, northwestern Montana, and northeastern Washington. The greatest lamb-feeding area in the nation is the valley of the South Platte in Colorado, which has hundreds of thousands of sheep on feed in winter.

Invariably sheep are to be found near mountains; for they can graze above the timberline in summer, utilizing the lush grasses of the brief summer. They then are driven in the fall into the deserts or into irrigated valleys to spend the winter. The usual pattern in the West is to graze the sheep on the sagebrush-grass vegetation in spring, progress toward higher country as the range becomes ready for grazing, spend the summers in the high-altitude range, and retire to sagebrush-grass in autumn. Livestock without winter range are taken to feed yards, where they eat alfalfa hay and some grain.

Sheep have persisted in a few areas in the Middle West—the central portion of the southern Peninsula of Michigan (sandy soils) and the Allegheny Plateau of western Pennsylvania, eastern Ohio, and the panhandle of West Virginia (infertile soils and rough terrain ill suited to most crops).

ARGENTINA (PATAGONIA)

Patagonia is one of the world's leading sheep lands; in the drier north, most of the animals are bred for wool. One third of Argentina's 50 million sheep graze throughout Patagonia, and it is they that supply most of the fine-apparel wools. All the way from the Río Colorado into Tierra del Fuego, the few scattered residents depend almost wholly upon sheep for their livelihood.

The best pastures and most of the mutton sheep are to be found in the extreme south—immediately north of the Strait of Magellan and on the island of Tierra del Fuego. Actually, despite its more southerly latitude, Tierra del Fuego's climate is less severe than central Patagonia's. Nor is water a problem, for fast-flowing streams are numerous. The better grasses in Tierra del Fuego are to be found on the grassy plain of the north. Here there is a carrying capacity of one sheep for each 2.5 acres, as contrasted with one sheep for 5 to 10 acres in dry Patagonia. Because of their hardiness and higher meat yields, Corriedale and Romney Marsh have replaced the merino as the predominant breeds.

ARGENTINA (SOUTHERN PAMPA) AND URUGUAY

Sheep have been crowded out of the better parts of the Pampa by beef cattle, which are more profitable and more popular. English breeds of sheep have persisted in the southeastern part, however, where they do well in the wetter areas where the water table is close to the surface. Here alfalfa does poorly, and beef cattle accordingly are far less numerous.

Uruguay ranks high in sheep. Eighty-three per cent of Uruguay is used as grass pasture, on which the carrying capacity is high—one **animal unit** per acre. Sheep are raised mostly in the northern portion of the country.

THE BALKANS, NORTH AFRICA, AND THE MIDDLE EAST

So limited is the rainfall and hence so sparse the pasturage in the Balkans, the Middle East, and North Africa that sheep are widespread and (with goats) the dominant animal. Sheep dare not venture into the true deserts because they cannot go without water for more than two or three days. Hence their grazing range is governed by distances between watering places. At times areas with good **browse** or grass cannot be grazed because of a dearth of water. In parts of the Middle East (e.g., Iran) sheep are the property of nomadic groups who drive their animals on long treks into and out of the mountains with the change in season. However, since little good grazing land is presently available outside the mountains, more animals must be fed on stubble of fields lying fallow or on the very scanty herbage of the desert margin. Almost everywhere throughout the region, the animals are raised for subsistence—for the immediate use of the peasant family.

It would be difficult indeed to overemphasize the role of this animal in the Balkans and in the great sweep of Arab-Moslem land of North Africa and Asia. In the interest of brevity, Greece is used to typify sheep raising in this part of the world.

Sheep have been important in Greece since Biblical times and are well adjusted to the dry summers, limited water supply, poor pasturage, and rugged terrain. In a typical year, sheep supply about 45 per cent of the total milk output and 47 per cent of the meat production. Sheep in Greece are raised primarily for milk; and of the total income from sheep, about one half is derived from milk and milk products. The bulk of the milk, at least 75 per cent, is converted into cheese.

Four systems of handling sheep are followed: (1) nomadic, in which considerable distances are covered; (2) transhumance, where several members of a family accompany the animals over a comparatively small area; (3) settled village type, where some of the people devote their time to sheep but others grow crops, the flocks depending upon pastures but also getting some feed from the cultivated fields; and (4) stabling, whereby improved strains are kept.

Greek sheep pastures are not good; many, in fact, are near exhaustion, having received little improvement since Homeric times. Moreover, they have been grazed continuously, often even overgrazed, thus preventing reseeding.

GREAT BRITAIN

Although Great Britain stands only about tenth in total sheep population, it ranks third in sheep density. Sheep are mentioned here because for centuries Britain was a leader, contributing many of the world's most illustrious breeds. Sheep are concentrated in three

Fig. 21-10. Goats browsing in argan tree, northern Morocco. The scarcity of browse on the ground results from serious erosion caused by overgrazing by large numbers of goats and by the cutting of trees for making charcoal. Not to be denied sustenance, the animals climb into the trees to feed. Though goats are the chief villains in the story of erosion over the globe, the people in backward areas cannot get along without them, for they supply milk, meat, butter, cheese, leather, and wool. (Photo by Major M. H. Baldwin, courtesy of B. J. Muccigrosso.)

main areas: (1) the southeastern Lowland, (2) the Midlands, and (3) the Highlands. Yet for some 80-odd years sheep numbers have been declining—mostly, however, in England. Present indications point to a continuing sharp decline in numbers in the southeast, perhaps to a lesser degree in the Midlands. The stronghold of the British sheep industry will be increasingly in the Highland portion.

GOATS

Goats rank among the more hardy of man's domestic animals; they can and do thrive on lands even too poor to support sheep. They are so nimble they can go almost anywhere —can even climb into trees (Fig. 21-10), and their digestive system enables them to eat just about anything that grows. They forage for themselves and survive when other animals die. Goats are generally found on the drier, browse-producing areas. They are by preference browsers, although they do graze many green, succulent grasses and weeds when these are available.

The goat has a bad reputation as a range destroyer and landscape changer; only the locust is believed to be more harmful to green vegetation. Dedicated conservationists regard the goat as Public Enemy No. 1. If goats are destroyers, one may ask why man keeps them. The principal answer seems to be that as pastures become poorer as a result of overgrazing, erosion becomes more widespread, and goats do better than either cattle or sheep. In some areas, as in the Ozarks and in the Pacific Coast states, goats are often used to clear pastures of undesirable brush. They are particularly important in arid and semiarid lands where farms are small and poor and population dense with respect to available water and arable land—as in Egypt, India, and Pakistan.

Though goats are found in most countries (except the colder lands), their distribution is densest in the Mediterranean Basin, particularly the eastern arm—Asia Minor and North Africa. India, however, ranks first in total numbers, though South Africa, East Africa, Brazil, Venezuela, and western United States all support large numbers.

THE WORLD'S ANIMAL INDUSTRIES : : 439

THE MEDITERRANEAN BASIN

In the countries surrounding the Mediterranean Sea, goats are the principal source of milk. Pastures are poor, the land is hilly to mountainous, and farms are mostly small. No other animal can compete with the goat in the domestic economy of the poor man. Three or four goats will supply as much milk as the average cow on half the rations. Moreover, a single cow supplies milk for but a portion of the year whereas with a few goats the farmer is assured a constant milk supply for his family. It is little wonder, then, that almost every farmer keeps goats.

INDIA

India leads all nations in the number of goats. Since nearly all small farmers keep goats, the animal is to be found throughout the greater part of the country. It is the favorite milk animal.

UNITED STATES

Goats are not popular in the United States, there being only about one tenth as many as sheep. Texas ranks first, with 70 per cent; but these are mostly Angoras, kept for their mohair. Other states maintaining goats are Arizona, New Mexico, California, Arkansas, Missouri, and Oregon (the Willamette Valley). The Indians of the Southwest, particularly the Navajos, raise considerable numbers.

SWINE

The pig is believed to be one of the first animals to be domesticated. Since it would eat almost any waste product, man early sensed its value once he became a farmer. The domestic breeds of swine are believed to descend from the European wild pig (*Sus scrofa*) and various forms of Asiatic wild pigs. Swine differ from all the animals considered so far, in that their digestive system cannot handle fibrous or bulky foods; therefore, they must have concentrated feed and hence are largely dependent on crops rather than pas-

ture. This is not to say that they cannot fend for themselves. The Hampshire breed, for instance, is a very good rustler. However, the hog is not a nomadic animal and does best under a system of sedentary agriculture. Yet throughout the world swine are maintained by different methods of feeding—on dairy by-products in Denmark, on corn in the United States, on mast in European and American forests, and on garbage in China. Swine are regarded as the most economical converters of feed into meat and fat among all the domesticated animals. The pig also is the most prolific of all the domesticated animals, bearing two litters (six to eight pigs in the first litter, ten to twelve every year thereafter).

Swine are not so universally distributed as are cattle and sheep. Not only do climate and feed affect their distribution but so also do human circumstances; for instance, as a result of Mohammedanism, swine are almost completely absent from much of the great sweep of land across North Africa and eastward to the Philippines. Only four swine regions stand out prominently: (1) the American Corn Belt, (2) Western Europe, (3) China, and (4) southern Brazil (Fig. 21-11).

UNITED STATES

Though swine are found in all parts of the nation, the Corn Belt (eight states from Minnesota to Ohio) produces 60 per cent of the total corn crop and has 69 per cent of the swine. It is traditional in the United States that corn is used to make hogs, about 50 per cent of the total corn crop being consumed by them (Fig. 21-12). Corn is excellent for fattening because of the high percentage of digestible nutrients and the high percentage of fats.

The system of raising swine in the Corn Belt differs from that of raising beef cattle. Swine are bred, farrowed, and fattened on farms within the region; they are not purchased from distant areas for fattening as are many beef cattle, but are an integral part of the agricultural system. The permanent hog population of the region consists of breeding stock whose numbers fluctuate but modestly.

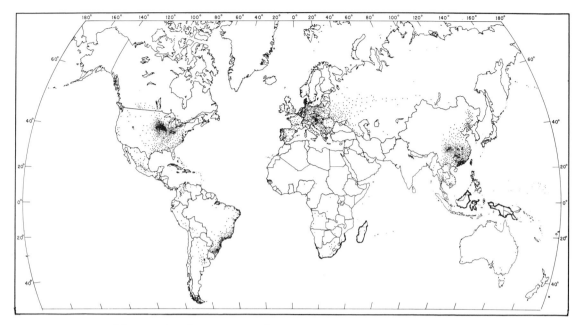

Fig. 21-11. *World swine distribution. More than 60 per cent of all the world's swine are in six nations—the United States, China, Brazil; the Soviet Union, West Germany, and Mexico. The absence of this animal from North Africa, the Near and Middle East, and Asia east of the Caspian Sea and north of the Himalayas results from religious taboos by the Moslems and Jews. (Courtesy of U.S. Department of Agriculture.)*

In short, the hog farmer carries on a "from-cradle-to-grave" or "from-breeding-pen-to-slaughterhouse" operation. He breeds his gelts and sows and keeps the litters until they reach market weight, when he sells them for slaughter. Hogs are maintained mostly in movable houses—a sow and litter to each house, row upon row of which are to be seen in the Corn Belt.

The Corn Belt is getting away from the fat cylindrical type of hog, for lard is no longer in heavy demand by modern housewives. Today the thicker the fat on the hog's back, the lower the grade of the animal. Grade No. 1 has a thin rim of back fat.

The Deep South ranks next to the Corn Belt in swine production, with about 18 per cent of the total of the nation. While many are carefully bred animals, many are semi-wild razorbacks.

WESTERN EUROPE

Swine densities are greatest in Central and Western Europe, from Denmark and the Netherlands eastward into western Poland and southward into the Great Hungarian Basin of Hungary, Yugoslavia, and western Romania (Fig. 21-11). Unlike the situation in the United States, swine are not fattened on corn; for, except in the Danubian Basin countries, corn does poorly—it does not ripen. Hence, the principal feeds are barley, rye, potatoes, and skim milk and whey.

DENMARK

Nearly all Danish farmers keep swine; the small size of the farms, about 40 acres, requires them to engage in dairying and hog raising, with poultry as a subsidiary enterprise.

The perfecting of a single breed leading to uniformity has strengthened the reputation of Danish pork products abroad. Ninety per cent of all Danish hogs are of the Landrace breed, which has relatively low feed requirements—an extremely important factor considering Denmark's heavy dependence upon imported feeds.

Fig. 21-12. Hogs eating corn, Marshall County, Iowa. Swine consume by far the largest proportion of the corn grown in the American Corn Belt, and the two great corn-growing states of Iowa and Illinois together produce more hogs each year than any foreign country exclusive of China, Brazil, and the U.S.S.R. Formerly, Corn Belt farmers reared lard-type hogs; now, with the lard market in eclipse, they specialize in meat-type hogs. (Courtesy of U.S. Department of Agriculture.)

GERMANY

No country's agriculture seems more intertwined with the rearing of swine than Germany's. Hogs contribute roughly two thirds of the total meat supply. Here the white potato is a major crop, and at least half the crop is fed to hogs. Potatoes contribute 40 to 50 per cent of the swine ration. In Germany, potatoes are steamed before being fed to hogs; they are never fed raw.

German hogs carry more fat than Danish hogs—apparently because Germany is deficient in fats and oils and thus wants to produce hogs that can supply lard.

THE NETHERLANDS

Almost every farm keeps swine, an economical way of utilizing many of the products and by-products of farming—whey in the cheese-making districts; skim milk in the butter-making districts; and rye, oats, and potatoes in the sandy lands in the eastern provinces. However, considerable feed must be imported for supplementing the diet of the hogs.

CHINA

It is believed that China leads all countries in the total number of swine—some 70 million.

Only in the northwest, where there is a considerable Moslem population, is the animal unimportant. The greatest concentrations are in the Szechwan Basin, the Canton Delta, the Central Lake Basin, the Yangtze Delta, and the North China Plain (Fig. 21-11).

Among the major reasons for the vast numbers of swine in a country so poor in most other large domesticated animals are the small farms and the teeming human population which makes imperative the utilization of every square foot of soil for food crops rather than for feed crops and pasture (swine are kept in pens); and swine are scavengers, can be fed garbage, and hence do not compete directly with man for food.

SOUTHERN BRAZIL

Brazil ranks fourth among all countries in the number of swine it supports. Almost all the hogs are to be found in the cooler southeast of the country—from Minas Gerais to the border with Uruguay (Fig. 21-11). The emphasis in this particular part of the country results from two circumstances: (1) the important German element in the population (as already noted, Germany ranks among the leading nations in the raising of this animal)

Fig. 21-13. Part of a flock of 1,400 pullets, Forsyth County, North Carolina. Few farm enterprises have changed so strikingly or have become so highly specialized as poultry raising. This has occurred in the past two decades. The trend is to larger flocks (7,500 is not an uncommon number of birds) and the use of labor-saving devices. Science has contributed advances in breeding, feeding, housing, and control of disease (especially coccidiosis, most serious disease affecting poultry). Chicken is no longer a specialty but a staple in the American market. (Courtesy of U.S. Department of Agriculture.)

and (2) the stress on corn in the farming system.

CHICKENS

The raising of chickens is probably the most widely distributed of all livestock enterprises. Chickens are found both in sparsely populated and densely populated areas. *Almost every farm the world over has its flock of laying hens.*

Chickens have proved to be highly adaptable not only to varied natural environmental conditions but also to space requirements and to type of feed. When necessary they can fend for themselves; they can even function as scavengers.

UNITED STATES

The United States is regarded as the world's leader in poultry. More than four fifths of all American farms are reported to keep them (Fig. 21-13). Outstanding areas are the Corn Belt; the Middle Atlantic states; the Hay and Dairy Belt; the Pacific Coast (the San Francisco Bay area, particularly in the vicinity of Petaluma, the Los Angeles Basin, the Willamette Valley, and the Puget Trough); and the Deep South, which in 1960 supplied 60 per cent of the national chicken output.

Southern farmers claim that their warm climate makes for low-cost production.

Two factors especially contribute to the distribution of chickens in the United States: (1) the plentiful supplies of grain produced on the farms and (2) proximity of most farms to large centers of population. Near most large cities, poultry raising is highly specialized. The number of fryers recently quadrupled (from 200 million to 800 million) in a ten-year period—an increase attributable in large measure to inclusion in the feeding ration of antibiotic drugs, such as terramycin and penicillin, which cure and prevent diseases. Feed too plays a role; in 1930 it required 15 pounds of feed and fifteen weeks of feeding to produce a 3-pound broiler. Today 7½ pounds of feed and less than nine weeks turn out a chicken of the same weight. Egg output per hen has been increased from 134 in 1940 to more than 200 in 1960. The zooming importance of poultry raising is indicated by the fact that poultry feed accounts for about two thirds of the formula-feed business's output (a 3.5-billion-dollar enterprise).

EUROPE

Although chickens are raised throughout Europe, they are most important in the western and central portions—Denmark, Belgium, the Netherlands, Ireland. Many hatcheries in these countries specialize in producing laying pullets; the yearly egg production per hen in 1958 was 200. One man can care for about 7,000 birds and an output of 4,000 eggs per day. A laying record is kept outside each cage; and when the number of eggs per hen drops, the pullet is sold for meat.

CHINA

Most Chinese farms keep chickens, but the number is small—about eight per family. Chickens are important for the same reasons as swine—they do not compete directly with man for the land (they live on garbage and help clean the threshing floors), and they fit very well into intensive subsistence farming, so characteristic of this land of teeming humanity.

WORLD OUTLOOK

Thousands of years ago, man domesticated a number of animal species. Some of these, such as the hog and chicken, he carefully husbanded, usually sharing with them the yield from his fields. Others, such as cattle, goats, and sheep, were made to depend on natural vegetation for sustenance. As man spread, he pressed into service every accessible area of natural grassland; when necessary, he did the same with brushland, forest land, and even desert. Over the centuries, the grazing animals have completely changed the vegetation—dangerously upsetting the ecological balance. Some lands—for instance, North Africa and the Middle East—have been grazed so long, for millennia, that we do not know what they were like originally.

In nearly every part of the world where grazing is a major pursuit, deterioration of the range is in progress, sometimes swiftly, sometimes slowly. Ultimately, however, the land promises to be destroyed as it was in North Africa, the Middle East, and elsewhere. What was the cause of the decadence of North Africa and the decline of its population? Some students suggest that the climate changed—that it got drier. Most, however, believe that nomads from Arabia introduced a grazing culture and that their animals so overgrazed the land that the region now stands as one of the world's worst examples of erosion.

There is also man's effort to control animal diseases. English authorities point out that as animals double in number, disease problems quadruple. Modern transportation and marketing multiply the dangers of exposure.

If man's numbers continue to skyrocket, more and more grazing land that is potentially arable will have to be pressed into farmland and used to grow *food rather than feed*. Meat will become increasingly a luxury item, even in developed countries. Even the amount of meat produced in the restrictive milieus of the world must be expected to diminish unless man adopts better management practices.

444 : : CHAPTER TWENTY-ONE

SELECTED REFERENCES

Boonstra, C. A. "Sheep Industry of Argentina's Patagonia," *Foreign Agriculture,* 15:143-145, July 1951.

Darling, F. Fraser. "Man's Ecological Dominance through Domesticated Animals on Wild Lands," in William L. Thomas, Jr. (ed.), *Man's Role in Changing the Face of the Earth.* Chicago, University of Chicago Press, 1956, pp. 778-787.

Davis, Charles M. "Merino Sheep on the Australian Riverina," *Geographical Review,* 44:475-494, October 1954.

De Graff, H. *Beef: Production and Distribution.* Norman, Oklahoma, University of Oklahoma Press, 1960.

Douglas, W. O. "The Bite of the Goat," *Land,* 11:25-28, Spring 1952.

Holscher, C. E., and D. A. Spencer. "Sheep, Goats, and Grasslands," in *Grass; Yearbook of Agriculture, 1948.* Washington, D. C., U.S. Department of Agriculture, 1948.

Peffer, E. Louise. "The Argentine Cattle Industry under Perón," *Food Research Institute Studies* (Stanford University), 1:151-184, May 1960.

Phillips, Ralph W. *Breeding Livestock Adapted to Unfavorable Environments.* Washington, D. C., Food and Agriculture Organization of the United Nations, January 1948. Agriculture Studies No. 1.

——————. "Cattle," *Scientific American,* 198:51-59, June 1958.

Post, L. C. "Cattle Breeds, An Aspect of Regional Geography," *Yearbook of the Association of Pacific Coast Geographers,* 21:51-58, 1959.

Sauer, Carl O. *Agricultural Origins and Dispersals.* New York, American Geographical Society, 1952, pp. 84-104.

Shaw, Earl B. "Swine Production in the Corn Belt of the United States," *Economic Geography,* 12:359-372, October 1936.

White, C. Langdon. "Cattle Raising: A Way of Life in the Venezuelan Llanos," *Scientific Monthly,* 83:122-129, September 1956.

SOME

PART FIVE ::

NONFOOD CROPS

CHAPTER TWENTY-TWO ::

In most economic-geography textbooks, hay and pasture are neglected; either they are left out altogether, or they receive but superficial treatment in the livestock chapter. This neglect results from two circumstances: (1) In the developed countries today, great emphasis is placed on urbanization and industrialization at the expense of rural living and agriculture. (2) Statistical reports on sources of farm income frequently are misinterpreted, so that hay and pasture are regarded as less important than corn, cotton, soybeans, wheat, cattle, hogs, and poultry as leading sources of agricultural wealth. *Yet about two thirds of the farm value of animal products in the United States, on the average, is the dollar value of the feed consumed, over 50 per cent of which is hay and pasture.*

Large parts of the earth (possibly 50 to 60 per cent) are destined by nature to

THE WORLD'S HAY,

serve as pasture or **browse** for domesticated animals (Fig. 22-1). These are the cold lands, the dry lands, the mountain lands, the infertile lands, and some lands that are too hot and rainy to sustain crops.

In addition to these marginal and submarginal lands, man in the Occident grows hay crops on millions of acres of land that are capable of yielding food crops. These hay crops help sustain livestock. Occidental man demands meat, poultry, and dairy products in his diet. Each American annually consumes about 700 pounds of milk and milk products, and almost 65 pounds of beef, in addition to other meat and poultry. All these items are costly types of food—costly in terms of arable land, for meat and milk animals utilize pasture grasses and forage crops that man cannot consume directly. Taking animal products as a whole, from three to four times as much land is required to produce the same number of calories as would be required if the cereals were consumed directly by man.

If the estimates of demographers are even reasonably accurate, the world population will reach 6 billion by the year 2000; to sustain such a population, most *good* land now growing *feed crops* will have to be used for producing *food crops*. If we consider the United States (exclusive of Alaska and Hawaii) in this respect, there are 707 million acres of nonforested pastureland, approximately 10 per cent of which is suitable for regular cultivation.

HAY

In this chapter hay will be regarded as any agricultural product (crop or grass) cut for

FORAGE CROPS, AND PASTURES

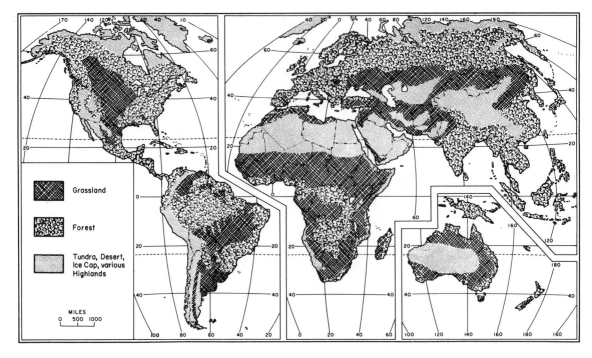

Fig. 22-1. Vegetation types (highly generalized). The four great plant formations of the earth's land surface are forest, grassland, desert shrub, and tundra. Grasslands include possibly one fourth of the area occupied by these types of vegetation and about one fifth of the earth's land surface. These four formations reflect chiefly climate. As a rule, humid lands are woodlands, dry lands are in desert shrub or waste, and grasslands occupy the lands of intermediate moisture supply. (After map by U.S. Department of Agriculture.)

fodder. Hay is extremely difficult to define; for it includes many items, depending on the particular area concerned. Thus, in the Lake states, timothy and clover are the principal hay crops; in New England, redtop and orchard grass; in the Corn Belt east of the Missouri River, timothy and clover, supplemented by corn silage; but west of the Missouri, alfalfa; in the South, grains cut green; in the northern Great Plains, wild or prairie grasses; in the central Great Plains, alfalfa; in the southern Great Plains, grain sorghums; and in California, grains (wheat, barley, and oats) cut green, together with alfalfa.

UNITED STATES: PRINCIPAL HAY CROPS

Hay and therefore livestock were unimportant in the English-speaking colonies during the 1700s. What animals there were foraged

and browsed in scattered clearings in the almost continuous forests. "The lack of grass was perhaps the greatest handicap of the early American farm, and this led to the importation of timothy, bluegrass, and clover." [1] Prior to the coming of the white man, the American Indians had no herbivorous domestic animals and therefore gave no attention to forage plants.

The total area in crops in the United States is roughly 335 million acres, of which about 75 million acres are in hay crops of various types. Another 1,000 million acres are in grass. Hay furnishes about 16 per cent of the total feed for livestock. The substitution of tractors and trucks and automobiles for horses (25.74 million horses and mules in the United States in 1920 but only 3.07 million in 1959) radically

[1] Lewis P. McCann, "The World Is Our Nursery," *Foreign Agriculture*, 14:53, March 1950.

Fig. 22-2. Baling hay in the American Middle West. One man with this machine gathers the cured hay, which has been windrowed, and bales it. The twine used has about three times the strength of ordinary binder twine. The bales may be tight or loose. As the hay is baled (at a rate up to 450 bales per hour), the bales may be dumped in the field as here or pushed onto a trailing truck on an extension of the baling chamber. (Courtesy of International Harvester Company.)

reduced the acreage given over to hay (Fig. 22-2).

No other American crops are so well distributed over the land as hay and forage (including pasture). Because hay and forage have low value per unit of bulk, they must for the most part be used locally or sold in nearby markets; ordinarily, they cannot stand the heavy expense of shipment to distant markets. Accordingly, maps of hay and forage and of pasture coincide well with maps of cattle, sheep, and goats. Approximately fifty species of grass and fifty species of **legumes** make up the hay production and cultivated pastures of the ·United States. Even soybeans are often grown for hay.

CLOVER

Crimson clover and Ladino clover are regarded as the best hay crops grown in the United States. They are particularly important in the northeastern portion of the country. This localization results primarily from the combination of fertile soils, adequate precipitation (40 to 50 inches), and moderate temperature, and the crops' ideal dovetailing in equalizing the **seasonal distribution of labor.** The clovers, which are both **perennial** and **annual**, thrive in a cool, moist climate.

TIMOTHY

Timothy was far more important in the past than it is at present, for it was considered superior as a hay for horses and mules. Baled, it was shipped to the big urban markets, where large numbers of horses were employed. Timothy does better on clay loams than on light-textured, sandy soils. It is well adapted to the cool, moist climate of the

Middle West. On many farms, timothy and clover are grown together.

ALFALFA

This important legume does best on fertile limestone soils under conditions of moderate rainfall and temperature. It does not thrive on acid soils or wet soils, or in places where the water table is near the surface. Alfalfa can stand considerable drought, sending its roots 15 or more inches into the soil. Because of its root structure, alfalfa possesses great power of survival. The crop first gained importance in this country in the West—California, Utah (where it is called lucerne), Kansas, and Nebraska. Much is grown now in the Upper Lake states. Alfalfa makes good hay, good pasture, and good silage. Much is dehydrated and used in connection with other feedstuffs to provide nutrition for livestock. Companies engaged in dehydrating purchase the alfalfa while it stands in the fields, cut it, and truck it to their plants, where it is placed in drums under intense heat.

Alfalfa is the most important single crop in the West, occupying more than half the irrigated land of the entire region. Some students of agriculture claim that alfalfa is the most perfectly balanced all-round single feed known. Also, being a legume, alfalfa is an excellent soil builder.

BERMUDA GRASSES

As timothy and clover are well suited to the northeastern part of the nation, alfalfa to the West and Upper Lake states, so Bermuda grasses are well suited to the Southeast. The Bermuda grasses, perennials, are native of India and are common in most tropical and subtropical parts of the world. They do well on the lighter, sandier soils and, during periods of hot weather, even on heavy soils. They produce most in July and August when other forages are failing because of hot, dry weather.

LESPEDEZA

Korean lespedeza is outstanding in the southern Mississippi Valley. This leguminous shrub, not a grass, is utilized both for hay and pasture. The lespedezas are especially useful on acid soils of low fertility.

THE WORLD'S GRASSLANDS

Grasslands are believed to occupy about one fifth of the earth's land surface. This floral form falls into three broad classifications: (1) the lands supporting tall grass (**prairie**); (2) those sustaining short grass (**steppe**); and (3) those tropical lands covered with **savanna**. It is the last two that comprise the great bulk of the earth's grasslands. Grasslands are areas where trees do not thrive because of unfavorable soil conditions (poor drainage or imperfect aeration), intense cold, strong winds, deficient moisture, or repeated fires.

TALL GRASS (PRAIRIE)

The prairie (a French word meaning "extensive meadow") found in the United States, from western Indiana to just west of the 20-inch isohyet and from the Canadian border to Texas, is regarded as the only area of its kind in the world.[2] During periods of wetter years, the prairie vegetation tends to migrate westward, partially replacing the short grasses of the steppe.

For untold ages the prairie endured. Then civilization arrived, and the onslaught began. Little of the prairie is left, for it comprised the best agricultural land in the nation; grasslands, flat to gently rolling, presented few topographic obstacles to the plow, and provided fertile soils. Some prairie still is to be seen (Fig. 22-3), but most of what remains lies alongside transcontinental railway tracks, where the tracks were placed in the middle of the right-of-way in original railway grants.

Prairies occupy both humid and subhumid lands. Areas that somewhat resemble the American prairie are the Argentine Pampa and

[2] Among plant geographers the term "prairie" is applied exclusively to the central North American region, the term "tall grass" to all other subhumid grasslands. A voluminous literature has grown up dealing with the question of why prairies were treeless. Climatic change, soil conditions, grassland as a true climax vegetation, and other causes have been advanced for the dominance of grass in the grassland areas of the world; but the conviction today is that these grasslands are wholly or partly man-made—the product of periodic burning.

Fig. 22-3. Tall-grass prairie. Prairie lies along the moister edge of the short-grass areas in central North America. The grasses shown here average 5 feet in height. Though the prairie was admirably suited for pasture, it was almost unequaled for crops; hence most of it was plowed up for crop use. (Courtesy of U.S. Department of Agriculture.)

nearby Uruguay and Brazil and portions of European Russia.

SHORT GRASS (STEPPE)

Steppe or short grass characterizes a large portion of the subhumid and semiarid mid-latitudes. Among the largest and best examples are the steppes of Eurasia ("steppe" is a Russian word meaning "grassy plain") and the Great Plains of North America.

Rainfall in the steppe fluctuates widely from year to year. Whereas the soils tend to be fertile, the precipitation is inadequate in most years for more than a haphazard agriculture. Though in the more favored lands wheat and grain sorghums do well, these lands generally are best suited for the grazing of livestock.

SAVANNA

Savannas are the extensive grasslands of the tropics (Fig. 22-1). In extent they exceed the tall-grass prairies and nearly, if not fully, equal the short-grass areas. Africa has more land in savanna than any other continent; in-

terior South America also boasts extensive tracts.

In the savanna the vegetation is dominantly grass; but there may be scattered trees, which tend to be small and scrubby, and grow singly or in groups (Fig. 22-4). These grasslands do not resemble those of middle latitudes. Tropical grasses in some areas grow quite tall (as high as 8 to 10 feet and occasionally 12 to 20 feet), corresponding to zones of greater or lesser moisture. They do not form sods as do the grasses of the steppes and prairies. Only a small part of the total area in savanna has been put under cultivation. Moreover, savannas are not natural pastures merely awaiting the herdsman (as the Spaniards, for example, believed when they introduced European cattle into the Llanos of Colombia and Venezuela).

Let us follow a group of cattle for a year over the Llanos. The dry season, which lasts from six to eight months, finds the animals completely exhausted from their constant search for water and grass. Then come the

Fig. 22-4. Tall-grass savanna in semiarid Africa. Savannas are the great grasslands of the tropics, and they cover more of Africa than any other plant formation. Characteristic of savannas are scattered trees—small and scrubby. (Courtesy of H. L. Shantz.)

rains with stands of grass that last for several weeks, at which time the feed situation becomes satisfactory. If the rains are heavy, the herd may drown or at least experience difficulty finding patches of dry land (Fig. 22-5). The rains, which last two to three months, are followed by a dry season; and the cycle starts anew.

The origin of the savanna, as of most grasslands, has long been a matter of study and of diverse opinion. Though there are still disagreements as to its cause, the conviction has grown that the savanna is a **fire climax**.

PASTURE IN EUROPE

Hay comprises one of the leading crops in Europe, particularly Northwestern Europe. Though there are many interesting aspects to the hay and pasture situation in several of the nations, because of space limitation only Britain is considered in this chapter.

Britain has long been a livestock country, and the wealth from its pastures in prewar days greatly exceeded that of any arable crop. The moist western part of Britain favors grass rather than crops. For so densely populated a country, almost every visitor is surprised to see so much land in pasture—permanent grass pasture: about 43 per cent of the total in England, 42 per cent in Wales. Although land un-

der grass is less productive than land under the plow, for many years prior to World War II the market for milk was sure because the price for milk was steady—contrasted with that for cereals, which oscillated widely. Moreover, the lower labor costs on grassland made it easier to be sure of an income. In 1938 the arable acreage was the lowest ever recorded. World War II changed this situation, for as German U-boats sank ships bringing food, a plow-up campaign was initiated; and some 6 million acres of grasslands were plowed up and planted to food crops. By 1943 Britain was between 70 and 80 per cent self-sustaining in food. It is believed that permanent pasture will not again assume its former importance.

AMERICAN PASTURES AND RANGES

American pasturelands and ranges constitute the largest acreage of land use in the nation—55 per cent of the total area. They supply the major part of the diet of the 94.5 million head of dairy cattle (50 per cent of the ration) and beef cattle (75 per cent of all feed consumed) in the country; they also provide an appreciable part of the feed of the nation's sheep and goats. Forage is the most abundant, the most easily grown, and the cheapest of all livestock feeds. However, these

Fig. 22-5. Criollo cattle caught on flooded land during river overflow in the rainy season in the Central Llanos. Many cattle drown when vast areas (possibly one third of the entire Llanos) become inundated. The flood lands, which take on the appearance of swamps, are soon clothed with a rank vegetation and with water-plant growth. (Courtesy of Consejo de Bienestar Rural.)

lands vary in their productivity and ability to sustain animals. In some parts of the country, 40 or more acres are required to provide sufficient herbage for one animal unit; in another area, a single acre will do so. Some dairy-farm pastures are so good that they enable a cow to produce 8,000 pounds of milk per year, whereas others do well to supply 1,000 pounds. Annual gross income of America's farms from meat and dairy products is about 10 billion dollars, of which grassland crops, either grazed or made into silage or hay, account for almost 6 billion dollars.

Though much of what is now the United States was originally in native grasses, for the most part these have been replaced. In almost every instance—over the nearly three fourths of all grazing lands in the United States (750 million acres), which are to be found in the seventeen states comprising the Great Plains and the West—the natural vegetative cover has degenerated.

The carrying capacity of pastures and browse lands depends upon climate, particularly rainfall; the character of the soil; and man's care. Nearly all soils in the humid parts of the nation are deficient in calcium, phosphorus, and nitrogen. Commercial fertilizers are relied upon to furnish plant food to pastures. The composition of the specific fertilizers to be used, of course, depends upon the local soils and climatic conditions. If pastures are overgrazed, they obviously can carry few livestock; if fertilized and rotated, they can sustain many. The plant species, too, are exceedingly varied to meet the conditions of soil and climate.

THE KENTUCKY BLUEGRASS

North-central Kentucky comprises a region characterized by a distinctive type of soil and terrain that sets it off as a garden spot— famous for its burley tobacco, sheep, cattle, and particularly its fine pastures and horses. Sound bones are the basis of fine horses, and such bones are best made on soils rich in lime and phosphate (maury silt loam). It is no coincidence that the winners at Churchill Downs are regularly Bluegrass animals.

AMERICAN GREAT PLAINS

The Great Plains, a semiarid land, receives 10 or 11 inches of precipitation in southern Alberta and up to 22 in southern Texas. The original vegetative cover in the central portion was short grass. Here in the heavy soils, percolation of rain water is restricted, and the runoff during sharp downpours is heavy; hence, for months or even years the subsoil may remain dry. To such a habitat the short grasses are best suited; for they make fullest use of the moisture in the topsoil, and their roots almost completely cover the area. The floral cover of the short-grass country looks like closely grazed pasture.

This was the land of the bison and antelope and of the Indian who hunted them. Later it became the land of beef cattle (and to a lesser extent of sheep) and still later of dry-farmed wheat. Cattle herding became the dominant enterprise on the Great Plains during the first three fourths of the nineteenth century; by 1880 the invasion was complete, and the fenced ranch was fast transforming the open range. Although sheep were as well suited to the short-grass country as were beef cattle, cattle became the dominant animals, because (1) Americans are primarily beef, not mutton, eaters; (2) there was a surplus of feed for finishing the animals in the Corn Belt; (3) feedlots began to spring up over wide areas in the Great Plains; and (4) quality sheep could be reared more cheaply in the mountain and desert areas to the west.

IMPROVEMENT IN AMERICAN PASTURES BY FERTILIZATION

For many years American pastures were the lands that for one reason or another were ill suited to crops and hence were set aside for pasture; or when land would no longer support grain, it was turned to pasture. Seldom were pastures fertilized, even with manure. As a result, their carrying capacity was low. In recent years research has proved that the productive capacity of the grasslands can be doubled, trebled, and even quadrupled through the planting of new strains of grasses and legumes adapted to a particular area and by stimulating their growth by proper management and use of adequate amounts of lime and fertilizer. A recent farm-management survey in a typical hill section of Vermont indicates that for every dollar invested in lime and fertilizer, a $5 return was realized. In the Middle West, it costs $20 to $40 per acre to correct soil-fertility deficiencies of permanent pasture but that an average return of about $50 per acre in extra milk and beef above the cost of treatment is common. In the South, there is much land in pasture. When such

lands are fertilized, sizable increases are obtained in the hay crop in pounds of beef.

THE ARGENTINE PAMPA

This extensive, potentially productive agricultural (for crops) area still is mostly in pasture. No part of the Pampa has less than 40 per cent of its area in pasture, and around the margins the percentage approaches 80. Cattle grazing still competes successfully with grain farming for land, even in the heart of the principal cereal zone. Pastures in the Pampa have a special significance not only because of their great extent but also because cattle are almost exclusively a grazing enterprise. Steers are finished on pasture.

The original native-grass pastures were composed of drought-resistant plants with hard, narrow leaves. Most of these pastures dried up for three or four months in the hot, relatively dry summer and again in winter; but in the rainier eastern Pampa such pastures remained green the year round. However, cattlemen came to realize that their animals and their business would do better if they shifted from a grazing industry based on uncultivated pastures to one based on cultivated pasture—alfalfa.

Alfalfa was introduced after 1890, and today Argentina (the Pampa) has the largest acreage in this crop of any nation on earth; moreover, alfalfa is Argentina's leading crop in acreage. Some of it is cut for hay, but most of it merely serves as pasture.

WORLD DESERTS AND NEAR-DESERTS: THEIR VEGETATION

Deserts—characterized by a fluctuating rainfall, where precipitation does not exceed the evaporating power of the air measured in inches of water—usually are not grassy but have a cover of shrubs and scrub spaced some distance from one another. In one county in Arizona, six forage types are recognized: desert shrub, desert grassland, grassland, piñon-juniper, chaparral, and ponderosa pine. These are areal groups with particular alti-

Fig. 22-6. Types of desert vegetation, Arizona. Southern desert shrub covers more than 50 million acres in the American Southwest, but it does intermingle with semi-desert grassland. Where the rainfall is less than 5 inches (e.g., in southeastern California and southwestern Arizona), such vegetation is almost valueless for grazing. In New Mexico and western Texas, where summer annuals are more plentiful, cattle are grazed on a yearlong basis. (Courtesy of U.S. Forest Service.)

tudinal, climatic, and edaphic connotations. In their ability to support a grazing enterprise, they range through the whole gamut—excellent to good, good to fair, and fair to poor (Fig. 22-6).

ARABIA AND NORTH AFRICA

The largest stretch of such vegetation extends across North Africa into western and central Asia (Fig. 22-1). It is referred to as a nomadic herding region where livestock are grazed on whatever grass or bush vegetation is available and where the animals are not fed on crops raised for the purpose. Although the vegetation varies from area to area, it is every-

where sparse because of the meager rainfall. The carrying capacity of such land is extremely low. The principal animals to be found on these grazing lands are sheep and goats (admirably suited to surviving on scanty forage and restricted water supply) and camels. The camel, a multipurpose animal, is of particular value in such lands and can go long distances without water and subsist on the poorest kind of vegetation. Asses, too, are well adapted to such lands. In Arabia during the months of migration the nomads change their tent grounds about every ten days because the sparse grass is grazed clean by the animals belonging to the tribe. Despite the impressive upward surge of science and engineering, it appears that nomadic herding will prevail over these deserts far into the future.

DRY AUSTRALIA

Australia, with 13 million head of cattle and 160 million head of sheep (five times the number in the United States), is essentially a pastoral country. It would be difficult indeed to overestimate the value of pastures to the Australian economy. Yet most of the country's grazing grounds are plagued by aridity. Sometimes droughts reduce sheep and cattle numbers drastically. However, the livestock industry is less vulnerable today than it was in the past, the result of pasture improvement; supplemental feed supplies; irrigation; widespread destruction of rabbits, dingoes, and other pests; and better transport.

The wide-open spaces of Australia encourage pastoral pursuits; even areas with low and erratic rainfall are utilized. Most of the cattle are maintained on the coarse pastures of the north—Queensland, Northern Territory, and the northern part of Western Australia. Most of the sheep are to be found south of the cattle lands—chiefly in the drier areas. In some sections the two types of animals graze the same areas—a good procedure because intestinal parasites are more easily controlled when sheep and cattle are raised together.

Because the unimproved pastures have only a fair carrying capacity and because of the huge numbers of livestock, the pastoralists wage unceasing warfare against rabbits, dingoes, kangaroos, emus, and cattle ticks—

all of which compete, either directly or indirectly, with livestock for pasturage and browse.

So much of Australia is desert and hence of minimal economic value that scientists are challenged to find ways of putting the dry lands to better use.

DRY SOUTH AFRICA

South Africa is one of the truly great grasslands on this earth; 85 to 90 per cent of its land area is in grass. In the Karroo area are many varieties of grasses, and hundreds of square miles of the region are grass covered. These hardy and drought-resistant plants—which vary in height from 3 or 4 inches to 2 or more feet, depending upon the soil and moisture conditions—are grazed by livestock, particularly by sheep but also by goats. During the driest years, hundreds of thousands of sheep die. Ranchers are beginning to rotate pastures in order to retard and prevent overgrazing and to permit seed to form, fall, and germinate so that young plants may become well established before grazing is permitted again. The great size of the ranches (10,000 to 30,000 acres) makes rotation economically feasible.

OUTER MONGOLIA

Since the days of Genghis Khan, and despite more than forty years of Communist rule, the way of life in this vast area of endless grass has changed almost not at all. For a thousand years Mongolians have lived indirectly on the grass cover, on which their livestock graze. Land cultivation is rare; only "barbarians till the soil."

VEGETATION OF THE NORTHLANDS: THE TUNDRA

Tundra, which in the original Russian means wasteland, includes all vegetation on the polar side of timberline and comprises a plant association of considerable variety. The tundra is a green and otherwise largely barren land (Fig. 22-7). In Eurasia, the dominant plants consist of mosses, in North America of lichens. A grassy tundra is not uncommon; it may have sedges and broadleaf plants but no trees.

Tundra vegetation does not die down in winter. Moreover, it possesses so much nourishment as to provide a complete ration for reindeer. Hence, it serves as pasturage for reindeer in Lapland, Canada, Alaska, and the Soviet Union. Actually only a small part of the tundra supports a grazing enterprise on a year-round basis. However, if such lands are not overgrazed, they could possibly support 30 million reindeer.

VEGETATION OF MOUNTAINS

No generalization applies to the vegetation of mountains on a world basis. The floral covering or lack of it depends upon latitude, altitude, distance from large water bodies, windward or leeward side of the mountain, and other conditions.

The example cited here is the *puna* of the central Andes of Peru and Bolivia. Between the mountain ranges are valleys and extensive plateaus, called *punas*, which lie at altitudes of 10,500 to 15,500 feet. Although they are rather uniform in their vegetative cover, they do display variations based largely upon availability of water. While there are many herbaceous plants in the *puna*, only the grass is mentioned here—ichu grass (*Stipa ichu*)—a coarse bunch grass that everywhere grows in hummocks or bunching cones. It reaches an approximate height of 20 inches. Ichu is well adapted to the rigors of the climate and changes little from summer to winter. The coarse upper blades are eaten by the llama and alpaca, and the more delicate parts by sheep.

WORLD OUTLOOK

During historic time the composition of the earth's natural vegetation has been substan-

Fig. 22-7. Tundra landscape, Northwest Territories, Canada. This vegetative cover consisting of lichens does not die in winter and possesses sufficient nourishment to provide a complete ration for reindeer. (Courtesy of Hudson's Bay Company.)

tially altered. This alteration has resulted from a variety of causes, mostly human, of which the two most noteworthy are fire and grazing by domesticated animals. Sometimes the changes have been so profound that scientists cannot reconstruct the original floral cover; no one knows what the range lands of North Africa and the Middle East were like originally, for they have been grazed for millennia. In few areas of the world today do nomadic pastoral graziers or even transhumants allow the grasses and other herbs sufficient time to recuperate between periods of heavy use.

In the next quarter of a century, grasslands are expected to show greater gains than crops. Already in the developed lands, through the use of better grasses and legumes and by more intensive fertilization, much progress is being made against overgrazing; and a beginning is being made even in some of the underdeveloped lands. Yet a negligible percentage of the world's grasslands is producing near potential capacity. Although many of the choicer lands now in pasture will have to be converted into fields for the production of food crops, the vast areas of desert, tundra, mountain, and even short grass and savanna must continue to support man through livestock. Thus, because the importance to man of the world's grasslands and deserts is great, man should strive toward a condition of equilibrium with the flora of his natural environment.

SELECTED REFERENCES

Cole, Monica M. "Vegetation Studies in South Africa," *Geography*, 41:114-122, April 1956.
Grass; Yearbook of Agriculture, 1948. Washington, D. C., U.S. Department of Agriculture, 1948.
King, G. H. *Pastures for the South.* Danville, Ill., The Interstate, 1950.
Llano, G. A. "Utilization of Lichens in the Arctic and Subarctic," *Economic Botany*, 10:367-392, October–December 1956.
Myers, W. M. "Need for Improving the World's Grasslands," *Foreign Agriculture*, 16:107-110, June 1952.
Nyhus, P. O. "Argentine Pastures and the Cattle-Grazing Industry," *Foreign Agriculture*, 4:3-30, January 1940.
Schmieder, O. "The Pampa—A Natural or Culturally Induced Grassland?" *University of California Publications in Geography*, 2:255-270, September 1927.
Sprague, H. B. (ed.). *Grasslands.* Washington, D. C., American Association for the Advancement of Science, 1959. Publication No. 53.
Watson, S. J. *Grassland and Grassland Products.* London, E. Arnold, 1951.
Weintraub, F. C. *Grasses Introduced into the United States.* Washington, D. C., U.S. Department of Agriculture, 1953.

CHAPTER TWENTY-THREE ::

Tobacco is used by mankind the world over. Its production, however, is much more restricted; for this crop has rather exacting natural environmental requirements. Even so, few commercial plants extend over so wide a range of the earth's surface. Though it is produced in at least sixty-four countries, three contribute more than half the world's commercial crop (Fig. 23-1).

TOBACCO AND NATURAL ENVIRONMENT

Tobacco faces the many hazards common to all crops, but it is more vulnerable than most. Frost takes its toll, hail can rip mature leaves to shreds, excessive rain makes the leaves too

THE WORLD'S

moist, and insufficient rain results in small leaves.

Tobacco derives its distinctive characteristics from the natural environment in which it grows—the soil, climate, terrain. Type of soil is believed to affect the aroma, flavor, and thinness of leaf more than any other physical factor. Though tobacco is grown on many different soil types, some soils are superior for its growth and demands. Climate, too, is extremely important—temperature, rainfall, humidity, and length of daylight. Very slight differences in climate are said to cause great variation in quality of the leaf.

Tobacco is reported to be hard on soil. Moreover, it is a **clean-tilled crop** and therefore induces soil erosion. Open winters (in many growing areas), torrential summer rains, and steeply sloping fields all facilitate soil erosion. Much of the burley tobacco crop, for example, is grown on rolling to rough terrain with only occasional fields of flat land. In the Smokies of Tennessee and North Carolina, tobacco is grown on slopes of 30 to 40 degrees.

Although tobacco can be grown over a wide range of soil types, excessive acidity harms both quality and yield. Flue-cured tobacco is grown on light-textured soils of the Piedmont and coastal plain, which are low in organic matter and nutrients (Fig. 23-2). They do serve as a medium, however, to which the proper amount of nutrients may be added. All tobacco soils must be well drained.

Only a relatively small number of the areas of the world capable of growing tobacco are sufficiently favored with the types of climate and soil to enable them to produce a leaf of superior quality. It is thus the qualities of soil

TOBACCO

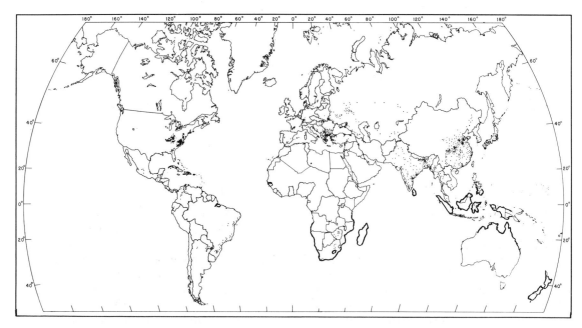

Fig. 23-1. World tobacco production. Note particularly the crop's great tolerance for different climatic and soil types. Nonetheless, slight differences in soil and weather markedly affect the quality of the leaves, as do methods of production and types of curing. As with so many other agricultural products, it is the Northern Hemisphere countries that contribute the bulk of the crop. (Courtesy of U.S. Department of Agriculture.)

and climate that give reputation to various types of tobacco, and these cannot be replaced by any known science.

CULTIVATION OF TOBACCO

Few crops require as much labor as does tobacco. Growers frequently refer to it as the "thirteen-month crop." Hence, the average tobacco farmer seldom devotes more than 2 to 10 acres of his land (the best) to tobacco; and often he grows almost nothing else, since there is little time left for other crops. He usually has a field of corn, which feeds not only his family but also the horses or mules that work his fields, the pigs that furnish his meat, and the chickens that supply his eggs and meat. Few tobacco farmers keep cows.

Tobacco requires more intensive cultivation than any other widely grown farm crop. It wears out human beings (the entire family

works) as well as soil. There is the seedbed, the preparation of the fields, transplanting, cultivation, topping (to prevent the growth of seeds), worming, suckering, spraying, harvesting, curing, stripping, and marketing. Obviously a crop that demands such prodigious human labor (495 man-hours per acre is not uncommon) does not lend itself advantageously to large-scale methods. Thus, a 100-acre farm need not have more than 2 or 3 acres in tobacco to make it an economic unit for a thrifty family. However, changes are occurring in the ways of growing the crop; mechanization is being adopted for certain tasks.

Most American tobacco growers are poor; it is reported that, despite acreage control and guarantees by the government, the monetary returns are not commensurate with the long hours spent on the crop. One wonders why they continue to grow tobacco if so many are poor. It is because they have been reared in a tobacco atmosphere and know all the intri-

Fig. 23-2. A typical field of bright flue-cured tobacco on North Carolina's light, sandy Atlantic Coastal Plain soils. Bright flue-cured tobacco outranks all other types in the manufacture of cigarettes both in America and Western European countries; it comprises 50 to 60 per cent of the American blend cigarette. (Courtesy of R. J. Reynolds Tobacco Company.)

cacies of its cultivation and marketing. At the same time, many know nothing of any other system of farming.

It would be inaccurate, however, to think that every farmer who grows tobacco grows it exclusively. Much tobacco is grown on general farms. Only when the farm income from the sale of tobacco reaches a defined percentage of the total farm income does the United States Census classify a particular farm a "tobacco farm." Hence, it is in the specialized districts that true tobacco farms stand out.

UNITED STATES TOBACCO PRODUCTION

From every standpoint the United States is the foremost name in tobacco; it produces the most, it manufactures the most, and it consumes the most. Tobacco was native to the New World—harsh *Nicotiana rustica* in the North (peace-pipe tobacco), *Nicotiana tabacum* (the tobacco in common use) in Central America and northern South America. In the American colonies, tobacco was the first major crop that served as an export to the mother country to pay for the imports of manufactured goods. The colonists tried to develop as staples other items, such as silk, wine, flax, and hemp, but to no avail.

MAJOR CLASSES OF TOBACCO

All manufactured tobacco products result from careful selection and blending of several different kinds and qualities of tobacco grown in different areas. American tobacco is, therefore, divided under government standards into

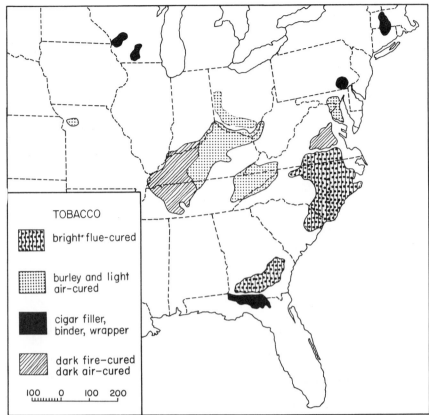

Fig. 23-3. *Major American tobacco-growing areas and the types of tobacco each grows. Though confined largely to the upper South, tobacco reaches into the North—Ohio, Wisconsin, Pennsylvania, Connecticut-Massachusetts.*

six major classes and twenty-six types. These may be grouped into those used for specific purposes: (1) for cigarettes and pipes (flue-cured, burley, and Maryland types); (2) for chewing and snuff (dark fire-cured and dark air-cured); and (3) for cigars (filler, binder, and wrapper types).[1]

The dominant quality sought by growers and manufacturers is aroma, but texture and

[1] The *filler*, the interior of the cigar, gives the cigar its principal characteristics. It is composed of loose leaves and cuttings and is held together by the *binder* or inner cover, a single leaf which holds the filler in shape and gives it style and appearance. All this is entirely covered by the *wrapper*, another single leaf, which gives external appearance, such as color. A specific type of tobacco has been developed for each part.

color of the leaf also are important—particularly in flue-cured leaves for cigarettes. Most strains of tobacco are developed by geneticists, both for special uses and for the best quality than can be produced on a specific soil.

THE CENTRAL PIEDMONT

This is one of the nation's outstanding tobacco-growing areas (Fig. 23-3). It is famous for dark fire-cured and air-cured leaf in Virginia and for bright flue-cured leaf in Virginia and the Carolinas. *Dark fire-cured* and *air-cured tobaccos* are grown on the heavier soils of the Virginia Piedmont—the former in the central part, the latter in the north-central portion. The fire-cured type has a cured leaf, dark in color, tough, oily, and high in nicotine.

Fig. 23-4. Flue-curing tobacco by indirect heat in the New Belt of North Carolina. No smoke comes in contact with the leaves. The resulting bright flue-cured leaf, yellow in color, is the most highly prized of all by the American cigarette industry. (Courtesy of U.S. Department of Agriculture.)

These types are used for pipe-smoking mixtures, snuff, and chewing. The fire-cured types have been grown primarily for export and the air-cured types for domestic manufacture. Both have been losing ground in recent years; present exports (about 43 million pounds) are only about half what they were before World War II.

Bright flue-cured tobacco is grown on the light, sandy soils of the Coastal Plain in eastern North and South Carolina, Virginia, and Georgia. This variety has been for many years the most important leaf grown for cigarettes, both for domestic use and for the export trade. Thus, of total exports of about 550 million pounds, the flue-cured variety accounts for about 433 million pounds. However, because of the notable switch from regular to filter-tip cigarettes, the light-colored, light-bodied, flue-

cured leaf used for regular cigarettes has given way to a darker, heavier-bodied, stronger, and cheaper leaf for filter tips. This sudden decline in popularity and demand has bewildered many light-tobacco growers.

The bright flue-cured leaf, light in both body and color, is grown in the New Belt of North Carolina on soils that in their natural condition are so infertile that in a sense they are virtually a neutral medium. Employing them, however, the experienced grower can apply the special blends of commercial fertilizers that give the tobacco precisely the qualities required. Accordingly, these soils, which would be almost valueless for most crops, are well suited to tobacco. This type of tobacco is cured by indirect heat. No smoke comes in contact with the leaves. Flue-curing hastens the curing process; after 24 to 36 hours at

Fig. 23-5. Growing broadleaf burley tobacco on terraced and contour-planted fields, near Georgetown, Kentucky. Burley is grown in the upper South—in the western counties of North and South Carolina, in eastern Tennessee, in mountainous eastern Kentucky, in the Kentucky Bluegrass Region, and in southwestern Ohio. One of America's chief types of tobacco, it is an essential ingredient (comprising about 30-40 per cent) of the high-quality American-type blended cigarette. (Courtesy of U.S. Department of Agriculture.)

temperatures ranging from 80°F to 120°F, a yellow leaf is produced (Fig. 23-4).

Burley tobacco is grown in the western and eastern mountain counties of Kentucky (Fig. 23-5) and most of eastern Tennessee, as well as the Kentucky Bluegrass, western North Carolina, southeastern Indiana, and southern Ohio (Fig. 23-3). Burley is grown largely on small farms where it is cultivated as a cash crop and is regarded as a necessity in the economy. After harvest it is air-cured by being hung in barns through which air is allowed to circulate (Fig. 23-6). Burley is used for cigarettes, pipe-smoking mixtures, and chewing tobacco and is one of the nation's most important classes of leaf; it is mild and flavorful and makes up about 35 per cent of the average cigarette.

Maryland tobacco, distinguished for its even burn, is mixed with other tobaccos for blending in cigarettes and pipe-smoking mixtures. It has been grown in the Chesapeake Bay area for more than two centuries (Fig. 23-3). The early growers here enjoyed the advantage of easy and direct relations with English merchants.

Farmers in the United States first became interested in growing *aromatic (Turkish) tobacco* commercially during World War II, when imports of foreign-grown leaf were seriously curtailed. More recently, as a result of the drop in popularity in bright flue-cured tobacco, they have again become interested in the aromatic tobacco. Also, Turkish tobacco is not included in the government's tobacco-acreage-control program; and it requires a relatively small investment, since the tiny leaves are air-cured. Moreover, the price of about $1 per pound is approximately double that of bright flue-cured.

Lands best suited for aromatic tobacco are the mountain and upper Piedmont areas of the two Carolinas, Georgia, and Virginia. Here farms are small, soil and climate are suitable, and the supply of labor is ample. The crop is grown on well-drained soils of medium fertility; phosphate and potash are raised to medium or even high levels, but nitrogen is kept at a low level. In addition, in order for the tobacco to be really aromatic, the plant population per unit area must be very high in comparison with traditional types of tobacco grown here.

THE CONNECTICUT VALLEY

The Connecticut Valley—from Middletown, Connecticut, on the south, to South Deerfield, Massachusetts, on the north (Fig. 23-3)—has been growing tobacco since about 1900. The product is today the area's most valuable agricultural product. The Connecticut Valley produces two kinds of tobacco: (1) the Havana seed and broadleaf binder crop, which is grown in the open; and (2) the Sumatra or shade tobacco, grown beneath vast expanses of cheesecloth (Fig. 23-7). The area is the source of about two thirds of the cigar binders used in the United States.

Fig. 23-6. *Air-curing burley tobacco. The stalks are cut in the fall and hung up in the barn. When the leaves are cured, they are stripped off, packed in bundles, and soon delivered to a warehouse for sale. (Courtesy of U.S. Department of Agriculture.)*

Most of the crop is grown in infertile sandy and sandy-loam soils of river terraces, which are generously treated with manure and commercial fertilizers. The valley's best shade tobacco is grown on fields on the deltas built into former glacial lakes. Though the deltas are sandy and gravelly, the topsoils are derived from a superficial layer of **loess.** The cheesecloth softens the rays of the sun, provides a more even temperature, minimizes wind movements, and protects the leaves from hailstones. However, growing tobacco under shade is extremely expensive. Much of the Sumatra tobacco is produced by large corpo-

rations under very scientific methods. Moreover, the crop is grown on holdings about twice the size of those elsewhere in the country.

LANCASTER COUNTY, PENNSYLVANIA

This famous agricultural area (Fig. 23-3) has about 30,000 acres in tobacco, the leaf of which serves as cigar filler. The crop is planted in seedbeds in spring or autumn. The leaf is mild in aroma and flavor. Yields are high— the result of planting only on the best soils and of scientific cultivation. The leaves are handled with great care after cutting. If the

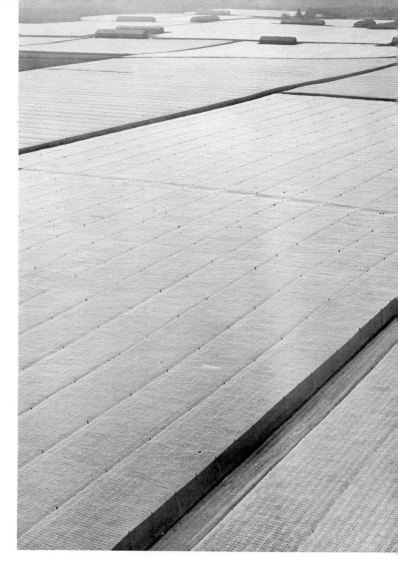

Fig. 23-7. Growing Sumatra leaf tobacco under cheesecloth in the Connecticut Valley, with tobacco barns visible in the background. The cheesecloth softens the rays of the sun, provides a more even temperature, minimizes wind movements, protects the leaves from the shredding effects of hailstones, and contributes to the production of thin, fine-textured leaves. The expense of producing this cigar-wrapper tobacco is justified usually by the high price paid for it. (Courtesy of United Aircraft Corporation.)

sun is intense and the leaf burns, the smoker can taste the burn and is apt to change his brand of cigars.

Lancaster County soils consist of heavy clays and clay loams, well suited to mixed farming. Only a small piece of the farmer's land is devoted to tobacco; the crop is merely one in a well-balanced rotation including winter wheat, clover, grass, corn, and tobacco. Beef cattle brought in during autumn from Virginia and West Virginia are fed during winter, consuming the county's corn, hay, and part of its wheat straw and providing manure for the fields of tobacco.

FOREIGN TOBACCO PRODUCTION

CANADA

Canada grows tobacco in several of its eastern areas. Flue-cured tobacco, Ontario's largest single cash crop, has made Canada self-sufficient in cigarette tobacco, except for a small amount of **latakia** and **perique** for blending. It has also brought great revenue to the Canadian government (more than 200 million dollars per annum).

Tobacco rescued a once distressed area in Ontario—Norfolk County, which lies just north of Lake Erie and about 90 miles west of Niagara Falls. Mixed farming and horticulture had been tried unsuccessfully on land that had become exhausted and badly eroded. However, the light, sandy soil is excellent for flue-cured tobacco. The climate, too, is favorable; killing frosts are rare after the first week in May and prior to the last week in September. Although the total output of tobacco is small, the crop is all-important to Norfolk County.

SOUTHERN RHODESIA

During recent years Southern Rhodesia has assumed a prominent place in the world tobacco industry. It is not only Africa's leading source of tobacco but is a world leader in production of light flue-cured leaf. Output has more than quadrupled since 1939. Most of the crop, grown by Europeans, is confined to an area within a 150-mile radius of Salisbury.

INDIA AND PAKISTAN

India ranks second or third in world tobacco production. The crop is grown throughout the subcontinent, but two thirds of the total acreage lies in the two states of Bombay and Madras (Fig. 23-1). The crop is planted at the end of the rainy period and harvested during the dry period. The quality of the leaf is low. Most of the output is consumed within the country.

The situation in Pakistan is similar to that in India; 70 per cent of the crop is grown in East Bengal. Here, too, the product is of low quality and is used mostly within the country.

CHINA

Tobacco is an important crop in China, though undeniably secondary to rice, which gets first choice of the land wherever soil and climate are favorable for it. Tobacco is grown on widely differing soil types, ranging from heavy clays to light sandy loams. There are five leading producing areas: the Weihsien Valley of central Shantung, the Central Honan Plain, the Chengtu Plain in Szechwan Basin,

southern Fukien and Kwangtung Province, and the North Hopei Plain.

Obviously, in so densely peopled a land, the acreage in tobacco per farm is small—a mere "garden" from the Western point of view. Total production, however, is enormous, because China is a large country, because much of its area is favorable for tobacco growing, and because so many millions of Chinese grow it (Fig. 23-1). Most of the crop, possibly all of it, is consumed within China.

INDONESIA

Indonesia is the fifth-ranking producer of tobacco in the world. About 80 per cent of the crop is grown on the two islands of Java and Madura (Fig. 23-1). However, the major producing district and one of the most important in the world is that surrounding Deli on the east coast of Sumatra, famous for its thin, highly elastic cigar-wrapper leaf. The crop here is grown scientifically and efficiently by large companies on residual soils of volcanic origin or on alluvium derived from volcanic materials. Java's crop is grown mostly in the eastern half of the island on young volcanic soils and in the wet and dry type of climate.

BRAZIL

Brazil is South America's leading producer of tobacco, accounting for approximately 60 per cent of the continent's output. Tobacco is grown in every state, but more than half the output comes from Rio Grande do Sul and Bahia. Minas Gerais and Santa Catarina also are impressive producers. An outstanding area in Bahia is that lying just west of Reconcava. Here rainfall is abundant, the soils are sandy and well drained, and the land is flat or nearly so. The crop is grown on small farms, and much fertilizer (mostly manure) is used—something unique for Brazil.

CUBA

Although the actual area devoted to tobacco in Cuba is small (Fig. 23-1), the country has long enjoyed an enviable reputation for the quality of its leaf. The tobacco, used both for fillers and wrappers, is grown on the rolling sandy plains of southwest Pinar del Rio just west of Havana. The crop, planted in seedbeds in November at the close of the rainy and hurricane seasons, grows during the cool winter. The sandy soils underlain by red clays provide an aromatic tobacco famous for expensive cigars. The entire economic life of the population in this segment of Cuba is inseparably bound up with tobacco. Much of the crop is grown under cheesecloth to protect it from the strong sun. Cuban tobacco is also a plantation crop. All land, including the tobacco plantations, was taken over by the government under the Agrarian Reform Law. The future of tobacco here is thus uncertain. Most of Cuba's tobacco has moved to export markets.

REPUBLIC OF THE PHILIPPINES

This archipelago ranks high in tobacco production. The crop is grown on most of the islands, but about 90 per cent of the total output emanates in the islands of Luzon and Cebu (Fig. 23-1).

BALKAN AND NEAR EAST COUNTRIES

The lands adjacent to the Black Sea and the Mediterranean Sea, and particularly to the Aegean Sea and the Adriatic Sea, comprise one of the world's leading tobacco-growing areas. These "Turkish" tobaccos are characterized by a very small and highly aromatic leaf that is much valued in the manufacture of high-grade cigarettes. Unlike most tobacco leaves (which are large—19 to 35 inches long with an average area of 1½ to 2½ square feet), Turkish tobacco leaves are scarcely larger than the leaves on an apple tree (Fig. 23-8); about 1,000 of them weigh 1 pound.

Although Greece, Bulgaria, Yugoslavia, and the Soviet Union are important producers, Turkey ranks highest in output. Particularly impressive is the area along the shores of the Sea of Marmara and along the middle and east coast of the Black Sea (Fig. 23-1). The tobacco grown here possesses smooth-burning qualities and is in such great demand abroad that most of it is exported, and less costly tobaccos are imported for home consumption.

As a high labor and income crop, Turkish tobacco is attractive to the poor farmers in these underdeveloped countries.

Oriental leaf accounts for about one eighth of world tobacco-leaf production. Turkey is reported to be a major trading competitor of the United States in the tobacco markets of the world.

THE SELLING OF TOBACCO

UNITED STATES

The American farmer sells his tobacco by auction in numerous cities scattered throughout the tobacco-growing areas. When the sale gets under way, the auctioneer proceeds to the first basket in a row, preceded by a warehouse official and followed by about a dozen buyers. The auctioneer's chant is monotonous and mostly incomprehensible to a visitor. The buyer must think fast and act fast; he has only about ten seconds to make his decision. In bidding, he merely signals. He may just rub his nose, nod, or wiggle a finger, or he may just glance; but the auctioneer understands every sign. The system employed has two purposes—speed and secrecy. A bidder frequently does not want his competitors to know what he is bidding, lest they run up the bid as they realize his interest in that grade.

SOUTHERN RHODESIA

Salisbury, Southern Rhodesia, ranks today as the world's largest tobacco-exporting market. Tobacco is auctioned off in the manner of the American South. Auctioneers strive to keep the bidding active; for if it should slow down, the price might fall too low.

In Rhodesia, sales take place on three competing floors. Bales weighing about 170 pounds are laid out in rows; open baskets are not employed, as they are in the United States, because the tobacco would dry out in the low relative humidity.

Fig. 23-8. Drying "Turkish" tobacco in the Near East. Much hand labor is required to harvest and manipulate a pound of such small leaves. (Courtesy of Turkish Information Office.)

WORLD TRADE IN TOBACCO LEAF

World trade is largely restricted to leaf tobacco—as a result of high tariffs on manufactured products and the desire of governments to manufacture leaves within their own boundaries. Taxes on tobacco consumption have been, since the seventeenth century, a favorite and dependable source of revenue for governments all over the world. The tobacco industry has become so highly specialized that the trade regularly looks to specific areas to meet the demand for various kinds of leaf. The principal countries engaged in selling tobacco are the United States, Southern Rhodesia, Canada, India, and the many nations in the eastern Mediterranean Basin.

In most years the United States is far and away the leading exporter. Flavor, aroma, and quality are high; and the leaf is well graded, packed, and shipped—all of which make American tobaccos popular the world over. The United States sends abroad about a fourth of its total production. Tobacco ranks third among American agricultural exports. Bright flue-cured accounts for 80 to 85 per cent of United States exports, burley for about 6 per cent. Approximately three fourths of the leaf exports move to Western Europe, about 15 per cent to Asia, and 10 per cent to Africa and Latin America.

Western Europe is the world's largest tobacco-importing area, normally taking more than 60 per cent of all the leaf tobacco entering world trade. Chief importer is the United Kingdom.

The United States also imports tobacco, mostly "Turkish," for blending—about 7 per cent of such leaf entering cigarette consumption. In addition, it imports cigar tobaccos from Puerto Rico, the Dominican Republic, the Philippines, and Indonesia. Even these small imports enable the United States to rank second or third among world importers.

American foreign trade in leaf tobacco fluctuates as a result of foreign restrictions imposed to save dollar exchange, even when American tobaccos are preferred. This situation has encouraged much expansion of tobacco growing in foreign lands. The United States accordingly is experiencing stiffer competition in world tobacco markets than at any time in its history. Southern Rhodesia and Canada have greatly increased their sales of flue-cured leaf in foreign markets, particularly those of Western Europe, whose countries are most eager to purchase as much tobacco as possible in soft-currency areas. With the exception of foreign-grown flue-cured, the Turkish tobaccos are America's strongest competitors in the world's tobacco markets.

MANUFACTURE OF TOBACCO PRODUCTS

Tobacco manufacture consists of two divisions: (1) a simple industry in which the tobacco leaf purchased at the auctions is reworked and prepared for the companies engaged in the manufacture of tobacco products, and (2) a complex industry that actually makes the products.

The tobacco from the auction warehouses is aged for two to three years at the factory. When the aging has been accomplished, the hogsheads in which the tobacco is stored are broken apart; and the tobacco leaves are passed through a steam bath to make them moist and pliable, and then to a stemming machine, which removes the leaves from the stems. The tobacco then is taken to blending tables where numerous varieties of tobacco are blended. The leaves next pass through a cutter, which shreds them, and on to vast drums where the tobacco is sprayed with flavoring solutions, particularly rum and maple sugar but also a dozen others.

The tobacco industry is largely the story of the manufacture of cigarettes because for many years the market for this product has soared, whereas that for most other tobacco products has remained stationary or declined. Today cigarettes account for about 80 per cent of the leaf tobacco used in the United States; in 1961, 490 billion cigarettes were consumed.

DISTRIBUTION OF THE AMERICAN INDUSTRY

In the early days in the United States, hundreds of little manufacturing plants, individually owned and operated by hand, sprang up throughout the tobacco-growing areas, and their products were peddled by wagon. This pattern largely continued in the manufacture of cigars and to some extent even in the manufacture of chewing and smoking tobaccos, but not in that of cigarettes. There are in the United States 381 factories making chewing and smoking tobaccos and snuff, 2,441 producing cigars, but only 60 making cigarettes; and the bulk of cigarettes is made in large factories.

The manufacture of chewing and pipe-smoking tobacco took place close to the tobacco-growing areas, but cigar making became widespread. In 1846, with lowered tariff duties on imported cigars, Cuba came to the fore, but American manufacturers countered by making cigars of Cuban tobacco filler and domestic-grown wrapper in the North. By 1860 Philadelphia had become the premier cigar-manufacturing city. Tobacco products other than cigars—that is, smoking tobacco, chewing tobacco, snuff, and cigarettes—became more concentrated in the South. In 1840 Richmond alone made 41 per cent of all processed products, and Louisville and St. Louis were gaining in importance as tobacco growing spread westward to Kentucky and Tennessee.

The United States dwarfs all the rest of the world in the manufacture of tobacco products and within the United States the South is dominant, the region contributing 93 per cent of the nation's tobacco leaf and fabricating 60 per cent of its manufactured tobacco products. This rank has been maintained for many years with little if any change. The manufacture of tobacco is an outstanding example of a major industry's utilizing at home one of its major products.

Since tobacco manufacturing, *all but cigar making,* is located very close to the tobacco fields, the Piedmont of North Carolina and Virginia is particularly important, with Durham, Winston-Salem, Reidsville, Petersburg, and Richmond as the leading centers (Fig. 23-9). In fact, the area with Richmond on the north and Winston-Salem on the south accounts for 80 per cent of the cigarettes manufactured in the United States.

The Piedmont is the logical place for cigarette manufacture, since, for almost a century, thousands of men have studied and solved the intricate problems connected with the production of bright flue-cured and other kinds of tobacco. There is little likelihood of any drastic relocation of tobacco manufacturing, although a few factories are located west of the Piedmont in Louisville.

Among the states, North Carolina is by far the leader in the manufacture of tobacco products (53 per cent). Virginia also is important (27 per cent): in fact, these two alone contribute about 80 per cent of the nation's output. Kentucky follows with 13 per cent.

THE MANUFACTURE OF CIGARETTES

The manufacture of cigarettes is the principal branch of the world's tobacco business. World output reaches into fantastic figures —1,971 billion in 1958.

The growth of this industry in the United States has been phenomenal; and the cigarette is now in a predominant position, in output, number of users, tax returns to the government, and in acreage devoted to the culture of tobacco.

The cigarette, which is now almost synonymous with tobacco, was invented by an Egyptian in 1821 and did not come into vogue in the United States until the post-Civil War period. The first cigarettes made

Fig. 23-9. *The Piedmont of North Carolina and Virginia—major tobacco-manufacturing area in the United States.*

for sale were hand-rolled—a slow and expensive process and one requiring much skill. The hand-rolled cigarettes were replaced by machine-rolled ones in the early 1880s. By the end of the decade both the product and the manufacturing process had become standardized. New York City became the first important cigarette-manufacturing center, but after 1890 it was replaced by Durham and Winston (later to become Winston-Salem) and by Richmond.

In the cigarette industry, domestic tobaccos are blended with imported aromatic leaves. To the expert these various types, even those domestically grown, are as different as day and night. Thus the Maryland variety, distinguished for its even burn, is mixed with bright-yellow leaf, known as flue-cured, that is grown in Virginia, the two Carolinas, and Georgia, and with cream-colored burley from Kentucky, Ohio, Indiana, and Tennessee. Formerly burley was used only in smoking mixtures; it is now sweetened and allowed to sweat its flavor into that of other varieties of leaf. These domestic tobaccos are blended with "Turkish," grown mostly in Turkey, Greece, and Bulgaria. Domestic and imported tobaccos come together for the first time in the blending drums.

At first in the American cigarette industry only two types were made: (1) domestic cigarettes from bright flue-cured tobacco of the Piedmont, and (2) "Murad" cigarettes made from imported Turkish tobacco. With the advent of World War I, however, the companies could no longer get Turkish tobacco; and the manufacturers introduced blended cigarettes. The various companies assiduously guard the secret formulas of their brands.

Cigarettes are made mostly in four-story brick buildings, each structure occupying approximately the space of a city block. The factories are well lighted and air-conditioned, for the tobacco must be surrounded by air of a specific temperature and humidity. The industry is so highly mechanized that only about 25,000 workers comprise the labor force. The process demands speed, since volume is imperative where the profit per unit is small. All operations are synchronized. The machines, marvels of mechanical ingenuity, are capable of turning out 1,200 to 1,500 cigarettes per minute; the latest turns out more than 1,600 per minute and requires but a single operator. So automatic is the process that labor is a small item in the cost structure —5 per cent of the total. Filled trays move to packing machines, where with lightning speed twenty cigarettes are counted out and arranged in rows, packaged, and then wrapped in moisture-proof cellophane. These fantastic machines, which turn out 135 packs per minute, fill and seal millions of packs a day.

Three companies make about 80 per cent of all American cigarettes, and yet there is today no illegal monopoly because the companies operate separately. Several economic factors enable the large companies to maintain their positions and simultaneously to discourage the growth of competitors: (1) the heavy financing required to carry inventories of leaf tobacco necessary for volume production (nearly 80 per cent of the leading companies' tangible assets are represented by inventories); (2) the internal revenue taxes of 8 cents a pack, which must be paid by manufacturers; (3) the elaborate and expensive storage and manufacturing facilities; and (4) the cost of advertising and promotional work, which are necessary for establishing brands on a volume basis—the only basis that permits efficient and economical production and distribution. In a given year the cost of advertising exceeds 175 million dollars.

For many years American cigarettes were made mostly with bright flue-cured, light-colored, light-bodied tobacco. In the past several years, however, smokers by the millions have switched to filter-tips (now more than 50 per cent of the total cigarette market). This switch has resulted in an upheaval in the tobacco industry. Manufacturers have discovered that a darker, heavier-bodied, and stronger leaf is best for filter-tip cigarettes.

THE CIGAR INDUSTRY

In the beginning and until the end of World War I, cigars were entirely handmade, requiring much skill and selling for a high price. These are the conditions that invariably stimulate inventors to replace the human hand with a machine. In handmade brands, the filler is cut and the wrapper is rolled around it according to the veins of the leaf. Very few cigars are made by hand today, for hand labor is too costly. The machine cuts both filler and wrapper, and rolls the wrapper around the filler; and it can make 1 million cigars a year.

The tobaccos going into cigars differ from those going into cigarettes and are produced in different areas and often in different states. Thus, Connecticut and Massachusetts specialize in wrapper leaf along with binder and filler leaves; Ohio and Pennsylvania contribute filler leaf; and New York and Wisconsin, binder leaf. Florida specializes in a type of Sumatra wrapper. Some filler leaf is purchased from Cuba and Puerto Rico, and some wrapper leaf from Sumatra.

The cigar industry has been having troubles. The first of these troubles affects growers, since a new homogenization process has enabled manufacturers to use lower-grade tobacco rather than the whole, high-standard leaf; the process also permits less tobacco to be used (an acre of tobacco converted into sheet-tobacco binder will bind as many cigars as the natural binders produced on 3 acres used in the customary manner). A problem facing manufacturers is the horde of new state taxes, which obviously reduces the number of cigars smoked. Such taxes resulted in a drop of 200 million cigars in 1959. Some 6.4 billion cigars were smoked in 1958.

TOBACCO MANUFACTURE OUTSIDE THE UNITED STATES

Tobacco products are made in almost every nation to meet domestic requirements—home-grown leaf being utilized when it can be successfully grown, imported leaf serving where quality leaf cannot be produced.

The tobacco industry in most nations is a government monopoly. All tobacco products are highly vulnerable to governmental regulation and control, and hence are among the most heavily taxed of all manufactured items. Among the methods employed by governments to collect such revenue are (1) government tobacco monopolies, (2) import duties, (3) export taxation, and (4) internal-revenue taxation. So high are duties on tobacco products in most countries that foreign brands are unavailable to all but the well-to-do.

TRENDS IN THE TOBACCO INDUSTRY

The production of cigarettes increases year by year, whereas that of most other tobacco products steadily declines. The cigarette industry is relatively stable, and the product promises to remain in great and increasing demand for many years.[2] Cigarette smoking by a large segment of women beginning in the late 1920s greatly increased demand and production. Moreover, the manufacturers of cigarettes are lavish in their expenditures for advertising, which is credited with the more than tenfold increase in consumption during a period of thirty years. Sales drop whenever such expenditures are curtailed.

It seems certain that the cigarette branch will continue to be dominated by a few giant companies and that the cigar industry will follow the same trend. Economic conditions necessitate mass-production methods. The future of the cigar industry, however, is far less bright than that of the cigarette industry. Annual declines are to be expected in the use of pipe tobacco, chewing tobacco, and snuff.

[2] Perhaps this statement should be qualified. Though there appears to be proliferating evidence that cigarette smoking causes lung cancer, the tobacco industry declares that a causal connection has not been proved. As long as definite proof is lacking, the cigarette industry promises to advance and prosper. Nonetheless, lung cancer does pose a threat to the industry.

SELECTED REFERENCES

Alderfer, E. B., and H. E. Michl. *Economics of American Industry.* New York, McGraw-Hill Book Company, Inc., 1950, pp. 627-642.
Birkhead, James W. *Brazil's Tobacco Production and Trade.* Washington, D. C., U.S. Department of Agriculture, March 1955. Foreign Agriculture Service Report No. 82.
——————. "How Flue-Cured Tobacco Is Produced in Rhodesia," *Foreign Agriculture,* 18:218-222, December 1954.
Durand, Loyal, Jr., and Elsie T. Bird. "The Burley Tobacco Region of the Mountain South," *Economic Geography,* 26:274-300, October 1950.
Pike, Clarence E. "Tobacco in Western Europe," *Foreign Agriculture,* 14:57-61, March 1950.
Tobacco. New York, Food and Agriculture Organization of the United Nations, October 1952. Commodity Series, Bulletin No. 21.
"The Tobacco Industry of Turkey," *World Crops,* 4(9):311-313, 1952.
"Tobacco Production by Type in Specified Countries," *Foreign Agriculture Circular,* April 30, 1953.

MISCELLANEOUS
VEGETABLE

PART SIX ::

PRODUCTS—FIBERS AND OILS

CHAPTER TWENTY-FOUR::

Since man became man, he has sought cover for his naked body. At first he employed furs, barks, and grasses, depending upon the location of his habitat and upon the materials available. Later he learned how to use the more durable plant and animal fibers for clothing and a host of other purposes. All this, of course, required thousands of years. Finally, in this present Age of Science, he has, through laboratory research and experiment, learned how to make textiles from synthetic fibers that are as good as and sometimes (for specific uses) superior even to nature's own.

VEGETABLE FIBERS

Nearly 2,000 recognized species of plants yield useful fibers and fibrous materials. These

THE WORLD'S
AND

fall into three classes: (1) *seed fibers,* those formed inside seed pods, of which cotton is an excellent example; (2) *soft (bast) fibers,* those obtained from the inner bark of plants, exemplified by jute, flax, hemp, and kenaf; and (3) *hard fibers,* those which extend through the pulpy tissues of leaves and stems of leaves of certain plants, of which abacá, henequen, and sisal are good examples.

COTTON

Cotton is indisputably man's most important textile fiber. It enters into his daily life more than any other product except salt. No other natural fiber and no man-made fiber can match all its inherent characteristics—strength, durability, washability, facility for dyeing and spinning and weaving, and adaptability for clothing and industrial uses. Each of man's fibers employed for making cloth possesses outstanding special properties: wool is warm; silk is smooth; rayon is cheap; nylon is strong. Cotton differs from them all in that it *combines all these qualities.* And possibly better than any, it can make a fabric that feels good when worn. Since the Industrial Revolution, cotton has held its own as the great all-purpose fiber of civilization—practical, economical, suited to mass production. And though its share of the total textile output has been declining, the fiber still accounts for 65 per cent of world textile production.

Cotton is grown in some sixty nations (the annual crop reached almost 47 million bales of 500 pounds each in 1959-1960—an all-time high), and it leads all competing fibers in foreign trade—about 15 million bales in 1959-1960.

Because of cotton's usefulness, efforts were begun centuries ago to cultivate the plant and

VEGETABLE, ANIMAL, MAN-MADE FIBERS

to extend the limits of production beyond its natural habitat. Through the ages man, by careful selection, developed early-maturing forms adaptable as **annuals**. Primitive and laborious hand methods used for separating the fiber from seeds long thwarted cotton's development. Not until 1793, when Eli Whitney invented the cotton gin, did large-scale production and resultant low prices become possible. This machine completely revolutionized world cotton production; for it eliminated the tedium of pulling the fibers from the seed by hand, which required one person a whole day to free just 1 pound of fiber from the seeds.

LEADING COMMERCIAL TYPES

Cotton is commonly grouped into four general classes: (1) *Egyptian* or *extra-long staple*—1⅜ to 1¾ inches; (2) *upland long staple*—1⅛ to 1⅜ inches; (3) *upland short staple*—¾ to 1⅛ inches; and (4) *Asiatic* or *very short staple*—⅜ to ¾ inch. Most difficult and costly to grow is the extra-long staple, which is vulnerable to insects and requires almost ideal conditions. In the United States it costs roughly twice as much as the ordinary variety to grow a pound.

COTTON AND THE NATURAL ENVIRONMENT

The critical requirements of cotton are: (1) a mean annual temperature of more than 60°F; (2) a **growing season** of 180 to 200 days; (3) a minimum annual rainfall of 20 inches (or its equivalent in irrigation water), with suitable seasonal distribution; (4) minimum rainfall in autumn; and (5) open, sunny weather. Ideal type of rainfall is the thunderstorm variety, in which the sun shines between showers.

Soils should be deep and well drained and reasonably high in organic content. Flat or undulating land is superior to rough terrain, since cotton, a **clean-tilled crop**, induces soil erosion.

WORLD DISTRIBUTION OF COTTON

Cotton is grown mostly (85 to 90 per cent) in the Northern Hemisphere. However, eight countries—the United States, China, the Soviet Union, India, Egypt, Brazil, Pakistan, and Mexico—account for the bulk. Eight others—Argentina, Turkey, Peru, Sudan, Uganda, Congo (Leopoldville), Korea, and the Congo (Brazzaville)—contribute most of the remainder.

United States. The United States is far and away the leading world source of cotton. In 1920 it produced two thirds of the world crop; in 1960 it accounted for 31 per cent. Principal growing area is the Cotton Belt—a region 1,600 miles east–west and 300 miles north–south and occupying about one sixth of the nation's total area (Fig. 24-1). From 1800 to about 1930, production centered in the states east of the Mississippi River. Cotton in the South then was all-important; it got first choice of the land,[1] and it vied with corn for first place in acreage. However, even at its peak, cotton provided the principal source of income on scarcely more than half the region's farms, and as late as 1929 it was the source of only about half the South's cash farm income. Today it represents less than 25 per cent of total farm income in the Cotton Belt. In 1929 there were nearly 1 million cotton farms in the Cotton Belt—the Deep South; today there are about half a million.

Eight circumstances have contributed to this decline:

1. The invasion of the region by the boll weevil, which causes an annual monetary damage of more than 200 million dollars and has enforced much diversification in crops.[2]

---

[1] A principle of economic geography applicable to cotton in the Cotton Belt follows: *The crop or other agricultural product which is most restricted in its climatic range will, if the demand for it be sufficient, have first choice of the land, though not to the exclusion of certain bulky crops needed for local consumption.*

[2] The boll weevil slipped over the border from Mexico in 1892. Had American farmers refrained from growing cotton for a few years, the havoc would have stopped, for boll weevils eat only cotton; but the farmers did not desist. By 1921 the pest had infested every part of the Cotton Belt. Despite the forward march of science, the boll weevil has not been vanquished or even conquered. In fact, it is displaying increasing immunity to insecticides.

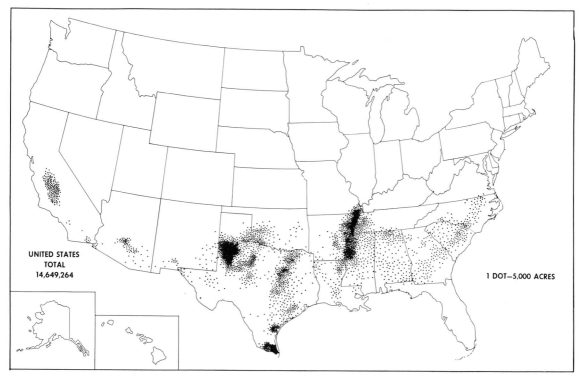

Fig. 24-1. Distribution of cotton production in the United States. Irrigated cotton areas in western and southern Texas, California, and Arizona are more conspicuous than most parts of the old "Cotton Belt." (Courtesy of U.S. Department of Commerce, Bureau of the Census.)

2. The enactment of acreage restrictions inaugurated by the great depression and designed to alleviate conditions for the cotton farmers; cotton growing spread west into Arizona and California and to foreign nations as the United States government maintained high prices.

3. Long-continuing low prices for cotton.

4. Depleted soils in the older and wetter cotton-growing areas.

5. Soil erosion.

6. Mechanization of production in the Southwest (Texas to California).

7. Competition of man-made fibers.

8. The rise of impressive output in Africa, Brazil, and the Soviet Union.

The New Cotton Belt. The old Cotton Belt has disappeared. Today eight cotton districts (Fig. 24-2) account for almost two thirds of the crop. These districts are expected to yield cotton for many years, since they enjoy a favorable combination of physical, economic, and cultural advantages. But even in these areas some other form of land use surpasses that allotted to cotton. *One-cropism is gone.*

Mechanization. The traditional picture that many Americans have of a typical Cotton Belt farm—one man, one mule, and forty acres—no longer holds true. The old order has changed; the area today is mechanized, and the gasoline age has put cotton farming on wheels.

Tractors swarm through the fields, hauling contrivances that break up the soil, drill seed into beds, pump fertilizer into the earth and chop up weeds, two or four rows at a time. Dare devil pilots in open-cockpit planes strafe the fields with poison dust to combat boll weevils. Mechanical pickers with revolving finger-like spindles lurch down the rows, pouring streams of cotton into big wire baskets. . . . Machines now harvest a fourth

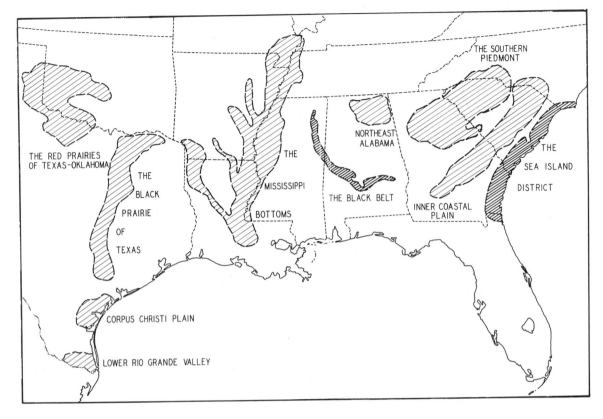

Fig. 24-2. American Cotton Belt—areas of intensive cotton production of importance today (light shaded) and those of historic significance only (dark shaded). (From C. Langdon White, Edwin J. Foscue, and Tom L. McKnight, Regional Geography of Anglo-America, *3rd ed., Englewood Cliffs, N.J.,Prentice-Hall, Inc., 1964.)*

of the crop, filling the gap left by the postwar exodus of farm hands to the cities.[3]

Mechanical pickers increase in numbers each year, but they increase in importance mostly in the West; for there the farms are larger and there are fewer of them, the population is much less dense, and the land is more level than on the farms of the Southeast. Also the farmers are less bound by tradition. Stripper-harvesters are used in the High Plains of West Texas and Oklahoma, picker-harvesters in the more humid areas—although picker-harvesters cannot be operated profitably on small (less than 100 acres) cotton acreages.

[3] "Cotton—That Fabulous Fiber," *Aramco World,* 9:10, January 1958.

Manual labor is becoming ever more scarce and costly. Since 1940, more than 5 million persons have left the cotton farms, mostly from the states in the eastern part of the belt; 4 million of these went to the congested cities of the North. Consequently, more and more mechanical pickers are being introduced to replace human pickers. The mechanical picker performs the work of at least forty human pickers: the average field hand can pick daily roughly half a bale of cotton (Fig. 24-3); by contrast, a mechanical picker—straddling two rows at a time at the steady rate of 3 miles per hour—can pick ten to twenty bales per day (Fig. 24-4). Hand-picked cotton costs $45 to $50 a bale, contrasted with $15 to $30 for machine-picked cotton. Although about one half of all United

States cotton still is picked by hand, many experts on cotton in the South declare that in just a few years nearly all the crop will be harvested by machines.

After picking, the cotton is hauled to a ginnery, where the fibers are separated from the seeds. Cotton harvested by "strippers" requires more processing than that harvested by hand or mechanical picker—for "strippers" gather up much trash, including the entire cotton boll. Also the mechanical picker gets more trash than the hand picker, thus calling for extra cleaning steps at the mill.

The Southwest. Cotton production has grown at a dizzy pace in the Southwest, until today this region accounts for roughly half the American crop. Here cotton units tend to be large, and mechanization is easier and more profitable. In Texas and Oklahoma, mechanization is associated with the decline in farm population, decrease in number of farms, and increase in the average size of farms.

The three states of New Mexico, Arizona, and California grow the crop under irrigation, employing different production methods and obtaining larger yields than the Cotton Belt —two bales per acre being not uncommon and one bale or more definitely expected. Cotton is California's leading crop. The center of production is the southern half of the San Joaquin Valley, where the entire crop is irrigated. The long, hot growing season and freedom from rains during harvest, the flat

land, and the absence of the cotton boll weevil (it does not thrive under arid conditions) are among the factors most favorable for production. Unlike most cotton-producing areas, California grows but a single variety, Acala, which was developed specifically for it; in fact, legislation prohibits planting any other kind in the San Joaquin Valley. It is a relatively long-staple variety, has good spinning qualities, and yields heavily—more than 1,050 pounds per acre in 1960. The bulk of the crop is machine picked because of the greater economy.

China. China is second among the nations of the world in cotton output. The principal areas of production, between 29° and 38° north latitude, are the fertile lower valleys of the Yangtze-Kiang and the Hwang-Ho. Cotton is usually planted as a second crop in the Yangtze Valley, whereas it is the main crop in some parts of North China. Six major cotton-growing districts are: (1) the Wei Valley of Shensi, (2) the central Hupei Basin, (3) the North China Plain, (4) the Yangtze Delta, (5) the Kiangsu Coast, and (6) the south-central Szechwan Basin.

Though climatic conditions favor cotton production, the fiber is of only medium to poor quality. Low quality over the years has resulted from inferior seed, inefficient methods, and the fact that in this country of 700 million people and miniscule farms the best land is given over to food crops; cotton invariably has been relegated to second-choice land. Some improvement in quality, however, has been made in recent years.

Traditionally China's cotton was used mainly at home—actually in the area where it was grown. Home spinning and weaving and the making of padded clothing still are important. The large population, the cold winters, and the general absence of fuel for heating necessitate the use of appreciable quantities of cotton for padding clothing.

Soviet Union. The Soviet Union has, since the turn of the century, become a major world source of cotton. Only the United States and China exceed her in output.

The cotton is grown both on irrigated and nonirrigated land, but the bulk is produced in the oasis country of Inner Asia—in areas that are hot and dry and possess annual rainfall totals of only 5 to 15 inches. The principal cotton oasis areas are Ashkhabad, Merv, Bukhara, and Samarkand, in the Tiflis district of Georgia, and in the Kura River Valley of Azerbaidzhan—between the Black Sea and the Caspian Sea on the west and the Mongolian and Sinkiang frontiers on the east.

Despite optimistic statements emanating from the Soviet Union regarding the progress in growing irrigated cotton, difficult and persistent problems are encountered: soil salinity, insufficient rotation with alfalfa, perennial labor troubles during harvest on collective farms. Moreover, the yields average only half to two thirds of those in Arizona and California. That the government is determined to approximate self-sufficiency in cotton, however, seems certain from the fact that fully 60 per cent of the newly irrigated land in southern Russia is being given over to long-staple cotton.

Some cotton is grown also, on the basis of natural rainfall, in the southern Ukraine, the Crimea, and the North Caucasus. Here the crop is being produced farther north than anywhere else on earth. However, both yield and quality suffer from the short growing season (less than 150 days).

India. India is regarded as the country where cotton has been cultivated longest. Commercial output, however, dates from the American Civil War, when the cotton famine in Manchester—resulting from the North's blockade of the cotton-growing South, whence came three fourths of the cotton Britain consumed—forced that nation in desperation to seek and develop new sources of supply and particularly to grow it within the Empire. Currently India ranks among the world leaders both in acreage and production, although she lost considerable cotton acreage to Pakistan as a result of partition. The government stimulates cotton growing by granting tax remittances on additional land brought under cultivation, by subsidizing supplies of improved strains, and by giving technical aid to farmers. However, with the population increasing at a rate of more than 8 million per annum and with countless numbers suffering from hunger, acreage restrictions may have to be imposed to use much of such land for food crops.

Though cotton is grown over a large part of India, the heart of production (on the fertile black *regur* soils) is the Deccan Plateau east of Bombay. In fact, Bombay state alone accounts for about half the total Indian crop. Farms and fields are small, and oxen provide the draft power for primitive implements. Thinning and picking are entirely by hand. Little fertilizer (either cow manure or commercial fertilizer) is used because of almost universal rural poverty. India suffers from the lowest per-acre yields in the world—about 79 pounds. The quality, too, is poor (65 to 70 per cent has a staple of ⅞ inch or less); and, although some improvement is being made in this respect, the quantity of long staple produced is negligible. Low yields and inferior quality result from adverse climatic conditions (the summer monsoon is fickle), the long time the land has been cultivated, the negligible use of soil enrichment, and the conservatism of the people. More than 90 per cent of India's cotton is rain-fed. When the crop is grown under irrigation, the yield jumps 100 per cent on the average.

India produces roughly 4 to 6 million bales per year, the bulk of which she converts into coarse yarns and fabrics to be used in making cheap clothing. She exports some half a million bales, Japan being the best customer. However, in some years so poor a crop is gleaned that imports are necessary. Also, to meet the quality requirements of her domestic textile industry, India annually imports a considerable amount of medium- and long-staple cottons.

Egypt. Egypt and long-staple cotton are synonymous in trade parlance. Yet one hundred years ago, Egypt produced little cotton. Grain was her mainstay as it had been for thousands of years. Today cotton is the chief export (80 to 90 per cent of total exports based on value), and it occupies a dominant role in the economy. Cotton is Egypt's major commercial link with the outside world.

Egypt's cottons (there are many varieties) have encountered little competition on the world market, since they are fine, strong, long-staple cottons, those in demand for the manufacture of yarns, threads, and fabrics in which fineness or strength, or both, are requisite qualities. Egypt, however, no longer holds a monopoly or even a near monopoly on such cottons; thus, in a recent year she accounted for 58 per cent of the Free World output of extra-long-staple cotton, Sudan 30 per cent, Peru 6 per cent, and the United States (California and Arizona) 5 per cent. In 1960 the supplies of extra-long-staple cotton exceeded world demand. Traditionally the exports have moved to the United Kingdom, France, Germany, India, Japan, Italy, and the United States. More recently, the Communist bloc has provided the chief markets.

Nine tenths of Egypt's cotton acreage is to be found on the rich soils of the Nile Delta, the remainder on the narrow sides of the Nile from Aswan to Cairo—a distance of 500 miles. The crop, which must be irrigated, is also grown **intensively**; 90 per cent of the landowners possess 5 acres or less, and 50 per cent till less than 1 acre.

Sudan. Though less impressive than Egypt in the production of long-staple cotton, Sudan nevertheless ranks among the eight top world producers; and, like Egypt, its entire economy is oriented around cotton. Sudan, which covers an area of nearly a million square miles— roughly the size of Western Europe—is a land of divisions and contrasts. Physically it ranges from desert and steppe in the north to tropical forest in the south. Stretching through the center is a wide belt bisected by the White and Blue Niles and comprising an outstanding cotton milieu. Most famous producing area is the Gezira, a rich, black, flat area between the White and Blue Niles south of Khartoum.

Sudan produces about 15 per cent of Africa's total cotton crop, which in 1959 exceeded 600,000 bales. Only high-grade long-staple cotton is grown under irrigation; and, by means of a carefully developed and rigidly enforced system involving every aspect of the industry, Sudan has been able to maintain the purity of this type. Virtually the entire crop is exported, the bulk going to the United Kingdom and India, the remainder to France, West Germany, Italy, and Czechoslovakia.

Brazil. Potentially, as far as the natural environment is concerned, Brazil is capable of competing for first place in world cotton output. In fact, at one time it was widely believed that southern Brazil might become the world's outstanding cotton-producing area. Moreover, cotton has been grown in Brazil even longer than in the United States. Until the early 1930s, Brazil's cotton was grown in the northeast—in the states of Bahia, Pernambuco, and Maranhão. Today, however, the bulk of the crop is produced in the southeast, in São Paulo. But although Brazil surpasses all other Southern Hemisphere nations, its output vacillates; during and for several years following World War II, it was the world's third largest exporter of cotton—ranking behind the United States and Mexico; in 1956-1957 it was sixth.

Currently the importance of cotton is influenced by the price of coffee, which usually is more profitable. However, when coffee prices drop or when coffee trees in considerable numbers are destroyed by abnormally severe freezes, cotton stages a comeback. It is influenced, too, by output and prices in the United States.

The crop is grown mainly in two areas: (1) inland in the hump (from the city of Natal); and (2) São Paulo state, which grows well over half the crop. As long as São Paulo leads both in coffee and cotton, cotton will move up and down as the world market price for these two commodities fluctuates. Additional factors that retard cotton expansion are (1) inadequate transport, (2) insufficient and inefficient labor, (3) poor cultural methods—only one farmer in four fertilizes his fields, (4) careless methods of picking, (5) scarcity of capital, (6) insect pests, and (7) occasional hazardous weather—exactly opposite of what

cotton needs. Yield per acre is very low—178 pounds on the average (about 100 pounds in the northeast, 340 in São Paulo). Paulista cotton is a short-staple variety that competes directly with cotton from the American Cotton Belt.

Mexico. Almost immediately after World War II, Mexico more than quadrupled cotton output and became one of the eight leading world producers. Significant, too, is the fact that Mexico is the second world exporter of cotton, a rank she is expected to retain into the foreseeable future. Annual cotton outshipments are valued at 200 to 300 million dollars. Cotton has become the country's leading export—doing what silver did between 1890 and 1910, petroleum from about 1915 to 1932, and industrial minerals (lead, zinc, and copper) from 1932 to 1946. Cotton exports increased by more than 100 per cent between 1950 and 1955. Most of the cotton goes to Japan, followed by West Germany, Belgium, the Netherlands, and the United Kingdom.

The bulk of the crop (95 per cent) is grown under irrigation and thus is restricted to about five important areas in the north and northwest. Here the climate (growing season, temperature, humidity), flat terrain, and alluvial soils (most of the cotton land is in river valleys, deltas, or old lake beds, where water is available but where the annual rainfall averages only 0 to 10 or 15 inches) are all favorable; actually the only important limiting factor to expansion is water.

The expansion of large irrigation projects and the drilling of wells provided the principal stimulus to expansion of cotton output. Leading states are Coahuila, Durango, Sinaloa, Baja California, and Sonora. In all, much of the cotton land is included in *ejidos*.

Mexican cotton is of the medium-staple American upland type and most is grown from United States seed—10 to 25 million pounds being imported annually. Mexican workers (many former **braceros**) have been trained in the handling of highly complex farm machinery and in using fertilizer and insecticides.

Pakistan. Pakistan ranks among the first eight world producers of cotton. In West Pakistan, where cotton is the leading crop, the principal cotton lands are in the Punjab and the lower Indus Valley lands (Bahawalpur and the Sind), which must be irrigated to sustain the crop. Cotton competes with wheat. American upland cotton (staple $^{15}/_{16}$ to $1^{1}/_{16}$ inches) prevails and is superior to the short-staple desi or Asiatic type characteristic of India. Much is grown on a sharecrop basis on farms 15 to 25 acres in size. Methods are backward. There is high insect and disease infestation, and considerable salting and waterlogging of the soil; and no commercial fertilizer is used. However, a rotation is followed, and some manure is put on the soil; yields per acre vary greatly even in the same district, but for the country as a whole are approximately twice those of India. Picking is performed by women and children, each harvesting 50 to 100 pounds per day.

Since Pakistan has little milling capacity, it can use only a small part of its total output and hence ranks among the leading raw-cotton exporters. Cotton production has declined steadily in recent years, the result of much loss of agricultural land through waterlogging and salinity and of the need to produce more food for a rapidly growing population.

Peru. Peru is included in the list not because of the extent of land in cotton or because the total output is large, but mainly because her cotton ranks with the world's best in quality and because cotton is the nation's principal agricultural export. The entire crop is grown in the irrigated coastal valleys, mostly north of Lima. Possibly the most important single area is in the far north near Piura. The crop is grown on large plantations, thriving as a result of rich soils heavily fertilized (200 pounds of guano per acre), high temperatures, much sunshine, and ample water when needed. There is, however, some trouble with insect pests; for, though these generally are scarce in desert areas, coastal Peru has a high humidity due to the presence of fogs that sweep in from the Pacific.

WORLD TRADE IN COTTON

The synthetic fibers have cut deeply into the supremacy of cotton, and yet cotton continues to be a major commodity in world trade. Roughly more than 15 million bales annually enter international markets. Although more than sixty nations produce cotton, five together account for three fourths of that getting into foreign trade—the United States, Mexico, Egypt, Brazil, and Pakistan. Leading importing nations are the United Kingdom, France, Italy, Japan, India, and West Germany.

The high-grade cottons of Egypt, Peru, and Sudan are in demand in countries with notable textile industries—even in some that grow cotton. Thus, both the United States and India are importers. The United States exports enormous quantities of upland cotton to European nations and to Japan and—in some years, when the price is low—small amounts to India. She imports long-staple cotton from Egypt and Peru. India exports short-staple cotton to East Asia and imports long-staple varieties to mix with her short-staple domestic cotton.

The United States—which in 1959-1960 produced 14.6 million bales, or 31 per cent of the world crop—exported 6 million bales, or roughly 40 per cent of its output. In that year cotton ranked as America's most valuable agricultural export. These exports went to more than fifty countries. The foreign Free World, which produced 16.9 million bales, exported 7.5 million bales; and the Communist countries, with an output of 15.1 million bales, exported 1.6 million. World cotton consumption in 1959-1960 amounted to about 47 million bales—a new record.

JUTE

Jute, cheapest of all the fibers, ranks second to cotton in quantity utilized. But it is a plebeian member of the plant-fiber family and hence does not move in the same circles as cotton and flax. It has many uses—burlaps, twilled sacking, and tarpaulin. Burlap is the most important; for bags made of it carry (or serve as covering for) potatoes, coffee, sugar, grain, cacao, castor beans, babassu kernels, feed, fertilizer, cotton, wool, and a host of other items. It is used also in upholstery for furniture and automobiles and as cloth backing for carpets and linoleum. In some of these fields it has no rivals. Such material is cheap and resistant to snagging. However, jute is weak and deteriorates rapidly upon exposure to moisture.

JUTE AND THE NATURAL ENVIRONMENT

Jute, a tropical crop, needs a hot, humid climate; in the area that accounts for 97 per cent of the world's production—India and East Pakistan—some 12 inches of rain fall each month of summer, and temperatures range from 70°F to 100°F. About 120 days are required for jute to mature. Alluvial soils (loams and sandy loams) serve well. Once the plant becomes established, it needs little attention, for its rapid growth soon chokes out weeds and grasses. It does well even when fields are inundated.

Although there are many other tropical deltas, only in South Asia is there the over-all favorable combination of humidity and heat, summer monsoon with consequent floods, and good soil drainage. However, the incomparable rank of the Ganges-Brahmaputra Delta of East Pakistan and India is not the result solely of the favorable natural environment. Equally important is the labor supply: with most of the work performed by hand, 1,000 persons are needed on each square mile for producing and marketing the crop. Labor is one commodity this region has in abundance, and it is cheap.

HANDLING OF THE CROP

Most of the world's jute is grown in the Ganges-Brahmaputra Delta (Fig. 24-5). Jute here is one of two major crops, the other being rice. Seldom on the small holdings are more than 2 or 3 acres in jute. Methods of production have changed little through the centuries. The fields are plowed in winter, and the seed is planted in April. By August the stalks stand 6 to 12 feet high and are ready to be harvested. This operation is done by hand, the stalks being cut several inches above the ground. The stalks are then tied into bundles and weighted down under water in a nearby pond to ret (rot). After ten to twenty-five days of retting, the fibers are free from the stalk, and workers standing waist-deep in the water beat them with wooden paddles; they then wash them and lay them on bamboo frames to dry and bleach. The individual farmer sells his crop to a middleman.

When the Indian subcontinent in 1947 was divided into two self-governing dominions, India and Pakistan, one of the knottiest problems created was that East Pakistan (Bengal) possessed virtually all the jute acreage and production but no spinning and weaving mills, whereas India, with almost no fiber, had all the mills. As a result, each strove to become self-sufficient in both the growing and manufacturing of jute. Both have made progress, though neither as yet has reached the goals set.

The only other countries that grow jute significantly are Communist China, Japan, and Brazil. In foreign trade in jute, Pakistan and India have no rivals. The United States is far and away the largest customer, annually importing jute valued at some 97 million dollars.

FLAX

The flax map (Fig. 24-5) can be misleading, for this crop is grown for *fiber* (linen) and for *seed* (linseed), and seldom does a single region grow it for both. Even the Soviet Union, the major exception, seldom grows the two in the same area. Actually flax as a fiber, despite its centuries-old service to man, has been slipping—giving way particularly to cotton. Especially has this been true in the United States, where, in colonial days, every farm grew its own flax and every household wove its own linen. Today virtually no flax is grown here.

Fiber flax is used for (1) fine linen and (2) thread, fire hose, and special-purpose cords, twines, and nets.

FLAX AND THE NATURAL ENVIRONMENT

Flax for fiber needs a moderate amount of precipitation well distributed over the

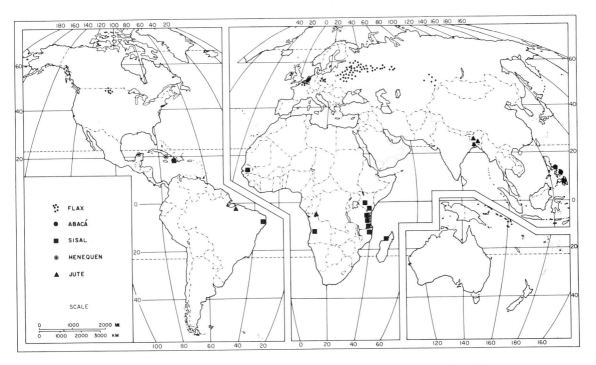

Fig. 24-5. World distribution of the vegetable fibers jute, flax, henequen, sisal, and abacá. Note that all save part of the flax are produced in the tropics or subtropics.

growing period, high humidity, and warm summer temperatures. Soils should be retentive of moisture, but at the same time drainage must be satisfactory; hence, sandy loams and clay loams are the principal flax soils. So difficult is the crop to grow that the better farmers sow it on the same ground not oftener than once in seven years. It does best when following sugar beets or grain (oats or wheat). About one hundred days are required to mature the crop.

LABOR REQUIREMENTS

Flax has exacting labor requirements. The crop first must be weeded when the plants are but a few inches high, and two or three subsequent weedings are necessary. Flax is generally pulled instead of cut (so as not to shorten the fibers). Formerly done by hand, this is now performed by machine. The flax is then tied into bundles, put in shocks to dry, and later retted in ponds, tanks, or streams, or, as in the Soviet Union, by dew. After retting, the stems are dried and **scutched**. All these

processes must be carried on by the farmer and his family before baling the crop for sale. Only lands with dense populations can afford to expend so much labor.

AREAS OF PRODUCTION

Virtually all the flax grown for fiber is confined to Europe: (1) the north-central plain of European Russia and (2) northwestern France, Belgium, and the Netherlands.

Most famous producer is Belgium, which possesses favorable soils and climate, parcelation of the land, the River Lys for retting, and an extremely dense population. Here flax has been grown for 1,200 years, the result of an edict by Charlemagne requiring every family in his realm to learn how to process and spin flax. Today the knowledge, handed down from father to son for centuries, has become an art.

Probably the linen of highest repute is "Irish linen," which in reality is made from Belgian, not Irish, fiber; Belgians grow and process the flax, the Irish spin and weave the fabric.

HEMP

The name hemp has been applied loosely to so many different hard and soft fibers that it and fiber have become synonymous. Thus people speak glibly of "Manila hemp" (abacá), "sisal hemp" (henequen), and "Indian hemp" (jute). However, in order to avoid confusion, the word hemp should be applied strictly to true hemp, one of the soft bast fibers. This long-stemmed annual, which attains heights of 3 to 18 feet, is grown mainly for fiber. It is one of man's oldest fibers, having been cultivated by the Chinese twenty-two centuries before Christ.

Hemp could be grown in virtually every middle-latitude country, but it is currently restricted to those in the Eastern Hemisphere—partly because of its narcotic and habit-forming properties, which have given rise to laws restricting production in many parts of the world; for example, in the United States, where it is known as marijuana, it can be produced, handled, and processed only under license. The plant requires a frostless season of at least 130 days, midsummer temperatures averaging between 60°F and 70°F, minimum annual precipitation of 27 inches (abundant moisture during germination of the seeds), and a fertile soil.

USES

Hemp is used mostly in making soft twines, cordage, and nets, and, in the European countries, for sacking, shoes, work garments, and clothing for peasants. Hemp has been losing out, on the one hand, to jute and cotton, which are produced at less cost; and, on the other, to such hard fibers as abacá and sisal, which have greater strength. Hemp does have special advantages, however, for use in making tarpaulins, sailcloth, and canvas.

AREAS OF PRODUCTION

Europe is the principal hemp-growing continent. Here the Soviet Union ranks highest, usually contributing half or more of the world crop. Most of the crop is grown south, southeast, and southwest of Moscow in an area

some 400 miles square. Italy ranks second and often is the principal exporter. The crop is centered north of Florence. Other producers are Yugoslavia, Romania, Hungary, Poland, and Turkey in Europe, and China and Japan in Asia.

KENAF

Kenaf is one of the lesser-known fiber plants in the Western Hemisphere but one that has grown in importance in recent years because of (1) its fast-growing qualities and (2) the Western Hemisphere's need, for security reasons, of a jute substitute. Kenaf has proved to be more productive per unit of land than any of the other fiber plants presented. In addition to gunny cloth, this fiber is used for ropes, cordage, fishing nets, floor matting, and rug backing.

Its original home is believed to be India. Like jute, kenaf grows 8 to 12 (on occasion 15) feet high, with stalks about ½ inch in diameter, and does so in about one hundred days. The plant resembles hollyhock. The soft fiber is in the stalk and is extracted either mechanically or by retting.

Kenaf is generally grown as an annual, occasionally as a perennial. Though adapted to wide variations in climate and soils, it is sensitive to frost and hence does best in the tropics. Nor can the crop stand strong winds or extremely heavy rain. Generally, 20 to 25 inches of rain well distributed over a period of four or five successive months gives good results. The wet period should be followed by a dry one. The number of hours of daylight (12½ hours or longer) is important for fiber production. A well-drained sandy-loam soil, neutral in reaction and containing considerable humus, is desirable.

In addition to its Indian habitat, kenaf is grown in other parts of Southeast Asia (Java), in the Middle East (Egypt and Iran), and in Africa (Senegal, Nigeria, and Natal in South Africa). Some is cultivated in the Soviet Union. Cuba, which normally uses 45 million bags (mostly jute) a year for its raw sugar, rice, and coffee, is now experimenting with kenaf.

HENEQUEN AND SISAL

Henequen and sisal ordinarily are considered together because they are close members of the same family (*Agave*), are to a certain extent used in the same manner for the same things, are grown (occasionally) in the same countries, and are both called "sisal" in trade parlance. Both are native of the Yucatan Peninsula and were being used by the Aztecs and Mayas when Cortez invaded Mexico in the sixteenth century. However, whereas sisal has traveled widely and is now grown in Africa and Asia, henequen has for the most part remained at home.

HENEQUEN

The greater part of the world's commercial crop of henequen is grown in northern Yucatan, south and southeast of Progreso and Mérida (Fig. 24-5). Production is centered here mainly because the climate and soil are extremely well suited to the crop. The climate is hot, dry, quite clear, and frost-free. Although the area receives annually more than 30 inches of rainfall, mostly from May to October, the effectiveness of precipitation is slight because of the excessive evaporation and because the water sinks almost immediately into the porous soils. The soil everywhere is stony.

Once planted, henequen needs little cultivation. The plant is long-lived, being replanted only at fifteen- to twenty-year intervals and bearing two crops of leaves annually. When the plant is six or seven years of age, the tier of lower leaves is cut after the inch-long terminal spine has been freed from the sword-like leaf, which reaches a length of 30 to 60 inches. Two tiers are harvested at one time, each tier containing fifteen to eighteen leaves. A worker cuts three or four thousand leaves daily and ties them into bundles, each of which contains forty to fifty leaves, for delivery to a mill. From 700 to 1,200 pounds of fiber are obtained from a planted acre.

Henequen cannot be produced profitably on a small scale, a minimum of 300 bearing acres being required to supply sufficient leaves to keep a fiber-cleaning machine operating.

The world normally produces about 270 million pounds of henequen, nine tenths of which is contributed by Mexico and the rest largely by Cuba. In Cuba henequen is relegated to rocky soils unfit for growing sugar cane. The United States is the largest importer, taking more than half the world total and using the fibers as binding and baler twines. Henequen is well suited for this purpose because it is (1) sufficiently strong to be tied by machine; (2) rot resistant; and (3) practically immune to insects, since the twine is treated with an oil that, in combination with the fiber, protects it to a great extent from destruction by insects.

SISAL

Sisal is regarded as the most important of the hard fibers and is the world's principal cordage fiber. From Mexico it was carried to Florida; then to Africa and Asia; and finally back to the Western Hemisphere, where it is now grown in Brazil and Haiti. Tanganyika leads in output, with one third of the world total (Fig. 24-5). Brazil, where the crop is heavily subsidized, ranks second, followed by Kenya, Angola, Haiti, Mozambique, and Indonesia. The largest importers are the United States, Canada, Japan, and the industrial countries of Europe. The United States uses as much sisal in car upholstery as for twine.

The sisal plant closely resembles the henequen plant. The physical conditions for sisal are almost a replica of those for henequen—the primary one being a tropical climate (there are no sisal plantations outside the tropics). However, though sisal does not stand drought so well as henequen, it endures excessive moisture better, growing in well-drained soils in Java with an annual rainfall of more than 100 inches. Sisal does well on a great variety of soils, but it must have good drainage.

ABACÁ

This fiber, often called Manila hemp, has long been the preferred one for rope for marine and industrial use. It combines strength, durability, and important resistance to salt water. However, in addition to uses in the maritime industry for mooring and towing, it also serves for cargo nets, cargo handling, slings, halyards, and lifeboat falls.

Abacá is a relative of the banana and is grown in the same manner. The fiber occurs in the outer portion of each successive leaf stem. Propagation is similar to that of the banana plant—rhizomes and suckers being planted in fairly deep holes. When the blossom appears, one and a half to two years after planting, the stem consists of twelve to thirty stalks in various stages of development, some ready for cutting. Two to four are harvested simultaneously, and subsequent cuttings are made every four to six months for ten to fifteen years.

The plant grows best where the annual rainfall exceeds 100 inches and is well distributed throughout the year; the humidity, too, should be high—78 to 88 per cent. In addition, abacá must have a tropical climate, an average temperature of 72°F to 80°F being essential. Though it thrives on a variety of soils, they should be deep, fertile, and well drained.

For decades the entire crop was supplied by the Philippines: it was an export crop— nine tenths moving into foreign markets, nearly a third to the United States. The crop has long been grown in thousands of small, primitively cultivated fields in the foothill area of southern Luzon, the eastern Visayan Islands (Leyte and Samar), in northern Mindanao (Fig. 24-5), and on many large and efficiently operated plantations in and around Davao in Mindanao.

In the past, many attempts were made to grow abacá in countries other than the Philippines, but most were unsuccessful. It was grown experimentally in Central America prior to the war and was produced in considerable quantity during hostilities, but at higher cost than in the Philippines.

The abacá industry has fallen on hard times, the result of (1) a mosaic disease that struck the southern section of Mindanao; (2) the evacuation of the Japanese, who had acquired 70 per cent of the plantations (on which they employed very scientific methods, which resulted in the highest-yielding, best-quality fiber) and had a monopoly on the industry;

and (3) rising competition of the synthetic, nylon, which, though far more expensive, is stronger, more elastic, lighter in weight, and longer wearing. However, unmanufactured abacá still ranks third among Philippine exports, being surpassed in value only by sugar and logs and lumber.

ANIMAL FIBERS

WOOL

Although wool in the form of **felt** (probably man's longest-used fiber) antedates all the vegetable fibers presented, it today ranks behind both cotton and rayon and is even feeling competition from the newer chemical fibers such as Acrilan, Dacron, and Orlon.

Wool's most desirable qualities are its warmth, durability, low heat conductivity, resilience, wrinkle resistance, water repellence, and special affinity for color.

Some wool is produced in nearly every country in the world, even in the tropics; but the bulk of the clothing wool entering international trade comes from five Southern Hemisphere lands: Australia (Fig. 24-6), New Zealand, Argentina, South Africa, and Uruguay. Together these five nations account for about 60 per cent of the total world output, 75 per cent of the apparel wool, and 85 per cent of the wool exports. The United States, though ranking fourth or fifth in wool output, is a deficit producer and the world's second leading importer.

THE REARING OF WOOL SHEEP

The sheep population of the world is put at about 750 million head, but only about half of these yield useful fleeces. There is considerable difference between wool and mutton sheep. Wool sheep are small in size, whereas mutton sheep are of large frame and yield large, fast-growing lambs. Mutton sheep generally produce wool of medium fineness, a coarser wool than true wool breeds. Wool sheep for the most part are to be found in the Southern Hemisphere, particularly in semiarid to arid lands. They are well suited to new and sparsely populated lands. Sheep pro-

Fig. 24-6. Merino ram, Australia; magnificent example of the type of sheep that has made that continent the world's leader in wool. Australia produces about half the wool entering international trade and about two thirds of the fine merino wool. (Courtesy of Australian News and Information Bureau.)

ducing lower-grade wool and raised by Indians are to be seen in the Andes of Bolivia, Ecuador, and Peru (Fig. 24-7).

The Australian wool crop, world's greatest, accounting for 1,600 million pounds for the 1960-1961 season out of a world total of 5,625 million pounds, grease basis,[4] fluctuates up to

[4] As the wool comes from the farm or the range it is "grease" wool—brown, matted, dirty (grass, burrs, dung), with much fatty or oily matter excreted from the glands of the sheep. In weight this foreign matter may run to as much as 40 to 70 per cent. It is from this grease that lanolin, a fat used for dressing leather and making cosmetics and soaps, is extracted. The wool must be cleaned and, before spinning, must go through a number of processes—scouring, carding, combing, gilling (removal of virtually all the grease and foreign matter)—all laborious and costly. Compare this with synthetics, which arrive at a mill exactly uniform, clean, ready for shipping.

5 per cent annually, depending largely upon rainfall conditions.

CLASSIFICATION OF WOOL

Wool varies widely in fineness and length of staple. There are two broad classifications: (1) *apparel wools* and (2) *carpet wools*. Standardization is far more complicated than might appear here; thus, the British Wool Control Board during World War II recognized more than 5,000 separate wool types—including 1,500 for Australia, 950 for New Zealand, and 350 for South Africa. Fibers vary as a result of breed, climate, type of pasture or **browse**, and management practices.

On a world basis, wool is divided—on the basis of fineness of the wool and the kind of sheep supplying the wool—into three broad types: *merino, crossbred,* and *native* or *carpet.*

Merino. The finest of all wools comes from the merino—a sheep native to Spain but today well adapted to the arid lands of Australia, South Africa, Argentina (Patagonia), and the United States. This breed, which is an industrious feeder and requires little water, shears a heavy fleece (40,000 to 48,000 fibers per square inch of skin) of high-quality wool, which commands a premium price. Except in the United States, the merino is reared for its wool. Merino production presently accounts for about 40 per cent of the total world wool output and is used almost exclusively for apparel.

Crossbred. This type of wool is derived from the sheep of English breeding, sheep that do best in areas of comparatively heavy rainfall —e.g., in New Zealand, Argentina (Eastern Pampa), and Uruguay. The sheep are reared for mutton and lamb as well as wool. The fiber is generally intermediate in fineness between the finer merino and the coarser unimproved wool (but Uruguayan wool is noted for its high quality and freedom from burrs and seeds that stick to the fleece).

Native or Carpet Wool. This class of wool is derived from native or unimproved breeds of sheep—that is, animals that have not been

Fig. 24-7. *Sheep in temporary corral made of tree trimmings, Peruvian Sierra. Much of the land here is far more suitable for grazing than for farming. Sheep, llamas, and alpacas all do well in the mountain cold, though the last two, native to the habitat, are far better adapted to the thin air of the higher elevations than are the introduced sheep. (Courtesy of A. Guillen M. and Allan Holmberg.)*

upbred with English or merino blood. Such sheep are to be found in extremely arid or mountainous lands, where the vegetation is so sparse as to be responsible for nomadism. Typical of such animals are the Barbary sheep living on the coarse pastures of semiarid Libya —pastures that are poor, dried and burned by the sun and wind, and practically devoid of water.

Fleece weights here are light, and the wool —coarse, harsh, wiry, and strong—is poor for apparel. Skins, meat, or milk may outweigh wool in importance. Such sheep lands are the Soviet Union (also a large producer of me-rino), interior China, East India, the Middle East, the Balkans, and North Africa.

WORLD TRADE IN WOOL

Wool is an important commodity in the trade of most middle-latitude countries. In the five major producing countries, wool plays a dominant role; a decline in wool consumption and prices can harm the entire economy of such nations. Thus, in Australia and Uruguay, wool provides two fifths of the total foreign-exchange earnings; in New Zealand, one third; and in Argentina and South Africa, one tenth each. Together these five supply more than

Fig. 24-8. Closeup of Angora goats, the animals that supply man with the long, lustrous, silky, white mohair, prized fiber for upholstery fabrics. (Courtesy of John Jeter.)

80 per cent of the wool entering world trade. Australia exports about 95 per cent of its total annual wool output.

Seven countries (the United Kingdom, the United States, France, West Germany, Italy, Belgium, and Japan) import in excess of 90 per cent of all wool entering foreign trade. The United Kingdom, though producing some wool itself, normally is the largest importer. The United States, generally ranking second in imports and first in consumption, purchases on the world market all of its carpet wool and from 40 to 50 per cent of its apparel wool. It does, however, produce wool on some 285,000 farms and ranches, about 20 per cent of the national output coming from Texas. At times

Japan becomes Australia's largest buyer, though Communist China has been moving up rapidly as a major market.

MOHAIR

Mohair, consisting of the long, lustrous fibers of the Angora goat, possesses characteristics of both hair and wool (Fig. 24-8). It averages about 4 inches in length, though it does on occasion grow longer; it is smooth and fine, and has considerable tensile strength, low elasticity, and no felting property. It is the basic raw material for many types of fabrics and is used for the upholstery in automobiles, trains, buses, airplanes, and home furniture.

Native of Asia Minor (Angora or Ankara Plateau, Turkey), the Angora goat is now important in South Africa and the United States, particularly the Edwards Plateau of Texas, which currently accounts for about 45 per cent of the world output; Turkey is second, with about 40 per cent, and South Africa third, with 10 per cent. The United Kingdom, the world's leading importer, takes half or more of all mohair exports, followed by Italy, France, and Japan.

SILK

Silk is a luxury item and hence is unable to compete in volume or price with cotton and wool. In the past several years it has been under pressure because of its high price in relation to cotton and the man-made fibers—particularly nylon, which in the United States has usurped 90 per cent of the market formerly enjoyed by silk for women's hosiery and lingerie.

SILK AND PHYSICAL CONDITIONS

Silk is the fine, soft filament extruded by the silkworm in forming its cocoon. It eats the leaves of the white mulberry, which thrives under a warm humid climate, particularly the Humid Subtropical, where leaves can grow over a long period. The tree occupies the less attractive land (rice tends to claim the best) —the paddy walls, sandy beach ridges, and riverbanks. Broods of worms are reared—in spring, summer, and autumn. The worms are fed on trays within the homes; fresh leaves in quantity must be always available, and the trays must be kept clean. Much labor is needed.

MAJOR SILK PRODUCERS

Japan, China, and Korea are the only major producers, followed by the Soviet Union, Turkey, and Italy. Japan dominates (80 per cent of the world output). Prior to World War II, silk contributed as much as 35 per cent of Japan's total exports based on value; today the figure stands at about 3 per cent. Notwith-

standing, some 800,000 Japanese farm families produce silk, relying upon it for a substantial part of their income—in some villages, as much as 70 per cent. Japan's prestige resulted originally from government stimulation; everything possible was done to improve and standardize quality and spur greater United States demand. Thus, Japan is reported to be a third of a century ahead of Communist China in techniques.

SYNTHETIC FIBERS

Man-made fibers well exemplify the extraordinary consequences of man's curiosity, scientific ingenuity, and determination to reshape substances. Man at first sought only to duplicate or replace the natural fibers; but with the passage of time and with the phenomenal growth of industrial chemistry, he shifted his emphasis and now makes fibers with specific characteristics to meet specific needs. He converts solids to liquids and back to solids. He uses as raw materials coal, water, air, cotton, wood, corn, corncobs, petroleum, and natural gas, to mention but a few. In every instance a liquid is changed into a fiber.

Strength, dyeability, easy washability, resistance to shrinkage, and minimum wrinkling are major characteristics of the newer synthetic fibers. Additional ones are uniformity, durability, and reasonable price.

COMPETITION BETWEEN NATURAL AND MAN-MADE FIBERS

Currently a real battle goes on between these two groups of fibers, with each fighting for as much of the market as possible. Representatives of the cotton, wool, and silk industries declare that synthetics never can replace their respective fibers, but as an outstanding chemist (not employed in industry) says, these people are completely unfamiliar with the potentialities of chemical research. Just as the automobile replaced the wagon, synthetic fibers will replace natural fibers.

Synthetics find many uses—for fabrics, clothing (including hosiery), rope and twine, draperies, rugs, and carpets. Moreover, the prices of synthetic fibers tend to decline with increased markets and greater efficiency in fabrication. The prices of cotton, wool, and silk gyrate considerably.

What promises to occur ultimately is a *textile* industry—not a cotton, a wool, a silk, or a synthetic one, but one that will draw on the entire field of fibers in the same way the steel-maker uses molten iron with the ferroalloy metals to produce precisely what is wanted.

TWO EXAMPLES OF MAN-MADE FIBERS

No hard-and-fast rules restrict the use of terminology in this industry, but the word "rayon" is best employed for fibers of cellulosic origin (viscose, cuprammonium, and cellulose acetate), and the term "synthetic fibers" for the true synthetics—nylon, Orlon, Dacron, etc. All of them, however, may accurately be called "artificial fibers" or "man-made fibers."

RAYON

Rayon and acetate fibers, the "bread and butter items" among the chemical fibers, currently account for about 90 per cent of all man-made-fiber output. Although first produced commercially around 1900, rayon achieved little importance until about 1925. It is made by chemically treating wood or cotton cellulose to produce a soluble solution capable of being made into a filament suitable for spinning into yarn.

Rayon is produced in thirty-nine nations, with four—the United States, West Germany, the United Kingdom, and Japan—accounting for 60 per cent of the world output. The fiber is particularly outstanding (far more so than either cotton or wool) in Western Europe—England, West Germany, Italy, the Netherlands, Belgium, France, and Spain. In total volume of rayon and other synthetic fibers, Western European production is about one third above that of the United States.

In Japan, which produces 13 to 15 per cent of the world's rayon, the fiber is a genuine threat to cotton. In 1956 Japan was the biggest rayon staple-fiber producer in the world. Japan produces the bulk of the raw materials, though about 20 per cent of the wood pulp is imported. Though Japanese raw-materials costs are relatively high, labor costs are low, and the government does much to favor the industry.

NYLON

The discovery of nylon, patented in 1938, represented the first financially successful major venture in synthetic fibers. Yet DuPont had spent 27 million dollars over a thirteen-year span before getting into commercial production. Because of the textile properties of this "new silk" made on a chemical base, it was immediately recognized as an ideal fiber for hosiery production. In the first year of manufacture, American women purchased 64 million pairs of nylon stockings.

When nylon hosiery yarn was introduced, it sold for $4.27 a pound; silk was selling for $2.79. To compete, nylon had to—and did—offer something that silk did not possess: longer wear per unit of sheerness. Demand outdistanced supply. Before the first plant at Seaford, Delaware, was a year old, a second yarn plant was begun. No other chemical product had ever leaped to fame so fast.

Nylon, in addition to its use in hosiery (the two are today virtually synonymous), has made a place for itself in the expanding field of automobile tires. Safety and long wear (not low cost) are the advantages. Nylon has gained prominence in still another field—marine cordage, where it competes with Manila hemp.

WORLD OUTLOOK

There is genuine competition among the vegetable, the animal, and the man-made fibers. There is also competition among the fibers within each of the three groups. Although each group is doing reasonably well, in each case one or more fibers is experiencing difficulty, even slipping; and all in the vegetable and animal categories are losing markets to the synthetics. Cotton is still the world's most important single fiber. If it is to hold its share of the market, however, it must lower prices to improve its competitive position. The synthetic industry offers sharp rivalry in research, efficiency, cost cutting, and market promotion.

As far as cotton is concerned—particularly in the United States—mechanization in production is being counted on to meet the inroads of the synthetic fibers. Lower costs of production are currently enabling the nation's cotton farmers to compete with those in foreign lands and simultaneously even with producers of synthetics. This is being accomplished in large measure by a shift in production into the Western areas, where mechanization means lower production costs. Carmical states that the southern cotton industry has emerged on a sounder basis than ever from the technological revolution that began more than twenty-five years ago.[5]

The outlook for some of the other natural fibers is a rather cloudy one. For example, in their competition with test tubes, the silkworm and the sheep appear to be fighting losing battles. The position of the natural-fiber industry, however, can be invigorated through increased blending of natural with synthetic fibers; the industry can benefit, too, from the vast amount of scientific experimentation so basic to the synthetic-fiber realm. Harmonious coexistence among all the fibers should culminate in not several textile industries but *a* textile industry, allowing adequate rewards for the three fiber worlds.

[5] J. H. Carmical, "Shift in Cotton about Complete," *New York Times*, October 23, 1960.

SELECTED REFERENCES

Airov, Joseph. *The Location of the Synthetic-Fiber Industry.* New York, John Wiley and Sons, Inc., 1959.

Anderson, R. N., and Elwyn F. Chase, Jr. "From Belgian Flax to Irish Linen," *Foreign Agriculture,* 16:127-133, July–August 1952.

Aull, G. H. "Changes in the Land of Cotton," in *Land; Yearbook of Agriculture, 1958.* Washington, D. C., U.S. Department of Agriculture, 1958, pp. 136-141.

Hornbeck, Bernice M. *Communist China's Cotton Textile Exports—Their Growth and Their Effect on World Markets.* Washington, D. C., Foreign Agricultural Service, U.S. Department of Agriculture, April 1959. FAS-M-52.

Prunty, M. "Land Occupance in the Southeast; Landmarks and Forecast," *Geographical Review,* 42:439-461 (specifically pp. 443-448), July 1952.

———————. "Recent Quantitative Changes in the Cotton Regions of the Southeastern States," *Economic Geography,* 27:189-208, July 1951.

Ramanhath, S. "The Cotton Industry of India," *World Crops,* 6:442-446, November 1954.

Welton, Richard S. *The World Carpet Wool Situation.* Washington, D. C., Foreign Agricultural Service, U.S. Department of Agriculture, December 1959. FAS-M-72.

CHAPTER TWENTY-FIVE::

The life and advancement of a nation are dependent on its supply of fats and oils to a degree little realized by the average person. For not only are these products essential items in the diets of men and animals, but also they are of great and ever growing importance to many industries. With every increase in population and with every discovery of new uses for fats and oils, the demand for them—in edible, industrial, and medicinal commodities —is greatly augmented.

The quantity of fats and oils procurable from animal and marine sources is, by and large, limited. Contrariwise, the production of oils of vegetable origin, through improvement of plant breeding and of agricultural methods, is clearly capable of great expansion, particularly in tropical lands but even in mid-latitude and subtropical areas. Vegetable oils, being a direct product, therefore promise to outrank by far the animal fats, which are the product

THE WORLD'S

of a two-stage agriculture. At present, vegetable sources account for three fifths of world production of oils and fats (Table 25-1).

Many plant families yield fatty oils, which are stored up generously in seeds and less abundantly in fruits, stems, tubers, and other vegetable organs. Vegetable fatty oils are similar to animal fats chemically, consisting of glycerin combined with fatty acid. At ordinary temperatures, oils are liquid and generally contain oleic acid, while fats are solid and contain stearic or palmitic acid. But because of differences in temperature, an oil in one country may be a fat in another. For example, in the tropics coconut oil is liquid; but when it is transported to the temperate zones and beyond, it solidifies into a fat unless it is maintained at a temperature above 74°F.

In recent years, the demand for edible oils has increased so sharply that science has rendered even formerly nonedible oils available as human food—primarily through the process of hardening or hydrogenation (adding hydrogen). Since the melting point rises with the hydrogen content, just a slight difference in hydrogen may determine whether a substance is an oil or fat at a given temperature.

Today, vegetable fats and oils from the far corners of the earth are competitive not only among themselves but also with animal fats, particularly butter and lard. Indeed, fats and oils represent possibly the choicest example of commodity competition; the ease of substitution keeps their prices low and comparatively steady. Relative price changes, which promptly influence the use of a given fat, are consequent upon a great number of factors: (1) inclement weather affecting the crop in a particular locality, (2) adaptation of crops to new areas, (3) development of new uses for certain oils, and (4) governmental economic controls and even direct prohibitions.

VEGETABLE OILS

TABLE 25-1

ESTIMATED WORLD PRODUCTION AND
EXPORTS OF FATS, OILS, AND
OILSEEDS, 1960
(in thousand short tons)

Commodity	Production	Exports
Edible vegetable oils		
Cottonseed	2,280	355
Peanut	2,315	740
Soybean	3,780	1,625
Sunflower	1,200	65
Rapeseed	1,235	100
Sesame	670	70
Olive	1,340	65
Total	12,820	3,020
Palm oils		
Coconut	2,125	1,175
Palm kernel	420	415
Palm	1,340	580
Babassu kernel	60	3
Total	3,945	2,173
Industrial oils		
Linseed	1,130	525
Castor	255	150
Oiticica	10	7
Tung	135	70
Perilla	5	*
Total	1,535	752
Animal fats		
Butter (fat content)	4,200	475
Lard	4,300	430
Tallow and grease	3,575	1,225
Total	12,075	2,130
Marine oils		
Whale	430	430
Sperm whale	115	115
Fish (including liver)	490	250
Total	1,035	795
Estimated world total	31,410	8,870

* Less than 500 tons.

SOURCE: Based on *World Exports and Production of Fats and Oils Set Record in 1960* (Washington, D. C., U.S. Department of Agriculture, Foreign Agricultural Service, October 24, 1960). Foreign Agriculture Circular, FFO 28-60, pp. 2-3.

Interregional competition is particularly notable between the animal industries of middle-latitude countries and the vegetable-oil industries of the tropics.

Since a high per capita fat consumption is one mark of a high living standard (fats are generally more expensive than either sugar or starches), it is not surprising that the advanced industrialized countries use a great percentage of fats and oils in the form of food. Many of the scientific innovations, agricultural experiments and expansion, and marketing changes in the vegetable-oils realm were stimulated or accelerated by World War II, when the industrialized nations were cut off from many of their sources of fats and oils.

CLASSES OF VEGETABLE OILS

Vegetable oils are generally classified as (1) *drying* (e.g., linseed oil), which rapidly absorb oxygen and are particularly valuable in the paint and varnish industries; (2) *semidrying* (e.g., cottonseed oil), which absorb oxygen more slowly and in limited amounts and can be utilized for food and/or nonfood products; (3) *nondrying* (e.g., olive oil), which are liquid at ordinary temperatures, are edible, and can also be used for lubricants, soaps, and other nonfood purposes; and (4) *fats* (e.g., coconut oil), which remain solid or semisolid at ordinary temperatures and are suitable for both edible and industrial uses.

For the purposes of this chapter, vegetable oils are treated according to genetic groupings: (1) tree crops, (2) field crops, and (3) by-products.

VEGETABLE OILS FROM TREE CROPS

COCONUT OIL

Coconut oil is one of the foremost vegetable oils entering international trade. The oil is procured from the dried meat of the coconut

(copra), half of which is fat and yields 65 to 70 per cent oil (80 per cent or more can be obtained when fresh meat is utilized in the presses). The natives along tropical coasts have for centuries boiled the crushed meats with water, skimming off the oil accumulated on the surface.

Since the oil is solid at ordinary temperatures, it is admirably suited for food products, particularly margarine; and it is practically indispensable for making candy bars and other confectionery. The oil, or its derivative, also is extensively utilized for toilet preparations, particularly soap (although, in industrialized countries, the manufacture of synthetic detergents based on mineral oils has sharply curtailed demand for this purpose), and for plastics, lubricating-oil additives, and a multitude of other industrial products. In the United States more than half of the imports are normally used in industrial commodities, while in Europe (particularly in the United Kingdom and West Germany) the bulk of the imports is utilized for margarine and other food items.

The coconut palm is possibly the most useful tree extant, filling more than a thousand specific needs and being literally indispensable in the tropical lands; it provides an easy life for natives of many small islands, which might be uninhabitable without it. The palm is limited almost exclusively to the wetter portions of the tropics, for it requires an annual rainfall of 60 to 100 inches well distributed throughout the year, abundant sunshine, and an annual average temperature of at least 78°F. Well-drained alluvial coastal plains, with light sandy soil, are not only physically but also economically ideal; for they offer the benefits of easy transport.

Mature, well-cared-for trees blossom about ten times during the year, producing a total of fifty to one hundred nuts. An estimated one thousand nuts will yield more than 500 pounds of copra (Fig. 25-1), from which 25 gallons of oil normally can be obtained. Two pressings are usually required to extract the oil, but some machines can remove it in one operation. The residue—coco-cake—retains 6 to 10 per cent of the oil and provides excellent stock feed. Whereas formerly the tropical producers shipped out only the copra, in recent years local mills have increasingly expressed the oil for export.

Cultivation is largely in the hands of natives, whose rather haphazard methods result in poorer quality and lesser yields than plantation operations (which are, for the most part, financed by American and European capital). Therefore, small-holding products often bring lower prices and are best used for inedible purposes.

Of the slightly more than half of total oil production normally entering world trade today, the bulk emanates from the Philippines, Indonesia, Ceylon, Malaysia, and Oceania. An important factor in making these heavily populated insular and peninsular lands the chief centers of production has been their supply of cheap and efficient labor. Since 1955, the Philippine Republic, the world's largest exporter of coconut products, has accounted for more than half of these commodities entering world trade. Coconut, occupying about 15 per cent of the total crop area, ranks third after rice and corn and normally provides more than a third of the nation's export earnings from all sources. Since the palm is ill adapted to long dry seasons or destructive winds, and cadang-cadang disease is a menace in some areas, plantings center chiefly on southern Luzon and the islands to the south.

Second to the Philippines as a commercial producer, and possibly first in total output, is Indonesia. The Celebes, Borneo, and the eastern islands, where plantation methods have been introduced, are the foci of production; and exports are destined primarily for Western Europe.

The coconut has long been of such importance to Ceylon that in certain areas a man's wealth is estimated by the number of coconut palms he possesses. Exports, chiefly from the western plains, go to India, Pakistan, and Western European nations.

Fourth-ranking exporter is Malaysia, where the two coasts of the Malay Peninsula provide the bulk of the nation's coconut oil, which moves primarily to India and Western Europe. As in Indonesia, plantation methods have been eminently successful, and under this system the palm has a very high yield of oil per acre —an average of 630 pounds. Southwest Pacific islands and Mozambique, in its lower Zambezi Valley, are the only other commercial producers of note.

In the four chief supply areas, the total annual exports regularly exceed 200 million dollars. When disease and/or adverse weather conditions cause a world shortage of coconut oil (as occurred in 1959), prices jump drastically.

PALM OIL AND PALM-KERNEL OIL

The oil palm yields so much oil per acre (up to 2 tons) that it is regarded as the most efficient producer of vegetable oils in the world.

It supplies two important commercial oils: (1) *palm oil*, a soft oil obtained from the pulp of the palm nut and utilized mainly for soap, tinning of sheet steel, metal working, and edible products, and (2) *palm-kernel oil*, a more valuable product (extensively utilized as a substitute for coconut oil), obtained from the kernel of the nut and used chiefly for soap, margarine, shortening, and detergents.

Indigenous to West Africa, the sun-loving oil palm requires climatic conditions similar to those of the coconut palm, but the extent and strength of its root system and its water-storing capacity allow it to withstand short periods of drought; however, it can also tolerate as much as 250 inches of rainfall. For best growth, the soil should be well drained; its fertility seems not of the greatest consequence, since some of the major palm belts flourish in heavily leached soils. The average palm starts to bear at 4 to 8 years of age, achieves full production between 30 and 50 years of age, and survives for more than a hundred years.

West Africa is by far the foremost producer of oil-palm products, its oil-palm belt stretching 200 to 300 miles inland from the coast from Gambia to Angola. Nigeria alone produces almost one third of the world's palm-oil products and more than two thirds of the palm kernels. Together these two commodities form the nation's most valuable exports. An increasing amount of these products is being retained for domestic use for both industrial and edible purposes. Although most growers in this area depend on nature for the success of their palm enterprises, some are benefiting from scientific cultural practices introduced through governmental extension work. Plantations are slowly gaining hold, for they can produce an average of 50 per cent more oil per tree than the wild palmeries.

The Congo is the second largest producer and generally the leading exporter of palm oil, having numerous big plantations where trees start to bear at a very early age.

In West Africa generally, land tenure presents a major hindrance to permanent land and crop improvements: rights of oil-palm fruit on a given plot are often vested in as

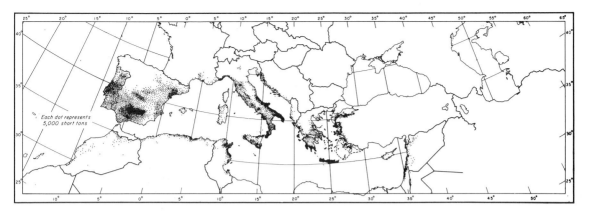

Fig. 25-2. The world's major olive-producing lands. Together the countries shown here contribute more than nine tenths of the world's olive crop and nearly all its olive oil. Not only is the olive one of the most, if not the most, typical of all Mediterranean crops, but it has for centuries supplied the people with oil, unobtainable to any extent from animal sources. (Courtesy of U.S. Department of Agriculture.)

many different families as there are trees. However, several factors—(1) improved transportation facilities, (2) the planting of government-sponsored palm estates, (3) availability of vast tracts of virgin land, (4) increasing population and consequent greater demand for cash crops, and (5) adoption of mechanical equipment—indicate that West Africa's oil-palm industry may well have its most profitable period in the near future.

Introduced into Indonesia and Malaysia as an ornamental plant, the oil palm has provided an important plantation industry in these areas, particularly Sumatra, in recent years. In Malaysia the industry was given pronounced impetus by increased demand for fats and oils following World War I and by the decline of rubber prices in 1921. Domestic consumption in these Southeast Asian areas is small.

The oil palms of Brazil have supplied increasing palm-oil exports to the United States in the past three decades, but tropical Africa and Southeast Asia (whose exports are about half those of Africa) continue to contribute about 95 per cent of total world shipments, which move primarily to Western Europe and the United States.

OLIVE OIL

Olive oil, procured from the fruit of the olive, has long been regarded as the finest of edible oils; it needs little or no refining and turns rancid only when exposed to air. Different-quality oils can be obtained by several, successively firmer, mechanical pressings: a gentle first pressing yields oil of the highest quality, which is used chiefly as a table and salad oil; the second pressing gives oils for cooking, sardine canning, and medicines; and a third, and sometimes fourth, pressing results in an inferior, greenish-tinged grade utilized mainly for soap and other nonedible purposes. The final residue, still holding 8 to 20 per cent oil, undergoes solvent extraction and yields the poorest grades, which are utilized for nonedible purposes.

Though it begins to bear significantly only after about ten years, the evergreen olive tree is extremely long-lived (in the Mediterranean Basin, trees 600 years old still yield some fruit). Almost the entire world production emanates from Mediterranean Subtropical lands—more than 95 per cent from the regions fringing the Mediterranean Sea (Fig. 25-2); for the drought-resisting tree thrives where summers are hot and dry (Fig. 25-3), winters mild and humid, and the mean annual temperature is not less than 57°F. Deep limestone soils produce high-quality fruits, and the trees are often planted on slopes to assure adequate drainage. A good crop one year is commonly followed by a medium to poor one the next, though inclement weather

Fig. 25-3. Olive trees by the tens of thousands, Andalusia, Spain. Nowhere else does one feel that the olive is so inextricably a part of the country and the way of life of the people. The trees are meticulously cared for; weeds are eliminated and the soil is harrowed. In this very dry land, every effort is made to conserve as much rainfall as is humanly possible. (Courtesy of Spanish Embassy in the United States.)

during pollination and the early set period can easily upset the cycle.

Spain, Italy, Greece, Portugal, Turkey, and Tunisia generally lead world production, in this order. Chief among the factors favoring olive culture in Mediterranean lands are (1) low-cost labor for the care, harvesting, and pickling of the olives and extraction of the oil—the finest oil coming from olives that are picked by hand (Fig. 25-4) and pressed with minimum delay; (2) rugged, stony, unirrigated terrain unsuitable for other crops; and (3) lack of summer pasturage, which discourages grazing and hence the production of animal fats, particularly butter.

Most Mediterranean countries import large quantities of olive oil. Spain and Italy alone absorb two thirds of total world production. However, several of these nations import low-priced oils, such as peanut oil, in order to send out their high-quality, high-priced olive oil. Spain imports a substantial quantity of seed oils, often blending them with olive oil and selling the resulting product as olive oil.

The United States, which purchases abroad about fifteen times as much olive oil as it produces, remains the chief importer outside of the Mediterranean lands—Italy in 1958 supplying 35 per cent; Spain, Tunisia, and Greece, about 20 per cent each.

In the Western Hemisphere, olives are cultivated on a limited scale. United States production is confined to California, where high labor costs cause the growers to concentrate on cultivating the larger varieties of olive for packing. Oil is expressed either from surplus olives or those unsuitable for table use. Several South American countries—Argentina, Chile, and Peru—have begun olive cultivation for oil, but only Argentina's industry is as yet of commercial importance.

TUNG OIL

Tung oil is a premium drying, and therefore a preeminently industrial, oil. It has unique properties of producing chemical- and water-resistant coatings and hence is of great value in paints and varnishes and in the linoleum,

Fig. 25-4. Farmer picking olives from a ladder, Andalusia, Spain. When quality is the major consideration, olives are picked by hand. Spain has long been the world's greatest producer, consumer, and (until recently) exporter of olive oil, and now is planting even more olive trees in an effort to reduce its increasing dependence on imported edible oils. (Associated Press photo. Courtesy of Spanish Embassy in the United States.)

oilcloth, and printing industries; it is useful also for brake linings, gaskets for steam pipes, abrasives, insulation for electrical equipment, and a host of other specialized applications.

The oil is procured from the seeds of two Chinese species: the tung-oil tree, a native of central and western China; and the mu tree of southwestern China. Since the oils from these trees are almost identical, imported tung oil is often a mixture of both. The handsome, frost-sensitive tree lives for some thirty-five years, thrives in a Humid Subtropical climate, and favors deep, well-drained, non-alkaline soils.

China, where tung oil has been used for centuries, remains by far the major producer and exporter, although—prior to World War II—outshipments decreased by about one third; increasing tonnages now go to the Soviet bloc. Most of China's commercial output emanates from Szechwan and other provinces along the Yangtze Valley, where, because of the pressure for food crops on the plains, hillside plantings are dominant. The ancient art of tung culture and processing has changed little through the centuries; almost everything is done by hand, and the oil is still recovered by primitive methods in small local mills numbering about 30,000.

The intermittently inferior quality, high price, and uncertain quantity of the Chinese product, plus the recognized importance of tung oil to the paint and varnish industries,

have compelled several other countries to cultivate the tung tree. The United States, Argentina, Paraguay, and Brazil have emerged as the most notable new producers.

Introduced into Florida in 1905, the tung tree was not commercially cultivated in the United States until 1932. It now prospers in a coastal plain belt, about 100 miles wide, stretching from southeastern Texas to southern Georgia and northern Florida, Mississippi being the foremost producer. The tung-oil industry has been of considerable importance to these southern areas, agriculturally as well as economically; for the tung trees, aided by liberal fertilization, do well on eroded and waste land unsuitable for other crops.

Argentina, where tung-tree cultivation is confined to the northeast, is the major South American producer. Since 1949 she has replaced China as the chief source of United States tung-oil imports; Paraguay and Brazil supply most of the remainder.

BABASSU OIL

Babassu oil is an exclusively Brazilian product and the most important of the New World palm oils, the babassu palm being one of the few wild oil-bearing palms to become an important source of commercial fat. The oil expressed from the kernels of the babassu-palm nut substitutes, when refined, for coconut oil in the margarine, confectionery, baking, and soap industries; it is also of value in manufacturing bullet-proof glass, lubricants, and explosives, and as a diesel-engine fuel.

The babassu palm grows most densely south and east of the mouth of the Amazon in the states of Maranhão and Piaui, the former alone having about 75,000 persons engaged in its production. Each palm can produce about 90 pounds of oil a year. It yields a lemon-sized nut, which is so hard to crack that as yet no completely satisfactory machine has been invented to do the job. Therefore, native women still patiently hack away at the shell, as has been the procedure for more than a century, each accumulating a daily maximum of 22 pounds of kernels. Since the babassu palm grows only in undeveloped areas, labor is scarce and transportation inadequate. Of the former billion trees in the producing areas, a large number have been wiped out by destructive and wasteful methods of collecting. Although the nut already contributes millions of dollars to Brazil's economy, it could be worth millions more. If a plantation system were to be established, 300,000 tons of oil might be produced annually.

OITICICA OIL

Oiticica oil, another exclusively northeast Brazilian product, is derived from the seeds (nuts) of a large evergreen tree that grows only on the alluvial riverbanks in the states of Rio Grande do Norte, Ceará, Maranhão, and Paraíba. Having outstanding drying properties, the semisolid oil, which is extracted by hydraulic presses or solvents, has uses similar to those of tung oil. For many years Brazilians have used the oil in medicine and as an illuminant. Entire production comes from wild trees, a full crop one year generally being followed by a small one the next.

The United States imports considerable quantities of the oil, using it as a substitute for tung oil. The oil's future, however, is a beclouded one, for it must compete not only with tung but also with dehydrated castor and linseed oil.

VEGETABLE OILS FROM FIELD CROPS

SOYBEAN OIL

Indigenous to China, where it has been grown for more than 5,000 years, the soybean has long been of supreme importance as a food plant to Eastern Asia and yields an extremely valuable oil, which today ranks first in volume of all fats and oils entering world trade.

Classified as either drying or semidrying, soybean oil, when refined, is used as a salad or cooking oil; its remarkable versatility renders it valuable in the manufacture of more than fifty food products, though chiefly for margarine and shortening. Moreover, the list of its industrial uses is constantly expanding; it is utilized, for example, to make soaps, paints and varnishes, rubber substitutes, linoleum, greases, insecticides, disinfectants, fertilizers, and cleaning compounds.

The several hundred varieties of soybeans are admirable drought and disease resisters and are adaptable to such a wide range of environments that the crop has become distinguished for the universality of its distribution—spreading from its Far Eastern home to every continent except Antarctica. However, the humid mid-latitude plains of the United States and China (including Manchuria) together contribute about 90 per cent of the world's soybean crop.

The bean or seed has an oil content ranging from 19 to 22 per cent in improved varieties. A bushel of soybeans yields 10 to 11 pounds of oil.

In the United States the soybean has been called the nation's "agricultural miracle." Introduced into America in the early nineteenth century, the soybean remained a relatively obscure crop until after World War I, when production and processing were accelerated. By 1956, production of this oil and feed crop had increased more than 7,000 per cent over that in 1925. In 1960 the United States was the world's outstanding producer and ex-

porter of soybeans and soybean oil, greatly overshadowing the traditional homeland, Mainland China. Soybeans now rank as the fifth most important cash crop. Though 31 states cultivate soybeans, more than 80 per cent is grown in the Corn Belt, with most of the remainder in the Atlantic Coastal Plain and the lower Mississippi Valley (Fig. 25-5). Decatur, Illinois (about 150 miles southwest of Chicago), with four modern processing plants, is today known as the soybean capital of the world. Almost 90 per cent of the oil is used as food, primarily shortening and margarine; but industrial consumption is slowly increasing.

Soybeans rank as China's fifth cultivated crop; but, in contrast to the United States, only about 27 per cent is processed. Political entanglements continue to hamper exports, and, too, there is a tendency toward greater use of grains as a staple food. Existing growing areas may undergo more intensive cultivation—particularly in Manchuria, about 80 per cent of whose agricultural exports consist of the soybean, its cake, and oil. China's exports move primarily to Western Europe and the Soviet Union.

PEANUT OIL

The peanut is not really a nut but rather a true legume, though its high oil content (40 to 50 per cent) renders it more nutlike than some other closely related legumes—e.g., beans and peas. Variously known as the groundnut, goober, earth nut, and by other names locally, the peanut, thanks to its high oil and protein content, is a staple food for many peoples, particularly in Africa and Asia. The refined, edible oil—expressed by hydraulic presses and expellers and, in Europe, also by solvents—is utilized as a salad oil, in cooking, for packing sardines, in the manufacture of margarine and shortening, and as an adulterant for olive oil. Manufacturers of soaps, cosmetics, pharmaceuticals, lubricants, and illuminants use the inferior, inedible grades, which can even serve as diesel fuel. Approximately two thirds of the world's 12 million tons of peanuts produced annually are crushed for oil. Contributing approximately one fifth of the world's edible-oil output, peanuts account for a third of the edible oils and oil-bearing commodities entering international trade. The pattern of world trade in peanut oil has changed markedly since before World War II.

Although virtually every tropical and subtropical country and even many mid-latitude lands grow peanuts, cultivation presents a number of difficulties. For optimum yields, the physiologically peculiar plant requires abundant sunshine, moderate rainfall, and sandy, friable soils; since it bears its fruits underground, harvesting is a long-drawn-out, laborious undertaking. Primarily because of its various drawbacks, the growing of peanuts is still limited—India, Communist China, and West Africa accounting for about 70 per cent of the crop (Fig. 25-6). Although a large producer, the United States definitely trails these areas. The major producing countries, with the notable exception of the United

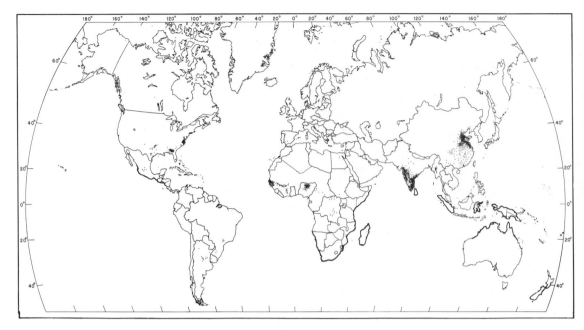

Fig. 25-6. World peanut production. India, North China, and West Africa harvest 70 per cent of the world crop. The peanut is truly vital to the economies and food supply of the major producing lands. (Courtesy of U.S. Department of Agriculture.)

States, cultivate the peanut mainly for oil.

Though accounting for only 4 per cent of total national crop acreage, India's peanut output ranks her as the world's paramount producer—about 5 million short tons annually. India's Monsoon Tropical climate, despite its capriciousness, is generally favorable for peanut culture. The long-time expansion in peanut acreage is primarily the result of the profitability of the crop: the gross return is higher than that of other nonirrigated crops whose cultivation costs are similar. Also the oil is the chief ingredient in a popular hydrogenated cooking oil called vanaspati. Low yields per acre (an average 678 pounds compared with 1,053 in the United States) are slowly being rectified as the government pushes improved agricultural practices.

China, the world's second largest producer, highly prizes the peanut, which it uses both as a cash crop and as oil for cooking. The sandy soils of the river valleys in Shantung, northern Kiangsu, and Anhwei are particularly favorable to peanut culture. Although acreage has been markedly expanded since

World War II, output has remained relatively stable. However, domestic shortage of fats and oils is a continuing problem as China's population relentlessly multiplies; hence, exports have been declining since 1956.

West Africa—principally Senegal, Ivory Coast, Nigeria, Gambia, and Portuguese Guinea—though ranking third as a producing region, has been the foremost exporter of peanuts and peanut oil since World War II. Though primitive methods prevail, in such specialized production areas as the Kano portion of Nigeria, Senegal, Niger, and Gambia, peanuts are the major source of cash income; for here many of the soils are unfit for alternate cash crops.

Nigeria is the world's largest exporter, supplying about 30 per cent of the total entering international trade (Fig. 25-7). Major markets are in Western Europe, particularly the United Kingdom. In West Germany and the Netherlands, Nigerian peanuts must compete with United States soybeans and cottonseeds as sources of oil for high-grade margarine and for oilcake for livestock.

Fig. 25-7. Peanuts bagged and stacked in pyramids for transport by rail in Kano, northern Nigeria. Peanuts and cotton are the region's major agricultural products and exports. These peanuts will be sent to Western Europe. (Courtesy of British Information Services.)

Though soil impoverishment has become a serious matter in some West African areas, the farmers, partially stimulated by the increase in population, continue to cultivate peanuts for cash at the expense of their own food supply. Aided by producer price-stabilization plans and government subsidies, by expansion of crushing operations, by improved quality of peanut products, and by new means of transportation, West Africa's industry has become increasingly profitable. Further acreage expansion and the possibility of higher yields should make secure West Africa's leading position in world peanut oil and oilcake exports, provided African farmers become less reluctant to utilize improved strains of seed and commercial fertilizers.

Peanut production in the United States has been marked by four periods of expansion: (1) during the Civil War, when soldiers campaigning in Virginia tasted the peanut, liked it, and proceeded to popularize it; (2) in the 1870s, when machinery was developed for picking, cleaning, and shelling peanuts; (3) in the early 1900s, when the ravages of the boll weevil forced many Southern farmers to turn from cotton to peanut cultivation; and (4) in the period after World War II, when Far Eastern vegetable-oil supplies were cut off. Today, peanuts, one of the South's leading cash crops, are grown along the coastal plain from Texas to Virginia.

SUNFLOWER OIL

Though native to the Americas, the sunflower has been exploited most prodigiously since the sixteenth century as a field crop in other lands, particularly in Russia. This enterprise was well founded, for the sunflower yields a seed containing 22 to 32 per cent high-quality oil, which vies with olive oil in its food and pharmaceutical value. The oil's semidrying properties render it useful, too, for paints, varnishes, and soaps.

The hardy sunflower adapts well to locales where most other oil crops are ill suited, and is cultivated not only in the tropics but also in many middle-latitude areas. But its drought-resisting qualities have made production most pronounced in warm-summer areas receiving an annual rainfall of 20 inches or less.

The Soviet Union cultivates the sunflower as its chief oil crop, annually accounting for about two thirds of the world's output of sunflower seeds. Production is concentrated in the southeastern portion of the Ukraine, in the central agricultural region, and in the middle and lower Volga Valley. Output fluctuates with annual variations in precipitation, since the sunflower is grown on unirrigated land.

Four Communist countries—Hungary, Bulgaria, Romania, and Yugoslavia—together with Turkey comprise the second major region of production. Hungary normally is the world's leading exporter of sunflower oil.

In South America, sunflowers usually are the major oilseed crop grown for edible oil; Argentina, Chile, and Uruguay are the principal producers. Argentina vies with Hungary for second place in world production and for first place as an exporter of sunflower oil, the two nations together contributing most of the oil entering world trade.

RAPESEED OIL

The rape plant, a member of the mustard family, yields seeds containing 30 to 45 per cent oil, which is extracted by expression or solvents. The cold-pressed crude oil is used for edible purposes in India and parts of Europe, being highly favored for greasing bread prior to baking; it is of value, too, as an illuminant, in making soap and rubber substitutes, and for tempering steel plates. The refined oil—called colza oil—in addition to being edible is particularly suitable for lubricating delicate machinery.

The crop does well in both cool and warm regions, being grown, according to locality, as a summer or winter crop. Some varieties thrive in areas receiving less than 20 inches of rainfall annually. Neutral, high-nitrogen soils are favored.

Asia accounts for about three fourths of the world output. China, which cultivates the crop throughout the Yangtze Basin, leads in world production, closely followed by India-Pakistan, whose acreages center in the Ganges Plain. Pakistan's rapeseed is her most important source of edible oil. India's yield per acre is the lowest of the major producing nations; but, because of the general demand for edible oils, acreage increases since 1947 have been substantial.

SESAME OIL

Cultivated since time immemorial, the sesame plant yields seeds containing about 50 per cent oil, which is easily extractable by cold pressure. Finer grades are added to margarine and other food products; poorer ones are utilized for soaps, insecticides, perfumes, rubber substitutes, lubricants, and illuminants.

The seeds are much in demand by the confectionery and baking industries and are relished in a wide variety of foods in the Orient and Africa.

Tropical, subtropical, and warm temperate regions favor the crop, which tends to be cultivated on the poorer soils and in areas where a peasant type of agriculture is dominant, since mechanized harvesting is as yet difficult. China provides about half the world crop, India one third, and Latin America and Africa the remainder. Though yearly average production of the oil nearly approaches that of olive oil, less than 8 per cent of total sesame output enters world markets, most of it as seeds.

In Africa the outturn of sesame seed has been increasing, Sudan since 1954 being the world's foremost exporter. Ethiopia, Nigeria, and Tanganyika have also become important exporters. Sesame provides Mexico with her chief vegetable oil; hence, little is exported. Colombia and Venezuela, too, are large-scale producers for domestic consumption.

LINSEED OIL

Linseed oil is procured from the seeds of the flax plant, which is indigenous to Central Asia and is one of the oldest plants known to man. The oil is extracted by hot or cold pressings and sometimes by solvents, the cold-pressed oil being used for edible purposes in Eastern Europe and Asia. Because of its superior drying qualities, linseed oil is used largely in paints and varnishes but is also of value for linoleum, oilcloth, printing inks, soaps, and as a binding agent.

Most of the world's flax grown for linseed is cultivated in higher mid-latitudes where much of the year is cold to cool, but summers may be hot. In northern latitudes flax is a spring-sown summer crop, in the subtropics a fall-sown winter crop; in all such areas, the maximum precipitation comes during the growing season. Either heavy or light soils are congenial provided they are sufficiently moist. In the Western Hemisphere, seed-flax cultivation is highly mechanized, being carried on with the same machinery utilized for wheat and other small grains.

Argentina, the Soviet Union, the United States, Canada, and India contribute most of the world's flaxseed. The only major exporters of flaxseed are Canada and the United States. Argentina is the outstanding exporter of linseed oil, being followed by the United States, Canada, India, and Uruguay. Western Europe, particularly the United Kingdom and West Germany, receive the bulk of world exports.

Argentina, which for many years prior to World War II invariably dominated production and exports, has recently seesawed with the United States for first place in flaxseed and linseed-oil output. Argentina's status has been jostled owing to a number of factors:

1. During World War II the government prohibited exports in order to use the oil domestically for power and heat.

2. At the end of the war, when demand for the commodities was large but world production was low, Argentina, assuming her leadership was secure, exported small quantities at high prices—a policy that boomeranged when traditional markets restricted imports and when the United States boosted domestic production.

3. Growers decreased flaxseed acreage as a protest against their reduced returns when the government retained the export margins.

4. Flaxseed must compete with more remunerative wheat and corn for the land.

5. Emphasis is being laid on industrialization, thus diverting resources away from agricultural production for exports. However, by 1959 Argentina had regained her status as the world's foremost exporter of linseed oil; and a large flaxseed crop in 1960 prompted the government to permit export of the seed for the first time since 1955.

Severance from her traditional sources of supply during World War II strongly stimulated the United States to increase flaxseed acreage. As a result, the nation has changed from the principal single prewar importer to the world's third-ranking exporter of flaxseed and linseed oil. More than 85 per cent of the national output emanates from the Dakotas and Minnesota—a segment of the Spring-Wheat Region.

Canada, the world's foremost exporter of flaxseed as such, retains a large part of her linseed oil for domestic consumption. Production centers in Manitoba and Saskatchewan—the Canadian portion of the Spring-Wheat Region—where crop acreage is determined largely by the relationship between flaxseed and wheat prices.

India ranks third in world flaxseed acreage (about 20 per cent of the world total). In some areas flaxseed has given way to peanuts, and in others it must compete with a variety of crops—particularly wheat, which brings in higher gross returns per acre. Approximately 90 per cent of the flaxseed is crushed for oil. In recent years, linseed-oil exports have fluctuated from a low of 3 per cent of production to a high of nearly 60 per cent.

SAFFLOWER OIL

The safflower plant has been cultivated since antiquity in parts of the Orient, northern Africa, and the Middle East, primarily for a pigment extracted from its flower buds and used in dyes. The seed, which is now the plant's chief claim to fame, has an oil content of about 38 per cent almost entirely recoverable by standard processing techniques. The oil's drying qualities and price are intermediate between soybean and linseed oil. Used today mainly for industrial purposes in paints, varnishes, enamels, and synthetic resins, the oil has long been prized also as a popular cooking fat in the Old World, particularly India. It is rapidly gaining enthusiasts in the United States as an edible oil because it is high in unsaturated fats.

Safflower thrives in localities favored with at least 125 frost-free days a year and tolerates semiarid conditions, doing best where good soil moisture is accompanied by hot, dry weather. The plant is grown both with and without irrigation; its yields on irrigated land far outstrip those on dry-farming land.

The most striking phase of the crop's recent history has been the emergence of safflower as a commercial farm crop in the United States. California in 1961 accounted for about half the total American acreage (which in little more than a decade leaped from almost zero to the equivalent of India's plantings—about a half million acres). Arizona ranks second in acreage and first in yields.

VEGETABLE OILS FROM BY-PRODUCTS

COTTONSEED OIL

Cottonseed oil ranks as the world's most important semidrying oil and has for generations served as the foremost vegetable oil in North America, being overshadowed only since the late 1950s by soybean oil. Since the seed (14 to 25 per cent oil content) is a by-product rather than a primary product of the cotton plant and has about one sixth the value of cotton fiber, its output is normally secondary to the fiber. Of the four products yielded by cottonseed—oil, cake or meal, hulls, and linters—the oil comprises only about 16 per cent by weight but brings in nearly 60 per cent of the market value. It takes about 1 ton of cottonseed to make 36 to 42 gallons of oil. Several processes are entailed in recovery of the oil: first, the seeds must be cleaned and freed from impurities and the linters and hulls are usually removed; the kernels are then crushed and heated, and subjected to hydraulic pressure, expeller presses, or solvent extraction; finally, the oil is pumped into tanks, where the impurities settle out. The pure refined oil, after bleaching and deodorizing, is widely used in the making of shortening and margarine and, after **winterization**, as a salad oil. The residue and also any oil unsuitable for refining have numerous industrial uses (e.g., in the manufacture of oilcloth, insulating materials, and nitroglycerin). Cottonseed meal is held in high regard as a fertilizer and livestock feed.

Of the principal cotton-producing lands—the United States, the Soviet Union, China, India, Egypt, Mexico, Pakistan, and Brazil—the United States (with nearly all of its mills in the Deep South) normally accounts for 35 to 45 per cent of total cottonseed output and for 75 per cent of the cottonseed oil entering international trade. This impressive figure results from the fact that nearly all of the American seed not needed for planting is crushed for oil, while in many other cotton-producing countries a smaller percentage is thus utilized. Since the yield of oil per acre approaches only about half that of other major oil-producing plants, cottonseed does not tolerate high transport costs between ginneries and crushing mills; hence, underdeveloped countries such as India, with inadequate transport and crushing facilities, tend to use the seed directly as cattle feed, manure, or fuel.

Outside the United States, chief exporters of the oil normally are China, Sudan, the Congo, Uganda, Syria, and Argentina; their largest markets being Canada, West Germany, the Netherlands, Egypt, and Israel.

CORN OIL

Corn, that versatile gift of the New World, yields an oil that is gaining prominence—particularly in the United States. The germ or embryo of the corn plant contains about 50 per cent oil, commonly expressed by expellers. Refining renders three fourths of the oil available for edible purposes, especially mayonnaise and salad dressing but also directly as a salad oil and liquid shortening. The crude, semidrying oil is used industrially in such commodities as soaps, rubber substitutes, textiles, paints, and insecticides.

Corn germ was long a waste product of the milling industries. The familiar "Mazola" oil, introduced in 1911, gradually gained acceptance, but its use has spurted most dramatically in recent years as a result of the controversy over fats in food and cholesterol (a waxy material carried in the bloodstream and suspected of being responsible for arterial blockage) as a cause of heart attacks. Many American medical authorities advocate a decrease in all types of dietary fat consumption; but they also recommend the substitution of vegetable oils and other unsaturated (liquid) fats for most of the saturated (solid), high-cholesterol fats of animal origin.

Yet of the more than 3 billion bushels of corn harvested annually in the United States, four fifths is usually fed to livestock; less than one fifth is processed, and of this only about 200 million pounds of corn oil have normally been turned out.

WORLD OUTLOOK

The important role of vegetable fats and oils in lubricating the world's trade channels becomes increasingly evident. Changes in total consumption stimulated by changes in economic and population conditions have been accompanied by notable developments in the utilization of oils and fats in recent years. The effects of war loom large in the remarkable shifts that have taken place in the vegetable-oil realm. A prime example is margarine, which, similar to innumerable other commodities, was a product of military history—invented in France to allay the severe fat shortage subsequent to the Napoleonic wars. Further developed during World War I, margarine manufacture emerged as a global industry by World War II. Significant, too, is the fact that whereas animal fats initially comprised the chief ingredients, vegetable fats do now.

The chemical conversion of fats into non-food products has made remarkable strides and promises to make many more. Improved and cheaper products to satisfy man's never ending wants will undoubtedly be created. Such oil crops as safflower, sesame, and sunflower may, indeed, duplicate the notable record of the soybean crop.

Ample future supplies of vegetable oils for all purposes seem virtually assured. The potentialities of vast equatorial and other tropical areas, tailor-made for oil crops but as yet minor contributors, are enormous, especially if scientific advances accompany increased cultivation. Undoubtedly Africa, which already is supplanting Asia as a surplus vegetable-oil area, presents the finest prospects for development and expansion of export vegetable-oil crops—provided the continent's political embroilments do not inhibit its potentialities.

SELECTED REFERENCES

Eckey, E. W. *Vegetable Fats and Oils.* New York, Reinhold Publishing Corporation, 1954.
The Fats and Oils Economy of India. Washington, D. C., Foreign Agricultural Service, U.S. Department of Agriculture, July 1960. FAS-M-89.
Francis, Helen. "Peanuts Around the World," *Foreign Agriculture,* 24:10-11, December 1960.
Goldblatt, L. A. "The Tung Industry: Processing and Utilization," *Economic Botany,* 13:343-364, October–December 1959.
Jamieson, George S. *Vegetable Fats and Oils,* 2nd ed. New York, Reinhold Publishing Corporation, 1943.
Knowles, P. F. "Safflower—Production, Processing and Utilization," *Economic Botany,* 9:273-299, July–September 1955.
Markley, Klare S. "Fat and Oil Resources and Industry of Brazil," *Economic Botany,* 11:91-125, April–June 1957.
Moore, Oscar K. "The Coconut Palm—Mankind's Greatest Provider in the Tropics," *Economic Botany,* 2:119-144, April–June 1948.
Mountjoy, Alan B. "Vegetable Oils and Oilseeds," *Geography,* 42 (Part 1):37-49, January 1957.
Reed, R. H. "The Miracle Crop—Soybeans," *Foreign Agriculture,* 25:3, 16, July 1961.
Yampolsky, Cecil. "Some Aspects of the Oil Palm in Indonesia," *Economic Botany,* 11:208-224, July–September 1957.

NONMINERAL

PART SEVEN

EXTRACTIVE INDUSTRIES

CHAPTER TWENTY-SIX::

The world's forests cover approximately one fourth to one third of the land surface of the earth (Fig. 26-1). The presence of forests in the tropics, subtropics, and so-called "temperate" lands has challenged man for millennia. His struggle against the forest has everywhere left its mark, sometimes in his now fruitful fields, sometimes in man-made deserts (Fig. 26-2), and sometimes in tiny agricultural clearings (e.g., **milpas**), as in the equatorial rain forest. Since man's attack began thousands of years ago—particularly since 1900, when world population really began to skyrocket—the forests increasingly have been felled to give way to cities, shopping centers, railroad rights-of-way, highways, airports, industrial complexes, and farm fields and pastures. Agriculture demands the removal of

THE WORLD'S

AND

natural vegetation. Consequently, the world's forests of the 1960s are to be found for the most part on the poorer lands—those unsuited to farming, because of unfavorable climate, infertile soils, inaccessibility, or remoteness of location.

FORESTS AND NATURAL ENVIRONMENT

Forests comprise indisputably the most important form of flora or natural vegetation. There are scientific reasons for the distribution of the world's forests; nonetheless, on a world map the distribution seems strikingly haphazard (Fig. 26-1). Although trees grow under a wide range of climatic conditions, they are in general limited to areas whose midsummer temperatures average 50°F or above. Along the equatorial margins of the high latitudes, approximately 15 inches of rainfall are required for forest growth; in the mid-latitudes, more than 30 inches with more than half falling during the warm months; and in the tropics, roughly 45 to 90 inches for deciduous and 90 to 150 inches for rain forest. Forests shun the low deserts, the true polar lands, and the highest parts of mountains and plateaus—those above **timberline**. However, climate certainly is not the only factor affecting growth and distribution. Other influential factors include (1) porous soils and bedrock; (2) fire; (3) grazing of animals, particularly sheep and goats; (4) parasites; and (5) logging.

FOREST RESOURCES INDUSTRIES

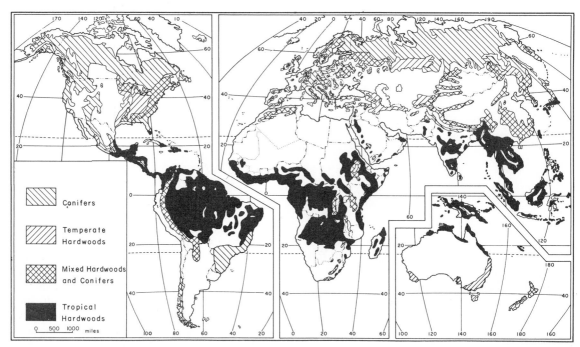

Fig. 26-1. The world's forested lands: major general classification. The forested area is destined to shrink as man's population explosion necessitates using every bit of potential arable land for food production.

Fig. 26-2. A timber-mined landscape in Michigan. Since being logged off, the area has been burned over many times. Careless burning of trash leads as the main cause, accounting for about 30 per cent of all forest fires; it is followed closely by incendiarism, 25 per cent; smokers, 16.5 per cent; lightning, 8.4 per cent; railroads and campers, 3.5 per cent each; lumbering operations, 1.5 per cent; miscellaneous causes, 11 per cent. (Courtesy of U.S. Forest Service.)

TABLE 26-1

DISTRIBUTION OF THE WORLD'S FORESTS

Region	Total forested area	Accessible	Conifers	Non-conifers	Forests in use	Forests as per cent of area	Forest area per inhabitant
	Million hectares					Per cent	Hectares
Europe	136	133	79	57	130	28.3	0.3
Soviet Union	743	425	580	163	350	33.9	3.8
North America	656	312	463	193	220	36.1	4.1
Latin America	890	329	27	863	83	39.7	5.2
Africa	801	284	3	798	108	27.0	3.9
Asia	525	311	120	405	232	19.8	0.4
Pacific Area	86	20	8	78	17	10.0	6.7
World total	3,837	1,814	1,280	2,557	1,140	29.1	1.6

SOURCE: Based on Food and Agriculture Organization of the United Nations, *World Forest Resources,* Rome, March 1955, p. 18.

CLASSIFICATION OF FORESTS

For this study of economic geography, we may classify forests as either *coniferous* (**softwood**) or *broadleaf* (**hardwood**). The conifers are the cone bearers whose leaves are needle-shaped; the broadleaf trees (either evergreen or deciduous) are precisely what the name connotes. The largest, though by no means the only, stands of conifers comprise the Boreal forest (see p. 522). The broadleaf trees grow in the wet tropics (evergreens), the wet and dry tropics (deciduous owing to a long dry season), and in middle latitudes (deciduous owing to winter cold or drought).

The softwood trees, which comprise about one third of the total forested area of the world, are in greater demand than the hardwoods; up to 40 per cent of the softwood lands have been exploited, contrasted with 25 per cent of the hardwood lands. Therefore, the location of the softwood forest is of considerable economic importance: 63 per cent of the exploited softwood forests are in the Soviet Union, 22 per cent in Anglo-America, and only 15 per cent in all the rest of the world (mostly in Europe). Thus, almost all of the softwood forests are to be found in the Northern Hemisphere (Fig. 26-1). The enormous forest areas of Africa and Latin America support almost exclusively hardwood forests.

THE WORLD'S FORESTS

NORTH AMERICA

North America (Fig. 26-3, Table 26-1) is a favored continent, 30 to 40 per cent being covered with forests. To be sure, much of the original stand was removed to make room for farms, and much has been destroyed by careless exploitation and repeated fires. Yet there still remain some 1,587.5 million acres, of which about half is presently **accessible**.

The expansion of land settlement at the expense of the forest appears to be nearing its end. Hence, if man adopts a sound long-term management plan, timber yields should increase.

CANADA

Canada ranks high in the proportion of its total area in forest and in acreage per capita. The total forested area covers approximately 1.6 million square miles, 60 per cent of which is capable of producing **merchantable timber**. A large area north of the more productive forest lands and south of the tundra grows trees too small and stunted to be commercial.

The Canadian forests contain more than 150 tree species, of which 31 are conifers: about 83 per cent of the volume of merchanta-

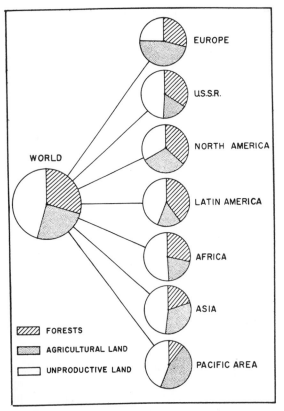

EUROPE

U.S.S.R.

NORTH AMERICA

WORLD

LATIN AMERICA

AFRICA

ASIA

FORESTS

AGRICULTURAL LAND

UNPRODUCTIVE LAND

PACIFIC AREA

Fig. 26-3. Land categories—world, continents, regions. Note particularly the relation of the forested area to population; thus Asia, with its enormous population, has the smallest forested area of any continent, whereas sparsely populated Latin America has the largest forested area. Note also the disproportionate share of unproductive land on the earth. (Courtesy of Food and Agriculture Organization.)

ble timber consists of softwood species. More than 90 per cent of the forested area consists of Crown land (held in the right of the federal and provincial governments).

The Canadian forests fall into eight regions, but only the four germane to economic geography are considered here.

The Boreal Forest.[1] This forest comprises the greater part of the total. It forms a con-

[1] The names employed here for the Canadian forest regions are those used by the Forestry Branch, Department of Northern Affairs and Natural Resources, Dominion of Canada.

tinuous belt from Newfoundland to the Rocky Mountains and northwestward to Alaska. Though white and black spruce are the characteristic species, balsam fir and jack pine range throughout and are particularly important in the eastern and central portions, whereas alpine fir and lodgepole pine are important in the western and northwestern parts. The Boreal forest is essentially, though not exclusively, coniferous (some admixture of white birch and poplar). In the northern part of this forest much **muskeg** and nonforested rock are encountered before the forest finally melts into the tundra. In the very southern extremity there is considerable intrusion by species from the Great Lakes–St. Lawrence region—white and red pine, yellow birch, sugar maple, and black ash.

The Montane Forest. This forest characterizes the uplands of British Columbia and a small area on the eastern side of the Rocky Mountains. Foresters regard the region as an extension of the Rocky Mountain forest of the United States. Among the typical trees are Douglas fir, lodgepole pine, and aspen. Ponderosa pine is important in the southern part.

Coast Forest. In this forest, a part of the same forest in the United States, conifers predominate—principally the western red cedar and western hemlock, though Douglas fir is important in the south (Fig. 26-4) and Sitka spruce in the north. The density of the timber stand per acre is five times that of the remaining accessible forest lands of the country.

Deciduous Forest. This forest, found in southwestern Ontario, is adjacent to the Lower Lakes. It closely resembles its counterpart south of the international border. Principal trees are the sugar maple, beech, white elm, basswood, red ash, and white oak, with a few conifers scattered throughout.

UNITED STATES

The original forest stand (**virgin forest**) was incomprehensible in its enormity—covering some 822 million acres. It was composed of more than 1,100 species of trees, of which

Fig. 26-4. Typical stand of virgin Douglas fir, Vancouver Island, British Columbia. The giant at the right measures 9 feet in diameter and stretches skyward for 150 feet to the first limb. It is believed that the root systems can supply water and minerals to the huge tops and allow the gigantic trees to grow so close together because rainfall is heavy (more than 100 inches), and because the late-summer rainless period is modified by high humidity and much fog. (Courtesy of National Film Board, Ottawa.)

more than 100 have been of economic value. So extensive was the virgin forested area that the early settlers regarded this resource as inexhaustible.

The history of lumbering in the United States is one of exploitation and migration. For many years Maine led the nation in output; with depletion of her virgin forests, New York became the leader, only to be superseded by Pennsylvania. About 1860 the industry began to migrate to the Lake states, which possessed some of the finest forests ever witnessed by man. However, ruthless cutting was the order of the day, and the sawdust flew from one end of the Lake states to the other. "Cut out and get out" was the slogan; "there is always more farther west." By 1880, when it became apparent to the operators that the

forests of the Lake states *were* exhaustible, their gaze fell on the magnificent pine forests of the South; and soon the trees there were being felled at an unbelievable rate. During the last of the 1880s, with the softwood timber of the Lake states exhausted and the end of the Southern pineries easily calculable, logging and lumbering leaped over the Great Plains, the Rockies, and the Great Basin to the redwood, fir, and pine forests of the Pacific Coast, the present center of the industry. This migration left economic chaos in its wake. After repeated fires, ghost towns and rural poverty settled down on the lands abandoned by the loggers.

The forests of the United States occur in five broad regions. So much of this forest has been culled, cut over, and burned that three

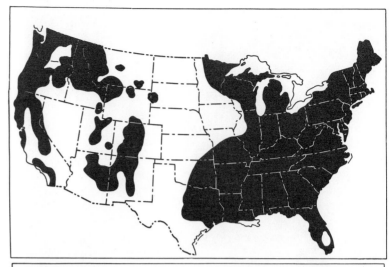

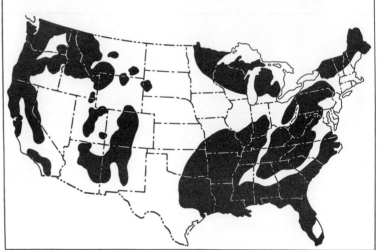

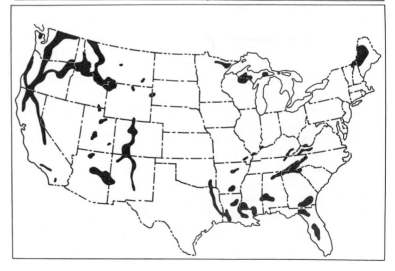

Fig. 26-5 (a, b, c). Virgin forests in the United States: 1620 (top), 1850 (middle), and 1940 (bottom). The original forest of 1620 is believed to have comprised 822 million acres. Man has whittled it away until today the acreage in virgin forest is negligible. (Courtesy of U.S. Forest Service.)

fourths of the original timber is gone (Fig. 26-5). Of the present forested area (647 million acres), the federal government owns approximately 89 million acres; and the states, counties, and municipalities own 11 million. Thus, about 100 million acres, or 21 per cent of the total, is publicly held. The remaining 79 per cent is still in private ownership.

The forests of the United States fall about equally into hardwood and softwood types. The West, including coastal Alaska, is almost exclusively a softwood area; the South, despite extensive pine (softwood) forests, is 58 per cent hardwood; and the East is largely hardwood.

The Northern Forest. This forest covers most of New England, New York, and the Upper Lake states, with southern extensions along the Appalachians reaching as far south as Georgia.

Over most of the region hemlock is associated with maple, beech, and yellow birch. Other hardwoods of note are black walnut, red oak, hickory, ash, and elm. The New England portion and the Lake states possess what may be called a transitional coniferous forest —an area of pine trees of various species interspersed with broadleaf deciduous trees.

Central Hardwoods Forest. This forest, consisting almost wholly of deciduous (hardwood) trees, originally was the outstanding hardwood forest of the world (Fig. 26-6). However, since much of it was on very fertile soils, it was sacrificed for farms. Today few stands of virgin forest remain.

Among the leading trees are the oaks (white, northern red, and black), American beech, soft maple, elm, sycamore, and cottonwood, but also wild black cherry, tulip, and hickory.

Southern Forest. This forest extends throughout the South, from the eastern half of Texas and Oklahoma to Virginia on the east and to the Gulf of Mexico on the south. Although it is not so large as the Central Hardwoods forest, it comprises some 197 million acres, on which approximately 18 per

Fig. 26-6. Stand of virgin mixed-hardwood timber, Wisconsin. The large trees are (left to right): maple, elm, black ash, and elm. Many of these trees attain heights of 125 to 175 feet and diameters of 4 to 10 feet. (Courtesy of U.S. Forest Service.)

cent of the country's saw timber is growing. It is composed of pines—longleaf, shortleaf, loblolly, and slash—on the sandy soils; a number of hardwoods—principally oaks, soft maple, ash, elm, and sycamore—on the heavier soils; and cypress and gums (red and black) in the swamps and bottomlands. Possibly most people think of the Southern forest as a coniferous or softwood forest; however, only 42 per cent of the land area is occupied by softwood timber.

The South, which currently produces about 27 per cent of the national lumber output, is favored by (1) proximity to its own large markets and to those of the Middle West and East, (2) rapid growth of trees, and (3) moderate relief. Since most of the trees utilized are second growth, and hence are small in size (diameter of 6 inches to 2 feet), the operations are less heavily mechanized than those, for example, along the Pacific Coast.

The Forest of the West. This forest falls into two segments—the Western and the West Coast. The bulk of the stand consists of softwoods.

The *Western forest* covers the mountains and higher plateaus of the West, exclusive of the Coast Ranges and the Cascade–Sierra Nevada. In the north it occupies both valleys and mountains; in the south, only the higher, well-watered elevations. This forest accounts for about 11 per cent of the total commercial forest land of the nation; yet it is not regarded highly, for it contains much land of low productivity—the result primarily of restricted rainfall. Only about half of this area has timber capable of being harvested. This Western forest accounts for about a quarter of the national softwood output.

The forest is composed principally of conifers, with ponderosa pine as the most common tree; but Engelmann spruce, Alpine fir, and Douglas fir are important at the higher elevations, and western white pine, western larch, and western hemlock at the lower elevations. Lodgepole pine occupies many of the burned-over areas.

Along the Pacific Coast north of San Francisco in the Temperate Marine climate—with its heavy rainfall, quite well distributed throughout the year, and mild temperatures for the latitude—stands the *West Coast forest.* This is one of the world's most majestic forests—one characterized by unusually tall, dense stands of trees—predominantly redwood, Douglas fir, sugar pine, western hemlock, western red cedar, Sitka spruce, and Pacific silver fir. Redwood trees commonly attain heights of 175 to 225 feet and are 3 to 10 feet in diameter, but some of these sylvan monarchs reach up to 300 feet and have diameters of 15 feet.

The West Coast forest includes both the California redwood forest and the Douglas fir forest of western Oregon and western Washington. The Douglas fir forest, which extends 480 miles from north to south and 100 to 150

Fig. 26-7. High-lead logging is typical in the Pacific Northwest. A "high-climber" prepares a spar tree by cutting off all the lower branches and the top. He then will fasten a cable network to the tree. The cables will be used to haul logs from where they have been felled to a central location for loading on trucks that will take the logs to a mill. (Courtesy of Weyerhaeuser Company.)

miles from east to west, contributes about 30 per cent of the nation's softwood lumber (Fig. 26-7).

The National Forests. The national forests (Fig. 26-8) came into being largely as a result of the outcry of a relatively small number of conservationists who bewailed the "wanton destruction" of the forest resource.

Under President Theodore Roosevelt the new Forest Service was placed under the Department of Agriculture, and a new concept developed under the able leadership of the Chief Forester, Gifford Pinchot. The Forest Service has been guided by three main concepts: (1) *sustained yield,* the concept that timber harvest and growth must be balanced

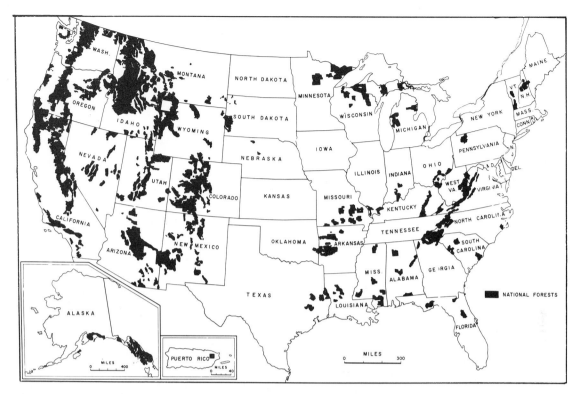

Fig. 26-8. *National Forests of the United States. Note that such forests are to be found in almost all the states, though most of the acreage is in the West—76 per cent of the commercial forest. These public forests, managed by the Forest Service, are for both economic and social use. Of the total acreage 80 per cent of that in the East was obtained by purchase, contrasted with only 3 per cent in the West. The forests of the West were former government lands located largely in high mountains and hence were uncut. (Courtesy of U.S. Forest Service.)*

over a period of time so that forest yield will be continued into perpetuity; (2) *multiple use*—that the forests should serve a variety of purposes (grazing, recreation, watershed protection, and soil conservation), not just as a source of forest products; and (3) *the greatest good for the greatest number over the long span of time*—i.e., avoidance of the short-term, high-profit philosophy that has been so persistent in the nation.

Much of the land comprising the national forests was of the poorest quality because it was acquired from the various states or private owners by purchase or reversion for nonpayment of taxes. The areas that had been in the **public domain** supported mature virgin forest, but those purchased from private owners had invariably been stripped of all useful timber

and often had been burned over several times. About one fourth of the lands included in the national forests capable of being managed for timber output are in the East; and three fourths are in the West, including Alaska. Generally speaking, the national forests have achieved the avowed purposes. They have been well managed to provide crops of timber, and yet maintain their other multiple-use values.

Growing Trees on a Crop Basis. The nomadic nature of the logging industry has been observed—how it started in New England, moved into the Lake states, then into the South, and finally into its last stand on the Pacific Coast. It was here that sustained-yield timber production received its greatest im-

Fig. 26-9. On Weyerhaeuser's White River Tree Farm, timber is cut in patches; this is called block-cutting or clear-cutting. All of the trees within a given area are logged, but none are removed in surrounding areas until subsequent years. In this way cutting can be balanced with growth. Mt. Rainier looms in the background. (Courtesy of Washington State Department of Commerce and Economic Development.)

petus. For example, about 1940, the Weyerhaeuser Company began to apply intensive forestry practices to a 120,000-acre, logged-out tract near Montesano, Washington. To teach the public that the company planned to grow another crop of trees, the area was advertised as a tree farm, the name implying forest management for the production of forest crops in perpetuity. So successful was the experiment that in 1941 the National Lumber Manufacturers Association initiated the tree-farm movement on a national scale (Fig. 26-9).

Tree farms now are to be found in thirty-eight states, and they vary from 3 acres to hundreds of thousands of acres. The states furnish planting stock, technical forestry assistance, or both. The woodland must be adequately protected against fire, insects, disease, and overgrazing. No revolutionary innovations are involved in tree farming, but the sustained-yield principle reaches its most intensive application in this area. By and large tree farming is paying off.

EUROPE

The forests of Europe are strikingly similar to those of North America. A coniferous forest extends eastward from Norway deep into Siberia, and a hardwood forest reaches from the Atlantic Coast of Western Europe to the Urals north of the treeless steppes. The western and central portions of Europe produce both hardwoods and softwoods. Mediterranean Europe, like all mediterranean lands, possesses open forest (*maquis;* called *chaparral* in other similar areas, such as California) made up of dense brushwood dominated by medium-height, evergreen shrubs. It is so poor that it produces only firewood and charcoal; and, once cleared, this forest has little regenerative power.

As early as classical times, much of this forest had disappeared by reason of war, pillage, fire, overgrazing, and erosion, leaving behind scrub and in some places even bare land. In Western and Central Europe, clearing began with the advent of agriculture in Neolithic times, being carried on partly by ax and partly by fire. By the sixteenth century complaints were already being made regarding shortages of wood. Most of Europe is today poor in forest, and the continent definitely is a deficit area: it possesses the smallest forest of any of the inhabited continents, as well as the smallest forest area per inhabitant. On the whole, however, Europe's forests are well and intensively managed and yield large quantities of wood considering the size of stand of commercial timber (Table 26-1).

Forest resources vary from country to country, the northern ones being better endowed than those in the west and south. Nearly all the countries of Western Europe are importers of wood.

FENNOSCANDIA

Fennoscandia, the principal forest-products region of Europe, is the most important export area in the world for lumber, pulp, and paper. The greater part of the forest is softwood (coniferous)—a forest that sweeps across Eurasia from northern Norway, Sweden, and Finland deep into Russia. The predominant trees are Scots pine and Norway spruce. The hardwoods that invade the conifer region are birches and aspen with some maple, elm, ash, and oak.

Norway, though important, is much less so than Sweden and Finland, whose forest industries on the shores of the Baltic Sea and the Gulf of Bothnia rank among the best in the world. The trees are cut in winter and hauled on ice roads to frozen rivers. When the ice breaks up in spring, the logs are river driven to sawmills, which are found at the mouth of virtually every Finnish and Swedish river. Water driving is the most economical method of transporting logs; thus, the cost of floating timber 80 miles is about the same as

for hauling it on a snow road a distance of 2 miles from the place of cutting to a river bank.

GERMANY

Germany stands among the world's leaders in forest management and, as a result, is one of the best forested countries in Europe. With 26 per cent of the area in forest, Germany meets the bulk of her wood requirements. The largest forest areas coincide with rugged relief and poor soils—lands least suited to agriculture. The proportion of total land area in forests increases from north to south. About 65 per cent of the West German forest is today composed of coniferous species—spruce and Scots pine; but there is also some silver fir, larch, and Douglas fir. The broadleaf species are predominantly beech and white oak.

Imports are mostly pulpwood from Fennoscandia and Austria; softwood logs and sawn timber from Czechoslovakia and Yugoslavia; and hardwood and veneer logs from Poland, Romania, and France.

POLAND

About 24 per cent of Poland is forested with the best timbered parts in the south—in the Carpathian Mountains, where fir comprises the principal species but where pine is to be seen on the sandy soils and spruce on the clays.

SOVIET UNION (EUROPE AND ASIA)

As Figure 26-3 and Table 26-1 show, the Soviet Union's land in forest is equivalent to that of all North America. It has the most extensive forests among all countries on earth, forests that cover almost one third of the country's vast extent. About 63 per cent of the exploited land is in softwood forest, contrasted with North America's 22 per cent. Yet the Soviet Union and the United States annually have about the same output. Wood production in the Soviet Union is hampered by slow growth (owing to the long, cold winters), small trees, economic inaccessibility of much of the forest (70 per cent is in Siberia and the Far East), reckless overcutting in the accessible areas, and poor transport by rail, by highway, and even by river (most of the major streams tapping the **taiga** flow from south to north into the ice-choked Arctic).

Since most of the people and hence the market have been in European Russia, the forest there was overcut even during czarist days, so that today the sawmilling industry is centered in the interior, though west of the Urals. East of these mountains, the center of activity is in the Yenisei Basin, but the marked continentality of the climate limits river flotation to a period of four to six months. Many sawmilling centers have sprung up in southern Siberia, where the Trans-Siberian Railway crosses the rivers.

The lumber industry is today centered in the north of European Russia, in the Urals, the Upper Volga, Siberia, and the Far East. Arkhangelsk, Leningrad, Volgograd, and Igarka are the leading centers of the sawmilling industry.

Felling of trees is essentially a winter pursuit, the logs being transported on horse-drawn sleds to stream courses preparatory to spring and summer drives.

The Russian taiga comprises about one third of the forested land of the world. In the European portion, pine and spruce are the most common species. Toward the Ural Mountains these species merge with stone pine, fir, and Siberian larch. Larch is the most widely distributed species in the Soviet Union. Pine, in second place, has some of its largest stands accessible to important markets; it is sent by rivers and railroads from the Urals and the European North to the timber-deficit areas of the center of the nation—the Donets Basin, the Volga, the North Caucasus, and the Ukraine.

Because of the size, quality, and location of its forests, the Soviet Union can play a vital role in the forestry situation of the entire world. Prior to World War II, she exported much lumber, because foreign exchange was needed. The heavy war damage to dwellings, factories, and communication systems changed this position; and for a number of years exports were negligible. However, the enormity of the Soviet forests and the fact that they contain the world's largest untapped softwood reserves would seem to indicate that the country may play a dominant role in the international trade of lumber in the future.

ASIA

Asia has a smaller percentage of her land in forests than any other continent (Fig. 26-3 and Table 26-1). Considering that at least half the world's people dwell here and that they are predominantly farmers, the small area in forest is understandable. Several of the countries (e.g., China, India, and Japan) import much wood, whereas Burma, Thailand, Malaysia, and Indonesia are primarily exporters.

CHINA

In few countries has deforestation gone as far as in China; yet her long history necessitated that the forests be ruthlessly pushed back by the constantly increasing demands of agriculture and population. Hence, forest has been virtually eliminated from the more densely populated areas. Yet much land could be devoted to growing trees, since 40 per cent of the area is not suitable for agriculture. Aside from the need for wood (millions of Chinese live without access to any supply whatsoever), China needs vast programs of reforestation to control stream flow and particularly to retard erosion. Silt is a major cause of disastrous floods in the Hwang-Ho and Yangtze-Kiang.

INDIA

Forest occupies about one fifth of the area of India, yet only half of it is considered worthy of profitable exploitation. On the whole, India is better off than China despite the fact that millions of Indians completely lack wood. The varied forest is of five types: (1) the monsoon forest, (2) the rain forest, (3) the beach and tidal (mangrove) forest, (4) the dry forest, and (5) the xerophytic forest. Only the monsoon forest is treated here, because its timber is in greatest demand in Europe and North America. It occurs throughout the western Deccan, where the rainfall varies from 40 to 80 inches and where the mean annual temperatures vacillate only slightly from 75°F to 80°F. The trees, which reach a height of 100 to 120 feet, are deciduous, being leafless during March and April. Several species, particularly teak and rosewood, are of great commercial importance. Teak has long been in demand. Even in pre-British times, the Arabs engaged in teak trade for building seagoing craft, and later the British cut heavily for logs for the British navy.

JAPAN

Despite her dense population, 68 per cent of Japan's total land area is in forest. The forests, which are quite evenly distributed over the four main islands, contain more tree species than most areas of comparable size. Parts of the forest, however, particularly in the broadleaf forests, are in inaccessible areas on steep mountain slopes and are most useful in protecting watersheds.

Exploitation is principally on slope lands of Honshu and Hokkaido, where *sugi* (a wood resembling western red cedar), pine, larch, fir, and spruce are cut. Although the coniferous forests occupy less than 15 per cent of the forest area, they yield 85 per cent of the saw logs cut each year.

BURMA

Burma has three types of forests: (1) the tidal (mangrove), (2) the evergreen rain forests, and (3) the mixed deciduous. Most important commercially is the last with its many precious trees, especially pyinkado and teak. Burma leads the world in production of teak, a large deciduous tree that loses its leaves during the dry season. In a narrow belt on either side of the Irawaddy River and the Salween River is the world's leading stand of teak. Teak does not grow in pure stands but normally comprises about 10 per cent of the forest.

In the logging of teak, the trees are girdled (a ring is cut through the sapwood around the base) three years before they are felled; this is essential in order for the sap to dry out so that the logs can be rafted to Rangoon and Moulmein, since green wood will not float and

there is no other effective way of getting the logs from the remote hilly forests (Fig. 26-10). Elephants are widely used in this forest enterprise. They drag logs in the forests and to streams, and they work in the timber yards and sawmills (Fig. 26-11). The elephant still is the most practical machine for handling teak in the jungle itself; but the truck is complementing, though certainly not competing with him in this work.

Prior to World War II, about 80 per cent of the Burmese output was in the hands of European concessionaires. Today the forests are nationalized.

Teak, popular as a fine cabinet wood, is much in demand for shipbuilding, furniture, flooring, and door and window frames. The heartwood is resistant to termites, though the sapwood is not. Burma exports principally to India and the United Kingdom, but also to South Africa, West Germany, and the United States.

LATIN AMERICA

In Latin America is to be found the world's greatest wood-surplus region (Fig. 26-3). Thirty-nine per cent of the region is in forest; yet very little has even been explored. Three Latin American forests are presented here.

THE RAIN FOREST

Like all tropical forests, this one is predominantly (probably 93 per cent) an area of hardwoods. The forest tends to be three-storied. The upper tier contains the giants—150 feet tall with diameters of 6 to 8 feet. Beneath this tier stands an intermediate story whose trees reach a height up to 100 feet and diameters up to 3 feet; and finally an understory of small trees able to stand heavy shade. In this forest the crowns intermesh, vines climb and interlace and hang down like great ropes, and underneath the canopy a twilight-like condition prevails even in midday. This forest, which is most extensive in Amazonia, contains probably 10,000 different species. However, about 200 species constitute the bulk of the forest. The trees also vary in wood density: some are lighter than cork, others are heavier than water; some are so hard they turn

Fig. 26-10. Teak raft moving down Burma's Irrawaddy River en route from Mandalay to Rangoon—a distance of about 400 miles. The raftsmen use bamboo poles to guide their valuable cargo downstream. (Courtesy of United Nations.)

Fig. 26-11. Elephant handling logs in teak forest. Teak is native of Southeast Asia from India to Indo-China. No mechanical machine has yet been perfected that is as practical or as efficient as the elephant for performing certain tasks in the handling of teak logs. In Burma alone 1,300 elephants are employed for extraction and haulage. (Courtesy of United Nations.)

Fig. 26-12. Scattered Paraná pine trees, state of Paraná, Brazil. The tree regenerates well only in its native climate. To date the Paraná pine forest has been of greater economic importance to Brazil than the thousands of square miles of hardwood forest comprising the Amazon Basin. (Courtesy of Hess.)

nails. In general, a third of the tropical woods found in this forest is composed of the hard, heavy type; another third is light and soft; and the remainder is intermediate.

The most abundant stands of timber are to be found in the river valleys—immense unbroken stretches reaching to the horizon on all sides. Thus, in Amazonia most of the settlements cling to the rivers; and here forest devastation is widespread. There are some treeless areas (savannas) within this forest and some areas where palms are the only trees.

"PINE" FOREST OF SOUTHEASTERN BRAZIL

Possibly the most important forested area from the standpoint of exploitation and utility is the Paraná pine forest found in the states of Paraná, Santa Catarina, and Rio Grande do Sul with small extensions into Uruguay, Paraguay, and Argentina. This is certainly the continent's most important stand of commercial softwood forest, and the Paraná pine is undeniably Brazil's most valuable timber tree (Fig. 26-12). Actually the Paraná pine is not a true pine since it has no resin ducts. In fact, no pines grow in the Western Hemisphere south of Nicaragua.

This forest supplies the bulk of Brazil's lumber and in excess of 70 per cent of the wood exports.

PINE AND BROADLEAF FOREST OF CHILE

A small area of Araucaria forest is to be found on both sides of the Andean divide, near latitude 42° south but mainly in Chile. Though standing only eighth among South American countries in total forest area, Chile ranks second in the value of wood exports.

The bulk of the forest is temperate-zone mixed broadleaf and deciduous forest—largely beech. Much of it has high utility value, but many useless species of trees are present. Much of this forest is inaccessible, transportation is largely lacking, and rainfall is heavy—all factors that hinder large-scale commercial exploitation. The most accessible portions have been badly exploited. Fires do much damage, too—so much, in fact, that they destroy annually four times as much timber as the entire nation uses.

AFRICA

As previously observed in Figure 26-3 and Table 26-1, Africa ranks second only to Latin America in total and in per capita forest area. Actually there are two types: rain forest and dry forest.

AFRICAN RAIN FOREST

This enormous forest covers nearly half of the forested area (Fig. 26-1). The richest segment extends from 12° north to about 5°

Fig. 26-13. Immense mahogany logs sorted, graded, and ready for shipment by rail from Kumasi to the port of Takoradi for export. Merchantable mahoganies, of great value as cabinet wood, have a low density per unit of area (an average of one tree per 20 to 25 acres) and command a high price in the major importing areas—Europe, South Africa, and the United States. (Courtesy of United Nations.)

south, chiefly along the west coast and into the Congo Basin. This forest has barely been scratched by logging operations, though a considerable portion has been cleared for agriculture. However, population in the entire area is increasing, with consequent deforestation for new subsistence crop-producing lands (shifting cultivation) and for new lands for the extension of commercial export crops—bananas, coffee, cacao, oil palms, and pineapples—and for the location of roads.

Today there is some exploitation of the forest for lumber. Various species of mahogany are logged and sawed into lumber from Liberia to the Congo. The trees grow to large size, frequently exceeding 150 feet with diameters of 6 to 10 feet. Mangrove extends in broad strips along the coast and inland up many waterways. Two of the most important logging centers are Kumasi and Takoradi in Ghana (Fig. 26-13). Stands of softwood species are small and limited in number. As in all tropical lands, so too here, logging is highly selective. Only the most valuable species and those light enough to float on rivers are commonly exploited. Such species are restricted, with but one or at most a few trees of merchantable size per acre. The cost of such logging is high, but is not likely to decrease as long as the current noncommercial species are not utilized.

Despite the enormity of the forest, Africa exports little timber; the bulk consists of cabinet woods. There is danger that the forest will disappear and be replaced by valueless secondary brush or by savanna.

THE DRY FOREST

This heterogeneous forest stands between the true rain forest and the thornbush steppes that border the deserts. No sharp line of cleavage separates the dry, open forest from the savanna forest. This area has been fired by man so often that it is almost impossible to reconstruct the original vegetative cover. Man has upset the former biological equilibria:

Nearly all dry Africa burns during the dry season; few parcels of soil are exempt from fires that sweep through the savannas and dry open forests, attack the edges of the dry dense forests, and make them retreat year after year. Some of the thornlands escape from the periodic fires either because the grassy vegetation is discontinuous or thin, or, more important, because there is generally no agriculture in these arid regions and therefore little reason for starting fires; the fires that do occur are accidental.[2]

This forest is of little value for more than local use (as a source of fruit, fat, tannin, kapok, copal, cork, and pasture), though occasionally in the **gallery forests** there are trunks of adequate shape and quality suitable for export. In general, Africa's dry forest appears condemned either to destruction or conversion into savannas.

THE PACIFIC AREA

As Figure 26-3 and Table 26-1 show, only about 10 per cent of the Pacific area is in forest. Australia and New Zealand, with about 93 per cent of the region's land area, together have about 31 per cent of the land in forest—25 per cent in New Zealand, 6 per cent in Australia.

AUSTRALIA

Australia's forest differs from that of the rest of the world, most of it (85 per cent) consisting of hardwoods of the eucalyptus family. Some of these trees rank with the redwoods

of California in size—both height and diameter.

The merchantable forests are restricted to the coastal areas with their reasonably heavy rainfall (about 30 inches). In the dry interior, only scrubby forms of vegetation grow—forms too poor to enter commerce.

It is estimated that Australia's forest area is about 20 million acres in size, 12.5 million acres of which may be classed as commercial. Some 85 per cent of the merchantable stand is owned by governments—federal and state.

NEW ZEALAND

Originally New Zealand, with its true forest climate, was covered with forests. The first Europeans on their arrival found the islands clothed with dense rain forest, though in South Island there was much land in tussock grass. Today, however, less than 20 per cent of the Commonwealth is forested, and this figure includes even the exotic species of the **forest (pine) plantations**.

During the past century more than half the virgin forest was destroyed directly or indirectly by man. Fire, ax, livestock, and plow—all hastened the changeover to grass. Today possibly less than 1 million acres of fully merchantable timber remains. However, more than 800,000 acres have been planted to exotic softwoods.

Beeches (6 to 8 million acres), either in pure stands or in mixed forest, are important; but they are, above all, watershed protection forests. (Beech-forest soils are unsuitable for agriculture or even for permanent grazing.) Best known to the outside world, despite the fact that they are no longer of importance as a source of timber, are the Kauri forests, whose trees grow to immense proportions and have timber of high value. Under proper management these forests could produce the greatest amount of timber in the nation. New Zealand must depend on modest imports of wood.

WOOD PULP

The first paper was probably made in China about 105 A.D. from rags, bamboo fiber, and

[2] Stephen Haden-Guest et al., *A World Geography of Forest Resources*, New York, Ronald Press Company, 1956, p. 379.

inner fiber of the mulberry tree. Centuries later, after the Moslem conquest of Samarkand, the Arabs brought paper to Baghdad about 800 A.D. and to Spain about 1150 A.D. It reached England in the 1300s.

In the early 1800s, an inquisitive observer, having watched a wasp making a nest of chewed-up wood, concluded that paper might be made from wood reduced to a pulp. In 1854, a method was developed, but not until 1866 did paper making become commercially successful. Today wood accounts for 80 to 90 per cent of the total pulp requirements of the paper industry.

Wood pulp is produced by mechanical and chemical means. About two thirds of the world pulp supply is made chemically, about a third mechanically.

CHEMICAL PULP

Three processes are in use—the *sulfite, sulfate,* and *soda.* In all three the logs, which are about 50 per cent cellulose in the form of fibers and 50 per cent lignin and other binding agents, are reduced to small chips and cooked under pressure in a chemical solution. The chemicals used determine the differences in the various pulps, but the purpose of the chemical process is to remove all nonfibrous matter. In this process the volume of the log is reduced by about half.

MECHANICAL PULP

In this process, which accounts for about 25 per cent of the pulp produced in the United States, the barked logs are ground into a pulp by revolving grindstones: hence the term "groundwood pulp." This pulp, low in strength, is regarded as inferior to that made by the chemical process, and is used in making low-grade paper such as newsprint.

LOCATION OF THE PULP-MAKING INDUSTRY

Pulp-making plants are a prime example of a *raw-materials* oriented industry. Such plants are located as near the source of wood as possible or on streams where the logs can be stream driven and thus cheaply assembled (Fig. 26-14). A company invariably finds it

necessary to buy outright sufficient timber holdings to ensure continuity of operations. Clean water in abundance also is a requirement, for pulp mills are among the four largest users of water in the United States—1.2 trillion gallons in 1953, or about 5 per cent of the total industrial intake of the United States. Sulfate pulp mills use about 64,000 gallons per ton of product; soda mills, 85,000 gallons; paperboard mills, about 15,000 gallons; and finished-paper mills, about 39,000 gallons. However, water is usually quite abundant in forested areas, where there is usually a dearth of other types of manufacturing. Thus the pulp industry has been expanding mostly in the Pacific Northwest and in the Southeast of the United States where tree growth is rapid and where there is a wide margin of water above the needs.

Transportation is a major consideration in locating pulp mills, for huge tonnages of raw materials must be assembled as well as fabricated materials sent to market. Still another location factor is power—cheap power—for driving the machinery; but electrical energy can be delivered via wire to the plant, provided the plant is not more than 300 miles distant.

As the world's peoples become more literate, and as general economic development rises, world production of pulp increases. The United States alone contributes about 47 per cent of the world total; and, together with Canada and Europe, produces about 90 per cent.

PAPER NEWSPRINT AND PAPERBOARD

PAPER

Paper, newsprint, and paperboard are made from pulp. The bulk of the world's paper is consumed in those countries having the highest living standards. Thus, the United States in a recent year had a per capita consumption of paper of 384 pounds; the United Kingdom, 163; West Germany, 115; Japan, 52; the Soviet Union, 26; India, 1; and China (where paper

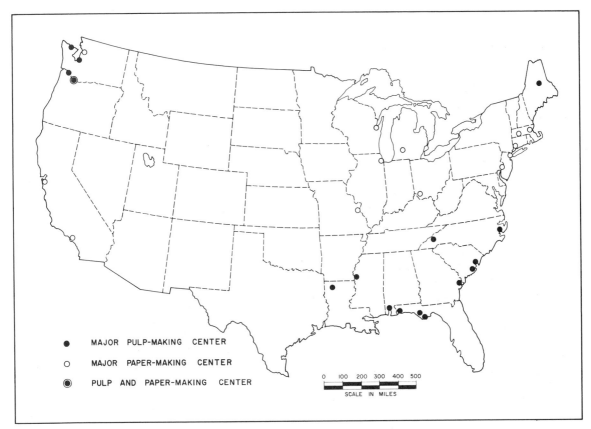

Fig. 26-14. Pulp and paper mills in the United States. (Courtesy of American Forest Products Industries, Inc.)

was invented), 2. The underdeveloped lands, with 70 per cent of the world population, consume only 8 per cent of the paper and make only 5½ per cent.

During the early years of paper production in the United States, paper was made from rags; and, since large population centers constituted the main source of supply of rags, paper mills were located in or near cities. With the development of wood as the principal raw material for paper, centers were located in or near the forests. Eventually the forests were cut down. However, the mills were too expensive to be moved; for their machinery comprised some of the biggest, most costly, most permanent, and most stationary in all industry. They have, accordingly, tended to remain in the original location, despite the higher cost of their raw materials by reason of the retreating timber supply. Hence,

over the years a sort of geographical obsolescence has attacked the mills.

NEWSPRINT

Newsprint comprises the largest unit of the industry—30 per cent of the total output of paper. It consists of a mixture of mechanical pulp (ground wood) and unbleached sulfite or semibleached sulfate in the ratio of about 80 to 15. The latter is added for strength. In 1960, United States mills met only about 25 per cent of domestic needs; the remaining 75 per cent was imported, mostly from Canada.

Newsprint plants are located in or near the forest and invariably are associated with pulp mills. They should also be near (1) an abundance of cheap power, (2) a large water supply, (3) waste-disposal facilities, and (4) good transport. An adequate labor supply, attractive community living, and receptiveness of the local population also enter into the selection of a plant site.

Since capital requirements are large, this industry in the United States is restricted to about a dozen plants strategically located so as to be assured of sufficient timber reserves to cover at least one half of normal requirements. The rest is usually purchased on the open market. Since long-distance transportation on this product (whose raw-material cost is a vital factor in the price of the finished product) is prohibitive, the pulp to be purchased must be available within a limited area—within 50 miles of the plant.

PAPERBOARD

Kraft paperboard constitutes a separate division. It goes into all kinds of boxes, containers, and cartons, serving as a corrugated board and a solid fiberboard. So popular has paperboard become, as a consequence of the growing scarcity of lumber and the savings in freight, that its consumption has doubled every decade since 1899.

This industry is raw-materials oriented, since there is much weight loss. In the United States it is located in the East, South, Middle West, and Far West. About a third of the plants are in New England and the Middle Atlantic states. The mills in the Middle West are mostly in Illinois, Indiana, Michigan, Ohio, and Wisconsin. The mills in the South, though among the latest to be built, show the largest percentage increase of production. The growing per capita consumption of paper has meant a large amount of waste paper in large cities, a source of raw material for paperboard plants that located there to use the waste. Such plants are also close to their markets.

PAPER MANUFACTURE

UNITED STATES

The United States leads all countries in the manufacture of paper, contributing about 60 per cent of the total world output. Moreover, the industry, the fifth ranking in the United States, uses more than 20 million cords of wood per annum. A single edition of the Sunday *New York Times* uses up the yield from

20 acres of trees. In the fabrication of paper, the nation falls into four regions.

THE NORTHEAST

The industry here mushroomed in the period 1865 to 1925. Massachusetts and New York (particularly the Adirondacks) became famous for their high-grade paper—some of it so good it was used as superior book paper. With the progressive depletion of the spruce stand, the industry shifted to the Lake states. However, Penobscot County, Maine, still is important.

THE LAKE STATES

With the decline of the Northeast, the Lake states became outstanding, producing largely high-grade paper. Little newsprint is produced because spruce is both scarce and costly.

The region is far from being self-sufficient in its local sources of raw material. In recent years it has been obliged to import from Canada up to one fourth of its pulp. The industry here uses about 40 per cent wastepaper, rags, and straw, and about 60 per cent new wood pulp.

However, the region is strategically located with respect to markets; it enjoys the momentum of an early start (the cost of mills is now so great that the plants tend to be immovable even when far away from their sources of pulp); and it possesses plenty of clean, cold water and considerable hydroelectric power. Moreover, its people understand the industry.

Wisconsin, leading state in the region, is likewise the leader in the nation—in number of persons employed, mill investment, and total sales volume. The industry is concentrated along 35 miles of the Fox River between Green Bay and Lake Winnebago and also along the Wisconsin River.

THE SOUTH

The South, sometimes called "the greatest natural tree farm in the world," has become the center of gravity of the entire United States paper industry. Since 1928 the number of pulp and paper mills has increased from 27 to 63. The replacement value of these plants is almost 3 billion dollars. Nearly 50 per cent

Fig. 26-15. *Air view of the world's largest integrated forest-products manufacturing center. It includes 3 sawmills, 1 plywood mill, 4 pulp mills, a bark-products plant, a fabricating plant, a chemical plant, and research facilities. This industrial complex involves so enormous an investment that the plants may be safely regarded as immobile— even fixed. This complex at Longview, Washington, exemplifies scientific plant location. (Courtesy of Weyerhaeuser Company.)*

of the nation's pulp and about 40 per cent of its paper are manufactured in the South.

Southern mills are more modern and more efficient than the mills in the East. Moreover, there is the great advantage in raw material: the trees grow so rapidly that they become economic raw material in 25 to 35 years or even less; copious rainfall, abundant sunshine, and long open winters enable Southern conifers to grow two to three times faster than do those in New England and the Lake states. Also, *timber cropping* is replacing *timber mining;* through this type of intelligent tree farming (222 million seedlings are planted each year), the supply of timber for pulping in the South can be made inexhaustible. There is a plentiful supply of labor and water, a year-long operating period, and nearness to major consuming markets. The region claims to produce paper products at lower cost than any other part of the United States. The South is especially outstanding in the production of kraft or strong paper and board (for sacks, bags, and wrapping paper).

THE PACIFIC COAST

The first mill, a rag-paper mill, was built in 1866-1867 at Oregon City. Today the paper mills, based upon wood, are mostly integrated —that is, they are a combination of pulp and paper mills (Fig. 26-15). In one respect this region is unique: it is self-contained, and it

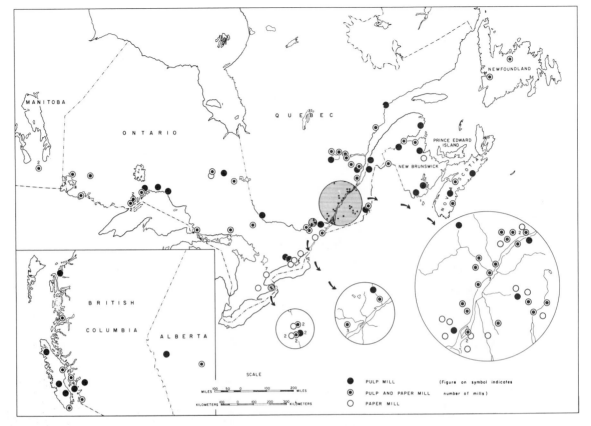

Fig. 26-16. Pulp and paper mills in Canada. (Courtesy of Dominion Bureau of Statistics.)

makes all classes of paper and paperboard from its own forests.

Probably nowhere else in the world does virgin timber produce such quantities of usable pulpwood—the average being sixty to seventy cords per acre as compared with about twenty cords in eastern United States, eastern Canada, Fennoscandia, and Russia. The reproducing capacity also is in excess of these other regions.

An important resource in addition to the forest is plentiful water of good quality. Most of the water is soft and, after treatment, is well suited to the industry. Since both the Columbia and the Willamette are navigable, most of the logs are rafted to the mills.

As the New England region leads in making finer paper, and the South in kraft papers and newsprint, the Pacific Coast is supreme in making bleached and unbleached sulfite

pulp, which is well suited for making high-grade paper.

CANADA

Canada leads the world in the manufacture of pulp and newsprint, and the industry is the principal factor in the nation's industrial life. The pulp and paper industry ranks first in employment, in total wages paid, in export values (22 per cent), and in capital invested; in short, it is Canada's leading industry.

Scattered over the Dominion in remote areas, often deep in the forests, are some 108 mills—35 devoted to making newsprint (Fig. 26-16). This industry has played a major role in the development of the Dominion's water power, for it uses about half of all the power generated for industry and mining. A string of mills, all water driven, lines the southern edge of the forest from the mouth of the St.

Lawrence to Lake Winnipeg. Especially important is the north shore of the St. Lawrence between Montreal and the city of Quebec and along such tributaries as the St. Maurice, Saguenay, and Ottawa. Among the leading advantages of this area for pulp and paper manufacture are (1) propinquity to the great forest; (2) navigability of the St. Lawrence, which enables deep-draft vessels to bring raw materials to the mills and take manufactured products to the markets of the world; and (3) numerous streams that descend from the Canadian Shield to the Great Lakes or the St. Lawrence River, which can provide both transportation for logs and hydroelectric-power development.

Canada ranks especially high in the manufacture of newsprint. To be specific, Canada supplies the equivalent of three out of every five newspaper pages printed throughout the world. Of the enormous tonnage of newsprint, about 95 per cent is exported—85 per cent to the United States. Europe and Latin America also are important markets. Since 1929, the United States has reduced its own newsprint output by one half because greater profit can be made by making other types of paper. There is no tariff on Canadian newsprint or pulp shipped into the United States, but there is a tariff on other paper products. This tariff, together with the relatively small market for paper in Canada, has played a major role in that country's concentration on newsprint.

The demand for wood for purposes other than paper manufacture (e.g., for rayon, plastics, and building and packaging materials) is increasing rapidly; consequently, many American firms—concerned that the supplies necessary to operate their American mills might become increasingly difficult to obtain —have acquired, by lease or license, large forested areas in Canada and have erected pulp mills from which they ship pulp to their own paper mills in the United States.

It is believed that the spruce-balsam forest is so extensive that it can meet the needs of the industry in perpetuity, provided reasonable conservation is practiced.

Newfoundland, peripheral to the heart of Canada's paper empire, is a major manufac-turer of newsprint. Almost 100 per cent of the output is destined for the export market, since the small population at home consumes a negligible amount. The United States regularly absorbs more than half.

NORTHWESTERN EUROPE

Particularly important in this industry are three of the Fennoscandic countries—Sweden, Finland, and Norway. Prior to the outbreak of World War II, they had only one rival in the exportation of newsprint—Canada.

SWEDEN

This country, a leader among world producers of pulp, newsprint, and paper, supplies about 10 per cent of the world output of wood pulp. Nowhere else on earth, except in Canada, does the pulp and paper industry consume so large a proportion of the annual forest cut. The trees do not attain great size, but they are suitable for pulp; streams are numerous for log floating; hydropower is abundant and accessible; and the important European market is close by. The interruption of shipping in winter on the Gulf of Bothnia has caused paper mills to locate farther south than pulp mills to permit year-around shipments.

The largest pulp-mill capacity is in the Sundsvall and Kramfors areas, though the latter, particularly the valley of the Ångermanälv with its older and smaller plants, is stagnating. The country's new mills are being located in southern Sweden, since wood from deciduous trees is now suitable for pulping. Mills producing mechanical pulp are invariably attached to those producing newsprint. Although the majority of the plants are situated at the mouths of rivers, there are exceptions as in the Örnsköldsvik area.

FINLAND

More than 70 per cent of Finland is heavily forested, and the forest is the bulwark of the nation's economy. Though Finland lost 25 per cent of its pulp-mill capacity with the war-ceded territory, the nation nevertheless is still outstanding; it increased its capacity by 45 per cent in the three-year period ending in

1962. Pulp and paper accounted for 42 per cent of the total exports in 1960.

The mills are closely tied to water—(1) rivers for stream driving, pulp processing, and power; and (2) ports for exporting pulp and paper. About half of all the electric energy in the country is used by pulp and paper mills. Most important pulp-making area is the Kymi River, whose major advantages are an early start, proximity to large forests, and ample supply of soft water. There are pulp mills also on the southeastern shore of Lake Saimaa and in the lake region on the railway lines that lead to winter export ports on the Gulf of Finland and the southern Gulf of Bothnia. Several newsprint mills, among them the largest in all Europe, are located in Finland east of Kotra. Western Europe provides the market for about 65 per cent of Finland's exports of pulp and paper.

NORWAY

Norway's pulp and paper industry, though far less impressive than those of her two neighbors to the east, is nonetheless important. Forest makes up one fifth of the total area of the country. The mountains facing the Atlantic, which one would expect to be clothed with fine forest because of the moisture-laden prevailing westerlies, are largely barren; the trees, cut long ago for export, have been replaced by grass and heather. The pulp and paper industry, concentrated in the south, is especially important on the rivers of Østandet and Sørlandet, where the usual favorable combination of conditions for this industry is to be found.

SOVIET UNION

The Soviet Union still is a small producer of pulp and paper (particularly on a per capita basis) compared with the United States and Canada. In 1950, Russia ranked sixth in world production. Since paper is a consumer good and the Soviet Union has emphasized capital goods (heavy industry), neglect of the paper industry is understandable.

As far as raw material is concerned, the Soviet Union possesses about one fifth of the accessible forest area of the world, a high per-

centage of the trees being pulpable. Three fourths consists of conifers; and more than half consists of spruce, fir, and pine. The distribution of this forest is less fortunate, however, more than three fourths being in Asiatic Russia—far from market. Moreover, the quality of this eastern forest is not outstanding for pulp and paper. Finally, the undeveloped transport net over much of Asiatic Russia is a retarding factor. Also, despite the fact that the Soviet Union has one of the longest systems of inland waterways in the world, the rivers by and large flow at cross currents to the channels of trade, running generally from south to north in the eastern and northern areas and from north to south in the western ones. There is also trouble with ice and floods in the lower courses of the north-flowing Siberian rivers.

Hence, the pulp and paper industry is located in northwestern European Russia, particularly in the Leningrad area, along with its satellite centers at Dubrovka, Parakhino, Svetogorsk, and Syassk. Many of the mills formerly belonged to the Baltic countries and to Finland. These acquisitions, rather than indigenous plant expansion, have accounted for much of the Soviet Union's growth in the pulp and paper industry. Russia's production is higher today than at any time in its history, but the country still must depend on imports.

ASIA

JAPAN

Paper is more important to the Japanese than to any other people in the world. Their homes have paper sliding doors and paper walls; and their umbrellas and raincoats, as well as many of their household articles, are made of oiled paper. Japan "westernized" her paper industry early. She makes two kinds of paper—Japanese style and foreign style. The latter is machine made, largely from wood pulp, and is used mostly for newsprint. The largest and most important pulp and paper mills are in Hokkaido, which has large stands of spruce and considerable hydroelectric power. Paper mills are also located in Honshu and Kyushu.

The Japanese-style paper continues to be fabricated by the traditional handicraft methods from the leaf of the mulberry tree, rice straw, and other plant fibers.

CHINA

China, the home of paper, still is a manufacturer but an unimportant one. Most of the paper is made from rice straw.

INDIA

India manufactures about half of her requirements of paper and boards but is wholly dependent upon imports for newsprint. India does, however, possess the requisites for an important industry—bamboo, grass, bagasse, wastepaper, and rags, besides spruce and fir. Only wood pulp must be imported. A modern newsprint and paper plant has recently been erected in the Central Provinces; it uses a mixture of bamboo pulp and pulp from a deciduous tree called *salai*.

SPECIAL FOREST PRODUCTS

LUMBER

The principal primary product of the world's natural-wood industries is lumber. It is made in establishments ranging from very primitive to very highly mechanized, and its manufacture constitutes one of the world's most important economic pursuits. Most of the lumber, both for world markets and domestic use, leaves the sawmills in square-edged form and is cut to standard thicknesses, lengths, and widths (Fig. 26-17). In 1957 the Soviet Union became the world's leading lumber producer, followed closely by the United States (Table 26-2).

Of such superior utility are the softwoods that, although they constitute only a little more than half the estimated growing stock of all the forests in use, they supply four fifths of the world's annual lumber supply. Broad-leaved species contribute relatively little to the volume of the world's lumber trade.

TABLE 26-2

WORLD LUMBER PRODUCTION
(HARDWOOD AND SOFTWOOD)
(figures in 1,000 cubic meters)

Country	Production (1957)
Soviet Union	79,000
United States	78,803
Japan	23,100
Canada	15,839
Sweden	7,325
Poland	7,043
France	7,000
West Germany	6,944
Finland	3,924
Brazil	3,425
China	3,120
Australia	3,101
Norway	1,892
New Zealand	1,409
Burma	440
Congo	321

SOURCE: "The World Picture," *The Timberman*, 60:4, May 29, 1959.

FUEL WOOD

The heaviest drain on the world's forests is for fuel. This has been true for thousands of years—long before man learned to use coal, oil, and natural gas. Even today more than half of all the wood consumed in the world is used for fuel. Based on value, however, the figure is a mere 15 per cent. In underdeveloped countries or regions where coal is lacking and petroleum costly, wood is employed both as untreated wood and as charcoal. Most fuel wood is used by farmers for their own use. In those parts of the world where the preferred fuels are scarce but where labor is cheap, as in many parts of Asia, wood is hauled considerable distances by cart or burro for sale in markets. And along some of the world's great rivers, boats burn wood—some from the natural forest, some from trees planted following deforestation (Fig. 26-18). One writer speaks of seeing hundreds of cords of mahogany and rosewood brought aboard Amazon River steamers for firewood, and another asserts that at least 75 million people in Latin America depend on the forest to provide firewood or charcoal.

Fig. 26-17. Many modern lumber mills blast the bark from the log by jets of high-pressure water. Thus, when the log is sawed into lumber, the slabs and edgings are already de-barked and can be converted to chips for pulp-making. (Courtesy of the Weyerhaeuser Company.)

CHARCOAL

Though charcoal, made from wood, is widely used, much is prepared by such primitive and wasteful methods that the valuable distillates are wasted. It is believed that charcoal burning has been the greatest single factor in forest destruction in Southwest Asia. Much good forest has similarly been burned for charcoal in various parts of Latin America (e.g., Mexico). Despite the fact that Japan has much hydropower and some coal, she supplements her coal in industry with charcoal.

CORK

Commercial cork is the outer bark of a species of oak which is to be found over some 5.3 million acres of cork forest in countries bordering the western arm of the Mediterranean Sea—particularly Portugal, Spain, and Algeria. Portugal, with about two thirds of the trees, leads in every phase of the business—number of persons engaged and in total tonnage of the crop (about half). The United States uses about half the annual world output.

The trees are carefully stripped every eight to ten years; poorest-quality bark is obtained from the first stripping, with each subsequent one improving during the 150- to 300-year life-span of the tree. The bark is dried in the open for several days, then delivered to market and sold. The product, because of its lightness and its resistance to moisture and

Fig. 26-18. Stop along the Amazon where river boats take on wood. The captain of the steamer decides where he will stop, since there are thousands of such places where wood is available. (Courtesy of Panair do Brasil.)

to penetration by liquids and sound, is valuable for flooring, life preservers, bottle stoppers, insulation, and compositions of various kinds.

TANNINS

Many species of trees yield **tannins.** In the United States (where tannins are obtained from the barks of eastern hemlock, chestnut, oak, and tanbark oak and the wood from chestnut) production at one time was very important; today, however, the nation imports possibly 90 per cent of the vegetable tannins it uses. Of the tannins imported, about 70 per cent is obtained from quebracho wood and about 20 per cent from wattle bark.

QUEBRACHO

The wood of this scrubby tree, which grows on the west side of the Paraguay-Paraná Rivers in the Gran Chaco of Argentina and Paraguay, contains a higher percentage of tannin content than any other tree. About 500,000 acres are cut over annually; yet at current rates of cutting the supply should last for 150 years. At riverside mills the logs are chipped and leached to yield an extract; more than 125,000 metric tons of this extract were exported in 1960. However, the world market and the price for quebracho have been declining since 1953.

WATTLE

Tanbark, with most of the same properties as quebracho, is obtained from wattle (acacia), which grows in Australia and in South Africa. Since wattle is produced at less cost than quebracho and may be used as a substitute, it, possibly more than anything else, has reduced the importance of quebracho.

NAVAL STORES

From the distillation of the pitch that exudes from the wounds made in living pine trees when they are tapped are procured turpentine and rosin, the two principal products that travel under the name "naval stores." They also are obtained from steam distillation of pine stumps in which all nonresinous portions have rotted away.

Principal forests supporting naval-stores industries are in the American South, the Soviet Union, France, Portugal, and Sweden. Those of the United States yield more than those of all the rest of the world combined, exclusive of the Soviet Union, which is believed to rank second.

WORLD TRADE

The world's annual forest harvest, outweighed only by coal, is estimated at 1,000 to 1,200 million tons. These forest products serve a greater variety of uses than any other material. Lumber leads the list of products, accounting with other structural uses for about one third of the annual world timber cut. Standard of living weighs most heavily on lumber consumption. Thus, the one fourth of the world's population living in Europe and North America consumes more than 60 per cent of the world's lumber, though only 21 per cent of the world's forests are there.

Foreign trade is dominated by the relation between weight and value. Obviously fuel wood cannot enter international trade; it is restricted to local use. Even lumber experiences some difficulty, less than one fifth of the world output getting into foreign trade. Pulp and paper, conversely, move freely over the world. (A cubic meter of wood converted to pulp contributes twice as much to national income as a cubic meter converted to lumber.)

The countries leading in foreign trade of lumber are Canada, Sweden, and Finland. The United States and the United Kingdom are the only major importers. Despite the Soviet Union's enormous forested area, the nation's growing needs—along with those of her satellites—keep down the volume of timber products available for export.

WORLD OUTLOOK

Some authorities forecast a wood famine for the underdeveloped lands that either possess poor forests or lack them altogether; equally well-informed authorities insist that no world shortage of timber is even in sight. In any event, the rapid, relentless increase in the world's population is making heavy drains on natural resources, including forests. The United States, Canada, and the countries of Western Europe consume more than 80 per cent of all the wood used; yet they possess only a small part of the world's total population. As peoples in the underdeveloped lands attain higher levels of living, they will need and demand more forest products; for, as has been noted, forests furnish the raw material for thousands of essential commodities.

Can the world's forests meet the staggering demands that are now being made and will increasingly be made on them? A world survey made in 1953 indicated that the world's forests are potentially capable of providing a flow of forest products for an expanding population, that less than one third of the present forest lands of the earth are being exploited. The survey also emphasized the marked contrast in man's use of softwood and hardwood forests. In the coniferous forests (if bark be included), growth and drain are roughly in balance, whereas in the hardwood forests growth exceeds drain. This underexploitation results in large measure from the unmarketability of many of the tropical and subtropical species.

In few countries on earth are forests receiving the attention they merit. Yet here is one of the few instances in natural-resources conservation where an optimistic viewpoint seems justifiable; for, fortunately, trees are a renewable resource—more can be grown on the same land, provided man employs more intelligence in his adjustment to the forest. Man can and must work on a world scale toward the goal of so increasing forest output that it keeps up with world needs.

SELECTED REFERENCES

America's Stake in World Forestry, Washington, D. C., U.S. Department of Agriculture, 1953. Report of the Chief of the Forest Service.

Calkin, John B. "The Pulp and Paper Industry," in Albert S. Carlson (ed.), *Economic Geography of Industrial Materials*. New York, Reinhold Publishing Corporation, 1956, pp. 310-331.

Clifford, Nicholas. *Commercial Hardwoods*. London, Sir Isaac Pitman & Sons, 1953.

Greeley, W. B. *Forests and Men*, Garden City, N. Y., Doubleday and Company, 1951.

Haden-Guest, Stephen, John K. Wright, and Eileen M. Teclaff (eds.). *A World Geography of Forest Resources*. New York, The Ronald Press Company, 1956.

Hills, Theo L. "New Zealand Forestry in Transition," *Journal of Geography*, 50:265-276, October 1951.

The Pulp and Paper Industry in Europe. Report by a Mission of European Experts, Published by the Organization for European Economic Cooperation, June 1959.

Richards, P. W. *The Tropical Rain Forest*, Cambridge, Cambridge University Press, 1952.

Rodgers, Allan. "Changing Locational Patterns in the Soviet Pulp and Paper Industry," *Annals of the Association of American Geographers*, 45:85-104, March 1955.

Sokolov, A. V. "The Map of the Forests of the U.S.S.R.," *Soviet Geography: Review and Translation*, 1:68-71, January–February 1960.

Timber Resources for America's Future. Washington, D. C., U.S. Department of Agriculture, January 1958. Forest Resource Report No. 14.

Trees; Yearbook of Agriculture, 1949. Washington, D. C., U.S. Department of Agriculture, Forest Service, 1949.

Yohe, R. S. "Forest Management in Sweden," *Foreign Agriculture*, 17:208-209, November–December 1953.

Zivnuska, J. A. "What's Ahead: Timber Surplus or Famine?" *Timberman*, 60:28-31, May 29, 1959.

CHAPTER TWENTY-SEVEN ::

Fishing is one of man's oldest and most wide-spread economic pursuits; however, it has not been one of his most progressive enterprises. An eminent biologist has gone so far as to say that the industry has advanced very little during the past thousand years—undoubtedly an exaggeration, but it is true that fishing has not been identified with the high degree of technological development that has charac-terized agriculture and manufacturing.

Although fishing supplies less than 4 per cent of the earth's food and gives employment to a minor proportion of the world's working force, the current world population explosion is forcing humanity to consider all possible sources of food. Animal proteins constitute the most serious food shortage, and these—now regarded as necessary in a well-balanced diet—come nine tenths from the land. With

THE WORLD'S

the rapid growth in world population, it seems hardly justifiable to be producing so many meat animals on lands capable of yielding food crops, since the raising of livestock is an inefficient way of utilizing good potential farmland. Fish would be the most easily available source for making up the deficiency. Thus, the fisheries may be the world's greatest undeveloped natural resource.

The biggest problem facing the fishing industry is that of bringing the riches of the oceans to man's table at a reasonable price. It was estimated recently that the total take has run no more than 1 pound of fish to the ocean acre the world over. This amount is expected to increase as a result of many new inventions, such as echo-sounding devices, electric fields, electronic barriers for the protection of valuable fish or the destruction of harmful ones, and electric traps for smaller fish.

PLANKTON: OCEAN PASTURES

Fish are the end product of a food chain that starts with plankton (from the Greek word meaning "wandering")—a vast living, swimming, drifting mass of tiny plants and animals that comprises the most abundant life forms in the oceans. A square mile of sea is reported to produce on the average 13,000 tons of vegetation per annum—five times the amount produced on land. Plankton, which forms the pastures of the sea, drifts passively with the ocean currents and tides.

COMMERCIAL FISHING ACTIVITIES

The single-celled diatoms and related microscopic plants tap the energy of the sun and conduct the major portion of the photosynthesis that goes on in the oceans—that is, they transform carbon dioxide and water into living material. Algae can carry on photosynthesis with much less light than other plants; they do so even in the long winter night of the polar regions. Under optimal conditions of light, temperature, and nutrient supply, they may multiply so abundantly as to actually cloud the water, giving it a green color and a slimy feel.

Algae are devoured by slightly larger protozoa; protozoa and algae are eaten by numerous tiny crustaceans; the crustaceans in turn serve as food for the herring, the most abundant fish of the ocean; and the herring finally is eaten by such carnivorous fish as cod, haddock, and tuna. Not only are algae the first link in the food chain, but they also give a foothold to plant and animal life in places where one would think no life could exist. . . .[1]

The minute algae, then, form the "grass of the sea" and are the base of a food pyramid, the apex of which is occupied by fishes or sea mammals (whales and seals) that serve as food for man. In short, they form the basis of the whole structure of marine life. They do best in cold water, which is richest in the nutriments they require.

FISH AS A RESOURCE

According to the Smithsonian Institution, there are 40,000 species and subspecies of fish. Through the ages these fish have evolved into a diverse group to fit the various habitats and to follow various ways of life. Some of them fly (but not like birds); some leap, walk, and burrow, as well as swim. Some fish, like the swordfish, can swim 60 miles per hour; whereas others, like the bass, do well to make 12 miles per hour.

Fish are more abundant, as far as number of species is concerned, in the tropics than in the colder waters of subpolar and polar seas or even of the cold currents in the tropics. This is a disadvantage for commercial fishermen, who prefer to capture large numbers of a single species when possible, since they can dispose of the catch more easily—often selling it to a single merchant.

Below relatively shallow depths, fish decrease. in number quite rapidly because the supply of dead and sinking food naturally diminishes with depth as it is eaten or decomposed. The fish that occupy the middle and lower depths of the ocean are sparsely distributed and specially adapted to conditions of darkness and high pressure. However, no part of the sea water is completely devoid of animal life.

THE OCEAN HABITAT

Surprisingly little is known in detail about the world oceans. The oceans are essentially a great wilderness full of secrets. At the same time, they are a vast treasure-house of unexplored riches. Only certain features are as yet understood: the sunlight conditions and the surface and near-surface temperatures for those parts frequented by vessels. However, more and more is being learned of the ocean depths, currents, and wind systems. Similarly, most of the fishing **banks** have now been mapped; and the charting of the shelf areas of the world is now virtually completed. Oceanography has added considerable knowledge of the world oceans during the past several years, but at the same time it has emphasized the vastness of the subject and the need to extend the scope of deep-sea research.

Most of the world's fish are caught on the **continental shelves**; the 100-fathom-depth contour (600 feet) is generally accepted as the approximate edge of the continental shelf and of the intensive shelf type of fishing. Beyond this depth the water usually deepens quite rapidly. The width of the continental shelf, therefore, is a major factor in the general intensity of fishing activity in an area; for it is on these shelves that the fish food is most abundant.

[1] F. J. Weiss, "The Useful Algae," *Scientific American*, 187:15, December 1952.

Fig. 27-1. *Beam trawling. The open-mouthed net bag, weighted at the bottom, entangles the fish and is pulled forward by the trawler, which scoops up fish in its path. (Courtesy of Lionel Walford and of U.S. Fish and Wildlife Service, Bureau of Commercial Fisheries.)*

METHODS OF FISHING

Methods of fishing are a response to (1) the habits of the fish, (2) the physical environment in which the fish are to be found, (3) spawning needs and food supply, (4) the cultural habits and technological level of the fishermen, and (5) the availability of capital.

Two principal methods of fishing—*demersal* and *pelagic*—are presented briefly.

DEMERSAL FISHING

Demersal fishing involves the seeking of fish that find their food on or near the sea floor. This means deep fishing—usually several hundred feet below the vessel. Such fishing calls for strong, bulky, costly equipment and large, expensive vessels to handle it. Demersal fish may dwell in quite dense association, though not to the extent of many pelagic species. Since most demersal fishes (e.g., cod, haddock, halibut) are predators, a major method of catching them is by baited hooks.

Trawls also are much used in demersal fishing. A trawl is a large, flattened, conical-shaped bag about 150 feet long with a mesh of about 3 inches square in the forward third of the bag; 1½ inches square in the central mesh, and a smaller, doubled mesh in the cod end of the trawl. The strength and size of the rope vary with the type of sea bed; a rocky bed requires a heavier and stronger trawl than a sandy one. The trawl is towed along the bottom by a **dragger** at the rate of 2 to 3 miles per hour (Fig. 27-1). A dragger, which may cost in excess of $75,000, is powered by diesel engines, whose compact power plant enables a few men with a winch to handle the great nets swiftly and smoothly.

Trawlers operate both in relatively shallow and deep waters. The more modern ones, which weigh up to 1,500 tons and are designed for expeditions up to thirty days, can fillet and deep-freeze the fish and even convert waste into fish meal.

The catching of shellfish is also a demersal activity, since shellfish have bottom-living habits. The simplest methods consist of using tongs or rakes operated by hand from vessels or small boats in shallow water, as in the catching of clams, oysters, scallops—all relatively immobile creatures (Fig. 27-2). Dredg-

Fig. 27-2. Tonging and dredging for oysters, Chesapeake Bay. Because the rich oyster beds were nearly destroyed by overfishing and pollution, oyster farming has become predominant; some 17,000 watermen from Maryland and Virginia are engaged in the business. (Courtesy of U.S. Department of Agriculture.)

ing is also resorted to, as is the suction pump. Traps of various types are used to catch crabs and lobsters; these traps or "pots" are laid on the sea bed where the inshore grounds are free from mud and where currents are weak. Prawns and shrimps also are caught from trawlers.

PELAGIC FISHING

Unlike demersal or botton fishing, pelagic fishing is concerned with capturing fish, such as mackerel, herring, and tuna, that travel in large schools close to the surface; such fish are found in greatest density on the continental shelves, though they are not limited to them. Pelagic fish are strong swimmers and are generally less tied to specific localities than are demersal fish. Moreover, they are more seasonal because they are more migratory. Some feed on plankton; others on fish. They are caught chiefly by drift net, floating gill net, purse-seine net, troll line, and other such gear adapted to efficient operation at or near the surface.

PRINCIPAL FISHING AREAS AND NATIONS

Figure 27-3 shows the major commercial fishing areas of the world. Most of it occurs relatively near the continents and in the Northern Hemisphere—mainly because the greater part of the world's population dwells there.

Eleven nations together account for well over half the world's annual commercial catch of some 30 million tons (Table 27-1).

JAPAN

On all accounts Japan ranks as the world's foremost fishing nation. Japan has more men engaged in fishing than any other nation—more than 3 million. Because Japan is only about the size of the state of California, because 75 per cent is mountainous, and because fodder is in short supply, livestock are not very important. Accordingly, seafood contributes about 85 per cent of the total animal

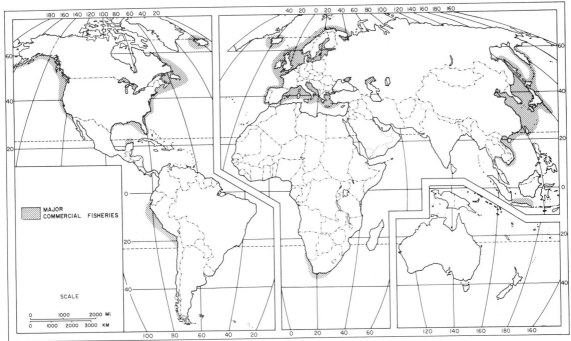

Fig. 27-3. World fisheries. Fishing, though latitudinally one of man's most widely distributed economic pursuits, is nonetheless mostly a Northern Hemisphere enterprise, the principal reason being the presence of the huge market for fish there. The map also emphasizes that most of the commercial fishing (except whaling) is confined to those portions of the seas relatively close to land. It is believed, though not yet proved, that the waters near land owe their greater productivity to the supply of some constituent derived from land drainage.

protein intake; and the country's per capita consumption of fish, about 100 pounds, is the highest in the world. The annual catch exceeds 22 billion pounds, or the equivalent of 9 pounds for every occupant of the earth. Most of the catch is consumed domestically —87 per cent as food. The value of the annual catch exceeds 700 million dollars, far above that for any other nation. The industry is a curious combination of ancient and modern— the result (partially) of the antiquity of the enterprise and of the great variety of the catch. The Japanese use tens of thousands of small fishing craft (Fig. 27-4), but they also have twelve times as many powered fishing vessels as the United States or the Soviet Union.

So vital is fishing to Japan that her vessels go far afield in the prosecution of the enterprise; thus Japanese fishing craft are regularly sighted in the Bering Sea, near American

TABLE 27-1

PRINCIPAL FISHING NATIONS, 1959

Country	Size of catch, in thousands of metric tons, live weight
Japan	5,875.0
China	5,020.0
United States	2,889.7
Soviet Union	2,756.0
Peru	2,000.0
Norway	1,607.2
Canada	1,050.6
United Kingdom	988.9
India	822.8
West Germany	765.0
Indonesia	723.3
Denmark	673.7
Iceland	639.9
Philippines	517.5
France (including Algeria)	511.0

SOURCE: Statistical Office of the United Nations, Department of Economic and Social Affairs, *Statistical Yearbook, 1960*, New York, 1960, pp. 122-123.

Fig. 27-4. Young fishermen drawing in net with its rich haul of yellowtail, at Kumanonada, one of Japan's three greatest fishing grounds. The young fishermen here are engaged in a fishing method unique to Japan. (Courtesy of Consulate General of Japan.)

Samoa and New Caledonia, and within a few hours of the New Zealand coast.

Japan is situated in possibly the most important fishing region in the world; for here converge cold and warm ocean currents, and the area of continental shelf is extensive. Moreover, the latitudinal extent of the insular nation gives the country access to waters of various temperatures, with resultant variation in the fish life. However, the fish caught near Japan are mainly warm-water species. The indented coastline affords numerous harbors and protection to fishing craft (Fig. 27-5).

Japanese fisheries are classified into *coastal, offshore, ocean, river,* and *lake.*

The waters near Japan, however, rich as they are, cannot meet the enormous fish needs of the 95 million Japanese. Hence, prior to World War II, Japanese fishermen went great distances in search of their quarry. Following World War II, the United States, the Soviet Union, Canada, China, Korea, and Australia excluded Japanese fishermen from many of their traditional fishing grounds. Most such restrictions, however, have since been relaxed.

It is difficult for the fisheries of Western nations to compete with those of Japan, for the differential in wages is substantial—$400 and up versus $100 per month. New Zealand fishermen assert, for example, that they cannot compete with Japan, that the Japanese can catch fish off the New Zealand Coast and land them in Kobe more cheaply than the New Zealanders can land catches in Auckland.

COMMUNIST CHINA

The Food and Agriculture Organization of the United Nations estimated in 1958 that China's catch was 6.6 million tons. If this figure were accurate (which may be unlikely

Fig. 27-5. Remote fishing village, Japan, where the fishermen-farmers still operate small wooden boats for part of the year and cultivate their fields during the off season. This type of coastline—so poorly adapted to commercial agriculture, yet so characteristic of much of Japan —naturally stimulates fishing. Japan, with more than 3 million persons engaged in this occupation, has about half the world's total fishermen. (Courtesy of Consulate General of Japan.)

because of the unreliability of Chinese statistics), it would have given China world leadership. With its long coastline bordering large shelf areas and its huge home demand for fish, China is believed to have as many as 2 million persons engaged in the enterprise.

Three types of fishing are carried on— *deep sea, inland waters,* and *inshore;* only the last is highly developed. The bulk of the catch is similar to that of Japan's subtropical fishes.

The leading fishing region lies along the southeast coast, where bays and inlets are numerous, agricultural land is scarce, and population is very dense. North China's regular coastline discourages large-scale fishing operations.

Like other peoples in Southeast Asia, the Chinese practice aquiculture, particularly in the rice-growing areas, where streams, canals, ponds, and even the rice paddies themselves provide the water milieu.

UNITED STATES

From the earliest days of settlement in Massachusetts, fishing has been important in what is now the United States. In the beginning a considerable proportion of all New Englanders lived from the sea. Today the United States ranks third in world catch, being surpassed by only Japan and China. More than a quarter of a million persons are involved, of whom 162,000 are bona fide fishermen. This is a small number compared with

Japan's 3 million, who obtain a catch just about double that of the United States (Table 27-1). Per capita consumption in the United States averages about 38½ pounds.

NEW ENGLAND

New England still boasts the largest total catch of all regions in the country. The commercial catch is currently about a billion pounds—roughly one fifth of total United States landings. The bulk of the tonnage consists of demersal fish—cod, haddock, flounder, hake, rosefish, and pollock. The cod catch, formerly the very sinew of the New England fishery, has slipped badly—sales at the Boston Fish Pier having slumped 70 per cent since World War II. Also the halibut here has been so reduced in numbers that fishing for it is no longer important.

THE BANKS

The principal areas for demersal fishing are the **banks**—broad expanses of relatively shallow continental shelf, which extend some distance out to sea from the coast. This area, from Georges Bank to the Grand Bank, is the largest shelf area within easy reach of the most densely populated part of the Americas. Ground fish are netted by diesel-powered trawlers.

Banks fishing is a dangerous business: the area is one of the foggiest in the world (the meeting place of the Labrador Current and the Gulf Stream), tropical hurricanes veer northeastward and often strike the fishing grounds, the northerly latitude increases the severity of winter weather, drifting icebergs present a navigational hazard, and the banks lie athwart the **Great Circle route** followed by trans-Atlantic vessels. However, with the adoption of draggers on the banks, the loss of life has tapered off to practically nothing —gales, fogs, and speeding liners no longer taking a terrible toll as in the past.

About two thirds of the total fish tonnage landed in New England is handled by four well-established ports—Boston, Gloucester, New Bedford, and Portland.

THE WARM ATLANTIC

This fishery differs markedly from that of New England. Here warm-water species comprise the catches; for the continental shelf is quite narrow, and hence less space is available for demersal fishing. This area leads in American pelagic fishing. The principal fish caught is the menhaden—a species allied to the herring. It is caught along the coasts of New Jersey, Delaware, Virginia, and North Carolina. Vast catches are possible because the surface schooling habits of the fish make it an easy prey to the purse seine. Menhaden are located by air search or by fish-finder and are caught in 1,200-foot nets in a great circle (Fig. 27-6). Though the menhaden catch is the largest of any single species (500,-000 tons per annum), this fish is not used for food; rather, it is converted into oil for paint, varnish, and soap, and into animal feed and fertilizers. Alewife, shad, croaker, butterfish, and scup also are taken along the coast and in estuaries by pound-net fishermen.

Most valuable fisheries of the Warm Atlantic are those concerned with shellfish—clams, crabs, and oysters. Chesapeake Bay ranks as the most intensive shell fishery in the world. The oyster predominates and is caught from Long Island Sound to North Carolina; but the Chesapeake Bay area, including the lower Potomac River, is the heart of the industry. Here about 17,000 men work the beds; and various methods, varying from tonging and dredging to suction, are employed. Unfortunately, Maryland and Virginia do not agree on how the oysters should be harvested. The cause of the trouble is less a matter of *where* to fish than of *how* to fish. On the Chesapeake itself, dredging is permitted by both states; but on the Potomac, Maryland, which controls the river up to Virginia's high-water mark under a treaty of 1785, restricts oystering to tongers and is determined to enforce the edict. Tonging is hard work and unrewarding; a dredge can bring up as many oysters in an hour or two as a tonger can in a whole day.

The oyster industry has declined from a yield of 17 million bushels in 1880 to about 10 million today—the result largely of over-fishing.

Fig. 27-6. *Pelagic fish often are caught in extensive nets, from which they must be dipped into the cargo hold of the fishing boat. This photograph shows menhaden being baled from a net off the coast of North Carolina. (Courtesy of North Carolina News Bureau, Department of Conservation and Development.)*

GULF OF MEXICO

This area is of much importance, particularly for shrimp and menhaden—menhaden dominating the catch based on weight, shrimp based on value. The Gulf has become the world's leading shrimp fishery. Shrimp fleets from Louisiana and Texas net most of the 100,000 tons that the nation consumes annually. The United States haul of shrimp now outweighs that of any other edible species.

THE WARM PACIFIC

California ranks very high in fishing; in fact, it registers the greatest landings of any state. Moreover, its industry is probably more diversified than that of any other state—about fifty species of fish and shellfish being exploited commercially. However, tuna and sardines (pilchards) have yielded the bulk of the income. California is the main base of the American tuna-fishing fleet that ranges from the state of Washington to Peru.

The continental shelf is so narrow off the California coast that most of the fishing is pelagic in nature. The cool California Current, along with the upwelling of deep, nutrient-rich water, also is an asset.

Tuna comprises the most valuable segment of the California fisheries; in some years its share in the total catch has passed 60 per cent.

Fig. 27-7. Fishing crew on a tuna clipper off the west coast of South America. As soon as a school of tuna is sighted, live anchovies are tossed from the bait tank into the sea. This attracts the tuna to the vessel; and, with heavy bamboo poles, short lines, and barbless hooks, the fishermen pull in the excited fish in rapid succession. (Courtesy of Breast-O'-Chicken Tuna, Inc.)

There are five types of tuna (mackerel family) —*albacore, yellowfin, bluefin, skipjack,* and *bonito.* Yellowfin is the most important of these based on tonnage. Tuna are caught by clippers, the fleet of which is based at San Diego, though the vessels operate as far south as Ecuador and Peru. It accounts for 70 per cent of the domestic catch. A modern clipper, costing half a million dollars, is large, 64 to 150 feet long with a capacity of 40 to 600 tons and capable of a 10,000 mile voyage of three to four months' duration. It is refrigerated and equipped with radar, radio, radio direction finders, automatic pilots, depth-sounding devices, radio telephones, and evaporators for converting salt water to fresh water.

More than 10 per cent of the fleet carries airplanes for spotting bait and schools of tuna. Actual fishing is done with hook and line (Fig. 27-7). Tuna fishing is carried on throughout the year. Nearly the entire catch is canned.

Until recently, the waters in the San Francisco–Monterey area were outstanding for their sardine fisheries. However, near the end of World War II, the fishery began to decline and has fallen catastrophically since 1952. Satisfactory explanation for this phenomenon has not been forthcoming. Presumably it is a complex involving overfishing and changing hydrographic conditions—current shifts leading to a fall in water temperature below the minimum for satisfactory spawning, a reduction in the amount of upwelling leading to a poorer growth of plankton, and changes in the food available to larvae.

THE COOL PACIFIC

Though there is no precise line separating the Warm and the Cool Pacific fishing regions, the mean annual surface isotherm of 55°F, which meets the Pacific Coast in Oregon south of Astoria, is regarded as a rough guide dividing the warm- and cool-water fisheries.

Fishing in this region is completely dominated by the salmon, a fish with strange habits: it is born in fresh water, spends much of its life in salt water (the ocean), and ascends the very river in which it was born to spawn and die.[2] The mortality of the fingerlings in stream and ocean is very high; for every ten fingerlings that go to sea, only about one adult salmon returns to the spawning beds, after the two or four or six years in the ocean (the length of time depending upon the species). Mature salmon are caught before they enter fresh water— that is, before they die and also before their flesh begins to deteriorate. The river mouths are thus the centers of salmon fishing.

Salmon are caught by gill net and purse seine (Fig. 27-8). Kings and silvers are caught also by trolling. Formerly about 60 per

[2] All *Pacific* salmon die after one spawning. *Atlantic* salmon do not.

cent of all Alaskan salmon were caught in traps, often called pound nets. However, traps are today almost completely outlawed in North America. A few continue to be utilized in British Columbia under a special legal dispensation and a few in certain Indian reservations that have thus far resisted state prohibitions against this form of gear. Catching salmon by trap was the cheapest method, but it resulted in depletion of this valuable resource and was regarded as favoring big-business interests over independent fishermen.

Of the five Pacific salmon species, the *king* or *Chinook* is largest (averages about 20 pounds) and is rated best in quality. Its greatest concentration is in the Columbia River. These salmon, which vary in age from four to six years, are sold fresh. The *red* or *sockeye*, a smaller fish, is particularly important in the Fraser River and is mostly canned. It returns after a four-year sojourn in the ocean. The *coho* or *silver* salmon is widespread over the region, is lower in quality than the other two, and is largely used fresh. The *pink* or *humpback* is the most abundant and is quite low in price. Its flesh is pale, and the individual fish averages only 4 pounds. It is caught mostly in the waters of southeastern Alaska. The *chum* salmon, with an average weight of 9 pounds, is the least valuable of all, its light yellow flesh being in small demand. It frequents particularly the waters of Alaska but also those of Oregon and Washington.

Another important fish caught here is the halibut; this area contributes about 75 per cent of the total world catch, all of which is shipped fresh or frozen. None is canned. Halibut, which live to twenty-five years, weigh up to 200 or even 300 pounds. American and Canadian halibut fishermen abide by the terms of the treaty of 1930, there being an annual quota of catch, restriction on type of gear, and definite opening and closing dates for the fishing season.

Giant crabs, some of which have a claw-to-claw span of 6 feet, are caught in increasing numbers in huge trawls dragged along the bottom of Bristol Bay, in the deep, cold waters north of the Aleutian Islands (Fig. 27-9).

SOVIET UNION

This huge country is so well known for its agriculture and other land activities that most persons are surprised to learn that it ranks fourth in world commercial fishing and threatens to displace the United States from the number-three position (Table 27-1). Russia has a long coast line, several seas (Black, Caspian, and Aral), and thousands of lakes and streams, which provide some of the finest fishing grounds in the world.

In the Soviet Union, fishing is a government operation, falling like agriculture into collective enterprises (*kolkhozes*) and state enterprises (*sovkhozes*). Five-year plans, which call for ever increasing catches, appear to be

Fig. 27-9. Catch of giant king crabs on deck of Japanese fishing boat, near Aleutian Islands. These crustaceans inhabit cold, deep waters (200 to 500 feet) and are caught in nets. They are then processed and frozen aboard. The largest crab ever caught here had a span of 6 feet and weighed 24.5 pounds. (Courtesy of Consulate General of Japan.)

successful, since fishing is an activity that lends itself well to detailed state control.

Under the Communists, fishing has spread to all the major fishing areas and even into international waters, particularly those in the North Atlantic. In the autumn of 1961 a fleet of fifty Soviet trawlers and two large mother ships were observed patrolling the fishing grounds barely 50 miles off Cape Cod. The grounds most assiduously fished are the Far East, the Caspian Sea, the Barents Sea, and the White Sea.

The Soviet fisheries are reported to employ about 600,000 men, but production per fisherman is small compared with that of an American or English fisherman—about a third as great. Murmansk today claims to be the greatest fishing port on earth. Russian fishing fleets are among the world's best. They employ freighter-sized factory trawlers capable of staying at sea for months at a time. They can process everything they catch and can store as many as 2 million pounds of frozen fish fillets.

The enormous land distances and relatively slow rail service limit the areas of fresh-fish consumption, so that about 80 per cent of the fish is salted. Of the remainder, a considerable percentage is chilled, canned, or reduced to oil and meal.

NORWAY

In any evaluation of the fishing industry, Norway must take high rank. Today Norway stands sixth among the major fishing nations. Fishing here is a venerable activity, known since the days of the Vikings. In the Middle Ages, dried cod, particularly from the Lofoten Islands, was a staple article of European trade; and through the ages fishing has been a vital source of livelihood for the "fishermen-farmers" of coastal Norway. Although only 6 per cent of the 3.587 million people comprising the population are classed as fishermen, the figure is far too low, since many farmers who live along the fiords spend as much time fishing as they do farming. Actually there are as many part-time as full-time fishermen; and there are another 40,000 spare-time fishermen—men employed in other occupations. The poverty of the Norwegian soil is counterbalanced by the richness of the adjacent sea. Temperature conditions are ideal for cod, herring, and allied species.

Norwegian fishermen are among the most advanced in adoption of scientific equipment. The use of the echo sounder for locating shoals and in opening up new fishing areas distant from the coast has enabled the herring catch to expand considerably since World War II.

Herring and cod are the two most important fishes landed, accounting together for about 85 per cent of the total catch. Though the herring catch varies widely from year to year, it dominates. Herring are salted and smoked, and canned as sardines.

The Lofoten Islands off the coast and north of the Arctic Circle are noteworthy. Millions of cod early in the year leave the Arctic and head for the Norwegian coast to spawn. Although foreign trawlers make large catches, it is believed that as many as 30 million cod reach their goal—the Lofoten Islands, where for spawning they find just the right conditions of sea and temperature during the period from February to April. Accordingly, some 15,000 to 32,000 fishermen and 4,000 to 7,000 boats of all sizes engage in the catch. The fish are caught mainly for export, though per capita consumption at home is high.

Norway's fishing industry is more decentralized than that of any other major fishing nation. This results from the great latitudinal range of the fishing grounds along the coast, the large number of harbors, and the small-scale financial units involved in the ownership of vessels.

CANADA

Canada ranks seventh among the nations in commercial fishing. Its east coast, oldest outpost in the New World, is inextricably associated with fishing in the minds of most people; in few lands are the inhabitants so dependent on fishing for subsistence as those of Labrador and Newfoundland. The soil over most of these two parts of Canada is so stubborn and the climate so severe that if man is to remain, he must lean heavily upon the adjacent ocean for much of his sustenance. Considering both the coastal area and the banks, nearly every variety of food fish found in the cold waters of the North Atlantic is present and caught (Fig. 27-10). Demersal, however, is more important than pelagic fishing. Cod, haddock, rosefish, ocean perch, pollock, and swordfish constitute the bulk of the catch, though such pelagic species as herring and mackerel are also found.

The banks south of Newfoundland lie at the meeting of two currents—the Labrador Current and the Gulf Stream. The "Cold Wall" marks the line of demarcation between them: north of it the ocean is a beautiful olive green; south of it, an indigo blue. The higher content of microscopic marine life gives the Labrador Current its olive-green tone, and heavy plankton density leads to good fish concentration.

A noticeable shift in Newfoundland production from salted groundfish to fresh and frozen forms began in the 1950s. Prior to World War II, Newfoundland exported to European markets, chiefly the Catholic countries of the south, up to 60 per cent of the landings as salted and dried fish. This she no longer does, since her postwar market has diminished as a result of greatly increased catches by French, Portuguese, and Spanish fishing fleets.

Fig. 27-10. A seine loaded
with fish is brought over the
side of a fishing boat off the
coast of Nova Scotia. (Courtesy
of Nova Scotia Information Service.)

The trend today is to power boats with fish-
freezing units aboard. A new laboratory at
St. John's devotes itself exclusively to the life
and habits of fish such as the cod.

Canada's Pacific Coast fisheries are important, too, ranking second only to Alaska's in
the combined salmon and halibut catch. All
conditions are similar to those presented for
the adjacent parts in the United States.

GREAT BRITAIN

Britain ranks eighth among world leaders
in fishing and was ahead of Norway until the
close of World War II. Fishing is more important to Scotland's economy than to England's.

The British industry, like that of the Japanese, depends to a marked extent on distant
waters, particularly the Barents Sea and the
shelves off Iceland and West Greenland.

Trawlers were formerly used to get more
fish in British waters, but these waters no
longer supply the quantity needed. Now about
70 per cent of the total catch comes from distant ocean areas. There are indications that
the North Sea, once the greatest herring
ground in the world, has been fished out—
mainly because too many immature fish were
taken.

Fishing is centered in a small number of
ports—Hull, Grimsby, Fleetwood, Yarmouth,
Lowestoft, and Milford Haven (in England);

and Aberdeen, Leith, Fraserbergh, and Peterhead (in Scotland). Principal species caught are cod and herring, but haddock and mackerel are also important.

Average production per fisherman in Britain is very high. Some 30,000 fishermen average about 35 tons per head, which exceeds the per capita output of Norway and the United States—the two runners-up. The British industry has long used advanced methods and has a high percentage of large vessels.

Per capita fish consumption in Britain averages about 55 pounds—nearly 7 pounds more than the per capita annual catch. This situation results from the small size of the islands, their dense population, and their inability to feed the people through agriculture and stock raising.

INDIA

Fishing is more important in India than most Westerners surmise, the country ranking ninth among the major fishing nations. Fish are utilized to supply certain parts of the country with animal protein. So densely populated is India and so agriculturally unrewarding over large areas that the country has turned to the sea as a partial compensation for the failure of the land. Actually the seas surrounding the subcontinent of India are warm and hence less rich in fish life than the colder waters off the coast of East Asia. New tuna grounds, however, were discovered recently in the Bay of Bengal.

Traditionally, the people of India, particularly the Hindus, have adjusted less readily to their nearby seas than have the peoples of Europe, East Asia, and North America to theirs. Their caste system, though presently weakening, long had a powerful effect in retarding the evolution of Indian fisheries.

The west coast, with its wider shelf, accounts for about 80 per cent of the total Indian catch, although the rough weather caused by the southwest monsoon virtually halts fishing activities during the summer months. Chief fishes caught are mackerel, oil sardine, and jewfish. Most Indian fishing craft are small and are without motors; they seldom venture more than 7 miles from the coast.

ICELAND

Possibly no other country is so economically dependent on fish as is Iceland, which ranks thirteenth in tonnage landed by all countries in the world. From 90 to 95 per cent of Iceland's exports consist of fish and fish products. The cool, short, cloudy summers and the ruggedness of the terrain restrict the amount of land that can be farmed to a mere ¼ *of 1 per cent*. The surrounding waters, however, are rich in fish—particularly cod and haddock and, in summer, herring.

Iceland's per capita annual income from the fishing industry is about $206—more than eight times greater than that in any other nation. The annual catch averages about 3 tons for each occupant of the island.

Lying at the meeting place of warm and cool ocean currents, the waters off Iceland's coasts afford rich fishing grounds—cod, herring, redfish, haddock, and plaice. It is not difficult to understand why Iceland is continuously concerned about foreign fishing fleets off her coast.

SOUTHERN HEMISPHERE FISHERIES

Along the west coast of South America is an equatorward-moving current of cold water. Along the immediate shore is a strong upwelling of water from great depths. This Peru Coastal Current (not to be confused with the Peru Oceanic Current to the west, which is less cold and much poorer in organisms) is remarkably uniform in temperature, averaging between 58°F and 64°F along the shore all the way from Chile to northern Peru. No waters in the world so abound in plankton. The richness of these waters in marine organisms results from the chemical composition of the water and from the almost perpetual haze and fog, which afford protection from too much sunlight.

All the fishing is pelagic, the narrow continental shelf offering little to the demersal fisherman. The tuna group dominates the Peruvian catch—the bonito being the principal species, followed by the swordfish, yellowfin tuna, and the skipjack tuna. Other important species are the anchovy, shad, mackerel, and pompano.

Chile, Peru, and Ecuador all are engaged in fishing these waters. However, it is Peru that takes the largest catch in all Latin America. In fact, in 1960 Peru became the fifth-ranking fishing nation (3.2 million tons) in the world and the leading producer of fish meal. The Peruvian coastal area falls into three distinct fishing areas, but the stretch between Chimbote and Pisco accounts for 80 per cent of the total catch.

In 1954 all three west coast South American countries fixed their maritime frontier at 200 miles from their coasts as a means of protecting the fisheries for their own use; accordingly, they seize any foreign fishing boats that come within the 200-mile limit without obtaining a goverment license and without agreeing to recognize official quotas limiting the possible catch. They have seized many tuna clippers and several whalers that moved inside this limit.

This west coast industry will surely rise in importance as a result of the fast-growing population, whose fish consumption is increasing substantially; the high cost of meat; the increasing interest on the part of American tuna-canning companies willing to locate their plants along the coast; and the abundance of fish life.

SEA HUNTING

Seals and whales are mammals; hence their capture is not, strictly speaking, fishing; particularly is this true of seals, which are killed on land.

SEALING

The sealing industry is largely in the hands of Americans and Russians in the neighborhood of the Pribilof and Commander Islands. The largest and the most important herd of fur seals in the world uses the Pribilof Islands in the Bering Sea as a breeding rookery. Here, by international agreement (July 7, 1911) among the United States, Canada, Japan, and Russia, pelagic sealing was prohibited; and a United States monopoly for killing Alaska seals was created, providing for a quota dis-

tribution of the skins taken. In the beginning no cows could be killed; only about 50,000 young bachelor seals were slaughtered. The bachelor seals could be spared without decreasing the birth rate, since they do not mingle with the breeding animals.

Before the treaty, the fur seal was in danger of extermination. The herd was being dangerously overexploited—decreasing from the original 3 million to 132,000 in 1910. However, as a result of the treaty, the number by 1950 had once again reached 3 million, and the rookeries were becoming overcrowded. Hence, for the good of the entire herd, some 30,000 cow seals are now killed annually in addition to young bachelor seals.

WHALING

Whales are the earth's largest living creatures, a full-grown blue whale weighing as much as 100 tons—more than twenty-five elephants. Whaling is conducted by men from a dozen countries, employing about 250 ships and 16,000 men. Though some whaling is carried on in the Arctic, Pacific, Atlantic, and Indian Oceans and in the Bering Sea, most of it takes place in the Antarctic—the whale's last and greatest sanctuary. The whaling industry is regulated by the International Whaling Commission, which sets the dates of the season, limits the catch, and regulates on size limits and on protection of calves.

Approximately 50,000 whales are caught annually. Whaling is the work of expeditions, each consisting of large floating factory ships accompanied by attendant whale catchers and tankers. Each year the ships bring back a total of about 2 million barrels of oil. Whales are hauled by winches and **flensed** and rendered down on board, thus eliminating the need for a shore base (Fig. 27-11). The ships are fantastic: the larger ones dispose of a 100-ton blue-whale carcass in less than ninety minutes and dispatch from 20 to 25 blue whales daily. The Russian *Sovietskaya Ukraina*, world's largest factory ship, can handle 65 whales a day or up to 4,000 a season. It can make its own fresh water, but *most important of all it is completely independent of land for a period of six months.*

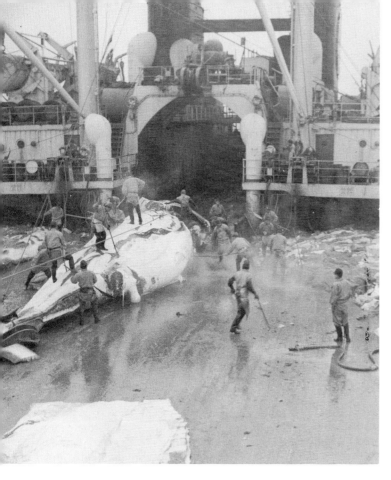

Whales feed largely on krill, a bright-red, shrimp-like crustacean that eats tiny plants and lives within 30 feet of the surface. Krill swarm in shoals of a few square yards to a half acre in size. Aggregates of such swarms may extend over hundreds of square miles. The whales browse in their midst. A whale requires more than a ton of krill per day—about a million calories.

The Norwegians are credited with being the world's foremost whalers. It was they who contributed most of the technological improvements—the basic, small, fast whale-catching vessel; the electric harpoon; the factory ship; and the echo whale finder. They even use helicopters to assist in locating their quarry. They account for two fifths of the world's annual catch.

Whale oil, the real reason for whaling, is used for margarine and soap, for tempering steel, for dressing leather, and for lubricants. In addition, whale meat is sold in countries having limited meat resources—Japan, China, Norway. Fertilizer also is a by-product of whaling.

FISH FARMING

Fish farming means raising fish in much the same manner as man raises livestock. In Eastern and Southern Asia, fish have been raised in fresh- and salt-water ponds and even in rice paddies for millennia. These are the lands where food needs are rising most rapidly. Fresh-water fish farming is well suited to land having poor transport; for it means cheap animal protein far from oceans, seas, or even large rivers. It is significant that until the post-World War II era, the oceans accounted for about 90 per cent of the total world catch. By 1958 this percentage had been reduced to 84 by reason of fresh-water fish culture, mostly in the Orient. The United Nations is trying to spread this practice more widely over the earth, especially in underdeveloped areas.

Oyster farming in Chesapeake Bay is also an example of fish farming. Here thousands of acres of useless bottom have been transformed into valuable food-producing areas.

WORLD FISHERIES AND THE POPULATION EXPLOSION

World population is increasing by more than 150,000 additional mouths every twenty-four hours. This fact, coupled with a decreasing per capita area of arable land, is a directly contributing factor to the discontent and strife that keep the world in constant ferment. As long as some 60 per cent of the world's population is chronically ill fed, the world must expect ideological, political, and military crises.

The ocean fisheries are increasingly mentioned as a panacea for meeting the protein deficiency of the peoples of the underdeveloped lands. Proponents assert that there are two promising lines of effort: (1) improve the efficiency of existing fisheries so as to lower the price of fish, thereby making it available to more people; and (2) develop new fisheries. These individuals insist that the potential of the ocean fisheries is very great.

Most scholars, however, believe that the harvests of the seas cannot be stepped up sufficiently to care for the needs of the lands most affected by the population explosion. Merely to maintain present per capita consumption in step with increasing population would require an additional annual catch of 8½ million tons over the next fifty years.[3] An addition of this size seems unrealistic.

WORLD OUTLOOK

The people in the economically underdeveloped nations need an inexpensive source of animal protein to help prevent malnutrition. However, in many such lands, transport is poorly developed and means of preservation are unavailable. One approach to the problem would be dehydration to prevent spoilage.

Man takes from the oceans 50 to 60 billion pounds of seafood each year; no one knows, however, what proportion of the total animal life of the oceans and seas this catch represents. The growth and numbers of fish are limited by the amount of food available to them. Thus, a plankton census would greatly help world fisheries.

A major problem facing the world is to prevent depletion of the best fishing grounds; almost every major fishing ground has either been overfished or is threatened by overfishing.

Greatest hope for the future of the world's ocean fisheries seems to be for greater advances in fundamental studies that might result in improved techniques for locating, identifying, and catching fish, and in techniques for maintaining, protecting, and enlarging their size and reproductive capacities (Fig. 27-12).

[3] Lionel A. Walford, *Living Resources of the Sea*, New York, Ronald Press, 1958.

Fig. 27-12. Big fish gets caught, little fish goes free. In 1959 the International Commission for the Northwest Atlantic Fisheries agreed to enlarge the mesh of nets to 4½ inches. This allows baby cod, haddock, and other food fish to escape and live long enough to be caught later as mature fish. (Courtesy of Lionel A. Walford and of U.S. Fish and Wildlife Service, Bureau of Commercial Fisheries.)

SELECTED REFERENCES

Barnett, Lincoln (ed.). "The Miracle of the Sea," in *The World We Live In*. New York, Time Incorporated, 1955, pp. 19-40.
Graham, Michael, and G. L. Kesteven. "Biological Possibilities in World Fisheries," *Fisheries Bulletin*, 7(1):1-13, Rome, Food and Agriculture Organization of the United Nations, 1954.
Highsmith, R. M. "Food from the Sea," *Foreign Agriculture*, 24:7-8, November 1960.
Koo, Ted S. Y. *Studies of Alaska Red Salmon*. Seattle, University of Washington Press, 1961.
Lee, Charles F. *Menhaden Industry—Past and Present*. Washington, D. C., U.S. Department of the Interior, Fish and Wildlife Service, June 1953. FL 412.
Merriman, Daniel. "Food Shortages and the Sea," *Yale Review*, 39:430-444, Spring 1950.
Minghi, Julian Vo. "The Problem of the Conservation of Salmon with Special Reference to Bristol Bay, Alaska," *Land Economics*, 36:380-386, November 1960.
Morgan, Robert. *World Sea Fisheries*. New York, Pitman, 1955.
Walford, Lionel A. *Living Resources of the Sea*. New York, Ronald Press, 1958.
Weiss, Francis J. "The Useful Algae," *Scientific American*, 187:15-17, December 1952.

THE WORLD'S

PART EIGHT::

TRANSPORTATION

CHAPTER TWENTY-EIGHT::

Transportation is inseparable from human progress. The world's most advanced and prosperous nations are the ones with the greatest facilities for the movement of people and goods; and the world's most backward nations are those with a paucity of transport. Thus, regions like the Ruhr or the American Manufacturing Region become unified and are linked with other regions by unsurpassed networks of waterways, railways, highways, and/or pipelines.

At first all transport, whether via land or water, was local. But with greater knowledge and improved means of locomotion, well-defined landways and waterways came into being. The citizens of developed countries—where fine highways, rivers, canals, railways, and pipelines now operate—seldom realize that primitive transport techniques still prevail over the larger portion of the earth; Asia,

THE WORLD'S SURFACE

Africa, and large sections of Central and South America and even of Eastern Europe and Anglo-America still are served by modern transport *only* at their borders and along navigable streams, so that these sections are essentially dependent on the most primitive forms of transport.

INLAND WATERWAYS

Irrespective of the stage of culture or of the stage of economic development, human beings like to see beyond their immediate milieu, and they feel the need to engage in barter or trade. Hence, the poorer the development of land and air communications within a given country, the greater the value of its waterways. Figure 28-1 shows the world's most-used inland waterways.

RIVERS

UNITED STATES

Ever since colonial days, much interest has been focused on the development of waterways. Rivers played a major role in the establishment of the nation and in the settlement pattern:

Waterways provided the main pathways which were followed in conquering the continental wilderness; and these same waterways, improved, developed, and maintained by private and governmental effort, have provided the basic framework on which has risen this great industrial nation.[1]

[1] C. H. Chorpening, "Waterway Growth in the United States," *Transactions of the American Society of Civil Engineers,* CT:976, 1953. Paper No. 2643.

TRANSPORTATION

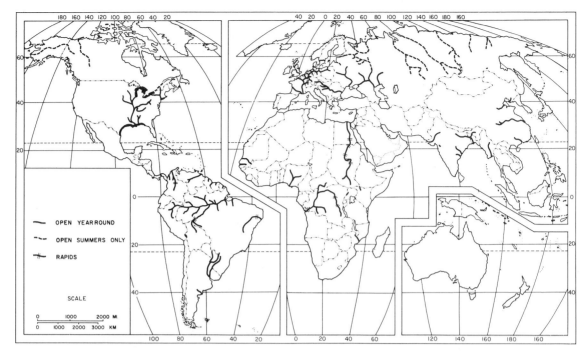

Fig. 28-1. The world's major inland waterways. Waterways may be of outstanding importance in backward and poorly developed regions, such as the Amazon Basin; but they may be of equal value in the most advanced and productive ones, such as North-western Europe.

Today there are some 23,170 miles of navigable waterways in the nation. The Mississippi River system, largest of all, provides more than 5,000 miles of waterway with depths of 9 feet or more, including the main river trunkline from Minneapolis to the Gulf of Mexico—a distance of more than 1,800 miles. The Illinois River is a link in the water connection between the Great Lakes and the Mississippi. The Ohio River links Pittsburgh (at its source) with Cairo (at its confluence with the Mississippi)—a distance of 981 miles. The Missouri is navigable for 760 miles to Sioux City, Iowa. Other much-used rivers are the Monongahela, the Kanawha, and the Tennessee.

On the Pacific Coast the outstanding rivers are the Columbia and the Sacramento. The former is a part of the comprehensive plan of development of the basin for navigation, flood control, irrigation, and hydroelectric power. When all structures are completed on the Columbia River and the Snake River, 9-foot slack-water navigation will be provided from the ocean to Lewiston, Idaho, 465 miles inland.

A Century of River Traffic. The past century witnessed both a decline and a resurgence of river transportation in the United States. Decline followed the rapid growth of the more versatile railroads—particularly during the 1870s, when the waterways, until then the backbone of the nation's transport, found it difficult to compete.

Revival of river development and commerce has come about in the past half century, particularly after World War II, as a result of unprecedented industrial development and the need to move vast quantities of bulk commodities cheaply rather than quickly—commodities like agricultural products (particularly grain), lumber, fertilizers, coal, iron ore, steel, paper, chemicals, sand and gravel, brick, sulfur, salt, and petroleum. Specially designed barges now haul molten sulfur, hot asphalt,

Fig. 28-2. Powerful towboat with barges of miscellaneous cargo on the Mississippi River near St. Louis. Towboats of this type may be powered by four diesel engines capable of developing a total of 8,500 horsepower. Tows may consist of as many as twenty-four large barges (or as many as forty of miscellaneous size), may cover approximately 7½ acres, and may carry up to 30,000 tons of general cargo. (Courtesy of Dorrill.)

even refrigerated products. More intensive improvements of rivers by the federal government stimulated the development of powerful floating equipment. Emphasis today is on power, compactness, and maneuverability. Modern towboats (a misnomer since the barges are pushed not towed) are twin-screw oil burners, which propel their string of barges upstream as well as down. The net result is that today's river traffic is ten times greater than that of the nostalgic packet-boat era, when the Ohio River from Pittsburgh to Cairo and the Mississippi from St. Louis to New Orleans were filled with boats. Some of the towboats today propel as many as twenty-four barges, each capable of carrying from 1,000 to 3,300 tons of freight, or a total of 24,000 tons or more—the equivalent of about seven average railroad freight trains (Fig. 28-2).

The Ohio River—Exemplary United States River. The Ohio River and its valley best illustrate the revival and boom in river traffic. The river enjoys the advantage of a strategic location with respect to important coal deposits and steel output; and a notable industrialization program has been conducted. Expanded chemical, steel, aluminum, and public-utility industries line the river today.

This stream ranks first in the nation in total freight traffic. In 1959 more than 80 million tons of commerce passed over its waters—half again as much as passed through the Panama Canal. Three commodity groups—coal and coke, petroleum and gasoline, and iron and steel—account for the bulk of the tonnage carried. Building materials, too, are important; but, unlike the other groups, they generally move only short distances.

SOUTH AMERICA

The countries of South America—particularly Colombia, Venezuela, Peru, Argentina, Paraguay, and Brazil—are uncommonly dependent on their rivers for transportation. Four river systems only are presented here: the Magdalena, the Orinoco, the Amazon, and the Paraguay-Paraná-La Plata.

Colombia: the Magdalena. No country in South America relies so completely upon river transportation as Colombia. However, Colombia has depended too heavily upon the Magdalena. Except for Buenaventura on the Pacific, there is surprisingly little settlement or economic development beyond the area touched by this river's influence. The lofty ranges of the Andes, which circle the basin on three sides, have hampered communication with other regions. The river's principal weaknesses—shifting sandbars, floods, and marked variations in the depth of the water—have resulted in uncertainties, delays, and high-cost transportation. Actually, aside from the fact that it flows in the right direction (that is, through the densely peopled sections) and connects the inland economic centers (Medellín, Bogotá, and Bucaramanga) with the important ports on the Caribbean (Barranquilla and Cartagena), it possesses few of the qualities of the ideal river for transportation. Frequently, for periods of six to eight weeks, traffic on the lower river practically comes to a standstill or a steamer must move from sandbar to sandbar as the water level is raised for a short period by a rainstorm in some of the upper tributaries. In flood season, the current is so strong that from three to five weeks may be required to get the boats upstream. The navigational channel is so fickle from season to season that even the most skillful river pilots at times are unable to prevent delays. Uprooted trees and other forms of vegetation are carried by tributaries into the river and menace traffic. Erosion is so serious that on the outside of meanders, huge chunks of soil and vegetation topple into the stream. Farther upstream the rapids at La Dorada impede navigation, so that freight must be trans-shipped by rail and later reloaded onto a shallow draft steamer. Finally, the craft comprising the river fleet are mostly old-fashioned paddleboats whose capacity is small but whose operational costs are high.

Venezuela: the Orinoco. Unlike the Magdalena, the Orinoco never has played a vital role in the life of the nation, for it drains the enormous Llanos—until recently devoted either to nothing at all or to a haphazard grazing enterprise. In the 1950s, however, two United States steel companies began mining and shipping millions of tons of iron ore out of the region. The ore shipped from Palua (Bethlehem Steel Corporation), on the right bank of the Caroní at its confluence with the Orinoco, moves downstream by barge or small river vessel across the Gulf of Paria to Puerto de Hierro on the Paria Peninsula, where it is stockpiled; then it is picked up by large ocean carriers and delivered to Sparrows Point, Maryland. Ore shipped from Puerto Ordaz (United States Steel Corporation), across the Caroní from Palua, moves via ocean vessel through the Boca Grande en route to Morrisville, Pennsylvania, and to Mobile, Alabama.

Brazil and Peru: the Amazon. Greatest of all rivers is the Amazon—207 miles wide at its mouth, discharging into the Atlantic 7 million cubic feet of water per second, and navigable for deep-sea ships for 2,300 miles—all the way to Iquitos, Peru. In the lower 1,000 miles of its course, the Amazon has an average

Fig. 28-3. Riverside market on the Rio Negro, Manaus, Brazil. Despite the great size of the river, few large vessels ply its waters. Most typical are the dugouts and other small craft seen here. (Courtesy of Panair do Brasil.)

depth of 100 feet. However, this fine waterway glides through a hot, humid, sparsely populated, and largely unproductive region. Only two lines of boats—one Brazilian, the other British—operate on the river. Otherwise, traffic is restricted to very small boats—even to dugouts (Fig. 28-3).

The Paraguay–Paraná–La Plata Rivers. This river system, because of its location rather than because of outstanding transport advantages, comprises the busiest waterway in all Latin America. The route extends some 1,800 miles from Corumbá, Brazil, to Buenos Aires. Oceangoing vessels ascend upstream only as far as Santa Fé, and most of these encounter considerable difficulty above Rosario. Smaller craft, those drawing 12 feet of water, navigate the Paraná and Paraguay as far north as Concepción, 180 miles north of Asunción; and still smaller boats (those drawing 6 to 7 feet) navigate from Concepción to Corumbá.

The Paraná, which is longer and carries more water than the Mississippi River, meanders badly; and at times it is so choked with sediment that the constant shifting of the channel impedes transport. Yet despite deficiencies, it, along with the Paraguay, provides an important lifeline to and from the outside world.

The La Plata is an estuary which receives so much silt from the Paraná River and the Uruguay River that the channels used for navigation must be dredged constantly. However, since it is the gateway for the foreign trade of both Argentina and Uruguay, it handles a very substantial commerce.

EUROPE

Europe is fortunate in its number of navigable rivers. Outstanding in Europe and very probably in the world is the Rhine, which, by the Treaty of Mannheim of 1871, is a free river. It serves the rich Westphalian coal region and the highly industrialized Ruhr. But besides Germany, the Rhine serves France, the Netherlands, and Switzerland. Via a productive valley, it reaches 513 miles to the head of navigation at Basel, Switzerland. So much labor and money have been expended on it that it is today regarded as a man-made river.

The Rhine is favored by gentle gradient and relatively uniform flow; for melting snow and ice give the upper course maximum flow in summer, whereas winter rains provide the high-water season for the middle and lower course. Hence, with two seasons of maximum supply, the flow in all except the upper course is quite steady.

Barge traffic is extremely heavy all the way to Switzerland. However, the heaviest tonnage plies the stretch downstream from the Ruhr, where the river throbs with activity. Such river ports as Duisburg-Ruhrort, at the junction of the Rhine and the Ruhr, handle in excess of 40 million tons of cargo annually; and Mannheim-Ludwigshafen accounts for more than 12 million tons. Rotterdam at the Rhine's mouth takes care of the heaviest transit trade of any seaport in the world.

Other important transport river arteries in Northwestern Europe are the Elbe (which ranks next to the Rhine), the Oder, and the Weser.

The Danube ranks first among the rivers of south-central Europe, though it handles only about one sixth as much freight as the Rhine. It taps no coal field or industrial region comparable with the Ruhr, it has no Rotterdam at its mouth, and it flows into no busy North Sea as does the Rhine.

SOVIET UNION

Rivers are much used in the Soviet Union; but, because of the long, cold winters, transport by river is restricted to eight months and in the far north to a matter of several weeks per year. There are other weaknesses, too: the rivers, by and large, flow at crosscurrents to the channels of trade, running generally from south to north in the eastern and northern areas and from north to south in the western ones. In Siberia, seasonal flooding, with ice thaws, poses real problems to transport operations. Hence, despite the fact that the navigable river system is believed to be the most extensive in the world, most of the streams are so deficient in one or more requirements for transport that they generate only about 11 per cent as much tonnage as the railroads.

The most important Russian river is the Volga; few world rivers have so influenced the life of the people or the history of a nation. The Volga carries about half the tonnage transported over all the inland waters. However, it serves no major coal–iron-and-steel agglomeration; and, unfortunately, it flows into the landlocked and shrinking Caspian Sea. From its source northwest of Moscow, it flows eastward through the taiga, then southward through one of the country's major grain areas, and still farther south through a pastoral region. Upstream traffic of oil, grain, and fish ordinarily exceeds downstream traffic of timber and lumber.

The Dnieper and Don have failed to generate any appreciable amount of traffic. And not one of Russia's navigable rivers is well located with regard to the basic mineral resources upon which the country's huge industrial development rests. Two North European rivers, the Dvina and Pechora, assume importance because railways are wanting. They handle numerous log rafts, and the Pechora in addition moves considerable coal from Vorkuta.

The north-flowing Siberian rivers accommodate a good deal of lumber traffic. Ships following the Northern Sea Route move under convoy aided by scouting aircraft and icebreakers; they proceed up the Yenesei, Khatanga, Ob-Irtysh, Lena, and Kolyma, delivering manufactures and taking on timber, lumber, minerals, and furs.

ASIA

In China, the largest rivers flow from west to east, thus permitting the tapping of the hinterland. Greatest of all Asiatic inland waterways is the 3,100-mile-long Yangtze-Kiang. The Yangtze gorge presents one of the greatest challenges to man for river transportation, for in places the current attains a velocity of 15 to 20 miles per hour. Yet through it passes virtually all the traffic between Szechwan and the Pacific. The Yangtze Basin accounts for 75 per cent of all cargo hauled. With its several major tributaries, the Yangtze serves roughly half the country, and its tributary area is said to contain about 250 million people.

The Si-Kiang is the great river of South China but is less important because it serves a more restricted area. Near its mouth are the important ports of Canton and Hong Kong.

In the past, China did not spend the vast sums on its rivers as did the United States, but under the Communists inland waterways reportedly are getting more attention and are being much improved.

In Southeast Asia—in Burma, Thailand, Laos, Vietnam, and Cambodia—most of the people live close to the rivers. The great trading cities are river ports—Rangoon at the mouth of the Irrawaddy, Bangkok at the mouth of the Menam, and Saigon on the delta of the Mekong. Since these rivers tap the world's Rice Bowl, there is a lively export trade in this cereal, which, together with teak, moves out in large quantities.

AFRICA

The greatest of African waterways is the Congo. Ocean vessels ascend the river to Matadi, 83 miles upstream from the mouth. Altogether there are 2,350 miles of steamer service from the sea. As with almost every tropical African stream emanating from the interior highlands, the Congo is interrupted by falls and rapids, which prevent continuous use of the stream by river craft and necessitate breaking bulk (Fig. 28-1). The navigable sections are joined by short railways around the rapids, thus making the river a combined rail and water transport system. Trans-shipment from water to rail and back again is, however, an extremely costly operation. Thus, for example, most copper of the Katanga moves to tidewater across other countries by all-rail routes.

The Niger, like the Congo, suffers from rapids. Only the lowest segment of the river is navigable at all seasons. The Gambia is navigable for 150 miles for small ocean vessels.

The Nile, world's longest river, is navigable for about 900 miles, except in low season. It does not significantly serve man for transport as do most other famous rivers.

CANALS

Canals, those man-made waterways through barriers in natural routes of travel, have existed since antiquity. Early canals were adjusted solely to level terrain, elevated land being shunned until the invention of the **chamber lock**. The main functions of most canals has been to shorten distances or to link together areas for mutual trade.

UNITED STATES

Canal construction got started in a small way in Virginia and New England shortly before 1800, but did not become important in the United States until the second quarter of the nineteenth century. The Erie Canal, completed in 1825, led to a period of very rapid canal development. Most successful of all American canals, it provided a water route to the trans-Appalachian region via the lowest route—a "water-level route." The canal system reached the apex of its development in the third quarter of the nineteenth century. Projects were being abandoned before the Civil War, and by 1880 most of the canals were not paying expenses Later, between 1903 and 1918, the old Erie Canal, now the New York State Barge Canal, was improved. The New York State Barge Canal is the only one built in the canal era that still has large commercial usage.

Outstanding of all American canals is the "Soo" (Sault Sainte-Marie) Canal, completed in 1855. Without this water segment connecting lakes Superior and Huron, the great bulk cargoes of iron ore, coal, limestone, cement, and wheat could not move in such quantity and at such low cost as they now do. In 1960 vessel passages totaled 16,606, and traffic exceeded 90 million long tons.

CANADA

Best known of the Canadian canals has been the reconstructed Welland. The first, which was completed in 1829, linked Lake Erie with Lake Ontario over a distance of 27½ miles; it had twenty-five locks and was used mainly to move grain expeditiously from the Prairie Provinces to market. However, the largest lake carriers could not use it. In 1931, a new Welland Canal, 30 feet deep and with eight locks, was completed. It could accommodate any ships plying the lakes. Today the Welland Canal, a segment of the new St. Lawrence Seaway, accommodates ocean vessels.

NORTHWESTERN EUROPE

In few parts of the world are canals so important as in Northwestern Europe, where, by interconnecting with major rivers, they seam the plain and provide the region with an enviable and unique source of inland water transport. The low relief of the North European Plain has facilitated construction, and a highly intricate pattern of inland waterways has thus been created.

In France, tributaries of the Seine lead canals through the entire area. In Germany the Dortmund-Ems Canal provides the country with an all-German waterway from the Ruhr to the North Sea; and the east-west Midland Canal penetrates the heart of Germany, connecting the Rhine and the Oder and making of Berlin an important inland port. The Netherlands is criss-crossed with canals; in fact, the country is unthinkable without canal transport. There are 70,000 canal dwellers in the country, people who go wherever there is trade. In many cities, as in Amsterdam, the canals are in effect extensions of the adjacent streets.

SOVIET UNION

Russia's rivers, for the most part, extend from north to south or from south to north, and therefore do not coincide with the major flow of traffic as determined by resource and population locations; canals, on the contrary, tend to go in an east–west direction. Canals thus became very important, particularly following the rise of the Bolsheviks. Canals now connect the Volga with Moscow, with the Don River, with the White Sea, and with Leningrad on the Gulf of Finland. With the completion of the Volga-Don Canal in 1952, landbound Moscow for the first time could lay claim to being a port of five seas—the White, Baltic, Black, Azov, and Caspian.

Construction of several of these canals literally ranks with such projects as building the pyramids in Egypt. For instance, most of the 140 miles of the Baltic–White Sea Canal were carved out of almost solid rock with picks and shovels. This canal shortened the stormy seventeen-day voyage around Norway by six days or less.

CHINA

No country in the world is reputed to rely so heavily upon canal transport as eastern China. The network in the Shanghai area, for example, is a maze of canals, the average distance between them being only 380 feet.

Fig. 28-4. Iron-ore docks, Duluth. Note that the ore vessels and the trains of loaded ore cars (right) seem very small when placed alongside these enormous peninsular docks. An ore carrier can be loaded in about four hours. (Courtesy of Robert Yarnall Richie and Fortune.)

For century upon century emperors and scholars ordered these canals to be built, so that in the neighborhood of the great rivers, the landscape resembled the network of arteries and veins in the human body.[2]

Greatest of all Chinese canals is the 1,056-mile-long Grand Canal. Begun in the fifth century B.C., it was extended several times and was completed in 1414. It fell into serious disrepair during the nineteenth century. Under the Communists, this canal is being rebuilt to link five important Chinese rivers—the Hwai, Yangtze, Yellow, Chientang, and

[2] Robert Payne, *The Canal Builders*, New York, The Macmillan Company, 1959, p. 62.

Hai. The Grand Canal is important to China because it flows in a north–south direction, whereas most Chinese rivers flow from west to east.

LAKES

THE GREAT LAKES

Greatest of all the world's inland waterways in volume of freight handled are the Great Lakes, through whose ports moves about 70 per cent as much cargo as through all Atlantic, Gulf, and Pacific ports combined. This eminent position results from (1) their combined great size (larger than Great Britain); (2) their great depth; (3) their strategic location in penetrating the heart of the North American continent, where bulk cargoes are available; (4) their east-west extension—the direction in which traffic naturally flows; (5) the paucity of severe storms and the absence of tides; and (6) the great number of important cities lining their shores.

They do, however, suffer from two weaknesses: (1) There is a dearth of first-class natural harbors; nearly all lie at the mouths of small rivers and must be protected by breakwaters. (2) Their transportation is interrupted by winter ice on the connecting rivers and straits. In an average year the Great Lakes navigation season lasts 250 days.

Great Lakes traffic consists largely of bulky products—iron ore, coal, limestone, cement, and wheat, most of which have low value for their weight (Fig. 28-4). Hence, to move them the hundreds of miles to market economically, man has devised a special type of vessel, which is a triumph of human design—a "glorified canal boat," built for capacity and speed. The largest ones attain lengths up to 730 feet and have capacities up to 22,600 tons. Some are self-unloaders.

Lake carriers average in excess of thirty round trips per season of navigation (approximately May 1 to December 15). Loading and unloading are facilitated by labor-saving devices which enable Great Lakes traffic to be the cheapest in the world when calculated on a ton-mile basis. In 1960, 70 million tons of iron ore were shipped down the lakes from Lake Superior ports.

THE ST. LAWRENCE SEAWAY

For almost half a century both Americans and Canadians dreamed of and discussed the possibility of improving the St. Lawrence River to enable oceangoing vessels to tap the Great Lakes as far west as Duluth and Superior in the United States and Fort William and Port Arthur in Canada—some 2,350 miles inland. However, the projected cost was so great (actual cost was 471 million dollars) and sectional interests so potent as to delay the project for decades. Following realization that the high-grade iron-ore deposits in the Lake Superior Region were becoming de-

pleted, the main argument for the Seaway was that the St. Lawrence was the most direct and the cheapest route between Canada's new Quebec-Labrador iron mines and America's hungry furnaces. The reduction in grain freight rates also entered the picture.

The Seaway consists essentially of a 27-foot channel and a system of seven locks. The locks accommodate vessels up to a length of 730 feet, with an average locking time of about thirty-five minutes.

The first few years of Seaway traffic did not live up to expectations; but the artery has already justified itself, and prospects for the future appear promising. However, the Seaway ordinarily cannot be used from December 1 (the winter closing date) until about March or April. During this period foreign ships move to salt-water ports.

RAILWAYS

Figure 28-5 portrays vividly the rail situation over the earth. Though drawn more than a third of a century ago, the pattern has changed hardly at all, nor is it expected to change in the future—although in several formerly backward lands now in the throes of their revolution of rising expectations (particularly the Soviet Union and China), some mileage is being added; and in areas of large-scale mineral development (e.g., Quebec, Venezuela, Peru, Brazil, Liberia, and the Rhodesias), new railroads have been and are being constructed.

Railroads emancipated transportation in large measure from the limitation imposed by topography and climate. They go almost anywhere, provided ample tonnages of goods are available for shipment at a profit. They lead directly from point of origin to destination; even in difficult terrain—mountains, deserts, lakes, swamps—they find a way.

ANGLO-AMERICA

UNITED STATES

The United States, with roughly 6 per cent of the world's population and land surface, has about 30 per cent of its railway mileage.

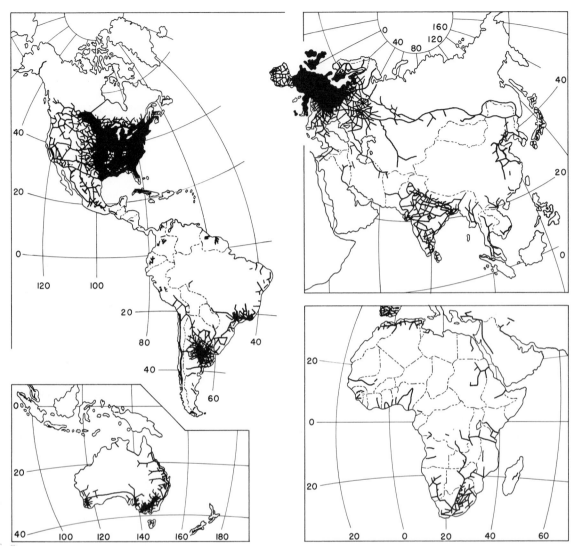

Fig. 28-5. Railway situation in the world at a glance.   (From Mark Jefferson and Economic Geography.)

The nation owes much to its railroads; industrial development would have been impossible without them. Over its 225,000 miles of line moves about 40 per cent of the nation's intercity freight traffic (Fig. 28-6). At the end of World War II, however, the railroads were carrying over 60 per cent of this traffic. The drop has resulted from motor-truck and inland-waterway competition.

The densest web reaches westward from the Atlantic Seaboard to the 20-inch isohyet (100th meridian), which marks the transition from humid to semiarid climate. Almost everywhere here, man is within 10 miles of a railroad. Chicago is the world's greatest railway center owing to a location on Lake Michigan where virtually all lines of communication focus. It serves as a terminal point for twenty-one trunk lines, which extend from Canada to Mexico and from the Atlantic to the Pacific.

In the South, the rail web is less dense and handles less than half as much freight. Here, in contrast with the rest of the nation, most railways extend north and south.

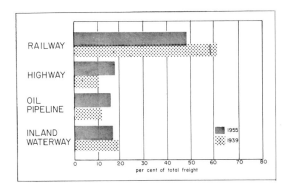

Fig. 28-6. *Percentage of total traffic carried by railway, highway, oil pipeline, and inland waterway in the United States, 1939-1955. Though rail traffic has declined, railways still move more freight than any single competitor. (Courtesy of Stanford Research Institute.)*

Figure 28-5 shows how the rail web falls off west of the 20-inch isohyet, where ranches are very large and crops partially give way to grazing; where cities are relatively scarce; and where population is sparse—so that little railway traffic is generated. Nevada, Arizona, New Mexico, and Wyoming are the poorest traffic producers in the West. Only seven railroads get beyond the Rocky Mountains and reach the Pacific Ocean.

One of the fastest-moving new developments is the "trailer-on-flatcar"—the so-called "piggy-back" service, whereby on long hauls loaded trailers are lifted onto freight cars and hauled by train to a distant city; there they are lifted back onto the ground and delivered by truck to their destination (Fig. 28-7).

CANADA

Despite Canada's huge size, nearly the entire population occupies that part of the country within 300 miles of its border with the United States. Ninety per cent of the country consists of tundra, mountain, forest, water, and wasteland—areas that railroads tend to avoid. Even in southern Canada, the rail net resembles that of the American West—a thin ribbon of communication spanning great distances through sparsely settled country with little available traffic.

Rail construction got under way when the scattered colonies in British North America could not form a larger and stronger unit and be effectively bound together economically, politically, and socially without cheap, reliable, year-round transportation. Thus, the promise of railway construction played a powerful part in the scheme for confederation in 1867. Today, new construction in Canada is mostly into the metallic mineral-rich areas of the Canadian Shield.

Two great railways, the Canadian Pacific and the Canadian National, serve this large nation, avoiding for the most part duplication of service. Unlike the situation in the United States, where there is no true transcontinental railroad, both Canadian lines reach from ocean to ocean. The assertion is often made that much of the trackage of the Canadian National Railways has no other reason for existence than the political one. It did indisputably inherit lines that never will pay and yet cannot be abandoned.

LATIN AMERICA

Latin America wholly lacks an internationally linked railway system. Indeed, only four of the twenty countries have anything even approaching a network. In most of the nations the railways are composed of disconnected fragments that are so poorly integrated with the settlement pattern as to make the movement of goods very costly. Because investment was often made without proper coordination, the result was dissipation of funds and a low yield for the capital utilized. Often, too, such investments were determined not by an order of priorities established at the national level but by local and circumstantial needs. This situation derives from the fact that most of the early railroads financed and constructed by British and French interests were designed principally for the transport of raw materials to seaports, and hence are not adequate to serve as a network for serving domestic needs. Moreover, there is no accepted standard **gauge** even in individual countries.

Figure 28-5 shows a unique pattern: the mileage is mostly along the periphery; there is nothing comparable with the great rail

Fig. 28-7. Solid train of Southern Pacific railway cars with trailers moving "piggy-back." On a solid "piggyback" train of one hundred cars, five crewmen can perform the work of two hundred truck drivers. "Piggyback" is convenient and economical, rates are competitive with highway carriers, and the service is virtually damage-free. (Courtesy of Southern Pacific Company.)

web to be found in the American Midlands. Obstructions are many and formidable: the volcanic ranges in Central America; the towering wall of the South American Andes, which forms the continent's backbone from the Panama-Colombia border to the Strait of Magellan; the rain forests; the floodlands; and the swamps. Only portions of Mexico, the Argentina-Uruguay area, the central plateau of eastern Brazil, and middle Chile possess rail nets even remotely comparable with those of northeastern United States and Western Europe.

COLOMBIA

Nowhere in South America is railway construction more difficult than in Colombia: mountainous topography, in those parts where most of the population dwells, necessitates layouts with steep grade, curves of small radius, and narrow roads and tracks—all of which entail high construction costs; jungle and swampy terrain also cause difficulties.

There are in Colombia two entirely unconnected networks and four isolated lines, with a total trackage of about 2,000 miles. The western network is the more important, for it carries 60 per cent of the goods and 50 per cent of the passengers. It links the cities of Cali, Medellín, and Manizales with the port of Buenaventura on the Pacific and with Puerto Berrío on the Magdalena. The eastern network is composed of four railways connecting Bogotá with the Magdalena towns.

A new system connecting Santa Marta on the Caribbean with Puerto Salgar in the central part of the country was completed in 1961. This meant the linking of a number of inland railways and the final realization of a modern transportation network within the country. Construction involved the conquest of almost impassable jungle interspersed with

Fig. 28-8. Freight cars on trains inbound and outbound on the Central Railway of Peru high up in the Andes. The ingots on the cars to the left are en route from the smelter at Oroya to the port of Callao for export; the oil-tank cars are en route from Callao to Oroya, Cerro de Pasco, and several montaña centers. The Central Railway is a vital link between the coast and the Andes and handles much of the country's mineral exports. (Courtesy of Runcie-Graphs.)

treacherous swamps, but the line is opening up a vast new area to agriculture.

PERU

Altogether Peru has a total rail trackage of only 2,076 miles, of which 114 miles were completed in late 1960, connecting the Toquepala copper mine in the western Andes with the port of Ilo and the smelter 12 miles north of the port. Peru's most famous line is the Central Railway, which climbs up the valley of the Rimac from Callao to Oroya, where one branch moves northwest to Cerro de Pasco, the other southward to Huancayo. As a standard-gauge line (4 feet, 8½ inches), it is reputed to be the world's greatest engineering achievement in a lofty mountain region. In short, of all the world's standard-gauge lines, it goes to the highest point—15,865 feet. It maintains a 4 per cent grade without rack or cable, it clings to almost vertical walls, it passes through 66 tunnels and over 58 bridges, and it has 21 switchbacks. It is completely rock **ballasted.** In one place it is built in the bed of the river, which is diverted through a boring to one side. It hauls copper, lead, zinc, vanadium, and other minerals (Fig. 28-8) down to the port of Callao for export and transports foodstuffs, oil, building materials, and other commodities up the long, hard pull to the mines and smelter.

Only slightly less spectacular than the Central is the Southern Railway, which operates from the ports of Mollendo and Matarani to Puno on Lake Titicaca and on to Cuzco. It climbs to an elevation of 14,668 feet. These two lines account for about two thirds of Peru's railroad trackage. Both were rehabilitated and modernized (including dieselization) in the late 1950s.

Though several of Peru's railroads breach the first range of the Andes, not one makes it over all of them. There is no longitudinal railroad along the coast.

ARGENTINA

Of all the countries in South America, only Argentina is well served by railways, but this is so in less than a quarter of the country—in the Pampa. In some respects, however, the Pampa *is* Argentina: it contains three fourths of the total population, four fifths of the cultivated land, three fourths of the manufacturing, and three fourths of the railway mileage. The rail web of some 27,000 miles covers approximately 100,000 square miles, extending westward from the Atlantic Coast to the drylands—about 64° west longitude. All major railway systems and their traffic in grain and livestock focus upon the great port and capital of Buenos Aires. Other points of convergence are Rosario, Santa Fé, and Bahia Blanca. Elsewhere the rail density is low; in huge Patagonia only an occasional line reaches inland from an Atlantic port.

Construction has been relatively simple—nothing comparable to that in Colombia and Peru. On the flat terrain, cuts, fills, bridges, tunnels, or even curves are not needed. However, ballast is scarce.

The Pampa from the standpoint of railways falls into four major zones, each served by the main line and branches of one of the large railroads. Most of the mileage is broad gauge.[3]

[3] The first railroad, 6 miles long, was built by the British in 1857. It was broad gauge—an interesting coincidence, since British railways are of standard gauge. Britain had on hand rolling stock built for use in Russia during the Crimean War but ill suited for her own gauge. Argentina, without a mile of railway, was a logical place to dispose of it. Once railroads started with this gauge, it was reasonable for the British and for the Argentines to continue with it.

Most of the Argentine railroads were built by British and French owners but were nationalized under Juan Perón.

BRAZIL

There is a real rail web in the so-called heart of Brazil—the area inland from Rio de Janeiro and Santos; but it thins out to the north, south, and west. Though this nucleus comprises only 11 per cent of Brazil's area, it has about half the nation's people and industry. It is also the chief center of coffee production. It is logical, therefore, that a high percentage of the railway mileage should be here. There is also a reasonably good distribution of railways in the hump, but they do not extend inland very far. In the gigantic Amazon Basin, there are altogether not more than 500 miles of railroad, 229 miles of which are included in the Madeira-Mamoré Railway around the falls in the Madeira River. This line was constructed to provide an outlet for wild rubber collected in Bolivia when Amazonia was the center of world rubber production. By those who know Latin American railways, the Madeira-Mamoré is considered one of the greatest achievements of all time.

A recently constructed route connects the Amazonian port of Macapá with the manganese mine at Amapá, 120 miles to the north. And in the far south there is a railway reaching inland all the way from São Paulo to Santa Cruz, Bolivia.

CHILE

This long, narrow country has a government-owned longitudinal railway encompassing about half the total railway mileage of the country and extending 1,500 miles from Arica on the north to Puerto Montt on the south. From it short lines extend west to port cities on the coast (the entire Chilean population dwells west of the Andes). However, there is no through traffic over this longitudinal railway, because its two major segments have different gauges and thus there can be no interchange of rolling stock.

In addition to the longitudinal railway, there are others such as the Arica-La Paz, the Chilean Transandine, and several lines operated by the big copper- and nitrate-mining companies.

EUROPE

Europe, literally laced with rail lines, is one of the best-served parts of the world, claiming about one third of the total mileage. The most concentrated distribution is to be found around the North Sea, where land and water routes converge and where vast numbers of cities and industries are located. Southern Norway and Sweden are included in the network. Eastward and southward the distribution thins out as industry gives way to agriculture. Only a few lines pierce the Pyrenees, the Alps, and the Carpathian Mountains and penetrate the rugged Balkans. The network thins out abruptly at the Iron Curtain (Fig. 28-5). Thus, whereas in Western Europe man need travel only 10 miles or less to reach the nearest railroad, in the peripheral portions he must travel 20 to 50 miles and even more.

Despite the prominence of railways in Western Europe, this mode of transport is relatively less important than that of east-central Anglo-America. The greater development and use of inland waterways, both rivers and canals, the importance of coastal shipping,[4] and the growing use of pipelines together divert much traffic that the railways would otherwise get. Particularly does this hold for the bulky, heavy, and low-value commodities. Important until recently, too, in impeding inter-country rail traffic were the man-made tariff rates and customs restrictions, which resulted from the fragmentation of the region into numerous political divisions. The formation of the European Common Market (the Six) and of the European Free Trade Association (the Outer Seven) has abolished most customs duties within each bloc but not between them.

[4] Europe stands alone among the continents for this type of trade. Most continents resemble solid blocks. But Europe may be considered one big peninsula, flanked by smaller peninsulas. It thus has 20,000 miles of seacoast, compared with only 5,200 for the United States.

SOVIET UNION

Probably no other country depends so greatly upon railways as does the Soviet Union (Fig. 28-5). The 1957 Soviet rail-freight traffic exceeded that for any year in United States history (even though the United States has considerably more total trackage), and its rail traffic increased thirteen times from 1913 through 1954. In the Soviet Union, the aim is to have railways move all traffic for which they can provide the fastest and most economical service; in the United States, the railways more and more handle only the traffic that cannot be moved by other means of transport.

Gauge differences seriously interfere with interchange between the Soviet Union and her satellites: thus, at the Soviet-Hungarian border, broad-gauge hopper cars of coal ride an elevated ramp to permit the contents to be dropped into Hungarian cars. It is reported that on lines connecting with the European satellites, the gauges are being broadened to conform with the Russian width in an effort to increase efficiency. Soviet railroads currently perform 80 per cent of the nation's freight haulage, measured in ton-miles.

The railroad plays a vital role as a carrier because vast distances separate the population centers and few physical barriers hamper railway construction—though climate imposes difficulties of operation in the polar and desert segments. The wide separation of mineral and other resources from the population and market areas has further aided the railroads, which qualify best as instruments of mass transport on the surface.

Moscow is the hub of the Russian rail system. All land west of the Volga and south of Leningrad lies within 35 miles of a railroad, with the maximum density in the Leningrad, Moscow, and Ukrainian industrial areas. Rail lines reach northward from the main rail net into the mineral and forest areas of the north and to their ports—e.g., to the ice-free port of Murmansk, to Archangel, and to the Pechora Basin. The mineral-rich Urals region supports a considerable network of trackage reaching out in all directions. Important lines extend to the Kuznetsk Basin; from north of Lake Baikal to the Pacific near Komsomolsk; and from Novosibirsk to Tashkent. Others connect Ulan-Ude with Peking, and Alma-Ata with Lanchow. Freight between Russia and China must be trans-shipped, since Soviet rails are of broad gauge; Chinese, of standard gauge.

The best-known Russian railroad—one that ranks among the world's greatest engineering achievements—is the Trans-Siberian, completed in 1904 and originally extending from Chelyabinsk to Vladivostok (via Harbin)—a distance of more than 4,000 miles. Today this railway, included as a part of the European Russian rail network, stretches 5,973 miles from the Baltic Sea (Leningrad) to the Pacific. It is the longest railway in the world.

The lonely Trans-Siberian line was built to help in the economic exploitation of the enormous Russian realm but also for strategic reasons. It was originally a single-track line, had no connection around Lake Baikal (a ferry transported trains over the 50-mile-wide lake), and crossed Manchuria direct from Chita to Harbin to Vladivostok. When, as the result of the Russo-Japanese War, Russia had to withdraw from Manchuria, the railway was extended from Chita to Khabarovsk to Vladivostok—a route which, though considerably longer, ensured that the railway would remain wholly within Russian territory. Rapid development of mineral production and of industrial centers under the Soviet regime necessitated strengthening this overworked line, which was double-tracked between 1928 and World War II. A second transcontinental route, the South Siberian Railway, is being extended slowly, as well as a Northern Trans-Siberian from Central Siberia north of Lake Baikal to the Pacific.

Since railroads are voracious consumers of fuel, absorbing from 25 to 30 per cent of the nation's coal, and since the coal bill accounts for about 20 per cent of the total railroad operating costs, the Soviet Union is giving much attention to substitute motive power—diesel and electric—with the idea of effect-

ing substantial fuel economy. It would seem that both the petroleum and water-power resources are adequate to validate the expansion planned for them by railways. Dieselization is projected mostly, though not exclusively, for the railways of European Russia; electric rail lines, for Asiatic Russia. Electrification of the Trans-Siberian Railroad from Moscow to Irkutsk was completed in 1961. High-cost electrification is possible in the Soviet Union only because of the heavy traffic.

ASIA

As the world's largest unbroken land mass, Asia has the greatest need for land transport. No large inland seas tap its interior, and few large rivers do. Figure 28-5 emphasizes the huge, relatively bare space that must be crossed by just a few very long railways. In fact, areas of unbelievable size have no railroads at all. Rail-line deficiency has been a major cause of economic underdevelopment.

The vast deserts and the lofty mountains create such barriers to efficient modern human mobility that commerce is reduced to small proportions. Here railway development is tentacular in form: the sole function is to connect certain productive inland localities with ocean ports.

JAPAN

Despite its small size, rugged terrain, and insularity, Japan has the densest rail net in Asia. Obviously, the maximum concentration is to be found on the small, heavily populated plains of eastern Honshu. Rail lines have a trackage of 12,254 miles, and they handle about 30 per cent of the freight traffic. In the south, Honshu and Kyushu are linked by a submarine railway tunnel under the Strait of Shimonoseki. In the north, however, Honshu and Hokkaido are connected by train ferries that shuttle across Tsugaru Strait.

INDIA AND PAKISTAN

India ranks fourth among all countries in the world in railway mileage. The Indian subcontinent was among the first to be well served by railway lines, these having been constructed by the British between Calcutta and Bombay and Madras and Karachi. The British set up a fine rail web in order to develop the economy; to benefit from trade, both import and export; to maintain peace by moving its small number of troops quickly into any area; and to keep down the toll of famine.

Today India and Pakistan together possess 33,011 miles of rail trackage—a striking contrast to the rest of Asia (Fig. 28-5). The network is thickest in the productive and populous Ganges Valley and thinnest in dry, sparsely populated Baluchistan, the Thar Desert, and the rugged eastern Deccan Plateau.

Orientation of traffic shifted as a result of partition: whereas traffic to and from northwest India formerly moved through Karachi, now it moves largely through Bombay and other Indian ports on the Arabian Sea. Similarly, traffic to and from East Bengal—which formerly moved through Calcutta—has shifted to Chittagong.

Some new lines have been constructed: in India, one linking Assam with the rest of the country; in Pakistan, one in East Pakistan, linking isolated Khulna with the main network of the Eastern Bengal Railway.

CHINA

China currently has a rail trackage of some 20,500 miles. Most of this was built by foreigners and hence was restricted to the eastern part of the country—between the Great Wall and the Yangtze-Kiang, especially in the north and northeast. Everywhere, except in Manchuria, there is a dearth of feeder lines. A good half of China lacks railways altogether, for the rugged terrain and the seriously eroded soil limit production and population and make construction of railways prohibitively high in cost. Railway lines radiate from Peking to its port (Tientsin), northeastward into Manchuria, westward into Suiyan, southwestward to Nanking and Shanghai, and thence to Hankow and Canton. New railways have been built westward and northwestward to connect with Russian lines.

As late as 1951 it was believed that the great day of railway expansion had passed.

Yet the program of the Communists to industrialize and to develop their large but widespread mineral resources must be based on the vital contribution of transportation, particularly that by rail. In 1960 the target was construction of 5,200 miles of new line, 500 miles more than the total mileage laid down during the decade 1949-1958.

AFRICA

The physical environment of Africa, possibly more so than that of the other continents, presents the greatest number of obstacles to rail transport. The high central tableland, the marked diversity in climates, the great rain forests, deserts, and savannas, the shortage of coal and of petroleum (except in the north), even the scarcity of water suitable for boilers—all have conspired to keep most of the continent from having even the beginning of a dense rail web. Aside from the strictly physical impediments are several human ones: (1) Africa lacks a common history—social, economic, or political. Although it is highly developed in the extreme north and south, there is no common interest between the two, and neither has played an important role in the development of tropical Africa. (2) Almost everything needed to construct a railway must be brought in from Europe, America, or East Asia and hence is costly. (3) Labor is expensive: foreign workers must be wooed from more congenial milieus, since native (local) workers have a low output. (4) Investors shy from a continent whose future is so uncertain. By no stretch of the imagination can the "investment climate" over most of the continent be regarded as good; and rail transportation is a long-term financial project.

In North Africa, small rail nets have evolved in Egypt, Tunisia, Algeria, and Morocco (Fig. 28-5).

In tropical Africa, though railroading began in 1885, the rail picture is far from impressive, considering the great size of the region. Most of the lines are of two types: (1) dead-end or (2) around falls and rapids. The former are essentially single tentacles that reach into the hinterland of an ocean port as far as an important mining community or an inland town. Most do not cross frontiers. In short, each exists solely to serve the specific territorial needs, and each runs at right angles to its coastline. In the Congo the early lines were in the nature of portages, around rapids and falls or from one river or lake to another (e.g., the railroad that circumvents the 220-mile stretch of rapids between Stanley Pool and the head of ocean-going navigation). Figure 28-5 indicates also that a few through lines have been built across tropical Africa.

The Cape-to-Cairo Railway, begun by Cecil Rhodes and Robert Williams in 1906 in an effort to penetrate the heart of Africa, was never completed.

Of all parts of the continent, South Africa has what most closely approaches a rail web, with a total trackage of about 13,371 miles. Yet, considering that it comprises some 473,-000 square miles (an area one sixth the size of the United States) but has a total population of only about 13 million, this is not a heavy mileage. Moreover, the population is highly concentrated into four areas—around Johannesburg, Cape Town, Durban, and Port Elizabeth—widely separated each from the other by very sparsely settled land.

The South African railways are regarded as the best 3-foot, 6-inch gauge railways in the world. They carry most of the freight, since navigable rivers are lacking and since they do not have the competition from highway traffic characteristic of many countries.

AUSTRALIA

The harsh physical environment over much of the continent, the limited arable area (13 per cent), and the concentrated distribution of population (nine tenths of the people live in the coastal area between Adelaide and Brisbane) have definitely restrained railway construction in Australia and have confined most of it to the better-watered east. Not one town or city of importance lies more than 50 miles from the ocean. One third of the nation is desert; another third is too dry for crops.

In the beginning, each state built its own railroads and, unfortunately, not of one specific gauge. The lack of a standard gauge necessitates extensive trans-shipment in the movement of freight; hence, interstate freight rates are high. Although much thought has been given to the possible unification of the gauges, cost for the most part has deterred it. Nor were the lines always located with regard to traffic potentialities. Only one transcontinental route exists: the Trans-Australian Railway, built by the Commonwealth Government 1,050 miles from Port Augusta to Kalgoorlie (Fig. 28-5). There is no such line extending north and south. A number of tentacles reach inland from ports, usually to mines, but are soon lost in the desert. Thinly populated northern Australia has but a meager rail trackage, and the northwestern quarter of the continent has none whatsoever.

Altogether, Australia has about 28,000 miles of rail lines. Most of the lines lose money—the result largely of great distances, small population, and the fact that only a minor part of the continent generates sufficient traffic to support modern rail services.

HIGHWAYS

Highways are not nineteenth- or twentieth-century phenomena. The Romans constructed roads as early as 350 B.C., extending them throughout their empire—roads that hold up under a type of traffic undreamed of at the time they were built. The Appian Way still is used as a thoroughfare into and out of Rome. The Egyptians, Carthaginians, and Etruscans were road builders, too. And in the New World, the Incas regularly conquered space by constructing fine highways throughout the Andes from present Ecuador to Argentina and Chile and along the coast of Peru. Such roads constituted a real advance over the primitive transport prevailing hitherto, for they largely eliminated natural obstacles to travel.

Today, in all *developed* countries, roads are vital to political integration and to social and economic progress. They give access to a country's untapped wealth. In many *underdeveloped* lands, crude trails still prevail, modern transport being found mostly at the borders and along navigable streams. The modern highway serves a nation most intimately. As civilization advances and the level of living of the populace rises, adequate transportation for delivering the commodities that make this progress possible must be made available.

UNITED STATES

During the seventeenth, eighteenth, and early nineteenth centuries, America was retarded by a lack of adequate roads. The settlements in the colonies were planted at sheltered harbors along the coast or along the banks of navigable streams. The crude roads were impassable in winter; they were dusty and rutted in summer; and in all rainy periods they were so muddy as to be virtually unusable. Hence, each settlement was circumscribed by a wall of isolation.

The development of the highway system falls into six periods, but only the last is presented here. More than anything else, the internal-combustion engine, used in the automobile, stimulated the building of good highways, for it emancipated man. He no longer had to live on or near a railroad line; the automobile enabled him to go where he wished, and it permitted the explosion of the big cities into suburbs. However, without good roads, the usefulness of the automobile and truck was limited. Until World War I, it was impossible to use trucks except in cities and their environs. The war, however, stimulated motorization; the railroads were overtaxed, and relief for them became imperative. By the war's end, an attempt was made to build and place roads on a national scale. Thousands of miles of modern highway were constructed that literally pulled the nation out of the mud. However, the growth in highways, particularly superior ones, has failed to keep up with demand, the nation having fallen behind in its building program during World War II. Moreover, it was not foreseen nor could it be expected that the number of motor vehicles would skyrocket to some 70 million by 1960; and there was no indication that the truck, a comparative novelty in the early 1920s, would become so vital a factor in the American transportation system as to reach 11.9 million by 1960.

The best highways are exemplified by such toll roads as the New Jersey, Pennsylvania (Fig. 28-9), Ohio, Indiana, and other turnpikes (used by both passenger cars and trucks) and by freeways such as the Gulf Freeway and the Nimitz Freeway. These are characterized by wide, divided traffic lanes, gentle grades, long sight distances, and limited access.

Today there are in the United States more than 3.5 million miles of roads and highways, of which 2.4 million miles are paved. The federal government, through the enactment of the Federal Aid Highway Act of 1956, is engaged in construction or improvement of interstate and defense highways at an estimated cost of 37 billion dollars, in addition to improvement of some 750,000 miles of feeder roads. Construction is expected to require about sixteen years for completion. The cost of these arteries is being defrayed in part by taxes on gasoline, oil, tires, etc. It is reported that the Interstate Highway System will connect 90 per cent of all cities of 50,000 persons and over.

CANADA

Despite Canada's great size, the nation has but a thin highway network, with most of the mileage lying within 200 miles of the southern border. As in the United States, there was little road building in Canada until after World War I. The little construction and maintenance that was conducted was essentially a municipal responsibility. Moreover, the demand was for construction and improvement of local roads and interregional roads within the provinces. Provincial grants were made to connect a farm-to-market road system. However, in the 1950s road building boomed, with more than 1 billion dollars spent on roads.

The need for a transcontinental highway, 5,000 miles in length and extending from the Maritime Provinces (St John's, Newfoundland) to British Columbia (Victoria), was early appreciated. The most spectacular of

Fig. 28-9. Segment of the Pennsylvania Turnpike (first of the modern state toll roads) in picturesque Bedford County. As a result of interconnections, it is now possible for through nonstop traffic to follow multilane expressways like this one from Portland, Maine, to Chicago, Illinois. (Courtesy of Pennsylvania Turnpike Commission.)

Canada's highways, it is not the most important economically; however, it represents the longest unbroken stretch of highway within a single country in the history of the world (Fig. 28-10). With its completion in the early 1960s, it enabled traffic for the first time to go from coast to coast through Canada.

There is at present much activity in constructing roads from the developed and populated south into the raw, almost empty, but mineral-rich arctic and sub-arctic areas. Some of these roads will be nothing more than "development roads."

LATIN AMERICA

Highway construction in Latin America is sporadic. In few countries and in few regions within countries is the highway situation what it should be. In some countries the airplane, railroad, waterway, mule, and ox move most of the cargo. In some the human carrier must be added. Nonetheless, road transportation is believed to have greater over-all potential for expansion than either rail or water transport, for (1) it is more flexible; (2) it offers lower rates; and (3) it costs the taxpayer less.

Yet the Incas had a system of stone-paved roads extending the entire length of their empire with crossroads at intervals leading from the *sierra* down to their cities in the *costa*. Over these roads traveled armies, fleet-footed couriers, and agricultural and mineral products. Even fresh fish were transported by courier to the capital, Cuzco. The Mayas in Yucatan also built paved roads; but—unlike the Incas, who had the llama—they had no beast of burden to use the routes.

On the brighter side of the present-day picture is the tremendous accomplishment of improved highways forming the backbone of Latin American economic development. Long-distance trucks now go over the ranges of the Andes and over Brazil's Serra do Mar and into the jungles.

The Pan American Highway, Latin America's outstanding highway, ultimately

Fig. 28-10. One of the most difficult sections in the construction of Canada's transcontinental highway: through Roger's Pass in British Columbia. (Courtesy of the National Film Board, Ottawa.)

will extend from Alaska to the tip of South America, traversing each continental nation. Of the 21,883 miles south of the Rio Grande, less than 4 per cent is impassable. The major bottlenecks are in Central America—mostly in Guatemala and Panamá.

MEXICO

Though there are extensive areas not penetrated by modern highways, Mexico must rank among the leaders in all Latin America in highways. From four gateway cities south of the United States border, good hard-surface roads stretch southward for hundreds of miles. There is also a gravel road southward in Baja California. And though north-south highways prevail, a number of east-west routes have been and are being built: Vera Cruz to Mexico City to Morelia to Guadalajara; Tampico to Antiguo Morelos to Lagos de Moreno; Mazatlan to Durango; and Monterrey to Torreón—to mention but a few. One of the most recent achievements is the highway linking Mexico City with towns in the northern Yucatan Peninsula.

One half of the Inter-American Highway of 3,200 miles—from Nuevo Laredo to the Panama Canal—lies in Mexico and is in good condition.

CENTRAL AMERICA

In this area a common market is being formed, thus making intercommunication more important than ever before. Highway expenditures in the past several years by Guatemala, Honduras, and Panamá have been among the highest in Latin America.

SOUTH AMERICA

Argentina. For decades Argentina ranked low in road mileage, particularly the hard-surface type; for she had the best railway network in all Latin America, a scarcity of materials for road building, a disproportionate share (more than a third) of the total population dwelling in Greater Buenos Aires, and a relatively small number of motor vehicles (even in 1960 only 440,000 automobiles, 315,-000 trucks, and 6,000 buses). During the Perón regime, road building came almost to a standstill. And in 1960, 80 per cent of the total highway network had been built prior to 1946. However, in 1960 the picture changed, and highway construction became one of the highest-priority projects in the government development plan. A ten-year program designed for completion in 1969 will give Argentina more than 12,000 miles of new all-weather roads. Though many new paved highways will be built, stress is primarily upon the upgrading of dirt roads—the farm-to-market and the farm-to-railhead roads. Some highways, however, will extend from Buenos Aires southward as far as Río Gallegos, near the Strait of Magellan, and northward as far as the Paraguayan and Bolivian borders.

Brazil. Brazil has about 58,000 miles of all-weather road. This is not much considering the vast size of the country; but seen against the background of the natural environment of bewildering variety (particularly jungle), which accounts for most of the immense north and northwest, the mileage is a human triumph.

Most of the roads are in the northeast ("the Hump") and the southeast (the heart of the nation)—those areas long occupied by Europeans and those most important for logging, mining, farming, and manufacturing. Hard-surface roads fan out from all the main port cities from Belém on the north to Porto Alegre on the south, but particularly from Rio de Janeiro and Santos. However, seldom do any of these roads reach far into the hinterland. The country's most modern highway is the 35-mile-long Via Anchiata between Santos and São Paulo. Another important artery, extending north and south, links Rio de Janeiro and Bahia.

An arterial-road pattern, including both a transverse and a longitudinal road system, is under way to aid in opening up the undeveloped lands and to facilitate internal trade. One of the first attempts in this respect is the 1,200-mile Trans-Brazilian Highway, connecting Belém with Brazília, and built through some of the densest jungle in the world. A road of this nature has been a dream for more than a century; for it is believed that if the north and south are connected, the isolation of the Amazon Basin will be ended forever.

Colombia. In no country in South America is land transport more difficult. The population nuclei, along with the major centers of production and consumption, are to be found on lofty plateaus or in valleys divided by the three prongs or fingers into which the Andes divide the nation. This situation, combined with the lack of integration and high costs of internal transport, has discouraged commercial transactions between regions. Interregional traffic is characterized by costly trans-shipments and long delays. There is virtually no highway transport where the population density is extremely low. Thus cattle are often flown by plane from the stock-breeding area around Villavicencio to the consumer center provided by greater Bogotá. In much of the mountain country, mule paths continue as an essential part of the communications system, mules picking their way slowly into places inaccessible to any other land transport. It is said that thousands of miles of these paths exist, leading to farms and houses that no modern highway has ever reached.

In recent years Buenaventura—the main port, handling 75 per cent of the coffee exports and a disproportionately large share of the imports—has become connected by highway with Cali, Popayán, Bogotá, Medellín, and other cities in the mountain region.

Peru. Considering that there are three Perus rather than one—desert, lofty mountains, and tropical rain forest—the highway situation is surprisingly good. A north-south hard-surface road stretches the full length of the nation in the narrow coastal area with offshoots eastward into all the agricultural valleys. There are several reasonably good roads in the hot, rainy Montaña east of the Andes, and a number of excellent hard-surface routes leading into and throughout portions of the *sierra*.

Bolivia. This backward, landlocked, poor, politically unstable country has long suffered from a dearth of traffic routes between the infertile but populous Altiplano and the fertile

Fig. 28-11. The Santa Cruz–Cochabamba Highway, reaching from Santa Cruz on the level plain and 300 miles west to Cochabamba, 7,000 feet in the mountains. The 300 miles separating the two cities are characterized by rugged and formidable mountains, wild streams, and dense rain forests. Highest point reached by the road is 12,050 feet about 47 miles east of Cochabamba. Travel over this highway is a harrowing, never-to-be-forgotten experience. (Courtesy of Macco Corporation.)

but undeveloped and almost empty Oriente —the broad lowland east of the Andes. Want of such a route destined Bolivia to regional isolation and a lack of national consciousness. To help solve the problem, the government negotiated a loan from the Export-Import Bank for completion of a paved highway from Santa Cruz to Cochabamba (Fig. 28-11). There are paved or at least all-weather highways from Santa Cruz southward to Villa Montes and Yacuiba, from Santa Cruz to Sucre, from La Paz to Lake Titicaca, and from Cochabamba to Potosí.

EUROPE

Highly industrialized, urbanized, densely populated Northwestern Europe, which possesses more than three fourths of the continent's motor vehicles, is served by a thick web of excellent hard-surface highways. The web thins out to the east and south.

Hitler recognized very early in his career the need for a national system of military superhighways. From Berlin, the center of the *Autobahnen*, roads were built to Falkenburg, 95 miles from the Polish Corridor; to Hamburg; to Saarbrücken, on the Franco-German frontier; to Munich; and to Vienna. By 1939, Germany had completed 1,900 miles of superhighway. Today, West Germany is continuing the construction of *Autobahnen*. It is now possible to travel by modern motor highways from the Baltic Sea to Basel, from the Benelux countries to East Germany, without any detours on secondary roads.

SOVIET UNION

Considering Russia's enormous size, its high rank as an industrial nation, and its large population, the highway system is one of the poorest in the world. It is probably true that in no other branch of transport was there such marked backwardness in tsarist Russia as in highways and, though steady progress has been made since World War I, the 100,000 miles of hard-surface roads are not impressive by Western standards.

The severe winter climate, the presence of **permafrost** over a large part of the northern half of the nation, and the poor drainage occasioned by the large area of plain conspire to make most Russian roads impassable for many months of the year. Thaws cost the nation hundreds of millions of rubles annually due to cessation of traffic. This situation, combined with the fact that until recently most of the population consisted of an agricultural peasantry living largely on a subsistence basis, limited (and still limits) highway transport to the cities and their environs and to local traffic. Railways and waterways accordingly handle long-distance freight, leaving only lightweight short-distance shipments to road transport. The Soviets, who have concluded that highway transport does not fulfill party objectives, regard it as superior to rail transport for distances only up to 25 miles. One is not, therefore, surprised to learn that motor carriers perform less than 5 per cent of Russia's freight haulage.

Geographical distribution of highways shows extreme concentration in European Russia, with Moscow functioning as the hub of a radiating pattern. Important highways connect Moscow with Leningrad and with cities in the Volga Basin. Yet even here there is nothing even remotely resembling the road pattern in the United States and Western Europe; American observers invariably comment on the absence of side roads, which, when present, slough off into ragged lanes and trails. Even the best highways are not built for heavy traffic.

There is no line-haul truck transport, the average haul being about 7 miles (which, by American standards, is local cartage) and confined mostly to urban and industrial centers.

There are vast expanses of territory—e.g., the extreme north, southern Siberia, and Central Asia—which are devoid of highways. Marked expansion of the highway system in the Soviet Union in the near future is not to be anticipated.

ASIA

This enormous continent is poor in total highway mileage and in hard-surface roads. Because this shortage has been a major snag in economic development, all governments have prepared comprehensive highway-development plans. However, progress is hampered by lack of funds, shortage of material, and scarcity of trained personnel.

JAPAN

Medieval Japan was linked together by a system of imperial roads that connected government centers and various shrines. Many roads radiated in various directions from Kyoto. Such roads obviously are ill suited to twentieth-century needs. Cross-country highways so typical of the United States are little developed. Only one ninth of the road mileage is outside cities and towns.

INDIA AND PAKISTAN

India and Pakistan lack good roads. The plains are almost devoid of road-building materials, and the summer monsoon makes travel by highway all but impossible.

India-Pakistan has but four major automotive highways: the Grand Trunk, most famous of all, extends eastward from the Khyber Pass to Calcutta via Delhi; the others connect Calcutta with Madras, Madras with Bombay, and Bombay with Delhi. Most of even these roads lack hard surface. There is a good road connecting Assam with Burma. The total length of all highways in India is 296,000 miles; in Pakistan, 46,000 miles.

Among the famous roads of Asia is the Burma Road, constructed during World War II to provide a surface lifeline from India to China. It exemplifies highway construction under almost insuperable difficulties and through extremely rugged terrain. The 200,-000 men, women, and children employed in constructing it used only human muscle, dynamite, and the crudest tools; 250 miles were cut through solid rock. The road extends from the railhead at Lashio, Burma, to Kunming, China, a distance of 726 miles. Unfortunately, it never was important as a supply line to war-time China; for it was captured by the Japanese. Another road was then built from India —the Ledo or Stilwell Road—to enable convoys of trucks to carry supplies to the Chinese.

CHINA

In 1921 Sun Yat-sen envisaged for China the construction of a million miles of road. In 1958, 248,000 miles—far short of Sun Yat-sen's dream—had been built. Except for a few remote areas, all counties are now served by motor transport; in pre-Communist days, less than half were reached by roads. Increase in mileage has been stimulated by the need to get fertilizer to farmers, the desire to develop minerals, and the rapid growth of the steel industry. Most of the highways, which serve mainly as feeders linking the main railways and river ports with the countryside, are involved only in short-distance transport.

Communist China, moving forward at a pace regarded as impossible a quarter century ago, still must be considered an underdeveloped country, and a major reason for this is the poor system of roads for quickening economic growth and for enabling a larger volume of goods to move cheaply within the nation.

When the Communists took over in 1949, the road network was inadequate for haulage of volume freight. Most of the roads were 20 feet wide or less, and only in the larger cities were any highways paved. Some were surfaced with crushed stone and were sufficiently well drained to be used throughout the year, but the majority (particularly in North China, where roads are merely beaten tracks wholly impassable in the rainy season) were unusable for at least three or four months.

There is little automotive traffic on the poor Chinese highways. However, the government leaders—wanting China to occupy a prominent place in the sun and realizing that therefore they will have to develop minerals and industrialization—are laying much emphasis

on transportation, both highway and railway. Inadequate transport has definitely retarded China's mining development.

Some connection by road is maintained between China and the Soviet Union via Sinkiang, but the distances are so staggering and the problem of providing fuel so great that little commerce is carried on. New roads have been built by the Chinese within Tibet and between Lhasa and Alma Ata in Soviet Central Asia and Irkutsk in Siberia.

AFRICA

Africa virtually lacked all-weather highways until after World War I. Until then it was the railroad that opened up the continent. The first roads were really feeders to the railroads, and even today the densest spread of roads and those of the highest quality are in areas where railways are located. The reason for this is obvious: only the most productive areas can support the cost of railways and highways. During World War II many roads were built in the battle areas; these roads became useful following the war. Secondary roads were also extended from the railways into additional farming areas to serve as feeder lines and to aid security and administration. Today the continent does have trunk roads and long-distance highways.

In North Africa, six north-south motorable roads span the Sahara, linking it with tropical Africa. It surprises most persons to learn that tropical Africa has more than a third of a million miles of motorable road. When present, laterite soil is used, because it is porous, dries quickly following rain, and is easy to handle. There are some gravel roads but very few hard-topped highways. During the dry season, most roads are usable by trucks and jeeps; but during the rainy seasons they are, over vast areas, impassable.

In addition to the roads spanning the Sahara, there are two longitudinal routes: "the high road" through East Africa, and "the low road" through the Congo Basin. There are also several latitudinal routes—mostly dirt roads. In isolated stretches in Middle Africa, so-called "improved roads" are only on the map.

South Africa has a reasonably good road system. There was considerable road construction during the years between the two world wars. The most famous road is the Great North Road, which is a segment of the highway extending from Cape Town to Algeria—usable in the dry seasons. The main highways are designated as "national roads," and ultimately all will be hard surfaced.

AUSTRALIA

Though Australia is nearly as large as the United States in size, her population is only about one seventeenth as great. The low density of population (three per square mile versus fifty for the United States) has retarded development of a highway system adequate to serve the nation. There is not yet sufficient volume of traffic to justify a road network of the American type. Yet, in total tons carried in the mid-1950s, highways accounted for 76 per cent; railways, for 19 per cent; and coastal shipping, for 5 per cent. Paved highways connect all the capital cities except for the Adelaide-Perth crossing of the uninhabited Nullarbor Plain.

PIPELINES

Transportation of petroleum and natural gas presents herculean problems because as minerals they are nearly always found far from the places where they are to be used (e.g., in Arabia, Iran, Bolivia, Venezuela, Algeria, and Sumatra, to mention but a few). Thus to move this oil and gas from where it is found to where it can be used is a great challenge.

PETROLEUM PIPELINES

The pipeline either fully or partially supplies the answer. Its sole reason for existence is to transport the oil or gas to refinery or to market. The first successful oil pipeline was completed in Pennsylvania in 1865. Previously all American oil went to market in barrels atop wagons; later it moved by rail (but not in the metal tank cars of today, which did not appear until 1907). Such methods were inefficient and costly, but so were the first pipe-

lines. Improvement followed improvement, until today pipeline transportation is the cheapest means of hauling petroleum overland. A unit for pipeline transportation includes branch feeders, trunk lines, initial and terminal storage tanks, and pumping stations. Pipe of 8- to almost 40-inch diameter is used for trunk lines; 2- to 4-inch for feeder lines. Oil is forced through the pipes by means of pumping stations spaced 2 to 50 miles apart—the precise distance depending on the terrain, the density of the oil, the size of the pipes, and the weather. At first, pipelines carried only crude oil, but many now carry petroleum products.

Pipelines are efficient transporters of liquid products because they employ the straight-line and the constant-flow principles. Though common carriers, they are free from the common-carrier obligation to transport a wide range of commodities. Because of low costs and efficiency, pipelines have advantages over railroads and trucks. Only the tanker transports oil at lower cost.

Crude-oil–gathering lines, laid on the surface, carry the output from individual wells to some central point—storage tank, or refinery, or a trunk line for further transport.

Crude-oil trunk lines, laid above or underground, transport crude oil from field or storage tanks to refineries, to seaboard, or to an inland-waterway terminal for handling by tankers or barges to refineries.

Refined-products trunk lines transport gasoline and other refined oils from refineries to centers of large consuming areas for local distribution.

The pipeline industry began in the United States in 1862 when a 2-inch wrought-iron line carried 800 barrels of crude oil 5 miles. But pipelines did not really come into their own until 1931, when the first long-distance line (1,000 miles) was built from Texas to Illinois. World War II stimulated oil-pipeline construction; for German U-boat packs infested the American Atlantic Coast, the Gulf of Mexico, and the Caribbean, and were successfully sinking large numbers of cargo carriers, including oceangoing tankers. Since the East had to have petroleum, the federal government in desperation constructed two pipelines, the world's biggest at the time—the "Big Inch" and the "Little Big Inch." The lines reached from Longview and Houston-Baytown, Texas, and lower Louisiana, to New York and Philadelphia. The "Big Inch," capacity 300,000 barrels daily and transporting only crudes, was opened in 1943; the "Little Big Inch," capacity 230,000 barrels daily, carried gasoline, kerosene, and fuel oils. So successful were they that they paid for their entire cost during the first two years. With the ending of the war, tankers once again could carry their burden safely and at lower cost; hence, both pipelines were converted into natural-gas carriers.

Today the United States, with about 200,000 miles of oil pipeline, leads the entire world. Principal movement is of crude oil from producing areas in the Midcontinent, West Texas, and Gulf Coast to refining centers along the Gulf Coast, in the Great Lakes region, and along the Atlantic Seaboard. Kansas, Oklahoma, and Texas together account for more than 60 per cent of the total American crude-oil-pipeline mileage. A number of long pipelines have been constructed in the West—most notably, from Salt Lake City into the Pacific Northwest; and eastward from Casper, Wyoming. The products lines have a somewhat wider geographical dispersion. Particularly are they outstanding from the great seaboard refineries in New Jersey and New York to markets in the Midwest.

CANADA

Canada has enjoyed a meteoric rise in oil production in recent years. But her oil fields are separated from her cities and markets by thousands of miles of almost wilderness. This has necessitated the laying of long-distance pipelines to refining centers in Ontario and British Columbia. The Interprovincial Line, reputed to be the world's longest, carries crude oil 1,930 miles from Edmonton, Alberta, to Sarnia, Ontario (via Minnesota, Wisconsin, and Michigan), and to Port Credit on the outskirts of Toronto.

A second important pipeline is the Trans-Mountain, constructed from Edmonton to Vancouver, British Columbia—a distance of 718 hard miles over mountains, across streams, through forests. It can handle 150,000 barrels per day. There are four pumping stations; ultimately, however, as demand permits, this number may be increased to thirteen capable of putting 300,000 barrels of crude into Vancouver.

Another and different type of line is the 200-mile-long line built from Portland, Maine, to Montreal. This line handles foreign, not Canadian, petroleum. Prior to construction of this pipeline, Montreal refineries depended on crude oil imported by ocean tanker via the St. Lawrence; and, since the river is icebound for an average of five months each year, the winter's supply had to be stored in advance. This pipeline largely solved that problem.

LATIN AMERICA

Although Latin America is well endowed with petroleum, most of the reserves appear to be concentrated in a small area close to the Caribbean—Mexico, Colombia, Venezuela, and Trinidad. Aside from Bolivia and Argentina, all the longer pipelines are in these four centers.

Mexico. The Mexican oil industry is geared essentially to supply the domestic market. A rather extensive pipeline network transports crude oil from remote jungles to ports and interior refineries. And refined products are piped to consumption centers. Principal concentration of pipelines is from the Poza Rica field in the New Golden Lane south of Tampico to inland refineries near Mexico City and westward to Salamanca.

Colombia. Colombia is active on the oil map of South America because of its favorable position on the Caribbean and because of attractive legislation and stable policies. Yet the entire production is won far from major domestic markets and from export ports. Connecting her producing fields with refineries and ports by pipelines ranks among the most heroic engineering tasks ever performed in the tropics and in mountainous terrain. Crude-oil trunk lines have been constructed from the producing fields in central Colombia near the Magdalena to a refinery at Barranca Bermeja on the river and to Mamoral Terminal on the Caribbean 10 miles across the bay from Cartagena; and from near the Venezuelan border to Coveñas, south of Cartagena.

Still another notable engineering feat is the 63-mile-long refined-products line connecting the seaport of Buenaventura (elevation 16 feet) with the inland terminal at Cali (elevation 3,142 feet). The gasoline making this journey by pipeline is brought from the refinery at Cartagena to Buenaventura by tanker every twenty days.

Venezuela. Venezuela is one of the best-served South American countries with respect to pipelines. In the west, which means Maracaibo (still the source of two thirds of the country's oil output), pipelines are located on the east and west shores and even on the floor of the lake (an estimated thousand miles of pipe). These lines feed the many tankers that enter the lake, and they carry crude to large refineries on the Paraguaná Peninsula at Amuay Bay and Puerto Cardón.

In the east (central and eastern oil fields), half a dozen crude trunk lines from the states of Guarico, Anzoategui, and Monagas focus on Puerto La Cruz, near Barcelona. Farther west is the pipeline connecting Barinas with Puerto Cabello.

Bolivia. Bolivia has pipelines that deliver crude oil from the Camiri field in the foothills east of the Andes up into the mountains to refineries at Sucre and Cochabamba. It has another that transports the oil 140 miles south to the Argentine border. There is also a products line to La Paz. In 1960 Bolivia's dream of an oil outlet to the sea was realized with completion of the first trans-Andean pipeline —a 12-million-dollar products line from Sicasica (southeast of La Paz), where there is a pumping station, to Arica, Chile, 218 miles distant, and over 14,000-foot mountains.

Argentina. In 1959 Argentina completed a 927-mile crude and condensate pipeline, from Campo Duran near the Bolivian frontier southward to San Lorenzo on the Paraná River, 250 miles northwest of Buenos Aires (San Lorenzo is Argentina's center for the manufacture of petrochemicals). Output from the important Comodoro Rivadavia fields in Chubut Territory, Patagonia, still is transported to Buenos Aires by tanker.

EUROPE

Since Europe is poor in crude-oil reserves, its pipelines until recently existed for the purpose of transporting crude oil from marine terminals to inland refineries and distribution centers. Only in Sicily, Germany, and the countries behind the Iron Curtain were there pipelines from wells or fields to refinery centers. Most of the lines were short and—compared with those in the United States, the Soviet Union, and Canada—unimpressive. However, there is presently a great spurt in pipelining. A 440-mile-long pipeline, constructed from Lavera, near Marseilles, to the upper Rhine Valley, supplies the French industrial area near Strasbourg and the new West German refining center near Karlsruhe with Algerian oil carried across the Mediterranean by tanker. This is the longest pipeline to date in Europe. It may be extended to Cologne, an important refining and petrochemical center, on which two pipelines focus from the North Sea. Another long line is the Rotterdam-Rhine, which extends from Pernis (Rotterdam) eastward to Venlo, where it divides into a north branch to Wesel and a south branch to Wesseling. Still another, the Wilhelmshaven-Cologne, serves seven oil refineries.

SOVIET UNION

The pipeline played an astonishingly minor role in Soviet transportation until after World War II, despite the fact that a 550-mile line had been constructed in Russia as early as 1905. Presently, great emphasis is being placed on pipeline transportation. This change results from a combination of circumstances: (1) the greatly increased production of oil and gas;

(2) the government's determination to depend more on oil and gas and less on coal than in the past; (3) the notable shift in oil production from the old Baku and North Caucasus centers to new ones in the Volga-Ural area; (4) expansion of the chemical industries, particularly the petrochemicals and plastics branches; (5) growing consumption of diesel fuel by railways, ships, agriculture, automobiles, and trucks; (6) a more widely distributed and larger population, which makes pipelines more economical than in the past; (7) overworked railroads; and (8) expanded oil exports.

Previously, petroleum was transported mostly by railways and waterways. A major flow line was across the Caspian, up the Volga, and across the Black Sea to the Ukraine. No longer is this the principal route of oil movement. Now and in the future, oil will move by pipeline from the Volga-Ural fields to the east (Omsk, Novosibirsk, Krasnoyarsk, and Irkutsk), to the northwest (Gorki and Yaroslavl), and to the west (Bryansk and Polotsk).

However, by American standards the Soviet's pipeline-construction program is not striking. The Russians are virtually starting from scratch: in 1950 the Soviet Union had less than 3,200 miles of trunk pipelines for oil and refined products; in 1955, only 4,600 miles of crude and 1,900 miles of products lines; and by the end of 1960, 10,000 miles of crude and 4,500 miles of products lines. In 1960 the United States had a total of nearly 200,000 miles.

In accordance with the seven-year plan (1958-1965), a 3,000-mile-long pipeline, the East European, was constructed from the Kuibyshev oil field on the Volga River to the satellite Iron Curtain countries. From Kuibyshev the line goes to Mozyr, Belorussia, where it divides, one branch reaching into Poland (refineries at Plock) and East Germany, and the other to refineries in Czechoslovakia and Hungary via Bratislava.

THE MIDDLE EAST

This, the world's richest oil region and one of its leading producers, makes full use of pipelines. Each producing country and sheikdom uses pipelines; but a nation like Arabia has a marked advantage over one like Iraq, in that it has alternative tanker routes. From the standpoint of pipeline charges, Iraq is at the mercy of the politicians in the three have-not countries (Jordan, Syria, and Lebanon) through which its pipelines move to ports on the Mediterranean. The three formerly were content with a minor share of the oil money, for their transit lands had been useless desert. This, however, is no longer true. The logical route for oil from the northern fields (Kirkuk) is to the Mediterranean. If this oil were to be piped to Kuwait and Basra, as has been proposed on a number of occasions, it would be traveling away from the European market and, after a 400-mile journey to the Persian Gulf, would have to compete with oil produced almost within sight of the sea. Oil from the Basra fields is expectably piped to that city.

Arabia's oil-producing areas are, of course, sufficiently close to the Persian Gulf so that they could, except for a very short journey to the Ras Tanura terminal and refinery, rely solely on ocean tankers. However, Aramco has constructed several pipelines (Fig. 28-12), its TAP-line being one of the world's greatest. TAP-line, which extends from Aramco's tank farm at Qaisumah to its marine terminal at Sidon, Lebanon, saves a 3,200-mile tanker voyage around Arabia.

Iran has an impressive pipeline network. Maps show pipelines snaking from the various fields down to Abadan and Khargu Island.

NORTH AFRICA

A pipeline has been constructed from the Hassi Messaoud field in central Algeria to the Mediterranean port of Bougie. Another extends from several fields in the Edjele area near the Libyan border through Tunisia to the port of La Skhirra on the Gulf of Gabés. In Libya pipelines reach from the Zelten field and from fields to the west of it to the Gulf of Sirte. Since the future output of these two areas appears bright and since Western Europe would like to break from the shackles held by the Middle East oil-producing coun-

Fig. 28-12. Oil pipelines transporting crude oil from the Abqaiq field to Damman and to the refinery and tanker terminal at Ras Tanura, Saudi Arabia. (Courtesy of Aramco.)

tries, much expansion in pipelines here is to be anticipated.

THE FAR EAST

In the Far East, responsible for 2.5 per cent of the world output of crude oil, most of the pipeline mileage is to be found in the country leading in production—Indonesia, mostly in Sumatra and Java. Though these pipelines have been built in lands of jungles and mountains, they are relatively short lines, mostly 200 miles or less.

NATURAL-GAS PIPELINES

Unlike crude oil and refined products, which can be transported by pipeline, tanker, barge, tank car, or truck, natural gas is transportable only by pipeline. Accordingly, in countries where both large reserves and markets are present, extensive pipeline networks have been laid down to handle natural gas. Some countries with much natural gas but extremely limited markets (e.g., Venezuela and Saudi Arabia) have wasted this valuable resource in the past by flaring. All countries are currently concerned about such waste and are taking steps to inaugurate drastic conservation practices.

Relatively few countries possess natural-gas pipelines, and only the United States has a true network. Canada, Mexico, Venezuela, Argentina, the Soviet Union, the Middle East, and Algeria exemplify the various stages from a very small to an impressive mileage.

UNITED STATES

Before the modern era of pipelines, there was no practical way of moving natural gas from the fields of the Southwest to the markets of the Middle West and East. Hence, the gas produced in conjunction with oil was flared, and that from gas wells either was flared or the wells were capped. Formidable obstacles had to be overcome before gas could be transported long distances.

Wide use of natural gas in the United States had to await the compressor, first used in 1890. But even it did not fully open the way. Natural gas did not become a major fuel until the 1920s with (1) the development of high-tensile-strength, thin-walled, large-diameter pipe; (2) the advent of electric welding of pipe joints in the field; (3) a heavy and enthusiastic demand for a superior fuel; and (4) a price that would be low in relation to other fuels. By 1931 natural gas was being piped 1,000 miles from Texas to Chicago, and four years later there were nineteen interstate systems.

Pipelines now transport gas from the Southwest—Texas, New Mexico, and the Four Corners Area—to nearly every part of the nation. Even Canadian gas reaches into the United States—into California and the "Upper Midwest." In Alaska a pipeline was completed in 1961 for transporting gas from Kenai on Cook Inlet to Anchorage. By 1961 the nation had more than 654,000 miles of natural-gas pipelines. Now the nation's fifth largest industry, the natural-gas industry is expected to double in size in a decade. Without the vast pipeline system, wide use of this superior fuel would not be possible.

CANADA

A new era in natural-gas pipelining is being created in Canada because (1) the reserves appear enormous and the Canadian market limited, and (2) in 1960 the Canadian Energy Board and the United States Federal Power Commission agreed one to export, the other to import, 850 million cubic feet of natural gas daily. The amount reached 1 billion cubic feet a day in 1961. Immediately following announcement by the two countries, pipeline construction got under way in Canada and the United States at five major points of contact, and hundreds of millions of dollars were expended.

Other lines have been built from the Western gas fields to Vancouver and into the states of Washington and Oregon. Most outstanding, however, is the Trans-Canada Pipeline, linking the Alberta fields with Toronto, Ottawa, and Montreal via Regina, Winnipeg, Fort William and Kapuskasing.

MEXICO

Mexico has oriented its natural-gas industry, which increased output 60 per cent between 1957 and 1958, to meet domestic needs and to supply some gas to the United States. Most of the gas is produced in the Frontera, Poza Rica, and Isthmus fields. An extensive pipeline network conveys gas from the important fields in the Northeast Zone to Monterrey, Torreón, and Monclova, and from the North Zone, the Vera Cruz Zone, and the South Zone to Mexico City.

VENEZUELA

Venezuela has vast natural-gas reserves. Very little is utilized, however, because (1) the total population in 1960 was only about 6½ million; (2) the climate is tropical, so that gas is not required for domestic heat; and (3) since the country is industrially immature, until recently most of the natural gas produced with crude oil was flared.

The picture is now changed. Much natural gas (more than 35 per cent in 1960) is injected under pressure into the oil reservoir; and a number of pipelines have been constructed from producing fields to cities: one line extends from central Guarico to Caracas, La Guaira, Arrecife, Santa Lucia, and Valencia; another from Anaco, south of Barcelona, northward to Puerto de la Cruz, westward to Caracas, and southward to Ciudad Bolívar and Puerto Ordaz on the Orinoco River; still another goes from La Paz west of Lake Maracaibo under the lake and eastward to the Paraguaná Peninsula. Yet, even as late as 1960, 56 per cent was flared.

ARGENTINA

Argentina has several very long natural-gas pipelines, one extending 1,090 miles from Campo Duran near the Bolivian border to Buenos Aires and paralleling the oil pipeline; the other extending 1,100 miles, from Comodoro Rivadavia in Patagonia to Buenos Aires.

SOVIET UNION

Prior to 1943, natural-gas pipelines were of only local importance in the Soviet Union. In that year the first long-distance line was constructed from the newly discovered fields near Saratov to Moscow. In early 1958, there were only 7,500 miles of gas pipeline in in the entirety of Russia. The seven-year plan (1958-1965), however, envisages monumental changes—the construction of forty main pipelines to reach 26,250 miles by 1965 and the increased use of natural gas for generating power (37 per cent by 1965) to free coal primarily for the iron and steel industry. This emphasis on natural gas does not appear to be out of line considering that reserves are estimated at double those in the United States. The new pipelines are being built from the main producing fields to the population and industrial areas, which lack a source of good cheap coal—that is, (1) from the North Caucasus fields, Saratov, and the Western Ukraine to the central industrial region, the Leningrad area, and the Baltic republics; (2) from the Central Asian fields, the Volga fields, the Komi A.S.S.R., and Berezovo along the lower Ob to the fuel-poor Urals (Sverdlovsk, Chelyabinsk, and Magnitogorsk); and (3) from the Bukhara field to all the larger cities along the northern slopes of the Tien Shan, as far east as Alma-Ata.

THE MIDDLE EAST

Like so many underdeveloped oil-and-gas-producing countries, those in the Middle East have almost no commercial use for natural gas; they do not need it for domestic fuel (they do not have cold winters), their overall population is small, and there is a dearth of manufacturing. Kuwait is following Venezuela's lead in injecting gas under pressure back into the oil reservoir. She also pipes gas 25 miles to a seawater distillation plant at Shuwaikh, which produces 5 million gallons of fresh water daily and is the world's largest installation of its kind. Kuwait also uses some natural gas for generating power. In Saudi Arabia Aramco is striving to promote greater use of gas, for which possible markets might be electrical-power generation, fertilizer, and lime plants.

ALGERIA

From Algeria's Hassi er R'Mel gas field in the Sahara to Western Europe has been projected and partly completed one of the boldest and most imaginative gas pipelines yet conceived by man. Part of the project involves a trans-Mediterranean Sea pipeline to Cartagena, Spain, from which terminus big-inch pipelines reach to France, Belgium, Luxembourg, and Germany.

WORLD OUTLOOK

For all-around performance, and despite the claims of rival forms of transport, the railway must be regarded as the best general carrier—at least in the developed nations. With few and diminishing exceptions, the railway is accessible; its terminals and stations are strategically sited for carrying on the most business; it is not subject to breakdown over long distances; and it can accommodate almost any weight or shape of load. Its charges, for the most part, are not excessive; and though competitors may claim to excel it in one or another of the advantages just mentioned, they positively cannot match the railroad in the *combination of advantages*. Hence, it is to be expected that the railway will continue to form the basis of civilized progress in any foreseeable future.

Transportation is growing apace also in the underdeveloped lands of the earth. To be sure, water transport has long been used in these lands, but few countries could progress far if dependent solely upon natural waterways.

Railroads are being extended in underdeveloped countries on all the continents but particularly in Asia, South America, and Africa. Even more than railways, highways are penetrating jungles, savannas, deserts, and mountains because they are cheaper to construct, they can go almost anywhere, and they are free to all who are near them. Finally, pipelines are snaking their way from oil fields to cities (markets) and to ports—e.g., in Venezuela, Colombia, Peru, Chile, Argentina, Algeria, Libya, Iraq, Iran, Kuwait, Saudi Arabia, and Indonesia. Even natural-gas pipelines are beginning to appear in Mexico, Venezuela, Argentina, Algeria, Saudi Arabia, Kuwait, and elsewhere. Wide development of transportation should immeasurably help such lands to raise their levels of living.

SELECTED REFERENCES

"The Asian Highway from Caravan Routes to Modern Roads," *United Nations Review*, 5:42-44, April 1959.

Carlson, Fred A. "Traffic on the Ohio River System," *Journal of Geography*, 59:357-360, November 1960.

Chang, Kuei-Sheng. "The Changing Railroad Pattern in Mainland China," *Geographical Review*, 51:534-548, October 1961.

Chorpening, C. H. "Waterway Growth in the United States," *Transactions, American Society of Civil Engineers*, CT:976-1041, 1953. Paper 2643.

Connole, W. R. "Future Prospects for International Pipelines," *Journal of the Pipeline Division, Proceedings of the American Society of Civil Engineers*, 83:1-6, June 1958. Proceedings Paper 1674.

Garbutt, P. E. *The Russian Railways*. London, Sampson, Low, Marston and Co., Ltd., 1949.

Gurley, Fred G. "Role of Railroads in United States History," *Transactions, American Society of Civil Engineers*, CT:891-903, 1953. Paper 2637.

Hall, J. W. "Pipeline Construction in the Past, Present, and Future," *Proceedings, American Society of Civil Engineers*, 85:9-25, January 1959.

Hastings, D. C. "Impact of the Federal Highway Program on the Nation and the Eighth District," *Monthly Review* (Federal Reserve Bank of St. Louis), 39:34-43, March 1957.

Hills, T. L. *The St. Lawrence Seaway*. London, Methuen and Company, Ltd., 1959.

—————————. "The St. Lawrence Seaway," *Focus*, 11:1-6, December 1960.

Hubbard, M. E. "Pipelines in Relation to Other Forms of Transport," *World Power Conference*, Madrid, 1960. Paper IIIA/8.

Jackson, W. A. D. "Transportation and Economic Development in Soviet Asia," *Geographical Review*, 46:574-576, October 1956.

Lydolph, P. E., and T. Shabad. "The Oil and Gas Industries in the U.S.S.R.," *Annals of the Association of American Geographers*, 50:461-486 (maps: petroleum pipelines, p. 479; gas pipelines, p. 482), December 1960.

Manners, G. "The Pipeline Revolution," *Geography*, 47:154-163, April 1962.

Murphey, R. "China's Transport Problem and Communist Planning," *Economic Geography*, 32:17-37, January 1956.

Patton, D. "The Traffic Pattern on American Inland Waterways," *Economic Geography*, 32:29-37, January 1956.

"Pipelining Is a Global Business," *Oil and Gas Journal*, 57:E-10–E-11, January 28, 1959 (*Petroleum Panorama*, 1859–1959).

Singer, S. R. "Transmission of Natural Gas," *Business Review* (Federal Reserve Bank of Dallas), 46:1-8, May 1961.

Ullman, E. L. "The Railroad Pattern of the United States," *Geographical Review*, 39:242-256, April 1949.

Wiedenfeld, K. "Transportation," in *Encyclopaedia of the Social Sciences*. New York, The Macmillan Company, 1950. 15:80-90.

Williams, G. B. "The Trans-Canada Highway," *Canadian Geographical Journal*, 54:42-67, February 1957.

Wilson, G. M. *Oil Across the World, The American Saga of Pipelines*, Longmans, Green and Co., New York, 1946.

CHAPTER TWENTY-NINE::

The oceans were long regarded as separating
men from each other, for man during most
of his history has been excluded from this
wilderness comprising nearly three fourths of
the earth's surface. When nautical enterprises
gradually developed, and the time needed to
cross these waterways was significantly reduced, man began to think of the oceans as
connecting links rather than separating gaps.
Each historical epoch has possessed its own
sea, and with each successive epoch the maritime field has been expanded. The geographic
stages of maritime development can thus be
traced from early exploitation of enclosed or
marginal seas, with their proximate opposite
shores and potentials for coastwise navigation,
to eventual outgrowth from inshore estuaries
or gulfs to the more challenging expanses of
the large oceans.

THE WORLD'S OCEAN

EARLY COMMERCIAL
OCEAN TRADERS

The first truly commercial mariners of antiquity were the Phoenicians, who inhabited a thin strip of coastline along the eastern Mediterranean. Their famed cedars of Lebanon gave them the raw materials for building ships. Developing great skill, they converted the Mediterranean into a veritable Phoenician lake and by 1000 B.C. had sailed beyond the Strait of Gibraltar to Britain and Scandinavia. The Greeks were next to reign over the seas. Then followed the Romans, who, though not a seafaring people, were pushed by their administrative and military skill into maritime trade. They thus bound together the empire which had absorbed all the maritime states fringing the Mediterranean. Later, with the decline of Rome, came the decline of maritime trade; and it did not flourish again until the Crusades, when Venice rose to prominence.

RISE OF MODERN
MARITIME TRADE

The development of ocean transportation came only with the invention of the mariner's compass, together with larger and more seaworthy sailing vessels. This paved the way for circumnavigation of the world during the fifteenth, sixteenth and seventeenth centuries by the Portuguese, Spanish, English, and Dutch. The invention of the steamship by Robert Fulton revolutionized maritime commerce.

Today a liner crosses the Atlantic in 4½ days, whereas 12½ days were required a cen-

TRANSPORTATION

tury ago. The switch from coal to oil wrought significant changes, saving loading time, labor, and storage space and permitting the generation of far more power per ton.

ADVANTAGES OF OCEAN TRANSPORTATION

Of the several factors favoring ocean transportation over other means of transport, cost is the most important. Water transportation is invariably cheaper than land transportation. The floating equipment is the only fixed capital demanded by an ocean carrier. No construction costs are involved on an ocean highway except at loading and unloading points (and these are usually paid by governments eager to obtain a greater share of sea commerce). The ocean routes need no maintenance crews for repair work. Steamer tracks are not taxed. Ocean carriers, handling up to 20,000 tons in one unit, lower the cost per ton through distribution of transport costs over large loads. Since the average ocean haul is much longer than that by rail or truck, a merchant buying goods in distant markets has a definite advantage because, once the ship is loaded, it is no more expensive to transport the cargo several thousand miles by sea than to haul it several hundred miles overland. An oceangoing cargo vessel can be built and operated much more cheaply than can its equivalent in freight cars and locomotives and trucks.

Additional advantages of ocean transport are (1) flexibility—the freedom of movement over the oceanic highway, (2) the high degree of safety with which heavy and bulky cargoes can be carried over long distances, and (3) the availability of numerous port facilities maintained by agencies not directly concerned with the operation of oceangoing vessels.

THE ROUTES

Most of the world's international trade moves by sea, except between the United States and Canada and between the countries of Western and Central Europe. The most important routes for this trade are located in middle latitudes by reason of the needs of their populations and the outstanding diversity of the goods produced and consumed. Natural conditions and greater industrialization account for the concentration of ocean tradeways in intermediate latitudes. One of the most notable features of the main ocean trade routes is their east–west direction.

Contrary to what the average person believes, the large, seemingly trackless oceans have definite, though invisible, great trunk roads supplemented by countless feeders and cross tracks. Wherever a great volume of trade moves between two or more points, there has emerged a well-defined route normally followed by vessels—a route determined by a number of economic and physical conditions. Economic factors include the size of the ship, volume of traffic, perishability of products, location of fueling stations, port facilities and charges, cargo-handling costs, and canal fees.

But certain physical factors have been most instrumental in establishing very definite routes over the seven seas:

1. Wind intensity and direction. The modern vessel can buck prevailing winds, but it prefers to move with them in order to maintain speed and reduce fuel costs. For example, ships in the tropical trades shift their routes with the shift of the winds.

2. Ocean currents. As with the winds, vessels try to move with rather than against currents. Thus, southbound freighters along the west Atlantic Coast hug the shore between the Florida coast and the Gulf Stream; northbound, they travel with the current. .

3. Dangerous shoals and rocks.

4. Prevalence of fogs, storms, and icebergs.

5. The sphericity of the earth—a phenomenon that makes the shortest distance between any two points on the earth's surface the arc of a great circle.

Figure 29-1 shows the world's major ocean routes, the most prominent being the (1) North Atlantic, (2) Mediterranean-Asiatic, (3) European–Eastern South America, (4) Panama Canal, (5) Cape of Good Hope, and (6) North Pacific.

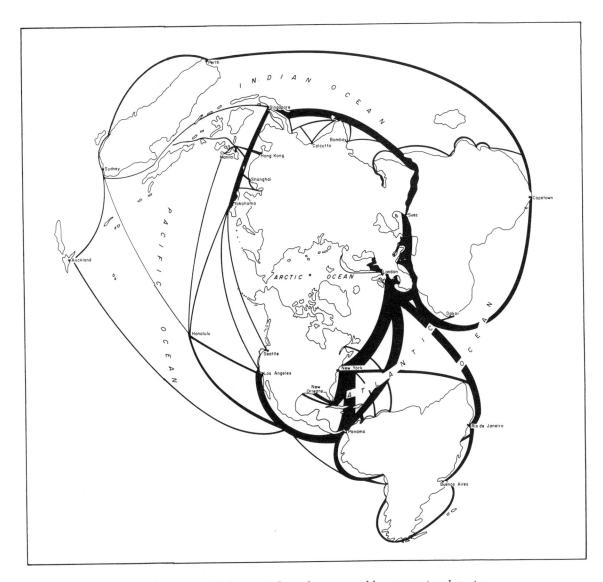

Fig. 29-1. Ocean trade routes, thickness of lines being roughly proportional to importance of the trade. Note particularly the North Atlantic route, which connects the two leading trading regions on earth (peoples with high levels of living, never ending wants, and hence incentives to trade). Plying this route are thousands of ships flying many flags and carrying an enormous variety and quantity of foodstuffs, minerals, forest products, and manufactured goods.

THE NORTH ATLANTIC ROUTE

Linking Western Europe and eastern North America, this route is the busiest of all shipping lanes; for it connects two continents that are the giants of the world in agriculture, in manufacturing, in trade, in finance, and in transportation. Since 1838, when the first transatlantic steamship line commenced operations in the North Atlantic Ocean, a carousel of commerce has evolved, until today nearly three hundred companies operate vessels over this route the year round.

At first, the sea lane served as the pathway of European emigrants to America and of European fisherman to the banks off the North American coast; traffic increased as raw materials moved to Europe, and as more people and manufactured goods moved to the United States; this trend was then partially reversed with the increasing industrialization of North America and the subsequent eastward movement of manufactured goods and American tourists.

The route's terminal branches reach from Central America to Newfoundland and from the Mediterranean to Scandinavia. As near as possible, the **great-circle route** is followed. Since the eastern North American coast line is virtually a part of the great-circle route to the British Isles, ships from the Caribbean area follow the coast and continue on approximately the same pathway used by ships from North American ports.

The great-circle route cannot, however, be followed precisely. Ships are forced southward of this course by (1) the protrusion of the northeastern North American landmass, (2) relative location of ports, (3) fog caused by the contact of the cold Labrador Current with the warm Gulf Stream, (4) reefs and shoals—at Sable Island east of the Maine coast and around the Grand Banks, (5) sandbars at Cape Hatteras along the North Carolina coast, and (6) icebergs.

The glaciers of the western coast of Greenland calve the icebergs, which constitute a serious menace to North Atlantic shipping. A typical berg, of which only one eighth is visible, measures 700 feet long, 250 feet wide, and 200 feet high. Radar waves do not easily bounce off one. The flood of icebergs begins in February, reaches a maximum in the latter part of April, and ebbs in late July. In the average season, about four hundred icebergs drift in this shipping lane. The extreme limit of the drift ice is the so-called "cold wall"— the boundary between the waters of the Labrador Current and the Gulf Stream—which serves as the southern boundary of the danger zone because icebergs rarely go much beyond.

In 1914, after the 1912 catastrophe of the superliner *Titanic*—which hit an iceberg and sank, carrying with it more than 1,500 persons—sixteen maritime nations inaugurated the International Ice Patrol. Since then, the shipping lanes have been shifted 2°30′ southward during the iceberg season. Information bulletins are broadcast twice daily, and every four hours shipmasters in the area furnish the patrol with data on their positions, course, speed, visibility, and weather. Not one ship has been sacrificed to icebergs since the patrol began its vigil.

The two major lanes of the North Atlantic Route (east to west and west to east) are 60 miles apart. Use of these tracks has always been voluntary, but collisions caused by failure to use the recommended lanes have incited representatives of the more than 65-year-old North Atlantic Track Agreement to make the use of certain tracks mandatory.

New York and London during the nineteenth century had a virtual monopoly on the trade passing over this route. However, though their total trade volume has increased, their relative position has been challenged by such ports as Boston, Philadelphia, Baltimore, Montreal, and Quebec on the North American side, and Southampton, Liverpool, Antwerp, Rotterdam, Hamburg, and Bremen on the European side.

Approximately one half of the world's freight, most of the world's ocean passengers, and more mail than on all other sea lanes combined transit this route. The nobility of the shipping industry—the luxurious, speedy passenger liners—follow this route more than any other. The world's major ship lines (except those operated by Japan and the Soviet Union) and more than four fifths of the deadweight tonnage of the world's merchant marine are owned by the countries rimming the Atlantic.

In addition to being generously served by oil-bunkering stations (oil today propels nearly all of the world merchant-vessel tonnage), the route surpasses all others in its access to abundant, cheap, and high-grade coal.

Eastbound freight tonnage is about four times larger than westbound; from Anglo-America a tremendous tonnage of foodstuffs, raw materials, and manufactures moves to Europe, while European shipments include primarily manufactured goods and other high-value and low-bulk commodities, which move by liners. Thus, a liner's cargo space on west-bound trips is practically empty—resulting in higher rates on eastbound cargo than would otherwise be the case. Rather than travel in **ballast**, many tramp ships carry, at very low rates, bulky cargo such as iron and steel, steel products, china clay, or even stone from Europe.

THE MEDITERRANEAN-ASIATIC ROUTE

This sea lane, the world's longest single trade route, penetrates what Mackinder called the "World Island," comprising more than half of the earth's land and the majority of its population. The enormous size and mountainous interior of Eurasia have forced its peoples to turn to the sea for much of their foreign trade. Connecting the civilizations of the West and the East, the seaway's trade is as varied as the peoples it serves, ranging from the crudest products to the most intricate manufactures.

The strategic link in this international chain is the Suez Canal, which opened in 1869. Born out of man's practical fondness for short-cuts, the 105-mile-long canal shortened the route from England to India by 44 per cent (about 6,000 miles) by eliminating the trip around the Cape of Good Hope, thereby tapping the huge Middle East oil reserve, lowering the prices of innumerable commodities, and immensely stimulating trade. Approximately 14,000 ships pass through the canal each year.

The economic health or illness of many nations is decidedly affected by the canal. In 1950 Egypt prohibited Israel from use of the internationally operated canal and in July 1956 seized full control. When in October of that year an Israeli-Egyptian military action of brief duration raged on the Sinai Peninsula, Britain, fearful that its "lifeline of the Empire" would be cut, and France attacked Egyptian bases; by November 7, when the United Nations had effected a cease-fire, the canal was completely blocked (a United Nations salvage group required 8 million dollars to clear it). World shipping, ever sensitive to international politics, strongly felt the repercussions of these developments: enormous tonnages of commodities had to be detoured thousands of miles; the canal's closure forced charter rates to rise rapidly. The main route now for shipping Middle East petroleum to Northwest Europe was via the Cape of Good Hope. Since no one knew how long the canal would be out of commission, supertankers by the wholesale were built to relieve the threatened oil shortage in Europe. When the canal reopened in May 1957, there was too much supertanker tonnage; hence, orders for new tankers were delayed and canceled, and charter rates fell to the lowest figure in ten years. Nor could the most modern supertankers transit the Suez Canal—they were too big. In the early 1960s, however, the canal was being widened and deepened for accommodating fully loaded tankers up to 47,000 tons.

The Mediterranean-Asiatic Route is characterized by an unusually large number of branch lines; every sea and gulf of Europe and Asia feeds into the main trunk route. Six traffic patterns distinguish the route:

1. Trade among the *countries around the Mediterranean and Black Seas*. The Mediterranean district imports, and the Black Sea district exports, foods and raw materials—a trade which in turn creates a vigorous exchange of Western manufactures for Eastern food and raw materials.

2. Trade between *Northwestern Europe and the Mediterranean*. Food and raw materials, including certain minerals, move westward, while return cargoes consist of manufactures and bulky commodities such as coal, lumber, and pulp.

3. Trade between *Europe and the Far East*. This, the oldest pathway of trade along the route, features a westward movement of a great variety of raw materials (e.g., mica and manganese, jute and other fibers, hides and skins, and oil seeds from India, rubber and tin from Malaysia and Indonesia, and teak from Burma and Thailand), food (e.g., rice destined for the great rice markets of London

and Bremen, and large quantities of spices), tea from India and Ceylon, and special manufactures; while the eastward movement consists of equally variegated manufactures.

4. Trade between *North America and the Mediterranean*. The trade over this route, while a greatly fluctuating one in volume and weight, is essentially from west to east, consisting of foods of many kinds, raw cotton, coal and some other minerals, steel scrap, iron and steel products, and a great variety of manufactured goods. Traffic from east to west is usually much lighter and consists of a number of minerals (e.g., Turkish chrome ore, Yugoslavian antimony, and Turkish manganese), Spanish and Portuguese cork, "Turkish" tobacco, Egyptian cotton, and a wide variety of subtropical agricultural products.

5. Trade between *Anglo-America and the Far East*. This exchange, which was far more active prior to the opening of the Panama Canal, is still lively with all but eastern coastal Asia. Again, eastbound trade consists primarily of manufactures but also much food, while spices from Southeast Asia and tea from India and Ceylon, together with raw materials (e.g., jute from India and Pakistan, mica and manganese from India, rubber and tin from Malaysia and Indonesia, teak from Burma and Thailand), move westward.

6. Trade between *nations of the Far East*. Japan's industrial expansion has stimulated a lively trade between herself and the tropical nations of Southern Asia. In return for food and raw materials (e.g., iron ore), she sends mostly a wide variety of manufactures and some re-exports. Should Communist China resume active trade relations with these nations, this already large traffic would increase notably.

The European–Eastern South America Route. The rich agricultural, pastoral, forest, and mining regions of eastern South America enjoy large markets for their products in highly industrialized Western Europe. Argentina, Brazil, and Uruguay ship enormous quantities of cereals, chilled and frozen meat, coffee, hides and skins, tropical and subtropical woods, wool, and minerals (especially iron ore and manganese from Brazil) eastward from a number of modern ports. The Rio de la Plata region is the chief focus of cargoes in South America. Return cargoes comprise much less in volume and weight. Indeed, they may be so scarce as to justify extremely low rates on such commodities as iron and steel and, at times, even stone. Many tramps are forced to leave in ballast.

THE PANAMA CANAL ROUTE

With its opening in 1914, the Panama Canal provided the key that opened the door to greatly accelerated trade not only between eastern United States and the west coast of both South America and the United States itself, but also between Australasia and Europe. By eliminating the long and often hazardous voyage around Cape Horn or through the Strait of Magellan, the canal shortened the nautical distance between New York and San Francisco by nearly 8,000 miles, that between Western Europe and western South American ports by about 2,000, and that between New York and Australian ports by about 4,000 miles. The competitive zone between the Panama Canal and the Suez Canal is reached in the Far East and Australia. Generally, therefore, European ships headed for the Far East and Australia travel via the Suez Canal, while those from eastern United States choose the Panama Canal as the shorter route.

The Canal Zone, which from its beginning has been controlled by the United States, is approximately 50 miles long and 10 miles wide. It is a major asset to the United States whose flagships carry about one quarter of the cargo tonnage annually passing through the locks (an estimated total of 66.5 million tons in 1962). The economic pulse of Latin America, especially the west-coast countries, has been incalculably strengthened by the commerce engendered since the birth of the canal.

Plying the canal westward are vessels carrying a great diversity of manufactures, food, and coal from eastern North America and

Western Europe, petroleum from Venezuela, and alumina from Jamaica (to Kitimat, British Columbia). Westbound from eastern United States to Japan are heavy shipments of coal, coke, iron and steel scrap, phosphates, and raw cotton.

Eastbound are ships with cargoes of minerals (South American iron ore, copper, antimony, lead, zinc, nitrate, and tin) and cargoes of tropical agricultural and forest products (bananas, cotton, cacao, coffee, sugar, and lumber). Other commodities moving east are softwoods from Chile and from the American Northwest, along with fibers, sugar, vegetable oils, spices, and tropical woods from the western Pacific.

THE CAPE OF GOOD HOPE ROUTE

This route, whose traffic declined considerably after the opening of the Suez Canal, is the focus of seaways linking eastern United States and Western Europe with the western, southern, and eastern coasts of Africa, and connecting Europe with Southeast Asia and Australia. The skirting nature of these routes is gradually being changed as new transportation nets are laid in the rich, developing interior of the continent, with resultant commercial expansion. Great-circle routes are rather closely followed except around the hump of northwestern Africa and on the Capetown-Melbourne circle, where the southern extent of the arc encounters ice and storms.

The Roaring Forties—strong westerly winds —are a boon to eastbound vessels between South Africa and Australia, but westbound vessels adhere to a more northerly course to evade the winds' full impact and thus save fuel. Cargo ships and refrigerator vessels often prefer the Cape of Good Hope Route to the Suez Route because it is cooler and less expensive.

Transiting this route are large tonnages of Australian and Southeast Asian food and raw materials in exchange for European manufactures. Gold tops the list of all South African exports in value; and it—together with some ferroalloys and nonferrous metals, and tropi-

cal and subtropical farm and pastoral products (e.g., sugar, hides and skins, wool, coffee, fruits) from South and East Africa—is exchanged primarily for European and American manufactures. Tropical west-coast Africa ships enormous quantities of mineral, agricultural, and forest products—cobalt, uranium, tin, copper, iron ore, lead, zinc, cacao, peanuts, rubber, lumber, and vegetable oils.

THE NORTH PACIFIC ROUTE

The Pacific, the world's largest ocean, was the last to have developed important trade routes over it. Although several densely populated countries rim the western Pacific, their productive capacity and purchasing power, for the most part, have been low. However, because of the zooming population and industrialization of the West Coast of the United States and the sprouting economies of several Southeast and East Asian nations, particularly Japan, trade along this route is being intensified. The great-circle route (4,300 miles from Puget Sound to Yokohama) via the Aleutians is frequently by-passed because (1) the Hawaiian Islands serve as a crossroads point, with refueling facilities at Honolulu; (2) the great circle connects sparsely settled Pacific North America with sparsely settled Northeastern Asia; and (3) though free of icebergs, the route is hampered by fog and severe winter storms.

Two traffic patterns characterize the North Pacific Route: (1) trade between the West Coast of North America and Eastern Asia; and (2) trade between American Gulf and Atlantic ports and the Far East (vessels often pick up way-cargo at West Coast ports en route). Eastbound cargo consists of food (primarily canned fish from Japan and sugar from the Philippines), raw materials (Manila hemp, copra, and tropical woods) and countless manufactures ranging from cameras to supertankers. Westbound tonnage consists of food (for example, cereals) and raw materials (chiefly lumber and wood pulp, raw cotton, steel scrap, and a wide variety of minerals) from the West Coast of North America, and primarily sulfur, phosphate, and cotton from Gulf ports, and iron and steel goods and numerous manufactures from Atlantic ports. Yokohama, Kobe, and Hong Kong are the primary destinations of westbound vessels. Tonnage of eastbound cargo is far less than westbound tonnage.

OCEAN CARRIERS

THE LINER

Liners are ships in a fleet or "line" which ply regularly between scheduled ports, regardless of the load available. They are of three types: (1) those that carry mainly passengers, mail, and express, with only slight cargo space and freight tonnage; (2) combination liners carrying passengers and high-value freight or special kinds of bulky freight that is clean to handle and can stand fairly high freight rates; and (3) cargo liners that carry only freight. More than 80 per cent of ocean traffic today is handled by liners. These aristocrats of all ocean carriers, weighing from 6,000 to more than 80,000 gross tons, represent the highest development in shipbuilding, offering the utmost in speed, luxury, and safety.

THE TRAMP VESSEL

The tramp is the slow drudge of the sea, carrying cumbersome cargoes of great weight or bulk in proportion to value, having no definite sailing schedules or fixed routes, and operating as a single unit of transport. The tramp is a free agent; it accepts cargo for any destination that promises a profit, and it acts as a regulator of freight rates when and where the demand for transportation exceeds the facilities offered by liners. The tramp's most lucrative markets are the big landmass areas.

Until the twentieth century, tramps were the principal ocean carriers. Their decline is attributable primarily to (1) the falling off of the coal-carrying trade; (2) the growing tendency to ship semi-manufactured or manu-

factured goods rather than raw materials; (3) the rise of industrial carriers; and (4) the demand for regularity of line service. Concerned over this decline, owners of tramp ships are now turning their "bums" into gentlemen; their vessels are today bigger, faster, and younger. The death knell of the tramp steamer is no longer forecast. Drudges in any field are always in demand; and wherever and whenever cheap, bulky, and heavy commodities can be shipped without much worry about great speed or regularity, the economical tramp will continue to ply its way over the seas.

THE TANKER

Most tankers, varying in size from less than 10,000 to more than 80,000 tons, carry either crude or refined petroleum in unbelievably large quantities. (For example, the supertanker *Universe Leader*, not the world's largest, carries 26 million gallons of oil.) To solve the problem of return cargo, several tanker lines have constructed some oil and combination ore carriers to eliminate nonpaying voyages in ballast. Thus the *Sinclair Petrolore* transports Kuwait oil to Marcus Hook, Pennsylvania, via the Cape of Good Hope; then picks up Venezuelan iron ore, which it delivers to Japan; and then sails empty to Kuwait. Standard of California tankers carry refined products from the San Francisco Bay area to Japan, then head southward in ballast for Dumai, Sumatra, where they take on a cargo of crude oil for refining in the San Francisco Bay area. There is thus a payload in both directions. Of the world's tanker fleet (3,146 ships in 1959), Liberia leads in registry,[1] followed by the United Kingdom, Norway, and the United States.

THE INDUSTRIAL CARRIER

This type of carrier is owned by a private company for the distribution of its own prod-

[1] Many United States tankers operate under Liberian, Panamanian, and other foreign registries because they simply cannot compete with foreign-owned tankers if operating under the American flag—the result of much higher wages, taxes, etc.

ucts. Oil tankers owned and operated by or for the big oil-producing and oil-refining companies, fruit ships, and ore-carrying vessels are handling more and more of the world's ocean freight.

THE WORLD'S MERCHANT FLEET

The merchant marine comprises the privately or publicly owned commercial ships of a nation, as distinct from the navy. The number of ships in the merchant fleets of the world are shown in Table 29-1. Although the United States and the United Kingdom owned almost a third of the tonnage in 1960, two points are significant: (1) 1,973 of the 2,996 United States vessels were government owned and were mostly obsolete; actually, then, the United States held fourth, not first, place; and (2) the United Kingdom's tonnage had dropped from 41 per cent in 1939 to 18 per cent in 1960.

TABLE 29-1

MERCHANT FLEETS OF THE WORLD, 1959
(ships of 1,000 gross tons and over)

Nation	Number of ships
United States	2,996
United Kingdom	2,466
Norway	1,332
Liberia	1,015
Japan	956
West Germany	892
Soviet Union	858
Italy	678
France	631
Netherlands	555
Denmark	356
Brazil	207
Argentina	146
India	136
Yugoslavia	117
Poland	115
Total all flags	17,185

SOURCE: *Marine Engineering/Log Yearbook, 19th Annual Maritime Review and Yearbook Issue,* 65:11, May 31, 1960.

The United States has bolstered foreign economies so well that foreign shipping today presents a very real competitive threat to American ships. Despite the fact that the United States foreign-aid program is administered under the "50-50 law"—by which 50 per cent of foreign-aid cargoes must be shipped in American vessels—the portion of United States foreign trade handled in American vessels is now down to about 10 per cent. The American Merchant Marine has always shown periods of ascendancy in wartime, periods of decline in peacetime. In 1959, ships registered in Panama, Liberia, and Honduras carried about 77 per cent of the country's foreign trade. Even in the tanker trade, Panamanian and Liberian bottoms accounted for 59 per cent of all cargoes going to and from the United States compared with 4 per cent for United States flag tankers. In tramp and industrial trade, ships registered under **flags of convenience** carried 37 per cent of all cargoes compared with 7 per cent for United States flagships.

The foremost maritime nations are those whose lifeblood is trade—insular Britain and Japan; peninsular and agriculturally poor Greece; the Netherlands—with a dense population, much land in pasture, and a poor minerals base; Norway, backed by a hinterland only 3 per cent arable. Greek and Norwegian ships, unlike those of the United States and Britain, seldom see home waters—they service chiefly global trade rather than the foreign trade of their homelands. If unified under one national flag, the Greek fleet would probably constitute the world's third largest merchant fleet; but Greek tonnage is largely under foreign flags, chief among them the American and British. An important difference should be noted between the merchant fleets of stable Norway and turbulent Greece: Norway's shipping industry is a strong source of revenue for its government, and of foreign exchange for its national economy; Greece's shipping industry (many of its ships were acquired from or financed by the governments under whose flags they sail), on the other hand, reaps profit largely for its highly resourceful shipowners, and sails so preponderantly under foreign flags as to lose its Hellenic identity.

The shipping trade, like the water it depends on, finds its own course, unless it is diverted by discriminatory tariffs, unfavorable treaties, wars, or curtains of iron and bamboo. Many man-made restrictions continue to hamstring international trade. But the developed industrial nations need raw materials, particularly minerals; and the underdeveloped countries need foreign exchange, fabricated products and even food. If the geographical division of labor can function and nuclear power can be substantially utilized for ocean vessels, it is impossible to even guess what the future may hold for world trade and ocean shipping.

SELECTED REFERENCES

Baldwin, Hanson W. "Storm over the Panama Canal," *New York Times Magazine,* pp. 27, 91-93, May 8, 1960.

Bross, S. R. *Ocean Shipping,* Cambridge, Maryland, Cornell Maritime Press, 1956.

Engel, L. "About Icebergs," *New York Times Magazine,* pp. 19-20, February 8, 1959.

Hardy, A. C. *Seaways and Sea Trade: A Maritime Geography.* New York, D. Van Nostrand Company, 1928.

McDowell, Carl E., and Helen M. Gibbs. *Ocean Transportation.* New York, McGraw-Hill Book Company, Inc., 1954.

Van Cleef, Eugene. *Trade Centers and Trade Routes.* New York, D. Appleton-Century Company, 1937.

Wheeler, Raymond A. "Clearing the Suez Canal," *Military Engineer,* 333:1-7, January–February 1958.

CHAPTER THIRTY ::

From earliest times man has dreamed of and speculated on the possibility of flight. During the past half century, he has made this dream come true; for in his very short span of existence he has gone aloft in balloons, airships, primitive airplanes, and twin- and four-engine ships, and is currently breaking records in jet planes. He has even succeeded in going aloft in rockets.

It is difficult to believe that in this brief time air routes can now girdle the entire earth (Fig. 30-1)—spanning the largest oceans, flying over the highest mountains, and hopping over pathless jungles, deserts, and tundras. Yet this accomplishment, which is taken for granted by nearly all air passengers, was paid for at a very high price by the air pioneers:

THE WORLD'S

For every second of the time we flash between the Atlantic and the Pacific a pilot has died to pave the way. For every mile we traverse, the airmen have flown a thousand hours to test and prove the techniques and the machines. For every feature of safety and dependability we enjoy, hundreds of young men have paid in the sweat of exhaustion and danger.[1]

THE AIR AGE

Pearl Harbor ushered in a new kind of geography—air-age geography. Since then, time and space have shrunk fantastically. No two places on the globe are today more than

[1] Gill R. Wilson, "With a Great Price" (editorial), *Flying*, 68:30, January 1961.

twenty-four hours apart by jet plane. Even this figure shrinks steadily. Distance is measured now as often in *hours* as in *miles;* no mode of human travel has so contracted our world as the airplane (Fig. 30-2).

CHARACTERISTICS OF AIR TRANSPORT

The airplane is characterized by (1) high unit operating costs, (2) high speed, and (3) relative independence of surface conditions. These features give it particular advantage in situations where speed is desired, where the size and weight of the object carried is small in relation to its value or importance, or where the surface conditions make transportation by

AIRWAYS

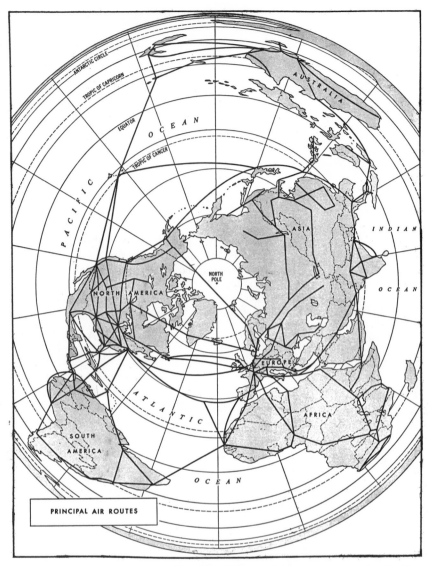

Fig. 30-1. The world airways map, duplicating in no small measure the world ocean-trade-route map. This results from the desire of the airlines to follow, at least in the early decades of flying, established traffic arteries. Primarily because of sheer expense, aviation is concentrated in the United States above all other countries, though Canada, Australia, New Zealand, Great Britain, Western Europe, and the Soviet Union are also important. (Published by permission of T. Y. Crowell; map from E. Willard Miller and Associates, Global Geography.)

Fig. 30-2. Our shrinking world. With the advent of steam, continents and oceans both began to shrink. However, only when man took to the skies in the airplane did distance and time really melt away. (Courtesy of E. I. du Pont de Nemours & Co., Inc.)

land or water slow, dangerous, or expensive. Because of the high cost of air transport, the airplane by and large has been most useful as a carrier of passengers and mail rather than of heavy freight. Yet there are situations in which air freight, even of the bulkier and heavier varieties, assumes considerable importance. The speed of air transportation has opened up new markets for highly perishable commodities, such as certain foodstuffs, drugs, and flowers. The low capital cost of airline facilities per route-mile compared with railways and highways [2] may make the airplane

the preferable means of transportation where the resources of an otherwise inaccessible region are to be opened up and where the traffic is expected to be light. In the past, air freight has had its most successful development in countries with natural barriers to surface transport, such as mountains, deserts, swamps, ice, or thick jungle, particularly if raw materials of high value and low bulk were available for extraction and export.

However, even where the resources destined for exploitation, such as petroleum or iron ore, are economically unavailable for transport by

[2] In 1955 the United States Foreign Operations Administration estimated that in Pakistan the capital cost per mile would be approximately $100,000 for rail- ways, $25,000 to $30,000 for highways, and only $2,- 000 to $3,000 for airline facilities. From the *New York Times*, May 10, 1955.

aircraft, air transportation may facilitate development. Personnel, construction materials, machinery, and supplies of all kinds may be flown in prior to the building of a highway or a railway—as was done, for example, in the recently discovered and developed iron-ore areas of Labrador and Quebec. In the Burnt Creek Development, the terrain was so difficult that during construction bulldozers and other heavy equipment, food, supplies, and, of course, employees were flown in. The 360-mile-long railway for hauling the ore cost $100,000 per mile to construct. In northern Canada, which is rich in many raw materials, future development awaits modern transport. It has been said that transportation, not climate, is the limiting factor in development of the 1.5 million square miles comprising the Yukon and Northwest Territories. Highways and railways are inching into the vast, remote, and climatically hostile area, but their cost of construction and maintenance is so high as to retard significant extension—particularly at a time when the economy still is heavily dependent on government spending. In such lands, with their dearth of railways and highways, the airplane is the cheapest form of transportation. It is no misstatement to say that the airplane is superior to every other form of transport in the initial stages of man's conquest of such a milieu. Thus, 20 million dollars were spent for improving the airport at Frobisher on Baffin Island as a supply center for the entire eastern Arctic.

For a number of years airlines, even in the United States, had to have government subsidy in order to exist. Thus in 1938 United States airlines received 42.1 per cent of their revenue from the government for flying the mail. By 1957 only 3.1 per cent of their revenue came from mail service. However, as a result of greatly increased speed, additional carrying capacity, and more effective utilization, the airlines are now able to make a profit. In the early 1960s, however, virtually all commercial airlines experienced severe financial difficulties. While their plight was attributable to a variety of factors, most important appeared to be the heavy expenditures for jet planes, too many of which were flying only partially filled.

AIR ROUTES

Four questions are dominant when companies are considering the location of an air route:

1. *How much traffic will there be?* This is the most important factor of all, because traffic is the key to the modern air route. There is concern not only over the number of persons but over the alternate routes already present or anticipated for the future. Can prospective travelers go by ship, train, or car? These same questions are applicable for freight.

2. *Which way must the route go?* This depends on whether the haul is a short one or a long one and on the existing political situation. If it is to be short, the route will be direct—that is, a **great-circle route.** If the route is to be long, it is customary to fly in convenient stages, the stops depending on (1) traffic to be picked up en route, (2) political restrictions (the aircraft of one nation is prohibited from using the airports of another nation outside the terms of special international agreements), and (3) operational problems. Thus, a jet requires extra-long runways, and night landing involves special problems. Regarding the political situation, it must be considered as of paramount importance. It is interesting to note that no international law exists defining territorial air limits and outer space. The sole law remains that of ancient Rome: "He who owns the ground owns everything to the heavens and to the depths." There is need for world accord on air space, but it is unlikely that any agreement will soon be reached, for the world of nations cannot even agree on defining territorial waters—a much less knotty problem.

3. *What kind of aircraft will be employed?* In this question airport accommodation and fuel range (safety margin of reserve fuel) must be considered, along with the volume and weight of the payload.

4. *What will it cost?* If the cost will exceed the anticipated income from the proposed route, the project will be possible under only one condition—that the government is so convinced of the value of the route to be flown

at a loss that it agrees to make up the difference.

The trade routes of the air have tended to follow the trade routes of the oceans and seas and of the land (railways and highways). This results from the fact that (1) the airplane is still developing (it takes five to seven years to design and build and test a new airplane) and (2) the cost of operating air transport service is very high. The present-day jet costs 6 to 8 million dollars; then there is the high cost of the maintenance organization with its highly skilled staff; the cost of maintaining stations all along the route to look after crew, passengers, and freight; the cost of actual flying; the cost of administration and sales organization; the cost of technical training; and aircraft depreciation and aircraft insurance. These expenses are reducible only when many people use the machine and help pay for it. Hence, the biggest airports are located in densely populated areas and those with the best bases for trade.

It is believed, however, that as air traffic becomes more mature, future air routes will more and more fly direct, cutting the corners off the old trade routes and establishing new routes. Thus North Africa's route across the Sahara to Nigeria now hops over the desert, whereas it formerly crawled around the coasts with stops at each port.

Air routes help create new centers of commerce, new inland ports, and new towns in hitherto backward areas. Natives who have never seen a train or an automobile are familiar with the airplane—their sole contact with the more highly civilized world.

AIRPORTS

The modern airport is a huge, busy, noisy, staggering place—a far cry from the large fields with their smooth, grassy surface used for landing and take-off in the early days of aviation (Fig. 30-3). The eye cannot take in the vastness, shapes, and colors of the world's greatest airports.

Today's airports have long, hard-surface runways, with sufficient buildings to house the multifarious services catering to passengers or freight. The airport may be and frequently is a city within a city. One of the latest additions to most big metropolitan airports is the fine hotel. Many travelers stay over briefly in transit, never seeing the nearby metropolis. The world's greatest airport is New York's Idlewild, which covers about 5,000 acres on the south side of Long Island on land reclaimed from Jamaica Bay. Built at a cost exceeding 330 million dollars, it has nine large hangars, seven runways (the longest of which exceed 10,500 feet), a million-dollar, eleven-story control tower containing more than $500,000 worth of complex electronic equipment, a fuel-storage installation capable of holding more than 4 million gallons, 10 miles of two-lane access roads, and five parking lots capable of handling 6,000 cars. The airport has its own police force and fire department, hospital, churches, government installations, restaurants, variety shops, and theater groups. However, any idea of completion of the airport would be illusory: in all probability Idlewild will never be finished.

Idlewild handles more than 210,000 planes annually—one landing or departing every 1½ minutes. In a few years the number is expected to reach 230,000—100,000 of them jets —which will process 12 million passengers. In 1959 there were ground positions for 75 aircraft; soon the number will be 140.

Airport sites are selected only after careful study. Most important factors are weather, distance from the major city, and the amount of traffic on the highways to and from the proposed airport (numerous freeways have been or are being built to speed access to the cities). Every effort is made to stay away from fog, other things being equal, for planes can be kept on the ground for many hours and incoming ones forced to seek more favored airports for landing. Yet most airports in middle latitudes are subjected to fog; those in both New York and San Francisco, for example, are at times completely immobilized by fog.

CARRIERS

Air routes over most parts of the world are covered by more or less similar types of air-

Fig. 30-3. John F. Kennedy International Airport, New York. World's most glittering airport showcase. It is the number one gateway to the United States, and perhaps the busiest airport on the globe. (Courtesy of The Port of New York Authority.)

craft, which vary in size and performance according to the sectors operated, traffic requirements, airports available, and other factors.

At any one time, three main classes of aircraft are in use: (1) standard types in production or in general service; (2) older aircraft, which have served for some time and are gradually being replaced by the standard types of the period; and (3) new types, which have been commissioned by certain lines but have not yet been adopted on a large scale.

This is the day of the jet-propelled transport plane. The British put into regular service the first "jetliner"—the De Haviland Comet—in 1952. With the opening of the jet age, eighty-seven world airlines in forty-two countries have ordered more than a thousand such craft.

The jet offers four major improvements over planes of the past: (1) a speed of 600 miles per hour—about double that of the piston-engine planes, which means cutting flying time in half; (2) nonstop flying, which eliminates the unnecessary multiplication of the dangers inherent in landing and taking off; (3) smoothness and lack of vibration and fatigue-causing noises inside the cabin; and

(4) a carrying capacity double that of piston-engine planes—170 versus 85.

The jet age caught the airports off guard; they were not ready to accommodate the big planes. The result is that all over the United States new and better airports have been scheduled for construction. The same thing is occurring in Europe. New runways are being hacked out of the jungle in South America, in Africa, and in Asia. Runways for jet planes must be 10,500 feet in length; in the United States the cost is $1,000 per foot.

AIR FREIGHT

Until a few years ago planes carried passengers and almost no freight, for freight was not profitable. A third of a century ago, pilots occasionally were handed a package, usually weighing less than 5 pounds, with the laconic instruction "Somebody will be waiting at the other end." From so humble a beginning has grown a worldwide service that today extends in and out of some 82 countries and which in 1959 had an international and domestic freight volume of 750 million ton-miles—a figure ex-

Fig. 30-4. Loading a Flying Tiger Line plane with miscellaneous freight. Air freight is growing rapidly and promises to expand more in the next decade than at any time since the organization of airlines. Through the use of airplanes, particularly the new cargo planes, packing costs are reduced, expensive transfers and reshipment charges are cut to a minimum, and insurance rates are lowered from 8 to 20 per cent (owing to lack of exposure to weather, water, high stacking in deep holds, or rough handling). (Courtesy of Flying Tiger Line and Watson Photo.)

pected to increase to 35 billion ton-miles at competitive rates by 1975.

The picture began to change in 1945, following World War II, when there was a surplus of cargo planes selling at low prices and great numbers of trained personnel recently released from the armed services. Equally important or perhaps even more so has been the advent of more modern planes, which have made this part of the business more attractive. Several American lines—e.g., Flying Tiger Line and Slick Airways, Inc.—are all-freight carriers (Fig. 30-4).

Today air freight is a recognized form of industrial transportation. It differs from its surface competitors in being much faster, but it is also more expensive. It is regarded, too, as a reliable form of transport. Stanley H. Brewer, an authority on air freight, projects a median industry growth of 30 per cent per year. This will mean penetration of markets now served by surface transport. Of the total freight movement in the United States in 1960 (1.4 trillion ton-miles), air cargo represented only 0.03 per cent. A rule-of-thumb comparison of average rates per ton-mile is air freight, 17–22 cents; railway express, 13–16 cents; truck, 5–8 cents, and rail, 3–6 cents.[3]

[3] H. T. Lewis and J. W. Culliton, "Characteristics of Air Freight and Its Market," Part I of *The Role of Air Freight in Physical Distribution*, Boston, Harvard University, Division of Research, Graduate School of Business Administration, 1956, p. 9.

Such figures take on real meaning, however, only when they are related to the value delivered in return for the differential in cost. Let us compare shipping costs on the same goods via air, rail, and truck. To ship 500 pounds of women's dresses from New York to Chicago by air freight costs $40.50, contrasted with $32.35 by railway express, and $32 by truck. To send 400 pounds of business machines from Los Angeles to Pittsburgh costs $98.80 by air freight, $92 by railway express, and $45.44 by truck.

The commodities making up most air freight include (1) automobile parts or accessories, (2) machinery, (3) electrical equipment, (4) wearing apparel (women's apparel at times comprises almost a third of the business; the right style must be in the right place at the right time), (5) cut flowers—a business made possible only by the airplane; (6) machine parts, (7) printed matter, (8) films, (9) aircraft parts or accessories, and (10) drugs and biologicals. Most of these commodities have high value in relation to weight; also they may be perishable, fragile, or damageable under rough handling. Thus a costly IBM 704 electronic data processor, easily damaged if jostled, weighing 30,425 pounds, was flown from Poughkeepsie, New York, to Paris in just a little over a day. By vessel, ten days to two weeks would have been required, and crating and packing costs would have been high. By air, the machine merely had to be bolted to a wooden platform and covered with padding and plastic. The machine did not even have to be tilted. Hence there was no danger of harming the delicate mechanism.

EXOTIC FREIGHT

Many wild animals are shipped by air for zoos, circuses, aquariums, pharmaceutical firms, and research organizations. Thus a plane from Calcutta sets down in New York with half a dozen elephants. Dozens of monkeys arrive frequently by air in the United States, to be used in medical research. One airline ships as many as 500 birds per day for ten straight days. Tropical fish are carried in water inside plastic bags, stowed in cardboard boxes.

Also, increasing numbers of domesticated animals are being flown; new American breeds of cattle (developed purposely for the American Humid Subtropical Deep South, but equally well suited for the tropics) are shipped to Venezuela, Colombia, Ecuador, Peru, and Brazil.

EMERGENCY FREIGHT

Much American machinery is used all over the world. Shipment by rail, truck, and vessel is so slow that often a company loses thousands of dollars a day when a part no larger than a football needs replacing. Thus, one of the world's largest construction companies, employing four hundred men on a tunnel job in Venezuela, was faced with a $10,000-per-day loss when a chain broke on one of its machines. The nearest replacement for the part was in Denver, Colorado. By surface transport, the 300-pound chain could be obtained in two weeks at a shipping cost of $34. Shipping the part by air cost $130.40, but it saved the construction company $100,000 in workmen's time. Thousands of such emergencies occur annually over the earth.

PRESENT STATUS OF THE AIR-FREIGHT BUSINESS

American air traffic, actual and potential, is not well balanced in directional flow. Most of the items making up air freight—except for some wearing apparel, films, electrical equipment, and flowers—emanate from the American Manufacturing Region, which means that the predominant movement is to the west and south. How to correct this imbalance still perplexes the carriers.

It would be erroneous to believe that airlines currently derive any considerable portion of their revenue from air freight; actually it constitutes only 6 per cent, compared with 94 per cent from passengers. However, within a decade airline revenue from cargo is expected to equal, perhaps even surpass, passenger revenue. This optimism stems largely from the development of new turboprop air freighters, which, though still used in only small numbers, are nonetheless sharply reducing operating costs. If domestic air-cargo rates can be reduced from the present 21 cents to 10 cents per ton-mile, air-cargo volume should rise from 400 million ton-miles per year to 5.5 billion ton-miles. The turboprop air freighters are, however, costly—up to 6 million dollars each for the larger ones and about 1.5 million dollars for the smaller ones. Aviation experts declare that the differences between passenger and cargo planes are no less marked than those between Pullman cars and freight cars. The new cargo planes are also easier and cheaper to load and unload. Douglas analysts have learned that if the ground-handling time of a large transport can be reduced from six hours to one hour, aircraft utilization will double with a saving of $1,260 per trip. In 1961 the Flying Tiger Line, operating turbojet-engine air freighters, reduced loading and unloading time to fifty-three minutes—a saving of four hours over conventional side loading. Its planes, holding 65,000 pounds, are loaded and unloaded merely by swinging the tail open (Fig. 30-4). Some types are loaded and unloaded at both ends simultaneously. Savings in time, with resultant lower operating costs, have resulted in sharp rate reductions: 37 per cent on electrical equipment, auto parts, electric cable, scientific instruments, printed matter; 22 per cent on office machines, glass products, seafood, plastic medical supplies; and 8 per cent on dry goods, machinery and machinery parts, hides, furs, shoes, and metals.

New also, though hardly beyond the blueprint stage in most instances, are elaborate mechanized freight terminals. San Francisco's newest major project is a 7-million-dollar, 260-acre air-freight city, capable of handling up to forty air freighters simultaneously.

WORLD OUTLOOK

If the first half of the twentieth century belonged to Henry Ford, the second half promises to belong to Wilbur and Orville Wright, for air technologies are reshaping the economic and social geography of the United States and of the world. Air transport is not restricted in importance to the rich developed countries; in some respects it is even more important in the impoverished underdeveloped countries, for it is more *vital* to them. Thus landlocked Bolivia, Paraguay, Afghanistan; the archipelagoes of Indonesia and the Philippines; the mountain barriers of all South American west-coast countries; the tropical rain forests and jungles of South America, Africa, and Asia; the tundras of North America and of Eurasia; and the great deserts of Africa, Australia, and Asia—all are brought into the dizzy pace of the twentieth century by the airplane.

The plane is unique in that it is under no compulsion to follow a narrowly defined path in any one of the above restrictive environments. *It can go anywhere, but it cannot land everywhere.* Hence airways as a means of transportation in these backward lands becomes basically a matter of airfields, their ground facilities, and their areal distribution.

The year 1960 was notable for air traffic. And yet that year was surely but a harbinger of an ever greater contraction of the world rendered possible by an ever greater expansion of the world's airways. Flight promises a fluidity of geography never before attainable. For the airplane, looking down on the earth, possesses the potential power to change the economic, social, and political patterns of the world's peoples—for better or for worse.

SELECTED REFERENCES

Brewer, Stanley H. *Air Cargo—The Big Breakthrough.* Seattle, University of Washington, Bureau of Business Research, College of Business Administration, November 1959. Occasional Paper No. 8.
————————. *Vision in Air Cargo.* Seattle, University of Washington, Bureau of Business Research, College of Business Administration, June 1957. Occasional Paper No. 5.
Gentry, D. "Air Cargo Transportation and Marketing," *Journal of Marketing,* 17:1-10, July 1952.
Lewis, H. T., and J. W. Culliton. "Characteristics of Air Freight and Its Market," Part I in *The Role of Air Freight in Physical Distribution.* Boston, Harvard University, Division of Research, Graduate School of Business Administration, 1956, pp. 3-115.
Pearcy, G. E., and L. M. Alexander. "Pattern of Commercial Air Service Availability in the Western Hemisphere," *Economic Geography,* 27:316-320, October 1951.

PART NINE::

CONCLUSION

CHAPTER THIRTY-ONE::

It was the best of times, it was the worst of times, it was the age of wisdom, it was the age of foolishness, it was the epoch of belief, it was the epoch of incredulity, it was the season of Light, it was the season of Darkness, it was the spring of hope, it was the winter of despair, we had everything before us, we had nothing before us, we were all going direct to Heaven, we were all going direct the other way—in short, the period was so far like the present period, that some of its noisiest authorities insisted on its being received, for good or evil, in the superlative degree of comparison only.

These are the first lines of Charles Dickens's *A Tale of Two Cities.* The book was first published in 1859, slightly more than ten years after the beginning of the Industrial Revolution; it was concerned with the French Revolution of 1789. Yet Dickens might all too ac-

CONCLUSIONS

curately have been describing today's world; for basic human needs and fears and hopes perhaps will never change. They have been made only more acute by the acceleration of technological gains and of population growth, the two phenomena that are constantly reflected in every aspect of economic, political, and social life today.

All the preceding chapters have emphasized the differences and the relations between the developed and the underdeveloped lands. The division between the two groups has resulted largely from the impact of science and technology. While science and technology have notably contracted our world, they also have incalculably expanded its problems. They have given man immense power not only over nature, to some extent, but also over his fellow man, to a terrifying extent. The greater intimacy men now share has served only to underscore the vast differences among them—thus creating new desires, new frustrations, new hostilities.

Most of the underdeveloped lands are painfully handicapped by overpopulation, biting poverty, low life expectancy at birth, constant battle against disease, high illiteracy, and many other weaknesses. These countries make up much of Asia, Africa, and Latin America, comprising more than two thirds of the world's habitable area; Asia alone accounts for about two thirds of the world's people. These underdeveloped expanses of the planet are exceedingly diverse; here in every type of geographical environment are peoples with highly different creeds and cultures and in many stages of development. While most of them have a paltry share of material goods, some

AND OUTLOOK

inhabit areas whose wealth of resources has barely been tapped. Diverse as they are, these peoples have one experience in common: their traditional ways of life have been seriously disturbed by the impact of the West's industrial revolution.

Today they are apparently determined to share in the better life enjoyed by the peoples of North America, Western Europe, Australia, and New Zealand. There are stirrings of the common man everywhere. As a world force, this militant unrest is new, because for countless centuries the peoples in the underdeveloped lands accepted their lot stoically. Now, however, they refuse to regard their poverty as inevitable; they demand to have some control over their own destiny. It is often primarily the leaders rather than the majority of the people in these lands who have become aroused over the possibilities of transforming their societies through the technology and science that made the West wealthy and powerful. (As far as can be determined, most of the rural inhabitants have barely broadened their horizons beyond the elemental desire for sufficient land to sustain their families and for freedom from heavy debt.) But while these leaders want to imitate the Western economic and social advances, they insist on telescoping the transformation into a few decades, in contrast to the century-long, trial-and-error industrial advance of the West.

Thus, today a revolution of rising expectations is sweeping like a tidal wave over these lands. The leaders of some of the nations have a deep desire for economic self-sufficiency. Yet the interdependency of the world is an outstanding phenomenon of our time. Even the gigantic countries such as the Soviet Union, Brazil, Canada, China, Australia, and the United States cannot meet, economically at least, all their requirements for food and raw materials. Most of the underdeveloped countries, realizing they are powerless to raise themselves by their own bootstraps, call upon the developed nations to give them help. The plight of these people gives Communism its greatest weapon ("stomach Communism"). Hence, the Free World must heed the de-

mands—not only for humanitarian reasons but for national self-interest. (The United States' Alliance for Progress requires a transformation of Latin American society, governmental administration, and economy before it will make specific grants.)

The question arises as to how best to offer such aid, whether by international or national lending organizations or by private enterprise. Private enterprise very possibly would be best, but nationalism in these countries has reached such a high pitch that they often regard foreign investment as imperialism. There is also the other side of the coin: private investment tends to shy away from countries whose politics are unstable, where expropriation and confiscation are ever present threats, and where laws are constantly changed, making more difficult the task of operating at a profit. In short, private investment seeks a favorable investment climate. In any event, neither international or national organizations nor private enterprise singly can provide the needed capital; even combined, it is unlikely they could.

In the future, trade between the West and the underdeveloped lands will depend largely on what occurs in the underdeveloped world rather than in the Western world. Economic aid can, of course, greatly enhance trade. But economic development must not be an end in itself; to be successful, it must offer increased hope and opportunity for more and more persons.

Why are certain countries underdeveloped? A few but by no means all of the reasons follow: (1) Often their economies are tied to a single product of crop (monoculture). (2) Frequently, restrictive trade practices discourage governments from investing in new export lines as a means of earning more foreign exchange; the economies of these countries are, accordingly, subject to the ups and downs of a market determined elsewhere. (3) Underdeveloped countries often are overpopulated with respect to their natural-resources base. (4) They lack capital, machinery, and technological know-how. (5) The social system often is static and rigid.

Invariably, underdeveloped nations believe that improvement in their conditions lies in industrialization. Hence, all over the world efforts are being made to engage in manufacturing. Often national governments become involved; thus in Latin America no less than eight national basic-steel plants have been established. However, the leaders in these nations apparently do not realize that, without working capital, technological know-how, education, and organized experience, they cannot duplicate what the developed nations have done. The booming prosperity of the Western industrialized countries and of Japan is based upon many decades of slow economic and political development and upon investment of huge amounts of national savings over the years.

The population explosion has been emphasized as one of the most urgent problems facing mankind today—second in urgency only to the control of nuclear weapons. A population that increased slowly until 1900 now doubles about every forty years. The 3 billion persons of 1960 are expected to increase to more than 6 billion by the year 2000. The recent increases have resulted not from any significant rise in birth rates but because death rates throughout the world have been falling rapidly. This is in contrast with the past, when birth rates and death rates both were high and largely balanced each other. The swift growth of world population imposes a severe burden on those countries desirous of raising their levels of living—a goal almost impossible of attainment so long as their populations increase along current lines.

Then there is the question of food for the increasing population. Is the world capable of feeding its people with a reasonably good diet? Here authorities disagree. It appears logical, however, that if already two thirds of the world's people are hungry and poor, the chances are not good. In nearly all underdeveloped countries, increase in food supply has been and is falling behind the increase in population. It is indeed sobering to contemplate the consequences of the food problem of China; already plagued by persistent famines,

China has an annual population increase of 15 million, and, should the present trend continue, she will have a billion inhabitants in another two decades.

Is there a sufficiency of minerals to meet man's ever increasing, insatiable needs? Man draws heavily on his mineral heritage. He has used far more minerals since 1900 than in all preceding time. More thought and planning must go into conservation and conversion of these, particularly the irreplaceable ones. Still another aspect of minerals use is their location. Many of the "have" nations are rapidly becoming "have nots" as a result of a century or more of exploitation. Today underdeveloped nations possess a very considerable share of the world's remaining mineral wealth. The political implications of this situation are frightening for the developed nations, which are dependent on the underdeveloped lands for some, or in certain cases most, of their raw materials. Will the underdeveloped countries provide a favorable climate for foreign exploitation, or will they allow only nationals to engage in mining? Will they permit minerals to be exported as concentrates or smelted materials, or will they insist upon their being processed within the country of origin? It is, further, of considerable concern to the Free World that Communist China, while still industrially embryonic, has a minerals base presaging an industrial potential vying with that of any nation.

Over the earth the close relationship between energy and economic progress is striking. The utilization of inanimate energy—its wide adoption in the United States, for example, and its restricted use in Bolivia—can serve as a handy yardstick for measuring the development of nations in the future.

The student has been made aware that in the United States and the countries of Western Europe, agriculture is relatively less important than manufacturing—that the labor force engaged in agriculture in the United States in 1960 was only about 8 per cent, and in Western Europe about 25 per cent. Yet the United States has never had such bounteous harvests and such surplus stocks and so high a standard of living—a situation resulting from the widespread use of farm machinery, fertilizers, insecticides, inanimate energy, and scientific farming methods. And Western Europe, with only 3 per cent of the world's land surface and 10 per cent of the population, was producing about 20 per cent of the world's food.

Labor costs comprise an important facet of international economic competition. Of particular importance are comparisons of those in the United States with those in Western Europe, the Soviet Union, and Japan. The disproportionately higher wages in the United States made little difference as long as American machinery and plants were far more modern and efficient than those in other countries. Today, however, those in many competing nations are as efficient or even more so. Thus, many American corporations are establishing plants abroad and many American ships are flying **flags of convenience.** Yet, it must be noted, too, that in the United States automation has progressed most rapidly—duplicating not only the work of men's hands but also of men's minds, and frequently doing it faster, cheaper, and more accurately. By enhancing the nation's productivity, automation is expected to aid appreciably in overcoming foreign wage advantages. At the same time, automation creates its own problem—namely, how to employ today's automation refugees and the 15 to 20 million new workers who will join the labor force by 1971.

Walter Heller, Chairman of the President's Council of Economic Advisers, noted in 1961: "In the old days we used to say that when the United States economy sneezed, the rest of the world went to bed with pneumonia. Now when the United States economy sneezes, the other countries say 'Gesundheit.'" The most serious challenge the United States has faced in international trade has been the development in Europe of the Common Market (the Six) and the European Free Trade Association (the Seven). And, assuming that Great Britain and other members of the Seven join the Six, the United States will have to compete with an enormous and efficient Euro-

pean cooperative trade bloc, which not only would erect tariff walls against the United States and other countries but also would be a competitive threat in those areas which have normally been supplied chiefly by the United States. Because of this prospect, the United States, together with other nations, is considering association with an enlarged Common Market. This would mean, of course, giving up a certain degree of American freedom of action in the economic realm, but it would immeasurably enhance economic growth, production, trade, and the level of living in other countries of the Free World.

Throughout this book the economic strength of both the United States and the Soviet Union has been demonstrated. The latter is determined to catch up with the United States in the economic contest by the magic year 1970 and to surpass it by 1972. In labor productivity (output per man) the Russians lag well behind the United States in almost every field. Whether the Russians will reach their objective is problematical: they do have a long way to go; yet they are narrowing the gap—doing so by concentrating on measures for strengthening the economic, political, and military potential of the nation rather than on production of consumer goods. All this poses a threat to the United States domestic economy through possible severe losses in the export trade. The American advantage is greater in agricultural than in industrial performance.

In 1961 a widely, if perhaps not wisely, publicized statement comparing the levels of living in the two nations was made by Bryce N. Harlow, a former deputy assistant to ex-President Eisenhower. He observed:

In order to enjoy the glories of the present Soviet system, we would have to abandon three fifths of our steel capacity, two thirds of our petroleum capacity, 95 per cent of our electric-motor output, destroy two of every three of our hydroelectric plants, and get along on a tenth of our present volume of natural gas.

We would have to rip up 14 of every 15 miles of our paved highways and two out of every three miles of our mainline railway tracks. We'd sink eight out of every nine ocean-going ships, scrap 19 out of every 20 cars and trucks, and shrink our civilian air fleet to a shadow of its present size.

We would have to cut our living standard by three fourths, destroy 40 million TV sets, nine out of every 10 telephones, and seven out of every 11 houses; and we would have to put about 60 million people back on farms.[1]

Statisticians claim that even in the early 1970s total Soviet production will not be more than 60 to 75 per cent of that of the United States. But account must be taken of the rate of Soviet economic growth: the Russians assert that this is 8 to 10 per cent yearly, compared with about 3½ per cent in the United States. Further, it would be folly to minimize the pace of Soviet industrial development: since 1917, production in heavy industry has increased by 8,500 per cent; since 1953, by 112 per cent. And most important of all is steel production, the basis of any nation's industrial strength: in the United States, output averages about 100 million tons a year; in the Soviet Union, production soared from 18 million in 1940, to 55 million in 1958, and to 72 million in 1960.

Naturally, the United States has an enormous lead in consumer goods and in the so-called "luxury market." It is a nation which in 1960 spent, for example, 7.4 billion dollars on tobacco, 2.3 billion dollars on photography, 323 million dollars on chewing gum, 100 million dollars on lipsticks, and 20 million dollars on power puffs. The great contrast in the use of productive capacity in these two heavyweight powers is the Russians' understandable aim at national effort and the Americans' equally understandable tendency toward private indulgence. It is worthy of note that in recent years the high United States standard of living has been made possible largely through the excessive exploitation of its own resources and those of numerous underdeveloped lands. In order to support 6 per cent of the world's population, the United States has been using more than 50 per cent of the Free World's nonfood raw materials.

It is all too easy to make a black and white contrast between the Free World and the Communist world; and people in both blocs are guilty of this habit. Yet today, more than ever before, mutual forbearance is an absolute necessity. It is, as someone has said, a matter of coexistence or no existence. And both groups, as they make their machines go faster and faster, seem to be forgetting that no amount of material success can serve as a substitute for a purposeful life based on a humane scale of values. Important as is the physical interchange of goods, it is secondary to cultural understanding.

The consequences of economic development have been most cogently remarked upon by Eugene R. Black of the World Bank:

It is not that there is any certain and established relationship between economic progress and the values of freedom and tolerance. There is no such relationship; economic development is a fickle process; it destroys old habits and attitudes toward life even as it creates the wherewithal for a better material life; it creates human desires often much faster than it provides the means for their gratification; its one continual and overriding requirement is change; by itself it leads nowhere in particular and may lead anywhere in general.

But part of facing the realities of this world is recognizing that economic development, while not sufficient, is necessary for progress towards all of the political, economic, and humanitarian aims which the free peoples believe in and seek beyond their shores.[2]

As recently as a century ago, life in many parts of the world was a never ending, tragic struggle for the bare essentials of existence. No longer should this, nor need this, be so. World production, consumption, and trade must now be concerned with fairer and more positive advantages for all human beings.

A few frontiers still exist. Seemingly intolerable milieus remain as challenges, but

[1] Bryce N. Harlow, "Who's Ahead of Whom?" *Ethyl News*, January–February 1961, p. 4.

[2] Eugene R. Black, *The Diplomacy of Economic Development*, Cambridge, Massachusetts: Harvard University Press, 1960, p. 19.

possibly not insuperable ones. Those who scoff at the idea of additional frontiers might do well to remember that only a century ago an eminent British historian confidently predicted that with a climate suitable only "for the reindeer, the elk, and musk ox," seven eighths of Canada was foredoomed to perpetual sterility; and, with similar conviction, a report on Arizona to the American Congress in 1858 observed, "The region is altogether valueless. After entering it there is nothing to do but leave."

Today's citizen must be well informed about his own physical and cultural environments as well as those of his fellow men; he must know where the various natural resources are to be found and how they are being exploited, and where they are processed and utilized. He must understand the wise use of the earth and its resources so as to contribute to the fight against waste, for, to a great degree, wise use has become the price of survival. His in-

tellectual curiosity, in the words of Lewis Mumford, "must be attached to social responsibility." We hope that this book will help the student to question and analyze the economic, not to mention the political and social, changes occurring in this restless world. What is behind a new economic and political measure? Does it prophesy a balance or imbalance of trade, cooperation or chaos? Above all, what is the goal of a new industrial enterprise: only the production of material goods, or also the production of good will and good men?

Crisis is symbolized in Chinese by two characters, one signifying danger and the other opportunity. The dangers man faces today are far greater than ever before, but so are the opportunities. The balance is most precarious. And it is well-educated people who can tip the scales one way or the other. Here, economic geography is an asset. As the *London Times* stated in 1848, "A man needs to rub up his geography these days."

SELECTED REFERENCES

Deevey, E. S. "The Human Population," *Scientific American*, 203:195-204, September 1960.

Fryer, D. W. "World Income and Types of Economies: The Pattern of World Economic Development," *Economic Geography*, 34:283-303, October 1958.

Just, Evan. "Foreign Private Investment—A Boon to Developing Countries," *Mining Engineering*, 9:641-645, June 1957.

Nehru, B. K. "$2,700 a Year or $70 a Year," *New York Times Magazine*, April 16, 1961, pp. 22, 116-117.

Pehrson, Elmer W. "Minerals in National and International Affairs," in *Economics of the Mineral Industries*. New York, American Institute of Mining, Metallurgical, and Petroleum Engineers, 1959, pp. 497-554.

White, C. Langdon. "The World's Underdeveloped Lands," *Focus*, 10:1-6, September 1959.

——————. "Industrialization: A Panacea for Underdeveloped Nations?" *Yearbook of the Association of Pacific Coast Geographers*, 17:3-18, 1955.

Willard, C. J. "Will We Have Enough Food and Fiber?" *Ohio Journal of Science*, 60:215-217, July 1960.

Wolf, C. *Capital Formation and Foreign Investment in Underdeveloped Areas*. Syracuse, Syracuse University Press, 1955.

GLOSSARY

Accessible forest. One that is within reach of economic management or exploitation as a source of forest products.

Acre-foot of water. The volume of water covering 1 acre to a depth of 1 foot; equivalent to 325,850 gallons.

Air drainage. The collecting, in valleys and lowlands, of dense, cold air flowing down from adjacent uplands during calm, clear nights.

Alloy steel. The name applied to several steels in which are incorporated one or more of the ferroalloy metals, in addition to carbon. These alloying metals impart to the steel certain desirable qualities, such as additional hardness; greater toughness; increased elasticity; and resistance to heat, stain, and rust.

Animal unit. A unit represented by as many animals as consume an equivalent amount of feed: one cow or steer, one horse or mule, five hogs, seven sheep, one hundred poultry.

Annual. A crop that is restricted in its growth to the frostless season; specifically, a plant that completes its growth in a single year.

Asphalt base. Descriptive of petroleum that yields asphalt but little or no paraffin.

Autobahn (pl. **autobahnen**). In Germany, a high-speed, four-lane highway with park strip down the middle to separate traffic moving in opposite directions.

Automation. An advanced form of mechanization, using instrumentation and electronic controls, which builds self-evaluating and self-correcting devices into operating equipment; increases output and, usually, quality of product at lower cost; but does not (as widely believed) nullify human judgments.

Ballast (for railroads). Gravel or broken stone laid in the roadbed of a railroad to make it solid for placing of the ties.

Ballast (for ships). Any relatively heavy substance used to maintain a vessel at its proper draft. Often, when a ship carries a cargo, it experiences difficulty in getting a profitable return cargo. Hence, rather than return with unprofitable water ballast, it returns with some item, such as iron ore, coal, stone, china clay, or steel, even though the profit made on the return trip is much lower than that on the original trip. An example is the Lake carrier, which transports iron ore to Lower Lake ports and returns with coal.

Banks. Uplands in the sea, generally near coastlines and 600 to 900 feet below the surface of the water, where fish congregate.

Barrel (cement). Equivalent to four bags or 376 pounds.

Barrel (oil). The standard measure for oil. A barrel holds 42 liquid gallons, 2 of which are in the buyer's favor.

Bayou. An abandoned channel of a river, in flat country, which remains swampy owing to river seepage, floods, and lack of drainage.

Beneficiation. Any process—crushing, roasting, sintering, and concentration—for improving the structure or grade of iron ore for blast-furnace use.

Blister copper. An impure form of copper, produced by air blown through molten copper matte. As the metal cools, the sulfur dioxide dissolved in it is expelled, giving the metal a blistered appearance.

Bracero. A day laborer, or one who works with his arms (Spanish: *brazos*). The term has lately been used to designate Mexican workers legally contracted for seasonal agricultural employment in the United States.

Browse. Tender shoots, twigs, and leaves of trees and shrubs (not grass), on which domesticated animals (cattle, goats, sheep) are allowed to graze.

BTU (British thermal unit). The amount of heat required to raise the temperature of 1 pound of water 1°F. The temperature range is generally from 60°F to 61°F.

Carbon steel. Ordinary steel, as contrasted with special or alloy steels (those containing nickel, chromium, molybdenum, tungsten, and vanadium).

Carrying capacity. The number of animal units that 1 acre of vegetation can sustain.

Chamber lock. An enclosure in a canal or river with gates at each end, used for raising and lowering vessels or boats as they pass from level to level.

Clean-tilled crop. A row crop, where soil between rows is cultivated to kill weeds and disrupt capillary movement of water. If clean-tilling is practiced on a slope and if rainfall is of the torrential type, soil erosion is pronounced.

Compost. A fertilizing mixture composed of rotted vegetable matter, especially manure and litter. The bottom layer is made up of an absorbent, such as leaves or straw, on which the farm refuse is dumped. During dry weather, the pile is kept moist.

Continental shelf. A shallow submarine plain of varying width which forms a border to almost every continent.

Cottrell process. A method of precipitating the solid matter from the smoke or fume of smelting furnaces, blast furnaces, etc. The fume is passed into a chamber in which hang insulated conductors. These latter are charged to about 70,000 volts above the potential of the floor of the chamber. The solid matter is deposited on the walls and floor of the chamber and is removed from the former by tapping with a hammer. Without the Cottrell process, the smelter fumes and gases affect crops adversely.

Crop rotation. The system of rotating four, six, or eight different crops in order to preserve or improve fertility of the soil and maintain the yields of the principal crop. In the past, con-

tinuous cropping of a single species, even where conditions have been most favorable for it, has resulted in lower and lower yields. However, techniques now being developed may permit single cropping year after year with high yields.

Crude (oil). Unrefined petroleum, or petroleum in its natural state—not altered, refined, or processed in any way for use.

Dragger. A type of motor fishing vessel used chiefly in the Atlantic, particularly in the Canadian Maritimes and in New England, whence the main demersal fishing takes place. The vessel is about 100 feet long and diesel-propelled; the foremast is often rigged to carry a small sail to diminish rolling when fishing.

Dry farming. Nonirrigated, water-conservation farming in areas that do not receive adequate rainfall to grow a crop every year. The land is treated so that its moisture is conserved (see *fallow*); a crop is grown every other year or, in areas receiving slightly more precipitation, two years in three.

Dumping. The sale of goods in quantity on the market, particularly remote markets, at abnormally low prices in order either to dispose of a surplus or to suppress competition.

Durum wheat. A high-yielding, high-gluten, hard wheat, winter or spring, quite drought- and rust-resistant, and used largely in making semolina, macaroni, and spaghetti.

Duster. An unproductive gas or oil well.

Ejido. A farming community in Mexico, which has received land in accordance with the procedures set up under the 1917 constitution. In these farm villages, averaging seventy families each, the lands have been divided into private farms. However, the land thus parceled out cannot be sold; and, if the family moves away, the title to the property remains with the *ejido*.

Equatorial forest (tropical rain forest). The hot, wet, broadleaved evergreen forest of the equatorial region; rainfall heavy; no dry season. Owing to extreme heat and moisture, growth is dense and luxuriant, containing an abundance of heavy vines and epiphytes. Individual species of trees are very scattered.

Extensive agriculture. Cultivation that results in high returns per man. Labor and capital are spread thin on the soil.

Fallow. In dry farming, that half of the farm land not in crops but plowed and cultivated in order to keep down weeds and conserve moisture.

Fellah (pl. **fellahin**). A peasant in Arabic-speaking countries, particularly Egypt; in Arabic, literally "a plowman."

Felt. A cloth composed of matted fibers of wool, made by beating rather than by spinning or weaving.

Fennoscandia. The region composed of the Scandinavian countries and Finland.

Fire climax. The result of persistent burning of the forest, which creates conditions unfit for future tree growth; a matted jungle of tall grass (savanna), against which young tree seedlings contend with great difficulty.

Flags of convenience (also called **flags of necessity**). The term used when a nation operates appreciable numbers of its vessels under flags of other nations in order to effect greater economies than would be possible under its own flag. United States maritime unions call such ships "runaways." The United States operates ships under the flags of Liberia, Honduras, and Panama; these vessels are kept as a part of the American fleet for defense purposes and are composed primarily of comparatively large, new bulk carriers.

Flaring (natural gas). Burning dry gas. When no immediate market exists for dry gas found with oil, it is burned in flares in the oil field.

Flense. To strip the blubber or skin from a whale or seal.

Flushing (tea). The production of new shoots; occurs particularly during the rains, when growth is luxuriant.

Flux. A material (e.g., limestone), added to the blast-furnace charge to combine with the gangue and form a fusible slag, thus facilitating the separation of impurities from the reduced metal.

Forest litter. The deposit of vegetable matter on the ground in a forest—twigs, leaves, and humus.

Forest (pine) plantation. Unique to New Zealand, where land-settlement laws (province of Canterbury) provided for free grants of land if plantations were established—a measure to forestall prospective timber shortages. The introduction of many Northern Hemisphere conifers,

which grow rapidly and do not require replanting, has helped rank these plantation forests among the fastest growing in the world.

Gallery forest. The woody vegetation prevailing on the edges of streams in savannas.

Gauge (railway). The distance between the inside edges of the steel rail. Rolling stock is restricted to the gauge—*standard* (4'8½"), *meter* (3'6"), and *broad* (5' or more).

Geographical division of labor. Whereby each part of the earth specializes on what it is best equipped by nature to do (e.g., the Palouse area of Idaho and Washington on wheat; the Butte district of Montana on copper; the Salinas Valley of California on lettuce; Sparrows Point, Maryland, on steel). This division is partly a product of rapid transportation and of the growth of human numbers.

Gluten. The sticky protein substance, especially in hard-wheat flour, which gives adhesiveness to dough.

Great-circle route. The shortest distance between two points on the curved surface of the globe, found by following the arc of a great circle.

Groundwater. Subsurface water occupying the zone of saturation. In a strict sense, the term applies only to water below the water table.

Growing (frostless) season. The period of plant growth between the last killing frost in spring and the first killing frost in autumn.

Guano. Accumulated droppings of millions of birds (cormorants, pelicans, lancers, guanays) on islands off the coast of Peru. Guano, rich in nitrogen, is collected for use as fertilizer in coastal oases. Mining and distribution are controlled by the government to avoid overexploitation.

Hardwood. Trees of the angiosperm group, commonly called broadleaved or hardwood trees. However, the wood of some trees of the gymnosperm group (conifers or softwoods) is considerably harder than that of some angiosperms.

Igneous rock. Solidified from a molten condition, having originated fairly deep down in the earth and been forced by strong internal pressures to erupt through the earth's outer crust. Igneous rock occurs in two forms: (1) *intrusive*, which does not reach the surface but solidifies in cavities or cracks; and (2) *extrusive*, which reaches the ground surface through a pipe or crack and then solidifies.

Industrial inertia (sometimes called "momentum of an early start"). The strong force tending to perpetuate manufacturing in a given place once it is established, despite the trend toward decentralization. The trend is strongest in those industries that are not "footloose"—e.g., iron and steel, petroleum refining, pulp and paper.

Insolation. Radiant energy from the sun, showing considerable variation over different areas of the earth's surface. It exhibits the least variation at the equator throughout the year.

Integrated plant (steel). One whose facilities cover the whole gamut of steelmaking operations, from the mining and quarrying of raw materials to the manufacture of finished products.

Intensive agriculture. A system of farming a given area to obtain the highest possible yields per acre. As population becomes especially dense and resort to new lands becomes difficult, there is a gradual transition toward intensive farming: a more elaborate rotation of crops, a more continuous use of each tract, deeper plowing, more frequent harrowing, systematic drainage, more carefully selected seed, and more abundant fertilizing.

Jet piercer. Equipment which uses an oxygen and kerosene mixture and water to sink holes for dynamiting hard taconite rock.

Kimberlite pipe. Tunnel-like intrusions of igneous rock in the diamond fields of South Africa.

Kwh (kilowatt hour). A unit of electrical energy equal to 1,000 watt hours.

Latakia. A superior grade of Turkish tobacco. It takes its name from Latakia, Syria, a growing, manufacturing, and trading tobacco area.

Legumes. Certain crops (e.g., beans, peas, clover, and alfalfa) containing nitrogen-fixing bacteria, which store nitrogen in tiny nodules on the roots of the crop. Such crops also help maintain the supply of humus.

Lodging. Beating down of standing grain by rain and/or wind, usually when stalks are mature and hence high and when heads are heavy with grain.

Loess. Deposit of wind-transported dust which,

over thousands of years, settled out to form a fine, extremely porous, fertile soil. China has the greatest deposits of loess.

Matte. An impure metallic sulfide product obtained during the smelting of metallic sulfide ores —e.g., copper, nickel, lead.

Merchantable saw timber. The portion of the bole of saw-timber trees above which a minimum merchantable saw log (as regionally defined) cannot be produced.

Metamorphic rock. Originally igneous or sedimentary rock but changed in character and appearance by heat, pressure, or the action of water.

Milling-in-bond. Descriptive of wheat milled in transit, the flour being destined solely for foreign markets.

Milpa. A type of primitive cultivation in the tropics, involving the girdling of the larger trees and the burning of underbrush, after which crops are planted crudely in the ashes. The practice is destructive of both vegetation and soils, and produces only one or a few crops from the same field. The land is abandoned, usually after the second year, for as many as twenty years.

Multiple-basing-point system. A modification of the "Pittsburgh Plus" system of marketing steel used by the industry from 1924 to 1948. In this delivered-price system, a seller quoted a "delivered" price to the buyer. The "delivered" price was composed of the price at the basing point (not necessarily the location of the seller's plant) plus freight charges from the basing point to the point of delivery. The seller used the basing point that gave his prospective customer the lowest "delivered" price.

Muskeg. Swampy areas in the forests of northern North America. Muskeg does not extend over one continuous area but is a vegetation having a physiognomy distinct from that of the surrounding kind owing to a waterlogged substratum.

Native copper. Metallic copper which occasionally contains small amounts of silver and bismuth and which fills cracks and forms the cement of sandstone and conglomerate.

Night soil. Natural waste of humans used for fertilizing agricultural fields, particularly in the Far East.

Oil pool. A buried layer of porous rock (called

the "reservoir rock") of varying thickness, which is saturated with oil and gas. The oil is under pressure. When the drill penetrates an oil sand, the pressure is released, and the gas expands and propels the oil to the surface.

Oil province. Loosely, a group of oil pools and fields producing under similar geological conditions.

Oil sand. Porous sandstone that contains petroleum; to oilfielders, any porous oil stratum.

Open-cast mining. Term used by the British to designate open-pit mining.

Ore. Solid, naturally occurring mineral aggregate of economic interest, from which one or more valuable constituents may be recovered by treatment.

Oxygen process. A process gaining in popularity for making pig iron and steel. The injection of an enriched (up to 50 per cent) blast or jet of oxygen into the working space of the furnace provides (a) a saving in heat and hence in coke consumption, (b) greater furnace efficiency, and (c) a reduction in the time required to refine molten metal in the furnace. Also the capital cost of the oxygen furnace needed to produce an equivalent tonnage is lower than that of the open-hearth furnace.

Paddy rice. The term commonly applied in Oriental countries to the rice plant as it grows in the field, to the cut and harvested stalks, and to the grains detached by threshing. Also "paddy" is the name given the flooded field.

Paraffin base. Descriptive of a crude oil that contains solid paraffins but practically no asphalt.

Pedalfers. A major division of mature soils, found in humid areas, usually in forests but also in humid prairies; generally high in iron and aluminum, and inclined to be acid except on limestone rock.

Pedocals. A major division of mature soils in subhumid, semiarid, and arid areas—grasslands and deserts; generally rich in calcium or lime and hence alkaline.

Perennial. A plant or crop that lives from year to year. The term is usually applied to herbs or crops having roots that persist but stems that die down to the ground seasonally.

Perique. A very high grade of tobacco grown in Louisiana. It is strong in flavor and used chiefly in smoking mixtures.

Permafrost. Permanently frozen ground in arctic and sub-arctic regions; lies at a shallow depth below the surface layer, which thaws for a few weeks in summer. Permafrost covers approximately 47 per cent of the area of the Soviet Union.

pH factor. A measure of hydrogen-ion concentration used to express acidity or alkalinity.

Pig iron. Crude iron produced by the reduction of iron ore in a blast furnace and cast into pigs for making steel, cast iron, or wrought iron. The principal impurities are carbon (2.5 to 5 per cent) and varying amounts of silicon, manganese, sulfur, and phosphorus. The composition varies according to type of ore, smelting practice, and purpose for which the iron is to be used.

Pittsburgh Plus. A system of selling steel in the United States prior to 1924; a careful combination of economic and geographic elements in a selling program. The steel consumer paid the Pittsburgh price plus the amount of freight from Pittsburgh, regardless of where the steel was manufactured. In this way, Pittsburgh steelmakers protected themselves from competition of more economical producers and from competition of manufacturers located closer to the consumer.

Placer deposits. Gravelly or sandy material, containing such metals as gold, platinum, and tin, formed by the action of running streams and found where the velocity and hence the carrying power of the water has decreased.

Plow sole. A compacted layer of soil formed at the bottom of a furrow by the passage of the plow, particularly when plowing is continuous at the same depth. Sometimes called "hardpan."

Podsols. Coarse, acidic, poor agricultural soils formed in high latitudes, chiefly under coniferous forests, and farther south on sands; podsols develop where precipitation is considerable but evaporation limited. The grayish-white A horizon (upper layer) contains little or no humus; the B horizon is brown, richer in minerals, and contains some humus.

Porphyry. A general term for igneous rocks containing relatively large isolated crystals set in a fine-grained ground mass; a variety of feldspar.

Prairie. The great grassland region of central North America, roughly from western Kansas to western Indiana and from central Alberta to Texas. The term is sometimes used to refer to any tall-grass area but is customarily reserved for the vast grasslands in the heart of the North American continent, while the term "tall grass" is applied to a grassland in a subhumid area anywhere in the world.

Public domain. Public land in the United States, consisting of three types: (1) land reserved permanently for specific purposes—national forests and national parks; (2) Indian reservations; and (3) lands recently withdrawn pending classification and further consideration of their utilization (this includes nearly all arid and semiarid land and all land usually classed as "unappropriated public land open to settlement").

Pure stand. Consisting almost entirely of trees belonging to a single species.

Ranch. From the Spanish *rancho*, a grazier's land holding. In the American West, the term is loosely used to denote a farm of large size utilized primarily for the raising of cattle, horses, or sheep. In the Pacific Coast states, however, any farm may be called a ranch (e.g., a fruit ranch, chicken ranch). The Texan, accustomed to ranches of 3,000 acres and more, is amazed at the Californian's ranch of 2 or 3 acres.

Ratoons. In sugar-cane cultivation, the successive crops from one planting following the first harvest. Each ratoon is lower yielding than the previous one.

Reduction (iron ore). The reverse of oxidation; the chemical reaction by which iron is produced in the blast furnace through removal of oxygen from the ore.

Reserve. The sum total of a given mineral in a mine, state, country, continent, or in the world as a whole. Reserves are ever changing; advancing technology enables man to work minerals of such low grade that at one time they would have been regarded as uneconomical.

Restrictive environment. Type of physical milieu (e.g., the polar lands, the deserts, the highest mountains, and the hot, humid lands) which offers limited economic opportunities to *civilized* man and sharply limits his numbers.

Room and pillar mining. In underground mining, coal is extracted from the seams. The "rooms" are the places from which the coal is removed; the "pillars" are the walls separating the rooms. The pillars thus help to support the roof. Mining by this method is wasteful because considerable coal is left in the mine.

Savanna. Tropical grassland usually bordering the equatorial forest in each hemisphere, though some savannas occur within the rain forest itself. Vegetation consists mostly of grass with scattered trees, for there are distinct wet and dry seasons and the lack of rainfall during the latter is not conducive to tree growth.

Scour. To pass a plow through the ground, turning a furrow without any soil clinging to the smooth polished blade.

Scutch. To separate the woody parts from the valuable fiber (e.g., flax) by beating.

Seasonal distribution of labor. Effort on the part of the farmer to so distribute his labor as to keep busy throughout the year. Rotation of crops, which requires labor at different times, helps much; so does the raising of livestock.

Self-fluxing ore. Ore containing natural impurities, which on heating act as adequate flux during smelting.

Selva. Dense equatorial forest in the basin of the Amazon River. Trees strain skyward, crowns intermesh; sunlight experiences difficulty penetrating the canopy and reaching the ground. Hence, no dense vegetation hampers movement by animal or man.

Slag dumps. Sites, often in bodies of water (e.g., a lake or bay), where new land is being made from slag. Slag is the material resulting from reaction of limestone (the flux) and the gangue of the ore and which floats on the surface of the molten pig iron in the blast furnace and must be tapped from time to time.

Softwood. Coniferous, evergreen trees of commercial species. The many species differ considerably one from another, but in all the wood is light-textured, easily worked, and nonresistant.

Steppe. Vast, level, generally treeless grasslands (short grass) reaching from the Danubian lowland to Soviet Central Asia. The term sometimes refers to corresponding subhumid or semiarid grasslands in other continental interiors.

Strategic material. As defined by the Army and Navy Munitions Board of the United States during World War II, a material the nation had to have to win the war but which it lacked within its continental confines and for which there was no effective substitute.

Strip cropping. Growing clean-tilled and close-growing crops on alternating strips, usually on slopes. Contour plowing prevails. When permanent, close-growing contour strips of legumes, legume-grass mixtures, or grass checks erosion.

Stripper well. A marginal well that produces a comparatively small quantity of oil and is generally pumped empty once or twice daily.

Taiga. Vast forests, predominantly coniferous, in the Northern Hemisphere spanning the earth in high latitudes south of the tundra. The southern limit is a zone of transition toward broadleaf forests or grasslands.

Tailing piles. Piles of the worthless portion (gangue) of a crushed ore, separated during concentration.

Tannin. A vegetable product converted into an astringent extract and employed to tan perishable hides and skins in such a manner as to make them durable and flexible.

Timberline. The altitudinal limit for tree growth on a mountain; elevation varies with exposure and latitude; a lower tree line may result from deficiency in precipitation.

Trap. The portion of reservoir rocks in which oil collects and is retained by water in the lower pore spaces.

Tundra. Area on the polar side of the taiga with vegetation composed primarily of lichens (especially in North America), mosses (especially in Eurasia), and low bushes.

Upland rice. A low-yielding dryland crop grown without irrigation; also called "hill" or "mountain" rice. It accounts for only a very small portion of the world's rice crop.

Valorization scheme. Brazilian government device for artificially controlling the coffee market when world production greatly exceeds consumption.

Virgin forest. Original forest as it existed before man began to cut its timber.

Water table. The upper limit of the part of the soil or underlying material wholly saturated with water; also called the level of saturation.

Wildcat. Any well drilled for oil or gas in virgin territory.

Winterization. Removal of a portion of the more saturated glycerides from a fatty vegetable oil so that the oil will not solidify at low temperatures.

INDEX

INDEX :: 651